PUBLIC ADMINISTRATION
AND
PUBLIC AFFAIRS

fifth edition

NICHOLAS HENRY
Georgia Southern University

PRENTICE HALL
Englewood Cliffs, New Jersey 07632

Library of Congress Cataloging-in-Publication Data

Henry, Nicholas, (date)
    Public administration and public affairs / Nicholas Henry. -- 5th
ed.
        p.   cm.
    Includes bibliographical references and index.
    ISBN 0-13-737560-3
    1. Public adminisration.   I. Title.
JF1351.H45   1992
350--dc20   91-8896
                                                             CIP

Production Editor: KERRY REARDON
Acquisitions Editor: KAREN HORTON
Copy Editor: STEPHEN HOPKINS
Cover Designer: FRANKLIN GRAPHICS
Prepress Buyer: KELLY BEHR
Manufacturing Buyer: MARY ANN GLORIANDE
Page Layout: JOH LISA
Editorial Assistant: DELORES MARS

To Muriel

© 1992, 1989, 1986, 1980, 1975 by Prentice-Hall, Inc.
A Simon & Schuster Company
Englewood Cliffs, New Jersey 07632

Printed in the United States of America

10 9 8 7 6 5 4 3 2 1

ISBN 0-13-737560-3

PRENTICE-HALL INTERNATIONAL (UK) LIMITED, LONDON
PRENTICE-HALL OF AUSTRALIA PTY. LIMITED, SYDNEY
PRENTICE-HALL CANADA INC., TORONTO
PRENTICE-HALL HISPANOAMERICANA, S.A., MEXICO
PRENTICE-HALL OF INDIA PRIVATE LIMITED, NEW DELHI
PRENTICE-HALL OF JAPAN, INC., TOKYO
SIMON & SCHUSTER ASIA PTE. LTD., SINGAPORE
EDITORA PRENTICE-HALL DO BRASIL, LTDA., RIO DE JANEIRO

CONTENTS

PART TWO: Public Organizations: Theories, Concepts, and People

3   THE THREADS OF ORGANIZATION THEORY   49

4   CONCEPTS OF ORGANIZATION THEORY   81

5   PEOPLE IN PUBLIC ORGANIZATIONS   113

PART FOUR: Implementation

10 APPROACHES TO PUBLIC POLICY AND ITS IMPLEMENTATION   285

11 GOVERNMENT CONTRACTING AND THE PUBLIC AUTHORITY   311

12 INTERGOVERNMENTAL ADMINISTRATION   353

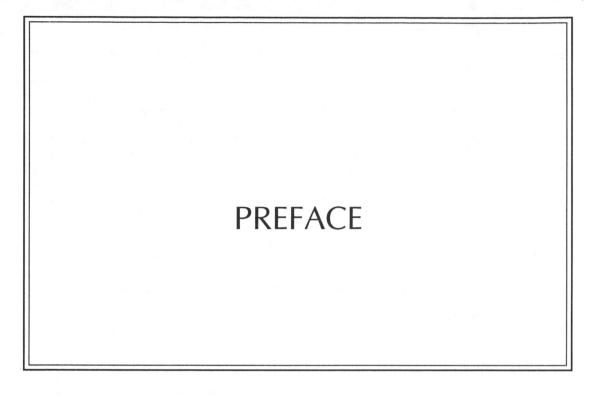

PREFACE

The fifth edition of *Public Administration and Public Affairs* traces the exciting evolution of public administration and presents a good deal of new and significantly augmented information about the field, particularly in the area of organization theory.

The new and significantly expanded discussions contained in the fifth edition include the following:

- The problem of bureaucratic power in a democracy.
- The behavioral differences between public administrators and private-sector managers.
- The unique qualities of public organizations, particularly the role of the task environment on the behavior of public organizations.
- Adult psychology and its importance to public organizations.
- Target budgeting, cutback management, and strategic planning in the public sector.
- The differences between leadership and management and how they function together in public agencies.
- The dramatic case of Robert Moses, as the master manager of public corporations in New York, and his death-struggle with Governor Nelson Rockefeller.

- The public's opinion of public leaders, and its implications for the health of the public service.
- The distinct differences between the public and private sectors in regard to the evaluation of executive performance, employee satisfaction and motivation, and decision-making styles and techniques.
- Ethical questions surrounding the field of organization development.
- The ambivalent organizational benefits of individual loyalty and commitment to the organization.
- Government contracting with the private sector.
- Intergovernmental administration within local governments, focusing on neighborhood associations and organizations.
- Material on the practice of ethical administration in the public sector.

Also given a new treatment in the fifth edition are the extensive appendices that have made *Public Administration and Public Affairs* a useful reference work for both students and practitioners since its initial publication in 1975. Appendix A is a compendium of annotated information sources in public administration and related fields. Not only are bibliographies, dictionaries, directories, encyclopedias, and guides in public administration explained, but so are comparable works in political science, management, American government, law, statistics, and the social sciences. As in the last edition, Library of Congress call numbers for each work are listed, a feature that should ease library searches. Similarly, Appendix B, which is an expanded list of selected journals relevant to public administration, also features Library of Congress call numbers as well as brief explanations of the journals listed. Appendix C lists selected academic, professional, and public interest organizations, with descriptions and addresses, and Appendix D provides the correct form of address for public officials. Appendix E explains what kinds of jobs are available in the public sector, suggests the best prospects for specialization in terms of acquiring a good job in government, lists the salaries that one might expect at all levels of government for certain kinds of administrative positions, and presents sample resumés to assist the reader in putting his or her best foot forward in applying for jobs.

Public Administration and Public Affairs reflects the continuing evolution and growing self-confidence of the field. The fifth edition reports are developments that betoken a field that is maturing, growing more intellectually powerful, and making greater contributions to the society that supports it. Writing the fifth edition of *Public Administration and Public Affairs* has been, as was the case with previous editions, a happy exercise.

ACKNOWLEDGMENTS

In the first edition of this book, I stated that I owed an intellectual debt to at least three of my teachers: Lynton Keith Caldwell, Jack T. Johnson, and York Y. Wilbern. I further noted that they taught me most of what I know about public administration, politics, and how to survive in a bureaucracy. I still owe my teachers that intellectual debt, and it is one that I will continue to acknowledge. Although it has been quite a while since I sat in their classrooms, their impact has waxed, not waned, over the years. This is especially true for Jack T. Johnson, who continues to advise me on matters managerial, even if by long distance.

In this fifth edition, I add a fourth person to this select circle: Frank J. Sackton. Professor Sackton (also Lieutenant General Sackton, retired) introduced me to the classroom of the practical world during the dozen years that I spent at Arizona State University. It was a rare education indeed, and one that I shall always treasure.

I am indebted to my editor at Prentice Hall, Karen Horton, who has been as unflagging in her support as she has been persistent in her constructive criticism. Beginning with the last edition, Karen revised the production schedule for *Public Administration and Public Affairs* so that new editions now appear every three instead of five years. For this, I am grateful.

Jennifer Graham, the chief word processor in the Office of the President at Georgia Southern University, did a superb job in producing the significantly revised manuscript for the fifth edition, and I am genuinely grateful. Peggy Beachum, Jo Ann Marsh, Ruth Ann Rogers, and Angie Waters of my immediate staff warrant high accolades for keeping my administrative days on track, and the office in order. I am indebted to my colleagues, students, and the following Prentice Hall reviewers: Charles Barrilleaux, *University of New Orleans*; James D. Slack, *Cleveland State University*; and Paula McClain, *Arizona State University*. All have had a constructive impact on the continuing evolution of *Public Administration and Public Affairs*.

As always, my wife Muriel, and my children, Adrienne and Miles, provided the deepest level of support. The book is for them.

N.H.

Statesboro, Georgia

CHAPTER

1

BIG DEMOCRACY, BIG BUREAUCRACY

Consider the dilemmas of two presidents in dealing with the government bureaucracy.

Almost three decades ago, President John F. Kennedy was pestered by his brother, Attorney General Robert Kennedy, over the fact that there was a large sign directing drivers to the Central Intelligence Agency's Langley, Virginia, headquarters. The Attorney General saw this sign every day that he commuted to work, and grew increasingly irked; he believed that its presence was in violation of federal policy because it advertised the address of the super secret spy agency. After listening to the intensifying complaints of his brother, President Kennedy ordered an aide to have the sign removed, who, in turn, directed the Interior Department to remove it. Nothing happened. A few days later, the president repeated his order. Again, nothing happened. Aggravated by both the bureaucracy and his brother's persistence, the president personally called the official in charge of signs: "This is Jack Kennedy. It's eleven o'clock in the morning. I want that sign down by the time the attorney general goes home tonight, and I'm holding you personally responsible." The sign was removed and the president had learned a lesson: "I now understand that for a president to get something done in this country, he's got to say it three times."[1]

Such an understanding of supposed bureaucratic inertia is held, in fact, by most presidents. But quite the opposite can occur. Consider the experience of President Jimmy Carter. President Carter's daughter, Amy, was having difficulty one Friday afternoon on a homework problem about the Industrial Revolution. Amy asked for help from her mother, who asked an aide if she knew the answer. The aide called the Labor Department for assistance. Labor was pleased to oblige. On Sunday, a truck pulled up to the White House with Amy's answer: a massive computer printout, costing several hundred thousand dollars and requiring a special team of analysts to work overtime. The department thought it was responding to an order from the president. Amy received a "C" for her homework assignment.[2]

GOVERNMENT AND THE HOSTILE AMERICAN

These episodes, trivial in and of themselves, symbolize the problem of public bureaucracy. It is not that government is too lethargic or too efficient, too futile or too effective: The public bureaucracy is, in the view of some, simply unresponsive to the directives of the citizenry and its elected executives.

This viewpoint is reflected in various polls. The people's trust in government has declined precipitously from around 80 percent in the late 1950s to levels ranging from as low as 17 percent to as high as 23 percent in the 1980s, depending upon the type of government (*i.e.*, the executive branch of the federal government, a state government, or a local government).[3]

An important point, however, is worth noting in these depressing statistics: Much of the decline in public confidence in government, as well as in many other institutions of society, seems to be more a distrust of the leadership of those institutions than a loss of faith in the institutions themselves. For example, the Gallup Poll, which has measured public confidence in institutions since 1973, found that the confidence in institutions in 1985 was 50 percent to 70 percent higher than was public confidence in the leadership of those institutions, and, while faith in leadership has fallen dramatically, the levels of confidence in the institutions which those leaders head have remained relatively unchanged since 1973.[4] As two observers put it, "In the past, American ideals of appropriate leader behavior have been fairly high and constant despite frequent disillusionments. This may be changing....[perhaps] the American mentality is reaching a point in a couple of decades that it took the French mentality several centuries to cultivate."[5]

Interestingly, public administrators themselves seem to share a faith in the institution of government, but question its leadership. Gregory B. Lewis pulled the responses of 513 government employees from a larger sample of 6,753 respondents to surveys undertaken in 1982 and 1988 by the National Opinion Research Center, and compared the responses of the government employees to these surveys with those of the general population. He found that public employees have no more confidence in the people running governmental institutions than the average citizen, and are no less likely to have confidence in the people running other social institutions. The same pattern

essentially held true for top public bureaucrats culled from the surveys, although this group (177 respondents) held the leaders of the military, organized labor, and the medical community in significantly less esteem than did either all government employees or the general public.[6]

Figure 1-1 indicates the level of distrust that Americans have in government and its leaders. It compares the threat of the rise of Big Government relative to Big Labor and Big Business as it is perceived by Americans. Clearly, Big Government is far more worrisome to the average American than either of the other two institutions.

Fiscal reality has reflected these trends in popular opinion, and this is particularly true at the grass-roots levels of government. Although California's notorious Proposition 13 of 1978, which was voted in by a two-to-one popular margin and which slashed property taxes in the state, became the symbol of the revolt against government and taxes in the popular mind, it is clear that the real revolt had begun years earlier. Between 1942 and 1976, the public sector at the state and local levels was a high-growth industry. For thirty-four years, state and local spending burgeoned at a rate almost three times faster than the economy. But after 1976, combined state and local spending in real terms began a decline that has yet to be reversed. (The decline began in 1974 for local governments, and in 1976 for state governments.)

The revolt continues, although signs of entropy are increasingly evident. Of the 116 fiscal restrictions that state governments have imposed upon their local governments or upon themselves— restrictions ranging from requiring full disclosure of financial records to limiting expenditures—about two-thirds have been enacted since 1970. A third were enacted prior to 1970, 26 percent were imposed between 1970 and 1977, but most—41 percent— were mandated in 1978 (the year of Proposition 13) and thereafter. However, the propensity of many states during the years of the tax revolt to increase user fees—notably the successful referendum of 1990 in California to double the gasoline tax over a period of five years—indicates to many that the last days of the tax revolt may be in sight.

Whether or not the state and local tax revolt is in its final days, Americans' distaste for Big Government has also made itself known to the federal level.[7]

FIGURE 1-1   The Public's Perception of the "Biggest Threat to the Country in the Future," Selected Years, 1959-1985

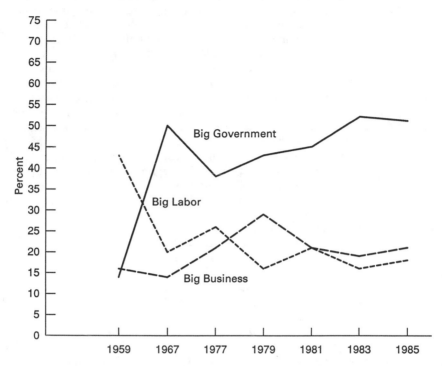

Source: Data derived from George Gallup, *The Gallup Poll: Public Opinion, 1983* (Wilmington, Del.: Scholarly Resources, 1984), pp. 127–128, and *1987*, p. 25.

The election of Ronald Reagan in 1980, who had campaigned for president for two decades on the promise to "get government off the backs of the people," was a major augury. So was the election of Reagan's loyal Vice President, George Bush, in 1988, whose famous campaign statement, "Read my lips. No new taxes!" may have got him elected. But these words would return to haunt him when fiscal realities forced Bush as president to renege on his pledge. Another omen is the spectre of the "balanced budget amendment." Surveys consistently find that Americans favor a constitutional amendment requiring a balanced federal budget by about six to one,[8] and in 1982 the U.S. Senate, with White House backing, voted to enact such an amendment, only to have it die in the House; thirty-one of the thirty-four states needed have called for a constitutional convention to enact a balanced budget amendment.

BIG GOVERNMENT

Americans, in short, have made it clear that they are fed up with something called Big Government, or at least the leadership of Big Government. But is the cause of their frustration actual or illusory? Is American Government really all that huge? Yes, it is, although how huge depends to a degree on one's perspective. Despite grassroots efforts to rein in government, it nonetheless continues to expand in harness. At all levels, government spending (but not, by any means, government revenues—at least not at the federal level) now exceeds $1.8 trillion, and government expenditures account for almost 40 percent of the Gross National Product.[9] The real tax burden on the middle class has increased by more than 90 percent since 1953, although this burden likely has decreased since the federal tax reforms of

1986 were enacted.[10] The number of full and part-time public employees at all levels of government stands at considerably more than 17 million, or one-fourth of the nation's civilian labor force. This figure does not include an estimated 3 million employees who work in the private sector, but who are paid entirely through federal contracts; nor does it include another 2.1 million military personnel.[11]

These are impressive figures. Even so, however, it is worth keeping in mind that American governments appear to loom less large in the lives of their citizens than do their counterparts elsewhere. In 1987, the revenues collected by all American governments amounted to 30 percent of the Gross National Product. But the revenues collected at all levels by the governments of the seventeen Western European democracies, Australia, Canada, Japan, New Zealand, and Turkey amounted to 39.1 percent of their respective GNPs, on the average[12]—a considerably higher take than in the United States.

Relatively speaking, perhaps, American governments do not amount to Big Government. But they do seem big in the eyes of most Americans. The surveys taken during the 1980s indicate that two-thirds of the general public believed that their own taxes were too high, and when asked whether they would favor more spending by government on eleven items dealing with foreign and domestic concerns, only five items were identified as policy areas worthy of greater public funding. (These areas were, in order of support, funding to fight crime, support education, provide health care, fight drug use, and preserve the environment; 61 percent to 65 percent of the general public thought that the government was spending too little on these areas.) The responses of public administrators to these questions were almost identical to those of the general public.[13] Americans, in short, including public administrators themselves, clearly have reservations about how big American governments have grown.

BUREAUCRATS AND THE APPROVING AMERICAN

Yet, when we scratch the surface of this hostility, and examine the one-on-one relationships that citizens have with their bureaucrats, we find quite different results. For example, a Harris poll of nearly 1,600 respondents in 200 locations around the country asked Americans if they had ever gone to a federal, state, or local agency to get "the government" to do something that was not related to routine matters, such as applying for a drivers' license or paying taxes. Among those who indicated that they had sought some kind of personal objective within the public bureaucracy about two-thirds stated that they had found their public bureaucrats to be helpful, and most were satisfied with the services that they received (46 percent, in fact, were highly satisfied with their treatment by federal civil servants).[14] Table 1-1 indicates the results of the survey by levels of government and citizen satisfaction.

TABLE 1-1 Public Opinions on Helpfulness of and Satisfaction with Public Bureaucrats

Did you find the people you went to at (the federal/your state/your local) government helpful or not helpful?

	Federal	State	Local
Helpful	73%	66%	64%
Not helpful	24	29	34
Not sure	3	5	2

Did you come away from that experience with (the federal/your state/your local) government highly satisfied, only somewhat satisfied, or not satisfied at all?

	Federal	State	Local
Highly Satisfied	46%	39%	39%
Only somewhat satisfied	29	26	26
Not satisfied at all	24	34	35
Not sure	1	1	0

Source: Confidence and Concern: Citizens View American Government, A Survey of Public Attitudes by the Subcommittee on Intergovernmental Relations on the Committee on Government Operations, U.S. Senate (Washington, D.C.: U.S. Government Printing Office, 1973), p. 315.

Another national poll conducted at approximately the same time by the University of Michigan Survey Research Center was designed to probe more deeply into the levels of satisfaction obtained by the average citizen when dealing with the government bureaucracy. These respondents were asked if they had ever gone to a government agency for help in several areas, ranging from looking for a job to obtaining retirement benefits. Sixty-nine percent of these respondents pronounced themselves to be very satisfied or fairly well satisfied with the way the government office had handled their problems. Sixteen percent said that the people in the office did more than they had to do to help them, and another 57 percent said that the level of effort to resolve their problem was about right. Nearly three quarters of the respondents said that the government office was very efficient or fairly efficient in handling their problems, and more than three-fourths said that they were treated fairly; only 12 percent, in fact, said that they were treated unfairly.[15] Table 1-2 indicates the results of this survey. There are additional surveys, both national and local, that have found results similar to these.[16]

TABLE 1-2 Public Satisfaction with Public Bureaucrats and Related Opinions

How satisfied were you with the way the office handled your problem? Would you say you were very satisfied, fairly well satisfied, somewhat dissatisfied, or very dissatisfied?

Very satisfied	43%
Fairly well satisfied	26
Somewhat dissatisfied	12
Very dissatisfied	14
Don't know, no answer	5

How much effort did the people at the office make to help you? Would you say it was more than they had to, about right, less than they should have, or no effort at all?

More than they had to	16%
About right	57
Less than they should have	12
No effort	9
Don't know, no answer	6

How efficient did you think the office was in handling your problem? Was it very efficient, fairly efficient, rather inefficient, or very inefficient?

Very efficient	43%
Fairly efficient	31
Rather inefficient	9
Very inefficient	11
Don't know, no answer	6

Do you feel you were treated fairly or unfairly by the office?

Fairly	76%
Unfairly	12
Mixed	5
Don't know, no answer	7

Source: Daniel Katz, Barbara A. Gutek, Robert L. Kahn, and Eugenia Barton, *Bureaucratic Encounters* (Ann Arbor: Institute for Social Research, University of Michigan, 1975), p. 64. Copyright © 1975 Institute for Social Research. Reprinted with permission.

What we seem to have are two different streams of thought running parallel to each other. On the one hand, there is a clear and genuine disaffection with "Big Government." On the other hand, however, there is a remarkably positive attitude found among Americans who have dealt with their public bureaucrats on a person-to-person basis. As one reviewer of the data concluded, "When queried in certain ways, the American public does not appear as disdainful of bureaucrats as the projected media image would indicate."[17]

There is a third facet of the role of government and the government bureaucrat in American democracy: the attitude of elected officials toward the public bureaucracy.

The opinions held by elected officials about public administrators are mixed. As Table 1-3 (which summarizes a national survey) indicates, politicians view bureaucrats as unimaginative,

TABLE 1-3 How the Public and Elected Officials View Public Bureaucrats

Description	Public (percentage agreeing)	Elected Officials (percentage agreeing)
Do things by the book	23%	60%
Play it safe	21	48
Bureaucratic	14	58
Make red tape	12	25
Dull	6	14
Corrupt	4	0
Honest	16	34

Source: Confidence and Concern: Citizens View American Government, A Survey of Public Attitudes by the Subcommittee on Intergovernmental Relations on the Committee on Government Operations, U.S. Senate (Washington, D.C.: U.S. Government Printing Office, 1973), p. 310.

prim, dull, and (unsurprisingly) "bureaucratic." Citizens are much less critical on these dimensions. But elected office holders are far more positive about bureaucrats when it comes to such basic matters as their honesty and incorruptibility; in these areas, citizens are more skeptical than are elected officials, although even on these dimensions Americans can hardly be categorized as critical.

Consider, then, the dilemma of both the public administrator and the citizen. Public administrators in American democracy must deal with a citizenry that seems pleased with their professional abilities, yet is distrustful of the institutions where public administrators work, and the officials who head those institutions. The citizenry's elected representatives, unlike the people who elected them, seem to hold public administrators in low-key contempt—a difficult situation for public administrators who are ultimately responsible to these elected officials. And, despite their best efforts, American citizens have not really shrunk the government. With the exception of a modest downturn in public employment levels in the early 1980s, government continues to grow. Why?

A Parable of Mice and Men

The following incident really happened in 1977 and 1978. It is offered without comment:

It is not only Congress but also the White House mice that have been teaching Jimmy Carter the limits of Presidential power.

When the members of the Carter entourage arrived from their country homes in Plains, Georgia, they were surprised to discover that their new city mansion at 1600 Pennsylvania Avenue was plagued with mice.

Indeed, the story goes that one night when President Carter was deep in conference with Frank B. Moore, his Congressional liaison chief, in his little hideaway office, two mice scampered across the carpet. The alarm went out to the General Services Administration, which does the housekeeping for Federal buildings, and the President turned to more weighty affairs.

But the mouse problem proved intractable. Just before the Latin American heads of government arrived in Washington for the signing of the Panama Canal treaties, one small gray creature climbed up the inside of a White House wall and died. The Oval Office was bathed with the odor of dead mouse.

Desperately, the President called the GSA. again. But the agency insisted that it had killed all the mice inside the White House and that therefore this mouse must have come from outside the building.

According to the agency, this meant that the offensive mouse was an "outside" mouse, a wayward ward of the Interior Department, which tends the grounds around the White House.

But the Interior Department demurred. It must be an "inside" mouse, said Interior officials. Moreover, regardless of its origins, it was obviously now the GSA.'s worry because the carcass was imbedded inside a White House wall.

"I can't even get a damned mouse out of my office," the President moaned to Jody Powell, his press secretary.

In frustration, he summoned two officials from each agency and lined them up before him in the stench of the Oval Office to break the bureaucratic deadlock. As a compromise solution, one aide quipped, "It took an interagency task force to get that mouse out of here."

Now, vigilant against future crises, the White House has gone on the offensive. As Mr. Powell remarked, "You can't open a desk drawer around here without getting your hand caught in a rat trap."

WHY BUREAUCRACY?

Although many explanations about why government grows have been put forth (including the guile of bureaucrats themselves), we shall review only the principal ones: political pluralism, the displacement/concentration hypothesis, and technological complexity.

Political Pluralism

Our first explanation is one that is favored by political scientists.[18] Although it is not usually employed to explain the growth of government, but rather to demonstrate how the political process is supposed to work, the pluralist model nonetheless has some utility as an explanation of why government has burgeoned in society. The basic model is this: Society is composed of a number of competing groups that have a broad range of interests, which may or may not be compatible with one another. Thus, blacks, for instance, may wish to wrest certain concessions from policymakers to accomplish their own particular ends (for example, bussing children to achieve integrated school districts). But such a gain for one group is achieved ultimately at the cost of other groups—or so it is perceived by other groups—(for instance, the inconvenience to whites that bussing may create). Hence, in the classic pluralist model one group's gain becomes another group's loss. Pluralists believe that such a process results in a social "good" on the grounds that the majority of people benefit from this contention of interest groups—provided, of course, that the basic human rights of a group or individual are not destroyed by the process. And government is the institution charged with society's responsibilities to protect these rights.

But how does the pluralist interpretation of the political process relate to a theory concerning the growth of government? The intellectual jump is not a difficult one to make, but it is worth some explanation. If government has an increasingly expanding economy from which to draw resources (*i.e.*, taxes), it becomes increasingly easier for policymakers to placate any given group, but not necessarily at the expense of other groups. With larger tax bases, more and more demands can be met by government, but without employing the traditional and necessary device of reallocating resources to do so.[19] When government's resources are scarce, and policymakers must take away resources from one program to provide funding to another program, it follows that what one group gains in the form of a new or expanded policy, another group consequently loses. With a growing economy, however, reallocative decision making is not required, or, at least, less required. Old programs can be maintained and new programs started by virtue of an increasingly expanding resource base in the form of growing industrialization, productivity, and employment—and the concomitant tax increases that these provide. Therefore, government can meet, for example, the traditional demand for an adequate national defense by letting lucrative contracts to businesses in the defense industries, and simultaneously it can assure the adequate safety of workers in those industries by setting up such devices as an Occupational Safety and Health Administration, thus meeting the demands of other groups whose values are not necessarily motivated by profit.

A secondary consequence of such a situation is that demands for government services by various groups have resulted in more government services that are wanted by some groups but not by others, and the tensions resulting from this situation may have contributed to the popular distrust and dislike of government. Nevertheless, it is this basic dynamic of competing interest groups demanding more and more resources from government—but only in the context of more available and growing resources—that serves as the basic pluralist theory explaining the growth of government.

The Displacement/Concentration Hypothesis

The traditional pluralist model of political scientists as an explanation of the growth of government is not particularly satisfying. This is not to say that the model is "wrong" but it is to say that it is awfully simple, and a more sophisticated interpretation of the growth of government is provided by economists.[20] As Alan T. Peacock and

Jack Wiseman observe in this context, economists, for the most part at least, do not base their theories on "any all-embracing theory of the state," as the political scientists implicitly do. Indeed, the assumptions of the economists in explaining the growth of government are that: "Governments like to spend more money, citizens do not like to pay more taxes, governments need to pay some attention to the wishes of their citizens."[21]

Peacock and Wiseman, for example, argue cogently that the growth of government may be attributed to two distinct features in the twentieth century. One is that certain major disturbances, such as wars, shift public revenues and expenditures to new and heretofore unimagined levels. When the disturbance has run its course, new ideas emerge as to what a tolerable tax level is, and higher plateaus of government activity in the economy are achieved and maintained; invariably, these plateaus represent a higher portion of the Gross National Product than was the case prior to the social disturbance. It is this phenomenon that Peacock and Wiseman call "the displacement effect." Economists do not assert that all social disturbances inevitably are accompanied by lasting increases in governmental expenditures, nor that the more permanent influences on the behavior of government, such as population shifts and growth, are irrelevant, but it is inescapable that the growth of government has been a reality in the twentieth century and can be traced, using economic statistics, to major periods of social disturbance. As Peacock and Wiseman observe, in Great Britain also the upward displacement of government revenues and expenditures came during and after two major disturbances, namely, World War I and World War II.

The displacement effect often is followed by an "inspection process" in society. The disturbance calls to the attention of citizens and governments new knowledge about their own society. Thus, for example, public education was seen as a desirable and social goal when the Napoleonic wars first exposed the educational deficiencies in the European lower classes. More recently, the development of British social services during World War II were the result of wartime bombing that had made the replacement of voluntary hospital services necessary; these social services eventually grew into the National Health Service after the war.[22]

Concomitant with the displacement effect and the ensuing inspection process, at least in some societies, is the "concentration process." The concentration process does not refer so much to increases in the total volume of government expenditures, but rather to the "concentration" of those expenditures at *higher* levels of government. Obviously, the concentration process can occur only in societies that have a federal form of government, such as the United States; thus, the national government acquires responsibility for public services, such as welfare, that traditionally have been the preserve of state or local governments. As we shall see in our chapter on federalism, such a concentration process has been occurring in the United States with particular rapidity during the last twenty years.

The concentration process is quite distinct from the displacement effect in the view of most economists. Economic reality, rather than social disturbance, works toward the increasing centralization of economic power by the national government relative to the state and local units. Thus, "local autonomy usually has many defenders, and its preservation is frequently a matter of political importance. At the same time, economic development produces changes in the technically efficient level of government, and also produces demands for equality of treatment (*e.g.*, in services such as education) over wider geographical areas.... Clearly, this evolution is distinct from the displacement effect, since the forces just described operate in normal as well as disturbed times."[23]

Even so, social disturbances that displace the level of government of expenditures upward also are going to have some bearing on the concentration process. Traditional political considerations often are swept aside during periods of major disturbance in a society, and some of these traditional political considerations may concern certain functions of government that "always" have been the exclusive preserve of subnational jurisdictions. As Peacock and Wiseman observe, "Periods of displacement are also going to be periods of interest from the viewpoint of the concentration process."[24]

Technobureaucracy: Bureaucracy as Interpreter of Technology

There is a third theory (there are many more, of course, but we are considering only the major explanations in this chapter), and one that owes much of its intellectual development to the futurists as opposed to the political scientists and economists.[25] Like the pluralist and displacement/concentration models, this explanation does not contradict any of the others; instead it merely amplifies the preceding two, and it will serve as this book's primary explanation of the burgeoning bureaucracy. It holds that bureaucracy is the inescapable political expression of technology. Technology, in this sense, refers to the growing complexity of society that has been brought about not merely by scientific discoveries of profound social significance, but also by the proliferating economic and social interrelationships that are associated with industrialization. Not only are purely technical complexities evident, but new and varied social relationships become apparent. "Technology," in this context, has certain conceptual relationships to what economists call "technical efficiency," and to what political scientists call "values," which are represented to policymakers by interest groups competing for resources in a pluralist political system; thus, in the political scientist's sense, both "technology" and "efficiency" are but two of many "values" to be "represented" by groups in the political process.

But the futurists' argument that technology lies behind the growth of government goes further and perhaps has more power as an explanation than either the theories of the political scientists or the economists, and one of the best empirical examples of the futurists' interpretation is provided by America itself. Ours is a technological society; indeed, the United States may be the archetype of technological societies. Computers, automation, and advanced modes of transportation and communication are developed in America first. The rest of the world adopts our technologies as experiments when they are already commonplace here. But technology brings with it new and interesting political problems. ("May you live in interesting times" is considered a curse in China.) Consider a simple one—highways.

Highway technology is one that most people can understand. The Romans, indeed, understood supremely well highways as a technology 2,500 years ago. Yet American society has grown so complex that highways have taken on new meanings as a technology. For example, in the late 1960s the U.S. Department of Housing and Urban Development (HUD) found that large and disproportionate numbers of urban rioters, notably in the Watts section of Los Angeles and in Newark, had lived in the riot areas for a year or less. Moreover, these people had recently moved to the riot-torn areas because they had been displaced from their original homes by such projects as urban renewal and highway construction. As a result, neighborhood "fabrics" were torn and former residents scattered—people became new residents in other areas; they had nothing to lose and no neighborhood to protect. Hence, building large highways through large urban areas, according to HUD officials, may have influenced the intensity of the urban riots of the late 1960s. Similarly, the interstate highway program has also spawned a major national debate over what is known as a "balanced" transportation policy. The central question in this debate is, "Do we want the automobile to remain the central mode of transportation in America at the expense of other alternative forms of transit, such as buses, trains, and subways?"

In sum, although most of us consider the highway to be relatively simple technology, it has resulted in complicated social and political problems that ultimately must be settled by the public at large. But how is the public to understand the more complex aspects of technological problems? Highways provide only one example; there are many others. Consider the problem of the computer and its role in the protection of privacy and in the gathering of social data on which to form public policy—where is the line to be drawn between the right to privacy, and the need for information and the right to know? Or consider the environment and its relationship with the energy dilemma—where does full employment end and the potential degradation of the earth begin? Still another problem is the population explosion—where does the right to life of the fetus end and the rights of the individual woman begin? Of course, these are not merely technological questions; they are also deeply moral and ethical ones. Technology, in the forms of industrialization, "the pill," and electronic data processing techniques, to mention only a few, has injected new layers of complexity that are only beginning to be understood by experts in their respective fields. Yet the political questions and the public problems that these technologies and others raise require that policies concerning them be formulated in the most broadly public sense conceivable. Nevertheless, the question stands: How is the public in a democracy to understand such issues as they pertain to these extraordinarily complex and technical questions?

The answer that has emerged in fact, if not necessarily in theory, is the public bureaucracy. Bureaucrats are hired to be specialists. They are, in a sense, experts in their particular fields. Because technology requires expertise, bureaucrats have been saddled with the responsibility of interpreting complex technological and political problems so that as many Americans as possible might understand the issues involved. Whether or not the bureaucrats do a particularly good job at this chore is another question altogether. But their abilities as specialists are one reason why they are there.

We have been suggesting in the preceding paragraphs that bureaucracy grows in large measure because technology requires expertise, and bureaucrats are the political actors who have been saddled with the responsibility of interpreting and translating complex technological and social problems into policy. By adopting this explanation of the *raison d'être* of the bureaucratic phenomenon as our primary thesis, we have posited a fundamental tension between bureaucracy and democracy. On the one hand are the bureaucrats-as-experts, the specialists with knowledge about particular professions and techniques. On the other hand are "the people," those who represent what are considered human values. To carry this dichotomy even further, we have the "computers"—the "technocrats"—squaring off against "humanity." This dichotomization, which obviously is grossly overdrawn, is nonetheless representative of the root tension between "the bureaucrats" and "the people." We consider this tension in upcoming chapters on organization theory, but for now it is enough to note that there is an inherent gap in any society between expertise, including the expertise of public administration, and populist democratic values.

BUREAUCRATIC POWER

Regardless of why the bureaucracy exists, and irrespective of why the number of bureaucrats has grown, the fact remains that the bureaucracy has power. The Founding Fathers of our nation never really addressed this "fourth branch" of government, nor did most of the founders of other nations. Karl Marx, for example, never comprehended the power of bureaucracy, and, despite the dramatic changes sweeping the Soviet Union, it remains as fine an example as any of a nation that has created a dictatorship of the bureaucrats that will likely never "wither away" in favor of a "dictatorship of the proletariat," as Marx predicted.

Staying Power

One major form of power that the bureaucracy has is simply its staying power. Perhaps the most infamous example of the staying power of public bureaucracies is the International Screwthread Commission, which one observer called the "commission that will not die."[26] Formed in 1918 by Congress with the stipulation that its life span would not exceed sixty days, it survived until 1933, when President Franklin Roosevelt ordered it abolished. But the Commission simply reformed itself as the Interdepartmental Screwthread Commission, which eventually was reestablished as the present Commission. Although most observers agree that the Commission's work was accomplished many years ago, it is still going strong.

Herbert Kaufman completed the first empirical research on the staying power of public bureaucracies and concluded, reluctantly, that it was awesome. Kaufman wanted to find out whether or not government organizations, in effect, "lived forever." To ascertain this, Kaufman determined how many U.S. government agencies had "died" (*i.e.*, were actually terminated, not just changed in name) between 1923 and 1973. He found 175 identifiably separate agencies within the government in 1923, and by 1973, not only were 109 of these same agencies still in operation, but the government agency "population" had exploded to 394 separate agencies. Only 15 percent of the original 175 had disappeared. When Kaufman compared the "death rate" of government agencies with the rate of business failures over the fifty-year period, he found that in any given year the rate of business failure exceeded the rate of agency death.[27]

Subsequent research has questioned Kaufman's conclusions about the relative immortality of government agencies, arguing that Kaufman's analysis was based on a sample of organizations which was incomplete, that his methodology was flawed in that it ignored, among other items, the large number of federal agencies that were created during the New Deal and World War II, and which were terminated following the resolution of those crises. Some have said that his definition of what would constitute a "dead" agency was far too stringent, and that if one were to adopt a more flexible concept of agency succession, then a far greater "death rate" of federal agencies would be evident.

B. Guy Peters and Bryan W. Hogwood took precisely this approach, and found that from the 1930s through the 1970s, 2,245 initiations, terminations, and various kinds of successions involving 889 federal organizations occurred over the course of this fifty-year period. As the authors concluded, "there has been a great deal of change in government over the fifty-year period we investigated. This change has included the birth of new organizations, the death of many more than might have been expected, and the metamorphoses of even more." Among other findings, Peters and Hogwood determined that "having a basis in an act of Congress does not protect an organization from termination or succession."[28]

In a sense, it is difficult to argue with either approach, in that Kaufman's approach is in many ways more straightforward, whereas Peters and Hogwood's tack is more flexible, and in many ways more complete. Nevertheless, it is a reasonable conclusion that most Americans believe, regardless of what evidence may be provided to them, that government organizations are indeed "immortal." Whether or not agencies outlive their usefulness is a question that the researchers of agency life cycles have not addressed.

Political Power

Perhaps even more important than staying power is policy-making power. It is increasingly obvious in the twentieth century that bureaucracy is the major policy-making arm of government. Consider some examples: Two little black girls are sterilized by family planning officials in Alabama. The U.S. Food and Drug Administration reverses past policy and bans cyclamates because of a single but determined biologist in its employ. A vice president of the United States resigns as the unanticipated but ultimate consequence of an investigation by a lone Justice Department lawyer in Maryland. The Pentagon Papers are released by a conscience-stricken analyst in the air force's Rand Corporation. The Watergate scandal erupts as the result of premeditated law-breaking by members of the cabinet, the White House staff, and a former president of the United States.

The preceding instances are examples of public policy being made by public administrators. Some of these policies are good, others bad. Some are confined in their social impact, others are reweaving the fabric of the American polity. All of these public policies, however, were made primarily by bureaucrats, with little or no influence from legislators or judges, and all affect the lives of people.

One should place, however, the power of bureaucrats to make public policy in perspective. In a careful, empirical, and original analysis of the federal policy-making process, John W. Kingdon found that while "no one set of actors dominates the process" of agenda setting and policymaking, "elected politicians and their appointees come closer than any other."[29] Kingdon, in fact, concluded from his study that the president and members of Congress were quite important in the initiation of new ideas and in the formation of the policy agenda for the nation. Almost equally important were top presidential appointees (who actually were ranked higher than the president in their agenda-setting influence), White House staffers, and congressional staffs. Of course, these latter groups are not elected officials, and may be considered public administrators (although they are not in the career civil service). Career civil servants, on the other hand, were considerably less important in originating new ideas for public policy and setting the national agenda, but they were extremely significant in structuring the alternative solutions that could be applied to recognized public problems. Kingdon found that "the customary distinction between line and staff bureaucrats is . . . important, because line people are particularly preoccupied with administering existing programs while staff people might have more time to concentrate on policy changes. Thus one does find staff people . . . who concentrate on legislative proposals, studies of future problems, and thinking about the directions public policy might take. . . . The career civil servants [on the other hand] may have more impact on the specification of alternatives. . . . With respect to agenda setting, then, a top-down model of the executive branch seems to be surprisingly accurate."[30]

BUREAUCRATIC SOVEREIGNTY

Public administrators also appear to have wrested control over critical policy areas from elected officials, both legislators and chief executives. A number of empirical analyses of city council members and city managers, for example, have concluded that the city manager plays a significant policy-making role in the urban political context, despite an image of being an apolitical administrator. A detailed study of San Francisco Bay Area city managers found that most of the city managers responding perceived clear political roles for themselves.[31]

Interestingly, the amount of education that city managers have attained has tended to determine whether they view themselves as "politicians" or as "administrators." Those managers who saw themselves in a highly political context tended to have majored in the social sciences or to have pursued master's degrees in public administration, but all of the responding managers felt that they should (and did) participate in the initiation, formulation, and presentation of policy proposals to their councils.

Bureaucrats and Legislators

In a much larger national study conducted by the International City Management Association,[32]

nearly 90 percent of city managers indicated that they always or nearly always participated in forming municipal policy, and this percentage was even higher in the larger cities. More than 60 percent of the managers felt that they played a leading role in making policy and, in an unusual aside, more than 12 percent reported that they always or nearly always gave political help to incumbent candidates who were up for reelection to the city council. Indeed, members of the city councils often readily accept this policy-making role by a nonelected administrator. In her study of city councils, Betty A. Zisk found that most councilmembers depended heavily upon the advice of the professional bureaucrats in making policy.[33]

Significant numbers of city managers perceive their political influence over their councilmembers to be increasing. One study indicated that 47 percent of local public managers anticipated that their policy recommendations and their role in the formulation of local policy would gain greater influence over time, in contrast to only 10 percent who thought they would lose influence as policymakers in the foreseeable future. Forty-four percent saw themselves as taking greater leadership positions in the formulation of local public opinion, compared to only 11 percent of local managers who thought that their leadership of community opinion would decline.[34]

Studies of other governmental bodies also tend to validate the hypothesis that public administrators are the policymakers. For example, in a classic study of policymaking in school boards, which are usually composed of members elected by the community, it was found that the professional school superintendent was the major formulator of board policy: "School governance has never completely fallen under the sway of the superintendent's office, but there is no question that the first half of the twentieth century saw enormous gains of power for the office."[35] In fact, the researchers concluded that in comparison with city managers in council-manager governments, superintendents exercised relatively more power over their boards than did managers over their councils.[36] A later study of school boards and superintendents found that boards adopted the policies recommended by their superintendents an astonishing 99 percent of the time; "the superintendent—far more than the board—is identified publicly as the 'governor' of education. Although superintendents are rarely selected by public election, they are, because of the expectations placed upon them, the symbol of school government."[37]

One might expect that chief executive officers who are appointed by elected officials would, at least to some degree, "naturally" assume the reigns of power in their organizations. But it also seems to be the case that bureaucrats who are appointed merely as staff assistants are also becoming increasingly influential in legislative bodies. Legislative staffs at both the state and national levels have burgeoned precipitously.

In 1960, no state legislature staffed its standing committees in either chambers, and only nine legislatures accorded their own legislative leaderships even partial staff assistance. By 1980, however, thirty-six legislatures staffed their standing committees in both chambers, and all states had a standing legislative bureaucracy. Almost two-fifths of the legislatures fund personal staffs year round and the remainder do so when the legislature is in session.[38] Currently, the nation's 7,482 state legislators pay more than 16,000 full-time legislative employees year round, a number that balloons to 25,000 employees when the legislatures are in session.[39]

A parallel growth is evident at the national level. In 1947, there were fewer than 2,500 personal and committee congressional staffers. Today, there are approximately 19,000 personal and committee congressional staffers, or about thirty-five staff members for each senator and representative, and the annual cost of Congress, in large part as a consequence of staff salaries, is nearly $1.5 billion per year.[40] So valued are these staffers that it is estimated that possibly more than 300 of them earn more than the senators and congressmen who employ them.[41]

About a quarter of these 19,000 staffers and other employees serve congressional committees; the remainder work for individual members of Congress. In addition to these personal and committee staffs, there is a growing legislative bureaucracy to which members of Congress have exclusive access. This bureaucracy includes the powerful Congressional Budget Office, which em-

ploys more than 200 people; the General Accounting Office, with more than 5,300 employees; the Office of Technology Assessment, which employs more nearly 150 people; and the Library of Congress, which has about 5,400 employees, including the Congressional Research Center with some 850 employees. These are only the principal nonpartisan staffs of the legislative bureaucracy in Washington, and they number approximately 20,000 people. When combined with Congress's 19,000 personal and committee staffers, the congressional bureaucracy totals about 40,000 employees.

We noted earlier that Kingdon's study of the policy-making process in Washington concluded that congressional staffers had significant levels of influence in the policy-making process.[42] Other studies confirm this. For example, one, an especially thorough examination of congressional staffing, observed that "staffers exert a strong influence on material with which they deal because of their position astride the office communications process, their control of factual data, and the expertise and professional judgment which they bring to their jobs . . . today's staff are more expert and are becoming increasingly specialized. . . . On occasion, they argue vigorously for or against a certain policy position."[43]

Occasionally these staffs can become extraordinarily powerful. For example, the so-called Madison group, a conservative, bipartisan collection of about a dozen congressional staff men and one woman, has been accredited with scuttling the Salt II Accords with the Soviet Union, cutting foreign aid to Nicaragua, increasing the defense budget, and initiating other policies—and this was done with no direction from the congressmen for whom they work.[44] Similarly, the experience of the House Armed Services Committee's thirty staffers indicates that when intelligent and savvy staff members are working for less informed and experienced legislators, their influence can become exceptional. The staff of the House Arms Services Committee is considered to be "among the strongest and most powerful committee staffs on Capitol Hill and. . . There is widespread agreement that members of the committee staff have more influence on military budgets, weapons and research and development than do members of the committee itself."[45]

The role of staffs at the state level, particularly in such heavily staffed legislatures as those in California, New York, and Illinois, indicates a similar experience. As a former staffer in the highly professionalized legislature in California put it, "The most remarkable discovery that I made during my tenure as a staff member was the amount of power I had over the bills on which I worked. The members relied almost entirely on staff to accurately summarize the legislation and also to develop compromises among the many interests which were brought into conflict by these bills."[46]

Bureaucrats and the Elected Executive

Just as the public bureaucrats have gained and are gaining autonomy as policymakers at the expense of legislators, public administrators also have encroached on the political independence of elected chief executives. Elected chief executives, notably presidents, are deeply aware of this encroachment. Consider some of the following comments made by presidents of the United States about "their" bureaucracy.

- Franklin Delano Roosevelt, who lamented his condition "under the shadow of the bureaucrat," bemoaned the impossibilities inherent in changing the U.S. Navy: "To change anything in the Na-a-v-y is like punching a feather bed. You punch it with your right, and you punch it with your left, until you are finally exhausted, and then you find the damn bed just as it was before you started punching." [47]
- Harry Truman: "I thought I was the president, but when it comes to these bureaucrats, I can't do a damn thing." [48]
- Dwight D. Eisenhower expressed himself as "amazed" over the naivete of his successor in dealing with the bureaucracy, who "seemed unaware of the limitations on presidential power to enforce decisions." [49]
- John F. Kennedy, Ike's successor, soon lost his innocence, and told a caller, "I agree with you, but I don't know if the government will."[50]
- Richard Nixon: "We have no discipline in this bureaucracy! We never fire anybody! We never reprimand anybody! We never demote anybody!"[51]
- Jimmy Carter, who, in the final year of his presidency, remarked, "Before I became president, I realized and was warned that dealing with the federal

bureaucracy would be one of the worst problems I would have to face. It has been worse than I had anticipated." [52]

The frustrations that elected chief executives endure in dealing with their own bureaucracies are legion, and it is little wonder that a primary objective of elected chief executives, particularly presidents, has been to gain control over their bureaucracies. Most presidents fail in this attempt.

In an enlightening analysis of "the administrative presidency," Richard P. Nathan analyzes how recent presidents have attempted to gain control over their bureaucracies, and how they have, by and large, failed. Lyndon B. Johnson, for example, thought that he had found the sole solution to the problem of controlling the bureaucracy, which Nathan calls the "single-solution syndrome," and he relied on a single professional group—economists—to implement a management control system for all of the federal government. The crux of his management control system was a budgeting technique (which we discuss in Chapter 8) called Programming-Planning-Budgeting (PPB). One day (August 25th, 1965, to be precise), and with no forewarning, Johnson dictated that the entire government was now on a PPB footing, and, while the idea may have been a grand one, its efficacy in terms of gaining presidential control over the federal bureaucracy was dubious at best. With the exception of the Department of Defense, the federal government (and many state and local governments, which were too quick to adopt it in the first place) abandoned PPB about as soon as Johnson departed the White House.

Johnson's successor, Richard Nixon, took an entirely different approach to gaining control over the bureaucracy, but also failed. At first, Nixon adopted a legislative strategy, in which he tried to push laws through Congress that would give him more control over the federal administrative apparatus, and, when that approach proved futile, he switched to an administrative strategy, in which he attempted to replace his initial appointments with Nixon loyalists. That tactic also was doomed to failure, and, as Nathan notes, "Although Nixon was on the right track, true to form he proceeded in a heavy-handed way that might well have failed even without Watergate."[53]

Jimmy Carter, who introduced a highly centralized and personal style of management to the White House, attempted to, in effect, implement his policies almost single-handedly, and became heavily involved in the details of agency operations. As one speech-writer in the Carter White House noted, Carter was a "perfectionist and accustomed to thinking that to do the job right you must do it yourself."[54] Obviously, that approach, too, failed.

These examples of presidential failure in controlling the federal bureaucracy seemed to constitute the rule of the administrative presidency, but, like any rule, there are exceptions, and among the most notable exception to this rule was the administration of Ronald Reagan, whose strategy has been largely emulated by his successor, George Bush. Like Nixon, Reagan used both a legislative and an administrative approach to gaining managerial control of the bureaucracy, but, unlike Nixon, the "Reaganauts" employed a dual approach to gaining control of the federal bureaucracy (with the notable exception of the Department of Defense) by combining both the legislative and administrative strategies, rather than using first one tack, and then the other, as Nixon had tried. Moreover, Reagan initiated his attempts to control the federal administrative apparatus immediately upon entering the White House, whereas Nixon made his attempt well into his presidency. As Nathan observes, Reagan "avoided the pitfalls of Nixon's heavy-handedness, Johnson's grand design, and Carter's atomic-submarine approach to management."[55]

Because Reagan was more successful than many elected chief executives in gaining control over the public bureaucracy, we shall devote some discussion to his tactics and why they worked. Nevertheless, it is important to keep in mind how difficult Reagan's successes were to achieve, and how limited they were.

Reagan's approach to controlling the bureaucracy was composed of five ingredients. The first was to choose cabinet officers who were loyal to both Reagan personally and to the ideology that he brought to the White House. Although appointing politically loyal men and women to cabinet positions would seem to be an obvious move, a far more typical presidential approach to cabinet appointments is to reach out to former (the president hopes) rivals, and appoint people of disparate political views and differing constituencies in an effort to heal the wounds of the campaign. When appointments such as these are made, the result frequently is an intense and immediate level of bureaucratic infighting among the cabinet secretaries and their subordinates.

A second ingredient of Reagan's administrative presidency focused on the appointment of subcabinet officials. Jimmy Carter had left such appointments to his cabinet secretaries, and this soon proved to be a serious error. Consider the following quotation from one assistant secretary who served under Carter: "There is a belief that some assistant secretaries are in business for themselves. Officially, when they testify on the Hill, they say the right thing in respect to the President's budget and legislative program, but privately, they tell committee staff members, 'I don't really think that.'"[56] Reagan did not permit this kind of administrative undermining of his agenda. Instead, his strategy was "one of having his most doctrinaire supporters in these [subcabinet] positions instead of in the more visible and exposed cabinet positions where they are more likely to be lightening rods for public criticism."[57]

A third component of Reagan's administrative presidency was how he motivated public officials. More so than most presidents, Reagan understood the more subtle levers of managerial power in Washington. Invitations to state dinners, favorable or unfavorable rumors emanating from the White House about an appointee's actions, an upbeat mention at a press conference, phone calls, notes, and favorable budget decisions, among other motivators, play an enormous role in Washington, and in government generally, relative to the private sector. Reagan also placed a greater stock than most presidents in making sure that his political appointees stayed home, rather than travelling abroad, so that they would have a better understanding of their own agencies, and he often communicated with them directly, avoiding middlemen as much as possible.

Another tactic that Reagan used in gaining control of the federal bureaucracy involved the budget, and we discuss this approach more thoroughly in Chapter 8. Suffice it to note here, however, that

Reagan was extraordinarily successful in implementing a budgetary process that enabled the president to gain more control over the bureaucracy than any of his predecessors.

Finally, Reagan understood that to truly control the bureaucracy, one had to decentralize. Nixon and Carter, perhaps more so than any other presidents, did not comprehend this admittedly paradoxical rule of bureaucratic control. Nixon provides an especially telling case in point. Rather than delegating authority to loyal subcabinet officials, Nixon, at the beginning of his second term, attempted to concentrate authority in a small group of senior advisors. This group rapidly became entangled in a miasma of details, and, as a consequence, the powers of subcabinet career officials were enhanced, rather than reduced. This strengthening of subcabinet careerists was precisely what Nixon wanted to avoid, but Nixon was late in learning that "the penetration of political officials into administrative processes is not a job that can be done, or even supervised, from the White House." [58]

We have reviewed these components of how Reagan gained control over his bureaucracy because they appeared to have worked, at least when compared with other approaches, and because they have been used so infrequently in the past. Reagan, as we have noted, in bringing the public bureaucracy to heel, provided the exception that proves the rule, but even in his administration there were spectacular failures of administrative control. Consider, for example, the grotesque cost overruns in the Department of Defense; corruption and blatant political favoritism in the Department of Housing and Urban Development that eventually cost the taxpayers millions of dollars; and, in what may turn out to be the most far-reaching example of irresponsible administration by the federal government in the history of the nation, the failure of the savings and loan associations. In the early 1990s, economists were projecting that the final bill for the losses incurred by the savings and loan associations (which were supposedly regulated, and certainly insured, by the federal government) could, over a forty-year period, exceed $500 billion including interest—a sum that amounts to more than a fourth of the annual public spending at *all* levels of American government. [59]

Control of the public bureaucracy by elected chief executives, it appears, is a highly relative notion.

Whether it is hemming in elected legislators or elected executives, it is clear that the public bureaucracy has waxed into a policy-making power of no mean proportion. Is this development "good" or "bad" for the public? We will not attempt to answer that question here, but the point stands that bureaucratic power is real and growing; and this is, in the views of many, worrisome.

KNOWLEDGE MANAGEMENT: THE BASE OF BUREAUCRATIC POWER

How has the bureaucracy grown so in political importance in modern America? The fundamental response must be that, in a highly complex and technologically oriented society such as ours, those who control and manipulate information gain power. The old saw that "knowledge is power" never has been more true than it is today. As Max Weber, the famous theorist on bureaucracy observed nearly a century ago:

The pure interest of the bureaucracy in power, however, is efficacious far beyond those areas where purely functional interests make for secrecy. . . . in facing a parliament, a bureaucracy, out of a sure power instinct, fights every attempt of the parliament to gain knowledge by means of its own experts or from interest groups. . . . bureaucracy naturally welcomes a poorly informed and hence a powerless parliament—at least insofar as ignorance somehow agrees with the bureaucracy's interests . . . [60]

More modern administrative theorists, though usually less savage in their assessments, have not seen fit to counter Weber's basic statement and, indeed, have reinforced it. One contributor to a symposium on this very topic summarized in *Public Administration Review* (the field's major journal) that, "Administration is knowledge. Knowledge is power. Administration is power," and that "this simplistic syllogism" is a major reality of our postindustrial age. [61] In a more empirical mode, investigators have noted the relationship between organizational complexity in political settings and the subsequent control that appointed administrators appear to gain. In the study of school boards cited earlier, it was found that the professional school superintendent had far more power relative to members of the school board in the big cities, substantially less power in the suburbs, and even less power in the small towns, indicating that as the more complex the political system, the more power administrators can gain.[62]

A similar conclusion can be drawn from the study conducted by the International City Management Association of city managers and city councils. The most consistent finding in the study was that, in cities of all types, more than 60 percent of the managers voiced strong opposition to a full-time, professionally paid city council: "This item evoked the strongest expression of opinion in the entire series of questions."[63] Moreover, a majority of managers opposed the provision of a full-time separate staff for the mayor, and 77 percent of the respondents reported that they always or nearly always resisted council involvement in "management issues." These strongly held opinions on the part of city managers indicate that the appointed urban chief executive is well aware that one of his major bases of political power is the control of information. A full-time professional staff for the mayor and a full-time, hard-working city council that is interested in "management issues" are anathema to the typical city manager. (Richard Nixon's chief adviser for domestic affairs, John Ehrlichman, also showed an understanding of this point when he said, "operations is policy."[64]) The urban manager is an example of the politics of expertise, a peculiar kind of political control that provides the manager with an ability to have his policies adopted by elected officials primarily because he or she controls a major source of information, the city bureaucracy itself.

EXPLORING BUREAUCRACY, UNDERSTANDING GOVERNMENT

For the better part of the twentieth century, the public bureaucracy has been not only at the center of public policy formation and the major political determinant of where this country is going, but also it expresses more articulately than any other American institution the mounting tensions between the values of the technological and information elite and the democratic and populist mass. The government bureaucracy also is the biggest conglomerate of organizations and employs more highly educated professional people than any other institution in the United States. It appears, therefore, that the public bureaucracy is worthy of some study, whether as an intellectual enterprise (so that we may learn more about how our country works), as an altruistic endeavor (so that we may learn how to promote the public interest more effectively), or as a personal investment (so that we will be more qualified for a job in government). The study of the public bureaucracy and the practice of its special skills is called *public administration.* We examine the peculiar nature and evolution of public administration as a field of academic enterprise in the following chapter.

NOTES

[1] John F. Kennedy, as quoted in Peter Goldman, et al., "The Presidency: Can Anyone do the Job?" *Newsweek* (January 26, 1981), p. 41.

[2] United Press International, "Amy's Homework Aid Likely Costs Thousands," *The Arizona Republic* (February 9, 1981).

[3] Terrence R. Mitchell and William G. Scott, "Leadership Failures, the Distrusting Public, and Prospects of the Administrative State," *Public Administration Review*, 47 (November/December 1987), p. 445; Lewis Harris and Associates, *Public Opinion Survey: Confidence in Leaders of Social Institutions* (New York: 1980 and 1984); "Public More Trusting?" *I.S.R. Newsletter* (Autumn 1983), p. 4; and Linda L.M. Bennett and Stephen Earl Bennett, *Living with Leviathan: Americans Coming to Terms with Big Government* (Lawrence, Kansas: University Press of Kansas, 1990).

[4] *Gallup Report* (Princeton, N.J.: February 7, 1985).

[5] Mitchell and Scott, "Leadership Failures, the Distrusting Public, and Prospects of the Administrative State."

[6] Gregory B. Lewis, "In Search of Machiavellian Milquetoasts: Comparing Attitudes of Bureaucrats and Ordinary People," *Public Administration Review*, 50 (March/April 1990), p. 224.

[7] As derived from: Advisory Commission on Intergovernmental Relations, *Significant Features of Fiscal Federalism*, 1988 ed., Vol. II, M-155 II (Washington, D.C.: U.S. Government Printing Office, 1988), p. 102. Figures are as of 1985.

[8] George Gallup, "Polls Show Tremendous Support for Balanced Budget Amendment," *The Arizona Republic* (February 25, 1979). Gallup has conducted similar polls since 1976 with comparable results.

[9] Advisory Commission on Intergovernmental Relations, *Significant Features of Fiscal Federalism*, 1989 ed., Vol. I,

M-163 (Washington, D.C.: U.S. Government Printing Office, 1989), pp. 12, 2.

[10] Advisory Commission on Intergovernmental Relations, *Significant Features of Fiscal Federalism, 1980—81* (Washington, D.C.: U.S. Government Printing Office, 1982), p. 48. Between 1953 and 1980, the total tax burden on the American family with an average income ($21,500 in 1980) increased by 92 percent. Most of this hike was the result of tax increases by the federal government. However, it is not yet known how the federal tax reforms of 1986 will affect taxpayers overall.

[11] Advisory Commission on Intergovernmental Relations, *Significant Features of Fiscal Federalism*, 1989 ed., Vol. II, p. 112; and Barbara Blumenthal, "Uncle Sam's Invisible Army of Employees," *National Journal* (May 5, 1979), p. 732. Data are for 1988 except for the estimate of 3 million "indirect employees" who were paid through federal contracts during the years 1979–1980. In 1988, full- and part-time civilian public employees numbered 17,281,000. More than 3 million worked for the federal government, more than 4.1 million worked for state governments, and nearly 10.1 million worked for local governments.

[12] As derived from: U.S. Bureau of the Census, *Statistical Abstract of the United States, 1990*, p. 845, Table 1456.

[13] Lewis, "In Search of Machiavellian Milquetoasts," p. 222.

[14] Harris survey as cited in Charles T. Goodsell, *The Case for Bureaucracy: A Public Administration Polemic*, 2nd ed. (Chatham, N.J.: Chatham House, 1985), p. 22.

[15] University of Michigan Survey Research Center, as cited in *ibid.*, p. 24.

[16] Several of these additional studies are cited in *ibid.*, pp. 25—26. See also: Steven A. Peterson, "Sources of Citizens' Bureaucratic Contacts: A Multivariate Analysis," *Administration and Society*, 20 (August 1988), pp. 152–165.

[17] Goodsell, *The Case for Bureaucracy*, p. 106.

[18] The single best description of the pluralist model remains that put forth in *The Federalist*, particularly "No. 10" by James Madison, but L. Harmon Zeigler and G. Wayne Peak's *Interest Groups in American Society*, 2nd ed. (Englewood Cliffs, N.J.: Prentice-Hall, 1972) is a very good elaboration on the pluralist viewpoint in a more modern context.

[19] As noted in the text, we are now moving slightly away from the traditional pluralist model. By introducing the notion of resources to pluralism, we implicitly are expanding the concept to include game theory. Many contributors to the theory of games, however, identify with political science. Game theory is explained more amply in Chapter 6 on "The Systems Approach," but suffice it to note here that game theorists would call the situation described in the text a "non-zero-sum game," or a "win-win scenario."

[20] The bulk of this discussion is drawn from Alan T. Peacock and Jack Wiseman, assisted by Jindrich Veverka, *The Growth of Public Expenditure in the United Kingdom*. A study by the National Bureau of Economic Research (Princeton, N.J.: Princeton University Press, 1961), pp. xxi—xxxi.

The displacement/concentration hypothesis as developed by Peacock and Wiseman is a refinement of the theories originated by Adolph Wagner in the late nineteenth century. Wagner set forth the "law of increasing state activity" which, to phrase it very crudely, contended that with social progress (a less than objective term in and of itself) came increased activity by government, thus intensifying the government's impact on the national economy as a whole. To quote Wagner, "Historical comparisons of different countries, at different times and places, show that in the case of culturally progressive peoples ... we can point to a regular expansion of the activity of the state and of public agencies in general. . . . The central and local governments constantly undertake new functions while they perform both old and new functions more completely and efficiently. In this way, increasingly more of the economic needs of the people...are satisfied more fully and in a better manner by the state and these other public agents. The clear proof of this development is seen in the increase of the financial needs of the central and local governments." See: Adolph Wagner, *Grundlegung der Politichen Oekonomie*, 3rd ed. (Leipzig: C. F. Winter'sche Verlags Handlung, 1893), p. 893, as quoted in: Frederick C. Mosher and Orville F. Poland, *The Costs of American Governments: Facts, Trends, Myths* (New York: Dodd, Mead, 1964), p. 20.

[21] Peacock and Wiseman, *The Growth of Public Expenditure in the United Kingdom*, p. xxiii.

[22] R. M. Titmuss, "Problems of Social Policy," *History of the Second World War*, Civil Series (London, 1950), Chap. xv, as cited in Peacock and Wiseman, *The Growth of Public Expenditure in the United Kingdom*, p. xxviii.

[23] *Ibid.*, p. xxv.

[24] *Ibid.*, p. xxv.

[25] Actually, there is no single literature of which I am aware that explains the growth of bureaucracy in precisely the same terms that I am using in the text. Nevertheless, a number of authors identified with "futures research" seem to imply it or state the explanation in different ways. A popular example would be Theodore Roszak's *The Making of a Counter Culture* (Garden City, N.Y.: Doubleday, 1969).

[26] Jim Clark, "The International Screwthread Commission," *The Washington Monthly*, as reprinted in *Doing Public Administration: Exercises, Essays, and Cases*, Nicholas Henry, ed. (Boston: Allyn and Bacon, 1978) pp. 41–42.

[27] Herbert Kaufman, *Are Government Organizations Immortal?* (Washington, D.C.: Brookings Institution, 1976).

[28] B. Guy Peters and Bryan W. Hogwood, "The Death of Immortality: Births, Deaths, and Metamorphoses in the U.S. Federal Bureaucracy, 1933–1982," *American Review of Public Administration*, 18 (June 1988), p. 131.

[29] John W. Kingdon, *Agendas, Alternatives, and Public Policies* (Boston: Little Brown, 1984), p. 47.

[30] *Ibid.*, pp. 33—34.

[31] Ronald A. Loveridge, *The City Manager and Legislative Policy* (Indianapolis, Ind.: Bobbs-Merrill, 1971).

[32] Robert J. Huntley and Robert J. McDonald, "Urban Managers: Managerial Style and Social Roles," *Municipal Year Book, 1975* (Washington, D.C.: International City Management Association, 1975), pp. 149—159. Seventy percent, or 1,744 city managers responded to the survey.

[33] Betty A. Zisk, *Local Interest Politics: A One-Way Street* (Indianapolis, Ind.: Bobbs-Merrill, 1973), p. 58.

[34] Richard J. Stillman, II, "Local Public Management in Transition: A Report on the Current State of the Profession," *Municipal Year Book, 1982* (Washington, D.C.: International City Management Association, 1982), p. 171. The figures are for 1980. The term "local public managers" includes the top appointed executive officers of cities, counties, and councils of governments. Stillman polled 3,106 cities, 195 counties, 135 councils of government that used a council-manager type plan. Not quite two-thirds of these governments responded.

[35] Harmon Zeigler and M. Kent Jennings, with the assistance of G. Wayne Peak, *Governing American Schools: Political Interaction in Local School Districts* (North Scituate, Mass.: Duxbury, 1974), p. 27.

[36] *Ibid.*, p. 251.

[37] Harvey J. Tucker and L. Harmon Zeigler, *Professionals Versus the Public: Attitudes, Communication, and Response in School Districts* (New York: Longman, 1980), p. 143. The percentage figure is found on page 144.

[38] As derived from Table 30, Council of State Governments, *The Book of the States, 1980—81* (Lexington, Ky.: Council of State Governments, 1980), p. 128; and Council of State Governments, 1961 survey, as cited in Herbert L. Wiltsee, "Legislative Service Agencies," *The Book of the States, 1961–62* (Lexington, Ky.: Council of State Governments, 1962), p. 67.

[39] William Pound, "The State Legislatures," *The Book of the States, 1982—83* (Lexington, Ky.: Council of State Governments, 1982), p. 181. Figures are for 1980.

[40] Neal R. Peirce, "The Enemy is Us: The Bloating of Legislative Staff," *Baltimore Sun* (August 25, 1983). Figures are for 1983.

[41] "Many Aides Paid more than Senators," *Washington Times* (February 16, 1983). The estimate is for 1983.

[42] Kingdon, *Agendas, Alternatives, and Public Policies*, p. 34.

[43] Harrison W. Fox, Jr. and Susan Webb Hammond, *Congressional Staffs: The Invisible Force in American Law Making* (New York: The Free Press, 1977), p. 144.

[44] William Safire, "Republicans' Young Turks," *The Arizona Republic* (December 5, 1980).

[45] Richard Halloran, "Military Panel Staff: Routes of Power," *New York Times* (June 28, 1982).

[46] Michael J. BeVier, *Politics Backstage: Inside the California Legislature* (Philadelphia: Temple University Press, 1979), p. 229.

[47] Franklin D. Roosevelt, quoted in Marriner Eccles, *Beckoning Frontiers*, Sidney Hyman, ed. (New York: Knopf, 1951), p. 336.

[48] Clinton Rossiter, *The American Presidency* (New York: New American Library, 1956), p. 42.

[49] Dwight D. Eisenhower, *The White House Years: Volume II. Waging Peace, 1956–1961* (Garden City, N.Y.: Doubleday, 1965), p. 713.

[50] John F. Kennedy, as quoted in Richard P. Nathan, *The Administrative Presidency* (New York: Macmillan, 1983), p. 1.

[51] Richard Nixon, as quoted in Richard P. Nathan, *The Plot That Failed: Nixon and the Administrative Presidency* (New York: John Wiley, 1975), p. 69.

[52] Jimmy Carter, as quoted by Haynes Johnson, "Tests," *Washington Post* (April 30, 1978).

[53] Nathan, *The Administrative Presidency*, p. 87.

[54] James Fallows, "The Passionless President," *The Atlantic Monthly* (May 1979), p. 38.

[55] Nathan, *The Administrative Presidency*, p. 88.

[56] Dom Bonafede, "Carter Sounds Retreat from 'Cabinet' Government," *National Journal* (November 18, 1978), p. 1852.

[57] Nathan, *The Administrative Presidency*, p. 90.

[58] *Ibid.*, p. 93.

[59] Paulette Thomas, "Fraud Was Only A Small Factor in S&L Losses, Consultant Asserts," *Wall Street Journal* (July 20, 1990).

[60] Max Weber, *From Max Weber: Essays in Sociology*, H. H. Gerth and C. Wright Mills, eds. (New York: Oxford University Press, 1946), p. 233.

[61] James D. Carroll, "Service, Knowledge, and Choice: The Future as Post-Industrial Administration," *Public Administration Review*, 35 (November/December 1975), p. 578. It is recommended that the reader see the "Symposium on Knowledge Management," James D. Carroll and Nicholas Henry, symposium editors, in the same issue.

[62] Zeigler and Jennings, *Governing American Schools*, pp. 177—178.

[63] Huntley and McDonald, "Urban Managers," p. 150.

[64] John Ehrlichman, quoted in Nathan, *The Plot that Failed*, p. 62.

CHAPTER

2

PUBLIC ADMINISTRATION'S CENTURY IN A QUANDARY

Public administration is a broad-ranging and amorphous combination of theory and practice; its purpose is to promote a superior understanding of government and its relationship with the society it governs, as well as to encourage public policies that are more responsive to social needs and to institute managerial practices attuned to effectiveness, efficiency, and the deeper human requisites of the citizenry. Admittedly, the preceding sentence is itself rather broad-ranging and amorphous, but for our purposes it will suffice. There are, however, additional characteristics of public administration that fill out the model we shall be using in the following chapters.

As Stephen K. Bailey noted, public administration is (or should be) concerned with the development of four kinds of theories:[1]

1. *Descriptive theory*: descriptions of hierarchical structures and relationships with their sundry task environments.
2. *Normative theory*: the "value goals" of the field, that is, what public administrators (the practitioners) ought to do given their realm of decision alternatives, and what public administrationists (the scholars) ought to study and recommend to the practitioners in terms of policy.
3. *Assumptive theory*: a rigorous understanding of the reality of the administrative person—a theory that assumes neither angelic nor satanic models of the public bureaucrat.
4. *Instrumental theory*: the increasingly refined managerial techniques for the efficient and effective attainment of public objectives.

Taken together, Bailey's quartet of theories form three defining pillars of public administration: organizational behavior and the behavior of people in public organizations; the technology of management and the institutions of policy implementation; and the public interest as it relates to individual ethical choice and public affairs.

In this chapter we review the successive definitional crises of public administration—that is, how the field has "seen itself" in the past. These paradigms of public administration are worth knowing, first, because one must know where the field has been to understand its present status, and, second, because this book represents a departure from past paradigms. We contend that public administration is unique, that it differs significantly from both political science (public administration's "mother discipline") and management (public administration's traditional alter ego) in terms of developing certain facets of organization theory and techniques of management. Public administration differs from political science in its emphasis on bureaucratic structure and behavior and in its methodologies. Public administration differs from management in that the evaluative techniques used by nonprofit public organizations are not the same as those used by profit-making private organizations. Also profit-seeking organizations are considerably less constrained in considering the public interest in their decision-making ᵢ ᵤctures, and the behavior of their administrators reflects this lack of constraint.

Public administration has developed as an academic field through a succession of five overlapping paradigms. As Robert T. Golembiewski has noted in a perceptive essay,[2] each phase may be characterized according to whether it has *locus* or *focus*. *Locus* is the institutional "where" of the field. A recurring locus of public administration is the government bureaucracy, but this has not always been the case, and often this traditional locus has been blurred. Moreover, this traditional locus is changing. *Focus* is the specialized "what" of the field. One focus of public administration has been the study of certain "principles of administration," but again, the foci of the discipline have altered with the changing paradigms of public administration. As Golembiewski observes, the paradigms of public administration may be understood in terms of locus or focus; when one has been relatively sharply defined in academic circles, the other has been conceptually ignored and vice versa. We shall use the notion of locus and focus in reviewing the intellectual development of public administration.

THE BEGINNING

Woodrow Wilson largely set the tone for the early study of public administration in an essay entitled, "The Study of Administration," published in the *Political Science Quarterly* in 1887.

In it, Wilson observed that it "is getting harder to *run* a constitution than to frame one," and called for the use of more intellectual resources in the management of the state. [3]

Wilson's seminal article has been variously interpreted by later scholars. Some have insisted that Wilson originated the "politics/administration dichotomy"—the naive distinction between "political" activity and "administrative" activity in public organizations that would plague the field for years to come. Other scholars have countered that Wilson was well aware that public administration was innately political in nature, and he made this point clear in his article. In reality, Wilson seemed ambivalent about what public administration really was. Wilson failed,

…to amplify what the study of administration actually entails, what the proper relationship should be between the administrative and political realms, and whether or not administrative study could ever become an abstract science akin to the natural sciences. [4]

Nevertheless, Wilson unquestionably posited one unambiguous thesis in his article that has had a lasting impact on the field: Public administration was worth studying. Political scientists would later create the first identifiable paradigm of public administration around Wilson's contention.

PARADIGM 1:
THE POLITICS/ADMINISTRATION DICHOTOMY, 1900–1926

Our benchmark dates for the Paradigm 1 period correspond to the publication of books written by Frank J. Goodnow and Leonard D. White; these dates, like the years chosen as marking the later periods of the field, are only rough indicators. In *Politics and Administration* (1900), Goodnow contended that there were "two distinct functions of government," which he identified with the title of his book. "Politics," said Goodnow, "has to do with policies or expressions of the state will," while administration "has to do with the execution of these policies."[5] Separation of powers provided the basis of the distinction. The legislative branch, aided by the interpretive abilities of the judicial branch, expressed the will of the state and formed policy; the executive branch administered those policies impartially and apolitically.

The emphasis of Paradigm 1 was on locus—where public administration should be. Clearly, in the view of Goodnow and his fellow public administrationists, public administration should center in the government's bureaucracy. While the legislature and judiciary admittedly had their quanta of "administration," their primary responsibility and function remained the expression of the state will. The initial conceptual legitimation of this locus-centered definition of the field, and one that would wax increasingly problematic for academics and practitioners alike, became known as the politics/administration dichotomy.

The phrase that came to symbolize this distinction between politics and administration was, "there is no Republican way to build a road." The reasoning was that there could only be one "right" way to spread macadam—the administrative engineer's way. What was ignored in this statement, however, was that there was indeed a Republican way to decide whether the road needed building, a Republican way to choose the location for the road, a Republican way to purchase the land, a Republican way to displace the people living in the road's way, and most certainly a Republican way to let contracts for the road. There was also, and is, a Democratic way, a Socialist way, a Liberal way, even an Anarchist way to make these "administrative" decision as well. In retrospect, the politics/administration dichotomy posited by Goodnow and his academic progeny was, at best, naive. But many years would pass before this would be fully realized within public administration's ranks.

Public administration received its first serious attention from scholars during this period largely as a result of the "public service movement" that was taking place in American universities in the early part of this century. Political science, as a report issued in 1914 by the Committee on Instruction in Government of the American Political Science Association stated, was concerned with training for citizenship, for the professions, such as law and journalism, and for "experts and to prepare specialists for governmental positions," and for educating scholars for research

work.[6] Public administration, therefore, was something more than a significant subfield of political science; indeed, it was a principal reason of being for the discipline.

As an indication of public administration's importance to political science, a Committee on Practical Training for Public Service was established in 1912 by the American Political Science Association, and, in 1914, its report recommended with unusual foresight that special "professional schools" were needed to train public administrators, and that new technical degrees might also be necessary for this purpose.[7] This committee formed the nucleus of the Society for the Promotion of Training for the Public Service, founded in 1914—the forerunner of the American Society for Public Administration, which was established in 1939.

The relations between the "public administrationists" (i.e., the academics) and the public administrators (i.e., the practitioners) were at this time quite close—indeed, little distinction was made between the two. The New York Bureau of Municipal Research, founded in 1906 by public-spirited philanthropists, was created to improve the management of local government, and in 1911 it established (and ran) the nation's first school of public administration, the Training School for Public Service, with Charles A. Beard as its first director, later succeeded by Luther Gulick. In 1924, the School, which had produced the nation's first trained corps of public administrators, was transferred lock, stock, and student body to Syracuse University, where it became the nation's first public administration program to be associated with a university—the Maxwell School of Citizenship and Public Affairs.[8]

In 1915, the Bureau of Municipal Research created the Government Research Association as a means of bringing together its Training School's graduates for annual conferences, a practice that it continued until 1932, when the Depression struck. The Association was, along with the Society for the Promotion of Training for the Public Service, an early forebear of the American Society for Public Administration.[9]

Public administration began picking up academic legitimacy in the 1920s; notable in this regard was the publication of Leonard D. White's

Introduction to the Study of Public Administration in 1926, the first textbook entirely devoted to the field. As Waldo has pointed out, White's text was quintessentially American Progressive in character and, in its quintessence, reflected the general thrust of the field: Politics should not intrude on administration; management lends itself to scientific study; public administration is capable of becoming a "value-free" science in its own right; the mission of administration is economy and efficiency, period.[10]

The net result of Paradigm 1 was to strengthen the notion of a distinct politics/administration dichotomy by relating it to a corresponding value/fact dichotomy. Thus, everything that public administrationists scrutinized in the executive branch was imbued with the colorings and legitimacy of being somehow "factual" and "scientific," whereas the study of public policymaking and related matters was left to the political scientists. The carving up of analytical territory between public administrationists and political scientists during this locus-oriented stage can be seen today in universities: It is the public administrationists who teach organization theory, budgeting, and personnel; political scientists teach such subjects as American government, judicial behavior, the presidency, state and local politics, and legislative process, as well as such "non-American" fields as comparative politics and international relations.

A secondary implication of this locus-centered phase was the isolation of public administration from such other fields as business administration, which had unfortunate consequences when these fields began their own fruitful explorations into the nature of organizations. Finally, largely because of the emphasis on "science" and "facts" in public administration and the substantial contributions by public administrationists to the emerging field of organization theory, a foundation was laid for the later "discovery" of certain scientific "principles" of administration.

PARADIGM 2: THE PRINCIPLES OF ADMINISTRATION, 1927–1937

In 1927, W. F. Willoughby's, *Principles of Public Administration* was published as the second full-

fledged text in the field. Although Willoughby's *Principles* was as fully American Progressive in tone as White's *Introduction*, its title alone indicated the new thrust of public administration: That certain scientific principles of administration existed; they could be discovered; and that administrators would be expert in their work if they learned how to apply these principles.

It was during the phase represented by Paradigm 2 that public administration reached its reputational zenith. Public administrationists were courted by industry and government alike during the 1930s and early 1940s for their managerial knowledge. Thus the focus of the field—its essential expertise in the form of administrative principles—waxed, while no one thought too seriously about its locus. Indeed, the locus of public administration was everywhere, since principles were principles and administration was administration, at least according to the perceptions of Paradigm 2. By the very fact that the principles of administration were indeed *principles*—that is, by definition, they "worked" without exception in any administrative setting, regardless of culture, function, environment, mission, or institutional framework—it therefore followed that they could be applied successfully anywhere. Furthermore, because public administrationists had contributed as much if not more to the formulation of "administrative principles" as had researchers in any other field of inquiry, it also followed that public administrationists should lead the academic pack in applying them to "real-world" organizations, public or otherwise.

Among the more significant works relevant to this phase were Mary Parker Follet's *Creative Experience* (1924), Henri Fayol's *Industrial and General Management* (1930), and James D. Mooney and Alan C. Reiley's *Principles of Organization* (1939), all of which delineated varying numbers of overarching administrative principles. Organization theorists often dub this school of thought "administrative management," since it focused on the upper hierarchical echelons of organizations. A related literature that preceded the work in administrative management somewhat in time, but which was under continuing development in business schools, focused on the assembly line. Researchers in this stream, often called "scientific management," developed principles of efficient physical movement for optimal assembly-line efficiency. The most notable contributions to this literature were Frederick W. Taylor's *Principles of Scientific Management* (1911) and various works by Frank and Lillian Gilbreth. While obviously related in concept, scientific management had less effect on public administration during its principles phase because it focused on lower-level personnel in the organization.

The lack of locus, if not, perhaps, the sharpening new focus of public administration during this period, made itself evident within the university community. In 1935, the Public Administration Clearing House held a conference at Princeton University, and the conference's report was radically different from the report issued in 1914 by the Committee on Practical Training for Public Service of the American Political Science Association. Suddenly political scientists had great difficulties with the idea of founding separate schools of public administration and they believed instead that existing courses in political science departments and in other relevant disciplines, such as law, economics, and management, provided, if they were correctly combined, an education that was entirely adequate for budding government bureaucrats. The conference, therefore, found itself "unable to find any single formula which warrants the establishment of an isolated college or university program which alone will emphasize preparation exclusively for the public service." Only a "university-wide approach" would be satisfactory, since the problem of public administration education exceeded the "confines of any single department or special institute or school."[11]

As a more modern scholar has since observed, "A logical consequence of this reasoning" as expressed by the Princeton Conference of 1935, "could have been the elimination of public administration as a discrete field of study within the universities."[12] Such were the dangers of not having a firm and stationary intellectual locus on which to build a curriculum.

Despite these difficulties, however, scholars who identified with the study of public administration nonetheless found it useful to establish, four years after the publication of the Princeton report, the American Society for Public Administration

(ASPA), which continues to function as the nation's primary association of scholars and practitioners of public administration, and as the sponsoring organization of the field's premier journal, *Public Administration Review*. But the creation of ASPA was less a response to the difficulties that the field of public administration was having within universities generally, and more a reaction to what public administrationists were experiencing within political science departments specifically. As Dwight Waldo has put it, "The sense that political science as an academic discipline did not adequately represent and nurture the needs of those interested in improving performance in public administration was a strong motivating force in creating the new organization. In retrospect, it is clear that ASPA represented above all an attempt to loosen public administration from the restraints of political science....."[13]

But the founding of ASPA was more than that: It was also an attempt to loosen public administration from the restraints of the citizenry. ASPA was created by practitioners and scholars of public administration for practitioners and scholars of public administration; its founding also was a secession from the Government Research Association, which was composed not only of practitioners and scholars, but also of taxpayers, citizen-based government reform groups, elected politicians, and philanthropists. Darrell L. Pugh, ASPA's historian and archivist, puts it cogently: "ASPA's formation...symbolized an end to the historic union by facilitating its fragmentation in favor of a new coalition based on professionalism."[14] Professionalism is, by definition, a phenomenon predicated on planned career ladders, closely held in-group values, an eschewing of popular "politics," and intimate ties with the universities; ASPA was all of these.

As with any proposed secession, its execution was not easy. Public administrationist Donald C. Stone recalls the emotions involved at ASPA's founding: "Questions of loyalty, sedition, intrigue, separatism, and schism kindled emotions."[15] Golembiewski has summed it up: the birth of ASPA was "an expression of the felt needs of the burgeoning graduates and faculty of suddenly virile programs of public administration. So much was at stake, practically as well as intellectually."[16]

The secession succeeded, and it symbolized public administration's conscious need to become a profession and a discipline. But professions have their own orthodoxies, and the "high noon of orthodoxy," as it has often been called, of public administration was marked by the publication in 1937 of Luther H. Gulick and Lyndall Urwick's *Papers on the Science of Administration*. This landmark study also marked the high noon of prestige for public administration. Gulick and Urwick were confidantes of President Franklin D. Roosevelt and advised him on a variety of matters managerial; their *Papers* were a report to the President's Committee on Administrative Science.

Principles were important to Gulick and Urwick, but where those principles were applied was not; focus was favored over locus, and no bones were made about it. As they said in the *Papers*,

It is the general thesis of this paper that there are principles which can be arrived at inductively from the study of human organizations which should govern arrangements for human association of any kind. These principles can be studied as a technical question, irrespective of the purpose of the enterprise, the personnel comprising it, or any constitutional, political or social theory underlying its creation.[17]

Gulick and Urwick promoted seven principles of administration and, in so doing, gave students of public administration that snappy anagram, POSDCORB. POSDCORB was the final expression of administrative principles. It stood for:

P lanning
O rganizing
S taffing
D irecting
C
O ordinating
R eporting
B udgeting

That was public administration in 1937.

THE CHALLENGE, 1938–1947

In the following year, mainstream public administration received its first real hint of conceptual challenge. In 1938 Chester I. Barnard's *The Functions of the Executive* appeared. Its impact on public administration was not overwhelming at the time, but it later had considerable influence on Herbert A. Simon when he was writing his devastating critique of the field, *Administrative Behavior*. The impact of Barnard's book may have been delayed because, as a former president of New Jersey Bell Telephone, he was not a certified member of the public administration community.

Dissent from mainstream public administration accelerated in the 1940s in two mutually reinforcing directions. One objection was that politics and administration could never be separated in any remotely sensible fashion. The other was that the principles of administration were something less than the final expression of managerial rationality.

Demurring to the Dichotomy

Although inklings of dissent began in the 1930s, a book of readings in the field, *Elements of Public Administration*, edited in 1946 by Fritz Morstein Marx, was one of the first major volumes to question the assumption that politics and administration could be dichotomized. All fourteen articles in the book were written by practitioners and indicated a new awareness that what often appeared to be value-free "administration" was actually value-laden "politics." Was a technical decision on a budgetary emphasis or a personnel change really impersonal and apolitical, or was it actually highly personal, highly political, and highly preferential? Was it ever possible to discern the difference? Was it even worth attempting to discern the difference between politics and administration if, in reality, there was none? Was the underpinning belief in politics/administration dichotomy of the field, at best, naive? Many academics and practitioners alike were beginning to think so.

Allen Schick in his superb analysis, "The Trauma of Politics: Public Administration in the Sixties," observes that the intellectuals' abandonment of the politics/administration dichotomy in the 1940s has been overstated in more recent years, and that those advocating its abandonment never intended to argue that something called "administration" and something called "politics" were totally inseparable. The challengers of the 1940s only wished to emphasize that public administrators, as well as legislators, made political decisions and public policies:

Public administration always has served power and the powerful...the service of power was pro bono publico, to help power holders govern more effectively. The presumption was that everyone benefits from good government...the constant concern with power was masked by the celebrated dichotomy between politics and administration. But the dichotomy, rather than keeping them apart, really offered a framework for bringing politics and administration together...the dichotomy provided for the ascendancy of the administration over the political: efficiency over representation, rationality over self-interest. ...In the end, the dichotomy was rejected not because it separated politics and administration but because it joined them in a way that offended the pluralist norms of postwar political science.[18]

Puncturing the Principles

Arising simultaneously with the challenge to the traditional politics/administration dichotomy of the field was an even more basic contention: that there could be no such thing as a "principle" of administration. In 1946 Simon gave a foreshadowing of his *Administrative Behavior* in an article entitled, appropriately, "The Proverbs of Administration," published in *Public Administration Review*. The following year, in the same journal, Robert A. Dahl published a searching piece, "The Science of Public Administration: Three Problems." In it he argued that the development of universal principles of administration was hindered by the obstructions of values contending for preeminence in organizations, the differences in individual personalities, and the social frameworks that varied from culture to culture. Waldo's major work also reflected this theme. His *The Administrative State: A Study of the Political Theory of American Public Administration* (1948) attacked the notion of immutable principles of administration, the inconsistencies of the methodology used in determining them, and the narrowness of the "values" of economy and efficiency that dominated the field's thinking.

The most formidable dissection of the principles notion, however, appeared in 1947: Simon's *Administrative Behavior: A Study of Decision-Making Processes in Administration Organization.*

Simon showed that for every "principle" of administration there was a counterprinciple, thus rendering the whole idea of principles moot. For example, the traditional administrative literature argued that bureaucracies must have a narrow "span of control" if orders are to be communicated and carried out effectively. "Span of control" meant that a manager could properly "control" only a limited number of subordinates; after a certain number was exceeded (authorities differed on just what the number was), communication of commands became increasingly garbled and control became increasingly ineffective and "loose." An organization that followed the principle of narrow span of control would have a "tall" organization chart (see Figure 2-1).

Span of control made sense up to a point. Yet, as Simon observed, the literature on administration argued with equal vigor for another principle: If

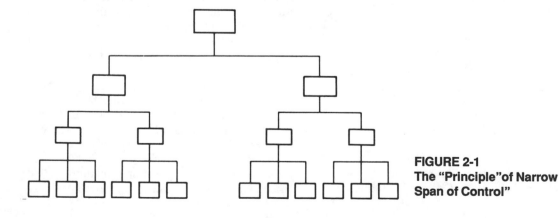

FIGURE 2-1
The "Principle" of Narrow Span of Control"

organizations were to maximize effective communication and to reduce distortion (thereby enhancing responsiveness and control), then there should be as few hierarchical layers as possible—that is, there should be a "flat" hierarchical structure. The logic behind this principle was that the fewer people who had to pass a message up or down the hierarchy, the more likely it would be that the message would arrive at its appointed destination relatively intact and undistorted. This, too, made sense up to a point. The "flat" hierarchy required to bring the bureaucracy into accord with this principle of administration would have an organization chart like that in Figure 2.2.

Obviously to Simon, and now to us, the two "principles" were mutually contradictory, and therefore by definition they could not be principles. This dilemma encompassed the whole of the traditional public administration literature, but it was never more than suspected of being so stark a case until Simon published his book.

But Simon went beyond merely pointing out inconsistencies in the traditional literature of public administration. More important, he reconceived the entire field.

Simon understood that administrative decision makers wanted to make rational choices (*i.e.*, the single "best" choice) but that there were a lot of variables standing in the way of locating the single most rational decision. In his book, Simon made the field aware that there were limits on information and computational abilities within any human institution. Where the purveyors of administrative principles had erred, in Simon's view, was in their assumptions that all alternatives were known, that the consequences of choosing any one of those alternatives were equally known, and that decision makers doggedly searched until they found the single best alternative from the standpoint of their own preferences. In questioning these assumptions, Simon argued that choices had to be discovered by searching for them; that typically only a relatively few alternatives could be considered;

that information also had to be sought through a search process; and that decision makers did not select the single best alternative, but instead "satisficed," or chose the alternative that both satisfied and sufficed from their point of view.

Simon's perspective was less economic than behavioral. In contrast to the literature that argued for principles of administration, Simon suggested a more human process of decision making. Hence, Simon argued that the constraints on organizational choices should include not only those external factors found in the task environment of organizations, but also those constraints that existed as part of the human condition, such as limits on memory, rationality, and information. These notions ultimately waxed into Simon's theory of "bounded rationality," or the idea that people are rational decision makers—within limits. The ultimate effect of Simon's *Administrative Behavior* (other than earning him the Nobel Prize in 1978) and related critiques appearing in the late 1940s was to bury the belief that principles of administration, public or otherwise, could be discovered in the same sense that laws of science and nature could be.[19]

By mid-century the two defining pillars of public administration—the politics/administration dichotomy and the principles of administration—had been abandoned by creative intellects in the field. This abandonment left public administration bereft of a distinct epistemological and intellectual identity.

REACTION TO THE CHALLENGE, 1947–1950

In the same year that Simon decimated the traditional foundations of public administration in *Administrative Behavior*, he offered an alternative to the old paradigms. For Simon, a new paradigm for public administration meant that there ought to be two kinds of public administrationists working in harmony and with reciprocal

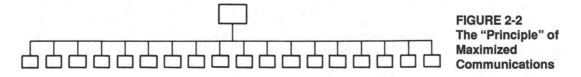

FIGURE 2-2
The "Principle" of
Maximized
Communications

intellectual stimulation: those scholars concerned with developing "a pure science of administration" based on "a thorough grounding in social psychology," and a larger group concerned with "prescribing for public policy." This latter enterprise was far-ranging indeed. In Simon's view, prescribing for public policy "cannot stop when it has swallowed up the whole of political science; it must attempt to absorb economics and sociology as well." Nevertheless, both a "pure science of administration" and "prescribing for public policy" would be mutually reinforcing components: "There does not appear to be any reason why these two developments in the field of public administration should not go on side by side, for they in no way conflict or contradict."[20]

Despite a proposal that was both rigorous and normative in its emphasis, Simon's call for a "pure science" put off many scholars in public administration. For one thing, there already existed a growing irritation in the field with POSDCORB and other "principles of administration" on the basis of their implicit claims of representing a "pure science"; the challengers of the late 1940s had shown that the "principles of administration" were hardly the final expression of science, and consequently public administrationists were increasingly skeptical that the administrative phenomenon could be understood in wholly scientific terms. Second, Simon's urging that social psychology provided the basis for understanding administrative behavior struck many public administrationists as foreign and discomfiting; most of them had no training in social psychology. Third, since science was perceived as being "value-free," it followed that a "science of administration" logically would ban public administrationists from what many of them perceived as their richest sources of inquiry: normative political theory, the concept of the public interest, and the entire spectrum of human values. While this interpretation may well have rested on a widespread misinterpretation of Simon's thinking (understandable, perhaps, given the wake of *Administrative Behavior*), as Golembiewski contends,[21] the reaction nonetheless was real.

The threat posed by Simon and his fellow challengers of the traditional paradigms was clear not only to most political scientists but to many public administrationists as well. For their part the public administrationists had both a carrot and a stick as inducements not only to remain within political science but also to strengthen the intellectual linkages between the fields. The carrot was the maintenance of the logical conceptual connection between public administration and political science—that is, the public policy-making process. Public administration considered the "internal" stages of that process: the formulation of public policies within public bureaucracies and their delivery to the polity. Political science was perceived as considering the "external" stages of the process: the pressures in the polity generating political and social change. There was a certain logic in retaining this linkage in terms of epistemological benefits to both fields. The stick, as we have noted, was the worrisome prospect of retooling only to become a technically oriented "pure science" that might then lose touch with political and social realities in an effort to cultivate an engineering mentality for public administration.

As we also have noted, political scientists, for their part, had begun to resist the growing independence of public administrationists and to question the field's action orientation as early as the mid-1930s. Political scientists, rather than advocating a public service and executive preparatory program as they had in 1914, began calling for, in the lucid and graceful phrases of Lynton K. Caldwell, the "intellectualized understanding" of the executive branch, rather than "knowledgeable action" on the part of public administrators.[22] In 1952 Roscoe Martin wrote an article appearing in the *American Political Science Review* calling for the continued "dominion of political science over public administration."[23]

By the post–World War II era political scientists were well under the gun, and could ill afford the breakaway of their most prestigious subfield. The discipline was in the throes of being shaken conceptually by the "behavioral revolution" that had occurred in other social sciences. The American Political Science Association was in financially tight straits. Political scientists were aware that not only had public administrationists threatened secession in the past, but now other subfields, such as international relations, were restive. And in terms of both science and social science, it was increasingly evident that political science was held in low esteem by scholars in other fields. The formation of the National Science Foundation in 1950 brought the message to all who cared to listen that the chief federal science agency considered political science to be the distinctly junior member of the social sciences, and in 1953 David Easton confronted this lack of status directly in his influential book, *The Political System*.[24]

The capitulation of the public administrationists to pressures brought on them by political scientists and their own self-doubt about where the field was and should be going was expressed beyond cavil in the major public administration journal in 1950. John Merriman Gaus, a prestigious public administration scholar, penned his oft quoted dictum in the tenth anniversary issue of *Public Administration Review*: "A theory of public administration means in our time a theory of politics also."[25] The die was cast.

PARADIGM 3: PUBLIC ADMINISTRATION AS POLITICAL SCIENCE, 1950–1970

As a result of these essentially political concerns and the icy intellectual critiques of the field, public administrationists leaped back with some alacrity into the mother discipline of political science. The result was a renewed definition of locus—the governmental bureaucracy—but a corresponding loss of focus. Should the mechanics of budgets and public personnel policies be studied exclusively? Or should public administrationists consider the grand philosophic schemata of the "administrative Platonists" (as one political scientist called them),[26] such as Paul Appelby? Or should they, as urged by Simon, explore quite new fields of inquiry such as sociology, business administration, and social psychology as they related to the analysis of organizations and decision making?

In brief, this third phase of definition was largely an exercise in reestablishing the conceptual linkages between public administration and political science. But the consequence of this exercise was to "define away" the field, at least in terms of its analytical focus, its essential "expertise." Thus, writings on public administration in the 1950s

spoke of the field as an "emphasis," an "area of interest," or even as a "synonym" of political science.[27] Even long-standing friends of public administration expressed their concern during this period. Frederick Mosher, for example, concluded, "Public administration stands in danger of…senescence",[28] while Martin Landau stated his deeply held worry that public administration, "that lusty young giant of a decade ago, may now 'evaporate' as a field."[29]

These concerns, which focused largely on the research agenda of the field, were reflected in the curriculum of public administration as well. A survey conducted in 1961 of graduate education in public administration found such enormous diversity of forms and emphases in university programs[30] that one observer could accurately state, "The study of public administration in the United States is characterized by the absence of any fully comprehensive intellectual framework."[31] Public administration, as an identifiable field of study, began a long, downhill spiral.

Things got relatively nasty by the end of the decade and, for that matter, well into the 1960s. In 1962 public administration was not included as a subfield of political science in the report of the Committee on Political Science as a Discipline of the American Political Science Association. In 1964, a major survey of political scientists indicated a decline in faculty interest in public administration generally.[32] In 1967, public administration disappeared as an organizing category in the program of the annual meeting of the American Political Science Association. Waldo wrote in 1968 that "many political scientists not identified with Public Administration are indifferent or even hostile; they would sooner be free of it," and added that the public administrationist has an "uncomfortable" and "second-class citizenship."[33] Between 1960 and 1970, only 4 percent of all the articles published in the five major political science journals dealt with public administration.[34] In the 1960s, "P.A. types," as they often were called in political science faculties, pretty much shuffled through political science departments.

At least two developments occurred during this period that reflect in quite different ways the gradually tightening tensions between public administrationists and political scientists: the growing use of the case study as an epistemological device, and the rise and fall of comparative and development administration as subfields of public administration.

Case Studies

The development of the case method began in the 1930s, largely under the aegis of the Committee on Public Administration of the Social Science Research Council.[35] Typically, cases were reports written by practicing public administrators on managerial problems and how they solved them. This framework gave way in the mid-1940s to a new version conceived in the Graduate School of Public Administration at Harvard University (as it was then called), which followed the lines of the public administration case study as we know it today. A joint, four-university program with foundation support resulted, called the Committee on Public Administration Cases. The Committee, in turn, engendered adequate interest in the case method to encourage the establishment in 1951 of the Inter-University Case Program.

The Inter-University Case Program published a spate of excellent public administration case studies, but began to falter in the 1970s; fortunately, the cause of the case study was taken up in 1977 by the newly formed Education for Public Service Clearing House Project, supported by grants from the Ford and Sloan Foundations. The Project lasted only a year, but succeeded in publishing a useful bibliography of public administration cases. In 1978, a successor organization, the Public Policy and Management Program for Case/Curriculum Development, was created via grants provided by the Sloan and Exxon Education Foundations, and was housed in the Intercollegiate Case Clearing House, a group that had been founded in 1957 with the purpose of developing case studies for business schools. The Intercollegiate Case Clearing House expired in 1980, but the Public Policy and Management Program for Case/Curriculum Development survived (and thrived) until 1985; it ultimately published three additional bibliographies of case studies, and developed a number of new cases. Currently, case development in public administration is conducted by the Association for

Public Policy and Management, which took over the activities (but not the grants, which terminated in 1985) of the Public Policy and Management Program for Case/Curriculum Development.[36]

The significance of the case study to the development of the field of public administration is a somewhat peculiar one, quite aside from the innate value of the case method as a simulation-based teaching device and as an extraordinarily effective vehicle for illuminating questions of moral choice and decision-making behavior in the administrative milieu. Waldo believes that the emergence of the case method in the late 1940s and its growth throughout the 1950s reflect the response of public administrationists to the "behavioral revolution" in the social sciences generally. On the one hand, the traditional public administrationists, particularly those who entered the field in the 1930s, welcomed the case method as a means of being empirical and "behavioral," and thus providing an additional way of reestablishing the linkages between their field and political science. The case study also offered a comfortable alternative to Simon's call for a rigorous, "pure science of administration" that could—probably would—necessitate a methodological retooling on their part. On the other hand, those public administrationists who entered the field later, and who had been academically reared in political science departments when behaviorism was very much in vogue, were not especially at home with the case study as public administration's answer to the challenge of the behaviorists, but they temporarily agreed to the case study method as an uneasy compromise. There was also a third grouping of public administrationists in the 1950s and 1960s who embraced the case study: the retired government bureaucrats, who were occasionally hired by political science departments when public administration was held in low academic esteem but was in relatively high student demand. This group appreciated an intellectual approach to the field that identified closely with administrative experience.

The scholarly uneasiness surrounding the use of the case method (which has never had the impact on public administration education that it has had in the business schools, although there are signs that use of the case method in public administration may now be making a comeback)

reflected the condition of public administration at that time: a band of dispirited scholars, isolated from their colleagues, but trying to cope in the only way they knew how. But this generalization did not apply to another group of "P. A. types": those who tilled the modish (and financially fertile) fields of comparative and development administration.

Comparative and Development Administration

Cross-cultural public administration, as the comparative approach also is called, is a fairly new development in the field. Prior to the abandonment of the principles of administration, it was assumed that cultural factors did not make any difference in administrative settings because principles, after all, were principles. As White said in 1936, a principle of administration "is as useful a guide to action in the public administration of Russia as of Great Britain, of Irak as of the United States."[37] But, as Dahl and Waldo, among others, would later point out, cultural factors could make public administration on one part of the globe quite a different animal from public administration on another part.[38] By the late 1940s, in fact, courses in comparative public administration were appearing in university catalogs, and by the early 1950s the American Political Science Association, the American Society for Public Administration, and the Public Administration Clearing House were forming special committees or sponsoring conferences on comparative public administration. The real impetus came in 1962 when the Comparative Administration Group (CAG, founded in 1960) of the American Society for Public Administration received financing from the Ford Foundation that eventually totaled about $500,000.

The Ford Foundation's support of comparative administration (which has since stopped) appears to have stemmed from an altruistic interest in bettering the lot of poor people in the Third World through the improvement of governmental efficiency in the developing nations, and from a political interest in arresting the "advance of communism," especially in Asia, by entrenching bureaucratic establishments composed of local elites—remember, the Ford Foundation's initial decision to support the field in a big way came at the height of the cold war.

The Foundation's emphasis on the Third World was especially enriching to a semiautonomous subfield of comparative public administration called development administration, which concentrates on the developing nations. Ironically, as we shall shortly see, the practical (if somewhat naive) motivations of the Ford Foundation underlying its funding of comparative and development administration were seldom shared by the recipients of the Foundation's grants.

Comparative public administration, as Ferrel Heady has explained, addresses five "motivating concerns" as an intellectual enterprise: the search for theory; the urge for practical application; the incidental contribution to the broader field of comparative politics; the interest of researchers trained in the tradition of administrative law; and the comparative analysis of ongoing problems of public administration.[39] Much of the work in comparative public administration revolves around the ideas of Fred W. Riggs, who "captured" (to quote one assessment)[40] the field's early interest in public administration in the developing nations, and who was simply a very prolific writer and substantial contributor to the theoretical development of the subfield in its early stages. From 1960 to 1970, when the subfield dominated comparative public administration, Riggs chaired ASPA's Comparative Administration Group.[41]

It was and is Riggs's intention and the intention of the comparative public administrationists generally to use their field as a vehicle for stiffening and strengthening theory in public administration. To borrow Riggs's terminology, comparative public administration is to do this by being empirical, nomothetic, and ecological; that is, put crudely, factual and scientific, abstracted and generalizable, systematic and nonparochial. In this emphasis, there always was a quantum of distaste in the ranks of CAG for studies that are rooted solely in the American experience.

Public administration has two differences with its comparative subfield. One is that the larger field is forthrightly and frankly culture bound. The defense of American public administration's "parochialism" is much the same as that for the "parochialism" of the behavioral sciences generally, and it is composed of four main points:

1. All empirical theory rests on the values of science that guide the conduct of the scientific method.
2. The choice of subjects to study usually reflects the researcher's socialization in and the needs of his or her own society.
3. Since humankind is the object of study in the behavioral sciences, then humanity's values, viewpoints, and culture must be included as part of the theory to be developed, notably as intervening variables in correlational analyses.
4. The uses to which public administration theory and data are put in practice inevitably must be culture bound.

A second difference that public administration generally has with comparative public administration specifically is the question of action versus theory. From its origins, American public administration has attempted to be "practitioner-oriented" and to be involved with the "real world," while comparative public administration, from its origins, has attempted to be "theory-building" and to seek knowledge for the sake of knowledge. Increasingly, this purely scholarly (as opposed to professional) thrust of comparative public administration has boded ill for the subfield. A spokesperson for the chief financier of CAG, the Ford Foundation, asked what "all this theorizing and all this study will amount to" in terms of improving the practice of public administration, and no one in comparative public administration ever really answered him.[42] In fact, the dominant theme among the members of CAG (although perhaps less emphatically among those involved in development administration) seemed to be to stick to their intellectual guns, and keep building theory as they perceived it. A survey of the CAG membership conducted in 1967 revealed that there was not a

...strongly stated appeal for linking the theoreticians with the practitioners...nor for an investment of resources in stimulating empirical research, nor for pursuing the work of the CAG into such practical realms as training and consulting.....[P]roposals to channel CAG efforts into the sphere of action received very short shrift among respondents.[43]

Not surprisingly, perhaps, the Ford Foundation terminated its support of CAG in 1971.

Comparative public administration has been productive and active as a subfield; reports of its death are premature, although comparative public administration does appear to have reached a critical point of development. Although CAG had achieved a membership of more than 500 by 1968, in 1973 it was disbanded and merged with the International Committee of the American Society for Public Administration. Relatedly, the field's major journal, *The Journal of Comparative Administration*, was terminated in 1974 after five years of publication. Analyses of core course requirements in Master of Public Administration degree programs across the country found that by the mid-1970s courses in comparative and development administration were virtually never required in the core MPA curriculum, and were almost never taken by students.[44]

Perhaps Golembiewski best sums up the dilemma (or what he calls the "fixation") of comparative and development administration by noting, that "public administration should take full notice of the fact that comparative administration's failure rests substantially on a self-imposed failure experience. It set an unattainable goal, that is, in its early and persisting choice to seek a comprehensive theory or model in terms of which to define itself."[45]

While this goal may be unattainable, there are signs that comparative public administration is continuing to make progress. Robert C. Fried sketches the challenges in developing a comprehensive theory of comparative public administration (and, implicitly, lets us know that the mainstream scholars of comparative public administration are still trying to construct such a theory). In his discussion of "Why Universal Theory Remains Elusive," he notes, among other problems, that national administrative systems are far more difficult to study than are other social institutions because there is difficulty in assessing their performance, their boundaries are difficult to pinpoint, there are cultural differences among nations, and there are other phenomena to consider.[46] On the other hand, one study of twenty journals conducted over a five year period found that the articles on comparative public administration were far more practitioner oriented, more empirically rooted, more likely to make policy recommendations, and more concerned with developing methodologies, than were articles on this topic in the past. Nevertheless, "the field as a whole...lacks features that give it clear identity...and thus the overall status of comparative public administration remains ambiguous."[47]

Political Science: The Impact of a Parent

Political science—the "biological parent," the "mother discipline" of public administration—clearly has had a profound affect on the character of the field. Public administration was born in the house of political science, and its early rearing occurred in its backyard. The fundamental precepts of American political science—the self-evident worth of democracy, a pluralistic polity, political participation, equality under law, and due process are examples of these precepts—continue to hold sway among even the most independently minded public administrationists. While it can be convincingly argued that the American civic culture inculcates these values among all its intellectuals, and that American public administrationists would cherish democratic values regardless of their experiences in political science, it nonetheless seems valid that the environment of political science sharpened and deepened the commitment of public administrationists to the country's core constitutional concepts. If, to indulge in speculation, public administration had been born and bred in the nation's business schools, would we have the same kind of academic field that we have today? Perhaps not. In any case, one can argue that, despite the disdain with which political science has often treated public administration, political science was a salutary former of the field in laying down its philosophic and normative foundations.

PARADIGM 4: PUBLIC ADMINISTRATION AS MANAGEMENT, 1956–1970

Partly because of their second-class citizenship status in a number of political science departments, some public administrationists began searching for an alternative. Although Paradigm 4 occurred roughly concurrently with Paradigm 3 in time, it never received the broadly based favor that political science garnered from public administrationists as a paradigm. Nonetheless, the management option (which sometimes is called "administrative science" or "generic management") was a viable alternative for a significant number of scholars in public administration, and, for some, it still is. But in both the political science and management paradigms, the essential thrust was one of public administration losing its identity and its uniqueness within the confines of some "larger" concept. Management is a field that covers organization theory and behavior, planning, decision making, various techniques of "management science" (such as path analysis and queuing theory), human resources management, leadership, motivation, communication, management information systems, budgeting, auditing, productivity, and, occasionally, marketing.

As a paradigm, management provides a focus but not a locus. It offers techniques, often highly sophisticated techniques, that require expertise and specialization, but the institutional setting in which that expertise is to be applied is undefined. As in Paradigm 2, administration is administration wherever it is found; focus is favored over locus.

A number of developments, many stemming from the country's business schools, fostered the alternative paradigm of management. In 1956 the important journal *Administrative Science Quarterly* was founded by a public administrationist on the premise that public, business, and institutional administration were false distinctions, and that administration was administration. Public administrationist Keith M. Henderson, among others, argued in the mid-1960s that organization theory was, or should be, the overarching focus of public administration.[48] And it cannot be denied that such works as James G. March and Herbert Simon's *Organizations* (1958), Richard Cyert and March's *A Behavioral Theory of the Firm* (1963), March's *Handbook of Organizations* (1965), and James D. Thompson's *Organizations in Action* (1967) gave solid theoretical reasons for choosing management, with an emphasis on organization theory, as the paradigm of public administration.

In the early 1960s, "organization development" began its rapid rise as a specialty of management. As a focus, organization development represented a particularly tempting alternative to political science for many public administrationists. Organization development as a field is grounded in social psychology and values the "democratization" of bureaucracies, whether public or private, and the "self-actualization" of the individual members of organizations. Because of these values, organization development was seen by many younger public administrationists as offering a very compatible area of research within the framework of management: democratic values could be considered, normative concerns could be broached, and intellectual rigor and scientific methodologies could be employed.

From the late 1950s through the mid-1960s, a spate of scholars writing in a variety of management journals accelerated the drumbeat of generic management as the logical successor to more "parochial" paradigms, such as public administration and business administration.[49] Weighing heavily in the value structure of these scholars was the interdisciplinary nature of management studies, and the necessity that university policymakers recognize this aspect and reorganize accordingly.

These intellectual currents had a genuine impact on the curricula of universities. A 1961 survey of graduate study in public administration in the United States found that, while the great majority of public administration programs were still located in political science departments, there was nonetheless "a groundswell development that tends to pervade all others," and this was the idea of "administration" (i.e., the field of management) as a unifying epistemology in the study of institutions and organizations, both public and private.[50] Similarly, by 1962, as many as a fifth of the business administration programs in the United States, Canada, and Mexico had joined the study of business administration with the study of economics, public administration, and other social sciences.[51]

The first institutional expression of the generic management "groundswell" came in the 1950s with the founding of the School of Business and Public Administration at Cornell University, and over the years three models of the generic management school developed.[52] The "purest" of these were those schools of administrative science that were created consciously (indeed, on occasion, ideologically) as generic, and which offer master's degrees only in "administration" or "management." The Graduate School of Management of the University of California at Irvine, founded in the mid-1960s, was the first edition cast in this mold, and the University of California at Riverside, Willamette University, and Yale University soon followed. Perhaps the most striking feature of these schools of administrative science is their size, or lack of it. The four extant examples have considerably fewer faculty than a typical department of political science or business administration at a major university.[53]

Closely related to the school of administrative science is the school of management. In this version, a business ethic prevails, and little or no attempt is made to understand the phenomenon of public administration, which is perceived as an extension of business management; education that is good for business is good for government. Master of Management or Master of Business Administration are the only graduate degrees offered, and "public management" is offered as a minor option within these degree programs. The University of California at Los Angeles, Stanford University, and Northwestern University are examples.

The third variant of the generic management model is seen in the combined school of business and public administration. Typically, these schools offer a common core curriculum for all students, but house separate departments of public administration that offer their own degree programs. Examples include the University of Alaska and the University Missouri at Kansas City.

During the 1960s and early 1970s in particular, the generic management concept was especially modish. Suddenly it seemed that a number of public administrationists were discovering the line in Woodrow Wilson's seminal essay of 1887 that state, "the field of administration is a field of business. It is removed from the hurry and strife of politics...."[54]

Perhaps it was this statement by Wilson that initially encouraged an attitude among some management scientists that strikingly paralleled the long-standing attitude held by political scientists about public administration, that is that public administration amounted to a subfield of their larger field. In the case of Paradigm 4, however, the "larger" field was management rather than political science. To some degree, such an attitude depends upon the perspective of the viewer. In a useful analysis, James L. Perry and Kenneth L. Kramer have clarified what this perspective means in terms of public administration and management.[55] If, for example, an analyst believes that the primary purpose of an organization is to achieve social goals (*e.g.*, education), as opposed to instrumental goals (*e.g.*, profits); that similarities and differences among organizations can best be understood by comparing organizations as a whole (*e.g.*, comparing the Department of the Interior with the Ford Motor Company), rather than parts of organizations (*e.g.*, comparing the accounting departments of different organizations); that selected similarities and differences among organizations carry more weight and are more important than others (*e.g.*, the influence of politics is more significant for public agencies than for private firms), as opposed to according equal importance to all similarities and differences; and that an analytical approach focusing on the discovery of patterns of organizational behavior (*e.g.*, technology and organizational change), rather than case studies (*e.g.*, "International Widget Markets in East Anglia: Lessons for Us All"), then that analyst likely will conclude that public administration is quite a bit different from private management. Analysts who hold opposite beliefs and approaches probably will contend that the supposed differences between the two are artificial: management is management is management. Table 2-1 summarizes these perspectives.

TABLE 2-1   Perspectives of Analysts Who Assess Similarities and Differences Between Public and Private Management

Issues raised in drawing comparisons	*Perspectives of analysts who conclude that public and private management are more similar than different*	*Perspectives of analysts who conclude that public and private management are more different that similar*
What is an organization's proper role toward its external environment	To achieve instrumental goals	To achieve social goals
Can similarities and differences in the management of organizations be understood by looking at the parts or at the whole of management.	The similarities and differences can be understood by looking at the parts.	The similarities and differences can only be understood by looking at the whole.
Are all similarities and differences of equal importance?	The similarities and differences ar weighted equally.	Some similarities and differences are more important than other similarities and differences.
Should proof of the existence of similarities and differences between organizations be based on case experiences or on dominant patterns within the entire population of organizations?	Case experiences	Dominant patterns

Source: James L. Perry and Kenneth L. Kraemer, "Part Three: Is Public Management Similar to or Different From Private Management?" in *Public Management: Public and Private Perspective,* James L. Perry and Kenneth L. Kraemer, eds. (Palo Alto, Calif.: Mayfield, 1983), p. 56.

Beyond the reality of differing belief sets among individual researchers, however, an even more serious problem exists with the argument that public and private management are indistinguishable. The generic management paradigm is predicated on the idea that a single literature exists that is relevant to managers in all kinds of institutional settings, including businesses and governments. To a degree, this is true. Organization theory, computer science, communication and information theory, statistics—in fact, all the topics listed earlier as composing the management field are pertinent to the study of public administration. What is often overlooked in this perspective, however, is that precisely the same claim can be made (and has been made) for political science: American government, state and local politics, and urban politics, for example, are all relevant to the study of public administration.

The point is that neither "truth" says very much. Neither field is adequate by itself as a paradigm for public administration. Public administration is simply larger than either management or political science.

Moreover, the literatures of both fields are biased in ways that reduce their usefulness to public administration. In the case of political science, as we have noted, the phenomena of government and politics require only "intellectualized understanding" among political scientists, not education for "knowledgeable action," as is needed by public administrationists and public administrators. In the case of management, and despite occasional protestations by management scientists to the contrary, the administrative phenomenon is typically cast in terms of the business world. A glance at virtually any introductory text in management brings this point home; government, when it is mentioned at all, is often treated as a "constraint" in the "organizational environment" of the corporation.

The admittedly fragmentary data indicate that the "real-world" skills needed by public administrators and business managers differ markedly. Little research has been done on this, but those successful businesspersons who have become public managers are among the first to deny that there are significant similarities between the public and private sectors, and public administrators who

enter the corporate world experience comparable difficulties of transition.[56] In addition, the growing research literature that empirically compares public and private organizations (reviewed in Part Two) casts doubt that the public and private administrative sectors can always be fruitfully approached as a single entity.[57] The emerging consensus of public administrationists increasingly appears to be that public and private management are, to cite Wallace Sayre's old saw, fundamentally alike in all unimportant respects.

It follows that if public and private management are alike in all unimportant respects, then those disciplines which attempt to understand these separate managerial sectors must rely to a significant degree on different sets of knowledge. And research indicates this to be the case. A careful study of eight major, representative generic schools of management found that there were a total of thirty different courses composing the "common" core of courses for a master's degree.[58] Although there was some limited agreement among the generic schools with regard to eight courses that emphasized operations research, statistics, economics, accounting, finance, and organization theory, there nonetheless remained a "substantial amount of disagreement about the commonality of administrative tools and techniques."[59]

The upshot of Paradigm 4 insofar as many public administrationists were and are concerned is that the field of public administration would exchange, at best, being an "emphasis" in political science departments, for being, at best, a subfield in generic schools of management.

Management: The Impact of a Foster Parent

If political science was profoundly influential on the evolution of public administration, management was less so. But, in many ways, the impact of management on public administration was more positive. In part, this was because management entered into the upbringing of public administration when the field was beginning its adolescence, and, unlike political science, it was not a blood relative; consequently, public administration was granted more independence and breathing room to grow and develop on its own. This is not to say that the household environment created by the field of management for public administration was one of warmth and succor. It was not. But instead of treating public administration like an abusive parent, as political science occasionally did, management, like an absent-minded aunt who was never quite sure who was living in which room and who often forgot to serve meals, at least let public administration stay in its house.

Management had at least three distinct and beneficial influences on public administration: It forced public administrationists to examine more closely what the "public" in "public administration" meant; it convinced many public administrationists that a whole new set of management methodologies was needed; and it provided public administration with a model of how to assess what, as a field, it was teaching and why.

Understanding the "Public" in Public Administration. One of the principal effects of the management paradigm on public administration concerned the distinction between "public" versus "private" administration. Defining the "public" in public administration has long been a knotty problem for academics. In part, this is because Western culture has never completely sorted out what Stanley I. Benn and Gerald F. Gaus call the "complex-structured concept" of "publicness" and "privateness" in society,[60] and this larger dilemma has had its effects on understanding what constitutes *public* administration.

Fortunately, Benn and Gaus provide one of the better analyses of the components of this complex-structured concept. They contend that publicness and privateness in society are composed of three dimensions: agency, interest, and access.

Agency, in this sense, refers to the "basic distinction...between an agent acting privately, that is, on his own account, or publicly, that is, as an officer of the city..... The public/private distinction is thus important in answering the questions: What is your standing as an agent? What significance do your actions and decisions have for the status of other people?"[61]

Interest "is concerned with the status of the people who will be better or worse off for whatever is in question."[62] Hence, it is in the interest of the private firm to benefit only the people in it and who

own it through salaries and profits. "By contrast, the supposed end of a public enterprise is to serve the public interest (providing a...service to any or every member of the community...)."[63]

Access refers to the degree of openness that distinguishes publicness from privateness. Access encompasses access to activities (*e.g.*, town meetings are public because they are open to all, but corporate board meetings are private because only board members have access to them), space (*e.g.*, the public town hall in contrast to the private corporate board room), information (*e.g.*, everyone may read the minutes of the town meeting, but only board members may peruse those of the board meeting), and resources ("access to lawnmowers is generally private; access to a...drinking fountain can be public in the sense that anyone may use it").[64]

These three dimensions of publicness and privateness are helpful in our understanding of how public administration's experience in its management paradigm has defined its public role, for agency, interest, and access all have a bearing on this role. We consider them in turn.

The institutional definition. Traditionally, when public administrationists thought about what the "public" in public administration meant at all, they thought about it in *institutional* terms, that is, the management of tax-supported agencies that appeared on government organization charts—the government bureaucracy. The bureaucracy—the agencies—constituted the "locus" of public administration that held sway over the field's focus during the periods of Paradigm 1 (the politics/administration dichotomy) and Paradigm 3 (public administration as political science). This bureaucratic locus amounts to an institutional definition of the "public" in public administration, and it is a virtual "match" with Benn and Gaus's thinking about the "agency" dimension of publicness and privateness. (Indeed, even the term "agency" seems to be uniquely suitable to public administration.)

The institutional definition of "public" still dominates thinking in the field. One review of some of the more important literature on public organizations concluded that the vast majority of writers (70 percent of the books reviewed) took an "agency" perspective, as opposed to an "interest" or "access" view in analyzing public organizations.[65]

Nevertheless, there are real problems with an agency, or institutional, definition, and public administration's experience with Paradigm 4 helped tease these out. The most notable problem, and one with which the better theorists in all fields are familiar, is that of the real world; the real world makes an institutionally centered definition of public administration problematic at best and untenable at worst. The research and development contract; the military-industrial complex; the roles of regulatory agencies and their relations with industry; the emergence of "third sector," or nonprofit and voluntary organizations; and the developing awareness of what one author has called "the margins of the state"[66] in reference to such phenomena as the expansive growth of government corporations and the privatization of public policy, all have conspired to make *public* administration an elusive entity, at least when attempts are made to define it in empirical terms that are based on an institutional construct.

The management paradigm was particularly useful in exposing these real-world deficiencies that are inherent to an institutional definition of public administration. Of course, the motivation of the management scientists to do so (occasionally with great glee) may have stemmed as much from a desire to claim public administration as an inseparable part of the management field as from a dedication to shed intellectual light on the problem. But understanding the shortcomings of defining public administration's locus as simply government agencies was nonetheless needed, and the management scientists provided it. So public administrationists began searching for an alternative framework for understanding the "public" in public administration.

The normative definition. During the 1970s, the alternative that emerged was a normative one, and it reflected Benn and Gaus's concept of "interest" as a dimension of the public/private concept. Inspired in part by the "new public administration" movement (which we explain in greater detail shortly) and its ethical overtones, the normative definition of public administration focused not on

government agencies as such, but on those phenomena that affected the public interest. This more dynamic philosophic approach could include not only government agencies and the actions of those agencies, but a plethora of other institutions, technologies, and interrelationships as well. Thus, rather than concentrating on the Department of Defense, for example, as its proper public locus, and leaving, say, Lockheed Corporation to students of business management, public administrationists began to understand that the department's contractual and political relationships with Lockheed should now be their central object of study, since these relationships clearly involved the public interest. This new, noninstitutional and normative definition of the "public" in public administration was brought about in large part by the difficulties encountered by public administrationists who were working within the confines of generic schools of management in explaining their field to their academic colleagues—colleagues who, on occasion, were somewhat less than sympathetic to the role of government in society and even to the notion of the public interest.[67]

The organizational definition. The normative definition of public administration clearly had advantages over the institutional one, but there were problems with it, too. It was, after all, not terribly precise; one person's idea of the public interest might not be shared by others. For example, the president of Lockheed, the secretary of defense, and a pacifist might have very different views of what constituted the public interest; they might even disagree whether the relationships between Lockheed and the Department of Defense were a proper subject of study for those who wished to discern what the public interest was.

Hence, a third option for defining the "public" in public administration presented itself: the organization. Specifically, were public organizations, such as government agencies, public authorities, voluntary associations, and nonprofit corporations, different from private organizations, such as IBM, and if so, how?

Public administrationists had muddled around for years with the notion that public and private organizations were distinctly different, but many of them drew this conclusion more from ideological beliefs than from empirical research. During the late 1970s and 1980s, however, a spate of new research appeared that focused on the public organization. As we explain in Part Two, this research is relatively unambiguous in concluding that there is at least one absolutely critical difference between the public organization and its private counterpart, and from which many other important differences derive: the difference lies in the impact of the organization's task environment on its inner workings and general behavior. The "task environment" of an organization is that "outside" milieu of other organizations and forces with which the organization must deal to survive. For General Motors, for example, the task environment is the marketplace; for the Interstate Commerce Commission it is a welter of political, economic, social, and market forces. What the new (and, for that matter, the old) literature on public organizations is contending is that the task environment is much more influential and critical for the behavior of public organizations than for private ones.

This idea that the impact of the task environment is central to the unique properties of public organizations corresponds nicely with Benn and Gaus's idea of "access" as a dimension of the public/private concept. In contrast to private firms, public agencies are exceptionally accessible. Private citizens, legislators, special interests, other organizations, and many other groups can and do involve themselves in the workings of public organizations far more readily than in private ones. They can determine or significantly influence the level of a public organization's resources (*e.g.*, its annual budget), how those resources will be used (*e.g.*, its enabling legislation), and can second-guess (or even reverse) the decisions made by its administrators in much more detail and more authoritatively because they have vastly greater access to the information relied upon by the public organization's administrators to make decisions than they have for private organizations.

These realities of organizational access render the public organization (and its administration) a very different creature from the private one, and constitute our third definition of the "public" in public administration.

Our definitions of *public* administration—institutional, normative, and organizational—are in no way mutually exclusive; rather, like Benn and Gaus's dimensions of "publicness" and "privateness" (agency, interest, and access), they are mutually reinforcing. Together, they form the "public" in public administration, the locus of both the field and the profession.

The New Methodologies. A second impact that Paradigm 4 had on public administration was methodological. Public administrationists associated with political science departments had long known (or at least it was dawning on them with accelerating speed) that the methodologies of political science were inappropriate for the concerns of public administration. Often these scholars looked to the management schools for illumination and guidance. In many cases, because the public administrationists of Paradigm 3 did not fully understand the methodologies employed by the management scientists, they put great (and frequently inappropriate) stock in their potential utility. In other instances, public administrationists of the Paradigm 3 mode rejected the methodologies of management out of hand because they found them threatening, or were ignorant of them.

The combined consequence of these reactions to the management methodologies was the ultimate recognition by the more committed public administrationists (whether they were found in political science departments or in management schools) that wholly new methodologies were needed for the field. Indeed, the development of these methodologies was central to the emergence of "self-aware" public administration.

In some cases, adapting on a selective basis the existing methodologies of both political science and administrative science was appropriate, such as survey research (from political science) and operations research (from management). But, by and large, new methods were needed, and "evaluation research" or "program evaluation" have become the terms that we presently associate with many of the developing bundles of methodologies that public administration calls its own.[68] The emphasis in these methodologies is on determining whether public programs are effective, efficient and, increasingly, whether they are needed. They borrow techniques from a variety of disciplines, and have a clearly "applied research" cast.

Closely related to evaluation research are the continually evolving methods of budgeting, ranging from line-item to Zero-Base methods. Increasingly, these "budgetary" concepts are becoming management control strategies that use the methodologies of program evaluation in determining budget allocations.[69]

Finally, there are existing quantitative techniques that fall under the general (and unsatisfactory) rubrics of "public decision making" or "public management," and which are being increasingly transformed and adapted to a governmental context. These include probability theory, statistical comparisons, linear correlations and linear programming (particularly, sensitivity analysis and the simplex method), government accounting, critical path method, cost-benefit analysis, decision trees, queuing theory, public choice theory, simulations, and management information systems, among others. There have been a number of recent works that do a fine job in applying these and other methods to problems of the public sector.[70]

Learning How to Take Oneself Seriously. A final aspect of the management paradigm that influenced the evolution of public administration as a field of study was the relatively serious way in which the business schools took their enterprise. Compared with political science departments, at least, the process of educating students in generic schools of management and in business schools was and is far more focused, self-analytical, systematic and, well, *serious*. This is not to say that individual political scientists or public administrationists take their classroom responsibilities lightly; by and large, they do not. But as a field, political science has never put itself through the long-term self-examination and critical assessment that business education has.

During the decade of the 1950s, business educators inflicted upon themselves a well-financed and searching examination of their curricula and instructional programs. The resulting reports—two thick volumes often containing sharp criticism of current practices—had profound effects on business education.[71] By contrast, the only comparable effort conducted by political science during this period resulted in a book that has been dismissed by political scientists themselves as one whose "very triteness and superficiality...made it important."[72] A later attempt to redress this problem focused more specifically on public administration education, but as it was still conducted within the environment of political science, the results were much the same.[73] Public administrationists criticized the report as dealing with "venerable and eminently fatiguing issues,"[74] and its only lasting impact seems to have been that it led to the field's concern with a "new public administration."[75] The major opus born by the "new public administration" (Frank Marini's *Toward a New Public Administration* of 1971), however, ultimately had little impact on the public administration curriculum, beyond, perhaps, sensitizing the field to the importance of educating for ethics.

These reports on education for the public service appeared in 1951 and 1967, when public administration was dominated by political science, and their superficiality in dealing with the problems they sought to address was rendered all the more stark when compared with the reports of 1958 that had been prepared by business educators. This lesson has not been lost on the current generation of public administrationists. A proliferating number of analyses of all aspects of public administration education by individual scholars have appeared since the mid-1970s (only a few of which have been cited in this chapter), indicating a renewed concern with the problem. More significantly, however, the National Association of Schools of Public Affairs and Administration has grown into a body of more than 220 member institutions, is enviably well funded, and is maturing into an organization that has the greatest likelihood of producing a self-evaluation of public administration education that parallels in scope and quality the analyses of business education conducted in the 1950s.[76] The model of a searching and systemic self-assessment that has been provided by the business education community may, perhaps, become the single most constructive effect that

Paradigm 4 ultimately has on the field of public administration.

THE FORCES OF SEPARATISM: "SCIENCE AND PUBLIC POLICY" AND THE "NEW PUBLIC ADMINISTRATION," 1965–1970

Even at its nadir, during the period of Paradigms 3 and 4, public administration was sowing the seeds of its own renaissance. This process—quite an unconscious one at the time—took at least two distinct but complementary forms: One was the development of interdisciplinary programs in "science, technology, and public policy," and "science and society," or programs with similar titles in major universities, and the other was the appearance of the "new public administration."

"Science, Technology, and Public Policy"

The evolution of "science, technology, and public policy" curricula in universities occurred largely during the late 1960s, and they were the intellectual forerunners of a later and deeper scholarly interest in the relationships between knowledge and power, bureaucracy and democracy, technology and management, and related "technobureaucratic" dimensions.[77] These programs, although broadly interdisciplinary, often were dominated by public administrationists located in political science departments. By the late 1960s, there were about fifty such programs and they were situated for the most part in the top academic institutions of the country. It was largely this new focus of science, technology, and public policy that gave those public administrationists connected with political science departments any claim to intellectual distinction during the 1960s, and it helped offset the loss of a disciplinary identity that then beset public administration. This renewed identity came in part because the focus of science, technology, and public policy did not (and does not) rely conceptually on the pluralist thesis favored by political science. Instead, the focus is elitist rather than pluralist, synthesizing rather than specializing, and hierarchical rather than communal.

"The New Public Administration"

The second development was that of the "new public administration." In 1968, Waldo, as Albert Schweitzer Professor in Humanities of Syracuse University, sponsored a conference of young public administrationists on the new public administration, the proceedings of which were subsequently published as a book in 1971, titled *Toward a New Public Administration: The Minnowbrook Perspective*. The volume remains the key work in this focus.

The focus was disinclined to examine such traditional phenomena as efficiency, effectiveness, budgeting, and administrative techniques. Conversely, the new public administration was very much aware of normative theory, philosophy, and activism. The questions it raised dealt with values, ethics, the development of the individual member in the organization, the relation of the client with the bureaucracy, and the broad problems of urbanism, technology, and violence. If there was an overriding tone to the new public administration, it was a moral tone. Nevertheless, with hindsight the "new P.A." can be viewed as a call for independence from both political science (it was not, after all, ever called the "new politics of bureaucracy") and management (since management always had been emphatically technical rather than normative in approach).

The science, technology, and public policy and the new public administration movements were short lived. Science, technology, and public policy programs eventually devolved into specialized courses on such topics as information systems, growth management, and environmental administration, while the new public administration never lived up to its ambitions of revolutionizing the discipline. Nevertheless, both movements had a lasting impact on public administration in that they nudged public administrationists into reconsidering their traditional intellectual ties with both political science and management, and contemplating the prospects of academic autonomy. By 1970, the separatist movement was underway.

Public Administration as Neither Management nor Political Science

The old question of whether public administration is a subfield of management or political science is considered in the following two selections. The selection discusses why public administration differs significantly from management. In it, Luther Gulick, public administrationist and confidante of President Franklin D. Roosevelt, suggests that the "politico-administrative system" is unique and warrants a unique educational treatment.

My point is best illustrated by a lesson I learned from President Franklin D. Roosevelt. In January 1937, Brownlow, Merriam and I finished our report to the president on the administrative management of the government. He sent it to the Congress in January. Some months later the hearings began and dragged on into that long, hot summer. Unfortunately, Brownlow and Merriam had to go abroad for conferences in Paris and left me with Joe Harris in Washington, to wrestle with Jimmy Byrnes and Congress over the "reorganization bill." As the only member of the committee "in residence," I had a number of sessions with President Roosevelt to test our further ideas on which we were then at work, in our search for greater efficiency and economy in national administration.

One of our technical teams had reached the tentative conclusion that the whole accounting system under social security was meaningless and highly wasteful. As you will remember, both the old age pension and the unemployment laws provided for contributions by the employer and the employee and the setting up of individual accounts under the name of each man and women covered. Millions of personal accounts were involved, with many more millions of accounts to come, and in those days, with electronic accounting still in its infancy, such accounting was very complex.

When it comes to making payments to those who retired or were unemployed, however, payments were to be made on the basis of legally defined amounts, which had little or no relation to the cash balances in the individual accounts.

Thus the individual cash accounts were quite superfluous for the administration of the system. Moreover the grand total of assets in the several funds were not invested as such. They were not even segregated in the treasury.

The technical experts thus reached the conclusion that individual accounts were totally unnecessary, and were a great administrative waste. I presented the idea to Frank Bane, Arthur Altmeyer, Harry Hopkins, Henry Morgenthau, Beardsley Ruml, Alvin Hanson and others, and then to the president. He asked a number of questions, and said to come back. Something apparently troubled him about the suggestion.

Some days later he had me up to his room where he generally had breakfast in bed. He asked me to restate the proposition, and then said: "I don't see any hole in the argument, but the conclusion is dead wrong. The purpose of the accounts for Tom, Dick, and Harry is not to figure what we collect or pay. It is to make it impossible when I am gone for the...Republicans to abolish the system. They would never dare wipe out the personal savings accounts of millions. You can't do that in America!"

Immediately I knew he was right. His reasoning rested not solely on the dramatic political insight stated so simply, but also on the psychological impact of personal accounts on the recipients and on those who paid into the social security account.

The error we technical management and accounting experts almost fell into was the inadequate definition of the system which we were analyzing. We did a good job on the law, on the bookkeeping, on administrative mechanics, and the fiscal and cost analysis. But we missed two dimensions of the problem, the political and the psychological, and we overlooked the prob-

lem of strategy which was always so important in the mind of the president.

Luther Gulick
Public Administration Review

PARADIGM 5: PUBLIC ADMINISTRATION AS PUBLIC ADMINISTRATION: 1970–?

In 1970, the National Association of Schools of Public Affairs and Administration (NASPAA) was founded. The formation of NASPAA represented not only an act of secession by public administrationists, but also a rise of self-confidence as well.

NASPAA's origins lay in the Council on Graduate Education for Public Administration, which had been founded in 1958 by the public administrationists in a small number of graduate programs in the field. The decision in 1970 to dramatically expand the scope of this somewhat cozy group (and later, in 1983, to decide to become a formal professional accrediting agency for public administration programs) indicated a determination by public administration educators to take public responsibility for upgrading the educational backgrounds and technical competence of the nation's government managers. By 1970, as represented by the founding of the National Association of Schools of Public Affairs and Administration, public administration could properly call itself, and increasingly be recognized as, a separate, "self-aware" field of study.

The profile of public administration as a "self-aware" field reflects in many ways what Simon predicted it would become in 1947. Although there is not yet a focus for the field in the form of a "pure science of administration," progress, particularly in the area of organization theory and information science, has been made in this direction. Additionally, considerable progress has been made in refining the applied techniques and methodologies of public administration. There has been, perhaps, less movement toward delineating a locus for the field, or what Simon called "prescribing for public policy." Nevertheless, public administration does appear to be emphasizing such

areas as state and local government, executive management, administrative law, and trying to answer all those questions that pertain to what "the public interest" is in a technobureaucratic, "Big Democracy."

The emerging curriculum of graduate public administration education reflects these emphases. A more or less agreed upon core curriculum seems to have developed for public administration education at the graduate level, and it centers on the environment of public administration (*i.e.*, general introductory courses that focus on the role of the bureaucracy in a democracy), quantitative methods, public budgeting, financial management, organization theory, and human resources administration in the public sector. The average number of required hours in these core areas has grown, with the primary expansion being in quantitative methods, public budgeting, and financial management. It appears that this increase in the required number of hours taken in the core curriculum has occurred at the cost of electives that students otherwise take.[78]

The increase in required courses in the core curriculum reflects to some degree the growing clout of the National Association of Schools of Public Affairs and Administration, which strongly favors a common core curriculum at the graduate level. Some ninety universities and colleges have been accredited by NASPAA, and accreditation by NASPAA is increasingly held in high esteem by academics, students, and employers alike. Surveys indicate that administrators of Master of Public Administration degree programs find that accreditation by NASPAA brings with it a higher prestige for the MPA program, a more effective program, and an enhanced ability to recruit higher quality faculty and students.[79]

As Table 2-2 shows, 1985, was the first year in which national surveys have been conducted that public administration programs within political science departments did not constitute a plurality

TABLE 2-2   Organizational Patterns of Public Administration Programs, Selected Years, 1973–1989

Organizational Pattern		1973	1977	1981	1985	1989
		N=101	N=156	N=192	N=193	N=220
1.	SEPARATE PROFESSIONAL SCHOOLS	25%	21%	17%	14%	13%
2.	SEPARATE DEPARTMENTS IN LARGE UNITS	23	31	33	34	34
3.	P.A. PROGRAMS COMBINED WITH ANOTHER PROFESSIONAL SCHOOL OR DEPARTMENT (e.g.,BUSINESS ADMINISTRATION)*	17	8	10	15	10
4.	P.A. PROGRAMS WITHIN POLITICAL SCIENCE DEPARTMENTS	36	40	39	31	37
5.	UNCLASSIFIED ORGANIZATION**	0	0	1	6	6
	TOTAL	100	100	100	100	100

*Includes professional school of public administration combined with another professional school (6 percent in 1989) and departments of public administration combined with another department (3 percent).

**Includes interdisciplinary programs and institutes reporting to the central university administration and other organizational structures.

Source: Derived from *NASPAA 1990 Directory*, pp. 19–20. Percentages have been rounded.

among the possible organizational patterns available for public administration programs in the universities. Instead, for the first time, separate departments of public administration constituted a plurality. While this position slipped slightly in 1987 and 1989 (apparently as a result of more political science departments joining NASPAA), the percentage of separate departments of public administration remained constant at better than a third of all possible organizational arrangements. The number of separate departments of public administration has more than tripled since 1973, and between them, separate schools and departments of public administration amount to nearly half of all the university public administration programs that are members of NASPAA. The secession, in short, is real.

Beyond the reality of that secession are some interesting patterns. For one, the number of public administration programs that are housed within professional schools or departments, such as business administration or management programs, has declined precipitously over the years, from 17 percent in 1973 to less than 10 percent in 1989—yet another aspect of the secession, but in this case, a secession from business schools rather than from political science departments. Nevertheless, the major move toward autonomy remains that of public administration pulling away from political science, and this appears to have been good for the field of public administration. Research indicates that the most effective MPA programs are those that are administered by schools of public affairs and administration and departments of public administration.[80]

There are more than 23,000 students enrolled in master's degree programs in public administration and public affairs, up from fewer than 11,000 in 1973.[81] Of these students, 48 percent are women, 12 percent are black, and 4 percent are of Hispanic origin.

Students in MPA programs are an unusual group. Three-fourths have jobs, and 64 percent are part-time students. Twenty-two percent of MPA graduates go to work for local governments following graduation, 16 percent are placed in state government positions, 21 percent in the national government, 11 percent in the nonprofit sector, and 9 percent end up working in the private sector.

There are about 7,800 undergraduate students who are majoring in public administration, and enrollments in undergraduate majors are rising. However, an undergraduate major in public administration is not a large variable; although seventy-three colleges and universities offer undergraduate degrees in public administration, fully one-half of these enrollments are concentrated in only seven institutions. In addition, there are nearly 1,800 students who are enrolled in doctoral programs in public administration, and enrollments in doctoral programs are increasing.

Meeting the educational needs of these students, whether graduate or undergraduate, and, in the process, supplying the public with capable managers, is no easy task. As the president of Harvard University, which houses the John F. Kennedy School of Government, put it:

...The universities have a major opportunity and responsibility to set about the task of training a corps of able people to occupy influential positions in public life. What is needed is nothing less than the education of a new profession. ...I can scarcely overemphasize the importance of this effort. ...Since universities are primarily responsible for advanced training in our society, they share a unique opportunity and obligation to prepare a profession of public servants equipped to discharge these heavy responsibilities to the nation.[82]

NOTES

[1] Stephen K. Bailey, "Objectives of the Theory of Public Administration," in *Theory and Practice of Public Administration: Scope, Objectives, and Methods*, James C. Charlesworth, ed. Monograph 8 (Philadelphia: American Academy of Political and Social Science, 1968), pp. 128–29.

[2] Robert T. Golembiewski, *Public Administration as a Developing Discipline, Part I: Perspectives on Past and Present* (New York: Marcel Dekker, 1977).

[3] Woodrow Wilson, "The Study of Administration," *Political Science Quarterly*, 2 (June 1887), pp. 197–222; reprinted 50 (December 1941), pp. 481–506.

[4] Richard J. Stillman, II. "Woodrow Wilson and the Study of Administration: A New Look at an Old Essay," *American Political Science Review*, 67 (June 1973), p. 587. More accurately, in formulating his politics/administration dichotomy, Wilson apparently misinterpreted some of the German literature that he read on public administration. In any event, the politics/administration dichotomy clearly had an impact on the early evolution of public administration. See, for example: Paul Van Riper, "The American Administrative State: Wilson and the Founders—An Unorthodox View," *Public Administration Review*, 43 (November/December 1983), pp. 477-490, and Daniel W. Martin, "The Fading Legacy of Woodrow Wilson," *Public Administration Review*, 48 (March/April 1988), pp. 631–636.

[5] Frank J. Goodnow, *Politics and Administration* (New York: Macmillan, 1900), pp. 10–11.

[6] *Proceedings of the American Political Science Association, 1913–1914*, p. 264, as cited in Lynton K. Caldwell, "Public Administration and the Universities: A Half-Century of Development," *Public Administration Review*, 25 (March 1965), p. 54.

[7] Committee on Practical Training for Public Service, American Political Science Association, *Proposed Plan for Training Schools for Public Service* (Madison, Wis.: American Political Science Association, 1914), p. 3.

[8] The financier of the Bureau's Training School for Public Service was Mrs. E. H. Harriman, who raised some $250,000 and turned it over to the Bureau of Municipal Research for a school. Ms. Harriman had preferred that her school be in a university in the first place, but could find no takers; the presidents of Harvard, Yale, and Columbia were approached by her, but she found them to be "polite but amused" by her proposal. See Luther Gulick, "George Maxwell Had a Dream," *American Public Administration: Past, Present, Future*, Frederick C. Mosher, ed. (Syracuse, N.Y.: Maxwell School of Citizenship and Public Affairs and the National Association of Schools of Public Affairs and Administration, 1975), p. 257.

[9] Darrell L. Pugh, "ASPA's History: Prologue!" *Public Administration Review*, 45 (July/August 1985), p. 475.

[10] Dwight Waldo, "Public Administration," in *Political Science: Advance of the Discipline*, Marian D. Irish, ed. (Englewood Cliffs, N.J.: Prentice-Hall, 1968), pp. 153–189.

[11] Morris B. Lambie, ed. *Training for the Public Service: The Report and Recommendations of a Conference Sponsored by the Public Administration Clearing House* (Chicago: Public Administration Clearing House, 1935).

[12] Caldwell, "Public Administration and the Universities," p. 57.

[13] Dwight Waldo, "Introduction: Trends and Issues in Education for Public Administration," in *Education for Public Service: 1979*, Guthrie S. Birkhead and James D. Carroll, eds. (Syracuse, N.Y.: Maxwell School of Citizenship and Public Affairs, Syracuse University Press, 1979), p. 15.

[14] Pugh, "ASPA's History," p. 476.

[15] Donald C. Stone, "Birth of ASPA—Elective Effort in Institution Building," *Public Administration Review*, 35 (January 1975), p. 87.

[16] Golembiewski, *Public Administration as a Developing Discipline*, p. 23.

[17] Lyndall Urwick, "Organization as a Technical Problem," in *Papers on the Science of Administration*, Luther Gulick and L. Urwick, eds. (New York: Institute of Public Administration, 1937), p. 49.

[18] Allen Schick, "The Trauma of Politics: Public Administration in the Sixties," in Mosher, ed., *American Public Administration*, p. 152.

[19] Ironically, the notion of "principles" of public administration has been quashed so thoroughly, that there is some scholarly activity underway to bring principles back. As one writer in the field has contended, "The utility of tested administrative principles . . . is as great as it was in 1939." However, this author, as well as others, argues that we should define the concept of administrative principle in considerably less rigid terms than did the field's intellectual forebears, and has suggested that, "A principle is a generalized normative statement based on experience and does not purport to be have the universality of a theory or law." See, Ronald C. Moe, "Traditional Organizational Principles and the Managerial Presidency: From Phoenix to Ashes," *Public Administration Review*, 50 (March/April, 1990), p. 136.

While I agree that there are some general precepts that public administrators would be well advised to follow (*e.g.*, authority should match accountability), and that it is the responsibility of the academics to, in conjunction with the practitioners, develop these precepts, I do not believe that changing the definition of the word "principle" is the way to do it. The first condition in any field of academic and professional endeavor should be to retain the clarity and precision of language; hence, redefining or fogging up what "principle" means is not a particularly fruitful way of advancing the discipline.

[20] Herbert A. Simon, "A Comment on 'The Science of Public Administration,'" *Public Administration Review*, 7 (Summer 1947) p. 202.

[21] Golembiewski, *Public Administration as a Developing Discipline*, pp. 20–22.

[22] Caldwell, "Public Administration and the Universities," p. 57.

[23] Roscoe Martin, "Political Science and Public Administration— A Note on the State of the Union," *American Political Science Review*, 46 (September 1952), p. 665.

[24] David Easton, *The Political System* (New York: Knopf, 1953). Easton pulled no punches in his appraisal of the status of political science. As he noted (pp. 38–40), "With the exception of public administration, formal education in political science has not achieved the recognition in government circles accorded, say, economics or psychology," or, "However much students of political life may seek to escape the taint, if they were to eavesdrop on the whisperings of their fellow social scientists, they would find that they are almost generally stigmatized as the least advanced."

[25] John Merriman Gaus, "Trends in the Theory of Public Administration," *Public Administration Review*, 10 (Summer 1950), p. 168.

[26] Glendon A. Schubert, Jr., "'The Public Interest' in Administrative Decision Making," *American Political Science Review*, 51 (June 1957), pp. 346–368.

[27] Martin Landau reviews this aspect of the field's development cogently in his "The Concept of Decision-Making in the 'Field' of Public Administration," *Concepts and Issues in Administrative Behavior*, Sidney Mailick and Edward H. Van Ness, eds. (Englewood Cliffs, N.J.: Prentice-Hall, 1962), pp. 1–29. Landau writes (p. 9), "Public administration is neither a subfield of political science, nor does it comprehend it; it simply becomes a synonym."

[28] Frederick C. Mosher, "Research in Public Administration," *Public Administration Review*, 16 (Summer 1956), p. 171.

[29] Landau, "The Concept of Decision-Making in the 'Field' of Public Administration," p. 2.

[30] Ward Stewart, *Graduate Study in Public Administration* (Washington, D.C.: U.S. Office of Education, 1961).

[31] William J. Siffin, "The New Public Administration: Its Study in the United States," *Public Administration*, 34 (Winter 1956), p. 357.

[32] Albert Somit and Joseph Tanenhaus, *American Political Science: A Profile of a Discipline* (New York: Atherton, 1964), especially pp. 49–62 and 86–98.

[33] Dwight Waldo, "Scope of the Theory of Public Administration," in *Theory and Practice of Public Administration*, Charlesworth, ed., p. 8.

[34] Contrast this figure with the percentage of articles in other categories published during the 1960–1970 period: "political parties," 13 percent; "public opinion," 12 percent; "legislatures," 12 percent; and "elections/voting," 11 percent. Even those categories dealing peripherally with "bureaucratic politics" and public administration evidently received short shrift among the editors of the major political science journals. "Region/federal government" received 4 percent, "chief executives" won 3 percent, and "urban/metropolitan government" received 2 percent. The percentages are in Jack L. Walker, "Brother, Can You Paradigm?" *PS*, 5 (Fall 1972), pp. 419–422. The journals surveyed were *American Political Science Review*, *Journal of Politics*, *Western Political Quarterly*, *Midwest Political Science Journal*, and *Polity*.

[35] This discussion relies largely on Waldo, "Public Administration," pp. 176–179.

[36] Christopher E. Nugent, "Introduction," *Cases in Public Policy and Management: Spring, 1979* (Boston: Intercollegiate Case Clearing House, 1979), p. v; and Colin S. Diver, "PPMP's Swan Song," *Public Policy and Management Newsletter*, 7 (May 1985), p. 1.

[37] Leonard D. White, "The Meaning of Principles of Public Administration," in *The Frontier of Public Administration*, John M. Gaus, Leonard D. White, and Marshall E. Dimock, eds. (Chicago: University of Chicago Press, 1936), p. 22

[38] See, for example, Robert A. Dahl, "The Science of Public Administration: Three Problems," *Public Administration Review*, 7 (Winter 1947), pp. 1–11, and Dwight Waldo, *The Administrative State* (New York: Ronald Press, 1948).

[39] Ferrel Heady, "Comparative Public Administration: Concerns and Priorities," in *Papers in Comparative Public Administration*, Ferrel Heady and Sybil Stokes, eds. (Ann Arbor, Mich.: Institute of Public Administration, 1962), p. 3. But see Heady's excellent work, *Public Administration: A Comparative Perspective*, 3rd ed. (New York: Marcel Dekker), 1984, especially chap. 1.

[40] Keith M. Henderson, "A New Comparative Public Administration?" in *Toward a New Public Administration: The Minnowbrook Perspective*, Frank Marini, ed. (Scranton, Pa.: Chandler, 1971), p. 236.

[41] Heady, *Public Administration*, pp. 15–16. Riggs's classic work in development administration remains his *Administration in Developing Countries: The Theory of Prismatic Society* (Boston: Houghton-Mifflin, 1964), but see also Riggs's *Prismatic Society Revisited* (Morristown, N.J.: General Learning Press, 1973).

[42] George Grant, as quoted in Henderson, "A New Comparative Public Administration?" p. 239.

[43] *CAG Newsletter* (June 1967), pp. 12–13.

[44] Nicholas Henry, "The Relevance Question," in , *Education for Public Service: 1979*, Birkhead and Carroll, eds., p. 42.

[45] Golembiewski, *Public Administration as a Developing Discipline*, p. 147.

[46] Robert C. Fried, "Comparative Public Administration: The Search for Theories," in *Public Administration: The State of the Discipline* , Naomi B. Lynn and Aaron Wildavsky, eds.,(Chatham, N.J.: Chatham House, 1990), pp. 322–325.

[47] Montgomery Van Wart and N. Joseph Cayer, "Comparative Public Administration: Defunct, Dispersed, or Redefined?" *Public Administration Review*, 50 (March/April 1990), p. 238. The authors surveyed twenty "likely journals" published between 1982 and 1986, and analyzed 256 articles on comparative public administration.

[48] Keith M. Henderson, *Emerging Synthesis in American Public Administration* (New York: Asia Publishing House, 1966).

[49] See, for example: Edward H. Litchfield, "Notes on a General Theory of Administration," *Administrative Science Quarterly*, 1 (June 1956), pp. 3–29; John D. Millett, "A Critical Appraisal of the Study of Public Administration," *Administrative Science Quarterly*, 1 (September 1956), pp. 177–188; William A. Robson, "The Present State of Teaching and Research in Public Administration," *Public Administration*, 39 (Autumn 1961), pp. 217–222; Andre Molitor, "Public Administration Towards the Future," *International Review of Administrative Sciences*, 27, No. 4 (1961), pp. 375–384; Ivan Hinderaker, "The Study of Administration: Interdisciplinary Dimensions," *Summary of Proceedings of the Western Political Science Association*, supplement to *Western Political Quarterly*, 16 (September 1963), pp. 5–12; Paul J. Gordon, "Transcend the Current Debate in Administration Theory," *Journal of the Academy of Management*, 6 (December 1963), pp. 290–312; and Lynton K. Caldwell, "The Study of Administration in the Organization of the University," *Chinese Journal of Administration* (July 1965), pp. 8–16.

[50] Stewart, *Graduate Education in Public Administration*, p. 39.

[51] Delta Sigma Pi, *Eighteenth Biennial Survey of Universities Offering an Organized Curriculum in Commerce and Business Administration* (Oxford, Ohio: Educational Foundation of Delta Sigma Pi, 1962).

[52] Much of the following discussion is drawn from Kenneth L. Kraemer and James L. Perry, "Camelot Revisited: Public Administration Education in a Generic School," *Education for Public Service: 1980*, Guthrie S. Birkhead and James D. Carroll, eds. (Syracuse, N.Y.: Maxwell School of Citizenship and Public Affairs, Syracuse University Press, 1980), pp. 87–102.

[53] National Association of Schools of Public Affairs and Administration, *1982 Directory: Programs in Public Affairs and Administration* (Washington, D.C.: NASPAA, 1982), pp. 28, 30, and 178; and the 1982 Yale *Catalog*. Yale is not included in the NASPAA *Directory*.

[54] Wilson, "The Study of Administration," p. 209.

[55] James L. Perry and Kenneth L. Kramer, "Part Three: Is Public Management Similar or Different From Private Management?" in *Public Management: Public and Private Perspectives*, James L. Perry and Kenneth L. Kramer, eds. (Palo Alto, Calif.: Mayfield, 1983), p. 56.

[56] See, for example, Michael Blumenthal, "Candid Reflections of a Businessman in Washington," *Fortune* (January 29, 1979); Donald Rumsfeld, "A Politician Turned Executive," *Fortune* (September 10, 1979); A. J. Cervantes, "Memoirs of a Businessman-Mayor," *Business Week* (December 8, 1973); and James M. Kouzes, "Why Businessmen Fail in Government," *New York Times* (March 8, 1987).

[57] Graham T. Allison, Jr. observes the slimness of research comparing public and private management, stating there is "virtually none." However, Allison does a good job in describing what there is. See his "Public and Private Management: Are They Fundamentally Alike in All Unimportant Respects?" (Paper presented to the Pubic Management Research Conference, Washington, D.C.: Brookings Institution, November 1979). More important, as we explain in Part Two, there have been some significant additions to this literature, at least as it applies to organization theory, since Allison wrote his evaluation.

[58] Kraemer and Perry, "Camelot Revisited," p. 92. The investigators found twenty-two universities by their own count that used a generic model in teaching management.

[59] *Ibid*.

[60] Stanley I. Benn and Gerald F. Gaus, "The Public and the Private: Concepts and Action," in *Public and Private in Social Life*, S. I. Benn and G. F. Gaus, eds. (New York: St. Martin's Press, 1983), p. 5.

[61] *Ibid*., p. 9.

[62] *Ibid*., p. 10.

[63] *Ibid.*, p. 10.

[64] *Ibid.*, p. 9.

[65] James L. Perry, Hal G. Rainey, and Barry Bozeman, "The Public-Private Distinction in Organization Theory: A Critique and Research Strategy" (Paper presented at the 1985 Annual Meeting of the American Political Science Association, New Orleans, August 29–September 1, 1985), Table 1.

[66] Ira Sharkansky, *Wither the State? Politics and Public Enterprise in Three Countries* (Chatham, N.J.: Chatham House, 1979), p. 11.

[67] An admittedly unfair (and possibly fictitious) example of this problem is provided by a university, at which I was once a faculty member. It allegedly housed "the largest business school in the Free World." (It then had some 12,000 students.) The story goes that a lone student stood up in the back of a lecture hall containing several hundred business administration students and asked the instructor, "Sir, what is the social responsibility of business?" The professor replied unhesitatingly, "Son, business has no social responsibility." On hearing the answer, the class burst into applause.

[68] Perhaps the seminal statement of evaluation research as it has been adopted by the field of public administration is found in Carol H. Weiss, *Evaluation Research: Methods of Assessing Programs* (Englewood Cliffs, N.J.: Prentice-Hall, 1972).

[69] A detailed and excellent study of this process at the federal level is contained in: Hugh Heclo, "Executive Budget Making" (Paper presented to the Urban Institute Conference on Federal Budget Policy in the 1980s, Washington D.C.: September 29–30, 1983). But see also: Joseph White, "Much Ado About Everything: Making Sense of Federal Budgeting," *Public Administration Review*, 45 (September/October 1985), pp. 623–630.

[70] Five good examples of this emerging literature are: Susan Welch and John C. Comer, *Quantitative Methods for Public Administration: Techniques and Applications*, 2nd ed.(Homewood, Ill.: Dorsey Press, 1988); E. S. Quade, *Analysis for Public Decisions*, 2nd ed. (New York: North Holland, 1982); Christopher K. McKenna, *Quantitative Methods for Public Decision Making* (New York: McGraw-Hill, 1980); Richard D. Bingham and Marcus E. Etheridge, eds., *Reaching Decisions in Public Policy and Administration: Methods and Applications* (New York: Longman, 1982); and John Kenneth Gohagan, *Quantitative Analysis for Public Policy* (New York: McGraw-Hill, 1980). For an applied version of some of these techniques, see: Nicholas Henry, ed., *Doing Public Administration: Exercises in Public Management*, 3rd ed. (DuBuque, Iowa: William C. Brown, 1991).

[71] Robert Aaron Gordon and James E. Howell, *Higher Education for Business* (New York: Columbia University Press, 1959); and Frank Pierson, *The Education of American Businessmen* (New York: Carnegie Corporation, 1959).

[72] Albert Somit and Joseph Tannenhaus, *The Development of Political Science* (Boston: Allyn and Bacon, 1967), p. 188.

Somit and Tannenhaus are referring to: Committee for the Advancement of Teaching, American Political Science Association, *Goals for Political Science* (New York: Sloane, 1951).

[73] John C. Honey, "A Report: Higher Education for Public Service, *Public Administration Review*, 27 (November 1967), pp. 301–319.

[74] Peter Savage, "What Am I Bid for Public Administration?" *Public Administration Review*, 28 (July 1968), p. 391. See also James S. Bowman and Jeremy F. Plant, "Institutional Problems of Public Administration Programs: A House Without a Home," *Public Administration Education in Transition*, Thomas Vocino and Richard Heimovics, eds. (New York: Marcel Dekker, 1982), p. 40.

[75] Schick, "The Trauma of Politics", p. 162.

[76] As this is written, in fact, NASPAA continues to struggle with an in-depth examination of the public administration curriculum. The funding for this project is provided by the Mellon Foundation and is being conducted largely at Princeton University's Woodrow Wilson School of Public and International Affairs. However, it is unclear at this point if the final product will be comparable in depth and thoroughness to the studies of business education conducted in the 1950s.

[77] Representative works of the Science, Technology, and Public Policy movement that had lasting impacts include: Michael D. Reagan, *Science and the Federal Patron* (New York: Oxford University Press, 1969) and Lynton Keith Caldwell, *Environment: A Challenge to Modern Society* (Garden City, N.Y.: Natural History Press, 1970).

[78] Khi V. Thai, "Does NASPAA Peer Review Improve the Quality of PA/A Education?" *Public Administration Quarterly*, 8 (Winter 1985), pp. 446, 450.

[79] Mark R. Daniels, "Public Administration as an Emergent Profession: A Survey of Attitudes About the Review and Accreditation Programs" (Paper presented at the National Conference of the American Society for Public Administration, New York, April 1983); and J. Norman Baldwin, "Comparison of Perceived Effectiveness of MPA Programs Administered Under Different Institutional Arrangements," *Public Administration Review*, 48 (September/October 1988) pp. 876–884.

[80] Baldwin, "Comparison of Perceived Effectiveness of MPA Programs Administered Under Different Institutional Arrangements," p. 876. Baldwin surveyed 207 MPA program directors, and received responses from 158, over a 76 percent response rate.

[81] National Association of Schools of Public Affairs and Administration, *Programs in Public Affairs and Administration: 1990 Directory* (Washington, D.C.: National Association of Schools and Public Affairs, 1990), p. 20. All the following data are taken from this source, pp. 20–21.

[82] Derek Bok, "The President's Report, 1973–74," *Harvard Today*, 18 (Winter 1975); pp. 4–5, 10.

PART TWO: *Public Organizations: Theories, Concepts, and People*

CHAPTER

3

THE THREADS OF ORGANIZATION THEORY

In this and the following chapters, we shall examine various perspectives on organizations, pertinent concepts about how organizations work, and the kinds of people one finds in organizations.

MODELS, DEFINITIONS, AND ORGANIZATIONS

The notion of "models," a useful epistemological device in the social sciences, has considerable utility in discussing what an organization is. A model is a tentative definition that fits the data available about a particular object. Unlike a definition, a model does not represent an attempt to express the basic, irreducible nature of the object, and it is a freer approach that can be adapted to situations as needed. Thus, physicists treat electrons in one theoretical situation as infinitesimal particles and in another as invisible waves. The theoretical models of electrons permits both treatments, chiefly because no one knows exactly what an electron is (*i.e.*, no one knows its definition).

So it is with organizations. Organizations are different creatures to different people, and this phenomenon is unavoidable. Thus, organizations are "defined" according to the contexts and perspectives peculiar to the person doing the defining. For example, Victor A. Thompson states that an organization is "a highly rationalized and impersonal integration of a large number of specialists cooperating to achieve some announced specific objective"; Chester I. Barnard defines an organization as "a system of consciously coordinated personal activities or forces of two or more persons"; E. Wight Bakke says an organization is "a continuing system of differentiated and coordinated human activities utilizing, transforming, and welding together a specific set of human material, capital, ideational and natural resources into a unique, problem-solving whole whose function is to satisfy particular human needs in interaction with other systems of human activities and resources in its particular environment."[1]

These models of organizations are all quite different and lead to quite different conclusions on the part of their proponents. Bakke, a social psychologist, has constructed a model of organizations that allows him to dwell on the human effects organizations engender, which he does at length and with little regard for how organizations get their tasks accomplished. Conversely, Barnard's model permitted him to write about what interested him in organizations as a retired president of New Jersey Bell Telephone Company; that is, how cooperation and coordination were achieved in organizations. Thompson's model, with its emphasis on rationality, impersonality, and specialization, ultimately leads to his taking the radical stance that organizations should have no administrators whatever, only coldly efficient "specialists." Yet, none of these models is "wrong"; they only facilitate the viewpoint they are used to illustrate.

Even though organizations represent different things to different people, it is not enough to "define" organizations, as James G. March and Herbert A. Simon once did, with the phrase "organizations are more earthworm than ape."[2] As an indication of their simplicity, March and Simon are correct, to be sure, but it is possible to ascertain additional characteristics of organizations that will be useful in our model for the remainder of this book. It may be said, therefore, that organizations

1. are purposeful, complex human collectivities;
2. are characterized by secondary (or impersonal) relationships;
3. have specialized and limited goals;
4. are characterized by sustained cooperative activity;
5. are integrated within a larger social system;
6. provide services and products to their environment;
7. are dependent upon exchanges with their environment.

These seven features make up our working model of organizations. To them we might add an eighth that is applicable only to public organizations: Public organizations draw their resources (their taxes and legitimacy) from the polity and are mediated by the institutions of the state.

Organization theorists, using essentially this list of characteristics but stressing different features of it, have produced a vast body of literature on the nature of organizations. The literature can be trisected into these major streams: the closed model, the open model, and what the late James D. Thompson called "the newer tradition," which at-

tempts to synthesize both models.[3] These three streams, each with its own "schools" and substreams, represent the threads of organization theory. The remainder of this chapter considers each literary stream, the thinking of its principal contributors, and the relationships and distinctions between streams.

THE CLOSED MODEL OF ORGANIZATIONS

Traditionally, the closed model of organizations has perhaps had the largest influence on the thought of public administrationists. The model goes by many names: bureaucratic, hierarchical, formal, rational, and mechanistic are some of them. And there are at least three permutations, or schools, that have thrived within its framework: bureaucratic theory, scientific management, and administrative management (sometimes called generic management).

Characteristics

Tom Burns and G. M. Stalker have provided a useful listing of the principal features of the closed model of organizations that will suffice for our purpose:[4]

1. Routine tasks occur in stable conditions.
2. Task specialization (*i.e.*, a division of labor).
3. Means (or the proper way to do a job) are emphasized.
4. Conflict within the organization is adjudicated from the top.
5. "Responsibility" (or what one is supposed to do, one's formal job description) is emphasized.
6. One's primary sense of responsibility and loyalty are to the bureaucratic subunit to which one is assigned (*e.g.*, the accounting department).
7. The organization is perceived as a hierarchic structure (*i.e.*, schematically, the structure "looks" like a pyramid).

8. Knowledge is inclusive only at the top of the hierarchy (*i.e.*, only the chief executive knows everything).
9. Interaction between people in the organization tends to be vertical (*i.e.*, one takes orders from above and transmits orders below).
10. The style of interaction is directed toward obedience, command, and clear superordinate-subordinate relationships.
11. Loyalty and obedience to one's superior and the organization generally are emphasized.
12. Prestige is "internalized," that is, personal status in the organization is determined largely by one's office and rank.

So runs our closed model of organizations. One should recall that, like any model, it is what Max Weber called an "ideal type."[5] An ideal type is what an organization (or any other phenomenon) tries to be. Once we know what something wants to become (such as a little girl who wants to become a fire fighter), we can predict with some accuracy how it will behave (the same little girl probably will want a toy fire engine for her birthday). In this logic, closed-model organizations behave in such a way as to fulfill the twelve characteristics posited by Burns and Stalker, although this is not to say that any actual organization meets all twelve features in practice. For example, of organizations that are widely known, the Pentagon and the American military organization likely come closest to accomplishing the requisites of the closed model, but the Pentagon's exceptions to the model are obvious: nonroutine tasks, unstable conditions, and externalized prestige are frequent facts of organizational life in the military. Nevertheless, the military behaves in such a way as to minimize these exceptions to the closed model, along which it is basically patterned.

Bureaucratic Theory

The first school of the closed model that warrants consideration is that of bureaucratic theory. Its chief theorist and best known representative was Max Weber, a remarkable German sociologist who also gave us the sociology of religion, a theory of leadership, and, along with them, those phrases familiar to scholars and practitioners in public administration: "the Protestant work ethic" and "charisma." In what is perhaps a too succinct summary of Weber's model of bureaucracy, the features of bureaucracy amount to the following:

1. a hierarchy,
2. promotion based on professional merit and skill,
3. the development of a career service in the bureaucracy,
4. a reliance on and use of rules and regulations,
5. an impersonality of relationships among career professionals in the bureaucracy and with their clientele.

Organization theorists working in the open-model stream of organization theory have been most critical of Weberian bureaucratic theory, largely because it has been the most influential of all the schools in the closed model and most clearly represents the values of the closed model. Open-model theorists dislike the rigidity, the inflexibility, the emphasis on means rather than ends, and the manipulative and antihumanist overtones of Weberian bureaucratic theory. But, in Weber's defense, these criticisms have often been overdrawn and certainly have not been leveled with Weber's own social context in mind. Although the origins of bureaucracy can be traced at least as far back as Cardinal Richelieu's machinations to unify the French kingdom and Frederick the Great's project to turn poverty-ridden, land-locked Prussia into an efficient, military nation, Weber was writing at a time when "Blood and Iron" Bismarck was in the final stages of engineering his consolidation of the German states and when positions of public trust were still assigned on the basis of class rather than ability. To Weber, an impersonal, rule-abiding, efficient, merit-based career service provided the surest way of fulfilling the public interest in the case of a politically fragmented but culturally unified Germany and an arrogant, powerful, yet somewhat silly *Junker* class. Justice based on rational law would replace what Weber called "*Kadijustice*," or justice based on the whim of a charismatic leader; the rationalism of the bureaucracy would offset the romanticism of the polity, and this was to the good of society. In short, Weber, in a large sense, was not antihumanist in his thinking, but the effects of the bureaucracy that he so loudly touted often were, both to the citizen clients and to the bureaucrats themselves.

Scientific Management

Another major literary stream encompassed by the closed model is represented by the theories of scientific management. Scientific management refers to what is more popularly known as time-motion studies; it flourished at the beginning of the twentieth century, and remains very much in use today in industry.

Scientific management had (and has) its intellectual home in America's business schools. Its motivating concern was to improve organizational efficiency and economy for the sake of increased production. Perhaps the most firmly entrenched characteristic of scientific management was its view of humanity. Human beings were perceived as being adjuncts of the machine, and the primary objective of scientific management was to make them as efficient as the machines they operated. This view of humanity applied solely to workers on the assembly line and in the lower organizational echelons; it did not apply to upper-echelon managers—it was to them that the scientific management literature was addressed.

The key representatives of the scientific management school are Frederick Taylor (who gave the school its name with his 1911 volume titled *Principles of Scientific Management*) and Frank and Lillian Gilbreth.[6] The person-as-machine conception, replete with all its discomfiting moral overtones, are on clear display in the writings of Taylor and the Gilbreths. A notorious example of the conception occurs in Taylor's (likely fictional[7]) story of Schmidt, the pig-iron hauler, whom Taylor unabashedly declared to be "stupid . . . phlegmatic . . . [and] more nearly resembles in his mental make-up the ox than any other type."[8] After Taylor analyzed Schmidt's physical movements, he ordered him to change how he moved his body, and, as a result of these "scientific" alterations in Schmidt's physical behaviors, Schmidt's production went up from twelve and a half tons of pig-iron hauled per day to forty-seven tons. Taylor is obviously proud of his feat in rendering Schmidt a more efficient, machinelike man, and because of

such feats he was eminently successful as a time-motion expert in his day. Similarly, Frank and Lillian Gilbreth developed the concept of the "therblig," each one of which represented a category of eighteen basic human motions—all physical activity fell into a therblig class of one type or another. (The scientific management experts rarely were constrained by false modesty; try reading "therblig" backwards.)

The person-as-machine model of scientific management doubtless has a distasteful aura. People are not machines. They do not have an array of buttons on their backs that merely need pressing for them to be activated. This distaste with the person-as-machine conception, however, has often been extended by some critics to include a distaste for the notion of efficiency, or "getting the biggest bang for the buck," to borrow the former Secretary of Defense Robert McNamara's phrase. Outside the realms of theory, few are against efficiency in government, least of all the governed. So one must be wary of dismissing the value of efficiency along with "Taylorism" (as scientific management also is called), as has occasionally been done by humanist critics of the school.

One also should be cautious of relegating Taylorism to the intellectual slag heap on the assumption that its scholar/practitioners were consciously tools of the robber barons and premeditated exploiters of the working class. To a degree they were, but Taylor and the Gilbreths would likely be shocked by the suggestion. Taylor's Schmidt, it should be recalled, was employed according to the standard industrial system of the age: the piece-work method. For every ton Schmidt hauled, he was paid accordingly. Thus, to increase his daily production meant that Schmidt, as well as his bosses, was better off. Moreover, Taylor himself had served as an apprentice workman in a steel company and knew what that side of life was like. For their part the Gilbreths applied their therbligs to surgery techniques in hospitals, and the sharply ordered "Scalpel! Sponge!" we watch being slapped into a surgeon's palm by a superefficient nurse on television is a direct result of the Gilbreths's operating-room studies. Prior to the Gilbreths's analysis surgeons rustled around for their own instruments with one hand, evidently holding open the incision with the other. Efficiency can serve humanism as well as any other value, and this aspect sometimes is overlooked by open-model critics.

As a final note, it is worth observing that Taylorism has been used—and is being used—by the federal government, occasionally in such a way as to render the person-as-machine model painfully apparent. One example is the use of "psychotechnology" by the National Aeronautics and Space Administration (NASA) in its training of astronauts. The objective of NASA's use of psychotechnology is to "integrate" the astronaut with the technological environment of his space capsule, both mentally and physically, in order to reduce his or her response time. Psychotechnology is essentially scientific management updated, but with the added fillip of psychoemotional as well as physical conditioning being practiced.

Administrative Management

The final literature based on the closed model is administrative management, which also is called generic management. Luther Gulick and Lyndall Urwick's *Papers on the Science of Administration* is an outstanding example of administrative management in public administration, although James D. Mooney and Alan C. Reiley's *Principles of Organization* is more frequently cited as exemplary.[9]

Administrative management presumed that administration is administration, wherever it was found (hence, its other title, "generic"), and therefore devoted its energies to the discovery of "principles" of management that could be applied anywhere. Once an administrative principle was found, it logically should work in any kind of administrative institution: government bureaucracies, business management settings, hospitals, schools, universities, prisons, libraries, public health centers, and international institutions— wherever. Thus, Gulick and Urwick gave us POSDCORB, and Mooney and Reiley contributed four principles of organization: the coordinative principle, the scalar principle (or hierarchial structure), the functional principle (or division of labor), and the staff/line principle. There were other proponents, of course, such as Mary Parker Follet and Henri Fayol.[10] Their impact on public administration has been detailed in Chapter 2.

Administrative management is closer in concept and perceptions to Weberian bureaucratic theory than to Taylorian scientific management. The major reason for this is that bureaucracies are less concerned with time-motion economies than are assembly lines, and both bureaucratic theorists and administrative management analysts were primarily concerned with the optimal organization of administrators rather than production workers. But, like both bureaucratic theory and scientific management, administrative management holds economic efficiency (or "rationalism") as its ultimate criterion.

The difference between traditional bureaucratic theory and administrative management is largely one of theory as opposed to implementation. Weber and his academic peers were interested in learning how bureaucracies functioned, why they functioned as they did, and what their implications for larger society were. Mooney and Reiley, Gulick and Urwick, Follett, Fayol, and their colleagues thought they knew how bureaucracies functioned and why, and they were interested in applying the principles of administration they had derived from their knowledge to actual administrative organizations to enable administrators to operate more efficiently and effectively.

There also was a second, more subtle difference between bureaucratic theory and administrative management, one that provides a linkage between the closed and open models of organizations. Weber and Taylor did not think much about underlings and toilers in organizations beyond their capacities for obedience (in Weber's case) and production (in Taylor's case), and they felt that both capacities were almost limitless, provided managers took their respective writings to heart. But with the emergence of the theorists on administrative management, a hint surfaced that underlings and toilers in organizations might conceivably have minds of their own. Indeed, it was not much of a hint, barely an inkling. But it was there, and it is noticeable in Mooney and Reiley's contention that the "indoctrination" of subordinates is vital to well-managed organizations. In fact, Mooney and Reiley attributed the durability of the Roman Catholic Church to its doctrine and its indoctrination—a function which has maintained a viable, continuing organization for nearly 2,000 years. Furthermore, in their view, both the doctrine and the indoctrination constitute a highly praiseworthy method of organizational control and survival.

Such a grudging concession to the thinking powers of subordinates did not amount to much in terms of high esteem for the subordinates' mental prowess generally. But it represented a recognition that subordinates were people (like managers) and could think (almost like managers). It was left for certain writers using the open model to assert that underlings and toilers could indeed think, feel, and behave on their own, and often differently from the ways they were supposed to. Some of these writers would argue that subordinates could outthink, outsmart, and outfox their superordinates—and did—with ease.

THE OPEN MODEL OF ORGANIZATIONS

The open model of organizations traditionally has had a greater influence on business administration than on public administration, although this situation has been changing in recent years. Like the closed model, the open model goes by many names. Collegial, competitive, freemarket, informal, natural, and organic are some of them, and, like the closed model, three literary streams run through the model's overarching framework. These streams, or schools, are, first, the human relations school; second, the (newer) field of organization development; and third, the literature that views the organization as a unit functioning in its environment. It is this final stream that has a unique utility to public administration.

The historical origins of the open model precede the intellectual roots of the closed model, originally developed by Max Weber, by more than a century and a half. In a perceptive essay, sociologist Alvin W. Gouldner[11] attributes the open model's original conceptualization to Count Louis de Rouvroy Saint-Simon, the brilliant French social thinker, and to his protégé Auguste Comte, the "father of sociology." Saint-Simon and Comte wrote during a span of time that began in the corrupt *ancien regime* of Louis XIV, continued through the bloody French Revolution and the rule of the military despot and national hero, Napoleon Bonaparte, and ended under the reign of Louis Napoleon. Partly as a reaction to the administrative stultification of the last days of the French kings and the explosiveness of the Revolution, Saint-Simon, and later Comte, speculated on what the administration of the future would be like. They thought that it would be predicated on skill rather than heredity; "cosmopolitanism" (by which Saint-Simon meant the development of new professions based on technology) would be the order of the day and organizations themselves would be a liberating force for man. Throughout, Saint-Simon and Comte stressed the value of spontaneously created organizations that developed "naturally" as they were needed. On reflection, Saint-Simon and Comte's views on organizations and society sound like a seventeenth-century version of Alvin Toffler's concept of "Ad Hocracy" in his book, *Future Shock*.[12]

Characteristics

Once again we rely on Burns and Stalker's research for a listing of the principal features of the open model.[13]

1. Nonroutine tasks occur in unstable conditions.
2. Specialized knowledge contributes to common tasks (thus differing from the closed model's specialized *task* notion in that the specialized *knowledge* possessed by any one member of the organization may be applied profitably to a variety of tasks undertaken by various other members of the organization).
3. Ends (or getting the job done) are emphasized.
4. Conflict within the organization is adjusted by interaction with peers.
5. "Shedding of responsibility" is emphasized (*i.e.,* formal job descriptions are discarded in favor of all organization members contributing to all organizational problems).
6. One's sense of responsibility and loyalty are to the organization as a whole.
7. The organization is perceived as a fluidic network structure (*i.e.,* the organization schematically "looks" like an amoeba).

8. Knowledge can be located anywhere in the organization (*i.e.*, everybody knows something relevant about the organization, but no one, including the chief executive, knows everything).

9. Interaction between people in the organization tends to be horizontal as well as vertical (*i.e.*, everyone interacts with everyone else).

10. The style of interaction is directed toward accomplishment, "advice" (rather than commands), and it is characterized by a "myth of peerage," which envelops even the most obvious superordinate-subordinate relationships (*e.g.*, a first-name "familiarity" exists even between the president and the office boy, on the logic that the maintenance of an image of intimacy is somehow "friendlier").

11. Task achievement and excellence of performance in accomplishing a task are emphasized.

12. Prestige is "externalized" (*i.e.*, personal status in the organization is determined largely by one's professional ability and reputation).

So runs our open model of organizations, which, like the closed model, is an ideal type. It seldom if ever exists in actuality, although a major university might come close (which is why the open model is occasionally called the "collegial" model). A Big Ten or Ivy League university could meet many of the requisites of the open model, notably specialized knowledge located throughout the organization, large horizontal interaction, and externalized prestige. But exceptions to the model also are apparent; tasks (*e.g.*, teaching, research, and studying) are relatively routine and, at least among the faculty, one is likely to find a higher degree of loyalty to the subunit (*i.e.*, the academic department) than to the organization as a whole.

Human Relations

Human relations, the first of three schools of the open model, focuses on organizational variables never considered in the closed model: cliques, informal norms, emotions, and personal motivations, among others. Paradoxically, this focus resulted from what originally was intended to be a research undertaking in scientific management, a literature at the opposite end of the continuum in terms of the values held by its theorists.

In 1924 Elton Mayo and Fritz J. Roethlisberger began a series of studies (later known as the "Haw-

thorne studies," so named for the location of the factory) of working conditions and worker behavior at a Western Electric factory. Their experiment was predicated on the then plausible Taylorian hypothesis that workers would respond like machines to changes in working conditions. To test their hypothesis they intended to alter the intensity of light available to a group of randomly selected workers. The idea—that when the light became brighter, production would increase, and that when the light became dimmer, production would decrease—is all very common-sensical, of course. The workers were told they would be observed as an experimental group. The lights were turned up and production went up. The lights turned down and production went *up*. Mayo and Roethlisberger were disconcerted. They dimmed the lights to near darkness, and production kept climbing.

Among the explanations of this phenomenon that later came forth were:

1. Human workers probably are not entirely like machines.

2. The Western Electric workers were responding to some motivating variable other than the lighting, or despite the lack of lighting.

3. They likely kept producing more in spite of poor working conditions because they knew they were being watched.

Mayo and his colleagues were so impressed by these initial findings that they ultimately conducted a total of six interrelated experiments over an eight-year period. In part because of the massive size of the undertaking, the Hawthorne studies number among the most influential empirical researches ever conducted by social scientists. Most notably they produced the famous term "Hawthorne effect," or the tendency of people to change their behavior when they know that they are being observed. But even more important, the studies were interpreted by succeeding generations of management scientists as validating the idea that unquantifiable relationships (or "human relations") between workers and managers, and among workers themselves, were primary determinants of workers' efficiency; conversely, material incentives and working conditions, while relevant, were less significant as motivators of productivity.

A reinterpretation of the Hawthorne data, using statistical techniques that were unavailable to Mayo and Roethlisberger, has turned the "human relations" interpretation upside down. In an important new analysis of the original data, Richard Herbert Franke and James D. Kaul concluded that human relations were *not* the reasons behind worker efficiency, but that the real reasons underlying increased productivity were such traditional motivators as "managerial discipline," fear (in the form of anxiety over the possibility of losing one's job during the Depression), reduction of fatigue (the experimental groups were given rest periods), and money (the groups were also given group pay incentives).[14]

Although the notion that the Hawthorne study workers produced more because of the relations among themselves and management has been recently and seriously questioned, the Hawthorne studies nonetheless marked the continuation of the Saint-Simonian tradition after a century-long gap and the beginning of human relations school as we know it.

Much of human relations has concerned itself with the informal work group at the assembly-line level. What makes them work or not work? How do they behave and why? Yet increasingly, human relations has had the managerial echelons as its investigative object, and this has contributed to the study of public administration.

Notable in terms of the impact of the human relationists on public administration is their research on motivation and job satisfaction. Much of this research centers around the "hierarchy of human needs" developed by A. H. Maslow. Maslow perceived human desires to be based first on the greatest need, (1) physiological essentials, which provided the foundation for the human's next greatest need, (2) security, then (3) love or belongingness, (4) then self-esteem, and finally (5) self-actualization. For the record, Maslow later added a sixth and highest need, "metamotivation,"[15] but Maslow's self-actualization need has spawned the most analysis in public administration. Self-actualization refers to the individual growing, maturing, and achieving a deep inner sense of self-worth as he or she relates to his or her job and organization. In terms of the person and the organization, Maslow wrote that these "highly evolved" self-actualized individuals assimilated "their work into the identity, into the self, *i.e.*, work actually becomes part of the self, part of the individual's definition of himself."[16]

Frederick Herzberg stimulated much of the empirical research that related to Maslow's hierarchy of needs. Herzberg developed the concepts of "motivators," which referred to direct determiners of job satisfaction (*e.g.*, "responsibility"), and "hygienic" or "intrinsic" factors, which related to psychological satisfactions derived from the task environment (*e.g.*, salary).[17] Although, as we describe in Chapter 5, Maslow's hierarchy of needs does not appear to apply as well in cultures other than that of the United States, limited testing in other cultures of Herzberg's motivation theory indicates that his theory does appear to work in different cultural contexts. In a comparative study of American and Korean public employees, it was found that "Herzberg's two-factor theory of job motivation applies with equal force in both national settings."[18]

Herzberg's framework (itself a derivative of Maslow's hierarchy of needs) and various modifications of it have produced a voluminous body of literature that attempts to test such hypotheses as the idea that "participative decision-making, interesting jobs, and related organization variables correlate positively with job satisfaction," and that "job satisfaction correlates positively with job performance." But, when one reviews this literature, as Frank K. Gibson and Clyde E. Teasley have done, there is not a clear-cut body of empirical results that relates organizational effectiveness to what Gibson and Teasley call "the humanistic model of organizational motivation."[19]

Organization Development

An important subfield of the open model is called organization development (OD). The overlappings of OD with the human relations literature are manifold, but it nonetheless can be considered a separate school because it attempts to go beyond the locus of small group theory and is almost missionary in its zeal to "democratize" bureaucracies.

Organization development is a planned, organizationwide attempt directed from the top that is designed to increase organizational effectiveness and viability through calculated interventions in the active workings of the organization using knowledge from the behavioral sciences. This intervention often is accomplished through third-party consultants. The stress in this definition of OD is on planned change, systemic analysis, top management, and the objectives of organizational effectiveness and "health." Richard Beckhard argues that these emphases distinguish OD from other kinds of efforts to change organizations, such as sensitivity training or "management development," which are not action oriented, and operations research, which is not human value oriented.[20]

Organization development can be viewed as having evolved along two distinct if intertwining branches, both of which owe much of their initial impetus to the social psychologist, Kurt Lewin. Wendell L. French and Cecil H. Bell, Jr., call these branches the "laboratory-training stem" and the "survey research feedback stem."[21] The laboratory approach focuses on small group methods; its origins may be traced to conferences held in 1946 and 1947, headed by Lewin, Kenneth Benne, Leland Bradford, and Ronald Lippitt. These meetings were sponsored by the Office of Naval Research, the National Education Association, and the Research Center for Group Dynamics. Elements of these organizations later formed the National Training Laboratories for Group Development, which became a significant force in the development of T-group (therapy group) and sensitivity training techniques. By the early 1960s it was becoming apparent that the laboratory approach could be used for entire organizations, not just small groups. Douglas McGregor, working for Union Carbide, and J. S. Mouton and Robert Blake, working for Esso Standard Oil, used the first versions of a "managerial grid" concept.[22] These efforts represented the initial attempt to involve top management in the human development of the organization, to take measurements of individual behaviors, to trace feedback effects, and to use "third-party" outside consultants to foster organizational innovation. These exercises in *intergroup* development represented a real departure from the standard T-group approach.

The survey research feedback stem can be traced to Lewin's Research Center for Group Dynamics at the Massachusetts Institute of Technology, which he founded in 1945. On Lewin's death in 1947, the Center's senior staff (including Lippitt, McGregor, and Leon Festinger) moved to the Survey Research Center at the University of Michigan and formed the Institute for Social Research. The people involved in the Institute began the initial studies of measuring employee and management attitudes concerning their organization. Feedback from these surveys was maximized through the use of interlocking group conferences. Thus, as these techniques developed, the individual participant in the organization was given a sense of the whole and of his or her particular role and of the roles of others as they pertained to the organization.

Since its beginnings in the late 1940s, OD has been used in a number of ways. While many of its applications have been in business organizations, its influence in public bureaucracies and in the broad-ranging field of community development has been accelerating since the early 1960s. Chris Argyris applied OD techniques in 1967 to the United States Department of State in an effort to resolve intergroup conflicts between Foreign Service officers and administrative officers. OD has been used for such diverse purposes as maximizing communications between a Community Action Agency and an Indian tribe, and for facilitating the organization of a new junior high school. The goals of these and many other OD projects have been and are broadly humanistic and reflect the underlying values of the field. The mission of organization development is to

1. improve the individual member's ability to get along with other members (which the field calls "interpersonal competence"),
2. legitimate human emotions in the organization,
3. increase mutual understanding among members,
4. reduce tensions,
5. enhance "team management" and intergroup cooperation,
6. develop more effective techniques for conflict resolution through nonauthoritarian and interactive methods, and
7. evolve less structured and more "organic" organizations.

OD advocates strongly believe that achieving these goals of the field will render organizations more effective in the rapidly changing environ-ment of technological societies. "The basic value underlying all organization-development theory and practice is that of *choice*. Through focused attention and through the collection and feedback of relevant data to relevant people, more choices become available and hence better decisions are made."[23] The techniques used by OD to maximize organizational choice include the use of confrontation groups, T-groups, sensi-tivity training, attitude questionnaires, third-party change agents in the form of outside consultants, data feedback, and the "education" of organizational members in the values of open-ness and participatory decision making.

Although it is commonly believed that OD is used primarily by the private sector, it may be that as many as half of all the applications of organization development conducted between 1945 and 1980 were conducted in government agencies—574 of them by one count.[24] In a study of 270 of these applications, or 47 percent of all known public-sector applications, it was found that these exercises, for the most part, were far-reaching and successful: "public-sector OD inter-ventions tend to hunt the bigger game: racial tension; conflict . . .; basic reorganization."[25] Moreover, 84 percent of the respondents in this survey reported that organization development had had "highly positive and intended effects" on their agencies, or that there had been a "definite balance of positive and intended effects"; only 9 percent reported negative effects.[26] These rates were quite comparable to the private sector's experience with OD.[27]

Human Relations and Organization Development: A Humanistic Caveat—and a Managerial One

Both the human relations and organization de-velopment schools of the open model draw on, and have been heavily influenced by, a branch of psy-chology called humanistic psychology, or *third force* psychology. Humanistic psychology, like OD, emerged in the 1940s in the United States, and in many ways its aims and values are identical to those of organization development: the flowering of the human being into his or her full potential, or a kind of self-actualization. Maslow, in fact, is considered to be at least as much a central contrib-utor to humanistic psychology as he is to human relations and OD. Other major figures in third force psychology are Carl Rogers (who is closely identified with the growth movement and with encounter groups), Arthur Janov (the originator of primal scream therapy), Ida P. Rolf (of "rolfing" fame), Alexander Lowen (promoter of bioenerget-ics), Fritz Perls (of Gestalt therapy), R. D. Laing, and Werner Erhard.[28] There are, of course, others.

A humanistic caveat. Most of the third force psychologists are therapists—what would be known in public administration circles as practi-tioners. They believe that psychology can be a much more positive force in society than its tradi-tional use of merely helping the neurotic would indicate. And, perhaps because they are practi-tioners rather than theorists, they are more inter-ested in developing and applying techniques of intervention (such as rolfing, primal scream ther-apy, and encounter groups) that are designed to "open up" people and free them of the psycholog-ical repressions of civilization than they are in developing and testing theory.

This bias toward action, as opposed to analysis, which is implicit in humanistic psychology, is clearly reflected in the practice of organization development. As one theorist of organization de-velopment noted, "The point is not to analyze [organizations] *but to change them!*"[29] More fully expressed, the goal of the humanistic psycholo-gists is to create a spiritually aware, happy, loving person who is unencumbered by society's hang ups. How such a "primal man"—a twentieth-cen-tury version of Jean Jacque Rousseau's natural man—might relate to the institutions of society does not concern the humanistic psychologists; society is not their field, people are, and simply because civilization is neurotic, it does not follow that people must be, too. Nevertheless, the inter-vention techniques created and used by the human-istic psychologists seem to be powerful; people often do appear to be altered after having experi-enced them. But what those changes really mean to both the individuals undergoing them and to others who later must relate to these new, rolfed, bioenergized, primal people is unclear.

The third force psychologists have deliberately set themselves apart from the field's more established traditions, notably the behaviorists and the Freudians. These traditions are insufficiently upbeat, visionary, and change oriented for their tastes. But whether the humanistic psychologists have been able to offer a serious alternative to mainstream psychology is an open question, and at least one observer has noted that most of the literature of third force psychology is "more or less pop psychology marked by carelessness and a lack of concern for the scientific method."[30] (It should be noted, however, that, in the views of many humanistic psychologists, their lack of scientific rigor is not a criticism, since they typically see themselves as practicing something beyond science, or at least something irrelevant to it.)

There is, certainly, a bright side to humanistic psychology: in its rejection of the behaviorists (at least as represented by B. F. Skinner), it overtly rejects on ethical grounds the idea that controlling the behavior of others through the manipulation of their immediate environment is acceptable. As Rogers puts it,

Who will be controlled? Who will exercise control? What type of control will be exercised? Most important of all, toward what end . . . will control be exercised? It is on questions of this sort that there exist . . . deep differences [between the humanistic psychologists and the behavioral psychologists].[31]

The third force psychologists, in sum, may argue that there is human salvation beyond science, but they would never suggest that there is human happiness (as Skinner contends) "beyond freedom and dignity,"[32] and this is likely to their credit.

There is, however, a dark side of the (third) force. In their dismissal of the Freudians, the third force psychologists risk dismissing the ego as well.

Sigmund Freud posited four dimensions of personality structure: the id, the libido, the ego, and the superego.[33] The *id* is the oldest and most basic element of personality; it is inherited, unconscious, utterly amoral, has no direct relationship to the external world, and exists solely to satisfy its own needs. The *libido* is the id's energy, its tension-release mechanism; the id functions through the libido. The *ego* is the conscious and preconscious part of personality, and is formed by a person's experiences; unlike the id, which is guided by the pleasure principle, the ego is directed by the reality principle, relates to the external world, and acts as a check on the id and libido. It is the ego that does such "unnatural" things to us as make us sublimate, repress, and fall in love. Finally, the *superego* is our conscience. It is a specialized part of the ego, is entirely conscious, and is that portion of the ego that is on the front line of its ongoing battle with the id and libido. (Obviously, we have grossly simplified Freud's theory of personality, but then this is not a book about psychology.)

Where the humanistic psychologists differ from the Freudians is on the question of whether the id and libido are less or more important than the ego and superego; the humanistic psychologists take a considerably greater interest in the former, and hold the id and libido in significantly higher esteem than the Freudians. Ego and superego, in their view, are associated with the repressiveness of society, while the id and libido relate to the holistic, primal person that they are trying to release from the forces of repression and guilt through their therapy techniques.

This emphasis seems to relate to a perspective held by the third force psychologists that humanity is fundamentally better (in moral terms) than the Freudians believe; the id is not all that bad. As a distinguished humanistic psychologist said, "So when a Freudian . . . tells me . . . that he perceives man as 'innately evil' or more precisely, 'innately destructive,' I can only shake my head in wonderment. . . . How could it be that [we], working with such a similar purpose in such intimate relationships with individuals in distress, experience people so differently?"[34] As one writer astutely observes, the humanistic psychologist's greater faith in the goodness of humanity leads to a greater emphasis on the idea that the ego and superego are indistinguishably integrated with—are part and parcel of—the id and libido. "For Freud, the id was basic; for [the humanistic psychologists] it existed simultaneously and equally with the superego."[35] This conception by the humanistic psychologists of the *inseparability* of the amoral id and the conscience-stricken superego, in contrast to the Freudian view of the virile id and lusty libido being held in tenuous and not-always-successful check by a repressed ego and guilty superego, made for much nicer people.

Nicer? Nicer in terms of being at peace with themselves, nicer in terms of being freed from the repressions of a neurotic society, nicer in terms of feeling good and feeling free to express themselves. The third force psychologists believe that nicer people—peaceful, unrepressed, happy people—are more moral people, and this is a logical conclusion if one believes, as the third force psychologists do, that people are inherently good, that they are not "innately evil" or "innately destructive." But "moral" to the humanistic psychologists is not an interactive concept, as it is to the Freudians and the behaviorists. To be loving and happy is moral, and that seems to be about it. Morality is not defined in external and social terms (society, after all, is perceived as repressive, neurotic, and part of the problem), but in internal and individual terms; to be happy is to be moral.

By contrast, the Freudians and the behaviorists do define morality in external and social terms. One can be unhappy—indeed, a curmudgeon—and still be moral. Morality is defined by the Freudians and behaviorists in terms of the individual and the external world, of a reality "out there," of behavior.

The humanistic psychologists are less concerned than the Freudians and behaviorists with developing people who fit in well with society, and are more interested in helping people fit in well with themselves. Releasing the personality from the forces of repression is releasing people's inherent goodness. And, because the ego and superego are the personality's vessels of society's repression, it follows that the id and libido should be granted greater freedom from them. The intervention techniques practiced by the third force psychologists are designed to do just that. Ultimately, the ego and superego lose.

Recall, however, that the ego is that part of the personality which is directed by the reality principle. When it goes (or so the Freudians believe), so does a person's ability to make his or her own choices on the basis of experiences with the external world. The result is a vacuum into which many substitutes may enter. But when the reality check provided by the ego is diminished, the resulting vacuum is not "filled" by the pleasure-loving id (which is off having a good time on its own); it is filled instead by some other reality check, a substitute ego provided by the external world that defines reality in terms of *its* own experience. These substitutes for the ego can be authority figures who may be "good" (at least as defined by society), such as the Pope, or "evil," such as the demagogic Jim Jones of Jonestown, Guyana, who in 1977 persuaded more than 900 of his followers to commit mass suicide because they accepted his version of reality.

It is of note in this regard that 22 percent of the followers of Bhagwan Shree Rajneesh, who resided in the commune of Rajneeshpuram in central Oregon (all of whom had turned over all their worldly goods to the Bhagwan and worked full time for him) during the early 1980s, had university degrees in psychiatry or psychology, and half of these held advanced degrees in these disciplines. Yet, according to one observer who studied the commune over a period of years, "with all the years of academic training represented, there was not, as far as I could determine, a single straight Freudian or straight behaviorist" among the Bhagwan's followers; all ascribed to third force psychology.[36]

So what? Consider this statement, made by a Rajneeshee named Ava, after the Bhagwan had fled the country and Rajneeshpuram's leaders had been imprisoned for fraud, for poisoning their fellow Rajneeshees (including Ava) and a number of outsiders, for bugging the quarters of most of the Bhagwan's followers (and the Bhagwan himself), and for attempted murder:

"I conveniently forgot things because they seemed impossible to remember. . . . I forgot the tape. . . of a conversation with Bhagwan which showed he was involved, well, in things he said he wasn't. . . . For three days, I was just so *angry* at Bhagwan. But I'm over that now."

Ava called in a third time to say that she hoped that she had not sounded too negative before. She had been in a bad space, but now she had accepted everything and Bhagwan was still her Master.[37]

One might infer that such is the fate of those who release their egos to others, and release of the ego is implicit in humanistic psychology, and, to a lesser extent, in human relations and organization development. One does not necessarily have to substitute another person—a "master"—for one's ego. One can substitute one's organization and one's work for it instead. This is, recall, what Maslow meant by self-actualization: "work actually becomes part of the self."[38]

A Managerial Caveat. To move from bureaucracy to commune, as we have done in this discussion, may seem to wander too far afield. This is, after all, a book about making public organizations and public administrators more effective, not about opening up the id and libido of public employees.

True, but here our apparent digression leads us to another aspect of human relations and organization development that is worth positing as a managerial caveat, as opposed to a humanistic one, about OD in particular. The third force psychologists seem to have convinced some of those third-party change agents (*i.e.*, OD consultants), who are hired by managers to make their organizations more effective, that helping organizations become more productive should not necessarily be at the top of their agendas; instead, making the organization's employees more self-actualized, fulfilled, and liberated human beings should top the OD consultants' agendas. Attaining this objective, of course, is not why OD consultants are hired by managers; they are hired by managers to make their organizations more effective and productive in their organizational environments, and if happier, more self-actualized employees are the means to this end, then all is well and good. But, from the manager's viewpoint, the means are not the end; the end is the end, and management's end is a more productive and effective organization, but not necessarily happier employees.

We are not suggesting that OD consultants and the values they represent are not useful to organizations and, indeed, to the public interest; they are. But the possible disconnection between the agendas and objectives of the practitioners of organization development and the practitioners of administration, both public and private, is worthy of note as a managerial caveat.

In a revealing article about this potential difference in agendas of third-party change agents in the OD tradition and of public administrators, Thomas H. Fitzgerald questions the propriety and morality of third-party change agents taking the side of the executives who hire them, and facilitating their interests. He writes that some OD consultants

...often share the mindset of management.... More than a decade ago, feminist writers pointed out male body language and condescending gestures, their special idiom for keeping women defined in pejorative ways—but people in the rank and file see these behaviors all the time in managers and executives.

Some consultants display similar managerial bearing. They are breezy, self-assured, and excessively articulate, and they take charge of the discussion. Employees soon figure out whose side they are on.... That style... permits consultants to gloss over the grubby realities of worklife....[39]

If this quotation is representative of the values, objectives, and agendas held by third-party change agents in dealing with the problems of managers, then perhaps managers, including public administrators, should be at least aware of them.

The Public Organization as a Unit in its Environment

A third school of the open model has a less bulky literature, but nonetheless is separate and identifiable. Notable among its early contributors are Chester I. Barnard, Philip Selznick, and Burton Clark.[40] This literary stream is currently undergoing a significant revitalization. It is characterized by its use of the organization as a whole as its analytical unit (in contrast to the other schools' preferences for the small group), its theme of the organizational pressures and constraints emanating from the environment, and its organizational strategies designed to cope with environmentally spawned problems.

Because this literary stream emphasizes so heavily the organization's relations with its task environment, a word of explanation about what the term *environment* means in the context of organization theory may be helpful. Herbert Kaufman explains the concept well:

Speaking metaphorically, you might liken the [organization's task] environment to a reticular pattern of incessant waves constituting a perpetually varying net or screen sweeping continuously through the total aggregation of interlocked organizations that form in the human population. The openings in the ever-changing screen constantly assume different shapes and sizes. At the same time, the organizations themselves are always changing as they try to avoid being swept away. If the two sets of changes are such that an organization can "fit" through the "holes" when the screen passes, the organization survives; if not, it is carried off.[41]

Kaufman's vivid description of the impact of the task environment on the organization—a description that implies the task environment is far more important to the success or failure of an organization than are such "internal" variables an organizational leadership or managerial competence—"goes double" for public organizations. Unlike private organizations, whose environment amounts to little more than the marketplace itself, public organizations must endure in an environment composed of far more complex, aggressive, and intrusive forces, among them politics, culture, law, economics, and organizational interdependencies not present in the corporate world. Perhaps because of this reality, organization theorists who are interested in such issues as strategic management and planning find themselves studying business firms (to manage, plan, and strategize require, after all, some independence from outside forces), whereas scholars more interested in the organization's relations with its task environment incline more toward the study of government agencies (where the impact of the environment on the inner workings of the organization is considerably more apparent than in private companies).

It is with this appreciation of the relationship between an organization and its task environment in mind that Selznick, for example, developed his "co-optation" concept in his book on the establishment of the Tennessee Valley Authority (TVA). The term *co-optation* referred to the strategy employed by the TVA Board of Directors in gaining the acceptance, and ultimately the strong support, of initially hostile local interests by granting their representatives membership on the board. The TVA, as a result, influenced and cajoled the local interests far more profoundly than the local interests influenced the TVA; in short, the TVA co-opted the local interests, but was required to modify slightly its own purposes in so doing.

There may have been a "sleeper effect" in the TVA's board's co-optation of local interests. In a more recent analysis of the TVA at the grass roots, Richard A. Couto found that those local interests that had been co-opted by the top administrators of the Tennessee Valley Authority had, nearly forty years later, become considerably more powerful, and, in fact, were able to develop a sufficient level of power that they could "foster new operative goals for TVA and to prevent TVA initiated modifications of those goals."[42] Couto concludes that, while Selznick was essentially correct in his description of co-optation, co-optation is a more dynamic process than Selznick initially posited, and Couto found that co-optation was, in reality, a "process of participation and representation rather than a stable, enduring outcome of bureaucratic process."[43] Most significantly, co-optation legitimated an agency's leadership in the eyes of both the agency and the co-opted groups (as Selznick found), but, in contrast to Selznick's findings, the supposedly co-opted groups, under certain conditions, could acquire real power over the agency. Co-optation also often functioned as a very effective form of participation and representation for some groups that traditionally had been relatively powerless.

Given its relatively small numbers, the theoretical school, in dealing with organizations as units in their environment, has had a disproportionate impact on public administration. This is understandable, however, for the stream is primarily concerned about the "public" (*i.e.*, the "environment"), and its political relationship with the organization. In this emphasis, the organization-environment literature is uniquely concerned with the problems of public administration.

Perhaps it is predictable, then, that more recent organization theorists in this stream have begun to address directly the unique aspects of public organizations, and the emphasis of their thinking is on how the task environment of public organizations differs from that of private organizations, and how these differences affect public organizations.[44] Although one may categorize these distinctions along many dimensions, the following are reasonably straightforward: the high importance of the demands being made on the public organization by its task environment relative to internal management needs; the unique impact of the task environment on the public organization's structure and bureaucracy; its decision making; the motivation of public managers; their satisfaction with their work; the public organization's internal management; and even the performance of its administrators.

Internal needs versus external demands. If the literature on the differences between public and private organizations agrees on anything, it is that upper-echelon public administrators must spend considerably more time and attention on their agency's external environment, and less on matters of internal management, than their counterparts in business.[45]

This reality brings with it several corollaries. On the one hand, public bureaucrats, for example, must deal with far more constraints and controls (most typically in the form of legal requirements) over their organizations than must private managers.[46] However, these constraints can be "informal" and political, as well as legal, and at least as equally controlling.[47]

On the other hand, the political environment (which is a specialized type of the task environment in which all organizations find themselves) in which public organizations must work provides opportunities and challenges as well as limitations. Support for the public agency is "out there," often waiting to be mobilized, in the forms of clients (or prospective clients), interest groups, other organizations sympathetic to the agency's goals, legislators, and other constituents.[48] It is this condition that forces public executives, as noted earlier, to expend considerably more effort on their organization's external relations, and that accords them a more political and expository role than their colleagues in the private sector.[49]

Structure and bureaucracy. Perhaps the most notable impact of the relative importance of environmental demands on public organizations is seen in how they alter organizational structure. Anthony Downs was among the first to assess the impact of the public organization's task environment on its internal structure. In *Inside Bureaucracy*, Downs argued that organizations (*i.e.*, government agencies) deprived of free market conditions in their environments were more pres-

sured to create additional layers of hierarchy than were organizations that functioned in the marketplace. Because it was so much more difficult for public organizations to measure output than it was for private organizations (which had an "automatic" measure of output called the profit margin), internal rules were needed to control spending, assure fair treatment of clients, and coordinate large-scale activities. The presence of these rules, in turn, demanded extensive monitoring to ensure compliance, and such monitoring meant more reports, and more effort spent on internal communications. Thus, Downs's "law of hierarchy" is a function of an organization's task environment, and whether or not that environment provides market mechanisms.[50]

Donald P. Warwick later expanded on Downs's main points by explicating those elements in the environment that shape the internal structure of public organizations: legislatures may do so by statute, accounting and budgeting bureaus may mandate highly bureaucratized record-keeping procedures, interest groups may pressure for internal changes, and so forth.[51]

A somewhat different conception of the role that environmental factors play in the dynamics of public organizations is provided by Marshall W. Meyer. Meyer agrees that the task environment has an unusually salient impact on public organizations, and also concurs that public organizations react to these impacts by "bureaucratizing"—that is, by adding on increasingly complex mechanisms. But, in contrast to the implications of Downs and Warwick, Meyer contends that such bureaucratization is not a sign of resistance to new demands from the environment, but is instead one of eagerness to accommodate those demands; additional layers of bureaucracy in a public organization may be used not only to control but also to serve, and they connote a desire to deliver more programs to more people in more ways: "contrary to stereotypes, bureaus tend to be very open and vulnerable to their immediate environments . . . increasing the bureaucratization of public agencies through additional rules and layers of hierarchy results in part from their openness to their environments."[52]

Although Meyer is more upbeat than are Downs and Warwick in his assessment of how the task environment affects the structure of a public organization, these and other analysts agree that, because of the public organization's greater vulnerability and openness to its task environment relative to its counterpart in the private sector, the public organization is significantly different in additional ways from the private organization. Certainly these differences include those found in the areas of decision making, motivation, satisfaction, management, and performance evaluation.

Decision making. The unique qualities of the public organization's exchanges with its task environment result in some unique qualities of decision making and management within public organizations. Decision making in the public organization is less autonomous than in the private sector,[53] and procedures are more constricting.[54] Practitioners who have served in both the public and private sectors at high levels note that legislators (who are equivalent to the members of a board of directors in the business world) are less likely to agree with public administrators on organizational goals, are less expert and less informed on substantive issues, and are less likely to be consistent in dealing with government executives and external constituents than are the board members found in the private sector.[55] Such phenomena have a distinct impact on the decision-making process of public organizations. Decision makers must be more aware of their symbolic leadership role and of "image management." They must deal with vastly more decision criteria and decision-making participants, and they must have a broader scope and make a decision of greater complexity; as a consequence, decision making in the public sector is slower than in the private sector.[56]

In one of the largest empirical and systematic studies of public and private decision-making, it was found that decision-makers in public organizations did not necessarily make decisions slowly as a conscious act, but there seemed to be a clear tendency toward a "vortex-sporadic" style of decision making, by which was meant that decision makers in public organizations tended to intermittently swirl through a series of intense meetings and conversations with each other when making decisions. The study, which involved intensive longitudinal research of strategic decision processes in thirty British public and private service and manufacturing organizations, also found that decision makers in public organizations were much more likely than those in private organizations to engage in formal and informal interaction with other members of the organization when making decisions.[57]

An even larger survey of 210 upper managers in thirty-nine public and private organizations in Syracuse, New York, substantiated the findings of other studies that decision making is more particpative and sporadic in the public sector than in the private sector: publicness is associated with greater decision participation but not smoothness.[58]

In further support of the notion that the impact of the task environment affects decision making in public organizations more than in private ones, it was found, in a study of more than fifty federal agencies which were headed by boards, that the Federal Government in the Sunshine Act of 1976, in the opinions of the members of those boards, had adversely affected the level of collegiality in agency decision making; many agency officials felt "that the strictures of the law weakened them in executing their responsibilities and weakened agency performance, especially in policy development."[59] In the views of the officials heading those agencies, the more collegiality was reduced, the more of the quality of agency decision making suffered.

It would appear from this literature that not only do public organizations have a unique style of decision making—intense, spastic, highly interactive, collegial, and slow—but that the impact of the outside environment, which is considerably stronger than it is in the private sector, can disrupt even these unique features of decision making in the public sector, and, in the view of the decision makers themselves, reduce the quality of decision making in public organizations.

Motivation. What turns public administrators on? Is what turns them on different from what turns on managers in the private sector?

The answer to the latter question is yes. Public administrators have a very different set of motivations than do their private counterparts (although there are exceptions), and these differences result in the very different ways in which executives in the public and private sectors lead their administrative staffs.

James F. Guyot compared federal managers with those in business, and concluded that middle managers in the federal service had higher needs for achievement than did their private-sector colleagues (a finding that runs directly counter to the popular stereotype of security-obsessed, indolent government bureaucrats), about the same needs for power as business managers, and lower affiliation needs (*i.e.*, their concern with acceptance or rejection by their colleagues).[60]

Guyot's research has never been precisely replicated, but evidence supporting his findings has been forwarded in other research. For example, studies of students who were about to enter management careers have found that there were no important differences between students just entering the "nonprofit sector" (mostly, but not exclusively, government agencies) and students beginning business careers when it came to their needs for power and security—a finding more or less supportive of Guyot's research. However, students entering the nonprofit sector had a greater need to dominate, were more flexible, had a higher capacity for status, and lower needs for wealth than students entering the profit-seeking sector.[61]

Most of the research agrees that "public managers, as compared to comparable groups in business, give lower ratings to the importance of high financial rewards as career goals and higher ratings to the importance of worthwhile social or public service."[62] Despite these differences in motivation among administrators in the two sectors, however, both groups work hard, and effort levels are roughly equal for both groups.[63] "The findings. . . do not indicate a terrible malaise in the public sector if the private sector is used as a baseline."[64]

It appears from this literature that government may be attracting people who are more difficult to manage than is business. Public administrators seem to have a higher need to achieve program objectives, are more likely to be loners, have more dominant personalities, are wilier (or what the literature euphemistically calls "flexible"), and are more demanding of status than are their counterparts in commerce. Moreover, although public administrators have power drives comparable to those of business managers, they may be less vulnerable to being bought off with monetary bonuses, since the available research suggests that government bureaucrats are less interested in growing wealthy and more committed to achieving results than are business executives. While these motivations may indeed be in the public interest, they do bring with them unique problems of public management.

Satisfaction. In light of the peculiar composition of the motivations underlying the organizational behavior of public administrators, it is perhaps not too surprising that many public administrators derive little satisfaction from their work. A relatively large body of literature has appeared indicating that public administrators are considerably less satisfied, and less loyal to their organizations, than are private managers.[65] Surveys taken of public administrators and private managers, particularly during the 1960s, indicate that public administrators are much less likely to feel that pay in their organizations depends upon performance, and that their own pay represents a reward for good performance. Public managers generally express feelings that they have less security, less autonomy, and are less "self-actualized" than are their counterparts in the private sector.[66] As a rule, it does seem that the typical public manager in the United States is more frustrated and dissatisfied in his or her work than is the typical private manager.

This generalization is brought home, at least to some degree, when we compare similar dimensions between public and private managers in other countries. Two independently conducted studies of public and private executives in Israel are quite striking in this regard. One, which compared 125 top managers in public enterprises to 125 top managers in private enterprises in Israel, concluded that there were no differences in terms of the perceived relations between rewards and the aspects of performance, personal freedom, delegation, and participation.[67] The other study, which focused on chief executives in ninety-one private firms and forty public enterprises in Israel, did find the public administrators to have a somewhat lower level of satisfaction with financial rewards and challenge (although the researcher concluded that these differences were not important statistically). But this study also found no differences between public and private managers in terms of how public chief executives perceived the impact external influences on their decision processes—and this is a striking difference with studies that have compared public and private administrators in the United States on the decision-making dimension.[68]

Nevertheless, most of the research indicates that many—perhaps most—public administrators in the United States experience less satisfaction with work than do most private managers in the United States. But there are some significant exceptions to this possible rule. ("Possible" because the exceptions that have been found in the research are so large that the rule may not be valid.) For example, it has been found that, while federal administrators typically register very low levels of satisfaction with their work on the various surveys that have been taken of them, this generality seems to break down when the type of federal worker is taken into account. In an extensive study undertaken in the early 1960s, it was found that, whereas college graduates and certain kinds of professionals, such as scientists and engineers, were less satisfied with their work than were their counterparts in the private sector, federal executives were quite comparable to business executives in terms of job satisfaction.[69] It also seems that blue-collar workers in the public sector are more satisfied with most of their work than are blue-collar workers in the private sector. On the other hand, white-collar public sector workers are much less satisfied with co-workers, supervision, and a general interest in their work, than are their counterparts in business.[70]

There also may be differences in satisfaction with work by level of government. For example, state workers may be more satisfied with their work than are both their corporate and federal counterparts. In a study that compared 150 mid-level public administrators to 125 counterparts in the private sector, it was found that, whereas the public administrators reported lower levels of satisfaction with co-workers, promotions, and rewards, there was no difference between the two groups in terms of role conflict, ambiguity, clarity of goals, motivation, and job involvement. The 150 public administrators were drawn from four state agencies and one federal defense installation,

but were not distinguished along state and federal lines in the research. However, it appears that there were far more state respondents than federal ones, and this may explain the somewhat more upbeat response among public administrators in this survey relative to private managers. This seems particularly true in surveys that compare the attitudes of only federal administrators with private managers; in those surveys federal managers are typically lower in satisfaction levels on all items than are private managers.[71]

But perhaps the most intriguing finding is that local public administrators seem to defy most completely and consistently the despondency and dissatisfaction found among federal managers when compared with executives in the corporate sector. In a study of three different surveys taken of private sector managers, federal career executives, and city managers in California, the differences among the three sets of respondents were quite striking. A remarkable 72 percent of the U.S. government executives stated that they did not feel that they would ever fulfill their life's ambition, compared to only 17 percent of the city managers and 18 percent of the private sector executives who also did not feel that they would ever fulfill their life's ambition. City managers and private sector executives were quite consistent in the level of optimism that they felt about economic, social, and political trends, and organizational and personal prospects; both city managers and private sector administrators were consistently more optimistic on all these variables than were federal executives. Fully two-thirds of the city managers would advise bright young people to seek careers in local government, while less than a fourth of federal executives would advise bright young people to seek careers in the federal government.[72]

While there is reason for concern about the relative dissatisfaction of public administrators with their jobs in comparison with their counterparts in the private sector, this concern seems to concentrate at the federal level, rather than at the state and local levels. Moreover, there are indications that the level of satisfaction of federal employees with their work may have deteriorated over time.

Why many public administrators are relatively dissatisfied with their careers remains an

enigma. Their dissatisfaction may be a consequence of particularly high psychological needs
among public administrators for achievement
and status, as the research consistently verifies,
relative to private managers; or their dissatisfaction may be attributable to objective reality: the
low levels of their satisfaction, which seems to
concentrate in the areas of promotions and rewards for work well done, "could simply reflect
more stringent norms or expectations among
government managers" of their colleagues than
are held by corporate executives.[73]

Management. These differences that we have
reviewed between the public and private administrators in decision making, motivation, and satisfaction correlate with differences in management.
Most obviously, public managers are faced with
"accomplishing" enormously complex but horren-
dously ill-defined objectives. Goals are vague,
and public organizations are appropriately sprawl-
ing as structures meant to achieve the vagaries of
large but poorly conceived organizational missions; performance criteria, consequently, are as
loosely construed as are the organization's goals
themselves. Again, these unique problems of
management in public organizations are attributable to forces in their highly politicized task environments, such as legislatures, pressure groups,
and elected chief executives, that constantly try to
use public organizations for political as well as
programmatic, economic, and social purposes.[74]

Although one draws short (far short) of describing the managerial milieu of public organizations
as chaotic, it does appear to be less bureaucratically rational (in Weber's sense of the word) than
private organizations. As a result, caution prevails, and innovation is less likely.[75] Studies of
executive behavior in the public and private sectors have found that public executives spend considerably more time in contact with the directors
of outside groups than do executives in the private
sector. Moreover, the style of interaction that the
public manager has with directors and external
interest groups is far more formal, as well as more
frequent, than the mode of interaction experienced
by private sector managers.[76]

It may be that more open management—open
in the sense that more people are dunning and

hassling the managers—may lead to less effective
management. In a survey of 20,000 students,
teachers, and principals in 500 public and private
high schools, it was found that the principals and
teachers in the public schools perceived outside
authorities as wielding a much stronger influence
on their management than did the principals and
teachers in private schools. This stronger influence in the public schools than in the private ones
by outside authorities was accompanied by weaker
parental involvement in the public schools, weaker
faculty influence on the curriculum, more managerial and less professional orientations among the
principals, less emphasis on academic excellence,
more formal constraints on personnel policy, and
less clarity of goals and disciplinary policies.[77]

As the foregoing discussion implies, subordinates are treated differently in public organizations, too. Delegating authority to subordinates
and controlling the behavior of subordinates are
more difficult in the public sector than in business,[78] in part because public executives are allowed to select significantly fewer of their own
subordinates than are corporate executives, and in
part because subordinates often can develop allies
to assist them in undermining their superiors in the
highly politicized task environment outside their
public agency.

It also appears that priority setting, planning,
and information management—all fundamental
tasks of management—differ markedly in the public sector. Planning and setting priorities are considerably more difficult because of less focused
organizational goals and more rapid turnover
among top executives.[79] The difficulties of setting
priorities and planning, accordingly, seem to exist
in an informational milieu that is unique to public
organizations. An empirical study of high-level
data managers in 622 public organizations and 383
private ones concluded that data managers in the
public sector had to deal with "greater levels of
interdependence across organizational boundaries...higher levels of red tape . . .[and] more
procedural steps for a specific management action" than did those in the private sector.[80] Although the planning for and the purchasing of
management information systems in public organizations appeared to be more difficult and complex than in private organizations, the directors of

public management information systems typically occupied a lower rung on the organizational hierarchy than did the directors of private management information systems.[81]

Evaluating executive performance. These differing realities affect administrators in the two sectors in different ways. Not only do managers in the two sectors behave differently, *but even what constitutes effective management can be polar opposites in each sector*! One study of executive work behavior compared forty managers in city governments with forty managers in industry, and concluded that the public managers believed— and, in fact, accurately so—that they had little control over how they used their time, and thus accorded scant effort to "time management," relative to the corporate managers. Urban managers were considerably more victimized by forces in their organizations' task environments than were their counterparts in the private sector; they spent less time alone in their offices, less time on planning, were more "rushed" to get things done, and spent nearly twice as much time on the telephone than did private managers.[82]

Other studies confirm this kind of office lifestyle. Research on U.S. Navy civilian executives and executives from a number of private service and manufacturing firms found that, while there were similarities in the work of the two kinds of managers, the public managers devoted far more time to crisis management than did the private managers.[83]

More significantly, *effective* managers display quite different work behaviors depending on whether they worked in the public or private sectors. In the study of urban and industrial managers, it was found that *more effective public administrators* were more flexible, planned less, and had less control over their time than did industrial managers. In fact, the *less effective public administrators* spent more time on planning their time than did the more effective public managers, whereas quite the reverse held true in the private sector: less effective industrial managers spent less time planning their time than did more effective industrial managers![84]

Other research substantiates the idea that because public administrators must deal with a more intrusive task environment than private managers both the nature of their work and the evaluation of their performance differ. A study of managers in four federal agencies and twelve large (Fortune 500) private corporations concluded that private managers performed better than public administrators when it came to expressing and achieving organizational goals. This superiority, however, was attributable to an absence of clear measures of performance (*e.g.*, profits) for public administrators. Because private managers were able to define organizational objectives more definitively than were public managers, and because intraorganizational procedures in the twelve companies were less subject to influence by outside interests than in the four agencies, more strategic planning was made possible in those companies and used more frequently by private managers. This greater freedom among private managers to engage in strategic decision making enabled them to score higher than their public counterparts on such measures of leadership as "conceptualization" and the "use of oral presentations." It is, after all, comparatively easy to articulate and drive home points when one is in a position to decide autonomously about an organization's future, with relatively little fear of being challenged by elements outside one's own organization.[85]

Perhaps because of these factors, public administrators express considerably greater frustration and dissatisfaction over how their performance and that of their co-workers is evaluated by their superiors than do private managers.[86] Similarly, public sector supervisors consistently state their concerns over constraints on their ability to reward and discipline subordinates.[87] Nor do public managers hold their co-workers in as high esteem as do their counterparts in the private sector;[88] in fact, they often do not think that their colleagues are very able, a jaundiced view that may be more a product of a disruptive task environment than of the innate abilities of public administrators.

Public administration, it appears, is different.

THE CLOSED AND OPEN MODELS: THE ESSENTIAL DIFFERENCES

We have reviewed two eminently disparate models of organizations and their respective literary emphases. In essence, their fundamental differences may be seen in four areas: (1) perceptions of the organization environment, (2) perceptions of the nature of human beings, (3) perceptions of the use of manipulation in organizations, and (4) perceptions of the role and significance of organizations in society. For purposes of review, we shall consider each of these differences.

Perceptions of the Organizational Environment

The closed model is predicated on a stable, routine environment, and the open model is predicated on an unstable environment, replete with surprises. Both models assume that organizations will act in order to survive and, ultimately, to thrive.

The beauty in these two differing perceptions of organizations is that both models work in the respective environments posited for them. That is, an open-model organization would likely "die" in a stable environment, and a closed-model organization probably would wither away in an unstable environment. To recall Kaufman on the task environment, one way or the other, an organization if it is to survive must adapt so that it can "fit" through the "holes" of the environmental screening equipment that sweeps incessantly through it. A variety of empirical studies have indicated this to be the case, notably Burns and Stalker's *The Management of Innovation*, and Michel Crozier's *The Bureaucratic Phenomenon*.[89]

Bureaucracy Versus Humanism: Two Views on the Human Being in the Closed and Open Models of Organizations

The following passages illustrate by contrast the differences between the closed and open models of organization theory. While closed-model theorist Max Weber and open-model theorist Frederick Herzberg address the plight of the bureaucrat in bureaucracies from vastly different perspectives, their basic agreement on the point that the individual remains in a genuine bind in bureaucratic settings is illuminating.

Once it is fully established, bureaucracy is among those social structures which are the hardest to destroy. Bureaucracy is the means of carrying "community action" over into rationally ordered "societal action." Therefore, as an instrument of "societalizing" relations of power, bureaucracy has been and is a power instrument of the first order—for the one who controls the bureaucratic apparatus.

Under otherwise equal conditions, a "societal action," which is methodically ordered and led, is superior to every resistance of "mass" or even of "communal action." And where the bureaucratization of administration has been completely carried through, a form of power relation is established that is practically unshatterable.

The individual bureaucrat cannot squirm out of the apparatus in which he is harnessed. In contrast to the honorific or avocational "notable," the professional bureaucrat is chained to his activity by his entire material and ideal existence. In the great majority of cases, he is only a single cog in an ever moving mechanism which prescribes to him an essentially fixed route of march. The official is entrusted with specialized tasks and normally the mechanism cannot be put into motion or arrested by him, but only from the very top. The individual bureaucrat is thus forged to the community of all the functionaries who are integrated into the mechanism. They have a common interest in seeing that the mechanism continues its functions and that the societally exercised authority carries on.

The ruled, for their part, cannot dispense with or replace the bureaucratic apparatus of authority once it exists. For this bureaucracy rests upon expert training, a functional specialization of work, and an attitude set for habitual and virtuoso-like mastery of single yet methodically integrated functions. If the official stops working, or if his work is forcefully interrupted, chaos results, and it is difficult to improvise replacements from among the governed who are fit to master such chaos. This holds for public administration as well as for private economic management. More and more the material fate of the masses depends upon the steady and correct functioning of the increasingly bureaucratic organiza-

tions of private capitalism. The idea of eliminating these organizations becomes more and more utopian.

Every audience contains the "direct action" manager who shouts, "Kick him!" And this type of manager is right. The surest and least circumlocuted way of getting someone to do something is to kick him in the pants—give him what might be called the KITA.

There are various forms of KITA, and here are some of them:

Negative Physical KITA

This is a literal application of the term and was frequently used in the past. It has, however, three major drawbacks:

(1) it is inelegant; (2) it contradicts the precious image of benevolence that most organizations cherish; and (3) since it is a physical attack, it directly stimulates the autonomic nervous system, and this often results in negative feedback—the employee may just kick you in return. These factors give rise to certain taboos against negative physical KITA.

The psychologist has come to the rescue of those who are no longer permitted to use negative physical KITA. He has uncovered infinite sources of psychological vulnerabilities and the appropriate methods to play tunes on them. "He took my rug away"; "I wonder what he meant by that"; "The boss is always going around me"— these symptomatic expressions of ego sores that have been rubbed raw are the result of application of:

Negative Psychological KITA

This has several advantages over negative physical KITA. First, the cruelty is not visible; the bleeding is internal and comes much later. Second, since it affects the higher cortical centers of the brain with its inhibitory powers, it reduces the possibility of physical backlash.

Third, since the number of psychological pains that a person can feel is almost infinite, the direction and site possibilities of the KITA are increased many times. Fourth, the person administering the kick can manage to be above it all and let the system accomplish the dirty work. Fifth, those who practice it receive some ego satisfaction (one-upmanship), whereas they would find drawing blood abhorrent. Finally, if the employee does complain, he can always be accused of being paranoid, since there is no tangible evidence of an actual attack.

Now, what does negative KITA accomplish? If I kick you in the rear (physically or psychologically), who is motivated? I am motivated; you move! Negative KITA does not lead to motivation, but to movement. So:

Positive KITA

Let us consider motivation. If I say to you, "Do this for me or the company, and in return I will give you a reward, an incentive, more status, a promotion, all the quid pro quos that exist in the industrial organization," am I motivating you? The overwhelming opinion I receive from management people is, "Yes, this is motivation."

I have a year-old Schnauzer. When it was a small puppy and I wanted it to move, I kicked it in the rear and it moved. Now that I have finished its obedience training, I hold up a dog biscuit when I want the Schnauzer to move. In this instance, who is motivated—I or the dog? The dog wants the biscuit, but it is I who want it to move. Again, I am the one who is motivated, and the dog is the one who moves. In this instance all I did was apply KITA frontally: I exerted a pull instead of a push. When industry wishes to use such positive KITAs, it has available an incredible number and variety of dog biscuits (jelly beans for humans) to wave in front of the employee to get him to jump.

Why is it that managerial audiences are quick to see that negative KITA is not motivation, while they are almost unanimous in their judgment that positive KITA is motivation? It is because negative KITA is rape, and positive KITA is seduction. But it is infinitely worse to be seduced than it to be raped; the latter is an unfortunate occurrence, while the former signifies that you were a party to your own downfall. This is why positive KITA is so popular; it is in the American way. The organization does not have to kick you; you kick yourself.

To elaborate, when an organization that is superbureaucratic, rigid, and routinized around long-standing patterns of well-ordered and predictable stimuli that have emanated from a habitually stable environment suddenly is confronted with a "new," unstable environment, the organization either must "loosen up" and adapt or die. For example, it is unlikely that a house of *haute couture*, which must be extremely sensitive to changes and trends in its task environment, would last long with a "tall" organizational structure staffed by Prussian officers who ran the fashion house along the lines of Kaiser Wilhelm's army.

Conversely, when an organization that is superfluidic and tackles each problem emanating from its environment as something unique, new, and fresh (which indeed may be the case), with no attempt to discover commonalities among tasks and to categorize and routinize them along "rational" lines, is suddenly confronted with a highly stable and structured environment, the organization either must adapt or die from its own inefficiency and absence of structure relative to its environment. For example, it is dubious that Bethlehem Steel Corporation, which functions in a relatively routinized market environment, would survive long if it were staffed by the volunteers who run "crash pads" for run-a-way youths in inner cities.

To summarize, in terms of matching environmental stability or lack of it, both the closed and open models make sense. From this perspective, it also makes sense that the closed model of organizations has traditionally had a greater impact on the study of public administration than the open model. When the nation was younger and simpler, the government smaller, and public bureaucracy less ambitious and complex, a closed model suited the American milieu. Lately, however, as the nation and government have grown, faced domestic upheavals, weathered technological change, and confronted future shock, the public bureaucracy has taken on new tasks, assumed new duties, and grasped new powers. The environment has changed and is changing rapidly, and the public bureaucracy must adapt to these changes or, if not die, become part of the problem. Thus, the literature of the open model seems destined to have growing influence on the thinking of public administration.

Perceptions of the Nature of the Human Beings

The second basic difference between the closed and open models parallels the first, in that their respective models of humanity match the models of organization. The late Douglas McGregor called these two models "Theory X" and "Theory Y." Theory X applies to the closed model, particularly to bureaucratic theory. Its underlying belief structure assumes that work is not liked by most people, most people prefer close and unrelenting supervision, most people cannot contribute creatively to the solution of organizational problems, motivation to work is an individual matter, and most people are motivated by the direct application of threat or punishment. It is apparent that organizations exemplifying the closed model not only would fit, but might possibly be appealing to Theory X people.

Theory Y, which goes by other titles as well, such as System 4, Self-Actualization, Intrinsic Motivation, and Eupsychian Management, has quite another underlying belief structure. Theory Y assumes that, given the right conditions, most people can enjoy work as much as play, most people can exercise self-control and prefer doing jobs in their own way, most people can solve organizational problems creatively, motivation to work is a group matter, and most people often are motivated by social and ego rewards. It is apparent that organizations predicated on the open model likely would attract Theory Y people.

There is another aspect to the nature of the human being posited by the open and closed models, and that is the problem of rationalism. In the closed model, *rational* means that everyone in the organization has the same goals and agrees on how to achieve those goals in an optimal fashion. Consider a hypothetical example. In International Widget, a closed-model organization, we may assume that (1) everyone wants to achieve the officially stated goals of the organization, which are to make widgets and profits; and (2) everyone agrees on how widgets should be made and profits reaped with maximum efficiency and economy.

In the open model, however, *rational* has quite a different meaning—it means that everyone in the organization has his or her own, personal goals and has his or her own, personal way to achieve those goals. If we turned our example of International Widget into an open-model organization, then the production of widgets and the reaping of profits would be incidental considerations at best to most members of the organization. Their real goals (*i.e.*, their "rationality") would revolve around such values as getting ahead, acquiring status (through salary, position, and reputation), and receiving various other psychological and social satisfactions. Some of these goals are in conflict (*e.g.*, several executives vying for the same promotion) and others are not, although they still may be quite disparate (*e.g.*, one member of the organization may have deeply set needs for organizational prestige, while another may want nothing more than the opportunity to do his or her own thing, such as auditing). The point is, however, that the official goals of the organization rarely are the real goals of the organization's people.

Moreover, people with the same goals in the organization will likely differ on how those goals should be fulfilled. Two executives competing for a promotion may have quite different means for

attaining the same end; one may prefer to cultivate those in influential positions and another may prefer to be judged on his or her merits, such as his or her sales record. It should be recalled, however, that in the open model even "merit" will mean different things to different people and, in certain organizational situations, "brown-nosing" may be regarded as a highly meritorious and rational activity. In sum, rationality in organization theory depends on what organization, group, or person you are talking about.

Perceptions of the Concept of Manipulation

Manipulation in an organizational context simply means getting people to do what you want them to do. Getting one's way, of course, may be accomplished through a wide variety of methods, ranging from brute force to no force at all, and the particular techniques of manipulation correspond with organizational perceptions on the nature of humanity.

The open model, most notably its organization development school, occasionally appears to argue against the practice of manipulation of people by other people. Manipulation is seen as dehumanizing, "dematurizing" (to use Argyis's term),[90] and generally nasty. Indeed, manipulation inhibits the self-actualization of organizational members and reduces their sense of self-worth. By contrast, the closed model, particularly its bureaucratic theory school, has no qualms about employing manipulative methods. It advocates "using" people for the sake of the organization's ends. Moreover, the callous use of authoritative coercion in manipulating people is seen as entirely legitimate.

The preceding paragraph may overstate the case, but it nonetheless is representative of the differing values of the two models concerning manipulation. In actuality, their difference over manipulation is one of style. In the ideal-type closed model, force is always a possibility; we can conceive of an administrator smashing the nearest chair over a subordinate's cranium in an effort to induce the underling to do things his or her way. In fact, similar incidents have happened; public administrators in the government of the Third Reich (as close to a prototype of a closed-model organization as one is likely to find) were known to level Lugers at the necks of subordinates when they displayed reluctance to follow orders and be a "good German." Conversely, the use of coercion in open-model organizations is considered reprehensible and is actively discouraged. Manipulation in the open model takes on a far more subtle hue; suggestions replace orders, persuasion supplants coercion, education is favored over obedience, socialization is used instead of force, and cooperation displaces authority. The fundamental idea is to so manipulate organizational members that they "want" to work for the organization.

An example of what this line of thought means in practice seen in Robert T. Golembiewski's discussion of the "inappropriate 'good morning'" in *Behavior and Organizations*. If administrators are to induce a feeling of supportive relationships among subordinates, goes the reasoning, then they must be aware of the more subtle requisites of the social context. It follows that one should not say "good morning" inappropriately when speaking to subordinates. An explosively cheery "good morning" is likely to put off, say, a secretary as being phony and overdrawn, while a snarled "good morning" or a grunt is likely to make him or her wary and sulky. "Good mornings" must be tailored appropriately in tone to the persons receiving them if individual self-actualization via supportive relationships is to be attained and thereby benefit organizational productivity.[91]

Not all the theorists of the open model are as straightforward in their acceptance of manipulation as Golembiewski. As Allen Schick accurately observes, Argyris, one of the intellectual leaders of organization development, "for two decades . . . has resisted his own findings that organization demands and individual needs are incongruent, and he still labors to develop models of compatibility."[92] Schick rightly perceives in this light that "the reconciliation of man and his organization has proved to be an essential but perhaps hopeless task. Either the individual is autonomous or the organization is dominant, for the very notion of individualism wars against even benevolent organization."[93]

In sum, manipulation is accepted as necessary by the open model as well as the closed-model of organizations. Only the techniques of manipulation differ. The closed model theorists, in the tradition of Weber, believed in orders and obedience, rules and regulations, punctuality and punctiliousness. The human dysfunctions of these manipulative techniques are obvious; rigidity, impersonality, narrowness, and stultification number among the human and organizational liabilities of authoritarian manipulation. But there are also human advantages to the crudities of the closed model's manipulative techniques: People in closed-model organizations "know where they stand." The authoritarianism of the closed model is for persons who like things straightforward and clearcut.

Just as the disadvantages of the closed model's manipulative techniques are apparent, so the advantages of the open model's methods of manipulation are clear; humanism, openness, communication, and innovation are enhanced by the use of OD concepts. But there are also liabilities to the social-psychological brand of manipulation employed by the open model. The more refined manipulative methods stemming from small-group theory, supportive relationships, myths of peerage, and appropriate "good mornings" tend to camouflage the unavoidable exercise of power in organizations. As a result people in open-model organizations may never be sure "where they stand." More significantly, if they think that they do know where they stand their knowledge may be the end-product of a manipulation of their psyches so subtle as to render them analogous to the "conditioned" human shell of the protagonist in George Orwell's *Nineteen Eighty-Four*, who uncontrollably shrieked "Long Live Big Brother!" even as he despised him. Eric Fromm expresses this idea more succinctly with his concept of "willing submissiveness"; that is, although organizational subordinates may appear to have "team spirit" (and actually may have been so successfully manipulated as to believe they have it), the psychological techniques used to create their willing submissiveness induces in reality a subliminal and deep internal resentment toward their superiors bordering on hatred.[94]

Perceptions of the Social Role of Organizations

The fourth principal difference between the closed and open models is particularly germane to the study of public administration, and centers on how the models' respective theorists have viewed the organization and its relationships with the larger society. In considering this dimension, we are examining from a different perspective the moral question of organizational manipulation.

Weber provides an especially solid example of a closed-model theorist who makes his values explicit in this regard. Weber believed a highly rational bureaucracy to be essential in achieving the goals of the tumultuous, charisma-dominated society that whirled beyond its confines. Without bureaucracy, society would achieve nothing; it would not "progress," it would not replace *Kadijustice* with the rule of rational law. To exaggerate, but to nonetheless state the point, bureaucracy, replete with its own internal injustices, dehumanizing rules, and monocrotic arbitrariness, was vital in its very rigidity and rationalism to the unorganized societal lunacy that it offset. If Weber's conception of the bureaucracy's station in society could be illustrated, it would look something like Figure 3-1.

Weber was not unsympathetic to the plight of the individual bureaucrat. In fact, he deplored what the mechanization and routinization of bureaucratic settings could do to the human spirit. But, when all was said and done, Weber could accept the dehumanization of society's social servants, who were somehow apart from the other citizens, on the grounds that the bureaucracy was essential to social progress and the elimination of injustice. There was, in sum, a higher morality that provided the *raison d'etre* of bureaucracy, and if a few unfortunates were hurt inside the bureaucracy, so be it.

In contrast to Weber, the open-model theorists have a completely different conception of the organization's role in society. To them, virtually everyone in society is encased in some sort of organization. Thus, for the public bureaucracy to manipulate and dehumanize its own bureaucrats in order to further society's goals and establish rational social justice is self-defeating because the bureaucrat and the citizen are one and the same. The open model's view of the role of the organization in society is a complex of interlocking and interacting organizations; society itself is a series of organizations, and there is no unorganized, nonrational society "out there," functioning beyond the organizations' boundaries. The open model's concept of society and the bureaucracy looks like Figure 3-2.

The contrast between the closed and open modelists is that the closed modelists distinguished between citizens and bureaucrats while the open modelists feel that essentially all citizens are bureaucrats—that is, all citizens belong to or are affected by organizations in some ways. The lack of distinction between citizens and bureaucrats, and between society and its organizations, has led the open-model theorists to see moral choice and the concept of the public interest as essentially intraorganizational phenomena. Thus, to treat a member of an organization, particularly a subordinate, badly is immoral because there is no higher morality to excuse such treatment, as there is in Weber's construct. In the open model, what is good for the individual is also good for the society.

THE LITERATURE OF MODEL SYNTHESIS

Students of organizations may be initially confused by the fundamentally different paradigms of organization theory represented by the closed

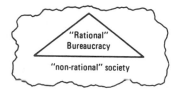

FIGURE 3-1. The Closed Model's View: Organizations *and* Society

FIGURE 3-2. The Open Model's View: Organizations *as* Society

and open models. One model assumes monolithic rationality, the other model assumes nonrationality, by which is meant a pluralist system of many unique rationalities. One model assumes a stable environment, the other assumes an unstable environment. One assumes a Theory X view of human beings, the other assumes a Theory Y view. One assumes that society is unstructured, the other assumes that society is highly structured. These are basic differences. Can they be reconciled and, if so, how?

The answer to the first part of the question is a qualified yes, and the attempt to do so is represented by the "newer tradition" of organization theory as exemplified by Herbert A. Simon's *Administrative Behavior*, James G. March and Simon's *Organizations*, Richard Cyert and March's *A Behavioral Theory of the Firm*, and James D. Thompson's *Organizations in Action*, although there is, of course, a much larger literature extant. Barnard's *The Functions of the Executive* can also properly be considered a key work in this stream, as well as a major contribution to the open model literature.

In terms of conceptually reconciling the two models, it first must be appreciated that our culture really does not facilitate our thinking of opposites as harmonious. It requires some hard concentration to think about something half closed, half open; half certain, half uncertain; half regulated, half spontaneous; and half rational, half nonrational. Yet, this is precisely what Simon, March, Cyert, Thompson, and others try to do, and they largely succeed.

The essence of the literature of model synthesis is that it starts with the open model (*i.e.*, it assumes that organizations are spontaneous collectivities of people with their own goals and drives operating in an uncertain environment), but explains organizational behavior as being motivated by a need to routinize and rationalize the organization's internal workings and its relationships with its environment whenever and wherever possible. This is essentially a Darwinian notion (adapt or die). Another way of saying the same thing is that organizations try to become rational. Consider the same concept from another perspective: Organizations try to make all variables (*e.g.*, member behavior, technological and environmental developments) predictable. Visualized differently, we can perceive that organizations try to achieve closure. Yet another (and perhaps the best) way of expressing the same idea is to say that organizations try to reduce uncertainty.

Thus, the two models are synthesized, and the synthesis is predicated on three very reasonable assumptions:

1. Organizations and their environments can and do change.
2. Organizations and the people in them act to survive.
3. Organizations and the people in them can and do learn from mistakes.

The key to understanding the literature of model synthesis is that all organizations must deal with uncertainty. Kaufman provides some useful insights in this regard. He suggests that organizations will try to grow as large as they can (since growth is seen as the basic stratagem for assuring organizational survival), and that the necessity of reducing uncertainty stands as the central problem in trying to grow; hence, "organizations are averse to uncertainty."[95]

Uncertainty may spring from two sources: those sources that are internal to the organization and those that are external to it. If the sources of organizational uncertainty are internal, then the organization will strive to reduce uncertainty by centralizing. Centralizing techniques include "control . . . of all communication to the members of the vexing suborganizations . . . so that nonconforming thought (and therefore deviant behavior) is prevented; intensifying surveillance to discourage nonconformity by increasing the probability of exposure and punishment; detaching key operations [such as taking away the control of funds and rewards from suborganizations] . . . thus reducing their self-containment and increasing their vulnerability to central direction; . . . indoctrinating all members . . . to respond only to commands from the central leadership and from no other source. . . [and finally, expelling] the offending suborganization, [an act amounting to] a contraction of boundaries constituting a withdrawal from internal sources of uncertainty."[96]

If, however, the sources of organizational uncertainty are external, then the organization will seek to expand its boundaries—to grow. For example, the organization will attempt to incorporate external sources of uncertainty into the organization. Selznick's co-optation, described earlier, is one form that this incorporation of external uncertainties might take; the effort by an organization to control some facet of the natural environment (for example, to engage in flood control or weather prediction) is another form; to merge or ally with competitive organizations is yet another.

If the expansion of an organization's boundaries is blocked, then the organization will seek to reduce its exchanges with its environment—"withdrawal from the source of uncertainty, as it were."[97] A firm uncertain about its future supplies or service needs might decide to stockpile or produce its own manufacturing components, or develop its own service staffs. Entire nations, such as China, have been known to reduce *their* external uncertainties by radically reducing exchanges with other nations and launching self-sufficiency policies; the invariable consequence, however, is an elevation of costs and a lowering of living standards.

The preceding points are important, and we shall be referring to them implicitly in the next chapter, which is about some concepts of organization theory. Before closing this chapter, however, let us summarize the three principal models of organization theory with Table 3-1.

NOTES

[1] See the following: Victor A. Thompson, *Modern Organization* (New York: Knopf, 1961), p. 5; Chester I. Barnard, *The Functions of the Executive* (Cambridge, Mass.: Harvard University Press, 1938), p. 11; and E. Wight Bakke, *Bond of Organization* (New York: Harper & Row, 1950), pp. 8–9.

[2] James G. March and Herbert A. Simon, *Organizations* (New York: John Wiley, 1958), p. 4.

[3] James D. Thompson, *Organizations in Action* (New York: McGraw-Hill, 1967).

[4] Tom Burns and G. M. Stalker, *The Management of Innovation* (London: Tavistock, 1961).

[5] Max Weber, *From Max Weber*, H. H. Gerth and C. Wright Mills, eds. (New York: Oxford University Press, 1946).

[6] See especially Frederick W. Taylor, *Principles of Scientific Management* (New York: Harper & Row, 1911); and Frank G. Gilbreth, *Primer of Scientific Management* (New York: Van Nostrand, 1912).

[7] Charles D. Wrege and Amedeo G. Perroni, "Taylor's Pig-Tale: A Historical Analysis of Frederick W. Taylor's Pig-Iron Experiment," *Academy of Management Journal*, 17 (March 1974), pp. 6–27.

[8] Taylor, *Principles of Scientific Management*, p. 59.

[9] See especially Luther Gulick and L. Urwick, eds., *Papers on the Science of Administration* (New York: Institute of Public Administration, 1937); and James D. Mooney and Alan C. Reiley, *The Principles of Organization* (New York: Harper & Row, 1939).

[10] See, for example, M. P. Follett, *Creative Experience* (New York: P. Smith Company, 1924); and Henri Fayol, *General and Industrial Management* (London: Pitmann, 1930).

[11] Alvin W. Gouldner, "Organizational Analysis," in *Sociology Today*, Robert K. Merton, Leonard Broom, and Leonard

TABLE 3-1   The Models of Organization Theory

The Closed Model	The Literature of Model Synthesis: Uncertainty Reduction	The Open Model
1. Bureaucratic theory (Weber)	(Barnard, Simon, March and Simon, Cyert and March, Thompson)	1. Human relations (Roethlisberger and Dickson, Maslow, Mayo, Herzberg)
2. Scientific management (Taylor, the Gilbreths)		2. Organization development (Lewin, McGregor, Bennis, Bechard, French and Bell, Lippitt, Shepard, Blake, Benne, Bradford, Argyris, Golembiewski)
3. Administrative, or generic management (Mooney and Reiley, Gulick and Urwick, Fayol, Follett)		3. The organization as a unit in its environment (Barnard, Selznick, Clark, Downs, Warwick, Meyer)

S. Cottrell, Jr., eds. (New York: Basic Books, 1959), pp. 400–428.

[12] Alvin Toffler, *Future Shock* (New York: Random House, 1970).

[13] Burns and Stalker, *The Management of Innovation*.

[14] The original Hawthorne studies are in: Fritz J. Roethlisberger and William J. Dickson, *Management and the Worker* (Cambridge, Mass.: Harvard University Press, 1939). The reinterpretation of the Hawthorne studies are in: Richard Herbert Franke and James D. Kaul, "The Hawthorne Experiments: First Statistical Interpretation," *American Sociological Review*, 43 (October 1978), 623–643.

[15] See Abraham Maslow, "A Theory of Metamotivation: The Biological Rooting of Value-Life," *Humanitas*, 4 (1969), pp. 301–343.

[16] Abraham Maslow, *Eupsychian Management: A Journal* (Homewood, Ill.: Dorsey Press, 1965), p. 1.

[17] See, for example, Frederick Herzberg, "One More Time: How Do You Motivate Employees?" *Harvard Business Review*, 46 (January/February 1968), pp. 53–62; and *Work and the Nature of Man* (Cleveland, Ohio: World Publishing, 1966).

[18] Chunoh Park, Nicholas P. Lobrich and Dennise L. Soden, "Testing Herzberg's Motivation Theory in a Comparative Study of U.S. and Korean Public Employees," *Review of Public Personnel Administration*, 8 (Summer 1988), p. 40.

[19] Frank K. Gibson and Clyde E. Teasley, "The Humanistic Model of Organizational Motivation: A Review of Research Support," *Public Administration Review*, 33 (January/February 1973), pp. 89–96.

[20] Richard Beckhard, *Organizational Development: Strategies and Models* (Reading, Mass.: Addison-Wesley, 1969), pp. 20–24.

[21] Wendell L. French and Cecil H. Bell, Jr., *Organization Development: Behavioral Science Interventions for Organization Improvement* (Englewood Cliffs, N.J.: Prentice-Hall, 1973).

[22] Douglas MacGregor, *The Professional Manager* (New York: McGraw-Hill, 1967); and Robert R. Blake and J. S. Mouton, *The Managerial Grid* (Houston, Tex.: Gulf, 1964).

[23] Warren G. Bennis, *Organizational Development: Its Nature, Origins, and Prospects* (Reading, Mass.: Addison-Wesley, 1969), p. 17.

[24] Robert T. Golembiewski, *Public Administration as a Developing Discipline, Part 2* (New York: Marcel Dekker, 1977), pp. 18–22.

[25] Robert T. Golembiewski, Carl W. Proehl, Jr., and David Sink, "Success of OD Applications in the Public Sector: Toting Up the Score for a Decade, More or Less," *Public Administration Review*, 41 (November/December 1981), p. 681.

[26] *Ibid.*

[27] Peggy Morrison, "Evaluation in OD: A Review and an Assessment," *Group and Organization Studies*, 3 (March 1978), pp. 42–70; and Jerry Porras, "The Comparative Impact of Different OD Techniques and Intervention Intensities," *Journal of Applied Behavioral Science*, 15 (April 1979), pp. 156–178.

[28] Representative works (besides Maslow's, cited earlier) include: Carl R. Rogers and Barry Stevens, *Person to Person: The Problem of Being Human* (Lafayette, Calif.: Real People Press, 1968); Carl R. Rogers, *On Encounter Groups* (New York: Harper & Row, 1970); Arthur Janov and E. Michael Holde, *Primal Man: The New Consciousness* (New York: Crowell, 1975); Ida P. Rolf, *Rolfing: The Integration of Human Structures* (Santa Monica, Calif.: Dennis-Landman, 1977); Alexander Lowen, *Bioenergetics* (New York: Penguin, 1975); R. D. Laing, *The Facts of Life: An Essay on Feelings, Facts, and Fantasy* (New York: Pantheon, 1976); and Walter Truett Anderson, *The Upstart Spring: Esalen and the American Awakening* (Reading, Mass.: Addison, 1983).

[29] Robert Kahn, quoted in Thomas H. Fitzgerald, "The O.D. Practitioner in the Business World: Theory vs. Reality," *Organizational Dynamics*, 16 (Summer 1987), p. 28. Emphasis is original.

[30] Frances Fitzgerald, *Cities on a Hill: A Journey through Contemporary American Cultures* (New York: Simon & Schuster, 1986), p. 284.

[31] Carl R. Rogers and B. F. Skinner, "Some Issues Concerning the Control of Human Behavior," *Science*, 124 (1956), pp. 1057–1065, as reprinted in Richard I. Evans, *Carl Rogers: The Man and His Ideas* (New York: E. P. Dutton, 1975), p. lxii.

[32] B. F. Skinner, *Beyond Freedom and Dignity* (New York: Bantam, 1972).

[33] Sigmund Freud, *The Ego and the Id* (London: Hogarth, 1947), and *Civilization and Its Discontents* (London: Liverwright, 1930).

[34] Carl Rogers, describing a conversation with the noted Freudian, Karl Menninger, and quoted in Howard Kirschenbaum, *On Becoming Carl Rogers* (New York: Delacorte, 1979), p. 250.

[35] *Ibid.*, p. 251.

[36] Fitzgerald, *Cities on a Hill*, p. 275.

[37] *Ibid.*, pp. 380–381.

[38] Maslow, *Eupsychian Management*, p. 1.

[39] Fitzgerald, "The O.D. Practitioner in the Business World," pp. 25, 27.

[40] See, for example, Chester L. Barnard, *The Functions of the Executive*; Philip Selznick, *TVA and the Grass Roots* (Berkeley, Calif.: University of California Press, 1949); and Burton R. Clark, *Adult Education in Transition* (Berkeley, Calif.: University of California Press, 1956).

[41] Herbert Kaufman, *Time, Chance, and Organizations: Natural Selection in a Perilous Environment* (Chatham, N.J.: Chatham House, 1985), p. 67.

[42] Richard A. Couto, "Co-optation in TVA: Selznick Updated" (Paper delivered at the 1981 Annual Meeting of the American Political Science Association, New York, September 3–6, 1981), abstract page.

[43] Richard A. Couto, "TVA's Old and New Grass Roots: A Reexamination of Cooptation," *Administration and Society*, 19 (February 1988), p. 453.

[44] Among the best reviews of this literature, and its manifold methodological problems are: Hal G. Rainey, "Public Organi-

zation Theory: Current Contributions and Research Directions" (Paper presented at the 1984 Annual Meeting of the American Political Science Association, Washington, D.C., August 30–September 2, 1984); Hal G. Rainey, "Public Management: Recent Research on the Political Context and Managerial Roles, Structures, and Behaviors," *Journal of Management*, 15 (April 1989), pp. 229–250; James L. Perry and Hal G. Rainey, "The Public-Private Distinction in Organization Theory: A Critique and Research Strategy," *Academy of Management Review*, 13 (April 1988), pp. 182–201; and Hal G. Rainey, "Public Management: Recent Developments and Current Prospects," in *Public Administration: The State of the Discipline*, Naomi B. Lynn and Aaron Wildavsky, eds. (Chatham, N.J.: Chatham House, 1990), pp. 157–184.

[45] Both the experiential and academic literatures agree on this point. For examples of the former, see: W. Michael Blumenthal, "Candid Reflections of a Businessman in Washington," *Fortune* (January 29, 1979), pp. 2, 6–49; and Donald Rumsfeld, "A Politician-Turned-Executive Surveys Both Worlds," *Fortune* (September 10, 1979), pp. 88–94. For examples of the latter, see: Bruce Buchanan II, "Red-Tape and the Service Ethic: Some Unexpected Differences Between Public and Private Managers," *Administration and Society*, 6 (February 1975), pp. 423–488; Louis C. Gawthrop, *Bureaucratic Behavior in the Executive Branch* (New York: The Free Press, 1969); Bruce Buchanan II, "Government Managers, Business Executives, and Organizational Commitment," *Public Administration Review*, 35 (July/August 1975), pp. 339–347; and Robert T. Golembiewski, *Humanizing Public Organizations* (Mt. Airy, Md.: Lomond, 1985).

[46] Lewis C. Mainzer, *Political Bureaucracy* (Glenview, Ill.: Scott, Foresman, 1973), p. 14; and John D. Millett, *Organization for the Public Service* (Princeton, N.J.: Van Nostrand, 1966). p. 10. The point is sufficiently basic that the list of sources supporting it could be expanded almost *ad infinitum*.

[47] Paul Appleby, *Big Democracy* (New York: Knopf, 1945); Gawthrop, *Bureaucratic Behavior*; Robert T. Golembiewski, "Organization Development in Public Agencies: Perspectives on Theory and Practice," *Public Administration Review*, 29 (July/August 1969), pp. 367–368.

[48] J. A. Stockfisch, *The Political Economy of Bureaucracy* (New York: General Learning Press, 1972); Gary L. Wamsley and Mayer N. Zald, *The Political Economy of Public Organizations* (Lexington, Mass.: D. C. Heath, 1973); and Herman L. Weiss, "Why Business and Government Exchange Executives," *Harvard Business Review* (July/August 1974), pp. 129–140.

[49] Stockfisch, *The Political Economy of Bureaucracy*; and Henry Mintzberg, *The Nature of Managerial Work* (New York: Harper & Row, 1973), p. 108.

[50] Anthony Downs, *Inside Bureaucracy* (Boston: Little, Brown, 1967), pp. 52–59, 145–146.

[51] Donald P. Warwick, *A Theory of Public Bureaucracy* (Cambridge, Mass.: Harvard University Press, 1975), pp. 73–80, 188–191.

[52] Marshall W. Meyer, *Change in Public Bureaucracies* (London: Cambridge University Press, 1979), p. 5.

[53] Buchanan, "Government Managers, Business Executives, and Organizational Commitment"; Louis C. Gawthrop, *Administrative Politics and Social Change* (New York: St. Martin's Press, 1971); and Mainzer, *Political Bureaucracy*.

[54] Mainzer, *Political Bureaucracy*; Millett, *Organization for the Public Service*; and Edward A. Holdaway, et al., "Dimensions of Organizations in Complex Societies: The Educational Sector," *Administrative Science Quarterly*, 20 (March 1975), pp. 37–58.

[55] Blumenthal, "Candid Reflections of a Businessman in Washington"; Rumsfeld, "A Politician-Turned-Executive Surveys Both Worlds"; and Weiss, "Why Business and Government Exchange Executives."

[56] *Ibid.*; Robert A. Dahl and Charles E. Lindblom, *Politics, Economics and Welfare* (New York: Harper & Row, 1953); and Golembiewski, *Humanizing Public Organizations*.

[57] D. J. Hickson, R. J. Butler, D. Cray, G. R. Mallory, and D. C. Wilson, *Top Decisions: Strategic Decision Making in Organizations* (San Francisco: Jossey-Bass, 1986).

[58] David Coursey and Barry Bozeman, "Decision Making in Public and Private Organizations: A Test of Alternative Concepts of 'Publicness'," *Public Administration Review*, 50 (September/October 1990), p. 525.

[59] David M. Welborn, William Lyons, and Larry W. Thomas, "The Federal Government in the Sunshine Act and Agency Decision Making," *Administration and Society*, 20 (February 1989), p. 483.

[60] James F. Guyot, "Government Bureaucrats *Are* Different," *Public Administration Review*, 22 (December 1962), pp. 195–202.

[61] James R. Rawls and Oscar T. Nelson, Jr., "Characteristics Associated with Preferences for Certain Managerial Positions," *Psychological Reports*, 36 (June 1975), pp. 911–918; James R. Rawls, Robert A. Ulrich, and Oscar T. Nelson, "A Comparison of Managers Entering or Reentering the Profit and Nonprofit Sectors," *Academy of Management Journal*, 18 (September 1975), pp. 616–622; and Warren H. Schmidt and Barry Z. Posner, "Values and Expectations of City Managers in California," *Public Administration Review*, 47 (September/October 1987), pp. 404–409.

[62] Hal G. Rainey, "Reward Preferences Among Public and Private Managers: In Search of the Service Ethic," *American Review of Public Administration*, 16 (Winter 1982), p. 290

[63] Hal G. Rainey, "Public Agencies and Private Firms: Incentive Structures, Goals, and Individual Roles," *Administration and Society*, 15 (August 1983), pp. 207–242; and U.S. Office of Personnel Management, *Federal Employee Attitudes* (Washington, D.C.: U.S. Government Printing Office, 1979).

[64] Hal G. Rainey, Carol Traut, and Barry Blunt, "Reward Expectancies and Other Work-Related Attitudes in Public and Private Organizations: A Review and Extension" (Paper presented at the 1985 Annual Meeting of the American Political Science Association, New Orleans, August 29–September 1, 1985), p. 9.

[65] Buchanan, "Government Managers, Business Executives, and Organizational Commitment"; and Buchanan, "Red Tap and the Public Service Ethic."

Although the literature that compares public and private managers by and large concludes that public administrators are less committed to their organizations than are private managers, this may not be an entirely negative factor insofar as the public interest is concerned. While it is generally assumed that a high level of personal commitment to one's organization is desirable, researchers in this area have argued that "high levels of commitment to the organization may have severe negative consequences where individuals within the organization are concerned, and for organizations themselves." See: Donna M. Randall, "Commitment and the Organization: The Organization Man Revisited," *Academy of Management Review*, 12 (September 1987), p. 460.

[66] Frank T. Paine, Stephen J. Carroll, and Burt A. Leete, "Need Satisfactions of Managerial Personnel in a Government Agency," *Journal of Applied Psychology*, 50 (June 1966) pp. 247–249; J. B. Rhinehart, et al., "Comparative Study of Need Satisfaction in Governmental and Business Hierarchies," *Journal of Applied Psychology*, 53 (June 1969), pp. 230–235; Lyman W. Porter and Edward E. Lawler, *Managerial Attitudes and Performance*, (Homewood, Ill.: Irwin, 1968); Buchanan, "Government Managers, Business Executives, and Organizational Commitment"; Buchanan, "Red Tape and the Service Ethic"; Hal G. Rainey, Carroll Traut, and Barrie Blunt, "Reward Expectancies and Other Work-Related Attitudes in Public and Private Organizations: A Review and Extension," *Review of Public Personnel Administration*, 6 (Summer 1986), pp. 50–72.

[67] E. Solomon and M. Greenberg, "Organizational Climate in the Public and Private Sectors" (Paper presented at the annual meeting of the Academy of Management, New York, 1982).

[68] Ran Lachman, "Public and Private Sector Differences: CEOs' Perceptions of their Role Environments," *Academy of Management Journal*, 28 (June 1985), pp. 671–679.

[69] F. P. Kilpatrick, M. C. Cummings, Jr., and M. K. Jennings, *The Image of the Federal Service* (Washington, D.C.: Brookings Institution, 1964).

[70] Michael P. Smith and Smith L. Nock, "Social Class and the Quality of Life in Public and Private Organizations," *Journal of Social Issues*, 36 (June 1980), pp. 59–75.

[71] Rainey, "Perceptions of Incentives in Business and Government," and Rainey, "Public Agencies and Private Firms." The studies that indicate lower federal scores on all dimensions are Rhinehart, et al., "Comparative Study of Satisfaction in Govermental and Business Hierarchies," and Paine, Carroll, and Leete, "Need Satisfactions of Managerial Personnel in a Government Agency." Both studies administered the same thirteen items in the Porter satisfaction scale, and found that federal administrators were lower on all thirteen items than were their counterparts in the private sector. Similarly Buchanan questioned only federal administrators in his public-sector sample, and found them to be lower than their counterparts in business on all items in his questionnaire. See, Buchanan, "Government Managers, Business Executives, and Organizational Commitment," and Buchanan, "Red Tape and the Service Ethic."

[72] Schmidt and Posner, "Values and Expectations of City Managers in California," p. 408. Schmidt and Posner compared surveys of 1,498 managers from the private sector taken in 1981, 803 career executives in the federal government taken in 1982, and 213 California city managers taken in 1983.

[73] James L. Perry and Lyman W. Porter, "Factors Affecting the Context for Motivation in Public Organizations," *Academy of Management Review*, 7 (January 1982) p. 96.

[74] See, for example: Laurence E. Lynn, *Managing the Public's Business* (New York: Basic Books, 1981); Herbert Kaufman, *The Administrative Behavior of Federal Bureau Chiefs* (Washington, D.C.: Brookings Institution, 1981); Richard Elling, "The Relationships Among Bureau Chiefs, Legislative Committees, and Interest Groups: A Multi-State Study" (Paper presented at the Annual Conference of the American Political Science Association, Chicago, September 1–4, 1983); and Randall B. Ripley and Grace A. Franklin, *Policy-Making in the Federal Executive Branch* (New York: The Free Press, 1975).

There are numerous examples of books and articles devoted to the unique problems of public management, but not very many with a perspective that is distinctively drawn from organization theory; most are written in the tradition of the literature of public policymaking.

[75] Charles L. Schultze, "The Role of Incentives, Penalties, and Rewards in Attaining Effective Policy," in *Public Expenditures and Policy Analysis*, Robert H. Haveman and Julius Margolis, eds. (Chicago: Markham, 1970), pp. 145–172; Golembiewski, "Organization Development in Public Agencies"; and Golembiewski, *Humanizing Public Organizations*.

[76] Henry Mintzberg, *The Structuring of Organizations* (Englewood Cliffs, N.J.: Prentice-Hall, 1979); and L. E. Kurke, and H. E. Aldrich, "Mintzberg Was Right? A Republication and Extension of *The Nature of Managerial Work*," *Management Science*, 29 (Winter 1983), pp. 975–984.

[77] John E. Chubb and Terry M. Moe, *Politics, Markets, and America's Schools*, (Washington, D.C.: Brookings Institution, 1990). See also, Chubb and Moe, "Politics, Markets, and the Organization of Schools" (Paper presented at the meeting of the American Political Science Association, New Orleans, September, 1985).

[78] Blumenthal, "Candid Reflections of a Businessman in Washington"; Rumsfeld, "A Politician-Turned-Executive Surveys Both Worlds"; Golembiewski, "Organization Development in Public Agencies"; Marshall W. Meyer, *Bureaucratic Structure and Authority: Coordination and Control in 254 Government Agencies* (New York: Harper & Row, 1972); and John W. Macy, *Public Service: The Human Side of Government* (New York: Harper & Row, 1971).

[79] Buchanan, "Government Managers, Business Executives, and Organizational Commitment"; and Gawthrop, *Bureaucratic Behavior in the Executive Branch*.

[80] Stuart Bretschneider, "Management Information Systems in Public and Private Organizations: An Empirical Test," *Public Administration Review*, 50 (September/October 1990), p. 537.

[81] *Ibid*. At least one observer has noted that, in his experience, once the information is available, candid discussion of

more sensitive points is less likely in government than in business. See: Blumenthal, "Candid Reflections of a Businessman in Washington."

[82] Lyman W. Porter and John Van Maanen, "Task Accomplishment and the Management of Time," in *Managing for Accomplishment*, Bernard Bass, ed. (Lexington, Mass.: Lexington Books, 1970), pp. 180–192.

[83] Alan W. Lau, Cynthia M. Pavett, and Arthur R. Newman, "The Nature of Managerial Work: A Comparison of Public and Private Sector Jobs," *Academy of Management Proceedings* (August 1980), pp. 339–343.

[84] Porter and Van Maanen, "Task Accomplishment and the Management of Time."

[85] Richard E. Boyatzis, *The Competent Manager* (New York: John Wiley, 1982).

[86] The research is quite consistent on this point. See, for example, Paine, Carroll, and Leete, "Need Satisfaction of Managerial Level Personnel in a Government Agency"; Porter and Lawler, *Managerial Attitudes and Behavior*; J. B. Rinehart, et al., "Comparative Need Satisfaction in Government and Business Hierarchies"; Ran Lachman, "Perceptions of Role-Environment Among Public and Private Sector Executives," *Academy of Management Proceedings* (August 1983), pp. 347–351; and Rainey, "Public Agencies and Private Firms."

[87] Macy, *Public Service*; and Alan K. Campbell, "Civil Service Reform: A New Commitment," *Public Administration Review*, 38 (March/April 1978), pp. 101–102.

[88] Buchanan, "Government Managers, Business Executives, and Organizational Commitment"; Buchanan, "Red Tape and the Service Ethic"; and Smith and Nock, "Social Class and the Quality of Life in Public and Private Organizations."

[89] Burns and Stalker, *The Management of Innovation*; and Michel Crozier, *The Bureaucratic Phenomenon* (Chicago: The University of Chicago Press, 1964).

[90] See, for example, Chris Argyris, *Organization and Innovation* (Homewood, Ill.: Irwin, 1965).

[91] Robert T. Golembiewski, *Behavior and Organizations* (Chicago: Rand McNally, 1962).

[92] Allen Schick, "The Trauma of Politics: Public Administration in the Sixties," in *American Public Administration: Past, Present, Future*, Frederick C. Mosher, ed. (Tuscaloosa, Ala.: University of Alabama Press, 1975), p. 171.

[93] *Ibid.*, p. 170.

[94] Eric Fromm, *The Art of Loving* (New York: Harper & Row, 1956).

[95] Kaufman, *Time, Chance, and Organizations*, p. 117.

[96] *Ibid.*, p. 44.

[97] *Ibid.*, p. 43.

CHAPTER
4

CONCEPTS OF ORGANIZATION THEORY

This chapter will review briefly some of the speculations and findings generated by organization theorists about organizations. Our review is hardly definitive; it concentrates on the literature of model synthesis explained in Chapter 3, and it emphasizes those concepts that seem especially germane to organizations in the public sector. The concepts covered are the following: change and innovation (particularly in regard to the roles of technology, task environment, and organizational members); information and intelligence; control, authority, and power; decision making; administration; and organizational assessment. These are not neat categories; their many conceptual overlappings are the result of the pervasive emphasis of decision-making theory in the study of organizations.

With the preceding sketch of the chapter's structure in mind, it is important to add three caveats about organization theory generally. First, organization theory is a broad but shallow field. It melds many concepts from many fields, but occasionally the propositions generated by organization theorists do not appear penetratingly insightful. Second, organization theory does not

attempt (at least, it rarely attempts) to tell you how to run your organization "better." That ability is normally the product of native intelligence, experience, and motivation. Organization theory does attempt to discover what makes organizations tick, how organizations behave, and what accounts for differences among organizations. This knowledge, it is hoped, may ultimately prove useful to students who eventually find themselves working in a public bureaucracy. Third, as we mentioned in Chapter 2, there are no "principles of organizations" that are worth anything. For every principle, there is a counterprinciple, or the principle itself may be tautological. There are, however, some enlightening perceptions in the literature about how organizations behave, and it is to a few of these that we now turn.

CHANGE AND INNOVATION

Obviously, being able to change, innovate, alter, and adapt (or however one labels it) is vital to any form of life, and organizations are no exception. Change in organizations is heavily influenced by at least three factors: (1) the technology of the organization (*i.e.*, what the organization does and how it does it—its official or formal goals, and its official or formal structure); (2) the task environment in which the organization must function; and (3) how the people in the organization react and interact to technology, environment, and each other.

Organizational Technologies

Theorists have attempted to categorize technologies and to relate these categories to other variables in the organization. As technology changes, so will the rest of the organization—that is, the organization's structure and the goals of the organization will alter.

For example, James D. Thompson[1] has classified organizational technologies into three types: *long-linked technology*, such as the assembly line; *mediating technology*, found in such institutions as the telephone company, which must deal with people and other variables both extensively and in standardized ways; and *intensive technology*, used by such organizations as hospitals and scientific laboratories, in which the object of the technology is often a human being and feedback from the technology itself is important to the organization. These three technologies correlate with at least three other organizational variables that are significant to change and adaptation: the *cost* of the operation in terms of decision, effort, and communication; the type of *interdependence* found among people and among parts of the organization; and the style of *coordination* necessary to the organization. To elaborate, a mediating technology would have low operating costs, "pooled" or "generalized" interdependence (*i.e.*, each unit of the telephone company, such as line personnel, contribute to the organization, but the company could continue functioning despite the elimination of one of its units), and standardization of parts and units would be the chief means of coordination. A long-linked technology would have intermediate costs, interdependence would be "sequential" (*i.e.*, no worker on the assembly line can work until the worker preceding him or her has completed his or her task), and planning would be the form of coordination favored. An intensive technology would have high costs, "reciprocal" interdependence (every part and person of the organization is dependent upon every other part and person), and would be coordinated through mutual adjustment of the parts. Thompson's view of technology and change in organizations is arranged in summary form in Table 4-1.

Charles Perrow[2] is even more adamant about the significance of technology for organizational change, and he empirically illustrates how technology affects the power structure of organizations. (Thompson only implies this, but, after all, interdependence and coordination are variants of power in any social setting.) Perrow's study of hospitals is intriguing in this regard. He notes that when hospitals used relatively simple technologies, boards of trustees tended to form the central power structure, but when medical technologies became more complex, physicians dominated hospital power relationships. Moreover, as medical technologies became more sophisticated, official hospital goals changed from a "humanistic" and charitable mission to a technically proficient and professionally remunerative mission. Finally, when hospital technologies began to require the

TABLE 4-1 Technology and Organizational Variables

Type of Technology	Type of Interdependence	Type of Coordination	Operating Costs
Mediating (telephone company)	Pooled	Standardization	Low
Long-linked (assembly line)	Sequential	Planning	Intermediate
Intensive (scientific laboratory)	Reciprocal	Mutual Adjustment	High

use of consultants, specialists, outside experts, and coordination among people and groups, administrators became the power elite. A change of goals also accompanied this change in technology, and the official hospital mission was suddenly perceived as including the social as well as the physical aspects of medicine.

There is little doubt that the technology of an organization can have a profound influence on organizational change. Despite methodological problems involving how "technology" and "organizational structure" are defined by different researchers, different levels of analysis, and different measures, the research is unusually consistent in concluding that when an organization's technology alters, so does the structure of the organization itself.[3]

No doubt, this relationship between technology and change pertains to public organizations as well as to private ones (although the literature on technology and organizational structure does not distinguish between public and private organizations). But technology, an "internal" factor affecting change, does not seem to be the primary force in changing public organizations. (We shall return to this point later.) That title, as we observed in Chapters 2 and 3, appears to be held by an "external" phenomenon: the organizational environment.

Organizational Environments

Environmental changes can have such profound effects that organizations will radically transform themselves to survive in an altered environment. Sheldon L. Messinger has noted how the Townsend Movement, for example, which originally was a politically activist plan to alleviate unemployment in the mid-1930s, gradually converted itself into a recreational club after the Social Security Act was enacted, which effectively knocked the ideological underpinnings from the Plan. Townsendites continued to pay lip service to their plan despite the presence of Social Security.[4]

In an effort to find out how organizational capacity for change related to the nature of the organization's task environment, Tom Burns and G. M. Stalker[5] conducted extensive empirical research at two fundamentally different organizations operating in highly dissimilar environments. Their study of a Scottish yarn company and a Scottish electrical engineering firm indicates radically different organizational structures as a function of environmental impacts. The engineering company had virtually continuous meetings, no written job descriptions, no rule book, and an informality surpassing that of the Israeli army, largely as the result of an unstable, rapidly changing task environment. The firm was quite successful in coping with fast-paced environmental changes because it was geared for them.

The yarn company was a well-established firm with a long tradition of industrial success. It had a massive rule book called the "Factory Bible" (which was followed scrupulously), highly formal and infrequent meetings, and painfully clear superordinate-subordinate relationships. But, because of recent changes in the historically hidebound task environment of the textile trade (e.g., the introduction of polyesters, blends, knits, and new marketing techniques), the firm was in trouble. Lack of structural response to a changing environment was hurting the organization financially.

Relatedly, William R. Dill has observed how the task environment can affect the autonomy and the capacity to effect changes in top management.[6] Dill's study of two Norwegian companies, "Alpha" (a clothing manufacturer) and "Beta" (an electronics firm) concluded that the Alpha management, operating in a stable environment subject to few unexpected contingencies, had far less autonomy than the Beta management. Alpha managers had relatively less freedom to make innovative decisions either in terms of the company's owners or relative to their fellow managers.

If this book's original hypothesis—that public administration increasingly is in a time of turbulence—is valid, then it also may follow that public administrators may increasingly find themselves possessing greater latitude and exercising greater power in dealing with that turbulence, at least if Perrow's and Dill's analyses are correct. Certainly the intellectual development of the field implies that this has been and will be the case. The belated recognition by public administrationists that public administrators do make political decisions would seem to be another way of saying that public bureaucrats, confronted with an increasingly unstable task environment (*i.e.*, the society), have gained increasing autonomy with which to deal with their environment.

The disproportionate impact of the task environment on public organizations has been noted, but the ways in which the environment causes organizational change is a subject of some debate, and different writers on this topic use different models, or metaphors, in explaining how the environment effects organizational change.[7]

The Biological Metaphor: The Organization as Organism. One model of organizational response to environmental change is *biological* (or, in the case of Herbert Kaufman, even prebiological[8]). The "population ecology" or "organizational ecology" writers are included in this model, and their ranks include Martin Landau, Howard E. Aldrich, and John Child, among others.[9]

The biological model is reasonably straightforward. The organization's task environment easily and intimately penetrates the organization, and changes in the organization occur with changes in its environment; stability in this extraordinarily open system of constant exchange between the organization and its environment occurs because all natural systems are ultimately self-regulating; and successful organizations achieve success by a process of natural selection that rewards the organization's ability to adapt to its environment.

There are problems with the biological model. For one, it assumes, as does the theory of natural selection, that perfect competition exists among organizations in the social world just as perfect competition is assumed among plants and animals in the natural world; this assumption is untenable. For another, adaptation in the natural world occurs for whole species, not individual organisms, but in the social world survival and extinction are perceived in terms of individual organizations. Organization theorists have developed a lot of taxonomies and classifications of organizations[10] that are based on all sorts of distinctions: their domain, structure, and function; the incentives offered to employees; whether they are regulated or unregulated, large or small, old or young, complex or simple, autocratic or democratic, and, of course, our old friend, public or private. But, as Kaufman

points out, these different classification schemes serve the personal purposes of different theorists, and, consequently, "What we are still groping toward . . . is a taxonomy [of organizations] that takes account of the developmental implications of evolution and calls attention to connections among the categories as well as to the distinctions between."[11] Finally, the ability to adapt in nature is determined by genetic sport, not exactly the thinking person's reaction to problems, while in society adaptability is a product of both luck (perhaps the social equivalent of genetic sport) and rational action—a quality not found in nature.

The Rational Metaphor: The Organization as Omniscient. It is this quality—that is, the thinking capacities unique to human beings—that is central to a second model of organizational response to the task environment: the *rational* model. It is difficult to list specific contributors to this model because its contributors' beliefs about the rational qualities of the organization as constituting the primary explanation of how organizations respond to their environments are implicit rather than stated up front; indeed, the critics of this model are far more readily ascertained than are its contributors.[12] But much of the business management literature, the contributors to the closed model of organizations described in Chapter 3, the research on leadership, and the writings on strategic planning implicitly accept the idea that the rational model best characterizes the organization's relations with its environment.[13]

The essence of the rational model is that people who direct organizations (and, hence, the organizations themselves) are, for all practical purposes, omniscient; they know everything that they need to know. They can discern and often accurately interpret events and trends in the environment, rank prospective organizational responses in order of their effectiveness in dealing with these events and trends, change the organization accordingly, and monitor and adjust to the results. This model has self-evident parallels with the belief sets expressed in the closed model of organizations (described in Chapter 3) and the rationalist model of public policy (described in Chapter 10).

Donald Chisholm perceptively points out that both the biological and rational models of the organization and its environment share a common blind spot: they "treat organizations as elementary, internally non-conflictual, elements within another conflict system."[14] This is a serious flaw because organizations are not happy families; they are, rather, pastiches of many aggressive (and passive) individuals and coalitions, each with their own agendas regarding organizational, coalitional, and individual objectives.

The Political Metaphor: The Organization as Actor. Thus, a third model of the organization's relations with its task environment presents itself: the *political* model. Contributors to the literature of this model include James G. March, Jeffrey Pfeffer, and James D. Thompson, among others.[15]

The political model is of unusual pertinence to public administration and, in a way, represents a compromise of sorts between the biological and rational models: neither the environment nor the "rational organization" is recognized as consistently dominant in determining organizational change; instead, organizational change is a product of unremitting political interaction among individuals and groups within the organization, who are cutting their own deals with each other *and* with other individuals and groups operating in the organization's external environment. The political model places considerable emphasis on *differentiation*, by which is meant the many divisions of labor, specializations, processes, and goals extant in large bureaucracies. And the political model emphasizes that most organizations are composed of members who can leave if they wish. It follows that many internal differences and few organizational sanctions soon lead to a situation in which organizational change is both "biological," in that the environment is impacting directly and discretely on elements within the organization (and not merely on the organization "as a whole"), and "rational" in that these internal elements, each in their own ways, are rationally dealing with that impact to further their individual goals and preferences about how their organization should change.

Organizational Members

The causal relationships between technology, environment, and organizational change are ob-

scure, but we do know that alterations in technology and environment are major factors in organizational innovation, and that these factors are "felt" by the organization through the people who make up the organization. For example, James G. March and Herbert A. Simon have noted that when an organization becomes stabilized in terms of technological and environmental change, the phenomenon of "goal displacement" often occurs.[16] That is, means become ends, or suboptimal goals become optimal goals for various parts of the organization. In the hypothetical organization of International Widget, for example, it may happen that the advertising department perceives the optimal end of the company to be creative marketing, rather than selling widgets. But to the president of International Widget, presumably, creative marketing—or, even more to the point, effective advertising—is simply a means of selling widgets. And to the corporation's stockholders, selling widgets is merely a means of making money. In each instance, goals have been displaced.

Change occurs in other ways, too. In an organization characterized by instability, change comes through (to borrow Richard Cyert's and March's term) organizational "drift."[17] *Drift* refers to the directions in which the organization flows as the result of various member coalitions being formed and reformed within its boundaries.

Of course, despite changes in technology and environment that affect human participants, organizational change can still be hindered by those members who are both powerful and conservative. Anthony Downs has noted the propensity of new organizations to be composed of "climbers," who are ambitious for the advancement that accompanies organizational innovation, and for old organizations to be dominated by "conservers," who feel more secure in stable, if possibly dying, organizations.[18] At the lower echelons, Michel Crozier has observed the inclination of French workers to resist changes that could be of obvious benefit to the organization's welfare, and ultimately their own, out of a deep psychological sense of *bon plaisir*, or the peculiarly French pride of having a recognizable, bureaucratic, and rational "place" in the organization's structure.[19]

Downs and Crozier oddly parallel each other's thoughts about how organizations change. Downs sees the process as related to an "age lump" phenomenon: organizations grow old and stultified just as their members do, and when the conservers retire they often do so as a "lump," making way for a resurgence of change-oriented climbers. Thus, organization change alternates between lethargic "drift" and "reorganizational catch-up."

Crozier sees essentially the same effect but with a slightly different dynamic. Because of the growing bureaucratic rigidity brought about by generally shared attitudes of *bon plaisir*, French organizations either must face collapse or revolutionary change from the top. The need to rationalize and bureaucratize is carried to the limit in French organizations, and with little regard for technological and environmental changes. Hence, change, when it comes, is revolutionary yet authoritarian, because it is long overdue and because the *bon plaisir* mentality of organizational members is one cultivated to resist cooperative innovation.

Downs's notion of an age lump in the life cycle of organizations and Crozier's concept that delayed change eventually means revolutionary change have some interesting applications in public administration. Public administration is facing an age lump of its own. The "Depression virtuosos"—those talented administrators who entered government service in the 1930s because they could not find better-paying jobs in business—have retired. Whether the upshot of this will amount to some sort of "revolutionary" change from the top in the public bureaucracy is a moot question, but it is notable that a new breed of climbers (women, ethnic groups, and highly educated youth) is knocking at the conservers' door with rising insistence.

Shaping Public Organizations: Technology, Environment, or People?

What is the most critical force in "causing" organizational change, particularly in public organizations: its technology, its environment, or its members? No one knows. However, some speculations have emerged in the research on organizations that are at least worth some discussion.

The (Probably) Limited Role of Technology. First, because the technologies of a public organiza-

tion—that is, what an organization does—seldom change, it follows that relatively little organizational change will occur because of technological change. The technologies of public organizations tend not to change because legislatures and other elements of the task environment generally inhibit it; the Social Security Administration, for example, is not likely to diversify and start manufacturing widgets, in addition to mailing Social Security checks. But this does not hold for private organizations; U.S. Steel, for example, can diversify, and it has done so to the point that manufacturing steel is now one of its lesser technologies, and it consequently has changed its name to USX.

This is not to say that public organizations are immune to the changes that accompany technological developments; the computer, for example, is a new technology that has altered virtually every other technology used by organizations, including those used by public organizations, and, as we describe in Chapter 6, significant organizational change has accompanied this new technology of the computer. Nevertheless, technology seems to be less a factor in changing public organizations than private ones.

Environmental Determinism versus Human Choice. This leaves the task environment and the members of organizations—its people—as the more important variables in motivating change in public organizations. Which is the more important? Kaufman argues in eloquent terms that the more significant factor is the environmental one, and not just for public organizations:

I anticipate . . . that comparisons between organizations that survive and those that expire will in the vast majority of instances disclose no significant differences in their respective levels of ability, intelligence, or leadership....[T]he Tolstoyan view of leaders as chips tossed about by the tides of history rather than masters of events cannot be rejected a priori.... [E]ven if leaders *do* appear to be as important as conventional opinions hold them to be, the quality of leadership will nevertheless prove to be randomly rather than systematically distributed among organizations, and chance will therefore remain the main factor in organizational survival.[20]

What, in sum, Kaufman and many of the leading organization theorists seem to be saying is that people do not count for much in shaping organizations.[21]

But not all organization theorists agree with this assessment; in fact, one exhaustive review of the literature identified the questions of whether the organization's environment or whether the people in it had the greater influence on an organization's destiny as two of the four "central perspectives" constituting the "debates in organization theory,"[22] and other analysts have described this issue as "one of the most pervasive and central arguments" in the field.[23]

As the theory of organizations grows more sophisticated, some tentative answers to this dilemma begin to emerge, and the answers center around not merely the "perspectives" (*i.e.*, the biases) of individual theorists, but the types of organizations that are being theorized about.[24] And here is where the public/private distinction in organization theory seems to have a special usefulness.

Table 4-2 is an attempt to categorize some of the more important ideas held by organization theorists regarding the impact of the task environment (or what is sometimes referred to by authors as "determinism"), and the impact of the organization's leaders, managers, and members (also known as "choice") on an organization's destiny. At one extreme, some theorists argue that the environment is all important, all pervasive, and that any decisions made by individuals or groups within an organization about the organization's future really make no difference. At the other extreme, some organization theorists, particularly those associated with the generic management field, argue that the human being is supreme and dominant over the forces of the environment; human choice, in this school, sets organizational destiny, not some social form of natural selection.

Quadrant 1 in Table 4-2 sketches the first extreme that we have described. Quadrant 1 lists some of the characteristics found in an organization that essentially is at the mercy of its task environment. Although an example of this kind of organization may be impossible to find in the real world, certainly some of the literature in political science suggests that, on occasion, federal regulatory agencies have been "captured" by the special interests that they are charged with regulating.[25]

The view held by those theorists who adhere to the paradigm expressed in Quadrant 1 is that environmental forces render organizationally autonomous and self-aware decision making by members of the organization moot, or at the very most, trivial. The organization's relationship with its environment is, to use the metaphor employed earlier, "biological." Change in the organization is achieved by random reactions to random, uncontrollable alterations in the task environment, and the organization's independent standing in society is low due to these environmental constraints. The political behavior of the organization can be characterized as low profile; conflict, both internally and externally, is not high.

The center of organizational control in Quadrant 1 is external to the organization since the environment has such a heavy impact on the organization's behavior. All managers in all organizations tend to have what some authors have called a "generic strategy," by which is meant the recurrent theme of their management posture. In the case of a Quadrant 1 organization, that strategy is a defensive one. Means are emphasized over ends because ends are determined by the task environment, and the role of the manager and the workings of the organization are passive or inactive. Organizational planning is very short-term and oriented toward the immediate solution of problems emerging from the task environment. Much of the literature of organizational ecology, economic history, and political systems has contributed to this view of the organization's relations with its task environment.

In Quadrant 2, we have a situation in which the impact of the task environment upon organizational behavior is strong, but the impact of the organization's members also is strong. Unlike an organization in Quadrant 1, in Quadrant 2 we have a contest among equals; these organizations function in conditions of perfect competition. An example of an organization in this situation might be any major corporation, such as General Motors or IBM, and the people in the organization are seen as being capable of rationally attaining the goals of the larger system. However, the situation described in Quadrant 2 does not envision some sort of Weberian monocrat directing and controlling the organization; rather, parts of the organization

TABLE 4-2 Relations Between Environmental Determinants of Organizational Behavior and Independent Organizational Choice

	Impact of Organization's Leaders, Managers, and Members ("Choice")	
Impact of Organization's Task Environment ("Determinism")	**Weak**	**Strong**
	Example: A government regulatory agency "captured" by the special interest that it is charged to regulate. *Worldview:* Environmental forces render organizationally autonomous and self-aware decision making moot. *Relation with environment:* "Biological." *Organizational change:* Achieved by random reactions to random, uncontrollable alterations in the task environment. *Organizational autonomy:* Low due to environmental constraints. *Political behavior:* Low, both externally and internally. *Center of organizational control:* External. *Generic strategy:* Defensive. *Decision emphases:* Means over ends. *Managerial role:* Inactive. *Planning:* Solution driven, short term *Contributing literatures:* Organizational ecology, economic history, political systems. *(Weak "choice," strong "determinism") Q1*	*Example:* A major automobile manufacturer. *Worldview:* Organizational individuals, departments, and hierarchical levels are capable of rationally attaining the goals of the larger system. *Relation with environment:* "Rational"/economic. *Organizational change:* Achieved by reordering of subsystems in the organization to adapt to changes in the environment, technology, and so forth. *Organizational autonomy:* Medium. *Political behavior:* Highly conflictual, externally directed, low profile. *Center of organizational control:* Shared. *Generic strategy:* Analytical/cautious. *Decision emphases:* Primarily means, with a secondary emphasis on efficiency-related ends. *Managerial role:* Reactive. *Planning:* Solution driven, short term, with some "slack search." *Contributing literatures:* Systems theory, structural/functionalism, contingency theory. *Q2 (Strong "choice," strong "determinism")*

	Impact of Organization's Leaders, Managers, and Members ("Choice")	
	Weak	**Strong**

Impact of Organization's Task Environment ("Determinism")

Weak		

(Weak "choice," weak "determinism") Q3

Example: A new non-profit, voluntary service organization.
Worldview: Organizations are collectivities of semiautonomous parts that constantly engage in bargaining with each other and outsiders to achieve ends.
Relation with environment: "Political."
  Organizational change: Achieved by bargaining, negotiating, and mutual political adjustment.
  Organizational autonomy: Low due to constraints within the organization.
  Political behavior: Low.
Center of organizational control: Latent.
Generic strategy: Reactive.
Decision emphases: Means and ends roughly equal.
Managerial role: Interactive.
Planning: Sporadic.
Contributing literatures: Public choice, political pluralism, organization development.

Q4 (Strong "choice," weak "determinism")

Example: A large government corporation.
Worldview: Organizations are hierarchically structured, rationally behaving, autonomous entities designed to implement the will of the people who head it.
Relation with environment: "Rational"/legal.
  Organizational change: Achieved by rationally deduced decisions made by top management and implemented by the organization's divisions of labor.
  Organizational autonomy: High.
  Political behavior: Highly conflictual, externally directed, low profile.
Center of organizational control: Internal.
Generic strategy: Creative/risk-taking.
Decision emphases: Primarily ends, with a secondary emphasis on effectiveness-related means.
Managerial role: Proactive.
Planning: "Slack search"
Contributing literatures: Decision theory, strategic planning, business management.

Strong		

Sources: Barton Wechsler and Hal Rainey, "Strategic Management in Political Environments," paper presented at the 1986 Annual Meeting of the American Political Science Association, Washington, D.C.: August 1986; Lawrence G. Hrebeniak and William F. Joyce, "Organizational Adaptation: Strategic Choice and Environmental Determinism," *Administrative Science Quarterly*, 30 (September 1985); and W. Graham Astley and Andrew H. Van de Ven, "Central Perspectives and Debates in Organizational Theory," *Administrative Science Quarterly*, 28 (June 1983).

and individuals within the organization recognize challenges to the organization surfacing in the environment and have the ability to respond to them. While some direction from the top is necessary to do this, various groups and individuals constituting the organization are rational actors in their own right, and can respond to the environment rationally in their own way. Hence, these organizational actors do not necessarily follow the wishes of the organization's leaders, but instead are capable of achieving the goals of the larger system (*e.g.*, surviving in the free market place) via their own judgments and actions. Hence, the organization's relationship with its environment is "rational" in the sense that we have used this term earlier, but with a distinctly economic emphasis.

Change in the Quadrant 2 organization is achieved by a rational reordering of subsystems within the organization to adapt to changes in the environment, technology, or whatever. Because of the tension between the deterministic forces in the environment and the capabilities for human choice within the organization, the organization is left with a medium level of autonomy. Political behavior is highly conflictual, but this behavior is largely externally directed; the organization is fighting to survive in a highly competitive environment.

The center of organizational control in Quadrant 2 is shared between the organization and its environment. Decisions tend to focus on means, but with a secondary emphasis on achieving efficiency-related ends. The manager's role is largely one of reacting to challenges coming from the environment. Planning, as in Quadrant 1, is short-term and solution-driven, but there is also some "slack search." *Slack search* is a term originated by James G. March and refers to planning activities that are not necessarily driven by the need for finding immediate solutions. Often slack search is not especially well connected with specific organizational needs. March describes it as a process of "dabbling" or nondirected activity.[26] And, in fact, many Quadrant 2 organizations do engage in this kind of slack search.[27] The literary schools that contribute to the Quadrant 2 concept in organization theory include systems theory, structural/functionalism, and contingency theory.

In Quadrant 3, organizations function in a situation in which there is little human choice and little environmental impact. Quadrant 3 is an unstable condition, both internally and externally, and one finds that Quadrant 3 organizations either die quickly or reform themselves in such a way as to move to another quadrant. An example of an organization functioning in a Quadrant 3 situation would be a nonprofit voluntary service organization, or any organization that is characterized by a decision process that has been described as "muddling through."[28] Lawrence G. Hrebeniak and William F. Joyce describe the situation expressed in Quadrant 3 as one in which organizations

have an array of internal strengths and competencies that are appropriate to external opportunities and conditions. . . . It is reasonable to argue that an appropriate mix or insufficient number of internal capabilities will prevent organizations from acting, despite the benignity, munificence, or lack of threat of the environment. In this view, the task of the organization is to develop the capabilities or distinctive competencies needed to take advantage of environmental conditions and thereby alter and escape from the conditions of [Quadrant 3].[29]

The view in Quadrant 3 is that organizations are federations of semiautonomous parts that constantly engage in bargaining with each other and outsiders to achieve their ends. The organization's relationship with its environment is "political" and organizational change is achieved by bargaining, negotiating, and by mutual political adjustment. Organizational autonomy is low and the level of political behavior is low. But these low levels of organizational independence and political activism are due less to forces in the environment influencing the organization than to constraints within the organization itself.

The center of organizational control in Quadrant 3 is latent because no real control of any kind has emerged. The organization's generic strategy is reactive; it tends to emphasize means and ends roughly equally. Its managers assume interactive roles with both the environment and with the internal parts of the organization; planning is rare, sporadic, and disjointed. Literatures that have had an impact on the thinking underlying a Quadrant 3 situation include public choice, political pluralism, and organization development.

Finally, Quadrant 4 posits a condition of strong organizational choice and weak environmental determinism. It is the extreme opposite of organizations in Quadrant 1. An example would be a large government corporation. We describe the power of the government corporation in Chapter 11. Suffice it to note for now that government corporations, which are corporations chartered by governments and often granted what amounts to both economic and political monopolies, have emerged during the past thirty years as important and independent economic and political policymakers. An example of this power is epitomized by the late Robert Moses, who headed a variety of government corporations in New York. As a biographer of Moses stated, "For thirty-four years, Moses played an important part in establishing [the City of New York's] priorities, and for seven years he established *all* the city's priorities."[30]

It is with this kind of dominance by organizational leaders over their task environments in mind that some writers have characterized organizations as being hierarchically structured, rationally behaving, autonomous entities that have the ability to implement the will of the people who head them. Thus, an organization with the characteristics of Quadrant 4 is eminently "rational," but instead of an economic orientation in this rationality (as is characteristic of organizations found in Quadrant 2), it has a much more legalistic one. Organizational change is achieved by rationally deduced decisions made by top management and implemented along rational lines by the appropriate divisions of labor within the organization. Organizational autonomy is high and the organization's political behavior is highly conflictual and externally directed against rivals in the environment; but this aggressive political behavior typically is characterized by a low profile.

The center of organizational control in Quadrant 4 is almost entirely internal, and the generic strategy employed by the organization is highly creative and risk taking. The organization emphasizes ends over means, although there is a secondary emphasis on those means that concern how to attain the organizations's ends most effectively. The role of the manager is highly proactive and slack search characterizes the planning function. Among the contributing literatures to a Quadrant 4 conception of organizations are decision theory, strategic planning, and business management.

These relationships between the organization's task environment and its capacity for organizational choice, as illustrated in Table 4-2, have a readily apparent bearing on public organizations. In fact, one could argue that the typology posited by Table 4-2 makes a credible case for arguing that public organizations are more diverse and are found in more types of environmental contexts than are private organizations. After all, as Table 4-2 shows, we find that public organizations (a term including "third sector" organizations) appear in three of the four quadrants (Quadrants 1, 3 and 4). While it is entirely possible that examples of private organizations could be used in these same quadrants, there is only one, Quadrant 2, that has obvious bearing on the private organization. One might infer from this that public organizations present a far richer source of study and inquiry than do private ones.

INFORMATION AND INTELLIGENCE IN ORGANIZATIONS

How information, intelligence, and knowledge are used, distorted, and transmitted has considerable significance for what we have just considered in the preceding section: change in organizations. Cybernetist and operations researcher Stafford Beer, in fact, defines information as "what changes us."[31] Additionally, the uses of intelligence have particular significance for the understanding of public bureaucracies, for it is on knowledge and feedback that public policy decisions are made and adjusted.

Hierarchy and Information

Perhaps the most focused research in the field of organizational intelligence has been done by Harold L. Wilensky.[32] Wilensky considered both private and public organizations, but it is clear that public bureaucracies stand to gain or lose the most from how information is used or abused. Wilensky's basic contention is that organizational change and control are achieved through the control of information. He observes that organizational change is hindered by such phenomena as "the significance of slogans," "the power of preconceptions," and, perhaps paramountly, secrecy.

In Wilensky's view, organizational conflict, informational control, and personal power are inextricably intertwined. Consider Wilensky's example of Nazi Foreign Minister Ribbentrop and his use of the notorious World War II spy "Cicero," who was the valet of the British ambassador at Ankara. Cicero sent astonishingly accurate and detailed intelligence concerning the Allied invasion plans to Ribbentrop. Although the Foreign Minister had his doubts as to the authenticity of Cicero's reports, his overriding reason for sitting on most of Cicero's information appears to have been interagency rivalry. Ribbentrop was involved in a bitter power struggle with the Reich Security Office, and he loathed von Papen, the German ambassador to Turkey. Because Cicero reported directly to one L. C. Moyzisch, an attaché on von Papen's staff employed by the Reich Security Office, Ribbentrop found it most expedient to dismiss Cicero's intelligence. Wilensky concludes from this and other instances that the use of secrecy exaggerates organizational pathologies that already may be present, such as conflict, authoritarianism, lack of feedback, and excessive personal power.

Wilensky also argues that information may be distorted and prevented from reaching the people who need it and can act on it by excessive centralization or decentralization of the organization. As an example of what happens to knowledge in a decentralized (or open model) organization, Wilensky cites the surprise of American troops at Pearl Harbor during the Japanese attack. The Japanese secret code had been broken, and there is substantial evidence showing that various elements in the military and foreign services knew approximately when and where the Japanese would attack. But the information failed to reach the forces at Pearl Harbor in time.

Partly as a response to the intelligence fiasco of Pearl Harbor, the aptly dubbed Central Intelligence Agency (CIA) was established. The idea was that important messages no longer would be lost in the interorganizational shuffle, as in the Pearl Harbor incident, but would be sent directly to the people, including the president, who were in a position to respond to new knowledge.

Nevertheless, information can be blocked in centralized (or closed model) organizations, too.

Wilensky cites the Cuban Bay of Pigs disaster as an example. In this instance, the CIA evidently approached the freshly elected President John F. Kennedy with what it represented as a long-standing, well-formulated, and superbly conceived (not to mention, sure-fire) plan for the overthrow of Premier Fidel Castro's revolutionary government in Cuba. Kennedy, who later implied he had been somewhat awed by the intelligence-gathering capabilities and expertise of the CIA and, in any event, had no comparable organization in terms of prestige to which he could turn for additional intelligence, decided to let the agency carry on, essentially in its own way. Among the other aspects of remarkably poor planning by the CIA, as it turned out, was the agency's ignorance of extensive swamps in the Bay of Pigs area, which entrapped the invasion force on the coastline and made the Cuban expatriates easy pickings for Castro's troops.

Gordon Tullock[33] has argued that organizational decentralization is more conducive than centralization to the preservation of information and the minimization of its distortion in organizations. Tullock constructs an arithmetic "model of hierarchical distortion," in which he reasons that the more an organization grows, the more effort and expense will be required for "internal" administration, to the detriment of the "external" achievements of organizational goals relative to the society. This pathology is unavoidable because the larger the bureaucracy, the more time must be devoted by its members to assuring that information reaches the right administrators relatively intact; in other words, the bigger the bureaucracy, the more people there will be who may stop, distort, take away from, or add to the same information bit, and hence greater effort must be generated to preserve "noise"-free intraorganizational communications. And this effort must be spent at the expense of accomplishing the organization's social mission. As a result of this reasoning, Tullock advocates that bureaucracies be vastly reduced in size so that the society may benefit more directly. Tullock believes that in small organizations the goals and rationalities of the organization (e.g., legal assistance for the poor) are more likely to complement the goals and rationalities of the individuals in the organization (e.g., getting ahead) because it is far easier to see causal relationships

Information, Intelligence, Organizations, and Four Dead Horses

Information and intelligence in organizations often exist only in the eye of the beholder. In the eyes of a number of beholders in Arizona, neither information nor intelligence characterized a senseless incident involving the Internal Revenue Service (IRS), the Arizona Livestock and Sanitary Board, and a herd of horses.

Carl J. Jatho was a free-wheeling entrepreneur from Kingman, Arizona, a small town in the northern part of the state, who headed a tax-preparation business called The Bookkeeper. For various reasons, Jatho and his bookkeeping ran into legal troubles. For example, he admitted in court to signing up customers for fictitious mining partnerships as part of his tax-shelter scheme. Ultimately, Jatho pleaded guilty to five counts of tax fraud that cheated the federal government out of an estimated $45 million in taxes owed by some 3,800 taxpayers. So many of these bilked taxpayers appeared in federal court *en masse* during Jatho's trial that the press took to calling them "The Jatho People." Ultimately Jatho was sentenced to three years in prison, fined $150,000, and ordered to pay $1.2 million for preparing fraudulent tax returns. Jatho was imprisoned in September 1986.

Among Jatho's remaining assets were thirty-five to forty horses that he kept fenced on his ranch in Kingman. Apparently no one thought too seriously about the fate of Jatho's horses until early January, 1987, when officials from the Arizona Livestock and Sanitary Board, the Internal Revenue Service, and some local agencies met to discuss what to do with them. What precisely occurred at this meeting is unclear. The IRS had the legal authorization to seize the horses as part of its civil case, but decided not to do so because its officials believed that only seventeen of the horses belonged to Jatho, and no one was sure which of the beasts were his. The Mohave County Animal Control Board and the Mohave County Sheriff's Office thought that the animals fell under the jurisdiction of the State Livestock Board, but the Livestock Board decided not to act on the grounds that it believed the IRS had jurisdiction. It did appear from subsequent press reports, however, that neither the IRS nor the Livestock Board had plans to take care of the horses, and that each

agency knew that the other was not going to assume responsibility for them either.

Five days after the meeting, the press reported that four of Jatho's horses had died from starvation. When questioned by the press about how and why this had occurred, IRS agent William Bronson stated that the horses were in such poor condition that they could not be sold, adding, "We are a tax collecting agency, not a humane society." At this point, the State Livestock Board acted and seized the horses, noting in the process that hay and other feed had been in the storage shed behind the Jatho house during the entire five months that had passed since Jatho entered prison. In an apparent effort to show that it was on top of the problem, the Livestock Board filed charges of willful neglect and cruelty to animals against Jatho, who had, of course, been in prison since September. Meanwhile, the Phoenix office of the Internal Revenue Service was besieged with phone calls from irate citizens.

At this point, the IRS and the Livestock Board began trading charges. A member of the Livestock Board stated that "It was the IRS that put the guy in jail. The IRS should have made some provision for those horses." The IRS contended, in turn, that it was the victim of a "cheap shot" by the media and other government agencies; the IRS suggested that the Livestock Board was well aware that it was not planning to take jurisdiction of the horses and thus the Livestock Board should have done so.

The senior Senator from Arizona, Dennis DeConcini, soon got into the act by writing the Commissioner of the IRS that the incident in Kingman was the "result of either a severely flawed policy by the agency or negligent actions taken by IRS personnel," and launched his own inquiry. As an aide to Senator DeConcini noted, "The word 'insane' is used rather frequently in news stories because news stories cover unusual and unexpected things, but I don't ever recall seeing a news story where the word 'insane' was more applicable....You don't just leave forty horses there to die. It's crazy. There's nothing rational about it." The state's largest newspaper, in an editorial, characterized the explanations from both the IRS and the Livestock Board as "lame and ludicrous."

Mohave County Supervisor Becky Foster, after noting that a number of citizens had offered to donate food or money for the benefit of the horses,

stated, "This restores your faith in humanity." Then she broke into tears as she watched workers dump the dead horses into a truck.

Sources: Steve Daniels, "Outraged Arizonans Rally to Rescue Starving Horses," *The Arizona Republic* (January 14, 1987); Andy Hall and Steve Daniels, "Agencies Trade Blame for Abandoned Horses," *The Arizona Republic* (January 15, 1987); and "The Cold Hands of the IRS," *The Arizona Republic* (January 16, 1987).

---

between individual acts and mission accomplishment in small organizations than in large organizations, and the evaluation of organizational performance is thus much easier. Tullock's recommendation is a radical one relative to the rest of organization theory, which tends to regard organizational growth as a sign of health.

March and Simon also have noticed that information tends to be distorted by multiple levels of hierarchy.[34] They note the pathology of "uncertainty absorption" in bureaucratic organizations, whereby data that initially are regarded as tentative, uncertain, and "soft" by the persons who collect them become increasingly final, certain, and "hard" as they are sent up through the decision-making hierarchy. Thus, we may assume that in the decision by Ford Motor Company to build the Edsel, the corporation's low-level market researchers concluded that there "might" be a market for a middle-range car in the United States, but by the time their findings reached Henry Ford it was being voiced in top management circles that there "was" such a market; uncertainty in the initial information had been absorbed by the various hierarchical levels that handled it on its way to upper management.

It also is worth observing that organizations can collapse because of too much information. Richard L. Meier conducted an intriguing study of a university library that was in the process of administratively breaking down because of too many demands and not enough resources. He examined how institutions without the benefits of functioning in a free-market environment, where information inputs could be adjusted through market mechanisms, responded to communications overload.[35] He delineated fourteen strategies used by

such organizations to cope with rising levels of informational stress, including queuing (*e.g.*, keeping library patrons in waiting rooms "outside" the organization); the creation of branch facilities; the creation of a mobile reserve (*i.e.*, having teams of personnel that are transferable to other units as needed); the evolvement of specific performance standards followed immediately by a reduction of those standards; having a "brainstorming" search for a "magic formula"; the promotion of self-service (*e.g.*, letting patrons into the stacks), which is a radical strategy because it represents a deliberate reduction of organizational sovereignty; the limitation of work to capacity as determined by rigid, ritualistic rules and as characterized by the denial of error and the refusal of challenge; and, ultimately, the dissolution of the organization. The library, in a very real sense, had no choice but to play out this scenario. It did not have the control over demands from its environment that, say, International Widget would have had. International Widget could simply boost the price of widgets, and thereby reduce demand (*i.e.*, communications overload). But the library—and, presumably, any public organization—did not have this option. It had to adjust internally.

These and other studies of informational dynamics in organizations are especially relevant to public administration for a number of reasons. Public organizations tend to be bureaucratic organizations, they do not operate in free-market environments, and they "produce" policies rather than products. Information is of unusual importance to these characteristics and functions. And recent developments in public administration indicate that information will be of even more importance to the public bureaucracy and the public than it is now. One such development is the growing professionalism and expertise of the public administrator.

Professionalism and Public Knowledge

The professionalization of public administration represents a second development that seems destined to affect the free flow of knowledge in the task milieu of the public bureaucrat. By *professionalization* is meant the evolution of a core of commonly shared and recognized knowledge and expertise held by members of a group. The rise of the MPA and DPA degrees, the establishment of professional schools of public administration and public affairs, and the appearance of new professional journals and associations all indicate that public administration is professionalizing as never before.

Paradoxically, professionalization of the public service has both benefits and liabilities for the public. As York Willbern noted in a seminal article on the subject,[36] professionalism in public bureaucracies brings

1. increased technical competence;
2. increased respect for technical expertise;
3. the enforcement of minimal ethical and technical standards;
4. insulation from pressure to discriminate against clients;
5. the avoidance of direct democratic control that might be of doubtful utility in some fields;
6. greater interchangeability of personnel among governmental units;
7. the incentive for officials to acquire more skills;
8. the creation of in-group loyalty; and
9. the provision of additional satisfactions to employees.

Conversely, however, professionalism also brings with it:

1. potential conflicts of interest between the professional group (*e.g.*, school teachers) and larger publics (*e.g.*, taxpayers);
2. the presence of undue influence wielded by special publics through professional ties (such as the medical profession's occasionally debatable impact on public health programs in some states through the American Medical Association);
3. the insulation of public servants from public control;
4. the lack of internal democracy often found in professional associations;
5. the limitation of public services by the professionals' insistence on the maintenance of unrealistic professional standards;
6. the diminishing of transferability of personnel among agencies because of overly specialized training;
7. the lack of interagency coordination because of professional specialization or jealousy;
8. the discouraging of citizen participation by the presence of a professional mystique.

Most if not all of the dysfunctions of professionalism listed by Willbern revolve around the control of knowledge and expertise—or what often passes for expertise. If knowledge is power, then how is professional knowledge (with its antidemocratic implications) to be used to further the goals of society? Obviously, it must be used carefully, for the very idea of being professional carries with it a dangerous footnote for democratic values: "We know more than you, therefore do as we say."

A homely example of how professional status, mystique, and expertise exercise a control over information that prevents and undermines the manifestation of democratic values is provided by Alan Altshuler in his study of a decision to locate a freeway in the Minneapolis-St. Paul area.[37] The local highway department made a conscious, internal decision to be inflexible on the proposed freeway's route and location and based this decision on the unsophisticated but "professional" criterion of a crude cost-benefit analysis. This analysis formed the core rationale of the department's justification of its decision. More profound, however, the department's sole, and quite effective, justification of its decision was that it was made on the basis of professional and technical values, and who could argue with "the facts"? This argument won the day, despite very legitimate pressures brought by black residents, white residents in some of the few remaining middle-class neighborhoods in downtown St. Paul (who had the quiet support of the governor), and retailers in the central business district, and by the existence of an alternative route developed by the city planner that would have satisfied these groups and answered their many protests. Expertise and the control of information took political precedence because they were presumed to be apolitical.

James D. Carroll has extended the concept of professionalism and has called it "noetic authority," or the power that derives from knowledge. He argues that the politics and administration of the future will be based on who controls information and knowledge rather than who controls wealth and power. Carroll cites the rise of a plethora of political and administrative issues involving the press, telecommunications, urban planning, the environment, education, transportation, and consumerism, among others, as disputes in which the old "politics of greed" is being displaced by the new "politics of knowledge."[38]

Information and Decision Making

As Carroll implies, information and knowledge are more important than ever before in organizational decision making. In light of this argument, however, how is it that "organizations seem to invest in information and information systems, but their investments often do not seem to make sense. They gather information and do not use it. They ask for reports and do not read them. They act first and receive requested information later, and do not seemed to be concerned about the order."[39]

These are important concerns. Few administrators have not both written and read the useless memorandum—useless, that is, in terms of its alleged relevance to making the decision at hand. The literature is rife with examples of information being generated so that managers might make better decisions, and yet that information has no apparent relationship to those decisions.[40] Why is this so?

Martha S. Feldman and James G. March have phrased the problem of information and decision making in organizations (what they call "a portrait of important features of information use") in a reasonably rigorous fashion:

1. Much of the information that is gathered and communicated by individuals and organizations has little decision relevance.

2. Much of the information that is used to justify a decision is collected and interpreted *after* the decision has been made, or substantially made.

3. Much of the information gathered in response to requests for information is not considered in the making of decisions for which it was requested.

4. Regardless of the quantity and quality of the information available at the time a decision is first considered, more information is requested.

5. Complaints that an organization does not have enough information to make a decision are voiced at the same time that available information is ignored.

6. The relevance of the information already being provided to decision makers is considerably less conspicuous than the unrelenting insistence by decision makers for more information.[41]

Organization theorists and decision scientists have provided two explanations for these pathologies. One is that "information overload" can occur, and organizations and the people in them simply are unable to process the information they have because of organizational and human limitations.[42] A second explanation often offered is that the information itself is poor or the wrong kind of information, and while there may be a great deal of information (*i.e.*, data), it is not information that we can use (*i.e.*, knowledge).[43]

Feldman and March offer a considerably more creative and original explanation, and one that is a genuine contribution to both organization theory and decision science. They contend that the apparent lack of a "match" between information and decision making in organizations does not, "in general, reflect stupidity on the part of organizations. Rather [these absences of matches between data and decisions] are symptoms of sophistication in understanding the role of information in organizational choice."[44]

Feldman and March go on to argue that the sophistication displayed by organizations that gather more information than they use or seem to need is not necessarily conscious. But the standard operating procedures of an organization that result in the production of such massive amounts of data may, in and of themselves, betoken a high quality of organizational decision making.

Feldman and March make three important points about the role of information in organizations. The first is that organizations tend to gather information in a "surveillance mode" rather than in a "decision mode." Information, in other words, is gathered for the sake of monitoring the environment and the internal workings of the organization on a routine basis. The kind of information gathered in this mode, which is the typical way in which information is gathered in organizations, is not related to specific decisions that are coming up on the organizational agenda.

Second, the standard operating procedures of organizations provide incentives for underestimating the costs of gathering the information relative to the returns that the information provides the organization. Typically, the information-gathering functions of an organization are separate from its information-using functions. Those who use the information are not those who gather it, and information users (*i.e.*, decision makers) seldom provide any particular set of guidelines to the information gatherers (*i.e.*, staffers and researchers). There is also a bias among information users that holds it is better to have more information than is necessary than less, and this also results in more information being gathered.

Finally, much of the information used in organizations is subject to "strategic misrepresentation." Information frequently is produced for the purpose of persuading someone to do something; when information is found that would undermine the process of persuasion, it is edited and discarded. At its worst, this process can result in a competition among liars, but organizations and the decision makers in them typically find ways of accounting for this pathology. "Decision makers learn not to trust overly clever people, and smart people learn not to be overly clever."[45]

These organizational realities result in information taking on its own value as a symbol and a signal in the political and decision-making life of an organization. The role of information as symbol and signal has been underestimated by decision theorists. Yet, these symbolic and signalling functions of information have great substantive importance. On the one hand, organizations underestimate the true cost of gathering information, yet on the other hand, they place a high value in using information to buttress preferred decisions:

Individuals and organizations will consistently over invest in information . . . because the acts of seeking and using information in decisions have important symbolic value to them and to the society....Decisions are orchestrated in such a way as to ensure that those making them and those observing them come to believe that they are reasonable—or even intelligent. The use of information, asking for information, and justifying decisions in terms of information have all come to be significant ways in which we signal that the process is legitimate, that we are good decision makers, and that our organizations are well managed....Since legitimacy is a necessary property of effective decisions, conspicuous consumption of information is a sensible strategy for decision makers. The strategy need not be chosen deliberately. It will characterize processes that work.[46]

By this logic, then, decisions that are information intensive have a greater legitimacy in organizations, and as a result it is ultimately easier to gain organizational acceptance of decisions and their smoother implementation if information has played a key role in the process. Because decision makers implicitly recognize this utility of information, it follows that better decision makers would invest more in gathering information than would poor decision makers, even if the information had nothing in particular to do with making the decision itself. Thus, "organizations that exhibit an elaborate information system and conspicuous consumption of information will . . . be more effective decision makers than those who do not."[47]

Organizations that are information-sensitive also will make their decisions more rapidly. A careful study of eight microcomputer manufacturing firms found that fast decision makers used more information in making their decisions than did slower decision makers. Fast decision makers also developed more alternatives in deciding how to deal with problems.[48]

Interestingly, fast decision makers also seemed to rely on counselling with respected colleagues more when making decisions than did slower decision makers. Recall, in this regard, our discussion in Chapter 3 about the differences in decision making in the public and private sectors: public decision makers indulged in a much more collegial style of decision making than did private decision makers. In the study of decision making in the microcomputer firms, it was found that a pattern of information reliant, advice-seeking, rapid decision making led to "superior performance" by executives.[49] Yet, in the public sector, decision making seems to have only one of these three components consistently present in the decision process: advice-seeking. Both information and rapidity often appear to be absent.

CONTROL, AUTHORITY, AND POWER IN ORGANIZATIONS

Organizational intelligence, noetic authority, information, and decision making as concepts overlap considerably with organizational control and authority. He or she who controls information possesses genuine power in the bureaucracy.

The analyst most noted for his argument that authority is the central variable in organizational behavior is Amitai Etzioni.[50] Etzioni contends that power is all, and that virtually all characteristics of the organization are determined by the kind of authority used in the organization. For example, a prison uses "coercive" power: its method of control is physical (e.g., solitary confinement); the organization acquires participants through the socialization of inmates; both officials (e.g., the warden) and information leaders (popularly respected or feared prisoners with no official position) are present; and "instrumental activities" (mechanical kinds of activities) predominate as the organization's chief technology. At the other extreme of Etzioni's power continuum, a political party uses "identitive," or "normative" power: its method of control is symbolic (e.g., appeals to patriotism); the organization acquires participants both through the socialization of its members and the selection of applicants; only "formal leaders" (or leaders who have both real and official power) are present, and "expressive activities" (or interpersonal activities) predominate as the organization's chief activity. Finally, in the middle ranges of Etzioni's continuum, a business corporation uses "utilitarian" power: its method of control is material (e.g., a salary); participants are acquired chiefly through a selection process; leadership comprises all types (officials, information leaders, and formal leaders), and activities may be both instrumental and expressive. Etzioni's concept is diagrammed in Table 4-3.

Public organizations commonly are a hybrid combining Etzioni's normative and utilitarian forms of organizational power. There is a certain "calling" involved in working for the public service and nonprofit agencies (thus yielding them some identitive power), but there is also a recognized necessity among those wishing to join public organizations that it would also be nice to earn a regular paycheck (thus giving public organizations some utilitarian power). It follows that public organizations would attract (and want) employees with an unusual set of attitudes about how they would like to spend their working lives; Herbert A. Simon has called these attitudes "decision premises."[51]

The Decision Premise: The Objective of Organizational Authority

A *decision premise* refers to the values and perceptions held by each member of the organization,

TABLE 4-3   A Continuum of Organizational Power and Authority

	Type of Power	Method of Control	Acquisition of Participants	Type of Leadership	Type of Activities
A u t h o r i t y	Coercive (a prison)	Physical	Socialization	Officials and informal leaders	Instrumental
	Utilitarian (a business corporation)	Material	Selection	Officials, informal leaders and formal leaders	Instrumental and Expressive
	Indentitive or normative (a political party)	Symbolic	Selection and socialization	Formal leaders	Expressive

on which he or she bases every decision he or she makes regarding the organization. These individual values and perceptions are unique to the individual, but many can be altered and influenced through the use of organizational means and sanctions available to those in positions of control, the division of labor in the organization and how it affects the individual, the standard operating procedures used in the organizations, the socialization and training of new members of the organization, and the kinds of people who are selected to join the organization. Together, these techniques can mold each individual's decision premise in a way that reduces organizational uncertainty by making the individual's decisions predictable. When uncertainty is low (*e.g.*, "I trust Mary to do the right thing...."), authority and control often are relinquished or "decentralized" ("... so I've made her responsible for the job").

Many organizations attempt to control, or at least filter, the decision premises of applicants even before they enter the organization. Some businesses prefer applicants who are business majors and fraternity or sorority members over applicants who majored in sociology and were independents. The rationale is that "B-school" joiners are more likely to cultivate a corporate team spirit than are socially aware loners. After entry, subordinates' decision premises are formed more fully by superordinates through "management training" classes and the more subtle socialization techniques extant in most large organizations.

There is an astonishing range of resources and techniques that organizations, particularly business organizations, have available to form the decision premises of their members more to their liking. In addressing the topic of "organizational seduction," Roy J. Lewicki suggests that "matching" the values of the organization and those of applicants to the organization is only the first step. Others include providing employees with an opportunity to work for a high-status organization (or at least with opportunities for attaining status within the organization), providing challenges, and providing a pleasant, even luxurious, work environment.[52]

In contrast to business administration, however, public administration has been far less able to control the decision premises of decision-making participants in public bureaucracies. True, there is a selection and socialization process in public bureaucracies but, more than other bureaucracies, public bureaucracies make decisions in situations characterized by unusual degrees of participation from the task environment. Public administrators, especially in recent years that have been characterized by a social milieu advocating "power to the people," increasingly find themselves asking "client-members" of their organizations to participate in the decision-making process. A client-member is a person who is both a "customer" and a member of an organization, such as a student in a university or an inmate in a prison. And, it is worth adding that other techniques available to the business organization for forming members' decision premises, such as providing a luxurious work environment, are less available to public organizations. In any event, public administrators often find that they lack the authority and control possessed by administrators in other institutional settings. This situation may well be to the benefit of the polity, but it often does not seem so to the frustrated public administrator confronting what occasionally appears to be organizational and environmental chaos.

Slack, Side Payments and Bargaining: The Milieu of Organizational Power

Organization theorists agree that the exercise of control, authority, and power in organizations is a complex, political phenomenon. Cyert and March, Downs, and Thompson more or less share the same concept of how control and authority are achieved in organizations. In their view, "slack," bargaining, "side payments," and coalition formation represent the dynamics of organizational control. *Slack* refers to those "nonrational" interstices present in even the most rigid bureaucracies that represent opportunities for what is known in the military as "scrounging" (*e.g.*, an unused computer in the accounting department mysteriously and "unofficially" finds its way to the advertising department where it receives considerable use). *Side payments* in organizations would not be possible without organizational slack. Side payments can be made in the form of status (*e.g.*, a new "unofficial" carpet for an individual's office or a promotion in name only, with no increase in salary or authority) or in the form of material rewards (*e.g.*, a salary increment). Side payments are usually made on the basis of discreet bargaining between the representatives of coalitions (*e.g.*, "young Turks," "old guard," whatever) in the organization, and genuine authority in the organization is determined by who represents what coalitions.

Styles of authority and control must change as the organization changes. Thus, the military sociologist Morris Janowitz[53] suggests that the old, closed-model style of authority traditionally favored in the military, that of "domination," is no longer suitable for an organization characterized by such technological and environmental changes as seen in new weapons systems, the adoption of deterrence as a strategy, the routinization of innovation, and the blurring of historic soldier/civilian distinctions. Janowitz urges that a "fraternal type authority" based on the open model's techniques of manipulation should replace the domineering techniques normally used in the military.

The "Two-Wayness" of Organizational Control

The notion of styles of authority leads us to the problem of the legitimacy—indeed, even the morality—of authority. Chester Barnard was perhaps the first theorist to appreciate that there was more to authority than a boss giving orders to an underling; Barnard pointed out that a subordinate had to *accept* a superior's directive before that superior could ever have something called authority, or power. Even more profoundly, Barnard contended that, before an order would be accepted by a subordinate, the superior first had to penetrate the subordinate's "zone of indifference." Most of the time, Barnard said, underlings really could care less about what a boss directed. Thus, authority was conceived as a two-way process between subordinate and superior, and this "two-wayness" added to the legitimacy of authority.[54]

Simon, whose early work was intensely influenced by Barnard, extended Barnard's concept of authority by devising a "zone of acceptance" and positing four basic motivations of subordinates to accept the will of a superior: rewards and sanctions, legitimacy, social approval, and the subordinate's

confidence in the superior's ability.[55] Of these motivations, those of rewards and sanctions are the most interesting, if for no other reason than that Simon thought the subordinate had more rewards and sanctions at his or her disposal than the superior! The superior had only three: the power to hire and fire; the power to promote and demote, and certain incentive rewards. But the subordinate had at least twice that number: the power to quit, to strike, to slow down, to perform minimally, to perform "literally" (or to do only what the jobs specified), and not to perform.

Organizational Power: The Place of Personal Skill

Simon's idea that the subordinate can have more power in an organization than his or her superior was revolutionary, and it had a lasting impact on the field of organization theory, particularly as it is applied to public organizations. For example, one study of the gubernatorial administrations in California of Ronald Reagan and Jerry Brown concluded that their organizational power was a direct result of their "obedience to [the] roles" expected of them by the organization (in this case, state government) that they led. As the authors put it,

This obligation to act within the bounds of a role does not decrease as one assumes high positions of authority; a role may grant more discretion in how it is enacted, but there are normative constraints to even the highest level position. The cabinet officers . . . no less than a clerk, were constrained to perform their roles in such a way as to demonstrate obeisance to norms. . . . One need only recall President Nixon's supposed abuse of office to recognize that no actor within a social system can ignore the rules of a system. To unseasoned actors, behaving capriciously...might seem the quintessential evidence of power. But such a strategy cannot endure in an organized setting.[56]

Nevertheless, superiors do retain some authority over subordinates. One review of the literature on organizational control identified six "major control mechanisms":[57]

Supervision, or the direct observation by a supervisor, who provides corrective feedback to the subordinate.

Input control, or the constraining of resources to subunits, a method favored especially by nonprofit organizations because they are limited (according to some analysts[58]) in their use of output controls relative to for-profit organizations.

Behavior control, or the structuring of individual and group activities via procedures, performance standards, and technology.

Output control, a type of control used extensively but not exclusively by for-profit organizations, it refers to the monitoring and evaluation of organizational outputs, such as market share, profits, or student test scores.

Selection-socialization, or a kind of control that exists when certain types of norms and values are internalized into the organization—"localized co-optation," discussed earlier, falls into this category.

Environmental control, is the constraint on the organization imposed by its task environment, although there are few studies illustrating how administrators capitalize on this constraint in terms of attaining their own organizational ends.

A study of how these six kinds of administrative control mechanisms were used by administrators to control 120 school principals in sixty elementary school districts found that district administrators used all six methods of control in a surprisingly broad and balanced way—at least when compared with studies of organizational control in private, for-profit enterprises. However, supervision was the least effective form of influence among the six; input control (largely in the form of budget allocations) was used extensively, as was behavior control (although the principals themselves did not perceive behavior control to be a major method used to control them). Output control was essentially restricted to student achievement, although the principals thought many more output controls were being used; selection-socialization controls appeared to be heavily present, as were environmental controls in the form of principals relying on the district office to provide them with feedback from their schools' communities.[59]

District administrators "zoned" their control of their principals, in that they tightly held the reigns over administrative matters, but only loosely over instructional ones. Similarly, ends were objects of tight central control, but the means for achieving those ends were not, and were left largely to the principals. The study concluded that "a more complex system of control" based on multiple sources of information "may be used for managers in not-for-profit organizations who have to supervise a workforce employing an unclear technology" (in this case, teaching), leading to greater managerial stress because these public managers are effectively "monitored by everyone around them."[60]

Organizational Power: The Role of Hierarchical Structure

As the study of public school principals implies, control and authority—in short, power—in organizations is a product of many factors besides that of personal skill. Most theorists agree that power is a matter of organizational structure as well as personal skill,[61] and the proposition appeals to common sense. Thus far, we by and large have been discussing qualities of skill, not hierarchy, in learning about organizational power, but this latter area warrants review, too.

Structure and Individual Power. Researchers increasingly suggest, in fact, that organizational structure may be more important than the skills of individuals in acquiring organizational power.[62] A complex study of a newspaper publishing company found that the "criticality" of a "task position" (*i.e.*, the removal of the position would result in a breakdown of work flow), the number of opportunities inherent to the occupant of a position to engage in transactions with people in many other positions, and access to the communication network of the coalition that dominated the organization had a strong, positive relationship with an individual's perceived power in the organization. Access to a variety of communication networks in the organization, particularly control of one's departmental communications, associated strongly with an individual's promotion to supervisory positions.[63] "While personal attributes and strategies may have an important effect on power acquisition," the study contended, "structure imposes the ultimate constraint on the individual."[64]

Structure and Group Power. Just as structural variables can affect the power of individual people in an organization, so they can influence the power of whole departments. Research indicates that the power of a subunit is a combination of three factors: the subunit's ability to copy with uncertainty; its "nonsubstitutability" (*i.e.*, no other department can do what it does); and its centrality to the larger organization.[65] Of these factors, that of centrality appears to be of greatest relevance to the public organization. But "centrality" can assume many meanings in this context, including a subunit's *immediacy*, or its ability to severely and quickly impact on the whole organization; its *pervasiveness*, or how much it interacts with other departments; and its *match*, or how closely its purpose corresponds to that of the larger organization.

One study of six universities found that the centrality factor, particularly as defined by the pervasiveness dimension, had the single greatest explanatory value in accounting for a subunit's power within the organization.[66] A later study of six other universities demonstrated that centrality, as defined by the department's match to the larger purpose of the organization, was critical in the subunit's power and its success in acquiring budgetary resources.[67] In fact, even if "peripheral" (*i.e.*, noncentral) departments developed their own outside constituencies and resources, their power within the university did not rise significantly (if at all) unless they focused "on broader institutional needs" and brought in "external resources that contribute to the whole."[68]

Studies of different kinds of organizations demonstrate different relationships. Research on five breweries, in stark contrast to the findings on universities, found that a subunit's ability to cope with uncertainty and its central immediacy to the entire organization yielded it a powerful position in the organization.[69] However, a study of four oil and gas companies found only a weak correlation between a subunit's capacity for dealing with uncertainty and its power, but relatively strong relations between high levels of power and the subunit's nonsubstitutability and centrality.[70] The authors of one review of the literature have suggested that "the findings can be used to argue that the relationships between power and its determinants vary with the industry studied,"[71] and, certainly, whether the "industry" is public or private would seem to have a bearing on these relationships.

DECISION MAKING IN ORGANIZATIONS

We noted that Simon's notion of decision premises is central to an understanding of power in organizations; it also provides a convenient introduction to the more general consideration of organizational decision making. Simon argues stringently for the concept that virtually all decisions in organizations are only "satisficing" decisions; that is, decisions do not maximize, they only satisfy and suffice, or (combined) "satisfice."[72] The satisficing idea ties in with the other concepts of the model-synthesis literature—organizational members are limited by their own "bounded rationality," slack characterizes even the "tightest" organizations, and so forth—but it is disconcerting nonetheless to conclude that organizations simply muddle through their problems and task environments, and that their members are almost incapable of making a perfect (or maximizing) decision. Yet this may well be the most realistic view of bureaucracy, and perhaps of the human condition generally.

James D. Thompson and Arthur Tuden,[73] accepting Simon's idea of satisficing, developed a "typology of decision issues," in which they matched decision-making strategies with whether organizational members agreed or disagreed about what causes what, and whether members agreed or disagreed about what the organization should do. For example, in a bureaucracy of specialists, in theory everyone would agree about causation ("If you fill out the form, then you will get your Social Security check"), and they would agree about decision outcomes ("Social Security is worthwhile to society"). In such a bureaucracy, decisions would be made "computationally"; that is, with little or no internal debate about values and with decisions made on the basis of shared technical perceptions. Other kinds of organizations necessitate other kinds of decision-making strategies; the matrix in Table 4-4 summarizes them.

In some ways Thompson and Tuden's typology of decision-making strategy seems a bit far-fetched. Some might argue, for instance, that finding very many "inspirational decision making" organizations in the real world would not be likely. Yet when we approach the area of public organizations, we find few agreements among organizational members.

TABLE 4-4   A Typology of Decision-Making Strategies

| Beliefs about Causation | Preferences about Outcomes | |
	Agreement	Disagreement
Agreement	Computational decision making (an organization of specialists)	Compromising decision making (Congress agrees that it facilitates social change, but disagrees about how society should be changed)
Disagreement	Judgmental decision making (a college agrees that students should learn, but disagrees on how to cause learning)	Inspirational decision making (an "atomic"organization, such as France in 1958— DeGaulle's Fifth Republic— represented inspirational and authoritarian decision making)

The Garbage Can Model of Decision Making

Michael Cohen, James G. March and Johan Olsen have given us a creative approach to this dilemma by analyzing what they called "organized anarchies."[74] They used universities as their example of organized anarchies, but with little alteration of their model, we find that governments provide fine examples, too.

Organized anarchies have three characteristics. First, members of the organization do not define their preferences about policies and goals very precisely, and on those rare occasions when preferences are defined in exact terms, they often are in conflict with each other. The organization is a "loose collection of ideas" instead of a coherent structure; "it discovers preferences through action more than it acts on the basis of preferences."[75]

A second characteristic of an organized anarchy is that the technology is as unclear as the preferences. Members do not understand what the organization does. For example, how familiar is the typical faculty member with the operations of the registrar's office? And vice versa?

Finally, participation in the decision-making process of the organization is extremely fluid, even erratic. Participants drift in and out of the decision-making process. Sometimes a member will attend a critical meeting, and sometimes not.

Cohen, March, and Olsen suggest that organized anarchies use a decision-making process that is composed of four separate streams: problems, solutions, participants, and choice opportunities. These streams rarely connect with each other. An organized anarchy "is a collection of choices looking for problems, issues and feelings looking for decision situations in which they might be aired, solutions looking for issues to which they might be the answer, and decision makers looking for work."[76]

When these four streams do connect with each other, however, the result is often a major decision. This connecting up of problems, solutions, participants, and choice opportunities is what Cohen, March, and Olsen describe as the "garbage can model." Thus, decisions are the function of a mix of problems, solutions, participants, and participants' resources (*i.e.*, the "garbage can"), and how that mix is processed. The "choice opportunity" is the mix that occurs within the garbage can. Hence, the structure of organized anarchies is a flow of separate streams or processes throughout the organization, with decision outcomes being heavily dependent upon the coupling of the streams at a given point in time.

Out of the Garbage Can: Decision Making by Objection

The garbage can model of organizational decision making seems to have unusual utility to public organizations; John W. Kingdon, for example, has noted its usefulness in describing the policymaking process (or decision-making writ large) of the federal government.[77] An analysis of the Cuban missile crisis of 1962 stated that "Although the Cuban missile crisis shared some characteristics of . . . [the] garbage can model, that model is not wholly appropriate for understanding the group decision-making process during the missile crisis."[78] The author's point is that, while the "missile crisis was in danger of becoming an organizational garbage can," it did not become one because top decision makers "controlled the issues that they allowed to be attached to the crisis," such as heading off the attachment of such side issues to the crisis as the removal of Fidel Castro as primier of Cuba.[79]

In this analysis, the garbage can model is extended to a model dubbed "decision making by objection." This model, like that of the garbage can, rejects (at least to a degree) the standard model of rational, step-by-step decision making: identify objectives, find alternatives, forecast and evaluate their consequences, and select the one best alternative. Also like the garbage can model, decision making by objection conceives a very large role for the task environment on the process of making decision, and thus accords it a special usefulness for public organizations.

The model of decision making by objection is as follows:

1. An objective is identified.
2. A way of attaining the objective is proposed.
3. This proposal will produce one of three results:
   (a) The proposed course of action will be ratified by the group;
   (b) It will die for want of a second (which was the fate of most proposed courses of action during the Cuban missile crisis); or
   (c) There will be an objection to the proposal. This objection will be framed (obviously enough) in terms of the undesirable consequences of the proposal, but the effect of the objection (and this is not so obvious) will be to further define the problem, or objective, and how it should be solved. "Goals are discovered through argumentation and debate."[80]
4. This argumentation can go on forever, unless "there is an imperative to act"[81] (such as in the missile crisis, the Soviet fleet steaming toward Cuba). In the case of such an imperative, a new and competing course of action will be suggested.

5. If no imperative to act emerges, the original course of action is usually abandoned after much debate, and a new one is proposed.

Decision making by objection not only emphasizes the role of the environment on decision makers, but stresses the self-defining nature of decision making, rather than the linear, rational, and sequential steps of decision making. Proposed courses of action provoke arguments that reveal new objectives (or refine understanding of the original objective), which, in turn, lead to proposals for alternative courses of action. Ambiguity, in this model, plays a fulsome role in decision making.

ADMINISTRATION IN PUBLIC ORGANIZATIONS

The ambivalency of decision making that is expressed by the garbage can and decision-making-by-objection models seems to extend to administration. This ambivalency of administration, however, is common to private as well as public organizations, because the art of administration rests on the concept of "coalition management." Every organization is a complex of coalitions and, while technologies, environments, and perceptions will always be unique, politically motivated coalitions will always be common. Thus, one way of expressing what an administrator does is to say that he or she manages coalitions that are contending, cooperating, and coalescing inside his or her organization.

James D. Thompson explains coalition management particularly well:

. . . in the highly complex organization, power is dispersed. . . . [and] for the organization to be decisive and dynamic, the dispersed power must be . . . exercised through an inner circle. Have we defined such an organization as inevitably lacking a central power symbol, a recognized leader? Certainly we are implying that unilateral power cannot fall to one man in such organizations. Yet we know that an individual can "cast the long shadow" over an organization....In the organization with dispersed power, the central power figure is the individual who can manage the coalition....[but he or she] can do so [only] with the consent and approval of the dominant coalition.[82]

Within the broad context of coalition management, a variety of administrative, or implementation, tactics are possible. Paul C. Nutt, in one of the few empirical investigations of organizational implementation tactics that attempt to assess their frequency of use and rates of success, identified four: persuasion, edict, intervention, and participation.[83] Nutt's study is a particularly useful one because it focuses on the active side of administration—implementing change in organizations, rather than maintaining the status quo—and on how the tactics of implementation affect "stakeholders" in the organization whose interests will be impacted by a proposed change.

Persuasion is by far the most commonly used tactic of implementation; of the 91 case studies analyzed by Nutt, 42 percent displayed this tactic. *Persuasion*, more than any other type of approach, involves the use of outside consultants, internal staff, or any persons identified as "experts" who attempt to sell a change or policy that they have devised to members of the organization. Persuasion seems to be particularly favored as an administrative tactic among public organizations. One examination of school administrators found that these administrators not only spent a great deal of their time talking with subordinates and peers, "and that this talk accomplishes administration, but that talk is used to do the work of tightening and loosening administrative control."[84]

The next most favored implementation tactic is that of the edict (it was used in 23 percent of the cases). Like the tactic of persuasion, implementing by *edict* is straightforward: the sponsor of the change—which can be an individual member, a part of the organization, the organization as a whole, or all of the foregoing—has a clearcut stake in implementing the change, and simply directs that it be done; the change itself has considerable significance to its sponsor. Using edicts to effect change requires that the sponsor has power in the organization and is prepared to risk it; if the change fails, the sponsor issuing the edict loses. Almost always, therefore, administration by edict involves managers, in contrast to persuasion which, in more than 40 percent of these cases, was used by experts who were not managers, but who had been delegated the task of implementing organizational change by managers.

Intervention (used in 19 percent of the cases) involves top managers (or any key executive with adequate authority) justifying a need for change, establishing new standards by which to judge performance in implementing the change, devising new ways to implement the change, and demonstrating the feasibility of the change and the improvements that result from it. In this tactic, administrators are not merely issuing edicts to change something, or wearing down the opponents of the change through unremitting talk; instead, they are personally pushing the change through, and altering the organization in virtually any way they can to accommodate the change they want.

Interestingly, managers using the intervention tactic were (with only one exception) unread in the literature of organization development (OD), as described in Chapter 3, which advocates "top down" intervention in the inner workings of the organization to achieve change. But the organization development literature also suggests that this top down intervention be implemented by "third-party change agents" (in other words, consultants). Yet, when third-party change agents were employed by managers to implement change, they never used the intervention tactic and were most frequently found using the persuasion approach. Perhaps because of the absence of outside OD consultants in the intervention tactic, "managers in this study were found to be far more aggressive than organizational development specialists acknowledge as either desirable or necessary."[85] Nevertheless, as we observe shortly, managers using the intervention tactic got things done.

Finally, implementation of change can be achieved by participation. *Participation* was the least used tactic in the study (it was recorded in only 17 percent of the cases), and refers to stakeholders in the change cooperatively implementing it. Participation can range from only token participation to comprehensive, with all members of the organization (or at least all stakeholders in the change) both framing possible solutions to a perceived problem and then, as a group, specifying the solution they will implement. Unlike the managers who used an intervention tactic, managers using a participatory approach were well informed about the organization development literature (which views employee participation in administration with favor), but drew short of allowing extensive participation; in more than 85 percent of the cases, managers used representatives of interested parties rather than all stakeholders as participants (amounting to a classic instance of what is meant by "coalition management"); in not one case did managers permit full, comprehensive participation by stakeholders.

Which tactic works? Without question, intervention (the approach used nearly the least frequently) is the most successful tactic of implementation: 100 percent of the managers who used it were successful in implementing the change they wanted, and, as a tactic, its resource demands were modest. It appears that there is something to be said for "hands-on" administration; the intervention tactic was deemed to be "highly desirable and worthy of active promotion among managers."[86]

By contrast, the other tactics were less effective. The next highest success rate went to the tactics of persuasion and participation, both of which recorded 75 percent success rates, but managers typically underestimated the budget and staff resources needed to make them more effective. Implementation by edict (the second most favored approach after persuasion) was clearly the least successful tactic; in only 42 percent of the cases was it used successfully.

Effective administration, it appears, is not accomplished by decree; it is done by the "down and dirty."

Effective administration, however, requires more than administrators who are willing and able to take a hands-on approach; effective administration also requires that administrators be granted the autonomy and freedom to administer in ways that they think will be the most effective, and here, as we discussed in this and the preceding chapter, public administrators have unique problems. The single most characteristic reality of the public sector is the overwhelming impact of the task environment (*i.e.*, "determinism") on the inner workings of the public organization.

Sadly, the heavy impact of the environment on the public organization, and the corresponding loss of autonomy suffered by its public administrators, seems to correlate with a lower quality of administration and decision making. A growing number of empirical investigations all point to this conclu-

sion. Greater organizational autonomy and independence, at least up to a point, associate with a higher quality of administration. To cite some of the more recent studies in this regard:

- A study of nine citizen advisory boards in Michigan concluded that a high level of autonomy of those boards had a direct and beneficial impact on the effectiveness of those boards. "The boards . . . were advisory boards, which do not have the legal power over program, budget, and staff. Rather, these boards made recommendations to the city commission which were acted on or not acted on at the prerogative of the commission. However, some of the citizen advisory boards were more effective than others in gaining their objectives and this was found to be related to the degree of independence which they attained." [87]

- A study of the impact of the Government in the Sunshine Act of 1976, which affected the meeting procedures of more than fifty federal agencies headed by boards of directors or similar collegial bodies, found indications that the law's opening up of the meetings of those boards diminished the quality of the decision-making process. Most agency officials felt "that the strictures of the law weakened them in executing their responsibilities and weakened agency performance, especially in policy development." [88]

- A ten-year study of the experiences of 20,000 students, teachers, and principals in some 500 public and private schools in the United States concluded that "the best determinate of the school's effectiveness was the degree of autonomy it enjoyed from bureaucracies and other outside interference. None of the other factors that usually preoccupied reformers, including class size, faculty salaries and spending per pupil, mattered as much." [89]

- An analysis of the safety records of twenty-four nuclear power plants in the United States, undertaken after the Three Mile Island nuclear crisis of 1979, found that the administrative autonomy of a nuclear plant correlated with a high safety record. "Autonomy is the outcome of a good safety record and contributes to a good safety record....If poor performers are given more autonomy, this analysis suggests, their safety record is likely to improve...." [90]

What the research indicates, in short, is that, within the American context of extreme openness, some enhancement of public agencies' administrative independence and organizational autonomy likely will result in more effective and responsive government, with little or no new resources being required.[91]

ASSESSING THE PERFORMANCE OF PUBLIC ORGANIZATIONS

Meier's research on the tribulations of a university library undergoing pressures from its environment was cited earlier as an example of the difficulty that a public organization has in dealing with a task environment that lacks the benefit of a market mechanism. On another plane, Meier's research shows that the problem is one of how to assess the performance and efficiency of all public organizations. As we explain in greater detail in Chapter 7, government agencies, unlike business corporations, normally cannot measure their performance by the fatness of their profits.

Thompson has framed the organizational assessment problem in a more rigorous manner. He observes that organizations may be evaluated according to one of three "tests"; the appropriateness of any one of these tests depends on the nature of the organization. Thompson posits efficiency, instrumental, and social tests as ways of assessing organizational performance,[92] and, in several ways, these tests represent a conceptual extension of Thompson and Tuden's earlier work on decision issues (see Table 4-3).

The *efficiency test* relates to Thompson and Tuden's notion of "computational decision making," and is applicable to organizations that have "crystallized standards of desirability," and whose members believe they fully comprehend the relationships between causes and effects. For example, executives in our hypothetical corporation of International Widget have a solid notion of what they want to do and how to do it: maximize profits (*i.e.*, their standards of desirability are quite firm and clear, or "crystallized") and manufacture widgets as cheaply as possible (*i.e.*, there is a clear causal connection between high profits and cheap production). Thus, assessing the performance of International Widget as an organization is both objective and easy; efficiency, or economic, tests are applicable.

The *instrumental test* is less objective, less easy to apply, and less optimal in evaluating organiza-

tional performance than the efficiency test. But it is the only kind of test that is appropriate for certain kinds of organizations, notably organizations that use "judgmental decision making." Instrumental tests are applicable to organizations that, like International Widget, have crystallized standards of desirability (*e.g.*, high profits) but, unlike International Widget, the organizational members are uncertain about what causes what. As a result of this situation, the efficiency test no longer is a suitable evaluative tool, because when no one is sure about causality there is no way of assessing the effects of what the organization is doing.

An example of such an organization might be a public agency. The Department of Defense, for instance, has a crystallized standard of desirability (providing an adequate nuclear deterrent), but its officers are unsure about whether their programs actually are establishing that deterrent. None of them knows if their defense policies are sufficient to deter a nuclear attack (until and unless, of course, one comes). Thus, unlike the officials of International Widget, the Pentagon brass always will be uneasy about whether its programs are maximizing its mission achievement. Hence, we see Defense asking for more money as a means of maximizing its standard of desirability (*i.e.*, its unproven nuclear deterrent capacity), but International Widget attempting to reduce its operational costs as a means of maximizing its standard of desirability (*i.e.*, profits).

The *social test* also is applicable to public bureaucracies, particularly those agencies that have ambiguous, rather than crystallized, standards of desirability. Whether or not members believe they understand cause-and-effect relationships does not matter, so the decision-making strategies of such an organization could range from one of compromise to inspiration. Such an agency might be a social service or a university; often, no one in these organizations can quantify, even remotely, the impact of their activities. What, for instance, is meant by "breaking the cycle of poverty"? What is "learning"?

Instrumental and, especially, social tests of organizational performance are the kinds of evaluational tools that public bureaucracies find themselves using. Neither test is especially effective, but at least the reasons for their ineffectuality are fairly clear; public organizations, like the polity they administer, lack specificity in expressing their goals and in comprehending the most efficient way to achieve those goals.

Because of this dilemma, organizations that are unclear about causality or standards of desirability have developed a number of variants of instrumental and social tests in an attempt to assess themselves and to prove their worth to their audience outside. Public organizations have been especially adept at this because their very survival depends on the monies and legitimacy that they draw from the polity. Put crassly, this means acquiring prestige. For an organization faced with the necessity of using instrumental or social tests as a method of assessment, prestige and status often become the operational yardsticks of performance.

One way of measuring prestige is by calculating the historical improvement of the agency. This calculation may be done in a number of ways: by assuring an increase in organizational visibility, by achieving budget increments, by obtaining favorable ratings from outside observers, by having a proliferation of programs, by an increase in the size of the clientele served, and so forth. Universities, for example, rely to a large degree on accrediting associations, faculty publications, and research grants (all of which are ratings by outside observers) as social tests of performance, while public agencies often rely on the relative size of their annually appropriated budget as an indication of prestige. It is not surprising that organizational growth is associated with high organizational prestige, which in turn relates to an inferred favorable assessment of organizational performance. This is an especially telling point for public bureaucracies. It indicates that we can expect public officials to try to acquire fatter budgets for their agencies in an effort to "prove" their agencies' high level of performance, and then rationalize that their fat budgets represent a measurement of high performance that already was there. Either way, it is the prestige factor that determines how public bureaucracies normally are assessed.

Unfortunately, the prestige factor can be carried to ludicrous lengths as a yardstick of organizational performance. Joseph W. Eaton found that the in-house research units in two "treatment-oriented" organizations were used primarily as a method of acquiring prestige rather than as a method of discovering more objective measurements of true organizational performance.[93] Any "substantive" research projects regarding organizational performance that could be potentially embarrassing were discouraged, while "symbolic" research—noncontroversial research that did not question the organizations' traditional goals nor threaten established power patterns and was essentially useless—was encouraged in the organizations. In this light, it is worth recalling that the government is generally regarded to have less prestige than business organizations by the American populace. This situation can affect relative organizational performance in the two spheres. A study of a public government hospital and a private volunteer hospital concluded that the private institution was better able to fulfill its official mission than the government hospital because of greater prestige in the community. The private hospital received more financial contributions, patients, and popular support.[94]

More recent and systematic studies substantiate how critical social tests can be to the very survival of public-sector organizations, particularly younger ones. (The literature of organization theory generally supports the proposition that newness is a liability among all organizations, and that new organizations are likelier to "die" than are established ones.[95]) An investigation of 389 newly founded, voluntary, nonprofit social service organizations in metropolitan Toronto[96] concluded that the acquisition of "external legitimacy" by these new social service organizations (typically in the forms of obtaining a *Community Directory* listing, a Charitable Registration Number, and a large and distinguished board) far outweighed the use of internal management changes within these organizations in predicting their long-term survival. Changes in the "internal coordination" of these organizations (a term encompassing changes in the organizations' service areas, chief executives, goals, client groups, and structure) bore no relationship (with one exception, that of changing the chief executive) to the survival rates of these nonprofit organizations. Social tests, then (and more precisely, the acquisition of social status), while often times less than measurable, appear to be vitally important to the success of public-sector organizations.

In this chapter, we have reviewed some of the more important ideas found floating in the vast ocean of organization theory. These ideas bob and bump into each other, depending on the prevailing currents. We have tried to point out those ideas that have a special utility to the public sector. In the next chapter, we move to a more lively part of organization theory: people.

NOTES

[1] James D. Thompson, *Organizations in Action: Social Science Bases of Administrative Theory* (New York: McGraw-Hill, 1967), pp. 14–82.

[2] Charles Perrow, "The Analysis of Goals in Complex Organizations," *American Sociological Review*, 26 (December 1961), pp. 854–866; and "Hospitals: Technology, Structure and Goals," in *Handbook of Organizations*, James G. March, ed. (New York: Rand McNally, 1965).

[3] Louis W. Fry, "Technology-Structure Research: Three Critical Issues," *Academy of Management Journal*, 25 (September 1982), pp. 532–552. Fry analyzed 140 articles and books on the subject published between 1965 and 1980 and found that nearly 49 percent of the works showed a statistically significant relationship between technological change and structural change, and that this significance was "roughly equal across different conceptions of technology and structure, different levels of analysis, and different types of measures" (p. 341).

[4] Sheldon L. Messinger, "Organizational Transformation: A Case Study of a Declining Social Movement," *American Sociological Review*, 20 (February 1955), pp. 3–10.

[5] Tom Burns and G. M. Stalker, *The Management of Innovation* (London: Tavistock, 1961).

[6] William R. Dill, "Environment as an Influence on Managerial Autonomy," *Administrative Science Quarterly*, 2 (March 1958), pp. 409–443.

[7] Many of the ideas in this discussion are drawn from: Donald Chisholm, "Organizational Response to Environmental Change" (Paper presented at the 1985 Annual Meeting of the American Political Science Association, New Orleans, La., August 29–September 1, 1985).

[8] Herbert Kaufman, *Time, Chance, and Organizations: Natural Selection in a Perilous Environment* (Chatham, N.J.: Chatham House, 1985). Kaufman likens the organization's relationship with its environment to "a process of 'chemical evolution'" that predates biological evolution (p. 91).

[9] See, for example, Martin Landau, "On the Concept of Self-Correcting Organizations," *Public Administration Review*, 33 (November/December 1973), pp. 533–542; Howard E. Aldrich, *Organizations and Environments* (Englewood Cliffs, N.J.: Prentice-Hall, 1979); and John Child, "Organization Structure, Environment, and Performance: The Role of Strategic Choice," *Sociology*, 6 (January 1972), pp. 1–22.

[10] Kaufman provides a nice overview of these. See: Kaufman, *Time, Chance, and Organizations*, p. 153.

[11] *Ibid.*, p. 150. One attempt to at least partially integrate the organizational taxonomies found in the literature of the biological model is: Douglas R. Wholey and Jack W. Brittain, "Organizational Ecology: Findings and Implications," *Academy of Management Review*, 11 (July 1986), pp. 513–533.

[12] Examples include: Herbert A. Simon, *Administrative Behavior* (New York: The Free Press, 1947); and James G. March and Herbert A. Simon, *Organizations* (New York: John Wiley, 1958). Virtually all the contributors to the open model of organizations and the literature of model synthesis, described in Chapter 3, could be listed in this respect.

[13] Perhaps the most straightforward, recent example of this view is: Thomas J. Peters and Robert H. Waterman, Jr., *In Search of Excellence: Lessons from America's Best-Run Companies* (New York: Warner, 1982).

[14] Chisholm, "Organizational Response to Environmental Change," p. 14.

[15] See, for example, James G. March, "The Business Firm as Political Coalition," *Journal of Politics*, 24 (November 1962), pp. 662–678; Jeffrey Pfeffer, *Power in Organizations* (Marshfield, Mass.: Pitman, 1981); and James D. Thompson and William J. McEwen, "Organizational Goals and Environment: Goal-Setting as an Interaction Process," *American Sociological Review*, 23 (February 1958), pp. 23–31.

[16] March and Simon, *Organizations*, p. 38.

[17] Richard M. Cyert and James G. March, *A Behavioral Theory of the Firm* (Englewood Cliffs, N.J.: Prentice-Hall, 1963).

[18] Anthony Downs, *Inside Bureaucracy* (Boston: Little, Brown, 1967), pp. 92–101.

[19] Michel Crozier, *The Bureaucratic Phenomenon* (Chicago: University of Chicago Press, 1964), pp. 220–224.

[20] Kaufman, *Time, Chance, and Organizations*, pp. 69, 150.

[21] For other examples, see: Aldrich, *Organizations and Environments*; and Child, "Organization Structure, Environment, and Performance."

[22] W. Graham Astley and Andrew H. Van de Ven, "Central Perspectives and Debates in Organization Theory," *Administrative Science Quarterly*, 28 (June 1983), p. 245.

[23] Lawrence G. Hrebeniak and William F. Joyce, "Organizational Adaptation: Strategic Choice and Environmental Determinism," *Administrative Science Quarterly*, 30 (September 1985), p. 336.

[24] Two important contributions to answering the question are: Barton Wechsler and Hal Rainey, "Strategic Management in Political Environments" (Paper presented at the 1986 Annual Meeting of the American Political Science Association, Washington, D.C., August 29–31, 1986); and Hrebeniak and Joyce, "Organizational Adaptation." Table 4-2 has been developed using several of the ideas contained in these pieces, as well as the thinking in Astley and Van de Ven, "Central Perspectives and Debates in Organization Theory."

[25] See, for example, Roger Miles Blough, *The Washington Embrace of Business* (New York: Columbia University Press,

1975); Mark J. Green, ed., *The Monopoly Makers: Ralph Nader's Study Group Report on Regulation and Competition* (New York: Grossman, 1973); Louis M. Kohlmeier, Jr., *The Regulators: Watchdog Agencies in the Public Interest* (New York: Harper & Row, 1969); Arthur S. Miller, *The Modern Corporate State: Private Governments and the American Constitution* (Westport, Conn.: Greenwood Press, 1976); and Robert Sobel, *The Age of Giant Corporations: A Microeconomic History of American Business, 1914–1970* (Westport, Conn.: Greenwood Press, 1972).

[26] James G. March, "Decisions in Organizations and Theories of Choice," in *Perspectives on Organization Design and Behavior*, Andrew H. Van de Ven and William F. Joyce, eds. (New York: Wiley Interscience, 1981), pp. 205–244.

[27] See, for example, Peters and Waterman, *In Search of Excellence*, pp. 200–234, in which they describe successes enjoyed by major companies that practice what amounts to slack search.

[28] Charles E. Lindblom, "The Science of Muddling Through," *Public Administration Review*, 19 (Spring 1959), pp. 79–88.

[29] Hrebeniak and Joyce, "Organizational Adaptation," p. 342.

[30] Robert A. Caro, *The Power Broker: Robert Moses and the Fall of New York* (New York: Knopf, 1974), p. 38. Emphasis is original.

[31] Stafford Beer, "Managing Modern Complexity," *The Management of Information and Knowledge.* Panel on Science and Technology (11th meeting). Proceedings before the Committee on Science and Astronautics, U.S. House of Representatives, 91st Congress, Second Session, January 27, 1970, No. 15 (Washington, D.C.: U.S. Government Printing Office, 1970).

[32] Harold L. Wilensky, *Organizational Intelligence* (New York: Basic Books, 1967). The saga of Cicero is on pp. 68–69.

[33] Gordon Tullock, *The Politics of Bureaucracy* (Washington, D.C.: Public Affairs Press, 1965).

[34] March and Simon, *Organizations*, p. 165.

[35] Richard L. Meier, "Communications Overload," *Administrative Science Quarterly*, 7 (March 1963), pp. 529–544.

[36] York Willbern, "Professionalization in the Public Service: Too Little or Too Much?" *Public Administration Review*, 14 (Winter 1954), pp. 13–21.

[37] Alan Altshuler, *The City Planning Process: A Political Analysis* (Ithaca, N.Y.: Cornell University Press, 1965).

[38] James D. Carroll, "Noetic Authority," *Public Administration Review*, 29 (September/October 1969), pp. 492–500.

[39] Martha S. Feldman and James G. March, "Information in Organizations as Signal and Symbol" (Paper presented at the Western Political Science Association in San Francisco, Calif., March 27–29, 1980). See also: Feldman and March, "Information in Organizations as Signal and Symbol," *Administrative Science Quarterly*, 26 (June 1981), pp. 171–186. The following quotations in the text are drawn from the paper first cited.

[40] See, for example, Thomas D. Clark, Jr., and William A. Shrode, "Public Sector Decision Structures: An Empirically Based Description," *Public Administration Review*, 39 (1979), pp. 343–354; Lindblom, "The Science of Muddling Through," pp. 79–88; Morton H. Halperin, *Bureaucratic Politics in Foreign Policy* (Washington, D.C.: Brookings Institution, 1974); and Michael D. Cohen and James G. March, *Leadership and Ambiguity: The American College President* (New York: McGraw-Hill, 1974).

[41] Feldman and March, "Information in Organizations as Signal and Symbol," pp. 12–13.

[42] See, for example, Steve Chan, "The Intelligence of Stupidity: Understanding Failures and Strategic Warning," *American Political Science Review*, 73 (1979), pp. 171–180.

[43] See, for example, Irving L. Janis and Leon Mann, *Decision Making* (New York: The Free Press, 1977).

[44] Feldman and March, "Information in Organizations as Signal and Symbol," pp. 15–16.

[45] *Ibid.*, p. 20.

[46] *Ibid.*, pp. 23–24.

[47] *Ibid.*, p. 25.

[48] Kathleen M. Eisenhardt, "Making Fast Strategic Decisions in High-Velocity Environments," *Academy of Management Journal*, 32 (September 1989), pp. 543–576.

[49] *Ibid.*, p. 543

[50] Amitai Etzioni, *Modern Organizations* (Englewood Cliffs, N.J.: Prentice-Hall, 1964).

[51] Simon, *Administrative Behavior*, pp. 48–52. For an interesting discussion of the decision premise in the context of ethical choice in the public sector, see: Debra W. Stewart, "The Decision Premise: A Basic Tool for Analyzing the Ethical Content of Organizational Behavior," *Public Administration Quarterly*, 8 (Fall 1988), pp. 315–328.

[52] Roy J. Lewicki, "Organizational Seduction: Building Commitment to Organizations," *Organizational Dynamics* (Autumn 1981), p. 7.

[53] Morris Janowitz, "Changing Patterns of Organizational Authority: The Military Establishment," *Administrative Science Quarterly*, 3 (March 1959), pp. 473–493.

[54] Chester I. Barnard, *The Functions of the Executive* (Cambridge, Mass.: Harvard University Press, 1938).

[55] Herbert A. Simon, *Administrative Behavior: A Study of Decision-Making Processes in Administrative Organizations*, 3rd ed. (New York: The Free Press, 1976), pp. 123–153. But see also the essay by Simon and Robert Bierstedt in *Studies in Managerial Process and Organizational Behavior*, John H. Turner, Alan C. Filley, and Robert J. House, eds. (Glenview, Ill.: Scott, Foresman, 1972), pp. 59–72; and J. Bernard Keys and Thomas L. Case, "How To Become an Influential Manager," *The Executive*, 4 (November 1990), pp. 38–51. Keys and Case summarize much of the research on this topic, and add their own, noting that because "of the increasing diversity of goals and values of employees and their increasing interdependence, the effectiveness of formal authority is diminishing" (p. 38).

[56] Nicole Wollsey Biggart and Gary G. Hamilton, "The Power of Obedience," *Administrative Science Quarterly*, 29 (December 1984), p. 548. In a critique of the authors' research,

one reviewer made a comment that amounted to a backhanded acceptance of the view that public organizations are different from private ones: "in making their case . . . [Biggart and Hamilton evoke] a somewhat oversocialized conception of power that may be typical of state government but is restrictive in its broader relevance." See: Walter W. Powell's review of Gary G. Hamilton and Nicole Woolsey Biggart, *Governor Reagan, Governor Brown: A Sociology of Executive Power* (New York: Columbia University Press, 1984), in *Administrative Science Quarterly*, 31 (March 1985), p. 134.

[57] Kent D. Peterson, "Mechanisms of Administrative Control over Managers in Educational Organizations," *Administrative Science Quarterly*, 29 (December 1984), pp. 576–581.

[58] See, for example, William H. Newman and Harvey W. Wallendar, "Managing Not-for-Profit Enterprises," *Academy of Management Review*, 3 (January 1978), pp. 24–31; and Mayer Zald, *The Political Economy of the YMCA* (Chicago: University of Chicago Press, 1970). This idea of the difficulties of achieving "output control" in nonprofit organizations is essentially another way of saying that public organizations do not have a profit margin with which to gauge performance.

[59] Peterson, "Mechanisms of Administrative Control," pp. 584–593.

[60] *Ibid.*, p. 595.

[61] See, for example, Pfeffer, *Power in Organizations* pp. 130–135.

[62] See, for example, Rosabeth M. Kanter, "Power Failures in Management Circuits," *Harvard Business Review* (July/August 1979), pp. 65–75; and Charles Perrow, "Departmental Power and Perspectives in Industrial Firms," in *Power in Organizations*, Mayer N. Zald, ed. (Nashville: Vanderbilt University Press, 1970), pp. 59–89.

[63] Daniel J. Brass, "Being in the Right Place: A Structural Analysis of Individual Influence in an Organization," *Administrative Science Quarterly*, 29 (December 1984), pp. 532–533.

[64] *Ibid.*, p. 518.

[65] David J. Hickson, et al., "The Strategic Contingencies' Theory of Intraorganizational Power," *Administrative Science Quarterly*, 16 (March 1971), pp. 216–229.

[66] Carol S. Saunders and Richard Scamell, "Intraorganizational Distributions of Power: Replication Research," *Academy of Management Journal*, 25 (March 1982), p. 194.

[67] Judith Dozier Hackman, "Power and Centrality in the Allocation of Resources in Colleges and Universities," *Administrative Science Quarterly*, 30 (March 1985), pp. 61–77.

[68] *Ibid.*, p. 75.

[69] C. R. Hinings, D. J. Hickson, J. M. Pennings, and R. E. Schneck, "Structural Conditions of Intraorganizational Power," *Administrative Science Quarterly*, 19 (January 1974), pp. 22–24; and Saunders and Scamell, "Intraorganizational Distributions of Power," p. 194.

[70] Saunders and Scamell, "Intraorganizational Distributions of Power," p. 198. Centrality as measured by immediacy and pervasiveness, but not its match, which was a concept not used in the study.

[71] *Ibid.*, p. 199.

[72] *Ibid.*, pp. 38–41, 240–244.

[73] James D. Thompson and Arthur Tuden, "Strategies, Structures and Processes of Organizational Decision," *Comparative Studies in Administration*, James D. Thompson, et al, eds. (Pittsburgh, Pa.: The University of Pittsburgh Press, 1959), pp. 195–216.

[74] Michael Cohen, James G. March, and Johan Olsen, "A Garbage Can Model of Organizational Choice," *Administrative Science Quarterly*, 17 (March 1972), pp. 1–25.

[75] *Ibid.*, p. 1.

[76] *Ibid.*, p. 2.

[77] John W. Kingdon, *Agendas, Alternatives, and Public Policies* (Boston: Little, Brown, 1984), p. 90.

[78] Paul A. Anderson, "Decision Making by Objection and the Cuban Missile Crisis," *Administrative Science Quarterly*, 28 (June 1983), p. 216.

[79] *Ibid.*

[80] *Ibid.*, p. 213.

[81] *Ibid.*, p. 217.

[82] Thompson, *Organizations in Action*, p. 142.

[83] Paul C. Nutt, "Tactics of Implementation," *Academy of Management Journal*, 29 (July 1986), pp. 230–261.

[84] Peter C. Gronn, "Talk as Work: The Accomplishment of School Administration," *Administrative Science Quarterly*, 28 (March 1983), p. 1.

[85] Nutt, "Tactics of Implementation," p. 255.

[86] *Ibid.*, p. 258.

[87] David G. Houghton, "Citizen Advisory Boards: Autonomy and Effectiveness," *American Review of Public Administration*, 18 (September 1988), p. 293.

[88] David M. Welborn, William Lyons, and Larry W. Thomas, "The Federal Government in the Sunshine Act and Agency Decision Making," *Administration and Society*, 20 (February 1989), p. 483.

[89] Don Wycliff, "Market System Urged as Way to Loosen Grip of School Bureaucracy," *New York Times* (June 6, 1990). Wycliff is reporting on the study: John E. Chubb and Terry M. Moe, *Politics, Markets, and America's Schools* (Washington, D.C.: Brookings Institution, 1990).

[90] Alfred A. Marcus, "Implementing Externally Induced Innovations: A Comparison of Rule-Bound and Autonomous Approaches," *Academy of Management Journal*, 31 (June 1988), p. 249.

[91] In a remarkable feature article in *Fortune*, one of the nation's foremost business magazines, precisely this point was argued, and strongly so. This could be an augury of reform, and movement toward a more autonomous public service. See: David Kirkpatrick, "It's Simply Not Working," *Fortune* (November 19, 1990), pp. 20–21.

[92] Thompson, *Organizations in Action*, pp. 83–98.

[93] Joseph W. Eaton, "Symbolic and Substantive Evaluation Research," *Administrative Science Quarterly*, 6 (March 1962), pp. 421–442.

[94] Ray H. Elling and Sandor Halebsky, "Organizational Differentiation and Support: A Conceptual Framework," *Administrative Science Quarterly*, 6 (September 1961), pp. 185–209.

[95] See, for example, Arthur L. Stinchcombe, "Organizations and Social Structure," in *Handbook of Organizations*, James G. March, ed. (Chicago: Rand McNally, 1965), pp. 153–193; Glenn R. Carroll and Jacques Delacroix, "Organizational Mortality in the Newspaper Industries of Argentina and Ireland: An Ecological Approach," *Administrative Science Quarterly*, 27 (June 1982), pp. 169–196; and John Freeman, Glenn R. Carroll, and Michael T. Hannan, "The Liability of Newness: Age Dependence in Organizational Death Rates," *American Sociological Review*, 48 (October 1983), pp. 692–710.

[96] Jitendra V. Singh, David J. Tucker, and Robert J. House, "Organizational Legitimacy and the Liability of Newness," *Administrative Science Quarterly*, 31 (June 1986), pp. 171–193.

CHAPTER
5

PEOPLE IN PUBLIC ORGANIZATIONS

We have seen that organizations are changed according to the ways in which technologies, task environments, and other people interact with one another in the organization. We know that people change organizations and this, in its way, is a comforting thought. Less comforting, however, is the thought that organizations change people—that organizations somehow, over time, alter personalities. Was the protagonist in *The Organization Man* by William H. Whyte[1] the same rigid automaton before he joined "the team," or was he originally a normal human being who was drastically altered by the organization once he was under its influence?

WHAT CAN ORGANIZATIONS DO TO YOU?

It appears that some organizations—what Erving Goffman calls "total institutions," such as prisons, orphanages, barracks, ships, asylums, sanitariums, monasteries, and certain types of schools—can change the people in them.[2] This is logical; the technology (*i.e.*, what the organiza-

tion does) of total institutions is altering people, and the mission of total institutions is to change the "client-members" inside them. The technology of prisons, for instance, is rehabilitation; the technology of schools is education.

Goffman has delineated the characteristics of total institutions as follows:

- All aspects of life are separated from the larger society and are conducted in the same place and under the same authority.
- The activities of client-members generally occur in "large batches" (*i.e.*, they do most things together, and client-members are treated equally).
- Each day's activities are tightly scheduled and regulated.
- Each activity is perceived as being part of an overall plan designed to achieve official goals.
- There is a staff/inmate (*e.g.*, guard/prisoner) split.

In his study of prisons, Goffman observed that life in the "inmate world" was characterized by (1) a "mortification process" that often was perpetrated unconsciously by the staff as the result of managing many people in a small space with limited resources, (2) a "privilege system" that amounted to nothing more than a lack of sanctions, and (3) various forms of adaptation by inmates to the mortification process. These adaptations could include situational withdrawal; rebellion; "colonization," in which inmates grew to prefer prison to the society outside; and "conversion" by those inmates, known as "square johns," who came to totally accept the official prison system. In the "staff world," Goffman noted that prison officials, who were pulled between the desires to maintain both humane standards and organizational efficiency, often developed a "theory" of human behavior that rationalized the inmates' hostility toward them.

Another kind of total institution may be closer to home to most readers: colleges and universities. Not all colleges, of course, have totalistic features, but many do. S. M. Dornbusch has written of the ethos prevalent in the United States Coast Guard Academy, which was designed to develop a "bureaucratic spirit" and a sense of solidarity in its students.[3] In this light, voluntary student resignations were speeded and hushed by academy officials, and questionable practices, such as hazing were justified with such slogans as "separating the men from the boys."

Charles E. Bidwell and Rebecca S. Vreeland[4] have developed a "typology of socializing organizations" for colleges that classifies a college's probability for successfully indoctrinating students for life according to the kinds of goals professed by college officials and the scope of student involvement in the institution. For instance, a "doctrinal- administered communal" college (i.e., a residential college with the goal of inculcating

certain ethical and philosophic beliefs in its students) would have a very strong and homogeneous moral impact on its client-members. An example might be Bennington College, which was founded in 1932 with the idea of liberalizing the daughters of wealthy and often conservative families. Studies by Theodore M. Newcomb[5] at Bennington indicated that, indeed, the college's students adopted more politically liberal attitudes during their college careers and retained these attitudes well into later life. Conversely, a "procedural-administered associational" college (e.g., a commuter college with "technical" goals, such as teaching its students a particular trade) would have no significant moral impact on its client-members. An example might be any public junior college.

Bidwell and Vreeland's conception of how organizations change their client-members is shown in Table 5-1.

If it is true that total institutions alter their client-members (and this contention is by no means conclusively validated by evidence), it does not necessarily follow that bureaucracies somehow change their members. Many (but not all) total institutions acquire their client-members by force, or at least by the application of social pressure (e.g., "Don't you want to go to Dad's alma mater?"). Bureaucracies rarely add to their memberships in these ways; people join bureaucracies relatively voluntarily. And when they do join, they are not client-members, such as a prisoner or a student. They are full-fledged members of the organization, such as a guard or a faculty member.

Some theorists, however, do argue that bureaucracies, particularly public bureaucracies, change the bureaucrats inside them. Perhaps the

TABLE 5-1 A Typology of Socializing Organizations

Goals	Scope of Involvement	
	Communal	Associational
Moral	Doctrinal-administered community: strong, homogeneous moral impact on client-members.	Doctrinal-administered association: moderate, homogeneous moral impact on client-members.
Technical	Procedural-administered community: strong, heterogeneous moral impact on client-members.	Procedural-administered association: no significant moral impact on client-members.

classic statement of this argument is Robert K. Merton's essay on the "bureaucratic personality." By the very drive of the bureaucracy to rationalize (and thus rigidify) its administrative techniques, the bureaucrats in it must be trained and socialized so that they begin to think along the lines and patterns mandated by those techniques. Thus, in Merton's words, the bureaucrat grows to personify "Veblen's concept of 'trained incapacity,' Dewey's notion of 'occupational psychosis,' or Warnotte's view of 'professional deformation.'"[6] Yet, after such training, a way of seeing also becomes a way of not seeing. It is an inescapable outcome that bureaucrats become methodical and prudent persons because they must if they are to survive in a bureaucracy that places "tremendous symbolic significance" on rules and adherence to those rules. In fact, the pressures to rationalize the bureaucracy work to produce "overconformity," because that assures a margin of safety in terms of reducing uncertainty in the organization. Additionally, the stress in bureaucracies to depersonalize relationships, combined with the "professional deformation" brought about by socialization, results in the unsympathetic, disinterested, and often uncomprehending bureaucrat perceived by the client who is concerned with his or her special problem and its several unique features. Because of such dynamics between social and organizational forces, the notorious bureaucratic personality who is petty, dense, and arrogant has emerged.

Other analysts are less positive that organizations change their members. Ivar Berg, in a methodologically careful empirical study, attempted to ascertain if organizations changed people by examining the attitudes and behavior of "old" and "new" organizational members; in Berg's words, "I tried to measure employees' propensities to accept and act upon their impulses."[7] After much analysis, Berg was forced to concede that he could not draw any final conclusions, although there was a "close fit" between senior members and their organizations. Problems involving personality change, self-selection, and organizational selection were too difficult to separate as intervening variables, and the thesis that the organization *caused* changes in its people was methodologically

impossible to "prove." Although research is continuing, whether or not bureaucracies change people must still remain a moot point.

We do know, however, that there are many different kinds of people in organizations, regardless of the forces that may have shaped their personalities. It is to some of these models that we now turn, in an effort to learn what our implicit assumptions about the nature of the administrative human being really are.

ADMINISTRATIVE HUMANITY: CLASSICISM VERSUS SOCIAL-PSYCHOLOGY

Throughout the preceding chapters, we have been implicitly contrasting the early, "classical" views of what people are like and how they behave in organizations with the more useful and more current perspectives derived from social-psychology on the nature of people in organizations. In this section, we do so more explicitly.

Administrative Humanity: The Classical View

Under the "classical view," we consider those early theorists who tended to ignore social and psychological variables in the constitutions of members of organizations, and who instead stressed their "rational" and physical dimensions.

The classical model of the bureaucrat was not drawn entirely from Douglas McGregor's Theory X (described in Chapter 3), which casts workers as stolid, uncreative types, but it was largely predicated on that concept. Max Weber, for example, perceived the key to getting things done in a bureaucracy to be primarily a matter of "rationalizing" the behavior of bureaucrats—getting each member to do his or her job in such a way that he or she optimally expedited the official goals of the bureaucracy. Frederick Taylor had essentially the same idea, but his theory rationalized the physical behaviors of workers.

Although the classical theorists had more highly refined models of administrative humanity than the preceding description may indicate, those models were nevertheless drawn from the basic conception that it expresses.

Administrative Humanity:
The Social-Psychological View

In contrast to the classical theorists, theorists relying principally on the open model of organizations, and McGregor's Theory Y conception of personality which views workers as self-motivated, creative people, focused less on rational, economic concerns and more on psychological and social ones. Representatives of a "pure" social-psychological view of the organization member would include Chester I. Barnard, Herbert A. Simon, James G. March, Richard M. Cyert, and James D. Thompson.[8] In this literary stream, the administrative human being is seen as a biological, physical, emotional, behavioral, and social creature who possesses limited cognitive abilities, but nonetheless has an occasional capacity, on the basis of his or her self-interest, to perceive, to act, to solve problems, and to bargain.

Simon provided a useful description of the social-psychological view in his *Models of Man.*[9] On the one hand, Simon posited *psychological man*, or *Freudian man*, who represented the model used by psychologists to predict the behavior of individual persons. Psychological man was beset by insecurities, quirks, motivations, and emotional needs; "rational" behavior was a totally individual phenomenon; every person had to do his or her own thing. On the other hand, Simon posited *rational man*, or *economic man*, who represented the model used by economists to predict the behavior of the economy as a whole. Economic man was totally rational in the sense that he not only understood thoroughly his own self-interest (*i.e.*, the acquisition of money), but was fully cognizant of all the options available to him and would act on the choice that brought him the most money. Thus, in contrast to psychological man who had his own unique and highly personal goals that were rational only to him, economic man had precisely the same goal as every other person in the economy, and would behave just like every other person to achieve it.

Administrative man, in Simon's view, provided a conceptual bridge between psychological man and economic man. While administrative man had his own private goals and rationality, he also understood the official goals and formal rationality of his organization. Moreover, he knew that his welfare and that of the organization were somehow related, although this was not to say that he believed what was good for the organization was necessarily good for him. Finally, administrative man could seldom if ever see all his possible options in making a decision, nor could he predict their consequences.

All these models of the human being work—that is, they yield accurate predictions—in their respective disciplines. The social-psychological model of the individual posited by the Barnard-Simon-March-Cyert-Thompson stream of literature works for organization theory.

Understanding the distinctions between the classical and social-psychological interpretations of the human condition in organizations is needed, but it does not take us very far in terms of comprehending the kinds of people with whom we must deal in public bureaucracies. There are at least three distinct literatures written in the social-psychological tradition that are of unique utility in this regard: models of adult development (which focus largely on psychological variables), models of cultural behavior, and models of political behavior (which, at the opposite end of the social-psychological continuum, focus largely on social variables). We consider these approaches in turn.

MODELS OF ADULT DEVELOPMENT

People change. How people change, and what effects those changes might have on the organizations in which they work, have been the subjects of psychological and social-psychological research since the 1930s.[10]

Turning Points

The adult development psychologists, taken together, have identified a series of psychological tasks that everyone must confront as a means of interpreting how people approach each stage of their lives, and with what attitudes. Erik Erikson, for example, posits a progressive mastery of psychological tasks that hinges on a series of critical turning points. From birth to year one, trust or mistrust can be inculcated into the psyche of the individual as a result of his or her early experiences with others; from one to six, the turning point becomes one of developing autonomy as an individual, or shame; from six to ten, initiative or guilt; from ten to fourteen, industry as opposed to inferiority; from fourteen to twenty, identity versus role confusion; from twenty to forty, intimacy or isolation; from forty to sixty-five, generativity and creativity, as opposed to stagnation; and from sixty-five until death, a strong sense of ego and integrity, as opposed to overwhelming despair.[11]

Different analysts have developed variations on this theme, but the theory is essentially the same: an individual is faced with critical turning points in his or her life, and these occur at specific ages. More important, a person can become mired in the negative option of any given phase, and fail to move beyond that phase. Thus, for example, a person could fall into a pattern of isolation, rather than intimacy, in his or her twenties or thirties, and fail to develop as an adult from that point.

The adult psychologists agree that when people are in their twenties and thirties, the most overriding psychological task is that of achieving personal intimacy. It is during this phase that a person shifts from his or her dependency on parents to an intimacy with (or isolation from) mates and peers in the work environment and society.

The next major phase is what is known popularly as the "mid-life crisis." How intense that crisis is varies from individual to individual, but people experience at least a "mid-life transition," if not a dramatic crisis. Mid-life transition is a period occurring from as early as the late thirties through as late as the early sixties, and women may experience more of a crisis during this phase than men.[12]

It is during mid-life that the individual chooses between such significant alternatives as looking at career options or resigning oneself to having attained all that one can attain professionally, and, on a personal level, accepting or becoming embittered over one's condition. George E. Vaillant refers to this period as one of determining whether an individual can "keep the meaning" of what his or her life or career has signified in reality, or become rigid and inflexible about a personal set of principles that may have grown hollow over time.[13]

Finally, an individual enters late adulthood, a period in which one reflects on what one's life has meant. These reflections focus either on the development of a sense of integrity about what he or she stands for, or on a sense of despair over what one has failed to accomplish.[14] One can, in sum, close one's life with serenity and contentment, or sadness and self-contempt.

Adult Development and the Public Organization

Manfred Kets de Vries and his colleagues conducted research that related the experience of Canadian executives in both the public and private sectors to the adult life span development.[15] Kets de Vries found a strong correlation between high and low levels of satisfaction with the organization and one's work and specific phases of adult development.

The first phase, which Kets de Vries calls "reality shock," and which occurs during the twenties when one enters one's first "real job," is characterized by very low levels of satisfaction. This shock was attributable to unrealistic expectations, and the anxiety-inducing search for a mentor among the senior executives—a search which might or might not be successful.

Organizational mentors become exceptionally important in the development of individuals as adults within the organization. The mentor is typically eight to fifteen years older than the person being mentored, takes the younger employee under his or her wing, and represents wisdom and authority to that person. Few people have as many as three or four mentors, and, more commonly, fewer.[16]

In a comparison of the mentoring function as found in public and private organizations, it was found that public administrators were more likely than were their counterparts in the private sector to find a mentor outside of the organization in which they worked; often, the mentor of a young public administrator is a former professor. Public administrators also are less likely than private managers to find mentors at the top rungs of the organization, a condition that may reflect the relatively frequent turnover of top political executives. Both public and private administrators, however, found the influence of mentors on their career development to be "substantial."[17] Daniel Levinson, who studied executives extensively within the framework of adult psychology, found that at about the age of thirty-seven the individual leaves the protection of the mentor and takes full charge of himself or herself.[18]

Leaving the mentor (if one has been found), and overcoming reality shock and dissatisfaction with the job, is followed by a period of socialization in the organization and personal growth, which occurs in the thirties. It is during this phase that the manager invests a sense of self in the organization and in his or her career. Levinson calls this period one of "settling down," and Vaillant refers to it as a period of "career consolidation."[19]

Not every one, however, is able to settle down. Levinson found that 45 percent of the individuals he studied "had major difficulties" during the "settling down" period, and, as a result, they could not create the basis for even a moderately satisfactory life in middle age.[20] Vaillant determined that 10 percent of his sample remained "perpetual boys," and never entered the successive stages of adult maturation. A larger proportion of his subjects never passed beyond the stage of career consolidation (or Levinson's time of "settling down"), and grew stagnant.[21]

If one is incapable of consolidating one's career, and then enters his or her late thirties through the mid-forties, job satisfaction takes a steep downward spiral. This is the most likely time that people are going to have a mid-life crisis, and consider the possibilities of new careers, new lifestyles, and new spouses. Michael Maccoby has concluded that today's executives are less egocentric and narcissistic than were the leaders of the public and private sectors of the past. The newer generation's characteristics of relative tolerance, flexibility, and openness appeared to be very important in weathering the mid-life transition, and in helping these people move on to a satisfying late adulthood.[22]

Job satisfaction typically rebounds during the late forties and fifties; Kets de Vries calls this period "acceptance," a notion that echoes Vaillant's concept of "keeping the meaning" of one's life and personal principles.

The roller coaster of job satisfaction takes yet another dip in the mid-to-late fifties, and continues to decline, although not as rapidly, through the early sixties as the individual nears retirement. Oddly, it appears that, while job satisfaction continues to decline, the individual's satisfaction with his or her organization appears to bounce back toward the end of his or her career.

The implications of the psychology of adult development for public organizations are several.[23] Obviously, young people entering the public bureaucracy in their twenties, like all young people entering the workforce, probably are going to experience a reality shock. Perhaps public organizations should be increasingly sensitive of this early phase of an individual's working life. Ironically, even though the individual is most vulnerable to "reality shock" when he or she first enters the public organization, the individual is also the most energetic and determined to succeed. This is the time to cultivate both organizational loyalty and individual ability by investing—in terms of responsibilities, training, and attention—in the new public administrator.

As those same public administrators enter their fifties, they, more often than not, will want to pass on their wisdom to the younger generation. This can be encouraged by top management, and perhaps should be. Both the new public administrators in their twenties and the more mature public administrators in their fifties apparently need to get in touch with each other—not only for the personal benefits involved, but also for the good of the organization in which they work. This matching up of the young and mature seems to be particularly needed in the public sector, where, as we have noted, finding mentors in the organization is more difficult than in the private sector.

The literature of adult development gives us a useful perspective on how people evolve throughout their organizational lives, and even how they evolve before they enter organizational life as young adults. So does another body of knowledge, if from an entirely different viewpoint, and that is the literary corpus of national culture.

MODELS OF CULTURAL BEHAVIOR

Although there is a vast literature on comparative and developmental public administration, which we mentioned in Chapter 2, relatively few theorists have considered the specific impact of national cultures (or "the collective mental programming of people in an environment"[24]) on organizational behavior, but some who have tackled this subject deserve mention.

Culture and Organizational Intelligence

Harold Wilensky, for one, has considered how cultural variables relate to attitudes about the organizational uses of information and the patterns of bureaucratic secrecy.[25] In his view, modern totalitarian governments based on technology (*e.g.*, Stalin's Russia, Hitler's Germany) were and are the most fully organized to protect secrecy. Information pathologies attained their ultimate expression in both states: huge sums were passed to "experts" of various kinds, antiintellectualism was rife, an immense intelligence-gathering apparatus was created, interagency sabotage was commonplace, and the general dysfunctions of bureaucracy were exaggerated. When these pathologies were combined with a dogma, such as proletarianism or racism, "grotesque intrigues," official paranoia, and spectacular intelligence failures (such as Hitler's strategy for the conduct of World War II) were the result.

Wilensky compares the administrative methods of developing radar employed by the British with those methods used by the Germans during World War II as an illustration of how differing sociopolitical cultures can affect organizations. Although the Germans may have had an earlier start than the British, they soon felt it necessary to bureaucratize their system of radar research by creating a Plenipotentiary for High Frequency Techniques. The Plenipotentiary established himself as a coordinator between a chain of new research laboratories that he had built and the Air Ministry. Abstract specifications of what the *Luftwaffe* wanted then were sent to the Plenipotentiary by the Air Ministry, who then checked his list of available laboratories and mailed the data to the one needing work. Because of an absence of interaction between fliers and scientists, German radar development eventually ground to a halt. In contrast, the British effort was characterized by continuous discussions between members of the Royal Air Force and the Telecommunications Research Establishment. A feature of this relatively open model approach was the frequent use of "Sunday Soviets," in which officials and experts of all ranks and designations discussed various aspects of radar development. Needless to add, it was the British use of radar that was instrumental in winning the Battle of Britain.[26]

Wilensky believes that the parliamentary democracies with traditions of aristocracy, such as Britain and France, fall midway between the pathologically secretive totalitarian nations and the publicity-hungry United States, which he feels has organizations that are the least constrained by secrecy. In the United States, news "leaks" are a common strategy of interagency rivalry, exposés of public figures are encouraged by the press, congressional investigations are favored, and the libel laws are loosely construed. In England, however, an administrator's first loyalty is to the Cabinet, and the Official Secrets Act is an effective cork on the leakage of secret information.

Unfortunately, in Wilensky's view, Americans display a love/hate syndrome for secrecy. Pressures for publicity provoke counterpressures for the reestablishment of "national security," and it is Wilensky's worry that the publicity consciousness of American culture may strengthen the power of secrecy via a kind of rebound effect; that is, "Let's not go too far with this publicity stuff, because we may sell ourselves down the river to our enemies abroad." The various investigations of the Watergate affair provide an example of America's love/hate syndrome for secrecy, particularly when the intense publicity that surrounded them is contrasted with the political defense of the accused: that a cover-up of the Watergate break-in was necessary for the sake of national security.

Culture and Organizational Failure

Unlike Wilensky, Michel Crozier has focused his research less on the effects of national culture on the organization's relationship with its political environment, and more on the influences that culture has on the internal workings of the organization.[27] Crozier's thesis is that each national culture has a unique effect on organizations operations in that culture, and this effect ultimately will constitute the primary pathology of the organizations. In France, as noted earlier, the culturally derived pathology is *bon plaisir* —that is, to quote Crozier, "it is considered better to restrict oneself and to remain free within the narrower limits one has fixed or even those one has had to accept."[28] *Bon plaisir*, a symptom long ingrained in the French culture, is a stubborn insistence on personal autonomy that inhibits cooperation in French organizations.

The Soviet Union, however, has quite an opposite cultural phenomenon that impinges on the workings of bureaucracy. This is the *blat*, which refers to an informal network of complicity entered into by middle managers as a means of assuring that the national production quotas set by the state are met. *Blat* is characterized by a high degree of mutual, almost familial, trust among middle managers. Middle managers are quite willing to enter into "illegal" deals with one another in order to fulfill the demands of "the plan," which rarely, if ever, provides the methods of its own success. As a result, hierarchy, suspicion, and control are emphasized by the top echelons of the Soviet bureaucracy, but often the otherwise destructive consequences of these pathologies do little to undermine the functioning of the *blat*.

In extreme contrast to Soviet organizations, American organizations are characterized by divisions of labor and the due process of law. These twin cultural factors bring about organizational pathologies unique to American bureaucracies. Functional specialization (which is almost another way of saying professionalization) results in an abnormally high number of jurisdictional disputes within and among American organizations, while the American passion for due process of law produces a plethora of impersonal bureaucratic rules designed to protect the individual from injustices. Both cultural traits tend to magnify the role of lawyers, or any official who is in a position to interpret organizational rules, jurisdictions, and prerogatives, and this aspect often impedes change in American organizations. British organizations, on the other hand, are permeated by a deference system based on class distinctions emanating from their culture that makes the use of impersonal rules to assure compliance by subordinates unnecessary, since the authority of superordinates possesses greater legitimacy than in American organizations. In France, peer-group resistance to authority acts as a substitute for impersonal rules and due process of law.

In Crozier's view, American organizations, on the whole, tend to protect the rights of individuals more effectively, are better attuned to reality, are characterized by more cooperation, and are generally more open than French, Russian, or British organizations. But the existence of many centers of authority in American organizations, and the difficulties that must be surmounted in coordinating them, pose problems of change for American organizations. Although American organizations are likely more open to innovation than the French, British, and Russian, Crozier notes that "Willful individuals can block the intentions of whole communities for a long time; numerous routines develop around local positions of influence; the feeble are not protected so well against the strong; and generally, a large number of vicious circles will protect and reinforce local conservatism."[29] These pathologies, like the bureaucratic dysfunctions of a differing nature in other countries, are the result of cultural factors unique to America that no organization can escape.

Culture and Managerial Behavior

Certainly the most systematic and massive attempt to categorize national cultures in ways that are potentially useful to managers is by Geert Hofstede, who collected more than 116,000 questionnaires (with an astounding 150 questions per questionnaire), which were administered in two waves to employees of an American-based multinational corporation in forty countries (mostly Western and large Third World nations). He also polled some 400 international managers from different public and private organizations. In addition, he analyzed all the other studies he could find that empirically compared national characteristics (Hofstede located thirteen of these studies, ranging in size from five to nineteen countries), and found that there was a "statistically significant" correlation between these investigations and his research.[30]

Hofstede identified four dimensions of national culture: power distance, uncertainty avoidance, individualism-collectivism, and masculinity-femininity. Specific national cultures can be any combination of these four dimensions.

Power distance refers to "the extent to which a society accepts the fact that power in institutions and organizations is distributed unequally."[31] Societies characterized by "small" power distance believe, among other things, that inequality should be minimized, superiors should be accessible, all should have equal rights, and that a latent harmony exists between the powerful and the powerless; cultures with a "large" power distance believe that a social order rightly assures proper inequalities in society, superiors should be inaccessible, power should have privileges, and latent conflict does exist between the powerful and the powerless. Some of the Western European nations, Australia, Canada, Israel, New Zealand, and the United States are small power distance cultures. All seven of the Latin American nations surveyed (Argentina, Brazil, Chile, Colombia, Mexico, Peru, and Venezuela), and all ten of the Asian countries polled (Hong Kong, India, Iran, Japan, Pakistan, the Philippines, Singapore, Taiwan, Thailand, and Turkey), plus Belgium, France, Greece, Italy, Portugal, Spain, South Africa, and Yugoslavia are large power distance cultures. (Socialist states, with the exception of Yugoslavia, were not studied.)

Uncertainty avoidance is the extent to which a culture feels threatened by ambiguity. Cultures with "weak" uncertainty avoidance are more accepting of uncertainty, live from day to day, have lower stress levels, believe time is free, accept dissent, are unthreatened by social deviations, are more risk prone, are not too nationalistic, are youth oriented, and are not enamored by a lot of rules. All ten of the English- speaking nations surveyed (Australia, Canada, Great Britain, Hong Kong, India, Ireland, New Zealand, the Philippines, South Africa, and the United States), all the Scandinavian countries (with the marginal exception of Finland), the Netherlands, and Singapore are weak uncertainty avoidance cultures. "Strong" uncertainty avoidance cultures perceive uncertainty to be a continuous threat, have greater stress levels, believe time is money, promote consensus over dissent, consider deviance to be dangerous, are security conscious, are highly nationalistic, are distrustful of the young, and like a lot of rules. Examples include all the Latin American countries, most of the Western European nations, Iran, Israel, Japan, Pakistan, Taiwan, Thailand, Turkey, and Yugoslavia.

Individualism-collectivism refers to a continuum of cultures. At one extreme of the continuum is individualism: society is seen as a loose grouping of people whose primary concern is caring for themselves. At the opposite extreme is collectivism, which reflects a tight social framework in which in-groups are distinguished from out-groups, and the in-group is expected to take care of the individual member in exchange for his or her total allegiance to it. In the individualist culture, identity is based on the individual, leadership is the ideal, and decisions are made by the individual. Individualist societies include Israel, most of the Western European countries, and all of the English-speaking nations surveyed, except those in Asia. In collectivist cultures, personal identity is based on the social system, membership in the organization or in-group is the ideal, and decisions are made by the group; examples of collectivist cultures are all the Asian and Latin American nations studied, plus Greece, Portugal, and Yugoslavia.

Finally, the *masculinity-femininity* dimension, like individualism-collectivism, is a continuum ranging from a masculine pole, in which assertiveness, performance, money, independence, ambition, machismo, and indifference to others are characteristic, to a feminine pole, in which nurturing, quality of life, people, the environment, interdependence, service, androgyny, and caring for others are the dominant values. Examples of masculine societies are most of the Asian and Latin American nations, all of the English-speaking countries, plus Austria, Belgium, Italy, Greece, West Germany (now Germany, but West Germany when Hofstede conducted his study), and Switzerland. Feminine cultures include all four of the Scandinavian states, Brazil, Chile, France, Iran, Israel, the Netherlands, Pakistan, Peru, Portugal, Singapore, Spain, Taiwan, Thailand, Turkey, and Yugoslavia.

The United States is a small power distance country (that is, its citizens value equality); a weak uncertainty avoidance nation (in fact, it is well below average, indicating high risk-taking propensities and a tolerance for dissent, among other characteristics); the single most individualistic society of the forty studied; and well above average as a masculine culture. Hofstede contends that these cultural dimensions shape thought and theory in any society, that the United States "has been the world's largest producer and exporter of management theories" for most of this century[32] (Germany and France were its immediate predecessors in this respect), and that American theories on organization and management have worked more effectively in some societies than in others.

Consider, for example, A. H. Maslow's "hierarchy of human needs," described in Chapter 3, which is central to mainstream organization theory, especially human relations and organization development. Maslow's theory, which culminates in the ultimate personal achievement, self-actualization, is predicated on the idea that certain, baser needs must be satisfied first, such as the need for security. Maslow's hierarchy is, at root, a theory of human motivation.

Hofstede's research indicates that Maslow's theory of motivation is less than universal and, in fact, is bound in the American cultural context. Self-actualization is a concept that can be supported only in a society that places a high premium on performance and achievement (or a society that is strongly individualistic and masculine, as is the United States), and on a willingness to take risks so that achievements may be made (or a culture that has weak uncertainty avoidance—again like the United States). But not all societies have these features. In fact, only the English-speaking cultures in Hofstede's study were identified as both masculine and weak uncertainty avoidance countries! Even more revealing, the "striking thing about the concept of achievement is that the word itself is hardly translatable into any language other than English"![33]

The United States and the other English speaking nations, in sum, are *achievement motivation* cultures, and thus can relate to a hierarchy of human needs that places achievement near the top and security near the bottom. But other cultures have different motivations. Some cultures, for example, may be masculine (like the United States) but also have strong needs to avoid uncertainty (such as Italy, Japan, Mexico, and Germany). These nations are *security motivated* (a combination of achievement and security), placing security

near the top of the pyramid of human needs and personal achievement (*i.e.*, self-actualization) near the bottom. Other nations may have weak uncertainty avoidance qualities, like the United States, but are feminine cultures (such as all the Scandinavian nations); and still others may be cultural polar opposites of the United States, being feminine societies that have strong uncertainty avoidance needs (such as France, Israel, and Thailand). In both these instances, *social motivation* explains individual behavior in organizations in these countries: quality of life plus risk taking in the former case (Scandinavian countries), and quality of life plus security in the latter (France, Israel, and Thailand). Thus, a theory of human behavior that presupposes a motivation to achieve the exclusion of other possibilities (as Maslow's hierarchy does) "is not the description of a universal human motivation process—it is the description of a value system, the value system of the U.S. middle class to which the author [Maslow] belonged."[34]

Cultural variables seem to call into question the whole open model of organization theory, at least when that model is cast into cultures which differ from that of the United States. For example, although the United States is a small power distance country, and equality and accessibility are valued, it does not score terribly high on this dimension, and a number of nations, such as Israel, Norway, and Sweden, have power distances that are even smaller. In these countries, organizational subordinates are much more likely to participate in decision making; the question in those countries is less one of top management taking a paternalistic initiative in "opening up" their organizations (as the organization development literature suggests), but more one of subordinates seizing the initiative. In fact, it is in those cultures with the smallest power distances that the "industrial democracy" movement is the strongest: "the very idea of management prerogatives is not accepted in the very low Power Distance countries."[35]

On the other hand, nations with large power distances, such as France and Italy, show little interest in participative decision making in the American style. "This suggests that subordinates in a large Power Distance culture feel even more comfortable with superiors who are real autocrats...."[36]

This is particularly true in France. "French people, from their early childhood onward, are accustomed to large Power Distances.... And in spite of all attempts to introduce Anglo-Saxon management methods, French superiors do not easily decentralize and do not stop short-circuiting intermediate hierarchical levels, nor do French subordinates expect them to."[37] When one multinational corporation issued a directive to all its worldwide subsidiaries that salary adjustment proposals should be initiated by each employee's immediate supervisor, the corporation's French managers interpreted this to mean that the supervisor *three levels above* should initiate salary adjustments![38] Organizational centralization in large Power Distance cultures is prized by superiors and subordinates alike, but decentralization is preferred in cultures with small Power Distances.

If power distance relates to centralization and decentralization, another cultural feature identified by Hofstede, that of uncertainty avoidance, bears on the use of formal rules—on "bureaucracy." Cultures with strong needs to avoid uncertainty are much more prone to rely on written regulations and procedures than are weak uncertainty avoidance countries. Confronted with the same problem, management students from France, what was then West Germany, and Britain recommended three different ways of solving it. The French students recommended referring the problem to a higher level; the Germans, from a culture with very strong uncertainty avoidance needs but (unlike France) relatively small power distances, blamed the lack of written rules as causing the problem, and recommended that they be drafted; the British, from a small power distance and strongly individualistic culture, ascribed the problem to poor communication, and proposed some sort of training program. For the French, the organization is a pyramid (it is both centralized and formal), for the Germans it is a well-oiled machine (formal, but not centralized), and for the British it is a village market (neither centralized nor formal).[39]

American culture seems to be relatively free of these particular mind-sets, and this may account for the comparative success of American corporations in other countries. Like the British students, American managers do not believe in hierarchy for its own sake (as in France) or in rules for their own

sake (as in Germany), but only in using (or not using) hierarchy and rules to achieve results. This orientation reflects the highly individualistic and masculine aspects of the United States. But the extreme individualism of American culture is fundamentally at odds with the collectivist traditions of other cultures, such as all of the nations surveyed in Latin America and Asia. These cultures believe in loyalty to the organization, and individuals do not calculate their behavior on the basis of what the organization can do for them.

MODELS OF POLITICAL BEHAVIOR

A third theme on the nature of the administrative human being that falls within the social-psychological framework deals with how administrators behave politically in organizations. The findings and speculations extant in this field of research have particular relevance to public administration, for politics influences the public administrative sector as no other. Five authors who are of particular note in this area are Gordon Tullock, Alvin Gouldner, Victor A. Thompson, Anthony Downs, and Dwaine Marvick.[40]

Bureaucrats as Medieval Politicians

Tullock posits an overarching conceptualization of how power is distributed in bureaucracies relative to a hypothetical reference politician. Tullock writes directly to the reader; he attempts to explain how he or she (the reference politician) can survive and thrive in the bureaucratic power setting.

Tullock visualizes bureaucracies in terms of modified feudal societies. Reference politicians are surrounded by "spectators" (who watch them but do not affect them), "allies," a "sovereign" (who is comparable to Weber's monocrat, but who lacks omniscience), "peers" (their hierarchical equals), "courtiers" (who make it a point to curry favor with organizational power figures), "followers" (who add to the reference politicians' power, but in a way different from that of their allies), and "barons" (powerful individuals in the bureaucracy who have cut out their own organizational domains and who operate within their domains quite independently from the rest of the organization—*e.g.*, J. Edgar

Culture and the Bureaucrat

The following selection discusses how national culture affects public bureaucrats. Its author is an Englishman and professor of English literature who is also assistant director- general of the United Nations Educational, Scientific, and Cultural Organization.

People, we assume, are much the same everywhere; personality will out, and the ups-and-downs of life are much the same everywhere too. Sure, but the ways these qualities and experiences express themselves differ in different societies. Each society has several ranges of typical face, and the distinctions between them become finer and finer as you look at them. There is a lean, quizzical, face one finds among clever men on the Eastern seaboard of the United States, the face of an intelligent man in a wide-open, mass-persuasive society who is not to be taken in, who has kept his cool and his irony. Such a face is not so likely to be found among its counterparts in Eastern Europe; the winds which beat on these men are different. Their faces are graver, more direct, and yet more reserved.

Because I have met them at some crossroads in my own life, I am particularly interested in a range of faces which cluster round the idea of a public man in Britain. At his most characteristic, this man is in his middle-fifties. His appearance is what the whiskey advertisements, giving it more of a gloss than it really has, call distinguished. His face is well-shaven but not scraped; it has a healthy bloom, but not an outdoor roughness; it is smooth, but not waxy. What is by now quite a full face is as solid as leather club-armchairs, and as decently groomed; it smells as good as the public rooms of those clubs. The hair is often marked by the appearance of Cabinet Minister's wings, that is, it is brushed straight back above the ears to plump out at the sides; it has a silvery sheen. The teeth are strong, one sees when the lips, as they readily do, curl back into a full, firm smile. They suggest someone who is used to talking in public and to deciding, to biting firmly into problems. They are wonderfully communicative

teeth, and remarkable evidence that from all the possible ways of using teeth, the ways we smile or grimace, we select only some: we select from the codebook of tooth-signals in our society.

The coherence of the style is rarely breached. I remember one occasion which, because of its oddness, underlined how consistent that style usually is. One such public man—one who was apparently such a man—said to me, as we stood around in the intervals of a meeting: "You see, Hoggart, I believe in the English people." As he said it, it sounded naive, a little self-important, touching, generous; but not sayable by a native English intellectual, least of all in that particular ambience. But he was a first generation European immigrant intellectual. His son is hardly likely to strike a false note like that.

Among the most striking in the line of public figures is the old-young man; and they are most often found in the higher reaches of education. These men are slim, with little trace of a paunch even at fifty-five; their faces still show the outlines formed when they were Head boys at their public schools or good day-schools. There is a French public type of about the same age who is in some ways similar; but the differences are interesting and, to me, unexpected. The French type is even leaner; he is also more elegant, better groomed, and more professional-looking than the Englishman. He is likely to have close-cropped hair and glasses with the thin gold rims. It all fits with being called a "haut fonctionnaire." The English type is more casual, looser in the limb...

Not long ago I was lost before a new kind of face. Or rather, I mistrusted my own reading of it; It was too easy and dismissive. This was a politician from the United States, a man who had been successful in oil or insurance well before he was forty and who now, in his middle forties, had an assured, thrusting, mercantile, tanned, smoothly smiling but tough look. To me the face, the whole manner, was two-dimensional, unmarked. It was like the face of a well-groomed dog. It said only: "Public acquaintance...manipulation...action"; not: "Friendliness...thought...feeling." Had such a man, you wondered, ever felt shabby or insecure? Oddly, it was easier to imagine him crying. There was probably within the rhetorics available to him a form of crying that would do. But I was probably wrong, unable to read the signals in a way which got me near his character, which made him three-dimensional, capable of real grief and joy, unpublic. I couldn't easily imagine him in his underwear, and when I did he looked like an advertisement in *Esquire*.

Richard Hoggart, *On Culture and Communication* (London: The Hogarth Press and Chalto and Windus Ltd., 1972). Reprinted by permission.

Hoover, as director of the Federal Bureau of Investigation during the mid-1960s, relative to the Justice Department and much of the rest of the federal bureaucracy). A reference politician may play any one or several of the roles that Tullock lists; few of them are mutually exclusive. But any reference politician will confront and deal with spectators, allies, sovereigns, peers, courtiers, followers, and barons in any public bureaucracy.

Locals versus Cosmopolitans and the Vexing Question of Loyalty

Gouldner also has itemized organizational roles, but along a different political dimension. In an empirical analysis of a small college's faculty and administration, Gouldner distinguished between "locals" and "cosmopolitans." *Locals* derive their power and sense of personal identity (their self-actualization, if you will), from internal organizational factors. There were several kinds of locals: the *dedicated locals*, who had a deep loyalty to the college, were committed to the idea of interdisciplinary studies, and were deployable from department to department; the *true bureaucrats*, who were satisfied with everything about the organization, including their own salaries, were suspicious of "outsiders" such as the American Association of University Professors (AAUP), and were prone to favor the strict use of rules and regulations; the *homeguard*, who were the least specialized and trained of the faculty, and were likely to be women administrators in the lower ranks; finally, the *elders*, who were oriented toward a particular faculty clique and a time period in the past.

Conversely, *cosmopolitans* related to factors external to the organization, such as their professional association. In contrast to the locals, cosmopolitans were measurably more likely to believe that lighter teaching loads would result in greater research productivity, valued their research time more, were more alienated from their colleagues in terms of their professional interests, were more likely to have a doctoral degree, published more, were less sociable, were less loyal to the organization, were acquainted with fewer of their fellow faculty members, were friendlier toward the AAUP, were likelier to be intellectually stimulated by sources outside the college, and were more dissatisfied with their salaries. There were two kinds of cosmopolitans: the *outsiders*, who were committed to specialization and were not particularly close to either students, colleagues, or the administration; and the *empire builders*, who perceived themselves as being economically independent, had a high commitment to their departments, preferred departmental autonomy, and disliked quality controls and checks, such as student ratings of teachers, and the central administration generally.

In terms of how localism and cosmopolitanism affected the organization directly, Gouldner found that central administrators tended to be high on the homeguard, dedicated, and true bureaucrat dimensions, and low on the outsider and empire builder dimensions. On the other hand, empire builders had considerable power in the organization (in the sense that they were comparable to Tullock's "barons"), and were less likely than locals to emphasize rules and regulations.

Gouldner's creative thinking about cosmopolitans and locals has spawned numerous replications, many of them useful. Later research has linked cosmopolitanism with heightened professionalism, innovation, and the early adoption of innovation by organizations.[41] Much of this research suggests that cosmopolitans are of greater utility than are locals to organizations facing an increasingly fast-paced and challenging task environment. Conversely, locals are perceived as having a unique claim as organizational stabilizers in this same task environment, and that this stabilizing quality derives directly from their greater loyalty to the organization.

This traditional distinction leads some writers to extol the worth of locals in terms of assuring organizational loyalty, and in emphasizing that individual commitment to the organization is good. No organization, after all, can be built on a cadre of employees who are disloyal to it and long survive. Hence, it is argued that the "localistic co-optation" of employees by top management is necessary because it assures the organizational loyalty of employees, and, thereby, organizational stability.

Localistic co-optation refers to management's efforts to isolate individual members from other centers of professionals in their field; to encourage interdisciplinary activities that push members into interacting with colleagues in fields other than their own; to discourage the emergence of "cells of latent cosmopolitans" by keeping resources artificially tight; to resist the entry of "outside" people into the middle and upper levels of the organization, since these people may have firmly formed cosmopolitan tendencies and loyalties that differ from those held by employees who have moved up from the bottom rungs of the organization's ladder; to reward the "unsophisticated impressionables" whenever possible, and to use them to socialize other members of the organization.[42]

No doubt, "localistic co-optation" may be a sure-fire way to develop exceptionally loyal employees. But an organizational loyalty that is redolent of, "My bureaucracy, right or wrong!" is not necessarily conducive to the long-term health, success, or even survival of the organization which commands it. No organization can succeed in the longer haul if it is populated by the organizational equivalents of Kamikaze pilots, just as no organization can long succeed if it is peopled by budding Benedict Arnolds.

While a low level of employee commitment to the organization brings with it problems of an unstable work force and hampered career opportunities for members, extreme levels of commitment among members, such as one occasionally finds in military units or athletic teams, can result in an organization losing its "flexibility and find itself burdened with overzealous employees, and it may become vulnerable to a variety of unethical and illegal behavior. In brief, the commonly assumed linear relationship between commitment and desirable consequences should be questioned."[43]

This digression on localistic co-optation, organizational commitment, and the organizational utility of employee loyalty reflects the traditional, if implicit, view of the literature on cosmopolitanism and localism that the (disloyal) cosmopolitans are the exclusive agents of change, while the (loyal) locals are the last bastions of stability. Increasingly, however, the research indicates that *organizational adaptability can be enhanced by locals*, as well as by cosmopolitans, and that *organizational stability can be enhanced by cosmopolitans*, as well as by locals. This is new.

Gouldner and many of his intellectual progeny implicitly assumed that an employee ultimately had to choose (consciously or not-so-consciously) between cosmopolitanism and localism, and that the strategically managed organization balanced these personality types as its chief means of balancing the need to adapt with the need to routinize. Now the research is suggesting that *both* types are needed to maximize the attainment of *each* objective.

Locals, for example, working with cosmopolitans, increase the chances of successful organizational innovation. A study of hospitals found that those hospitals demonstrating the greatest flair for innovation were characterized by a cosmopolitan professional, such as a physician, *and* a local administrator; working together, this combination seemed to be the most effective in making their organizations the most innovative. Less effective was a combination of two cosmopolitans; their outer-directed needs and ignorance of the local organization resulted in less innovative organizations. The least innovative hospitals were those characterized by a local professional and a local administrator. The researchers concluded that to maximize organizational innovation "it is necessary to include the bureaucratic [*i.e.*, local] and professional [*i.e.,* cosmopolitan] perspectives within an organization."[44]

Just as locals can help enhance organizational innovation, cosmopolitans can help develop organizational stability. A study of intercollegiate sports programs in the United States concluded that the inculcation of "intense loyalty" among members of the organization was useful if that loyalty were held by members who also reflected cosmopolitan traits—who were, in short, not only intensely loyal, but highly sensitive to the task environment, the need to adapt, and professional values. "To the extent that an organization is able to engineer the alignment of individuals' professional goals with those of the organization, it will have a greater likelihood of producing intense loyalty in its members," thereby enhancing organizational stability. "Thus, organizations...that are structured so that individuals are dependent on the success of the group for their own success will be more likely to produce intense loyalty."[45]

In other words, the best of both worlds is possible: deep personal commitment to the organization can equate with great personal success, both within the organization and in the marketplace, and deep personal commitment to professionalism and an understanding of the marketplace can equate with great organizational success.

The notion of cosmopolitanism and localism is increasingly significant to public administration because of the field's growing reliance on the use of expertise. As public bureaucracies fill with more highly trained and specialized experts, new patterns of personal loyalties, perceptions, and commitments may evolve that will present new kinds of organizational contingencies to the public administrator. It is probable that the functions of the public administrator will change as the personnel in his or her organization professionalize. We consider the implications of this development more thoroughly in Chapter 9.

Bureaucrats as Sycophants

Thompson argues that precisely because of the growing social necessity for highly educated specialists in organizations, private as well as public, the political power of the administrator ought to be reduced radically. In fact, Thompson thinks that

bureaucrats and administrators should be exorcised altogether from organizations because they are dysfunctional. In Thompson's opinion only *specialists,* such as scientists, lawyers, engineers, and accountants, get things done in organizations; bureaucrats only get in the way. *Bureaucrats* or *administrators* are nothing more than sycophants and parasites in any organization, according to Thompson, and he urges that we recognize this fact for what it is and toss out the rascals before it is too late. (A third type is also posited by Thompson: *bureautics*—or those persons who cannot accept organizations of any kind and drop out. Thompson does not think highly of bureautics and concentrates on bureaucrats and specialists.)

Thompson then asks rhetorically how bureaucrats have managed to featherbed so effectively in organizations for as long as they have and offers three explanations. One reason that bureaucrats have maintained their organizational power position is their shrewd use of "dramaturgy," or, to put it in the vernacular, their capacity for manufacturing "snow jobs." Bureaucratic dramaturgy is designed, like the other two strategies used by bureaucrats to justify their positions, to camouflage their lack of any knowledge that is truly useful to the organization. Dramaturgy consists of personal aloofness, firm handshakes, an unwavering eye, confidence, and winning smiles—in short, the Dale Carnegie method of executive development personified. Dramaturgy has gone far in keeping bureaucrats inside organizations, but the image that it creates is in reality insubstantial froth and fluff.

Equally insubstantial, but nonetheless effective in the preservation of bureaucratic power, is the bureaucrats' reliance on "ideology" and "bureaupathology" to justify their organizational existence. Ideology is simply tradition. Bureaucrats have always been around, and it has become an ideological rationale that they should stay around. Bureaupathology refers to the excessively rigid, even by bureaucratic standards, roles assumed by bureaucrats to maintain their power positions. Rules, obedience, loyalty (to themselves), and subservience are stressed as a means of heading off embarrassing, uncomfortable, and probing questions from the dispossessed specialists about why the organization is run in the way it is.

Thompson takes a radical stance on administrators: he considers them useless at best and dangerous at worst. He thinks administrators should be eliminated from organizations in order that the skill-possessing specialists can get together without interference and get the organization's job done more efficiently and effectively.

Obviously, in a book about public administration we cannot bring ourselves to accept Thompson's thesis. If we did, I would not have bothered writing this tract, and you (hopefully) would not have bothered taking this course. But the notion that Thompson articulates so straightforwardly—that administrators play psychological roles and political games in bureaucracies for their own ends—is well worth amplification, if for no other reason that you might stand a better chance of recognizing some roles and games for what they are and react to them accordingly. Two analysts who have pursued this line of thought are Downs and Dwaine Marvick.[46]

Zealots, Advocates, and Statesmen

It was mentioned earlier that Downs posited "conservers" and "climbers" in organizations and related these personality types to an "age lump" phenomenon that he associated with organizational change. Conservers and climbers are "pure" types that can be blended in different ways to produce: *zealots*, *advocates*, and *statesmen*. These personalities are distributed along a continuum that relates to the breadth or narrowness of their perceptual scope.

Zealots tend to have the most shallow perceptual base; they are effective founders of organizations but not very effective managers once the organization is established. They espouse the most narrow policy set, such as a particular pet project, and promote it with a zeal that warrants, in Downs's mind, the title with which he has dubbed them.

Advocates articulate broader policy sets than do zealots. They tend to see the organization as a whole and to understand its components; occasionally this results in advocates having a magnified view of themselves and their organizational roles. They believe in the organization and generally occupy its higher, nonroutinized offices. While advocates are highly partisan in defending the organization relative to its environment, they often are impartial arbiters of internal disputes and are sensitive to the long-range implications of organizational policies.

Statesmen have the broadest perceptual abilities of the three types; they see their society as a whole and their organization's role in it. Because of their greater loyalty to the entire society, however, statesmen often are misfits in their organizations. In theory, anyway, statesmen would be willing to sell their organizations down the proverbial river if they believed that their society would benefit as a result. Needless to say, there are few statesmen around, although they may be particularly needed in public organizations.

Career Types and their Political Motivations

A similar but more empirical study of the roles bureaucrats play in public organizations was undertaken by Marvick. Marvick asked, "What must management do in order to cope with persons having different career perspectives?" Marvick tried to place in broad categories the individual goals and rationalities of public bureaucrats that are assumed to exist in the open model.

This was an eminently worthwhile project, and his study has manifold uses for public administrators. It is one thing merely to say, as the open-model theorists often do, that everyone is unique in organizations and then stop. True enough, one must retort, but so what? How far can such a statement carry us in terms of understanding our organizations and our colleagues? Not very far. Yet it is quite another matter when we can type, no matter how roughly, the individual rationalities according to certain broad commonalities. This gives us an insight and a theory to work with. The writers whom we have reviewed in this chapter have tried to do just that and are therefore useful. But Marvick's study is especially useful, empirical, and not very well known.

Marvick trisected public bureaucrats by career style: *institutionalists, specialists*, and *hybrids*. Institutionalists were believers in the organization, but their career commitments were "a matter of 'sublimated' interest—ends in themselves." That is, institutionalists received their psychoemotional gratifications from the organization on the bases of very superficial criteria, such as unwarranted optimism and the shallow status rewards granted by the organization. As a group, institutionalists were relatively high in their demands for organizational advancement and unqualifiedly high in their quest for organizational prestige. They tended not to stress the task-oriented features of their jobs, but preferred to emphasize the job's benefits. And they tended to have spent most of their career lives in government, often in the military. Institutionalists generally were found to be mid-level bureaucrats, encumbered by few family ties, with relatively few formal educational attainments, and with short job histories—that is, they had changed positions (although they had not necessarily advanced) within the government frequently.

Institutionalists were very sociable people within the organization, and were extremely loyal to it and to their co-workers. In that light, they preferred being in on group decisions, wanted their decisions buttressed by their peers, and tended to compare their job performance with others on an *ad hominem* basis. In sum, institutionalists were "place- bound" (like Gouldner's locals), and committed to an executive career in the government. They had a superficial concern with achieving their agency's goals, were optimistic concerning their agency's performance (and their own), were gregarious and preferred working with others, felt relatively uninfluential in terms of their agency (and probably were), but nevertheless were complacent about their organizational role.

Specialists were at the opposite end of the spectrum from institutionalists. Unlike institutionalists, who occupied generalized managerial slots, specialists tended to be highly educated professionals, such as lawyers, scientists, engineers, and accountants. Specialists were not particularly concerned about personal advancement in the organization and had virtually no interest in organizational status rewards. What they did want very badly, however, was the freedom to do their own thing, to be in jobs that allowed them to use their professional skills on a daily basis. In terms of career histories, specialists tended to have experience both in public and private bureaucracies. They had less military experience than institutionalists and, while they were fairly well advanced in terms of their careers, specialists were seldom interested in executive positions, in stark contrast to institutionalists. Whereas institutionalists revealed a sublimated need for organizational status, specialists displayed an unconscious demand to use their specialties. Task orientation rather than place orientation was a key difference between specialists and institutionalists; specialists, like Gouldner's cosmopolitans, had no particular loyalty to the organization, nor did they indicate a desire for prestige as defined by position in the organization.

Interestingly, specialists resembled institutionalists in that they preferred to have their opinions supported by their peers, although they favored working alone and were less likely to be involved in group decisions than institutionalists. Yet, as individuals, specialists had more influence within the organization than did institutionalists. Finally, specialists were by far the most critical of the agency's performance and of bureaucratic methods generally; in this sense, Marvick felt that specialists were "manifestly maladjusted" in their working relationships.

Hybrids, or "politicized experts," had the characteristics of both institutionalists and specialists. Like specialists, hybrids were highly educated professionals, were advanced in organizational rank, had experience in both the public and private sectors, and were disinterested in organizational prestige. Like institutionalists, hybrids were very concerned with acquiring executive positions and charting a career in government. If there was a single group that could be called the realistic "loners," it was the hybrids. They were very keen on executive advancement and generally divorced themselves from any strong identification with particular groups in the organization. Marvick calls them "free agents," that is, they thought of *both* place and skill in quite detached terms. Hybrids were unconcerned with peer groups, organizational prestige, and the exercise of their skills; they were committed neither to their agency nor to their profession. Nevertheless, hybrids were very committed to money and advancement. Interestingly, in this light, hybrids tended to have far heavier family responsibilities than either institutionalists or specialists. Also of interest, hybrids had relatively low levels of influence in the bureaucracy, which may reflect their propensity for working alone; although their influence equalled that of institutionalists, it was lower than that of specialists. Hybrids, like institutionalists, were not especially critical of meetings and similar bureaucratic paraphernalia and were well adjusted to their jobs; on the other hand, they were likely to be disgruntled when they felt that they were being distracted from their work. Finally, hybrids had no sublimated goals, unlike either of the other two types. Hybrids' goals were explicit and personal, and they were quite amenable to using either place or skill criteria to advance their goals. Because of this, hybrids often were the organization's realists in Marvick's view.

All three groups possess perils and potentialities for public organizations. Institutionalists can become rule-oriented and inflexible; their sociability can degenerate into cliquishness, their loyalty into recalcitrance to change, and they resist performance evaluation along quantitative, measurable scales. Yet, institutionalists provide the bureaucracy with genuine organizational stability and furnish the needed lubrication for the interpersonal relationships in the agency.

Specialists tend to displace the agency's goals because their individual, professional projects are more important to them than the organization's welfare. This propensity can affect organizational performance generally. Moreover, their highly critical cast and lack of place commitment can cause sinking morale, disharmony, and high rates of turnover. In view of Marvick's findings, we might recall Thompson's advocacy of organizations staffed entirely by specialists and speculate on what such organizations might really be like. Yet, when properly placed, specialists can get things done in a most effective way, and they are not inclined to compete politically with other members of the bureaucracy.

Hybrids bring the most dangers and benefits to the organization. Their chief danger lies in their instability. Hybrids are fair-weather friends, "superficial and showy performers." Their lack of both place and skill commitments render them unpredictable. Yet, hybrids are the most likely people to assess accurately and holistically the dynamics and problems of the organization. Un-

like the other two groups, they possess no sublimated personal needs that might interfere with their realistic evaluation of the organization and where it is going. Nevertheless, hybrids must be watched, for they are prone to change the organization purely for their own self-betterment.

Marvick's typology has clear parallels with the constructs of Downs, Gouldner, Tullock, and others, but it is notable in that Marvick has associated his classifications with variables that can be found in any personnel file—educational attainments, job histories, family responsibilities, and so on. This is useful administrative knowledge, particularly when amplified by the analyses that have been reviewed in this chapter. Together, these studies aid us in understanding the political parts of people with whom we deal in organizations.

Who must deal with these people? One could proffer the mundane (and entirely accurate) answer, and state: the supervisor. Others, however, might provide a response more drama laden, and say instead: the leader.

LEADERSHIP: THE CLASSICAL VIEW

We noted earlier that, under the classical view of administrative humanity, the rational behavior of bureaucrats is emphasized, whether this behavior is cast in economic, systemic, or physical terms. But when these same writers in the classical tradition cast their eyes on a particular type of administrative human—the leader—rationality goes out the window and romance, drama, and mythic heroes fly in. No longer are we talking about the limitless capacities of clerks to cower and laborers to labor, but of dizzying social forces that must be brought to heel by leaders possessing transcendent qualities. "True leaders" (for the classical writers allowed for the possibility that charlatans could occupy leadership positions), in this perspective, are different; it is their destiny to command.

Weber, for example, delineated three kinds of leadership: *charismatic, traditional*, and *legal/rational*. A charismatic leader was a primitive, *Volksgeist* (folk spirit) sort, who embodied the spirit of the people. He (never *she* in this literature) led a *Gemeinschaft* type of society, or a society characterized by irrational romanticism. A traditional leader represented what Weber was resisting in the Germany of his day, that is, a person who was a leader by dint of heredity and class. A legal/rational leader was a monocrat, or any other bureaucratic leader, who fulfilled Weber's criterion of impersonal and rigid rationalism. A legal/rational leader led a *Gesellschaft* type society, or a society characterized by rationalism, regulations, impersonality, and bureaucracy. The monocrat (or the omniscient bureaucrat who headed the bureaucracy) was a legal/rational leader who should, in Weber's view, displace the incompetent, traditional leaders of German society and counter, with his *Gesellschaft* organization, the revolutionary tendencies represented by charismatic leaders that were rife in the larger *Gemeinschaft* culture.[47]

Similarly, James D. Mooney and Alan C. Reiley delineated three leadership types, although, unlike Weber's typology, their distinctions were more directly applicable to organizations than to society generally. Mooney and Reiley described leaders as being *titular leaders, controllers*, and *true organizers*, and these types were related to their staff/line principle of organization. A titular leader followed his staff's advice undeviatingly and hence was not much more than a figurehead; a controller was at the other extreme, he or she refused to delegate authority to line officers, and usually ignored staff advice; a true organizer was a leader who simply did everything right—including, of course, the correct application of Mooney and Reiley's principles of organization.[48]

It also is in the classical tradition that Amitai Etzioni and Philip Selznick develop their views on leadership. To Etzioni, as we noted in Chapter 4, leaders may be typed according to personal positional power: *officials* have authority only by virtue of their hierarchical position, *informal leaders* command because of their personal and charismatic qualities, and *formal leaders* combine the power features of both.[49] Selznick relates leadership to levels of political and social interaction. *Leaders* coalesce and mold elements of the society at an "institutional level" and are rather grandiose figures generally, while *administrators* fritter away the hours doing the mundane but necessary chores of a bureaucratic and technical nature that keep the organization running on a day-to-day basis.[50]

In an updated and expanded version of Selznick's thoughts on the differences between leaders and administrators, John P. Kotter provides a helpful framework that distinguishes the functions of leadership from those of management. Leadership, suggests Kotter, ultimately is about "coping with change," while management, at root, is about "coping with complexity." These two fundamental differences lead to quite different organizational roles between leaders and managers. But, in contrast to Selznick, Kotter argues that leadership and management are of equal importance to the organization, because "each system of action involves deciding what needs to be done, creating networks of people and relationships that can accomplish an agenda, and then trying to ensure that those people actually do the job. But each accomplishes these three tasks in different ways."[51]

Leadership's way of accomplishing these tasks is to *set a direction* —create a vision—for the organization. Next the leader must *communicate* that vision and *align people* in a way that they can implement that vision. Leaders must *motivate and inspire* people to attain the vision—in other words, *keep them moving in the right direction*. It is the responsibility of *management* to *plan and budget* for the direction set by leadership; to *organize and staff*—create the organizational structure—to implement the plan; and to *control activities and solve problems* in achieving the plan.

The relative importance of these functions of leadership and management to the organization depend on the conditions of the time. In periods of slow change, management is of greater significance; in times of rapid change, leadership is. Kotter offers "a simple military analogy" to make his point:

a peacetime army can usually survive with good...management up and down the hierarchy.... A wartime army, however, needs competent leadership at all levels. No one yet has figured out how to manage people effectively into battle; they must be *led*.[52]

Although Kotter's views on leadership and management are in the classical tradition, his thoughts constitute a bridge that links the classical perspective (leaders are different from managers) with the social-psychological one (leaders are not necessarily more important than managers). We consider the large literature on the social-psychology of leaders next.

LEADERSHIP: THE SOCIAL-PSYCHOLOGICAL VIEW

In contrast to the classical view, leaders do not emerge as transcendent figures in the social-psychological perspective; in fact, they barely emerge at all. Mainstream organization theorists in the social-psychological tradition largely abjured the very idea of organizational "leadership" because it was difficult to reconcile with the open model, which held that organizations were composed of unique individuals with unique rationalities, motivations, and behaviors. By implication, then, to study "leadership" meant that one accepted the proposition that some organization members had some characteristics—that is, "leadership" characteristics—in common, and this went against the grain of the open model. While a few analysts—notably Tullock, Gouldner, Downs, and Marvick—tried to find distinctions among classes of organizational actors and to isolate organizational types (although not leaders as such), these efforts were not the norm.[53] Today, this is changing.[54]

Leadership is now seen as but one of several roles that the executive plays in an organization, and Henry Mintzberg provides a useful listing of these roles.[55] In Mintzberg's perspective, *leadership* is one of only three *interpersonal roles*. The other two are the executive's *ceremonial role*, which involves attending ceremonies and so forth, and the *liaison role*, which entails giving and receiving information, thereby learning what is going on elsewhere in order to gain benefits for the organization. In addition, executives play at least three *informational roles*: that of *monitor*, which involves the routine search for information for the organization; *disseminator*, which involves transmitting information to relevant organizational members; and *spokesperson*, which involves transmitting information outside the or-

ganization. Finally, there are at least four *decision-making roles* played by executives: that of *entrepreneur*, which entails seeking opportunities, identifying problems, and initiating actions on behalf of the organization; *disturbance handler*, which requires resolving conflicts among individuals or units; *resource allocator*, which involves the executive in making choices within the organization about the allocation of resources; and *negotiator*, which entails representing the organization in third-party, formal negotiations.

A number of researchers have used Mintzberg's model in analyzing organizational executives, and have found that the importance of his executive roles can differ markedly depending upon the hierarchical level (*e.g.*, a chief executive officer may need to spend more time in his or her spokesperson's role than does a division chief) and functional area (*e.g.*, the executive in a labor intensive organization, such as a university, may find his or her role as a resource allocator to be more significant than does the executive in a capital intensive organization, such as a railroad).[56] However, it appears, according to analyses of executives in both the public and private sectors, that "public sector executives engage in activities that correspond to Mintzberg's managerial role descriptions, and that the major role functions are similar in both areas."[57] The researchers conclude that this similarity of managerial roles between the two sectors may exist because "the private sector is becoming more like the public sector" due to a growing task and environmental complexity being experienced by both sectors.[58] But it is important to keep in mind that executive decision-making behavior, motivation, satisfaction, and managerial constraints (which we discussed in Chapter 3) are different in government; executive work, perhaps in contrast to executive roles, appears to differ dramatically between the public and private sectors.[59]

Leaders have some impact on all of the executive roles listed by Mintzberg, regardless of whether they are in the public or private sector. Mintzberg defines *leadership* as the hiring, training, motivating, evaluating and rewarding of subordinates, and leadership requires that subordinates' needs be integrated with the needs of the organization.

THE EVOLUTION OF LEADERSHIP THEORY

Scholarship on the nature of leadership can be viewed as having progressed through four distinct phases: the *"trait" period*, from about 1910 to 1940; the *behavior period*, from 1940 through the late 1960s; the *contingency/transactional approach*, from the mid-1960s onward; and the *organizational leadership phase*, which had its origins in the mid-1960s but began a significant acceleration in the late 1970s. Both the trait and behavior periods were distinguished by their focus on the individual leader; the contingency/transactional approach expands the theory's unit of analysis to the leader's interactions with small groups; and the organizational leadership phase further broadens the scope of analysis and deals with the leader and the organization as a whole. Table 5-2 is an attempt to outline the theories of leadership that are in the tradition of social psychology, and you may wish to refer to it in the following discussion.

The Leader as an Individual, 1910–1965

Leadership Traits, 1910–1940. In the early literature on leadership, the emphasis was on who leads and who follows. The unit of analysis in this literature is the individual member of the organization. Hence, the point of much of the research in this phase was to identify those unusual features of the individual that were associated with "leadership." Researchers would compare "leaders" (as determined by the office they held in the organization) with "followers" on such dimensions as dominance, sensitivity, physical appearance, moodiness, masculinity, and other traits that were thought to relate to leadership. Then the scores of leaders and their subordinates on these measures would be compared.

Ralph Stogdill tried in 1948 to make some sense of these trait studies, and reviewed more than 120 of them in an effort to find some sort of pattern. He concluded that no pattern existed and this conclusion led him to argue that, because leadership situations can vary substantially from organization to organization, research was needed that matched personality traits with the characteristics of the organizational situation.[60]

Leadership Behaviors, 1940–1965. Other researchers had come to the same conclusions years earlier, if from different perspectives. In 1939, Kurt Lewin and his colleagues published their classic study of leadership. It was in this study that research assistants were trained in three styles of leadership: autocratic, democratic, and laissez-faire (meaning virtually no activity by the leader). Lewin then loosed his graduate assistants on groups of preadolescent boys, and began measuring the results. The conclusion that Lewin and his colleagues drew was that the democratic style of leadership seemed to be the most effective. But perhaps the lasting importance of this seminal work was that it took a behavioral approach to the study of leadership.[61]

During the 1950s, leadership theorists developed two major clusters of behaviors that they believed were useful (if for different reasons) in providing leadership.[62] One cluster was that of *consideration behaviors*, which related to interpersonal warmth, concern for the feelings of subordinates, and a participative/communicative style of leadership. This cluster of behaviors also was called "socio-emotional," or "employee-oriented" behavior.

The second cluster of behaviors was that of *task behaviors*. This grouping stressed such behaviors as directness, facilitation of goals, and the obtaining of task-related feedback. This configuration also was called the "initiation of structure," or "production-oriented" behavior.

As in the trait era, behavioral researchers were attempting to find the single best style of leadership. They failed. They could not determine whether consideration behavior or task behavior resulted in such outcomes as group productivity and satisfaction among followers.

The Leader and the Small Group, 1965–present

By the late 1960s, leadership theorists were moving away from the individual as the object of analysis, and began focusing on the small group. At least two major branches constituted this focus, and they appeared roughly concurrently in time. One is the "contingency" approach, and the other is the "transactional" approach. Both are mutually complimentary and quite interrelated.

TABLE 5-2 Social-Psychological Theories of Leadership

Theoretical School	Approximate Period	Analytical Scope	Principal Ideas	Comments
Traits	1910–1940	Individual leader	Leaders are born, not bred, and leadership traits can be scientifically identified.	
Behaviors	1940–1965	Individual leader	*Consideration behaviors* and *task behaviors* are the major clusters of leadership behaviors.	These behavioral categories are basic to later theory.
Contingency Approaches	1965–present	Small group	Fiedler's "scale of situational control" is composed of group trust, goal clarity, and leader's authority. "Relationship motivated" leaders and "task motivated" leaders are less or more effective depending on how high or low the group rates on the situational control scale.	Leaders can deliberately change styles and approaches to suit the leadership needs of the group.
Subschool: Normative decision theory			Leader's style may be "autocratic," "consultative," or "group-oriented" (and other designations), and the effectiveness of leader's style relates to group's support of leader and clarity of information. Leadership styles correspond to Fiedler's relationship and task motivated leaders.	Leadership style is so basic to self that leaders cannot change it to suit needs of group.
Transactional Approaches	1965–present	Small group	Graen's idea of "vertical dyadic linkage" holds that a leader's effectiveness depends on the level of trust between the leader and the group.	Transactional approaches focus on problems of the group, as well as on the problems facing the leader. (Contingency approaches concentrate primarily on the leader.)

TABLE 5-2 (continued)

Theoretical School	Approximate Period	Analytical Scope	Principal Ideas	Comments
Subschool: Path-goal theory			Leadership style relates to motivation and satisfaction of group. Leader's consideration behaviors are effective when task is distasteful and when subordinates are nondogmatic and display high personal growth needs. Task behaviors work better with groups dealing with unstructured tasks and with subordinates who are dogmatic and show little need for personal growth.	
Leadership and the Organization	1965–present	Organization and its environment	Leadership of large organizations is worthy of study.	Although it has earlier antecedents, organization-wide research on leadership accelerated dramatically beginning in the 1980s.
Subschools: Leadership Competencies and Hierarchy			Different leadership competencies are needed to best manage different levels of the organization.	
Contingency/Transactional Approaches			Demands, constraints, and choices form the leader's opportunities for action. The "multiple influence model" of leadership adds the complexities of environment, context, and structure to this mix.	The horizons and challenges of the leader are expanded to include not only small groups of subordinates but also superiors, peers, and forces outside the organization.
Charismatic/Symbol Approaches			Magnetic personal qualities of the leader and his or her use of organizational symbols are the important features of leadership.	Represents a return to the study of leadership traits and the perspectives of the classical writers on leadership.

Contingency Approaches. The contingency approach to the study of organizational leadership reflects mainstream thinking in organization theory generally: managers must deal with contingencies that can occur as a result of any number of factors, such as the organizational environment, new technologies, or different personalities. Fred Fiedler did much of the original work in contingency theory.[63] Fiedler developed a personality measure that represented a refinement of the concepts originated by the behaviorists. Through a scale that he titled "the esteem for the least preferred co-worker measure," Fiedler categorized individuals as "task motivated" or "relationship motivated." But Fiedler went beyond the behaviorists by developing a "scale of situational control," which was determined by the degree of trust and support that followers accorded their leader (what Fiedler called "leader-member relations"), by the clarity with which goals and procedures for accomplishing a group's task were given (called "task structure"), and by the degree to which the leader had formal authority to punish and reward his or her followers (called "position power").

Using this framework, Fiedler described a "high control" situation as one in which a leader had the trust of his or her followers, there was a clear task structure, and the leader had a high level of power to reward and punish. A situation of "moderate control" occurred when the task structure was ambivalent or the group was uncooperative. A "low control" situation was one in which followers were not supportive of the leader, the nature of the task was unclear, and the leader's authority to dispense rewards and punishments was ambiguous.

In a high control situation, a task-motivated leader functioned quite well. Task-motivated leaders were less effective in a moderate control situation because they frequently became anxious and moved, often inappropriately, to a quick solution; typically, they were critical and punitive toward their followers. In these moderate control situations, a relationship-motivated leader was found to be more effective. In a low control situation, which often amounts to a crisis situation, the task-motivated leader once again surfaces as the appropriate leader type. Participation by followers and consideration of followers by leaders are not particularly relevant under these low control conditions. Although Fiedler's contingency model has been the subject of some controversy, at least one review of empirical tests given over the years that used the contingency model found that the predictions generated by the model were largely accurate.[64]

A variation of the contingency model is called "normative decision theory."[65] In this theory, the concept of "autocratic decision making style," in which a leader makes a decision on his or her own without participation by followers, relates (more or less) to Fiedler's task-motivated leader. A "consultative decision making style" is one in which the leader makes the decisions but only after consulting with followers, and, to a lesser degree, it also relates to Fiedler's task-motivated leader. The "group oriented style" clearly corresponds to Fiedler's relationship-oriented leader, and it is one in which decision making responsibility is shared by members of the group. The group-oriented leadership style also parallels in concept Lewin's earlier notion of democratic leadership.

The normative decision theorists relate these decision-making styles to the level of support that subordinates accord their leader and the amount of structured and clear information available to the leader. If the situation scores highly for both characteristics, then an autocratic decision-making style is the most effective because it is the most economical and efficient. But if the structure and clarity of the information are insufficient, then a consultative style is preferred. If the leader lacks support from subordinates, then a participatory group decision-making style is the most effective until the leader can gain the subordinates' trust.

A somewhat different perspective on the autocratic, consultative, and group-oriented decision-making styles was taken by Bernard M. Bass and his colleagues.[66] In this construct, five decision-making styles were developed. The "negotiative" and "directive" styles related to Fiedler's task-motivated leader and to the normative decision theorists' autocratic decision-making style. Bass's "consultative," "participative," and "delegative" decision styles related more to Fiedler's relationship-motivated leader and to the normative decision theorists' group-oriented decision making style.

Bass and his colleagues' contribution in this stream of research was the idea that leadership decision-making styles did not function independently of each other, but did seem to cluster around two different sets of behaviors that Fiedler called "task" and "relationship."

Obviously, the contingency model and the normative decision theory are quite parallel. But they diverge on the issue of whether or not leaders can change their personal psychological stripes. On the one hand, the normative decision theorists appear to assume that a leader can move from an autocratic to a group style with little effort, if that is what the situation demands. Contingency modelists, on the other hand, see the task-motivated leader and the relationship-motivated leader as quite basic to the concept of self, and for a leader to be able to don one persona and forsake the other would be difficult at best, and perhaps impossible.

This issue has yet to be resolved, but it has some significant implications. For one, if the contingency modelists are correct, then it is in the best interest of leaders to find followers who match their own task or relationship motivations. If the normative decision theorists are correct, however, then the field of leadership training could experience a rejuvenation, for if decision-making styles can be changed to meet the requisites of a particular small-group situation, then leaders need only be trained in how to recognize various types of situations that occur in small groups, and change their behavior accordingly.

Transactional Approaches. A second major component of the small-group approach to leadership is transactional analysis. Unlike the contingency models, which concentrate only on the problems confronting the leader in dealing with a small group, transactional approaches also analyze the leader's subordinates and the problems confronting them.

The basis of transactional approaches is the "vertical dyad linkage theory," developed initially by George Graen and his colleagues.[67] Vertical dyad linkage theory emphasizes the relationship of the leader with each of his or her individual subordinates; Graen called this relationship the "dyadic linkage." Each subordinate develops a special "exchange relationship" with his or her leader; some subordinates are considered to be "in group subordinates," while others are "out group subordinates," who are less trusted by their leaders.

The vertical dyad linkage notion implicitly relies, as much of leadership theory does, on what social psychologists call "attribution theory." Attribution theory deals with those rational processes that form the basis of people's judgment of each other. One of the major aspects of these interpersonal judgments is the tendency of an observer to develop a causal explanation for someone else's behavior. These explanations will often center on whether the behavior was determined by factors that are internal to the person being judged, such as his or her ability and dedication, or factors external to the person, such as outside management pressures or "luck."[68]

Research indicates that when people make a judgment about someone else, they tend to attribute a person's behavior to internal causes.[69] These judgments are highly biased and personal, and often people are judged by others on the basis of circumstances over which they have no control. Studies indicate that supervisors render more negative judgments, and focus these negative judgments on a subordinate's internal attributes (*i.e.,* poor performance is the subordinate's "own fault") when the negative results of a subordinate's acts are more severe. For example, researchers in one study asked nursing supervisors to judge a hypothetical situation in which a nurse left a railing down on a patient's bed. The researchers found that if, in the hypothetical situation, the patient fell out of the bed, the nursing supervisors gave the nurse a much more negative rating than in those situations in which the patient did not fall out of the bed.[70]

Path-goal theory, another permutation of the literature on leadership, has evolved in part as the result of work in the areas of dyadic linkages and attribution theory. Path-goal theory deals with the effects that leader behavior has on the motivation and satisfaction of subordinates, rather than on larger issues of decision making and group performance. Researchers in this area have found that consideration behavior by a leader is most effective when a follower's job is distasteful or boring, while structuring or task oriented behavior by the leader is most effective when a subordinate's job is unstructured.[71] Studies in the path-goal tradition found that subordinates who scored relatively high on scales that measured the intensity of dogmatic beliefs responded better to leaders who engaged in high levels of task-oriented structuring behavior. But followers who scored relatively low on the same scales performed better when the leader displayed consideration behaviors.[72] A similar investigation found that subordinates who showed a high need for personal growth in their jobs did not like a structured, task- oriented approach under any conditions, even when the task at hand was quite unstructured. By contrast, followers who showed relatively low levels of need for personal growth did not respond to consideration behaviors on the part of a leader; this seemed to be the case because these kinds of subordinates were happy in what amounted to boring, routine work.[73]

The Leader and the Organization, 1965–present

In the late 1970s, after an extended hiatus, the problem of leading organizations (as opposed to individuals and small groups) began to surface as an object of research.

Organization theory, perhaps more than other social sciences, tends to reflect its times. In the early years of the twentieth century, its focus was on the production line and human productivity. Organization theory was, in many respects, an adjunct of American industrialism.

In the 1930s and 1940s, the field became enamored with science and psychology; scientific "principles" of management were constantly being "discovered," and the field of administration busied itself with writing the literature that later became known as "cow psychology." ("Cow psychology" is the disparaging term that has been applied to many studies in human relations on the grounds that such research assumes that workers in organizations are perceived by researchers as being comparable to a herd of cows, and "cow psychology" willingly provides management with the means of moving the "herd" in the direction it wishes.)

From the late 1950s through the early 1970s, organization theory emphasized such concepts as democratic decision making and participatory management. In this stream, all workers were seen as largely equal—each was an individual psycho-

logical and social actor possessing a unique set of motivations—and researchers, as a result of this assumption, found the concept of leadership to be largely passé, and possibly counterproductive. In retrospect, this emphasis can be seen as a reflection of an era in American history in which authority and leadership were questioned at all levels of society. One consequence, however, of ignoring the area of leadership (and, by inference, the notion of power and its exercise in organizations) was to leave the topic of organizational leadership to social psychologists interested in small-group behavior. Even today the concept of leadership is approached by organization theorists with circumspection, and is defined in passive terms. For example, leadership is "the degree to which the behavior of a group member is perceived as an acceptable attempt to influence the perceiver..."[74] Or another definition: "the process of leadership is the use of noncorrosive influence..."[75] Currently, however, the disinclination of organization theorists to examine the phenomenon of organizational leadership seems to be in remission.

Leadership Competencies and the Organizational Hierarchy. As with most generalizations, there are exceptions. For example, a few organization theorists, most of whom were associated with business administration, were attempting as early as the mid-1960s to link leadership competencies (*i.e.*, knowledge, abilities, and "traits") with concepts of organization hierarchy.[76] Perhaps the best known of these efforts is *The Social Psychology of Organizations*, by Daniel Katz and Robert Kahn, which appeared in 1966.[77] Katz and Kahn argued that different levels of the organizational hierarchy required different kinds of leadership talent. At the top, for instance, leaders were needed to make political and strategic decisions of large magnitude, and this required a far- ranging knowledge of the organization and a stylistic "gift of grace." Middle managers functioned largely as lawyers and teachers, interpreting directives and explaining them to other members of the organization. Here human relations skills were paramount. Lower-level managers dealt with the organization as it existed, and required technical knowledge of how it worked. Table 5-3 summarizes the basic concepts articulated by Katz and Kahn.

TABLE 5-3 Leadership/Management Function and Ability/Skill Emphases as a Function of Organizational Level

Level or Zone of Organization	Type of Leadership/Management Function or Pattern	Ability/Skill Emphases	
		Cognitive (Knowledge Based)	Affective (Attitudinally Based)
Top	Organization: Creations and alterations in strategic and policy decisions and organizational design	Total organization/ external and system control	Charisma: Gift of grace aura
Middle	Interpolation: Supplementing and "filling out" of top level strategy/ policy and organizational design decision	Subsystem perspective: Orientation upward to superiors and downward to subordinates	Integration of formal role requirements with face-to-face interactions: Human relations skills
Lower	Administration: Use of existing structure	Technical knowledge and understanding of policies and rules	Concern with equity in use of rewards and sanctions

Source: Barbara Kellerman, ed., *Leadership: Multidisciplinary Perspectives* (Englewood Cliffs, N.J.: Prentice-Hall, 1984), p. 122. Adapted from Daniel Katz and Robert Kahn, *The Social Psychology of Organizations*, 2nd ed. (New York: John Wiley, 1978), p. 539.

Another attempt to relate hierarchy to leadership deals with the leaders' competencies in the areas of administration, human relations, and technology. This approach is quite similar to that of Katz and Kahn's, and suggests that administrative skills are needed more by top-level managers, while human relations and technical competencies have greater utility for middle and lower- level managers.[78]

Contingency/Transactional Approaches and Organizational Leadership. A more recent approach undertaken by organization theorists working in the area of leadership has been to adopt the contingency model, originally developed by Fiedler, and expand it to the larger organizational setting. The work by Rosemary Stewart is especially useful in this respect.[79] She describes the kinds of contingencies with which leaders must deal in managing large organizations, they are the following: *demands*, or what anyone in the job must do in order to keep the job—that is, the minimum description of the manager's job; *constraints*, or factors both inside and outside the organization that limit what a leader can do, such as laws, unions, and technologies; and *choices*, or the opportunities extant for leaders in similar jobs to do different work and to do it in different ways

from their colleagues. Demands and constraints may limit choices, but if leaders modify existing demands and constraints, then new choices can be made available. Key choices include what Stewart calls "domain choices," or "the area in which the manager gets involved and seeks to have an influence," and "contact choices," or the kinds of people with whom the leader chooses to interact. The significance of Stewart's work is that she moves away from the leader's relations with a small group of subordinates, and expands the leader's role in dealing with outside groups, superiors, and organizational actors who are on the same hierarchical level as the leader.

A variation of Stewart's work is provided by John R. Schermerhorn, Jr., James G. Hunt, and Richard N. Osborn, who have developed what they call the "multiple influence model of leadership."[80] As with Stewart, an effort is made to conceptually capture a broader range of contingencies, and thus expand the contingency model from the small group to the whole organization. In addition to the subordinate, task, and group variables that are dealt with in the standard contingency model, Schermerhorn, Hunt, and Osborn mix in the organization's environment, context, and structure. Specifically, these new contingencies furnished by the multiple influence model includes *environmental complexity*, which refers to conditions outside the organization or work unit; *contextual complexity*, which deals with size and technology; and *structural complexity*, which refers to the structure of the organization and how demanding the requirements for control and coordination are. Schermerhorn, Hunt, and Osborn relate these contingencies to the various leader behaviors that have been identified by earlier theorists, such as task behaviors and consideration behaviors, but they go further by explaining how leadership influences organizational outcomes, and how leaders themselves are influenced by organizational contingencies. The multiple influence model of leadership also uses the notions of "required behavior" (which is analogous to Stewart's idea of "demands"), and "discretionary leadership" (which corresponds to Stewart's notion of "choices").

Resurrecting Max: Charisma and the Organization. Perhaps the newest area of research by organization theorists on leadership represents, in some ways, a return to the thinking of Max Weber. Increasingly, charisma and "symbols" are becoming a focus of scholarly concern. These efforts have little to do with the contingency model, but try to make sense of more mystical topics, such as the ability of a leader to transform organizations through a "gift of grace."[81]

Some of the more systematic work in this area has been written by Robert House. Leaders who have charisma, according to House, are those "who by force of their personal abilities are capable of having a profound and extraordinary effect on followers.... [and] is usually reserved for leaders who by their influence are able to cause followers to accomplish outstanding feats."[82] House lists the characteristics of charismatic leaders as being dominance, self-confidence, and a strong conviction in the moral righteousness of his or her beliefs. Charismatic leaders exhibit behaviors that focus on role modeling, image building, goal articulation, confidence, the making of demands that reflect high expectations, and the arousal of motivation in followers. The charismatic leader creates an organizational culture in which symbols, ranging from certain kinds of memoranda to certain kinds of carpets, play a prominent role.

In an effort to "demystify charisma," Jay A. Conger and Rabindra N. Kanungo tried to isolate the empirical differences between charismatic and noncharismatic leaders. In contrast to a noncharismatic leader, a charismatic leader is opposed to the status quo, possesses an "idealized vision" of the future, incurs great personal risk and cost, is expert in using unconventional means to transcend the existing order, is far more sensitive to the task environment, articulates goals strongly, is elitist and entrepreneurial, and can transform people in a way that they become committed to the radical changes he or she advocates.[83]

Welcome back, Max.

The theory of organizational leadership is taking new and interesting directions. One scholar sums up the situation neatly: "We can now look back on over seventy years of scientific research on leadership.... The various theories say much the same thing in slightly different ways, and advocates engage in quibbling over relatively minor differences.... The last twenty years of research has reinforced and clarified certain common threads, and the study of leadership stands poised for a thrust into a new era of growth."[84]

LEADING THE PUBLIC ORGANIZATION

The preceding discussion of leadership has been, admittedly, somewhat academic. How does one use the literature of leadership? Does that literature work for the public organization as well as the private one?

In a useful review, Mark A. Abramson reduces the literature of organizational leadership to a practical formula for the public administrator: leadership equals vision, communication, and hard work.[85] Certainly Abramson's formula reflects the research that we have reviewed here. But how well does it work in the public sector?

Vision—"the presentation of an alternative future to the status quo"[86]—is not all that easily formed in the public sector, where both the status quo and the agency's future are legislated. Perhaps more important, public agencies, at least at the federal level, are increasingly likely to be headed by short-term political appointees; rarely are such men and women visionaries. Career public administrators, by contrast, often do have a vision for their agency, but are frequently fated to be "number twos," not "number ones." "And 'number twos' do not have visions or, at least, do not go around shouting about them."[87] This "topping out" of many career public administrators at a rung short of the top position in an agency appears, it should be pointed out, to be less the case in local and state governments than in the federal one; at the subnational levels, the ability to articulate a vision for the public organization may be greater than at the national level.

Communicating the vision, as noted, can also be more difficult in the public sector than in the private one. Not only does the "number two" phenomenon impair communication, but so does much of the traditional lore of the public administrator—that is, the need to be "neutral," to be "removed from politics" (and politics are, in essence, communication), and, to recall Louis Brownlow's famous dictum, the need to cultivate "a passion for anonymity." These values have not enhanced the propensity of leaders of public organizations to communicate their vision of an alternative future, although many public administrators nonetheless have done so, and quite effectively.[88]

Abramson's third component of leadership is hard work, and here many public administrators excel, in part because public administration is intrinsically demanding and inspiring. Consider the example of James Forrestal, who, when secretary of defense, "worked his staff seven days straight. When he left his office at 10:30 p.m. on Sunday, he told them to have a nice weekend."[89]

Vision, communication, hard work. These are the elements of leadership, irrespective of sector, public or private. Nevertheless, as with other facets of public organizations, the chore of administrative leadership in the public sector seems to be more challenging and difficult than in the corporate world.

NOTES

[1] William H. Whyte, *The Organization Man* (New York: Simon & Schuster, 1956).

[2] Erving Goffman, "The Characteristics of Total Institutions," in *Symposium on Preventive and Social Psychiatry*, sponsored by the Walter Reed Institute of Research (Washington, D.C.: U.S. Government Printing Office, 1957), pp. 43–84.

[3] Sanford M. Dornbusch, "The Military Academy as an Assimilating Institution," *Social Forces*, 33 (May 1955), pp. 316–321.

[4] Charles E. Bidwell and Rebecca S. Vreeland, "College, Education and Moral Orientations: An Organization Approach," *Administrative Science Quarterly*, 8 (September 1963), pp. 166–191.

[5] Theodore M. Newcomb, "Attitude Development as a Function of Reference Groups: The Bennington Study," *Readings in Social Psychology*, 3rd ed., Eleanor E. Maccoby, Theodore M. Newcomb, Eugene L. Hartley, eds. (New York: Holt, Rinehart & Winston, 1958), pp. 265–275.

[6] Robert K. Merton, "Bureaucratic Structure and Personality," *Social Forces*, 18 (1940), p. 563.

[7] Ivar Berg, "Do Organizations Change People?" *Individualism and Big Business*, Leonard Sayles, ed. (New York: McGraw-Hill), p. 62.

[8] See, for example, the following works: Chester I. Barnard, *The Functions of the Executive* (Cambridge, Mass.: Harvard University Press, 1938); Herbert A. Simon, *Administrative Behavior: A Study of Decision-Making Processes in Administration Organizations*, 3rd ed. (New York: The Free Press, 1976); James G. March and Herbert A. Simon, *Organizations* New York: John Wiley, 1958); Richard M. Cyert and James G. March, *A Behavioral Theory of the Firm* (Englewood Cliffs, N.J.: Prentice-Hall, 1963); and James D. Thompson, *Organizations in Action: Social Science Bases of Administrative Theory* (New York: McGraw-Hill, 1967).

[9] Herbert A. Simon, *Models of Man, Social and Rational* (New York: John Wiley, 1957).

[10] Among the major contributors to the psychology of adult development are: Carl G. Jung, *The Integration of Personality* (London: Kegan Paul, 1940); Erik Erikson, *Childhood and Society* (New York: Norton, 1950); Daniel J. Levinson, et al, *The Seasons of a Man's Life* (Knopf, 1978); Roger Gould, *Transformations: Growth and Change in Adult Life* (Simon & Schuster, 1978); and George E. Vaillant, *Adaptation to Life* (Boston: Little, Brown, 1977).

The following discussion relies largely on these excellent synopses: Harry Levinson, "A Second Career: The Possible Dream," *Harvard Business Review*, 61 (May/June 1983), pp. 122–129; Harold L. Hodgkinson, "Adult Development: Implications for Faculty and Administrators," *Educational Record*, 55 (Fall 1974), pp. 263–274; and Richard L. Schott, "The Psychological Development of Adults: Implications for Public Administration," *Public Administration Review*, 46 (November/December 1986), pp. 657–667.

[11] Erikson, *Childhood and Society*, pp. 270–271.

[12] Gould, *Transformations*, p. 294.

[13] Vaillant, *Adaptation to Life*, p. 234.

[14] Erikson, *Childhood and Society*, p. 269.

[15] Manfred Kets de Vries, et al., "Using the Life Cycle to Anticipate Satisfaction at Work," *Journal of Forecasting* (Spring 1984), pp. 161–172; Manfred Kets de Vries and Danny Miller, *The Neurotic Organization* (San Francisco: Jossey-Bass, 1985); and Manfred Kets de Vries, ed., *The Irrational*

Executive: Psychoanalytic Studies in Management (New York: International Universities Press, 1984).

[16] Daniel Levinson, "The Psychosocial Development of Men in Early Adulthood and the Mid-Life Transition" (Mimeograph, New Haven, Conn.: Yale University, 1973), as quoted in Hodgkinson, "Adult Development," p. 266.

[17] Dee W. Henderson, "Enlightened Mentoring: A Characteristic of Public Administration Professionalism," *Public Administration Review*, 45 (November/December 1985), pp. 857–863.

[18] Levinson, et al., *The Seasons of a Man's Life* (New York: Knopf, 1978), p. 79.

[19] *Ibid.*, and Vaillant, *Adaptation to Life*.

[20] Levinson, et al., *The Seasons of a Man's Life*, p. 320.

[21] Vaillant, *Adaptations to Life*, p. 228.

[22] Michael Maccoby, *The Leader* (New York: Simon & Schuster, 1981), p. 221.

[23] Much of this discussion is based on Schott, "The Psychological Development of Adults," pp. 663–665.

[24] Geert Hofstede, "Motivation, Leadership, and Organization: Do American Theories Apply Abroad?" *Organizational Dynamics*, 9 (Summer 1980), p. 43.

[25] Harold L. Wilensky, *Organizational Intelligence* (New York: Basic Books, 1967), pp. 110–129.

[26] The failure of the Hubble Space Telescope provides an unfortunate reminder that organizations do not learn, people learn. Launched in 1990 at a cost of $1.5 billion, it soon became evident that much of what Hubble was designed to do could not be accomplished because the telescope's mirrors had been improperly ground and inadequately tested before launching. Like the Nazis' approach to radar development, the Hubble was designed and built at several different sites by different corporations, which appear to have been selected, in part, as a means of resolving turf wars within the National Aeronautics and Space Administration.

[27] Michel Crozier, *The Bureaucratic Phenomenon* (Chicago: University of Chicago Press, 1964).

[28] *Ibid.*, p. 223.

[29] *Ibid.*, p. 236.

[30] Hofstede, "Motivation, Leadership, and Organization," p. 44. But see also: Hofstede's *Culture's Consequences: International Differences in Work-Related Values* (Beverly Hills, Calif.: Sage, 1980).

In "Motivation, Leadership, and Organization," Hofstede observes (on p. 44), "The fact that data obtained within a single MNC [multinational corporation] have the power to uncover the secrets of entire national cultures can be understood when it's known that the respondents form well-matched samples from their nations: They are employed by the same firm...; their jobs are similar (I consistently compared the same occupations across the different countries); and their age categories and sex composition were similar—only their nationalities differed. Therefore...the [only] general factor that can account for the differences in the answers is national culture."

[31] *Ibid.*, p. 45.

[32] *Ibid.*, p. 49.

[33] *Ibid.*, p. 55.

[34] *Ibid.* A review of international applications of (American-originated) organization development (OD) techniques—techniques that are predicated on Maslow's assumptions about human needs—certainly lends credence to this conclusion. See: Alfred M. Jaeger, "Organization Development and National Culture: Where's the Fit?" *Academy of Management Review*, 11 (January 1986), pp. 178–190. In fact, "cultural" differences, in Jaeger's view, have accounted for the failure of OD applications *within* the United States! Jaeger cites studies (pp. 183–184) indicating that OD is more successful in Southern California than in New England, and that many of its operating premises are "not natural" in the U.S. State Department.

[35] Hofstede, "Motivation, Leadership, and Organization," p. 58.

[36] *Ibid.*, p. 57.

[37] *Ibid.*, p. 59.

[38] *Ibid.*, pp. 59–60.

[39] *Ibid.*, p. 60.

[40] Gordon Tullock, *The Politics of Bureaucracy* (Washington, D.C.: Public Affairs Press, 1965); Alvin W. Gouldner, "Cosmopolitans and Locals: Toward an Analysis of Latent Social Roles," *Administrative Science Quarterly*, 2 (December 1957 and March 1958), pp. 281–306 and 444–480; Victor A. Thompson, *Modern Organization* (New York: Knopf, 1961); Anthony Downs, *Inside Bureaucracy* (Boston: Little, Brown, 1967); and Dwaine Marvick, *Career Perspectives in a Bureaucratic Setting*, University of Michigan Governmental Studies No. 27 (Ann Arbor, Mich.: University of Michigan Press, 1954).

[41] See, for example, Jerald Hage and Robert Dewar, "Elite Values versus Organizational Structure in Predicting Innovation," *Administrative Science Quarterly*, 18 (September 1973), pp. 279–290; Jan L. Pierce and Andre I. Delbecq, "Organization Structure, Individual Attitudes, and Innovation," *Academy of Management Review*, 2 (January 1977), pp. 27–37; Everett M. Rogers, *Diffusion of Innovation*, 3rd ed. (New York: The Free Press, 1983); and John R. Kimberly and Michael J. Evanisko, "Organizational Innovation: The Influence of Individual, Organizational, and Contextual Factors on Hospital Adoption of Technological and Administrative Innovations," *Academy of Management Journal*, 24 (December 1981), pp. 689–712.

[42] Roy L. Lewicki, "Organizational Seduction: Building Commitment to Organizations," *Organizational Dynamics*, 10 (Autumn 1981), pp. 16–19.

[43] Donna M. Randall, "Commitment and the Organization: The Organization Man Revisited," *Academy of Management Review*, 12 (July 1987), p. 467. For a lucid discussion of how organizations are able to achieve intense levels of loyalty from their employees, see: Patricia A. Adler and Peter Adler, "Intense Loyalty in Organizations: A Case Study of College Athletics," *Administrative Science Quarterly*, 33 (September 1988), pp. 401–417.

[44] Thomas S. Robertson and Yoram Wind, "Organizational Cosmopolitanism and Innovativeness," *Academy of Management Journal*, 26 (June 1983), p. 337.

[45] Adler and Adler, "Intense Loyalty in Organizations," p. 415.

[46] Downs, *Inside Bureaucracy*; and Marvick, *Career Perspectives in a Bureaucratic Setting*.

[47] Max Weber, *From Max Weber*, H. H. Gerth and C. Wright Mills, eds. (New York: Oxford University Press, 1946).

[48] James D. Mooney and Alan C. Reiley, *The Principles of Organization* (New York: Harper & Row, 1939).

[49] Amitai Etzioni, *Modern Organizations* (Englewood Cliffs, N.J.: Prentice-Hall, 1964).

[50] Philip Selznick, *TVA and the Grass Roots* (Berkeley, Calif.: University of California Press, 1949).

[51] John P. Kotter, "What Leaders Really Do," *Harvard Business Review*, 68 (May/June 1990), p. 104. See also Kotter's *A Force for Change: How Leadership Differs from Management* (Glencoe, Ill.: The Free Press, 1990).

[52] Kotter, "What Leaders Really Do," p. 104.

[53] As we observe later in this discussion, there was another reason why organization theorists were slow to study leadership: the disinclination among social scientists generally from the late 1950s through the early 1970s to write dispassionately about the use of power and authority—phenomena that are conceptually inseparable from the phenomenon of leadership.

There is still a notable reluctance among social scientists to give leaders much credit for organizational performance one way or the other, although this is changing. See, for example, Alan Berkeley Thomas, "Does Leadership Make a Difference to Organizational Performance?" *Administrative Science Quarterly*, 33 (September 1988), pp. 388–400. Thomas's empirical study concludes that it does.

[54] Much of the following discussion is based on two excellent reviews of the literature on organizational leadership: Martin M. Chemers, "Social, Organizational, and Cultural Context of Effective Leadership," in *Leadership: Multidisciplinary Perspectives*, Barbara Kellerman, ed. (Englewood Cliffs, N.J.: Prentice-Hall, 1984), pp. 91–112; and James G. Hunt, "Organizational Leadership: The Contingency Paradigm and Its Challenges," in *ibid.*, pp. 113–138.

[55] Henry Mintzberg, *The Nature of Managerial Work* (New York: Harper & Row, 1973).

[56] Larry D. Alexander, "The Effect Level in the Hierarchy and Functional Area Have on the Extent Mintzberg's Roles Are Required by Managerial Jobs," *Academy of Management Proceedings* (August 1979), pp. 186–189.

[57] Alan W. Lau, Arthur R. Newman, and Laurie A. Broedling, "The Nature of Managerial Work in the Public Sector," *Public Administration Review*, 40 (September/October 1980), p. 519. The researchers studied 370 top-level (GS 16 through GS 18) civilian executives in the U.S. Navy, two-thirds of whom were in research and development. A comparable study of 225 private sector executives is found in Alexander, "The Effect Level in the Hierarchy and Functional Area Have on the Extent Mintzberg's Roles Are Required by Managerial Jobs."

[58] Lau, Newman, and Broedling, "The Nature of Managerial Work in the Public Sector," p. 519.

[59] See, for example the following research which distinguishes between the work of public executives and private executives: Lyman W. Porter and John Van Maanen, "Task Accomplishment and the Management of Time," in *Managing for Accomplishment*, Bernard Bass, ed. (Lexington, Mass.: Lexington Books, 1970), pp. 180–192; W. Michael Blumenthal, "Candid Reflections of a Businessman in Washington," *Fortune* (January 29, 1979), pp. 33–49; Herman L. Weiss, "Why Business and Government Exchange Executives," *Harvard Business Review*, (July/August 1974), pp. 129–140; Donald Rumsfeld, "A Politician Turned Executive Surveys Both Worlds," *Fortune* (September 10, 1979), pp. 88–94; Hal G. Rainey, Robert W. Backoff, and Charles H. Levine, "Comparing Public and Private Organizations," *Public Administration Review*, 36 (March/April 1976), pp. 233–244; Frank M. Patitucci, "Government Accounting and Financial Reporting: Some Urgent Problems," *Public Affairs Report*, 18 (June 1977), pp. 1–7; David Methé, Jerome Baesel, and David Shulman, "Applying Principles of Corporate Finance in the Public Sector," in *Public Management: Public and Private Perspectives*, James L. Perry and Kenneth L. Kraemer, eds. (Palo Alto, Calif.: Mayfield, 1983), pp. 243–255; Lee C. Shaw and R. Theodore Clark, Jr., "The Practical Differences Between Public and Private Sector Collective Bargaining," *UCLA Law Review*, 19 (August 1972), pp. 867–886; and A. J. Cervantes, "Memoirs of a Businessman-Mayor," *Business Week* (December 8, 1973), pp. 19–20.

[60] Ralph M. Stogdill, "Personal Factors Associated with Leadership: A Survey of the Literature," *Journal of Psychology*, 25 (1948), pp. 35–71.

[61] Kurt Lewin, Ronald Lippitt, and Ralph K. White, "Patterns of Aggressive Behavior in Experimentally Created Social Climates," *Journal of Social Psychology*, 10 (March 1939), pp. 271–299.

[62] For examples of this literature, see: Robert L. Kahn and Daniel O. Katz, "Leadership Practices and Relation to Productivity and Morale," in *Group Dynamics* Dorwin Cartwright and Alvin Zander, eds., (New York: Harper & Row, 1953); and Robert F. Bales and Paul E. Slater, "Role Differentiation in Small Decision Making Groups," in *Family, Localization, and Interaction Processes* Talcott Parsons and Robert F. Bales, eds. (New York: The Free Press, 1945).

[63] Fred E. Fiedler, "A Contingency Model of Leadership Effectiveness," in *Advances in Experimental Psychology*, Vol. 1, Leonard Berkowitz, ed. (New York: Academic Press, 1964); and Fred E. Fiedler, *A Theory of Leadership Effectiveness* (New York: McGraw-Hill, 1967).

[64] Michael J. Strube and Joseph E. Garcia, "A Meta-Analytical Investigation of Fiedler's Contingency Model of Leadership Effectiveness," *Psychological Bulletin*, 90 (September 1981), pp. 307–321.

[65] Victor H. Vroom and Paul W. Yetton, *Leadership and Decision Making* (Pittsburgh, Pa.: University of Pittsburgh Press, 1973); and Victor H. Vroom and Arthur G. Jago, "On the Validity of the Vroom-Yetton Model," *Journal of Applied Psychology*, 63 (April 1978), pp. 151–162.

[66] Bernard M. Bass, et al., "Management Styles Associated with Organizational, Task, Personal, and Interpersonal Contingencies," *Journal of Applied Psychology*, 60 (June 1975), pp. 720–729. See also: Karl W. Kuhnert and Philip Lewis, "Transactional and Transformational Leadership: A Constructive/Developmental Analysis," *Academy of Management Review*, 12

(November 1987), pp. 648–657; and Bernard M. Bass, *Leadership and Performance Beyond Expectations* (New York: The Free Press, 1985).

[67] George Graen and Steven Ginsburgh, "Job Resignation as a Function of Role Orientation and Leader Acceptance: A Longitudinal Investigation of Organizational Assimilation," *Organizational Behavior and Human Performance*, 19 (June 1977), pp. 1–17.

[68] Harold H. Kelley, "The Process of Causal Attribution," *American Psychologist*, 28 (February 1973), pp. 107–128.

[69] Edward E. Jones and Keith E. Davis, "From Acts to Dispositions," in *Advances in Experimental Social Psychology*, Vol. 2 , Leonard Berkowitz, ed. (New York: Academic Press, 1965).

[70] Terrance R. Mitchell and Robert E. Wood, "Supervisors' Responses to Subordinate Poor Performance: A Test of an Attributional Model," *Organizational Behavior and Human Performance*, 25 (February 1980), pp. 123–138.

[71] Robert J. House, "A Path-Goal Theory of Leadership," *Administrative Science Quarterly*, 16 (September 1971), pp. 321–338.

[72] Stanley E. Weed, Terrance R. Mitchell, and William Moffitt, "Leadership Style, Subordinate's Personality, and Task Type as Predictors of Performance and Satisfaction With Supervision," *Journal of Applied Psychology*, 61 (February 1976), pp. 58–66.

[73] Ricky N. Griffin, "Relationships Among Individual, Task Design, and Leader Behavior Variables," *Academy of Management Journal*, 23 (December 1980), pp. 665–683.

[74] Robert House and Mary Baetz, "Leadership: Some Empirical Generalizations and New Research Directions," in *Research in Organizational Behavior*, Vol. 1, Barry Staw, ed. (Greenwood, Conn.: JAI Press, 1979).

[75] Arthur Jago, "Leadership: Perspectives in Theory and Research," *Management Science*, 28 (March 1982), p. 315.

[76] See, for example, Floyd Mann, "Toward an Understanding of the Leadership Role in Formal Organizations," in *Leadership and Productivity* Robert Dubin, George Homans, Floyd Mann, and Delmar Miller, eds. (San Francisco: Chandler, 1965); and Robert Katz, "Skills of an Effective Administration," *Harvard Business Review*, 52 (September/October, 1974), pp. 90–102.

[77] Daniel Katz and Robert L. Kahn, *The Social Psychology of Organizations* (New York: John Wiley, 1966), and 2nd ed. (New York: John Wiley, 1978).

[78] Mann, "Toward an Understanding of the Leadership Role in Formal Organizations."

[79] Rosemary Stewart, *Choices for the Manager* (Englewood Cliffs, N.J.: Prentice-Hall, 1982).

[80] John R. Schermerhorn, Jr., James G. Hunt, and Richard N. Osborn, *Managing Organizational Behavior* (New York: John Wiley, 1982).

[81] Examples of some of this literature include: James MacGregor Burns, *Leadership* (New York: Harper & Row, 1978); Bernard Bass, *Stodgill's Handbook of Leadership* (New York: The Free Press, 1981); Robert Dubin, "Metaphors of Leadership: An Overview" in *Leadership: The Cutting Edge* James G. Hunt and Lars Larson, eds. (Carbondale, Ill.: Southern Illinois University Press, 1977); and Henry Tosi, "Toward a Paradigm Shift in the Study of Leadership," in *Leadership: Beyond Establishment Views* James G. Hunt, Uma Sekaran, and Chester Schreisheim, eds. (Carbondale, Ill.: Southern Illinois University Press, 1982).

[82] Robert House, "A 1976 Theory of Charismatic Leadership," in *Leadership: The Cutting Edge*, Hunt and Larson, eds.

[83] Jay A. Conger and Rabindra N. Kanungo, "Toward a Behavioral Theory of Charismatic Leadership in Organizational Settings," *Academy of Management Review*, 12 (November 1987), pp. 637–647.

[84] Chemers, "The Social, Organizational, and Cultural Context of Effective Leadership," p. 105.

[85] Mark A. Abramson, "The Leadership Factor," *Public Administration Review*, 49 (November/December 1989), p. 563.

[86] *Ibid.*, p. 563.

[87] *Ibid.*, p. 564.

[88] James W. Doig and Erwin C. Hargrove, eds., *Leadership and Innovation* (Baltimore, Md.: Johns Hopkins University Press, 1987). Fourteen profiles of career public administrators, who led both their organizations and the nation in their capacities as public administrators, are featured in the book, and all are notable in their skill and enthusiasm in communicating their personal visions through the media.

[89] Cecilia Cornell and Melvyn Leffler, in *ibid.*, p. 374.

PART THREE: Public Management

CHAPTER

6

THE SYSTEMS APPROACH AND MANAGEMENT SCIENCE

Public administration always has been concerned with the techniques of management—what Stephen Bailey called "instrumental theory,"[1] and what political scientists have occasionally referred to as the field's predilection for "nuts and bolts." Like any social science, public administration has its own corpus of methodologies, and since the late 1960s the field's methods have developed in an increasingly separatist and unique way.

There are two reasons for this trend. First, government has been in the forefront of management science in recent years. Planning- Programming-Budgeting received much of its impetus during the early 1960s in the Defense Department under Robert McNamara. Computer-based information storage and retrieval systems have been at least partially developed with the concentrated sponsorship of the National Science Foundation. Systems analysis and management science have been applied in new ways by the National Aeronautics and Space Administration. Operations Research and the Critical Path Method were originated largely as the result of interest displayed by the U.S. Navy. While the talents of business administrators, psychologists, and scientists have contributed significantly to the development of new and more refined administrative techniques, public administrators have been a key element in their evolution.

A second reason for this trend is that public administrationists are aware that the central methodologies of the "mother discipline," political science, are usually irrelevant to practicing government bureaucrats. True, some of the methodologies of political science have utility; an acquaintance with the rudiments of public opinion polling, for example, could be of some use. But it is difficult to see what use a public administrator would have for such techniques as legislative roll call analysis, content analysis, or international aggregate data analysis.

An underlying thesis of this book is that an effective public administrator needs to learn the languages and symbols of other people. By this reasoning, a white administrative analyst in the Equal Employment Opportunity Commission would be well advised to try to understand the languages, symbols, and cultures of African-Americans and Hispanics if he or she wishes to be effective. Similarly, administrators in the Office of Education would benefit both their agency and themselves by learning the jargon of education.

Equality of opportunity and education are fairly particularistic examples, however. When we approach the interrelated topics of systems theory, management science, budgeting, public personnel administration, performance assessment, and public policy analysis, we are dealing with new languages and symbols that *all* public administrators would be well advised to learn. Not to learn them, or attempting to ignore them, renders public administrators very vulnerable indeed. They can be placed in the unenviable position of trying to hide their ignorance (and probably making fools of themselves in the process). They become victims of the "snow jobs" and the jargon of those who are more facile in the idiom of the hour. To resurrect an old but nonetheless valid cliché, knowledge is power. It follows that, while an ability to synthesize and generalize will always be vital to public administrators, they can ill afford to permit administrative power to devolve to technical specialists by dint of their own ignorance of technologies, languages, and symbols.

This is not to say that every public administrator should be as fully steeped in Operations Research, systems theory, statistical analysis, computer science, or whatever, as are the full-time professionals in those fields. But the public administrator should know at least some of the basics of these subjects so that he or she will be able to cut through the verbiage of technical analysis and recognize the underlying value choices that the jargon often obscures. Politics pervades all endeavors, and to recognize the politics of expertise requires an understanding of the languages and the symbols of the experts. All too frequently public administrators have hidden behind the phrase, "We can leave that to the engineers." They can no longer afford to be so flippant, or if they are, then public administrators must accept the consequences of their having taken such a position: the social deficiencies that result when "engineering mentalities" are placed in positions of political power, the dangers of technocracy, the political disregard for human problems by a new managerial elite trained in science but not in social science, and—last but

not least—the undermining of their own usefulness in the governmental hierarchy.

The nuts-and-bolts techniques of public administration that we shall consider in Part Three are not only sophisticated but increasingly vital to the efficient and effective management of the public sector. As society becomes more complex, so must the methods used to regulate it become more sophisticated and complex. Indeed, biological, neurological, and cybernetic theories support this contention. Information theorist W. Ross Ashby's "law of requisite variety" states that regulatory mechanisms must equal in complexity the systems they are designed to control.[2] Thus, the growing sophistication of public administration's traditional hands-on orientation is hardly surprising in view of the country's growing social and technological variety.

A consideration of the methodologies of public administration follows. The emphasis accorded systems theory, its permutations, and the emerging area of program evaluation in public administration, is unusual but needed; it indicates the recent surge of intellectual effort by public administrationists to develop the tools they need to cope with the American social ecology. Budgeting and human resource management also are included in this section. Budgeting is perhaps the most traditional administrative technique of the field, but treating human resource management as a methodology may strike some readers as novel. Yet, it really is a methodology, a technique, an area of professionalized expertise. Finally, these methods have their own politics and values, and these facets shall be considered throughout Part Three.

THE SYSTEMS IDEA

A system is an entity in which everything relates to everything else. To put it another way, systems are composed of components that work together for the objectives of the whole, and the systems approach is merely a way of thinking about these components and their relationships.

In an extraordinarily lucid essay on the topic, C. West Churchman has noted that the management scientist keeps in mind five basic considerations when he or she thinks about systems:[3]

1. The total *objectives* of the system and, relatedly, the measures of performance of the system (in a government agency, the performance measure would be the level of service per dollar of appropriation).

2. The system's *environment*—its fixed constraints (in the same example, the environment would consist of the clients served by the agency, legislative relations, relations with other agencies, and interest groups, among other factors).

3. The system's *resources* (the dollars and personnel in the agency).

4. The system's *components*, and their activities, goals, and performance measures (those subsystems that develop and deliver public policies).

5. The *management* of the system (the decision making that concerns the amount of resources to make available to each subsystem).

Each of these concepts requires some hard, analytical thinking. Although, in one sense, the systems approach is simply common sense made rigorous, successfully analyzing a system is not always easy.

Consider, for example, the first concept, that of objectives. As we noted in Part Two on organization theory, determining the goals (or the rationality) of a system can become complicated. A person who proclaims his or her dedication to public service, for instance, yet seems to be found more often in private enterprise earning money, represents a "system" with two different kinds of objectives. His or her *stated*, or *official*, objective is public service; his or her *real*, or *operational*, objective is earning money. Measuring the performance of his or her operational goal would consist of counting how much money the person has earned. Such, at least, is the way a management scientist would view the situation.

In terms of public administration, one defines the system according to the problem that one wishes to resolve. Often this entails considerable coordination among and revision of disparate systems that have been developed for other kinds of problems. Senator Daniel P. Moynihan, when he was director of the President's Urban Affairs Council, confronted this dilemma in trying to formulate welfare policies for the poor.[4] After considerable analysis, Moynihan and his advisers concluded that the "system" of welfare worked

against its own objective—that of making the country's deprived population less deprived. In fact, Moynihan believed that the War on Poverty, the Aid to Families with Dependent Children program, the Office of Economic Opportunity, and the entire "service- dispensing class" of welfare's big bureaucracy worked far more beneficially for the middle class than for the lower class. The middle class received the jobs spawned by the numerous welfare programs, while the lower class paid with its income taxes, at least in part, the salaries of the welfare bureaucrats. Moreover, the welfare programs stigmatized the recipients, in Moynihan's opinion, by reducing their self-esteem, increasing their psychological and economic dependency on government, and encouraging (albeit unwittingly) an attitude of outright loathing toward welfare "bums" among lower middle-class whites. Moynihan concluded that a more disastrous piece of social engineering could not have been designed had one tried.

To alleviate this situation, Moynihan, in effect, redefined the "system" of social deprivation in America. He did so by including the income tax as a newly recognized variable in the system and by redefining poverty more as a matter of money and less as a matter of lifestyle, which had been the usual emphasis of the welfare bureaucrats and social workers. By redefining America's system of social deprivation to include these variables, Moynihan was able to see the problem in a new light. He proposed that the tax structure be so rigged as to provide every citizen with a minimum annual income. Partly as a result of his analysis, those citizens with annual incomes under the so- called poverty line were exempted from paying any income tax whatsoever. Moynihan also proposed a complicated negative income tax (the Family Assistance Plan), which would have had the Internal Revenue Service supplementing the income of those citizens under the poverty line so that they would have a guaranteed annual income.

The negative income tax was a radical idea; the systems approach tends to come up with politically radical notions on occasion. A Yugoslav Marxist stated that, were the guaranteed annual income to be enacted, it might become the most important piece of social legislation in history. (Partly because of its radicalism, Moynihan's

Family Assistance Plan was defeated twice in the Senate, with the help of both parties.)

Nevertheless, the point stands that very new and fresh solutions to very old and distressing problems can emerge as a result of analysis via the systems approach. Moreover, the example also indicates that any system inevitably is embedded in some larger system. Thus, while a system may work superbly as a discrete entity, it may not work at all in terms of a larger system. This is a common problem, for instance, in computer-based information storage and retrieval systems. Occasionally, an information system, by the nature of its programming, will "define out", that is, exclude, variables that can be of considerable importance to the organization as a larger system. This situation can produce severe organizational dysfunctions.

This leads us to the *Weltanschauung* problem. *Weltanschauung* is a German word meaning "world view," or the underlying belief structure held by a person about how the world works and what makes it go. For example, Theory X and Theory Y represent two different, partial *Weltanschauungen*. Similarly, the personnel in the U.S. Department of Commerce may have a different *Weltanschauung* than the personnel in the Department of Labor. The advantage of the systems approach is that it forces us to formally delineate the differences and similarities between world views. To do this aids in rationalizing the means and ends in an organization. Goals are clarified, means are focused, and efficiency and effectiveness are improved.

THE SYSTEMS DEBATE

The idea of defining the parameters of a system and the notion of a *Weltanschauung* lie at the center of the larger debate about systems theory generally. While we have been discussing the systems approach from the viewpoint of the management scientist (who obviously favors it), there are other points of view and other kinds of analysts who question its utility—who, indeed, are concerned about its dangers. Churchman has categorized these analysts as efficiency experts (primarily the scientific management crowd we reviewed in

Chapter 3), humanists, and antiplanners.[5] We shall consider their arguments in turn.

The Efficiency Approach

The crux of the notion behind efficiency is that there must be one best way to do a job. The words *a job* imply that the overriding concern of the efficiency expert is to complete a subsystemic task with maximum efficiency, and such, in fact, is the case.

The management scientist has no argument with the time-motion expert as far as he or she goes. Conflict arises when what is good for the subsystem becomes bad for the total system. In other words, the management scientist has the broader perspective, and the limited rationale of the efficiency approach is frequently in direct contradiction with the more comprehensive rationality of the systems approach. When the efficiency approach is favored over the systems approach under these circumstances, organizational dysfunctions can result.

Consider Churchman's example of the airport as a case in which the efficiency expert's cost-reduction policy leads to an increase in the total cost of the system. The objective of the efficiency expert is to reduce "wastage" by keeping every piece of equipment in continual operation; to let an airplane sit idle is "waste" in the efficiency expert's terms. Thus the time-motion expert will try to schedule an airplane takeoff and landing every minute (assuming such scheduling would be safe) on each airstrip; such a schedule would maximize the efficient use of airstrips, airplanes, and airport personnel. The subsystem that occupies the efficiency expert's attention in this case is the schedule for airplane use of each airstrip.

A problem exists beyond the vision of the time-motion expert, however, that will cause systemic inefficiency. The efficiency expert is assuming that planes are taking off and landing *every minute*, but in reality they are taking off and landing every minute *on the average*. It is this situation that concerns the management scientist. He or she realizes that wind conditions, differences in the engines of planes, and so forth, cause certain delays and speedups, and that, therefore, airstrip idleness must be balanced against airplane idleness. In the management scientist's view, the efficiency expert fails to note that one inefficiency in the system must be offset by another. Thus, the management scientist brings in probability theory and, by applying it to the airstrip/airplane mix, concludes that if the efficiency expert's one-plane-per-minute recommendation were to be followed, the waiting line of airplanes on each airstrip eventually would increase without limit. Although the airstrip is being used "efficiently," the waiting-time per plane grows increasingly inefficient. As a result, the management scientist might suggest the construction of a new airstrip, even though the existing one is not in use during certain times of the day. Probability theory indicates that the efficiency of the total system would be improved by such an addition.

The Humanist Approach

It is the larger systemic outlook that distinguishes the systems analyst, or management scientist, from the time-motion expert. With the humanist approach, we get the reverse effect. The humanist argues that it is the management scientist who is too narrow in his or her definition of "the system"—or any system. At root in this dispute is a question of values. This aspect distinguishes the humanist's approach from the fundamental difference between the approaches of the management scientist and the efficiency expert—in their case, the difference is one of systemic size, but both sides agree that economic efficiency and effectiveness are the prime values.

The humanist suggests that there is more to "life" (which is essentially the humanist's "system") than economics. He or she argues for human genius, triumph, despair, and all those uniquely human conditions that the system of life encompasses. These variables can never be included in the management scientist's or in the efficiency expert's system, and it is therefore incomplete according to the humanist.

Robert Boguslaw has extended this argument to warn us of the dangers that accompany the application of the systems approach to social problems. He states that the management scientists and the systems analysts are "the new utopians"—that is, they intend to create a theoretically "perfect" world, but one that may define out human prob-

lems in the process. The new utopians are concerned with "people-substitutes" that have neither "souls nor stomachs." Machines will limit human behavior; at best, the individual will become a conditioned, humanoid shell, molded by the use of economic and behavioral data, and designed to fit ever more tightly with the ever rationalizing system being perfected by the systems analysts who manages it.[6]

To this, the management scientist can but reply: I have to analyze on the basis of the data that I can use. True, systems analysis works best when the data are quantifiable, measurable, or weighable, and this condition by itself renders economic (and, to a lesser degree, behavioral) questions important. Economic and behavioral data are more feasible to examine, analyze, and reshuffle than are the less measurable, more elusive humanistic values represented by Boguslaw. In this sense, the planner and management scientist ultimately are concerned with—and limited by—what is feasible. It is not that the new utopians are necessarily antihumanist; rather, they cannot yet quantify those values that the humanist would like them to include as part of the system. When this is tried, the results can be somewhat pathetic. For example, a computer-based college search service once included "campus beauty" as a variable in finding "the right college for the right applicant." "Beauty," however, was determined by the number of trees per acre. That may be one person's definition of beauty, but it is not necessarily everyone's.

The Antiplanning Approach

There are several variants of the antiplanning approach; they all represent a repugnance toward the notions of both systems and analysis. In this aspect, the antiplanners differ from the efficiency experts and the humanists. The efficiency expert values both ideas of systems and analysis, but simply goes about the systems analysis in a more limited way than the management scientist. The humanist also values the concepts of systems and analysis, but wants more variables, usually nonquantifiable variables, included in the process. Not so the antiplanners. But at least they are easily identified, the most common variety is the experientialist. He or she believes that experience in the organization, combined with natural ability, native intelligence, and personal leadership, beats management science every time. This may be true occasionally, but it would be a difficult contention to "prove" either way. There are examples in industry of "experienced" executives who climbed to the top of their corporations (which often were characterized by rigid seniority rules), only to then reject newfangled management science techniques and lead their companies into bankruptcy.

A somewhat more serious version of antiplanning is held by the skeptic. The skeptic is a relativist who asks if anything is really "true." For instance, do Americans have a "better" quality of life now than fifty years ago, or vice versa? Is planning "better" than antiplanning? Both are worthy questions, but they also are sophomoric ones. While skepticism suggests good questions, it does not provide good answers. Perhaps in time answers will be found to these questions, but until that day skepticism does not go very far as an argument for (or against) antiplanning.

Still another proponent of antiplanning is the determinist. The determinist argues that any system is the result of various, often unidentifiable, social forces, and it therefore follows that decision makers in a system do not really make decisions at all, but merely ratify the inevitability of determinism as it affects their organization. Determinism relates to a number of concepts concerning decision making in public administration—for example, satisficing, muddling through, disjointed incrementalism, intuitionism, nondecision making, and the "technostructure." These notions basically argue that systemic decision making is not a reality in public bureaucracies, and they attempt to describe the policy-making process as it "really" is: incremental, fragmented, unanalytic, limited, and disjointed.

From this viewpoint, however, determinism is a statement of fact, not an argument against the systems approach. Thus, the determinist argument is not an argument *against* planning (as are the experiential and skeptical arguments); rather it merely asserts that the systems approach is not here yet. This, of course, may change, and, while it is a dubious proposition at best that human decision makers will ever become computers capable of measuring all systemic variables, it is nonetheless

fair to state that many decision makers would like to become more analytical in their work.

MANAGEMENT SCIENCE: THE PUBLIC EXPERIENCE

Although the evolution of management science techniques has been largely associated with the business schools, public administrationists, as we noted, are increasingly adapting and developing them to the needs of governments. As this process accelerates, governments, in turn, have begun adopting them. Although we tend to emphasize in this section the federal experience with certain techniques of management science, they are clearly making an impact at the local and state level as well; local governments in particular have made significant progress in using them. In part, the burgeoning popularity among local managers over the techniques of management science may have been motivated by a number of reports and studies issued (especially during the 1970s) on the need for more management science at the local level.7

Data indicate that local jurisdictions not only are adopting management science, but are becoming increasingly sophisticated in making judgments about the utility of selected management science techniques in the public sector. Table 6.1 indicates the growth in use of selected management tools by municipalities in 1976, 1982, and 1987. These tools may be categorized as falling under five general categories: techniques focusing on resource and expenditure control, such as Program Budgeting and Zero-Base Budgeting; techniques used to set broad-based goals and objectives, such as Management by Objectives; techniques involving the provision of information and administrative support functions, such as management information systems and performance monitoring systems; techniques aimed at raising the level of efficiency and effectiveness, such as productivity improvement programs; and techniques that focus on assuring individual and group performance, such as incentive programs and productivity bargaining.

As Table 6.1 shows, many of the techniques sampled in the survey are reported to be in use by two-thirds or more of the municipalities responding, and many have shown significantly higher

TABLE 6–1 Reported Use of Selected Management Science Techniques by U.S. Municipalities, 1976, 1982, and 1987

Technique	Percent Reporting Use		
	1976	*1982*	*1987*
	(N=404)	(N=460)	(N=451)
Techniques for Resources and Expenditure Control			
Program, Zero-Base, or Target-Base Budgeting	50%	77%	75%
Techniques for Achieving Broad-Based Goals and Objectives			
Management by Objectives	41	59	62
Techniques for Information Provision and Administrative Support			
Management Information Systems	42	67	76
Performance Monitoring	28	68	67
Techniques for Raising the Level of Efficiency and Effectiveness			
Productivity Improvement	43	67	54
Techniques Designed to Assure Individual and Group Performance			
Management Incentive Program	16	48	64
Productivity Bargaining	10	22	16

Sources: As derived from: Rackham S. Fukuhara, "Productivity Improvement in Cities," *The Municipal Year Book, 1977* (Washington, D.C.: International City Management Association, 1977), pp. 193–200 (for 1976 data); Theodore H. Poister and Robert P. McGowan, "The Use of Management Tools in Municipal Government: A National Survey," *Public Administration Review*, 44 (May/June 1984), p. 218 (for 1982 data); and Theodore H. Poister and Gregory Streib, "Management Tools in Municipal Government: Trends Over the Past Decade," *Public Administration Review*, 49 (May/June 1989), pp. 240–248.

levels of usage by cities over the eleven-year period. The studies from which the table is derived found that population size (cities ranging in population from 25,000 to 1 million were surveyed), region, and form of government did not seem to make any difference in whether a city was a heavy user of modern management science or not. Instead, each technique appears to be judged on its own merits and suitability, and some techniques are seen by the chief executives of the cities that use them as more effective and more easily implemented than others. Budgeting techniques, management information systems, Management by Objectives and revenue forecasting are rated as the most effective among the techniques employed. Productivity improvement programs, incentive systems productivity bargaining, and quality circles generally are considered to be the least effective. By far the most common correlation occurs when a city implements a management technique on a city-wide basis, rather than on a selective basis; when a technique is adopted city-wide, urban administrators are much more likely to view it as effective than when it is used only by a part of the municipal government.[8]

Management science techniques also are enjoying a growing acceptance among state administrators. Table 6.2 indicates the use of selected management science techniques among nearly 850 state administrators in ten states. (An effort has been made to make Table 6.2 comparable with Table 6.1, although the studies did not always use precisely the same categories.) Compared with local administrators, state administrators surpass municipal managers in their use of techniques for achieving broad-based goals and objectives, such as the use of Management by Objectives, but they lag behind local administrators in their use of techniques that are used for resource and expenditure control, for information provision and administrative support, for improving efficiency and effectiveness, and for providing incentives for individual and group performance.

State administrators who use the management science techniques listed in Table 6.2 say that they have garnered the most positive results from the following techniques: surveys of clients,

TABLE 6–2 Reported Use of Selected Management Science Techniques by Ten States, 1984

Technique	Percent Reporting Use[a]
Techniques for Resources and Expenditure Control	
Program Budgeting	41%
Zero-Base Budgeting	46
Inspector-General Units in Agencies	23
Techniques for Achieving Broad-Based Goals and Objectives	
Management by Objectives	66
Authority to Reprogram Funds	29
Techniques for Information Provision and Administrative Support	
Management Information Systems	60
Performance Evaluation and Review Technique	37
Performance Indicators	72
Techniques for Raising Level of Efficiency and Effectiveness	
Productivity Improvement Program	17
Cost/Benefit Analysis	50
Program Evaluation	72
Surveys of Clients	37
Operations Research	15
Project Management	17
Techniques Designed to Assure Individual and Group Performance	
Incentive Programs	
Performance Pay	8
Career Executive Systems	20
Less Civil Service Protection for Middle/Upper Managers	26
Job Enlargement	30
Evening/Saturday Hours	14
Flextime	58
Productivity Bargaining	3

Source: As derived from: Richard C. Elling, "Of Bandwagons and Bandaids: A Comparative Assessment of the Utilization and Efficacy of Management Techniques in State Bureaucracies," (Paper presented at the Annual Meeting of the American Political Science Association, Washington, D.C., August/September 1984), Table 7.

[a]Percentages are percentage of respondents indicating that a particular management science technique was used in their unit or affected their unit. The respondents were 847 middle-to-top-level state administrators in Arizona, California, Delaware, Indiana, Michigan, New York, South Dakota, Tennessee, Texas, and Vermont.

management information systems, Operations Research, professional training, program evaluations, job enlargement, the authority to reprogram funds, cost-benefit analysis, performance indicators, Performance Evaluation and Review Technique, productivity improvement programs, Management by Objectives, flextime, and career executive systems. Among the techniques that garnered the least positive results among state administrators were the following: the elimination of civil service coverage for middle and upper administrators, Zero-Base Budgeting, and users' fees.[9]

One can argue that neither local or state public administrators have adopted management science techniques to the extent that they should. But one should place the matter in perspective; one survey of the use of management science techniques by major corporations found that only 60 percent of management science projects had been "completely" or "mostly" implemented in the private sector.[10] The data indicate, in other words, that there are real impediments (although not necessarily insuperable ones) to the adoption of management science in both the private and public sectors. These include a shortage of time, inaccessibility of data, the usual resistance to change, a response time often necessitated by management science techniques that takes too long to meet management's needs, and a tendency to oversimplify managerial situations by relying solely on quantitative data.[11]

Nevertheless, management science techniques bring with them significant advantages to organizational decision making, including the ability to break down complex problems into smaller parts that can be more easily analyzed, the increased likelihood of making better decisions because of the systematic thought enforced by the use of management science techniques, and the ability to assess alternatives more clearly. But the limitations include frequent high costs, inapplicability to a number of problems, poor data bases, and a tendency to divorce technique from reality. Management science is most effectively implemented when top management sponsors it, when responsibility for the programs is clearly assigned, when managers have already participated in the implementation of management science techniques, when the technical aspects of management science are not permitted to dominate decision making, when data collection is done rapidly, and when record keeping is accurate.[12]

MANAGEMENT SCIENCE: AN OVERVIEW OF SELECTED TECHNIQUES

There is a variety of formats that can be used to sort out the various techniques of management science. In this section, we use our own method, but it is worth keeping in mind that all management science techniques rely on five basic steps:

1. Diagnosis of the problem, including the identification of the problem's central parts and an assessment of whether the application of management science techniques will justify the costs of applying them to the problem.

2. Formulation of the problem, or the defining of the problem in operational terms, and the identification of those variables in the problem that are subject to managerial control and those that are not.

3. Model building, or the relating of major elements of the problem to each other in terms of how the problem is diagnosed and defined.

4. Analysis of the model, including the combination of resources and values that best meet the objectives of management. Often, both the model and the analysis portion of management science involve computer applications.

5. Finally, the findings provided by management science must be implemented. In other words, the manager must accept the findings of the specialists of management science techniques if these techniques are to be effective. It helps if line managers participate in the first four steps of management science. One study found that the recommendations of management scientists were implemented four-fifths of the time when managers participated in the development of the recommendations, and only two-fifths of the time when the managers did not participate.[13]

Management science is often labeled Operations Research (OR); however, in this book, we place management science in a somewhat broader perspective so that we may not only address Operations Research as a separate technique, but may discuss as well other methodologies that have been of particular utility to public administration. We consider these in turn.

Operations Research

E. S. Quade has observed that Operations Research (and, for that matter, the other techniques of management science) differs from systems analysis in that it focuses on "efficiency problems in which one can maximize some 'payoff' function that clearly expresses what one is trying to accomplish," rather than trying to clarify alternative policy choices within the system as a whole.[14] Operations Research, in other words, comes into play only *after* value choices have been made. It is used to maximize systemic efficiency and effectiveness within the subsystems represented by those choices. Our prior example of the optimal airstrip/airplane mix problem is also an example of how the management scientist would apply Operations Research, for OR relies on the use of probability theory, queuing techniques, and mathematical model building to allocate and utilize resources maximally within a designated subsystem.

Operations Research got its start and its name in England, primarily during the development of

British radar in the late 1930s. Later OR was brought into the analysis of other kinds of war-related problems. In 1940, an early and elementary Operations Research analysis of British fighter plane losses over France persuaded the English to make the significant decision not to send any more fighters to France. Soon OR was being applied by the Allies in the analysis of bombing runs and their effectiveness and in the analysis of how to boost the "kill ratios" of Nazi submarines.

In the submarine analysis, it was simply a matter of applying rudimentary probability theory. The British were having considerable difficulty with German U-boats in the English Channel. Operations researchers observed that the depth charges of British submarine hunters never exploded until they had sunk at least thirty-five feet below the surface. As Churchman has noted, "what is especially interesting about this story is that the scientists kept asking stupid questions" and in the process recommended that the charges be set to go off closer to the surface. This was done, and the number of destroyed Nazi submarines in the English Channel rose significantly.

Because of these kinds of successes on a variety of battlefronts, by 1945 there was no major Allied command without an OR group of one kind or another. Since World War II, OR has been applied to the problems of bus scheduling, the U.S. Post Office, the Department of Defense, waste management, land use, urban planning, highway safety, education, agriculture, and even birth control. With the advent of computers possessing enormous analytical capacities, the uses and refinements of Operations Research have burgeoned, and its potential application to a variety of problems in public administration is almost limitless.

Operations Research is used most fruitfully in the solution of public administration problems that repeat themselves. Russell L. Ackoff and Patrick Rivett, while noting that there is no "one way" to classify these kinds of managerial problems, nonetheless provide a useful guide. They state that OR may be applied to at least eight kinds of problems.[15]

1. *Inventory*, which involves problems of idle resources—most training problems, for example, can be viewed as inventory problems.

2. *Allocation*, or finding the optimal mix of resources available, jobs to be done, and ways to do those jobs—most budget problems are problems of allocation.

3. *Queuing*, which considers how to get people or material through a service facility in the fastest, most efficient, and most effective way possible—problems relating to bus scheduling are an example.

4. *Sequencing*, which attempts to solve problems relating to performance in a queue—for example, minimizing the total time needed to service a priority group of waiting clients in a queue.

5. *Routing*, or the effort to minimize the distance, time, or cost involved between points. "The traveling salesperson problem" is the classic expression of a routing dilemma, and the objective is to find the shortest, most efficient route for a salesperson to take between cities. It is a simply stated problem, but a difficult one to solve: while there are only six possible routes between four cities, for eleven cities there are 3,700,000 possible routes.

6. *Replacement*, which is the attempt to minimize the costs of replacing items that degenerate or fail with the passage of time—such items may include everything from light bulbs to lathes to labor wastage.

7. *Competition*, or the problems of maximizing returns for one decision maker in the face of rivalry from other decision makers—in terms of public administration, competitive problems arise in the area of foreign policy.

8. *Search*, which involves the optimal method for finding the opportunities and resources needed by a decision maker. Operations Research has been used to routinize search procedures and reduce costs in auditing, in geological explorations, in inspections, and in other areas.

Most OR problems involve mixes of these classifications, and operations researchers have developed or adapted a number of statistical and computer techniques to solve them. Inventory problems, for instance, often employ the use of matrix algebra (in linear programming), and the calculus of variations (in dynamic programming)—and then computer-based simulations for their resolution. Mathematical programming also is used in the solution of allocation problems, notably linear, nonlinear, stochastic, parametric, and dynamic programming. Queuing problems also require some sophisticated mathematics, particularly probability theory and the use of differential and integral equations. Sequencing problems involve simulation, Performance Evaluation and Review Technique (PERT), and the Critical Path Method (CPM). Dynamic programming and relatively simple calculus often are used for replacement problems, and gaming is a favored type of simulation used in the analysis of competitive problems. We shall consider PERT, CPM, simulation, and game theory in greater detail in this chapter because they have been used to a significant extent in the solution of public administration problems.

Before continuing this brief review of Operations Research, it is worth reemphasizing that OR is "value-free." That is, it can be, and has been, used for virtually any purpose. While mail deliveries have been speeded by OR, Sir C. P. Snow has observed that Sir Winston Churchill used Operations Research in World War II to optimize the effects of British bombing strikes on the civilian population of Germany.[16] (Churchill wanted revenge, but, fortunately for the German people, his operations researchers overestimated the effects of British bombing raids.) Similarly, operations researchers were asked to calculate the effects that the first "firestorm" bombs would have on Tokyo. (Unfortunately for the Japanese, because the OR workers neglected to consider adequately the frailties of Japan's wood- and-paper domestic architecture, among other variables, operations researchers underestimated the awesome destruction wrought.) Finally, "kill ratios," "body counts," "overkill," and the other unsavory phrases of the more recent Vietnam conflict were derived from the concepts of Operations Research. Amorality is an inescapable facet of efficiency, and it is Operations Research that is used to maximize efficiency scientifically. Thus, it is useful to comprehend some of the overlapping techniques of OR and management science in order to enhance our capability of perceiving the values that underlie the jargon of administrative techniques. Path Analysis provides a useful example.

On Efficiency in Public Administration

Rudolph Hoess was a Nazi SS captain who, in his own words, "personally arranged the gassing of two million persons" during a two-and-a-half year period in the Auschwitz concentration camp. The following passage concerns Hoess's feelings about being "a good German," following orders, and being efficient in the execution of his duties. It illustrates that "value-free" management science can be used for any purpose.

So, as Hoess himself has written, "by the will of the Reichsfuhrer SS, Auschwitz became the greatest human extermination center of all time." He considered that Himmler's order was "extraordinary and monstrous." Nevertheless, the reasons behind the extermination program seemed to him to be right. He had been given an order, and had to carry it out. "Whether this mass extermination of Jews was necessary or not," he writes, "was something on which I could not allow myself to form an opinion, for I lacked the necessary breadth of view." Hoess felt that if the Fuhrer himself had given the order for the cold, calculated murder of millions of innocent men, women, and children then it was not for him to question its rightness.

What Hitler or Himmler ordered was always right. After all, he wrote, "Democratic England also has a basic national concept: 'My country, right or wrong!'" and what is more, Hoess really considered that was a convincing explanation. Moreover he thought it strange that "outsiders simply cannot understand that there was not a single SS officer who could disobey an order from the Reichsfuhrer SS."...His basic orders, issued in the name of the Fuhrer, were sacred. They brooked no consideration, no argument, no interpretation....it was not for nothing that during training the self-sacrifice of the Japanese for their country and their Emperor, who was also their god, was held up as a shining example to the SS....

Hoess's own account of his misdeeds is not only remarkable for what he has described but also for the way in which he has written it. The Nazis, Hoess among them, were experts in the use of euphemisms and when it came to killing they never called a spade a spade. Special treatment, extermination, liquidation, elimination, resettlement, and final solution were all synonyms for murder, and Hoess has added another gem to the collection, "the removal of racial-biological foreign bodies."...

Hoess was a very ordinary little man. He would never have been heard of by the general public had not fate decreed that he was to be, perhaps, the greatest executioner of all time. Yet to read about it in his autobiography makes it all seem quite ordinary. He had a job to do and he carried it out efficiently.

Although eventually he appears to have realized the enormity of what he did, he nevertheless took pride in doing it well....

Lord Russell of Liverpool
Commandant of Auschwitz

Path Analysis

There are several variations of Path Analysis. Performance Evaluation and Review Technique is one version that is used to coordinate complex projects; another variant is the Decision Tree, which is used to clarify policy options. We consider both in turn.

Performance Evaluation and Review Technique (PERT) and the Critical Path Method (CPM). PERT, or CPM, sometimes called "network analysis," goes by many names, but essentially it is the same technique. PERT was developed in the late 1950s by the Booz, Allen, and Hamilton consulting firm for the U.S. Navy as a method of assuring that the incredibly complex task of constructing the first Polaris missiles and their nuclear submarines would be completed on schedule. PERT more than fulfilled expectations; the Polaris system was completed almost two years ahead of the scheduled target date. Since then, PERT has been and is used by a variety of government agencies (particularly the research-and-development oriented agencies) for a variety of systems analysis and scheduling purposes. All of the U.S. military services, the National Aeronautics and Space Administration, the Federal Aviation Agency, the Nuclear Regulatory Commission, and the Office of Management and Budget among others, had adopted PERT by the early 1960s.

PERT is an effort to specify for the administrator how various parts of a particular project interrelate, especially what parts of the project must first be completed before the remaining parts of the project can be started. For instance, before we can open our front doors for a cocktail party, we first must have glasses and liquor. A PERT chart not only specifies and clarifies this sequence, but gives us the times at which each portion of the overall sequence must be finished in order to keep the whole project on schedule. In its most sophisticated (and computerized) form, a PERT chart can give the administrator the time *and cost* for each part of the project; it is simply a matter of developing a formula of the cost per each unit of time (*e.g.,* days, or hours).

Decision Trees. The purpose of a Performance Evaluation and Review Technique is one of project coordination. A variation of Path Analysis that is less concerned with coordination and focuses more on decision alternatives is called the *Decision Tree.* A Decision Tree assigns numerical values to preferences and to the manager's best judgments regarding the likelihood of certain events occurring in the future.

Let us consider a hypothetical example. A city manager wishes to build a park. He or she has the option of building a large park or a small park. Critical in deciding which size the park should be built is his or her estimate of the probability that the park will be used a great deal or not very much.

Just as Performance Evaluation and Review Technique ultimately rests on the average numerical value of some experts' guesses about how long it might take or how much it might cost to complete some activity, the probabilities used in Decision Trees ultimately rest on the best guesses of experts about how many people a park might serve, or the levels of productivity for any given project. Thus, for our park project, a city manager, after consulting with appropriate experts, might guess that a large park has a 60 percent probability of being used intensively, and a 40 percent probability of being used infrequently. By contrast, the manager might guess that a small park would have a 30 percent chance of being used intensively, and a 90 percent chance of being used infrequently.

These estimates would be displayed on a Decision Tree, as shown in Table 6.3. Note that the table also displays the costs of each decision and the anticipated revenues that would result if the assumptions about usage were proven valid. Again, the anticipated revenues are based on best guesses by the manager, and these best guesses about revenues are then combined with the manager's best guesses about prospective usage. Thus, if the manager built a large park that had a 60 percent chance of being used intensively, the annual revenue yield derived from that park would be $90,000. If the large park were not used intensively, the yield would be $32,000 (*i.e.,* $80,000 ξ .4 = $32,000).

At this juncture, the city manager has done the following:

- He or she has estimated what it will cost to build a large park or a small park.
- The manager has further estimated the probability of high or low usage for both a large park and a small park.
- A third estimate has been made about how much a small park and a large park will yield in the way of revenues, and these figures have been hedged, in effect, by marrying them with the estimated probability of high or low usage for each size of park.
- And finally, a likely figure for annual revenues to be derived from each size of park has been arrived at by adding together the two estimates (the high usage estimate plus the low usage estimate) to obtain a figure that represents the city manager's best guess about what the annual revenues for the park will be.

At this point, a fourth estimate is made by the city manager: what it will cost each year to maintain and run the park. The difference between the estimated annual yield and the estimated annual cost becomes the net cost or yield for maintaining the park. In the case we have used, the city manager will recommend to the city council that a large park be built on the grounds that it would lose less money over time than a small park.

TABLE 6–3 Decision Tree for a City Park

Fiscal Estimate Phase 1	Fiscal Estimate Phase 2	Fiscal Estimate Phase 3	Fiscal Estimate Phase 4	
Build a large park: $2 million	High Usage (probability = .6)	Annual Revenue Yield $150,000 × .6 = $ 90,000 + $ 80,000 × .4 = $ 32,000	· Annual Operating Costs	Net Yields (+) or Costs (−)
	Low usage (probability = .4)	$112,000	$125,000	− $13,000
Build a small park: $1 million	High usage (probability = .3)	$75,000 × .3 = $22,500 + $40,000 × .9 = $36,000		
	Low usage (probability = .9)	$58,500	$75,000	− $16,500

Path Analysis: A Contextual Caveat. Both the Performance Evaluation and Review Technique and the Decision Tree are variations of Path Analysis, and both have utility for the administrator. But keep in mind that all the arithmetic we have reviewed rests on out-of-the-hat estimates— educated guesses—nothing more. While Path Analysis is a very valuable tool for clarifying interdependencies in the system and allocating resources accordingly, it nonetheless rests on some person out in the field scratching his or her head and taking a shot at how much time it might take or how much it might cost to complete some activity. If the person in the field knows what he or she is doing, those optimistic (most likely) and pessimistic estimates may be superbly accurate; but if he or she does not know, and must rely on "guesstimates," no amount of algebra is going to help.

While Path Analysis may succeed in making those initial estimates look very impressive and scientific to the uninitiated, all the projections of Path Analysis go back to some people making guesses. At best, those guesses may be educated and based on experience; at worst, they may be fabricated from thin air. While Path Analysis can be extremely useful to the public administrator, its foundation of guesswork should never be obscured by its superstructure of techniques.

Simulations and Games

Another aspect of systems theory and management science involves simulations and games. Both are models of variables and their behavior in the system, and like Path Analysis they attempt to clarify for the decision maker how the system works by abstracting and simplifying it.

From War Games to Management Games. Modern simulations and games got their start in the early war games—chess may have been such a war game.[17] The first true war game was originated in 1798 in the German state of Schleswig, and during the course of the following century two forms of the *Neue Kriegspiel* (as the game was called) evolved: rigid and free. Both versions became popular in the Prussian military academies and had spread to the rest of Europe and to West Point by the end of the nineteenth century.

By World War II, all the major international powers were playing war games, and Japan and Germany were becoming especially adept. At the Total War Research Institute and Naval War College of Imperial Japan, Japan's future actions for the years 1941 to 1943 were gamed during a period of days. Roles were played by members of the military and government elite, and the roles represented included the Italo-German Axis, the Soviet Union, the United States, England, and various eastern powers, including Japan, which, interestingly, was played as a fragile coalition of military, government, and industrial interests. Japan's military groups proved more aggressive than the others in this game, winning most of the internal disputes, and plans for controlling Japan's consumer goods in wartime were developed during the course of the games that were identical to those actually put into effect in Japan on December 8, 1941. Similarly, prior to Hitler's ascension in 1933, the German Reichswehr gamed Germany's future relations with Poland, which was of grave concern to the Germans since their military strength was limited to 100,000 troops by the Treaty of Versailles. Previously, in 1929, Erich von Manstein (later General von Manstein) proposed that the standard war game be expanded to include a political game. The inventiveness of the player representing Poland in alleging German provocations dumbfounded the player representing the German Foreign Ministry, while the procrastination of the League of Nations in coming to German's diplomatic defense was also gloomily enlightening.

By the 1950s similar games and simulations were being played in the Soviet Foreign Office and the U.S. Air Force's Rand Corporation. The U.S. Joint Chiefs of Staff now have a Joint War Games Agency, which has developed TEMPER, for "Technological, Economic, Military, and Political Evaluation Routine," indicating the broadened scope of the historic *Neue Kriegspiel.*

More recently, the use of games and simulations has been extended to a diversity of new fields. Herbert A. Simon and Richard C. Snyder have used it to refine decision-making theory.[18] The American Management Association developed the first popular management game in 1956 after some of its members discovered the use of gaming at the Naval War College, and a number of private corporations have since developed their own variants. Sociology, economics, political science, education, psychology, law, and anthropology also have developed simulations.

Public administration has been using simulations peripherally for a number of years. The field of organization development (described in Chapter 3), in fact, relies on the use of person- to-person simulations and games in a major way as a means of "democratizing" and "opening up" organizations. But public administration's direct use of simulations and games has been fairly recent, although they now are a standard feature at the national conferences of the American Society for Public Administration. Such games have included the "Health Game," involving role playing in the field of providing health services, and "I'm OK—You're OK," which approaches bureaucratic problem solving through transactional analysis.

As we have observed, simulations and games are the playing out of scenarios and involve abstraction, simplification, and substitution; their advantages are economy, the clarification of the phenomena being simulated, reproducibility, and safety. Beyond these features, simulations and games can be categorized according to three distinct types: simple two-person games, computer games, and person-machine games. Each of these games has its own kind of usefulness, although, as we shall see, person-machine games would appear to combine and add to the best of the other two types.

Two-Person Games. Two-person games grew out of social science research in small group theory. As an area of study, small group theory has had a notable impact on public administration, and many of its propositions have been used by organization theorists in human relations and organization development.

Perhaps the most formal, mathematical statement of "the games people play" in small groups is the two-person game as developed by Anatol Rapoport.[19] Two-person games may be either "zero-sum" (one person may win only at the expense of the other), or "non-zero-sum" (both players win or both players lose). This is not quite so simple as it may sound, however, because there are a variety of mixes in terms of relative costs and benefits that are possible, and calculating the maximum win and minimum loss per player often requires the use of some fairly sophisticated mathematics. Thus, we hear such terms used in game theory as "maximin" or "minimax" (which mean the same thing) to denote these kinds of strategic thinking. As Sam Spade put it in *The Maltese Falcon*, "That's the trick, from my side...to make my play strong enough so that it ties you up, but yet not make you mad enough to bump me off against your better judgment."

Prisoner's Dilemma. There is a classic example often used to illustrate the Prisoner's Dilemma, which can be seen as either a zero-sum or a non-zero-sum two-person game: A prosecutor is convinced that two prisoners are partners in a crime, but he cannot prove the guilt of either one on the basis of the existing evidence and needs a confession of their mutual complicity. To get it, the prosecutor separates the prisoners and points out to each of them individually that they may confess or deny the crime. If neither prisoner confesses, both will be booked on some minor charge. If both prisoners confess, the prosecutor will recommend a lighter sentence. If one prisoner confesses and the other does not, the confessor will be freed for turning state's evidence, while the other will be prosecuted to the full extent that the law allows.

Thus, each prisoner can get a maximum payoff by double-crossing his or her partner—that is, by confessing—but only if the other prisoner does not also confess; this would be a zero-sum game, or one player winning at the expense of the other. But if both prisoners should elect to double-cross, both lose—hence, a non-zero-sum game. If both stand fast (*i.e.*, if they have adequate faith in one another to cooperate with each other), then both win something, but each wins less than if he or she had been the only double-crosser. This, too, is a non-zero-sum game. The prisoner's dilemma can be illustrated more formally by the payoff matrix posited in Table 6.4.

The subscript a's and the subscript b's next to each number in the matrix represent the payoff (or lack of it) to Prisoner A and Prisoner B, respectively. Each number stands for years in prison that the prisoner must face for each alternative. For example, if Prisoner A confessed everything and Prisoner B denied everything, then Prisoner A

TABLE 6–4 The Payoff Matrix of Prisoner's Dilemma

		Prisoner B			
		Deny Everything		Confess Everything	
	Deny Everything	I		II	
		2a	2b	10a	0b
Prisoner A					
	Confess Everything	III		IV	
		0a	10b	5a	5b

would get off scot-free and Prisoner B would get the book thrown at him or her, as Quadrant III indicates. Conversely, if both prisoners confessed everything, each would get five years (Quadrant IV), and if both denied everything, each would get only two years (Quadrant I).

The Payoff Matrix. We can understand how the payoff matrix of prisoner's dilemma becomes useful to practicing public administrators when we cast it into relatively everyday circumstances. Table 6.5 indicates how a payoff matrix would be used in a more normal situation of public management. Instead of positing the dilemmas of Prisoner A and Prisoner B, we use the concepts of choice and possible outcomes.

Once again, imagine that a city was considering building a park, and that the city had the choice of building a large park or a small park. The city manager, after investigating the possibilities, would want to array his or her choices regarding a large or small park, and match them with the possibilities of how frequently the park would be used, how much income the city could derive from users' fees, and how much it would cost to maintain the park. For example, if a city built a small

park that was used frequently by many people, the users would be unhappy, the users' fees derived from the park would be low, but then the cost of maintaining the park presumably would be low as well. On the other hand, if a small park were used infrequently, its users would be presumably happy and the cost would remain low, but the income from users' fees also would remain low. With a large park and low usage, the users are pleased with the park, but costs are high and income derived from the park is low. However, with high usage of a large park, the users are reasonably contented, and income is high, offsetting high cost.

Table 6.5 shows these possibilities graphically. It is this kind of clarification that game theory has provided the practicing public administrator.

N-Person Games. Game theory grows more sophisticated when we talk about "non-zero-sum, n-person games"—that is, life. With more than two people, the possibility of coalitions, deals, and bargains emerge, and our matrix waxes infinitely more complex. W. H. Riker[20] has done some of the theoretical work in this area, although Anthony Downs has considered the possibilities of non-zero-sum, n-person games in

TABLE 6–5 A Payoff Matrix in Public Administration

		Possible Outcomes	
		Low Usage	High Usage
C H O I C E S	Large Park	Happy park users; low income; high costs.	Happy park users; high income; high costs.
	Small Park	Happy park users; low income; low costs.	Unhappy park users; low income; low costs.

terms of organizations and in largely nonquantitative language. Downs brings in the "size principle" and contrasts it with the "information effect." The size principle refers to the desirability of the leader of a coalition acquiring only the bare majority needed to win. Such a coalition is optimal, because any members beyond those needed for a winning majority simply make the coalition less easily controlled; thus, the notion arises of the "minimum winning coalition." The information effect relates to the need for "padding": Since information is distorted in organizations, the coalition leader can never be sure that his or her coalition will be big enough to win, so the leader accepts the control of adding members to his or her coalition for the sake of assuring victory.[21]

These ways of thinking play a large role in the newly resurgent field of political economy, or public choice. Political economists ask, how do we measure what the polity "wants"? How do we determine what choice is in the public interest? How do we measure that choice and its alternatives? In this perspective, public policymaking can be viewed as a theory of games, just as the choices that the individual makes in terms of his organization may be seen as an array of zero-sum and non-zero-sum options. Public choice is considered in more detail in Chapter 10.

In the last two paragraphs, we have been digressing from our original two-person game, and instead have been considering more complicated situations. This is easy to do because the two-person game does not take us very far when it comes to developing theoretical models that pertain to real life. In other words, the chief disadvantage of the simple two-person game is just that—it is too simple; it cannot handle more than one or two propositions at once.

Computer Games. To simulate more complex models of society and organizations requires the enormous analytical capacities of the computer. Computer simulations often are used in connection with the problems and techniques associated with Operations Research. Instead of working with problems of human behavior and personality, computer games deal with the operation of large and complicated systems. Occasionally, the formal theorems of game theory are programmed on a computer, as is sometimes done with foreign policy questions: If the United States does this, will the Common Market do that? Obviously, the notions of zero-sum and non-zero-sum games play a significant role in such computer simulations.

Two-person games and computer games both have their uses. A two-person game has the great advantage of dealing directly with real life situations. Although there are elements of artificiality in the laboratory approach to people, the techniques of sensitivity training, T-groups, and role playing are nonetheless more likely to evoke "real" emotions and responses from players simply because they deal with real people. In this sense, the simulation—the model—gains in accuracy and predictive power.

Unfortunately, human-to-human games cannot cope with very complicated models. They cannot consider the nonhuman variables extant in any administrative system, such as office rules or an unanticipated urban riot. A computer simulation, however, can. The "traveling sales representative" simulation, for example, can tell us that there are 3,700,000 different ways to travel among eleven cities, and it can tell us the characteristics of each of these ways. These variables are too rich to be included within the limited theoretical confines of a simple person-to-person game. On the other hand, a computer simulation cannot tell us with very much accuracy just how human beings would react to such data—or, more important, how human and nonhuman variables would interact in the total system. Since all administrative systems include both kinds of components, the ability to model their interactions becomes a critical task for simulations, and it is for this task that person-machine games have been designed. Person-machine games represent an attempt to combine the best features of human-based and machine-based games.

Person-Machine Games. An example of a person-machine game is provided by the American air defense system. In refining this system, a person-machine game was used that simulated both the hardware complex (*i.e.*, radar, interceptor planes, communications, and so forth) and a team whose mission it was to decide whether or not to launch the interceptors on the basis of receiving and judging incoming signals under a variety of conditions. As a result of this simulation, the optimal conditions for the correct player response were discerned, and some of the hardware was modified.

Person-machine games also have been used for sensitizing public policymakers to their administrative environments. The Massachusetts Institute of Technology has, since 1959, conducted such games for high-ranking officials in the Departments of Defense and State, and a person-machine game has been developed at the University of North Carolina for training Peace Corp volunteers.

In sum, simulations and games are a technique of management science (as well as of social science) that can be used to clarify the interrelationships of variable in an administrative system and to expand the awareness of administrators in that system. In this orientation, simulations and games relate to and overlap with the other variants of the systems approach and management science.

Management Science: Some Less Numerate (and More Literate) Techniques

We have reviewed several of the more significant methods of management science, but there are other methods of management science that are less quantitative in their approaches. These include the Delphi exercise, scenarios, and simply the use of written guidelines.[22]

Delphi Exercise. Of particular interest among the nonquantitative techniques used in public administration is the Delphi exercise. The Delphi exercise relies on two kinds of sources of information: representative citizens and recognized experts. Originally, the Delphi exercise was used as a means of forecasting future events and difficulties, and it is receiving increasingly widespread use among public jurisdictions as a method of anticipating potential future problems in specific areas of the public interest. Often it is used by city governments, for example, to forecast future problems that might affect comprehensive urban planning.

The technique of the Delphi exercise is to send out series of questionnaires to both representative citizen groups and experts in a particular field.

With each succeeding wave of questionnaires (usually about three series are sent), the questionnaire itself is revised and refined to the point that policymakers can pinpoint prospective future problems and difficulties that will have to be confronted by relevant governments. The basic idea is to reconcile the opinions of knowledgeable experts with the feelings of the public. Typically, these questionnaires are answered anonymously and evaluated equally, so that organized interest groups or strong-willed individuals cannot dominate the responses.

Scenario Writing. Scenarios received much of their initial impetus from the Department of Defense in projecting the possible outcomes of various battlefield strategies. They are, in many respects, an informal version of Operations Research in that they systematically consider various kinds of philosophic, technological, social, political, economic, and physical factors, and then, by altering the original assumptions about each of those factors, attempt to predict possible outcomes.

The advantage of scenarios is that they pressure policymakers into thinking comprehensively and systematically about their assumptions (assuming that they have any) about the future. Among the more obvious areas that are relevant subjects for scenario writing in public administration are transportation, finance, and housing.

Written Guidelines. Finally, one of the more obvious but often overlooked management techniques of a nonquantitative nature is the use of written guidelines. The larger the government becomes, the more important it is that staff and other administrators charged with the gathering of information collect and present data in comparable ways so that policymakers may view the system and its component parts in a consistent manner.

For example, written guidelines can be applied to any kind of staff report forwarded to policymakers. Typically, these reports would be broken down into two parts: a preliminary analysis of the problem and an evaluation of the problem, including recommendations. The preliminary analysis would include problem identification; a description of the problem, including the current situation and the history of events leading up to it; a scope of analysis, including financial, legal, organizational, and administrative questions; an assembly of facts, again including financial, legal, organizational, and administrative questions; the assumptions used by the person gathering the data; and alternative solutions and their consequences. The evaluation section of the report would include public relations covering those groups and individuals affected by the problem; alternative solutions to the problem; press relations; and the action recommended.

THE COMPUTER: A NEW DAWN IN PUBLIC MANAGEMENT?

An important component of virtually all the techniques of management science is electronic data processing (EDP), also known as automatic data processing (ADP)—in short, the computer.

Computers and Governments

Computers: A Far-Reaching Federal Failure? It is often forgotten that electronic data processing originated in the public sector. A Census Bureau employee named Herman Hollerith invented a punch card and tabulation machine for use in the 1890 Census. Today, the federal government owns more than 100,000 microcomputers and at least 16,000 general purpose computers; it leases over 1,500 more. The government employs more than 200,000 full-time computer science personnel, and spends more than $20 billion a year to run them—an amount that represented a doubling of federal spending on computers between 1985 and 1990.[23]

To assure improved coordination among computer systems, Congress in 1980 passed the Paperwork Reduction Act, which authorized the General Services Administration to oversee the purchasing of the federal government's data processing and telecommunication equipment. The Act also empowered the National Bureau of Standards in the Department of Commerce to provide technical advice, created the Office of Information and Regulatory Affairs in the Office of Management and Budget to coordinate information management, and required each agency to designate an official to be responsible for information management and computer science. More recently, the General Services Administration has created an Office of Software, in an attempt to get all federal agencies to use compatible data bases. In 1983, the General Accounting Office (GAO) created its division of Information Management and Technology, in recognition of the fact that computers represent as much a managerial challenge as a technical one.

Despite these yeoman efforts to make the most of computers, however, the federal government's experience with computers has been as frustrating as the computers themselves are necessary. The Social Security Administration, the Internal Revenue Service, the air force, and the navy have all been plagued by enormous cost overruns and deadlines that require them to have new electronic information systems in place by certain dates. These deadlines have slipped by not only by years, but, in some cases, by decades. The General Accounting Office states that "not one major government computer system reviewed by GAO has come in under budget or on time."[24] It ascribes this "syndrome of failure"[25] to a lack of vision and commitment on the part of federal agency leaders, an absence of long-term strategic planning, an inability to recognize that EDP often brings with it new ways of managing, and a lack of advice from experts, either from outside or inside the agencies. In the view of the GAO, these problems seem likely to expand, not recede.[26]

Computers: Gratifying at the Grass Roots? Computers also have made themselves felt among the grass-roots governments. By the mid-1970s, at least 90 percent of cities and counties and all of the states were using computers in a systematic way.[27] Most of the local uses of computers revolve around the areas of finance, utilities, services, personnel records, administration office support, and law enforcement, although there are about 450 different computer applications at the city and county levels alone.[28]

Only 3 percent of American cities and counties do not have some sort of computer support (and 88 percent have their own in-house computer system, as opposed to having a joint-use arrangement with other governments or privatizing their computer services).[29] Ninety-six percent of local governments use at least one central system; 73 percent employ microcomputers; 77 percent have used some sort of computer for five or more years; more than two-thirds have a technical staff dedicated solely to computers; 57 percent of local governments have a separate data processing department; and, on the average, the data processing budget as a percentage of the total operating budget of local governments is only slightly more than 1 percent.[30] Microcomputers clearly are the rage among America's local governments. In 1982 only 18 percent of local governments (and even fewer small local governments) used microcomputers; three years later, this proportion had rocketed to about 84 percent.[31] Fifty percent of local government managers are very satisfied with their central computer systems and 41 percent are very satisfied with their microcomputer systems.[32] Indeed, only about 5 percent of local government managers are dissatisfied with their systems.[33] City and county administrators believe that their biggest problems with both central and microcomputer systems center on the acquisition of experienced and competent technical staff and on training problems; problems relating to hardware and software are not seen as major difficulties.[34]

The significant investment in computers by state and local governments seems to have (by and large) paid off in the long term, justifying the overall satisfaction of state and local administrators with their EDP systems. A survey of forty-six American cities that had committed to computers at a relatively early date found that, between 1976 and 1988, these metropolises had made major gains in the areas of fiscal control, cost avoidance, and improved relations with citizens. These gains were not immediately realized, however, and represented long-term payoffs over a period of years. On the other hand, it has remained problematic whether or not computers will ever deliver comparable benefits in the areas of planning and managerial control.[35]

From Data to Decisions

Increasingly, the literature distinguishes between two basic types of information systems in public management. The first is the *management information system* (or *MIS*), which is "an interconnected set of procedures and mechanisms for data accumulation storage and retrieval, which is designed to convert organizational data into information appropriate for managerial decision making." Generally, a management information system summarizes data on such areas as population, facilities, salaries, services provided, inventories, employees, and it provides data concerning these areas on demand to managers. By contrast, a *decision support system* (*DSS*) is "an interactive computer-based system that is structured around analytic decision models on a specialized management data base directly accessible to managers, that can be used to assist management at all levels of an organization with decisions about *unstructured* and *nonroutinized* problems."[36]

The key distinction between a management information system and a decision support system is that the management information system is merely a data base to be used by managers, while a decision support system provides decision-making assistance for unstructured problems and the incorporation of modeling techniques that are directly accessible to the decision maker. In other words, a decision support system can be designed to assist in "what if" kinds of inquiry, such as projecting possible increases in transit costs.

Clearly, public agencies are moving increasingly toward the supplementation of management information systems with decision support systems, A survey of state agencies in Colorado found that 57 percent of the agencies indicated that they had a decision support system in place. In most cases, decision support systems are used primarily by middle managers, and most of these administrators were quite pleased with the usefulness provided by decision support systems.[37]

More innovative governments have combined both types of information systems and used them to deliver services more effectively and efficiently. Wichita Falls, Texas, for example, has aggregated and stored data for purposes of equalizing property taxes, and automated its purchase order processing through the application of computer techniques borrowed from both types of systems.[38] Fort Lauderdale, Florida, by borrowing the Census Bureau's geographic data and combining it with its own management information system, was able to equalize crew work loads and ensure more efficient refuse service in its sanitation department.[39] Tulsa, Oklahoma, created the Tulsa Regional Automated Criminal Information System, which allows police officers to call in to headquarters on a twenty-four-hour-a-day basis to collect such information as a briefing on a car, a person, a stolen vehicle, and current warrants or arrest records.[40]

These examples indicate the several uses to which computers may be put in the public sector. Kenneth Kraemer and his colleagues have categorized these uses on a scale ranging from basic to sophisticated.[41] At the bottom of Kraemer's pyramid of governmental uses of computers is the performance of routine and repetitive administrative tasks, such as payroll calculations and licensing chores. Here is where management information systems are all that is needed. At a higher level of sophistication is the use of computers for the planning and control of internal management operations, such as scheduling, allocating, and monitoring traffic control and the use of emergency vehicles. In this usage, there is an emphasis on rapid response capability. At the top of the pyramid is the use of computers for strategic planning and scheduling, involving such techniques as the Performance Evaluation and Review Technique, which we covered earlier in this chapter; decision support systems come into play at this level.

The organizational and human implications of EDP, the systems approach, and management science run much deeper, and "the computer" symbolizes the threat of these techniques for many people. The concluding portion of this chapter will consider some of the ramifications of technology for organizations and for decision making.

TECHNOLOGY, THE PUBLIC BUREAUCRACY, AND THE PUBLIC

Herbert A. Simon has observed that popular views on the implications of computers and automation for human beings can be classified according to "economic" and "technological" dimensions, and by "conservative" and "radical" interpretations.[42] These are shown in Table 6.6.

Simon considers himself to be a technological radical and an economic conservative in his perceptions of computers and automation; that is, he foresees employment patterns similar to today's, and computers taking over the more mundane activities of humanity—in short, the best of both worlds. In this view, Simon argues that the computer will free people from the dispiriting and deadly routine chores that have burdened bureaucracies for too long, and that it will release the energies of human beings to pursue more fulfilling enterprises. Notably, people no longer will have to be clerks and assembly-line workers; instead they can work in jobs involving face-to-face, human-to-human interaction. In Simon's view this will be a far more gratifying experience than is possible in the unautomated present. Already, in fact, computers (in the form of the management information systems, noted earlier) have taken over the solving of "well-structured problems" (such as sending and collecting telephone bills). They are rapidly usurping "ill-structured problems" (through the use of decision support systems) and are slowly

TABLE 6–6 Views on the Human Implications of Computers and Automation

	Economic Dimension	Technological Dimension
Radical Perceptions	A "glut" of goods, widespread unemployment, the rise of a technocracy.	Computers can do anything that human beings can do, including thinking.
Conservative Perceptions	Rising production, full employment, with employment patterns similar to today's.	Computers can do only what human beings program them to do.

developing heuristic problem-solving techniques for application to supervisory duties.

Moreover, Simon contends, the fears of a "technocracy" (or a ruling class possessing the skills demanded by a technologically advanced society) developing along with the expanded use of computers are unfounded. As a technological radical, Simon argues that computers can be programmed to program themselves, thus preventing programmers and mathematicians from evolving into a powerful elite. He contends that as automation progresses, maintenance problems decrease.

Similarly, full employment should accompany automation, and as an argument Simon offers an analogy: The horse disappeared because of automation (in the form of the automobile), but human beings did not; the horse corresponds to the machine, but humanity does not. Thus, technology will increase real wages and capital per worker. In brief, Simon urges that we recognize the enormous significance of the computer in forming human kind's image of itself. Galileo and Copernicus showed us that human beings are not at the center of the universe; Darwin enlightened us with the knowledge that humanity is not created by God, not especially endowed with soul and reason; Freud demonstrated that the individual person is not completely rational; and the computer will yield us the insight that the human race is not uniquely capable of thinking, learning, and manipulating its environment.

There is, of course, a less optimistic view concerning computers and automation. Boguslaw, Jean Meynaud,[43] and Jacques Ellul,[44] among others, argue that technology will dehumanize mankind and possibly create economic chaos if carried to its automated extreme. Boguslaw phrases this view particularly succinctly. He suggests that "the automation revolution has *not* led to a world of happier and more vital people" because a basic tenet of the technological value structure is that work is stupid. This tenet goes against the grain of traditional Western (especially American) thought. "For example, fundamental to Max Weber's Protestant work ethic is the notion that hard labor—sweat-of-the-brow-type labor—is essentially a good and desirable thing." But the values of automation and technology contradict this historic value, and

have turned Max Weber's ethic on its head to read, "Hard work is simply a temporarily unautomated task. It is a necessary evil until we get a piece of gear, or a computer large enough, or a program checked out well enough to do the job economically. Until then, you working stiffs can hang around—but, for the long run, we really don't either want or need you."[45]

This value dissonance, combined with the ongoing popular glamorization of science, quantitative techniques, and professionalism, work to provoke deep-set anxiety and alienation among workers and managers alike. Boguslaw wonders what the successor to the Protestant work ethic might be:

Will the unspoken creed, which once could be verbalized as "I may not be a brain but I can always make a living with these hands; I am fundamentally the producer," be replaced by another, which when verbalized might say, "All these hands (or all this mind) can do is what some machine hasn't yet gotten around to doing....I am the one, in effect, who is doing the exploiting—why not do it deliberately and systematically?"[46]

Simon and Boguslaw are sufficiently representative of the two poles of the computer/planning/automation/technology/humanism/organiza tion/management debate. What is worth examining further at this juncture are the potential effects of the new technologies on the managerial echelons of organizations, particularly public organizations, and there are a few studies that have attempted to do this. In them, the investigative missions of the authors revolve around such questions as: Will middle management be displaced by machines? Will top management control all variables in the organization via computer technologies and management science, or will it, too, be displaced by automation? Will administrators generally be alienated by the new machinery, or will they become "true believers"? Will the authority relationships and the controlling abilities of administrators be altered by the use of computers? It is these kinds of concerns that characterize the studies that we shall review briefly in terms of the computer's impact on authority and control, organizational structure, "dehumanization" and alienation, decision making, and the special case of government data banks and citizen privacy.

Authority and Control

A frequent premise of investigators is that computers facilitate the concentration and centralization of authority in organizations. Although empirical findings are mixed in this area, the bulk of the research tends to support the proposition, but with some interesting variations.[47] A study by Thomas L. Whisler of twenty-three large insurance companies indicated that where computers were introduced in the organization, decision-making loci tended to move upward in the hierarchy; indeed, the most commonly reported phenomenon in the study was the centralizing of control after the introduction of computers. Computers tended to displace clerks in the companies; it was estimated that without EDP, the companies would have required a 60 percent increase in their clerical staff, but only a 9 percent hike in supervisory personnel, and a mere 2 percent increase in managerial jobs.[48] Simon's observations on the propensity of EDP to solve well-structured, ill-structured, and supervisory problems in an ascending order of rapidity and accuracy would seem to be substantiated by Whisler's research.

From another viewpoint, however, managers report a "decentralization" of authority attributable to computers, but only in the sense that managers are released from routine chores and are able to spend more time on authoritative decision making. In a study of fifty state employment agencies (plus agencies in Puerto Rico, the Virgin Islands, and Washington, D.C.), S. R. Klatzky observed a "cascade effect" in terms of authority as a result of computers. Computers created a "vacuum" of activity at the managerial levels by freeing these managers from many routine jobs; if top-level managers then *decided* to let their authority devolve after the introduction of EDP, the resulting "new" authority granted to each level of the hierarchy could be handled more effectively since computers had taken over routine tasks.[49] Thus, computers, together with a decision by top management to decentralize their authority, created a "cascade" of authority to lower levels that increased the mission effectiveness of the organization generally.

The cascade effect can also be seen in a study conducted by Donald R. Shaul of fifty-three middle managers and fourteen top managers in eight companies. Shaul found that after EDP had been adopted, 60 percent of the managers reported an increase in planning activities, a "high percentage" increased their directing activities. In addition, a greater propensity by managers to relinquish certain kinds of authority was observed. Interestingly, two-thirds of the managers reported less need to bother with "controlling" subordinates because the computer kept an adequate check on misuse of budgetary funds and work time, while opportunities for engaging in coordination activities increased.[50]

Withington observes in this regard the phenomenon of "flickering authority" in organizations enabled by the advent of EDP. Because the computer frees all managers from a plethora of mundane duties and furnishes them with information that they can use more potently than ever before, they have more time to develop their ideas and more information to substantiate them. Authority thus becomes more accessible to all managers. In Withington's words, "The effect is that the authority for originating and testing ideas for change 'flickers' within the management structure of the organization. He who has the idea is the one who temporarily has the authority to proceed with its analysis..."[51]

In a careful empirical analysis of nearly 1,500 employees in forty-two municipal governments, it was found that "greater employee control in the work place is attributed to the computer as the employee's role ascends the organizational hierarchy. This is the first empirical confirmation that computer technology enables the information elite to reap the greatest increases in control within organizations."[52]

The researchers in this study distinguished four role types of municipal professional service workers: managers (top administrators who typically rely on summaries of information to make decisions), staff professionals (data analysts who advise managers), "street level bureaucrats" (line personnel who directly provide city services to citizens), and "desk top bureaucrats" (who are extensively involved in processing information). Table 6.7 indicates the findings of this study.

TABLE 6–7 Summary of Findings About Relative Impacts of Computing on Control of Work

		Pervasiveness of Data-handling in Work[a]		
		High	*Low*	
				Actual Impacts[b]
Autonomy in the organization's hierarchy	High	Staff Professionals	Managers	+ *Influence over others*
	Low	Desk top bureaucrats	Street level bureaucrats	− Influence over others
Actual Impacts		−*Supervision of work by others* + *Time pressure*	+ *Supervision of work by others* − *Time pressure*	

[a]*High* means that data-handling tends to be direct, multi-modal, and continual; *low* means that data handling tends to be indirect, use-oriented (relative to generation and manipulation), and intermittent.

[b]*Impacts* are those effects on control of work attributed to computers. The table indicates those roles which have experienced an impact in a significantly different pattern than the roles with which it is contrasted.

Source: Kenneth L. Kraemer and James N. Danziger, "Computers and Control in the Work Environment," *Public Administration Review*, 44 (January–February 1984), p. 39. Reprinted with permission from Public Administration Review © 1984 by The American Society for Public Administration, Washington, D.C. All rights reserved.

Staff professionals, for example, experienced less supervision of their work by others, more influence over others, and an increase in time pressure as a consequence of the introduction of computers. Staff professionals, in short, were the most likely to gain more organizational authority as the result of their understanding and use of electronic data processing. However, intensifying time pressures accompanied this expansion of their authority.

Managers also were able to increase their influence over others, but found themselves to be more closely supervised by others as well. However, time pressures on managers were reduced by the introduction of computers.

The desk top and street level bureaucrats lost their influence over others, but beyond that commonality, the impact of the computer on their working roles varied. The desk top bureaucrats found that their work was less supervised by others, but that time pressures were increased, while street level bureaucrats (those who dealt with people and clients on an ongoing and continuous basis) found themselves to be more supervised by others, but also under fewer time constraints. As the table indicates, the computer affects the control of work

in the work place on the basis of how pervasive data handling is in one's work, and depending upon the level of autonomy that one possesses in the organization's hierarchy.

Organizational Structure

If computers have an effect on the exercise of authority in organizations, they have an equal impact on hierarchical structure. Most analysts agree that EDP will pressure the hierarchical pyramid to "flatten," and this pressure would appear to be the result of the increased organizational control made possible by computer technology.

Some two decades ago, John Pfiffner and Robert Presthus prophesied in their public administration textbook that the hierarchial pyramid would not so much flatten as a result of computer as spread into a "bell" shape. This, they believed, would occur because middle managers would be displaced by the new and evolving information technologies.[53]

Later research supports Pfiffner and Presthus's predictions. Rolf T. Wigand points out that a major function of middle managers is communication—transmitting orders from the top of the pyramid to the bottom, and providing feedback from the base to the peak. In large organizations, middle managers tend to evolve into an "organizational sponge," retaining and eventually squeezing upwards or downwards information that is provided to them by the top or bottom of the hierarchy. The "sponge" effect, which is created by middle management, is an organizational pathology in that information is distorted, delayed, or withheld. Computers and new communication and information technologies can and are slicing through (and slicing out) the sponge of middle management, and the process is so gradual that often it is not noticed. But it does seem to be real; by the mid-1980s, unemployment among managers and administrators in nonfarm industries occasionally was reaching levels that had not been seen since World War II.[54]

EDP-resultant changes in organizational structure present difficulties for public administrators. A study by Marshall W. Meyer, using data gathered from 254 state, county, and city finance departments and comptrollers' offices, found that tensions arose between superordinates inexpert in EDP and subordinates proficient in computer science because electronic data processing requirements forced superordinates and subordinates to cooperate in ways not provided for by the traditional bureaucratic structure. If the organization was able to adapt to the use of EDP, Meyer found, horizontal interaction increased and the normal vertical interaction of the closed model decreased; if the organization was too stultified to change, administrative pathologies quickly surfaced.[55] In this light, Whisler noted a blurring of traditional line-staff distinctions in organizations as a result of EDP; staff members with computer skills gained new organizational prestige.[56]

With the advent of microcomputers, the research on the impact of computers on organizational structure has moved from a consensus that computers tended to centralize organizations to a growing opinion among researchers that computers promote the decentralization of organizations.[57] Perhaps the best characterization of this research, however, is that computers centralize some decisions and decentralize others. As two researchers in the area note, computer "technol-

ogy supports either arrangement; which arrangement is followed in any particular instance is a function of organizational history, management, and politics."[58]

"Dehumanization" and Alienation

If clerks are the bureaucrats most often displaced by automation, those clerks who remain frequently find that their jobs become rigidly routinized, and occasionally they are transformed into key punch operators. Such, at least, was the conclusion of Albert A. Blum in a study of EDP and white-collar workers.[59] On the other hand, the promotion possibilities for those clerks remaining are about the same as they were prior to the introduction of EDP, and Whisler found that, while clerical responsibilities were not enlarged, salaries went up with the increased need for clerical precision.[60]

A survey of more than 2,000 secretaries conducted in twenty-one major American cities found unusually high levels of job satisfaction among secretaries concerning the use of office automation, particularly computers, and especially with regard to microcomputers and word processors. Eighty-seven percent felt that office automation had had a positive effect on the secretarial profession, and more than nine out of ten stated that secretaries could produce a higher volume of work as a result of automation, and that office automation allowed secretaries to be more efficient. A significant majority of secretaries stated that office automation had made their jobs more challenging, had allowed them to spend more time on more responsible activities, had made their jobs more fulfilling, had increased their productivity, and in fact, had increased the managerial productivity of executives.[61]

Older bureaucrats occasionally experience a sense of alienation when EDP is introduced. Meyer's findings imply this, but a study by H. S. Rhee specifically noted the presence of conflict between older, bureaucratically oriented locals and younger, professionally oriented cosmopolitans over the automation issue.[62]

Generally speaking, research on the impact of computers on work life agrees that job performance improves and the work environment is enhanced by the introduction of computers.[63] In a massive study of 2,400 people whose jobs had been affected by computers, it was found that three quarters of the respondents believed that computing had "provided them with a greater sense of accomplishment in their work."[64]

Computers and Decision Making

One of the more intriguing questions is determining how computers affect not only the quality of the working environment, but the quality of the work output itself. One study concluded that mid-level managers actually appear to make *different kinds* of decisions depending upon whether or not they are computer literate! Mid-level managers familiar with computers tend to make their decisions on the basis of computer-provided information rather than on information furnished by other sources, such as books and journals. Often, however, the kind of information provided by computers differs from the information gleaned from other sources. While it is an open question whether the kinds of decisions resulting from the use of computer-based information are "better" or "worse" than decisions that are based on information from other sources, it nonetheless is of note "that when computers are involved, computer literate decision makers choose different information than computer novices and that the selection of computer information has an effect on the outcome of the decision."[65]

Generally, most investigators seem to agree that EDP does not affect top-level decision makers very much one way or another. Rodney H. Brady, after interviewing more than 100 top managers and examining in detail the decision-making process in more than a dozen large companies, concluded that the computer has not had much impact on decision making at the top.[66] On the other hand, EDP has speeded the overall decision-making process in organizations by making more information more readily available to top managers. Rhee found that the concern over a computer- oriented technocratic elite eventually displacing top administrators was not a view shared by the top administrators themselves; in fact, highest-level decision makers did not consider a technical background to be a pre-

requisite for their positions.[67] Whisler reported that the organizational centralization accompanying the introduction of computers tended to increase the responsiveness and power of the topmost echelon,[68] while Shaul concluded that middle managers, too, believed that their responsibilities and capabilities had increased after the advent of EDP.[69]

Still, one wonders. There have been reports in business magazines of "deskless offices" in the presidential stratum of "progressive" multinational corporations. In these poshest of quarters, there are no desks, only chairs, lounges, and coffee tables. The underlying assumption is that the topmost corporate decision makers should be only that; he or she should do no more than listen, confer, and decide; he or she should be relieved of anything resembling paperwork—the brain is all. Similarly, the growing "fetish of the clean desk" refers to the propensity of top-level administrators to have no more than one sheet of paper on their desks at any one time, and betokens an emphasis on "thought" and decision making rather than on "paper shuffling"; the presidents of private foundations seem to favor this clean desk affectation. Continuing this line of thinking, a major company once introduced a "waterbed room" for use by its top-level executives (presumably on a one-at-a-time basis); the idea is that an executive could float, meditate, and ultimately decide the grand issues facing the company.

Do these developments reflect anything other than a desire to make the decision-making process more effective and, probably, more pretentious? It seems possible, at least, that top executives may be trying to manipulate their images (their "dramaturgy," to recall Victor Thompson's term) in such a way as to distinguish their functions from the functions of the computer. The more they are unlike the computer, the less paper they handle, the more they "think," the more essential they become as human beings. This, of course, is only specula tion, but the increasing obsequiousness displayed for the decision-making function in organizations may reflect a subliminal fear over the awesome, if as yet unrealized, cognitive powers of "The Computer."

Data Banks, Privacy, and Public Policy

As with other administrators, computers and the many overlapping techniques of management science have had an impact on public administrators. Paul Armer observes that governmental use of EDP could facilitate interagency sharing of information, reduce expensive duplication of information systems, improve planning, upgrade auditing (thus increasing revenues), and bring about more responsive services to the public generally. In Armer's view, EDP will increase the pressures for the consolidation of national, state, and local government, starting only with the consolidation of files through information-sharing systems but ultimately consolidating and centralizing governmental authority as well: cities will defer power to counties, counties to states, states to regions, and regions to the nation.[70]

Nevertheless, Armer desponds that governments are beset by factors that inhibit the optimal use of computer-based information storage and retrieval systems. Notable in this regard is the unfamiliarity of top-level government executives with EDP and management science. There is a lack of qualified personnel to perform the necessary kinds of systems analysis. There is a need to rewrite laws in order to permit the integration of files and information-sharing arrangements. A general lack of coordination among government agencies, the parochialism of many agencies, and finally, popular and official fears of invasions of privacy and of a *1984* variety of technocratic state all inhibit the best use of computer systems.

Armer's final caveat regarding computers and government is worth additional examination; the computer-and-privacy/computer-and- policy issue is one unique to *public* administration. In 1977, in *Whalen* v. *Roe*, the Supreme Court recognized for the first time the constitutionally protected "zone of privacy" of the individual, a concept that involved the right of people to prevent others (such as a government agency or a private firm) from disclosing personal data to the public. However, Congress had recognized the value of individual privacy even earlier by its passage of the Privacy Act of 1974, which restricted how federal agencies could use and distribute information that they had collected about private citizens.

As late as the mid-1970s, concerns over government's misuse of personal data seemed somewhat overdrawn. A federal study conducted in 1975 found that nearly three-quarters of the personal data systems subject to the provisions of the Privacy Act were not even on computers and were completely manual![71] By 1985, however, privacy concerns were intensifying. The Office of Technology Assessment reported that twelve cabinet departments and thirteen independent agencies maintained 539 record systems to which the Privacy Act applied. These record systems contained more than 3.5 billion records, or an average of fifteen files for every man, woman, and child in the United States.[72] Sixty percent of all these systems were fully computerized, and 78 percent of those systems that contained files on more than a half million people were computer based.[73] In fact, about eighty-five federal data bases contain some 288 million records on 114 million people.[74] Some forty states provide information to direct mail firms for a fee, using information provided by citizens when applying for a driver's license or registering a vehicle. And some 10 million centrally stored records of individual criminal histories are available to at least 64,000 law enforcement agencies, which employ more than 1 million officers who are authorized to request these records from the Federal National Crime Information Center.[75]

Of even graver concern is the accelerating trend among government data banks to "mix and match" information on individuals, and at least fifteen federal agencies engage in this practice.[76] *Computer matching* is the electronic comparison of two or more sets or systems of individual personal records. The federal government, through such legislation as the Deficit Reduction Act of 1984, the Debt Collection Act of 1982, the Federal Managers Financial Integrity Act of 1982, the Paperwork Reduction Act of 1980, the Social Security Amendments of 1977, the Food Stamp Amendments of 1977 and 1980, and other laws, has encouraged computer matching as a means of detecting fraud and other criminal activity, including the abuse of the welfare system and tax evasion, among other objectives. These new acts have resulted in the creation of such electronic dossiers as the Internal Revenue Service's Debtor Master File and the Medicaid Management Information System, among other federal systems that are extensively engaged in computer matching. It appears that the number of matches tripled from 1980 to 1984, and that more than 2 billion separate records were exchanged during those four years.[77] As one observer has noted, "No longer is information merely stored and retrieved by computer. Now, information is routinely collected on computer tapes, used within an agency in computer form, exchanged with and disclosed to regional offices or other agencies in computer form, manipulated and analyzed with sophisticated computer software, and archived on computer tapes. These disclosures and manipulations are currently performed for entire systems of records..."[78]

The worries of Americans over issues of personal privacy have grown as these trends have accelerated. In 1970, about 35 percent of Americans expressed themselves "concerned" over "threats to personal privacy"; by 1990, nearly 80 percent registered themselves as "concerned" or "very concerned" over these threats. Americans express considerably higher trust with regard to the government's potential use of personal files than they do with private firms' use of them, but 71 percent of Americans agree that "consumers have lost all control over how personal information about them is circulated and used by companies."[79]

In a useful summary of the computer-and-privacy/computer-and- policy issue, Alan F. Westin has observed that there are at least five kinds of data bank systems emerging in American society: statistical systems for policy studies, executive systems for general administration, systems designed to centralize data gathered by other agencies, individual agency data-bank systems, and mixed public-private systems.[80] All these data-bank systems bring with them new problems of public policy. If we are to learn more about our citizenry in order to develop more responsive and effective public policies, where do we draw the line with regard to privacy? At what point does the collection, storage, retrieval, and sharing of social information become an invasion of the citizen's privacy? Emerging from this fundamental dilemma concerning the government's use of computers are delicate political issues: Who will control this new technological capacity? Will new knowledge of old problems inspire brand-new problems in society (as may be the case with improved crime statistics, which have served to frighten many a formerly complacent citizen)? Where does the expertise and planning enabled by the computer end, and where does democratic participation by the public in public policymaking begin?

In any event, it seems unavoidable that the new knowledge of problems will undermine the justifications of past governmental inaction in attempting to resolve those problems. Knowledge is pressure, with or without pressure groups, and the computer makes all of us, whether private citizen or public bureaucrat, more knowledgeable about government, society, and our problems. In short, computers, systems analysis, and management science may serve not merely to centralize the administration of government, but to widen the scope of government activities beyond anything yet envisioned.

In this chapter, we have reviewed briefly the scientific techniques and political potentialities of the systems approach, management science, and the implications of technology and technique for public administrators, public organizations, and government. In so doing, some arbitrary conceptual distinctions and emphases necessarily have been made. In reality, systems analysis, Performance Evaluation and Review Technique, Operations Research, Critical Path Method, queuing theory, cybernetics, game theory, prisoner's dilemma, simulations, computer science, budgeting theory, linear and dynamic programming, information theory, and all the rest of it represents variations on the same theme: the efforts to clarify decision options and to measure program effectiveness. In reality, the overlapping between the techniques and technologies of public administration are manifold, just as are the overlapping between what is policy and what is program, what is politics and what is administration, and what is value and what is fact.

Many of these techniques have been bundled into a package called "program evaluation," which we consider in the next chapter.

NOTES

[1] Stephen K. Bailey, "Objectives of the Theory of Public Administration," in *Theory and Practice of Public Administration: Scope, Objectives, and Methods*, Monograph 8, James C. Charlesworth, ed. (Philadelphia: The American Academy of Political and Social Science, October 1968), pp. 128–139.

[2] W. Ross Ashby, *Introduction to Cybernetics* (London: Chapman and Hall, 1961).

[3] C. West Churchman, *The Systems Approach* (New York: Dell, 1968).

[4] Daniel P. Moynihan, *Maximum Feasible Misunderstanding: Community Action and the War on Poverty* (New York: The Free Press, 1969).

[5] Churchman, *The Systems Approach.*

[6] Robert Boguslaw, *The New Utopians: A Study of System Design and Social Change* (Englewood Cliffs, N.J.: Prentice-Hall, 1965), pp. 1–28.

[7] See, for example, Study Committee on Policy Management Assistance, Office of Management and Budget, *Strengthening Public Management in the Intergovernmental System* (Washington, D.C.: U.S. Government Printing Office, 1975); Advisory Commission on Intergovernmental Relations, *Improving Urban America: A Challenge to Federalism* (Washington, D.C.: U.S. Government Printing Office, 1976); Special Task Force on Intergovernmental Management, American Society for Public Administration, *Strengthening Intergovernmental Management: An Agenda for Reform* (Washington, D.C.: American Society for Public Administration, 1979); and Charles R. Warren and Leanne R. Aronson, "Sharing Management Capacity: Is There a Federal Responsibility?" *Public Administration Review*, 41 (May/June 1981), pp. 381–387.

[8] The surveys are: Theodore H. Poister and Gregory Streib, "Management Tools in Municipal Government: Trends Over the Past Decade," *Public Administration Review*, 49 (May/June 1989), pp. 240–248. Poister and Streib surveyed 1,060 cities ranging from 25,000 to 1 million people in 1987–1988, and received 451 usable responses, or a response rate of 43 percent. For 1982, see: Theodore H. Poister and Robert P. McGowan, "The Use of Management Tools in Municipal Government: A National Survey," *Public Administration Review*, 44 (May/June 1984), p. 221; and "Municipal Management Capacity: Productivity Improvement and Strategies for Handling Fiscal Stress," *The Municipal Year Book, 1984* (Washington, D.C.: International City Management Association, 1984), p. 208. Poister and McGowan surveyed 1,052 municipal jurisdictions with populations ranging from 25,000 to 1 million and received 460 usable responses, or a response rate of 44 percent. The 1976 survey can be found in Rackham Fukuhara, "Productivity Im-

provement in Cities," *The Municipal Year Book, 1977* (Washington, D.C.: International City Management Association, 1977) pp. 193–200. Fukuhara surveyed cities of the same population range as the later surveys and obtained usable responses from 404 cities, or a response rate of 43 percent.

[9] Richard C. Elling, "Of Bandwagons and Bandaids: A Comparative Assessment of the Utilization and Efficacy of Management Techniques in State Bureaucracies" (Paper presented at the Annual Meeting of the American Political Science Association, Washington, D.C., August–September), 1984, Tables 13 and 14.

[10] Efraim Turban, "A Sample Survey of Operations Research at the Corporate Level," *Operations Research*, 2 (May/June 1972), pp. 708–721.

[11] C. Jackson Grayson, Jr., "Management Science and Business Practice," *Harvard Business Review*, 51 (July/August 1973), pp. 41–48.

[12] Randall L. Schultz and Dennis P. Slevin, eds., *Implementing Operations Research/Management Science* (New York: Elsevier, 1975).

[13] Lars Lonnstedt, "Factors Related to the Implementation of Operations Research Solutions," *Interfaces*, 5 (February 1975), p. 24.

[14] E. S. Quade, "System Analysis Techniques for Planning-Programming-Budgeting," *Planning-Programming- Budgeting: A Systems Approach to Management*, Fremont J. Lyden and Ernest G. Miller, eds. (Chicago: Markham, 1972), p. 246.

[15] Russell L. Ackoff and Patrick Rivett, *A Manager's Guide to Operations Research* (New York: John Wiley, 1963), pp. 21–34.

[16] C. P. Snow, *Science and Government* (Cambridge, Mass.: Harvard University Press, 1961), pp. 47–53.

[17] The following discussion on war games is drawn largely from John R. Raser, *Simulation and Society: An Exploration of Scientific Gaming* (Boston: Allyn and Bacon, 1969), pp. 46–49.

[18] See, for example, Herbert A. Simon, Donald W. Smithburg, and Victor A. Thompson, *Public Administration* (New York: Knopf, 1950); and Richard C. Snyder, H. W. Bruck, and Burton Sapin, eds., *Foreign Policy Decision-Making: An Approach to the Study of International Politics* (Glencoe, Ill.: The Free Press, 1962).

[19] Anatol Rapoport, *Fights, Games, and Debates* (Ann Arbor, Mich.: University of Michigan Press, 1960).

[20] W. H. Riker, *The Theory of Political Coalitions* (New Haven, Conn.: Yale University Press, 1962).

[21] Anthony Downs, *Inside Bureaucracy* (Boston: Little, Brown, 1967), pp. 112–131.

[22] The source of much of this discussion is David R. Morgan, *Managing Urban America*, 2nd ed. (Monterey, Calif.: Brooks/Cole, 1984), pp. 105–110.

[23] Pete Earley, "Government Computer Network is Aging," *The Washington Post* (February 21, 1983); Kathryn Johnson, "Washington Catches Up To the Computer Age," *U.S. News and World Report* (April 2, 1984), pp. 27–28; Frank Reilly, "Information Technology and Government Operations," *The G.A.O. Journal*, 5 (Spring 1989), p. 42; and Sam Overman,

"When GAO Comes, Mind Your Bits and Bytes," *Government Executive* (September 1990), p. 30.

[24] "Bringing Order to Government Information Systems," *Facing Facts: Comptroller General's 1989 Annual Report* (Washington, D.C.: U.S. General Accounting Office, 1990), p. 27.

[25] Reilly, "Information Technology and Government Operations," p. 44.

[26] "Bringing Order to Government Information Systems," pp. 28–29.

[27] Rob Kling and Kenneth Kraemer, "Computing and Urban Services," in *Computers and Politics: High Technology in American Local Governments*, James N. Danziger, William Sutton, Rob Kling, and Kenneth Kraemer, eds. (New York: Columbia University Press, 1982), p. 200; and James N. Danziger, "Evaluating Computers: More Sophisticated EDP Uses," *Nation's Cities*, 13 (October 1975), pp. 31–32.

[28] Among the major surveys of local government uses of computers are the following: Kenneth L. Kraemer, *Evaluation of Policy-Related Research in Municipal Information Systems* (Irvine, Calif.: Public Policy Research Organization, University of California at Irvine, 1975); Donald F. Norris and Vincent J. Webb, *Microcomputers, Baseline Data Report*, Vol. 15, No. 7 (Washington, D.C.: International City Management Association, July 1983); James N. Danziger, William Sutton, Rob Kling, and Kenneth L. Kraemer, eds. *Computers and Politics: High Technology in American Local Governments* (New York: Columbia University Press, 1982); Kenneth L. Kraemer, et al., *Microcomputer Use and Policy, Baseline Data Report*, Vol. 17, No. 1 (Washington, D.C.: International City Management Association, 1985); John Scoggins, Thomas H. Tidrick, and Jill Auerback, "Computer Use in Local Government," *The Municipal Year Book, 1986* (Washington, D.C.: International City Management Association, 1986), pp. 33–45; Jeffrey L. Brudney, "Computers and Smaller Local Governments," *Public Productivity Review*, 12 (Winter 1988), pp. 179–192; and Alana Northrop, Kenneth L. Kraemer, Debora Dunkle, and John Leslie King, "Payoffs from Computerization: Lessons Over Time," *Public Administration Review*, 50 (September/October 1990), pp. 505–514. For a comparatively rare survey of state governments' management of computers, see: Sharon L. Caudle, "Managing Information Resources in State Government," *Public Administration Review*, 50 (September/October 1990), pp. 515–524.

[29] Scoggins, Tidrick, and Auerback, "Computer Use in Local Government," p. 34.

[30] *Ibid.*, pp. 34–35.

[31] *Ibid.*, p. 40; and Donald F. Norris and Vincent J. Webb, "Microcomputers: A Survey of Local Government Use," *The Municipal Year Book, 1984* (Washington, D.C.: International City Management Association, 1984), p. 195.

[32] Scoggins, Tidrick, and Auerback, "Computer Use in Local Government," p. 43.

[33] *Ibid.*

[34] *Ibid.*, p. 42.

[35] Northrop, Kraemer, Dunkle, and King, "Payoffs from Computerization," p. 505.

[36] All the quotations in this paragraph are from: James Senn, "Essential Principles of Information Systems Development," *MIS Quarterly*, 2 (June 1978), p. 17. Emphasis is original.

[37] Robert P. McGowan and Gary A. Lombardo, "Decision Support Systems in State Government: Promises and Pitfalls," *Public Administration Review*, 46 (November 1986), pp. 581–582.

[38] Gerald G. Fox, "Information Systems and Decision Making," *Public Management*, 53 (October 1971), pp. 9–11.

[39] Robert H. Bubier, "Modern Refuse Vehicle Routing," *Public Management*, 55 (August 1973), pp. 10–12.

[40] Carole H. Hicks, "The Broad Scope of Computer Usage in City Government," *Current Municipal Problems*, 7 (1980–1981), pp. 191–196.

[41] Kenneth Kraemer, et al., *Integrated Municipal Information Systems: The Use of Computers in Local Government* (New York: Praeger, 1974), pp. 50–51.

[42] Herbert A. Simon, *The Shape of Automation for Men and Management* (New York: Harper & Row, 1965).

[43] Jean Meynaud, *Technocracy* (London: Faber and Faber, 1968).

[44] Jacques Ellul, *The Technological Society* (New York: Knopf, 1967).

[45] Boguslaw, *The New Utopians*, p. 25.

[46] *Ibid.*, p. 26

[47] For reviews of this research, see: Kenneth L. Kraemer and John Leslie King, "Computing and Public Organizations," *Public Administration Review*, 46 (November 1986), pp. 488–496, but especially p. 492; and Rolf T. Wigand, "Integrated Communications and Work Efficiency: Impacts on Organizational Structure and Power," *Information Services and Use*, 5 (November 1985), pp. 241–258.

[48] Thomas L. Whisler, *The Impact of Computers on Organizations* (New York: Praeger, 1970).

[49] S. R. Klatzky, "Automation, Size, and Locus of Decision-Making: The Cascade Effect," *Journal of Business*, 43 (April 1970), pp. 141–151.

[50] Donald R. Shaul, "What's Really Ahead for Middle Management?" *Personnel*, 41 (November/December 1964), pp. 9–16.

[51] Withington, *The Real Computer*, p. 203.

[52] Kenneth L. Kraemer and James N. Danziger, "Computers and Control in the Work Environment," *Public Administration Review*, 44 (January/February 1984), p. 32.

[53] John M. Pfiffner and Robert Presthus, *Public Administration*, 5th ed. (New York: Ronald Press, 1967), p. 247.

[54] Rolf T. Wigand, "Integrated Communications and Work Efficiency," and U.S. Department of Labor statistics as cited in Kris Aaron, "Computers are Squeezing Out Many Middle Managers," *Scripps-Howard Business Journals* (December 1984), p. 2.

[55] Marshall W. Meyer, "Automation and Bureaucratic Structure," *American Journal of Sociology*, 74 (November 1968), pp. 256–264.

[56] Whisler, *The Impact of Computers on Organizations*.

[57] See, for example, Charles Myers, *The Impact of Computers on Management* (Cambridge, Mass.: MIT Press, 1967) for a view that computers tend to centralize management, in contrast to the perception that computers tend to decentralize management, as contained in, for example, Peter Blau, et al., "Technology and Organization in Manufacturing," *Social Science Quarterly*, 21 (March 1976), pp. 20–40.

[58] Kraemer and King, "Computing and Public Organizations," p. 49.

[59] Albert A. Blum, "White Collar Workers," *The Computer Impact*, Irene Taviss, ed. (Englewood Cliffs, N.J.: Prentice-Hall, 1970).

[60] Whisler, *The Impact of Computers on Organizations*.

[61] Anne-Marie Schiro, "Secretaries' Poll on Computers," *New York Times* (March 14, 1983). The study is titled, "The Evolving Role of the Secretary in the Information Age," and was conducted by the Minolta Corporation in cooperation with the Professional Secretaries International Association.

[62] H. A. Rhee, *Office Automation in Social Perspective* (Oxford: Basil Blackwell, 1968).

[63] See, for example, A. J. Jaffe and Joseph Froomkin, *Technology and Jobs: Automation and Perspective* (New York: Praeger, 1966); Russell Rumberger, "The Changing Skill Requirements of Jobs in the U.S. Economy," *Industrial and Labor Relations Review*, 34 (July 1981), pp. 578–590; and Jon Shepard, *Automation and Alienation: A Study of Office and Factory* (Cambridge, Mass.: MIT Press, 1971).

[64] James N. Danziger and Kenneth L. Kraemer, *People and Computers* (New York: Columbia University Press, 1986), p. 380.

[65] Ralph F. Shangraw, Jr., "How Public Managers Use Information: An Experiment Examining Choices of Computer and Printed Information," *Public Administration Review*, 46 (November 1986), p. 514.

[66] Rodney H. Brady, "Computers in Top Level Decision-Making," *Harvard Business Review*, 45 (July/August 1967), pp. 67–76.

[67] Rhee, *Office Automation in Social Perspective*

[68] Whisler, *The Impact of Computers on Organizations*

[69] Shaul, "What's Really Ahead for Middle Management?"

[70] Paul Armer, "Computer Applications in Government," in *The Computer Impact*, Taviss, ed.

[71] Office of the President, *Federal Personal Data Systems Subject to the Privacy Act of 1974: First Annual Report of the President, 1975* (Washington, D.C.: U.S. Government Printing Office, 1975), pp. 4–6. Nevertheless, the remaining systems were fully or partially computerized, and contained more than 80 percent of the total individual records owned by the federal government.

[72] These figures are for 1982, when the federal government's computerized files on individuals were last counted. See: Robert S. Boyd, "An Eagle's Eye," *Savannah News- Press* (July 22, 1990). No doubt, there are more such files now.

[73] U.S. Congress, Office of Technology Assessment, *Federal Government Information Technology: Electronic Record Systems and Individual Privacy*, OTA-CIT-296 (Washington, D.C.: U.S. Government Printing Office, 1986), p. 22.

[74] Anne R. Field, "'Big Brother, Inc.' May be Closer Than You Thought," *Business Week* (February 9, 1987), p. 27.

[75] *Ibid.*

[76] *Ibid.*; and Priscilla M. Regan, "Privacy, Government Information, and Technology," *Public Administration Review*, 46 (November/December 1986), p. 631.

[77] Field, "'Big Brother, Inc.' May be Closer Than You Thought," p. 28; and Regan, "Privacy, Government Information, and Technology," p. 631. New controls, however, are being introduced; from 1984 to 1989, when Congress stopped the practice, the Social Security Administration provided private credit bureaus with verification of citizens' Social Security numbers. See: Boyd, "An Eagle's Eye."

[78] Regan, "Privacy, Government Information, and Technology," p. 630.

[79] Harris Polls conducted in 1970, 1977, 1978, 1983, and 1990, as cited in Boyd, "An Eagle's Eye." Unless noted otherwise, all figures in the paragraph are for 1990.

[80] Alan F. Westin, "Civil Liberty and Computerized Data Systems," *Computers, Communications and the Public Interest*, Martin Greenberger, ed. (Baltimore: Johns Hopkins, 1971), pp. 151–168; and "Information Systems and Political Decision-Making," in Taviss, *The Computer Impact*, pp. 130–144.

PUBLIC PROGRAM EVALUATION AND PRODUCTIVITY

In 1984, the President's Private Sector Survey on Cost Control, known as the Grace Commission after its chair, J. Peter Grace, released 2,478 recommendations on 784 aspects of federal administration in the form of forty-seven reports made up of more than 12,000 pages bound in thirty-eight volumes, and the commission contended that, if its recommendations were followed, $424.4 billion could be saved in the federal budget in three years. The reports represented the work of some 2,000 volunteers over eighteen months who had been donated by 859 companies and other organizations that had contributed about $75 million in cash and services toward the project. The work of the Grace Commission represented, in the view of one observer, "probably the biggest army of outside help given the government since World War II," eclipsing in both its scope and in the number of people involved the reports of Roosevelt's Brownlow Commission, Truman's and Eisenhower's two Hoover Commissions, Nixon's Ash Council, and Carter's Reorganization Project.[1] It was, in sum, the largest public program evaluation ever undertaken.

THE ROOTS OF EVALUATION RESEARCH

One of the more exciting developments in public administration during the last few years has been the intellectual and professional evolution of what has come to be called program evaluation, evaluation research, or productivity improvement. Although the field is relatively new, its roots can be traced back at least as far as the early part of this century when Frederick Taylor began his time-motion studies, and more recently when Elton Mayo conducted his experiments among workers at the Western Electric plant, as described in Chapter 3.[2] In the 1940s, groundbreaking evaluative research was conducted on such topics as the effects of work relief programs and public housing,[3] and some observers have contended that Theodore Newcomb's research at Bennington College (reviewed in Chapter 5) is an early example of evaluative research.[4] It was also during the 1940s that the work of the pioneering experimenters in organization development (noted in Chapter 3) embodied some of the basic theoretical precepts of program evaluation, particularly in the initial work by Kurt Lewin, Ronald Lippitt, Leon Festinger, and Harold Kelley.[5]

With the inauguration of Lyndon Johnson's Great Society legislation in the 1960s, social scientists rediscovered poverty, education, and similar domestic issues, and evaluation researchers focused on public programs in these areas.[6] The Office of Economic Opportunity (later retitled the Community Services Administration in 1975, but ultimately eliminated in 1981) was especially aggressive in encouraging evaluation research components in its sundry projects, and the Elementary and Secondary Education Act of 1965 did much to promote evaluation research in education.

PROGRAM EVALUATION'S IMPACT ON PUBLIC ADMINISTRATION

Nevertheless, it was only in the 1970s that public administrators became aware of (and started using) evaluation research in any comprehensive sense.[7] Indeed, as late as 1971 a leading public administrationist could ask, as the title of an editorial in the field's leading journal, "Why Does Public Administration Ignore Evaluation?" The question was entirely justified; as the editorialist understated, "our literature, teaching, and research have not been overtly concerned with it,"[8] and even four years later this author could accurately observe that "the practice of evaluation in public administration remains in its formative stages."[9]

A 1970 study of federal evaluation practices conducted by the Urban Institute concluded that "the whole federal machinery for making policy and budget decisions suffers from a crucial weakness; it lacks a comprehensive system for measuring program effectiveness."[10] Similarly, program evaluation efforts at the state and local levels still were in their embryonic stages in the early 1970s. A national survey of all cities and counties with more than 50,000 people conducted in 1971 found that only 38 percent of the 354 responding governments had some form of a program evaluation unit in even one agency or more,[11] while a poll of state governments conducted the following year ascertained that only half of the forty-two responding states had a full-time program analyst in at least one agency.[12] Respondents in both surveys displayed a strong desire to learn more about program evaluation and to implement it more widely.

Federal Developments

By the mid-1970s, there were clear signs that public administrators in all levels of government were determined to use evaluation research in a significant way. In 1974, the Office of Management and Budget created its Evaluation and Program Implementation Division, which was specifically designed to evaluate federal domestic programs,[13] and the Congressional Budget and Impoundment Control Act of the same year directed the Comptroller General, as head of the General Accounting Office, to "develop and recommend to Congress methods for reviewing and evaluation of government programs carried on under the existing law."[14] The Office of Technology Assessment, the Congressional Budget Office, and the Congressional Research Service also have responsibilities for program evaluation.

In 1987, the General Accounting Office concluded that, despite a significant decline between 1980 and 1984 in the level of federal resources available for evaluation research, the number of program evaluations produced remained about the same as in the earlier years, "suggesting continued executive branch interest in obtaining evaluation information."[15]

State Progress

With the federal government setting the pace, state governments became more interested in improving their productivity. Perhaps this interest was tweaked by a federal study that appeared in 1978 indicating that state governments needed more evaluation research, but had some significant problems in acquiring it.[16] A 1980 survey of state governments found that, while most states did not have comprehensive, formal productivity improvement programs, there nonetheless was considerable interest in program evaluation,[17] and another poll discovered that by the mid-1980s legislatures in thirty-five states had expanded existing agencies or had created new ones charged with the evaluation of program effectiveness and efficiency.[18]

A study conducted in 1984 of all fifty states indicated that, while much remained to be done in the way of program evaluation, much progress had been made. Ten states had centralized—that is, they were responsible for improving productivity in all state agencies—productivity improvement programs. Most were located in the state budget office or department of administration, and focused on upgrading technology (especially computers and word- processing capabilities) and employee motivation systems (notably through merit pay, performance appraisals, and quality circle programs). Other options for improving productivity, such as reorganization of the agency, alternative delivery systems, better operating procedures, and training programs, were used only sporadically. However, the overall assessment of state-centralized productivity improvement efforts was one of a "lack of stability...an 'up and down' pattern."[19] The states' long-term commitment to systemwide productivity enhancement is, in short, unclear.

Local Efforts

Local efforts to improve productivity seem to be more intense than state efforts. In 1976 a major study conducted by the International City Management Association found that 64 percent of local governments were using program evaluations to improve productivity. The survey found that almost half of the cities, 46 percent, had organized special staffs to evaluate productivity in their cities and to identify better methods to improve the delivery of services. Most of these staffs were located in the cities' budget offices, and 338 cities reported that they were using outside resources, as well as their own employees, to improve productivity.[20] A survey conducted in 1987, which was designed to replicate the 1976 survey, found that 80 percent of local governments were using evaluation research—a "significant increase" over the less than two-thirds of municipalities that were using program evaluations eleven years earlier. In those cities where program evaluations were used on a city-wide basis (rather than in just selected munic-

ipal departments), 49 percent of the local officials pronounced program evaluation to be a "very effective" management tool.[21]

An analysis based on data collected in a national survey of local governments concentrated on four kinds of performance measures used by local governments in conducting program evaluations:[22] *workload*, or *output measures*—in other words, the amount of work performed or service provided, such as the amount of trash collected; *unit costs*, or *efficiency measures*—that is, the dollar costs per unit of output or workload, such as the cost per control hour; *effectiveness measures*, or the extent to which objectives are achieved and needs are met, such as the containment of the number of commercial burglaries or the reduction of substandard housing units; and *client*, or *citizen satisfaction measures*, meaning the extent to which clients feel their needs are met, ascertained by counting the number of complaints received about a program as measured over time, or by conducting surveys of citizens served. The study concluded that the first of these measures, that of workload or output measures, tends to be used most frequently in all functional areas of city government; this appears to be the case because workload-related information can be generated comparatively easily, particularly in contrast to the other three types of performance measures.

Police departments tend to use performance measures most frequently, and, in fact, were rated the highest in terms of using workload effectiveness and citizen satisfaction measures. Other functional areas that tend to be heavy users of performance measures at the municipal level include the services dealing with solid waste disposal and recovery, street maintenance, parks, and health.

One of the debates about using performance measures, as well as the other components of program evaluation, is that the results obtained are not worth the cost. In other words, the setting up of a government's information gathering capacities and evaluation bureaucracies is not justified by the kinds of productivity improvements that can be accomplished. However, municipal administrators seem to believe quite the opposite. Chief administrative officers of the communities surveyed in 1982 thought that performance measures had made a major contribution toward the evaluation of program performance and toward making subsequent budget allocations. Perhaps more important, these chief administrative officers agreed that performance measurement systems had resulted in more efficient service delivery, significant cost savings, and more effective programs. Sixty-one percent of the respondents felt that on balance "the positive payoff of the performance measures used in their jurisdictions were worth the cost and organizational strain of collecting these data. Less than one percent felt that it was not."[23] The larger the municipality, the stronger this correlation was likely to be.

It is not an easy task for any local government to adopt the techniques of performance evaluation and increased productivity; one exhaustive review of the literature identified no fewer than thirty-seven barriers to increased productivity in local governments, ranging from the lack of political appeal inherent in the techniques themselves to various "performance myths," such as the presumed advantages of certain, expensive police practices.[24] Nevertheless, some characteristics of local governments have emerged that bear strong relationships to the likelihood of whether or not a locality will successfully adopt productivity improvement measures. These characteristics include a participative management style in city government, relatively high levels of privatization, a local emphasis on economic development, department heads who have college educations, a comparatively low reliance on intergovernmental sources of revenue,[25] and extensive civil service reforms in city government, such as the decentralization of personnel decision-making authority, the creation of a senior executive service, and the elimination of a veterans' preference policy in hiring and promoting.[26]

Increased productivity measures, in short, seem to be associated with governments that are interested in improving all kinds of management, and the motivations behind this kind of activity in the fields of evaluation research and productivity improvement by all levels of government appear to stem from an underlying disaffection among citizens with the disappointing results of public programs. As Francis G. Caro notes,

there is every reason for dissatisfaction with the current state of intervention on problems of health, economic security, education, housing—indeed on the entire range of social disorders that confront our urban communities. Neither the rhetoric of politicians nor the pleas of do-gooders of various persuasions are sufficient to guide program development. Similarly, neither the theories of academicians nor the exaggerated statements of efficacy by practitioners are adequate bases for the support and expansion of various human service activities. Evaluation research, not a new but nevertheless an increasingly robust enterprise, can have a major impact on social problems.[27]

WHAT IS PROGRAM EVALUATION?

True, evaluation research seems to be making a political comeback in governmental circles, but what is it? Evaluation research has a number of possible definitions,[28] but perhaps the most useful one is provided by the Assistant Comptroller General of the Program Evaluation and Methodology Division of the U.S. General Accounting Office:

Program evaluation is a way of bringing to public decision makers the available knowledge about a problem, about the relative effectiveness of past strategies for addressing or reducing that problem, and about the observed effectiveness of particular programs.[29]

One review of the literature on the evaluation process noted that the more recent attempts to define evaluation reflect "concern with both information on the outcomes of programs and judgments regarding the desirability or value of programs."[30]

A final note: It is important to observe in defining evaluation research that *evaluation research* differs from *basic research. Evaluation research* is a form of applied or "action research" because it may contribute to social action, but without assessing by the researchers the effects of specific interventions in a program. It is concerned with basic theory and research design, but its chief function is to evaluate comprehensively a particular activity and, this is important, to meet an agency's deadline.

The Purposes of Program Evaluation

The emphasis that current definitions of evaluation research place on the effectiveness of programmatic outcomes (and on the desirability of even having those programs as social policy in the first place) leads us to ponder the real purposes of program evaluation. At one level, program evaluation allows policymakers to confront the problem of resource allocation. Policymakers obviously must choose among competing social objectives and among competing ways of achieving those objectives; moreover, these choices must give full consideration to the somewhat abstruse principles of justice, equity, and political reality. Thus, certain social questions can be raised that evaluation research often can clarify.[31] These policy queries include: What is the appropriate level of achieving a particular objective? Are there choices for reaching that level? What resources will be required to attain the program objective? Are there obstacles to the implementation of a particular alternative, and what would be the costs of attempting to overcome the obstacles? And finally, are there equity considerations connected with the leading alternative?

If resource allocation questions were the only purpose underlying program evaluation research, they would provide more than adequate justification for conducting it, but there is a deeper motivation initiating program evaluations, a motivation that is more political than economic. As one analyst notes,

evaluation research can be invoked for a variety of purposes, not only as a means of improving programs. Sometimes evaluation is undertaken to justify or endorse an ongoing program and sometimes to investigate or audit the program in order to lay blame for failure, abolish it, change its leadership, or curtail its activities.[32]

Kinds of Program Evaluation

Analysts have attempted to delineate various kinds of evaluation research and to match these techniques with the most suitable types of social programs. Among the most basic distinctions in the literature of evaluation research is that made between summative and formative research.[33] *Summative evaluation* is designed to assess a program's result after the program has been well established. *Formative evaluation* is meant to improve a program while it is still ongoing and fluid.

These very basic distinctions have since been refined, and a variety of taxonomies have been developed by specialists in evaluation research. For example, the now-defunct Community Services Administration distinguished among *program impact evaluation*, which assesses the impact and effectiveness of a program; *program strategy evaluation*, which evaluates the program's strategies to determine those that are most effective in delivering services; and, finally, *program monitoring*, which assesses the individual project in order to determine operational efficiency.[34] The Urban Institute modified these distinctions formulated by the Community Services Administration to include *project ranking*, which is an effort to rank the *relative* achievements of local projects.[35]

Conversely, the Rand Corporation developed a somewhat different series of distinctions for the Department of Health, Education, and Welfare (now the departments of Education and Health and of Human Services). It separated evaluation from compliance control and capability building. *Compliance control* is defined as "monitoring for compliance with legislative intent and administrative regulations," while *capability building* is attained through efforts to make a program more subject to evaluation techniques, including "increasing state and local decision makers' ability to carry out their own evaluations."[36]

One of the more useful categorizations of the evaluation literature is that devised by Orville F. Poland, in which the schemata of effectiveness evaluation, efficiency evaluation, and eclectic evaluation are offered.[37] *Effectiveness evaluation* uses controlled experiments to determine how well programmatic goals have been achieved. *Efficiency evaluation* uses cost effectiveness approaches to determine what the costs of the goals being achieved are. *Eclectic evaluation* analyzes a program's secondary criteria, such as its inputs, outputs, and processes, in an effort to identify programs needing greater attention; it can lead to a better understanding of how the program really works.

Given the various efforts at categorizing kinds of program evaluation (and there are many more than we have mentioned), perhaps the most straightforward approach is that offered by the Evaluation Research Society, which has listed six types of program evaluations that are conducted on a routine basis.[38] We shall review these kinds of program evaluation with an emphasis on identifying what sorts of information these evaluative approaches produce for the public administrator.[39]

Front-end analysis is evaluation research that is conducted before a decision is made to engage in a new program. Generally, it addresses policy formulation problems, often relying on the findings of prior evaluations, in an effort to estimate how feasible the program might be and its possible effects.

The kinds of information that front-end analyses produce are data relating to planning, and which can be used to provide a rational approach to a program and to its later evaluation. Front-end analysis also measures ongoing problems and the progress of programs that have been conducted in the past. An example of a front-end analysis is the General Accounting Office's study of teenage pregnancy, which was provided to Congress before legislation was introduced proposing service programs for pregnant teenagers.[40]

A second kind of evaluation research is *evaluability assessment*. Evaluability assessment is employed to answer questions of policy formulation and implementation. The policy assumptions underlying a program are compared with what the program says it is supposed to do (*i.e.*, its stated objectives), and an effort is made to assess the reasonableness of those assumptions and the probability that the program is able to attain its objectives. Evaluability assessment describes the characteristics of how the program is being implemented, and it is helpful in determining the practicality and utility of undertaking a later full-scale evaluation of the effectiveness of the program; if it is determined that a full-scale evaluation of the program would be in order, evaluability assessment typically provides the basis for such a large-scale evaluation. Fundamentally, evaluability assessment is retrospective in nature, and involves questions of accountability.

More than any other type of evaluation research, evaluability assessment provides the public administrator with information about the implementation and management of a public program. An example of an evaluability assessment is Bruce Buchanan's effort to assess whether the Senior Executive Service of the federal government has met its goals.[41]

Process evaluation is a kind of program evaluation that can either be used by itself or in combination with another kind of evaluation research. Like evaluability assessment, it employs a retrospective view of programs. The goal of process evaluation is to describe and assess the processes of discrete program activities, such as management, strategic planning, operations, costs, and the details of the implementation process. A process evaluation can be very helpful in determining the effects of a particular program on its clientele group.

In sum, the process evaluation not only can enlighten questions of policy implementation, but also it can be useful, especially when used in tandem with effectiveness evaluations (to be discussed next), in answering questions of accountability. Thus, the primary type of information that the process evaluation provides a public administrator is knowledge about the implementation and management of a program (which evaluability assessments also do), and about the effectiveness of the way in which the program is being implemented and managed (which the effectiveness evaluation also does). Examples of a process evaluation are those studies that focus on how innovations in the public sector are circulated and become routinized.[42]

The *effectiveness*, or *impact evaluation*, is perhaps the most appreciated by top agency executives and legislators, principally because it focuses on whether or not a public program is doing what it is supposed to be doing. Like process evaluations, an effectiveness evaluation is retrospective. In its effort to determine how well a program has been doing, it must face up to the very real problem of showing that changes observed in a particular problem area can be attributed to the impact of the program, rather than to the trends in the environment over which the program has no control. As a consequence of making this difficult distinction, effectiveness evaluations must be designed in such a way that an understanding can be obtained from the evaluation about what conditions might have been—or would have been—if the program had not been present. As Eleanor Chelinsky observes, "This, of course, is the quintessential accountability question." [43] Effectiveness evaluations, however, are also needed to address questions of implementation, since it is at the level of execution of a policy where the impact of that policy may or may not be made.

Effectiveness evaluations provide the public administrator with information regarding the impact of the program, its implementation, and its management; it also measures ongoing problems inherent in the program and the progress of the program. An example of a well known effectiveness evaluation is the Kansas City Police Department's study about the effectiveness of police patrols in preventing crime; this evaluation found that there were no statistically significant differences in crime rates, citizen attitudes, the reported number of crimes, citizen behavior, or even in the rate of traffic accidents among (1) areas where no police patrols were sent out, and police responded only to specific calls for help; (2) areas where patrols were maintained at previous levels; and (3) areas where patrols were doubled or tripled in size. [44]

A fifth kind of program evaluation is *program and problem monitoring*. Rather than using a single shot or retrospective approach, program and problem monitoring is continuous, and its purpose is to provide information on problems, or, at least, to track problems, in both the long term and the short term, in a variety of areas simultaneously. Program and problem monitoring attempts to focus on how the problem may have changed over time, whether or not the program is continuing to comply with public policy, how service delivery methods may have altered over time, and so forth. Program and problem monitoring can be used not only to address policy formulation and policy implementation questions, but also to answer accountability questions. Its unique value is that it enables administrators to follow the evolution of problems, and the impact of a program on those problems, over time. Frequently, program and

problem monitoring relies on time-series analysis, data systems, and forms to be filled out by public administrators who work far down the line from those public administrators who demand and use the forms.

The types of information that program and problem monitoring provides public administrators typically focuses on the planning and the designing of a program and its evaluation, the implementing and managing of the program, the justification and demonstration of program effectiveness, and, of course, most obviously, the measurement of ongoing problem resolution and program progress. Program and problem monitoring is capable of furnishing information in all these areas by itself, and not in conjunction with any other type of program evaluation. An example of a program and problem monitoring evaluation is the General Accounting Office's study of the effectiveness of the Comprehensive Employment and Training Act Program, which employed three different sets of monitoring data: data on characteristics of the participants (which addressed how well the program was targeted); financial data (which addressed how much the program was costing); and, status reports (which addressed the mix of services and how many participants were actually being placed in jobs). All these sets of data were provided by local public administrators to federal public administrators on a quarterly or yearly basis. [45]

Finally, *meta-evaluation*, or *evaluation synthesis*, constitutes our sixth form of evaluation research. Meta-evaluation reanalyzes findings from a number of previous evaluations (but occasionally from just one evaluation) to find out what has been learned in the past about a public policy. Meta-evaluation is the most comprehensive, and obviously retrospective, approach to evaluation research in that it synthesizes a number of findings for purposes of determining program effectiveness and what may be known about a given problem area. It is highly flexible, and can provide public administrators with information about all the major questions of public policy: Is the policy accountable? Is it effective? And what more about the policy area needs to be known?

Evaluation synthesis provides the public administrator with information on planning and evaluating programs, justifying the effectiveness of the program's implementation and management, and demonstrating the effectiveness of a program. An example of an evaluation synthesis is the General Accounting Office's study of drinking-age laws and their effects on highway safety.[46]

These six kinds of program evaluation constitute, in the words of one authority in the field, "the everyday repertoire of program evaluation."[47] As we noted earlier, these approaches are certainly not the only ways to classify program evaluations, but "it would be fair to say that they represent widespread agreement in the field with regard to common practice in program evaluation, and that they are relevant, in various degrees, to the needs of public administrators."[48]

THE EVALUATION PROCESS

As noted, the process of evaluation is far from simple, and Figure 7-1 illustrates this process. The chart shows four fundamentals of

the evaluation process: ascertaining decision makers' needs; defining the nature and scope of the problem; determining valid objectives; and specifying comprehensive measures.[49] Let us consider these in turn.

Four Fundamentals of Program Evaluation

To determine a decision maker's needs, we first must ask what *the decision maker's perceptions of the problem* are. Is he or she dissatisfied with the effectiveness or the results of the program—or with the lack of a program—to meet a particular social mission? How will the information brought out by a program evaluation be used? When is the final report needed?

Defining the nature and scope of the problem also is important, and it is vital that the people who are to use the results of the study (in other words, the decision makers themselves) understand the nature and scope of the issues at stake at least as thoroughly as the people responsible for conducting the study.

FIGURE 7–1 The Process of Program Evaluation

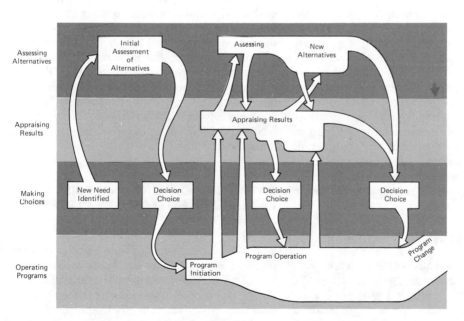

Source: U.S. General Accounting Office, *Evaluation and Analysis to Support Decision Making* (Washington, D.C.: U.S. Government Printing Office, 1976), p. 8.

This means that all persons involved in the evaluation should be aware of the study's origin, review legislative hearings and reports associated with the topic, be informed about the history of the program designed to deal with the problem, and examine together the past analyses and evaluations of the issue. The General Accounting Office (GAO) has noted that "there is often a trade-off between the breadth of a study and the precision of the results."[50]

Determining valid objectives is a third area of importance. To the extent possible, a statement of objectives should include a complete understanding of the intended benefits. It should include how many of those benefits are expected to be attained, identify possible recipients of adverse consequences and any unintended problems that cannot be avoided, include important qualitative features (although measuring qualitative attainments is hardly an easy task), and, finally, account for multiple objectives that may be in conflict with one another or, conversely, be in support of one another. As the GAO again notes in this regard, "the importance of taking such a comprehensive view of objectives cannot be overstated. Oversimplified statements (1) will not capture all essential aspects of the effects intended, and (2) may contain implied conflicting consequences for groups other than the intended beneficiaries."[51]

The final area of importance is that of *specifying comprehensive measures*. It should include quantifying the extent to which the program's goals are met—in other words, effectiveness measures. These comprehensive measures should involve capturing the qualitative aspects of the consequences, or *intangible measures*; quantifying to the degree possible unintended consequences, or *side effect measures*; and quantifying as much as possible the differences of impact on the beneficiaries and the bearers of the cost, or what are known as *distribution measures*.

Conducting a Program Evaluation

Once these fundamentals of the evaluation process are established, certain basic steps must be taken to successfully execute a program evaluation.[52] Among the first is *preparing a detailed study plan*. The plan should include a clear statement of the problem and a careful listing of built-in constraints and assumptions to be used in evaluating the problem. It should state the methods to be used and elaborate the resources to be committed in the study. It should include a report schedule, specified procedures for amending the study plan, and finally, it must have a time frame for completing the major components of the study, including a final deadline.

Next, *a study team should be selected, lines of communication established, and appropriate methods to conduct the study determined*. We shall return to the problem of method later, but suffice it to note here that in selecting appropriate methods the following criteria should be used: *level of validity* (how much confidence can a program manager have in the results of the study?); *relevance* (will the results be useful to decision makers?); *significance* (will the study results show the program manager substantially more than can be deducted from direct observation?); *efficiency* (does the value of the study exceed the cost?); and, finally, *timeliness* (will the analytical information be available in time to meet program objectives and legislative schedules?).

All evaluation plans should *specify procedures for using the results*. In other words, the evaluation's results must be communicated if they are to have any effect, and this means specifying the nature of the reports and to whom they are to be made; communicating those reports with clarity and with conciseness; and following up. The follow-up should include interpreting the report to decision makers, responding to questions that have not been answered by the report, and generally helping decision makers develop a logical reaction to the report.

DATA ENVELOPMENT ANALYSIS: FINDING THE BOTTOM LINE IN PUBLIC MANAGEMENT

One of the great potential utilities of evaluation research is that it may enable us to determine what the "bottom line" in public administration is. The private sector has long had "bottom line" measurements available to it, specifically the profit margin. But the nonprofit sector does not, and researchers in the field of program evaluation slowly are developing measurement techniques that enable them to determine their level of efficiency in the delivery of public services.

Efficiency is a term that can have several implications. As Roger B. Parks points out, "efficiency" often has meaning beyond the phrase of "the biggest bang for the buck." Such a definition does not necessarily take into account how many resources it takes to conduct a program, nor the corresponding potential prices of policy outputs. Nor does such a definition include other measures that might be attached to the value of the outputs produced by a public agency, such as the degree of importance that citizens and clients might attach to those outputs.

We are not considering these refined definitions here. Instead, we are talking in terms of what the field of program evaluation commonly calls "technical efficiency," or the attempt to maximize the difference between all benefits from all costs in an operation.[53]

Data Envelopment Analysis is one of the more recent techniques being used to measure technical efficiency—the "bottom line"—of the public sector.[54] In its simplest terms, Data Envelopment Analysis establishes measurable outputs for a particular "decision-making unit," such as a government agency or a corporation. For example, a police department (a "decision-making unit") would have certain obvious kinds of outputs, such as number of suspects arrested, number of officers assigned to patrol, and so forth. These outputs are then divided by pertinent inputs. In the case of the police department, the pertinent input would be the department's budget. This procedure is then done for a number of police departments and the results are compared. Those departments that do not measure up to the average performance (as determined by specific measures) of the other police departments are thus made aware that they are not performing at their potential efficiency.

In an effort to be fair, other factors are mixed into these measures of efficiency, such as environmental factors over which the decision-making unit may have no control. In the case of the police department, for example, such factors may include the percent of population below the poverty line, since poor populations are often afflicted with higher crime rates. In this fashion, the productivity

and efficiency of decision-making units can be compared on the basis of "fairness"; in other words, police departments that are working in high-crime areas, or in areas with large percentages of their populations below the poverty line, are compared only with those police departments that are working in areas afflicted by similar levels of crime and impoverishment. Or, if these kinds of comparisons are not possible (which is not uncommon), then those police departments that are in tougher areas than are other departments are granted advantages—"weights" along specific measurement areas—that are designed to render them comparable to their peers.

Data Envelopment Analysis has been applied with some success to school districts and police departments.[55] One study of police departments, which analyzed data from a set of 469 municipal police agencies, concluded, by using Data Envelopment Analysis, that some factors relating to police department efficiency were more controllable than were others. Among those factors not at all amenable to control were the proportion of citizens living below the poverty level and how long the police department had been functioning in the community. Factors more subject to control were those involving the utilization of resources, organizational structure, and personnel policies. The study found that the allocation of resources to the patrol division was associated with somewhat higher levels of efficiency among the more efficient police departments, although this relationship was not a strong one. However, the relative bureaucratization of the police department (*i.e.*, having several more hierarchical layers than the average) did associate strongly with lower levels of efficiency. Among personnel policies, unionization of the police force had a negative association with efficiency, whereas police departments that were unburdened with civil service and educational requirements showed a bimodal pattern. Departments without civil service or educational requirements were more likely to be found in the lowest *and* in the highest quartiles of the efficiency distribution of the study.[56]

Our point is not to delve into the details of what makes some police departments more efficient than others, but rather to convey a flavor of how Data Envelopment Analysis can work. Data

Envelopment Analysis may be as close as any of the program evaluation methodologies in being able to derive measures of technical efficiency for the public sector.

This review of the nuts and bolts of evaluation research in public administration does not address the human problems encountered in conducting a program evaluation. These problems are scientific and technical, administrative and political, and moral and ethical. We consider these next.

SCIENTIFIC AND TECHNICAL PROBLEMS IN EVALUATION RESEARCH

As Henry Riecken accurately observes,

The central scientific problems in evaluation are (a) the segregation of treatment effects per se from random variation on the one hand and from systematic biasing through uncontrolled factors that are extraneous to treatment on the other hand, and (b) the reliable measurement of these effects.[57]

Problems of Validity and Measurement

The first part of the problem, as Riecken phrases it, deals essentially with the question of validity. Evaluation researchers can use a number of methods to assure validity—selecting the appropriate experimental methods, using a nonrandom comparison group method, comparing similar programs using time series analysis, and using similar approaches.[58]

The other portion of Riecken's dilemma is that of measurement. Before a program evaluator can measure anything, however, he or she must identify the objectives of the program in a way that permits valid measuring. Such an identification of program goals includes perceiving the content of the objective (in other words, what is to be changed by the program), the target of the program, the time frame within which the change is expected to occur, the number of objectives if there are more than one, and finally, the extent of the expected effect.[59]

Once objectives are so defined, then distinctions can be made between immediate, intermediate, and ultimate objectives, and measurements can be developed accordingly. One type of mea-

surement, for example, is input measurement: What are the resources allocated by an agency for a particular program relative to the services actually received by the clients of that program? In this case, the resources would be the inputs. Original and secondary data also need to be measured. As Caro observes, "identification of variables is, of course, only a first step in the measurement process. Evaluators are often confronted with serious obstacles in seeking the valid, reliable, and sensitive measures they need." Caro goes on to note that agency records often are seriously deficient and the evaluator must collect his or her own original and secondary data; such data collection "may add enormously to the cost of evaluation."[60]

Caro also notes that the subjects of the evaluation (e.g., public administrators) may try to redirect their behavior in an effort to affect the evaluation's outcome, and that detecting this attempt becomes particularly difficult when evaluative criteria and data are incomplete. An example of the evaluative problems posed by incomplete data is provided by higher education. Who has not heard of the "publish or perish" dictum in universities and not wondered if the number of a professor's publications actually has anything to do with his or her teaching abilities? Relatedly, do grades indicate the real level of learning by a student?

Finally, there is the measurement problem of occasionally trying to measure the unmeasurable—a problem more common in the public sector than in the private one. Assigning a monetary worth to a human life is an example. Early cost-benefit analyses conducted by the government based the value of a human life on a person's projected earning power—a calculus that strikes some as a bit coldblooded. Still, determining the value of a human life is difficult to sidestep in many program evaluations, notably those in health, safety, defense, crime, transportation, the environment, and many other areas of basic governmental functions. The conclusion is inexorably, if reluctantly, drawn that, whether or not life can be measured, it nonetheless must be assigned some dollar value in many program evaluations, if the evaluations are to be useful.

Federal officials are doing precisely this, but without coherence. The U.S. Department of Agriculture low-balls a human life at $1.1 million; the

Office of Management and Budget pegs a life at $1 million to $2 million, and the Consumer Product Safety Commission agrees that a life tops out at $2 million. The Occupational Safety and Health Administration measures a really good human life at $3.5 million (and a poor one at a baseline of $2 million); the Nuclear Regulatory Commission says each and every life is worth $5 million (its figure, interestingly, is based on the hazard pay for fighter pilots in the Korean Conflict), while the Environmental Protection Agency says a life can be worth as much as $8 million—or as little as $1.6 million.[61]

Problems of Research Design

A final major problem of a scientific and technical nature in evaluation research is that of dealing with program research design. The design problem can be broken down and understood in terms of the following components: controlled interaction between program practitioners, interaction between recipients of the program, and the diffuse and unstable nature of many programs.

Achieving control over the variables in a program for purposes of evaluating that program is unusually difficult in an action setting. When a *control group* (*i.e.*, a group of clients who are excluded from receiving the benefits of a particular experimental program designed to improve services) is set aside for purposes of comparing it with an *experimental group* (*i.e.*, a group of clients who do receive the benefits of a particular program innovation), there is often a great deal of social and political pressure to provide the benefits of that experiment to both groups. Thus, both the program's administrators and the program's clients are reluctant to withhold services from a particular group that might benefit from those services, even though the evaluation study might be ruined by doing so. Relatedly, self-selection is a problem in a program evaluation in an action setting; "it is difficult to refuse service to those who seek it and provide service to those who resist it."[62]

In short, action settings simply inhibit evaluators from using a well-controlled experimental design. However, one of the real problems in developing a research design for program evaluation is more political than social; hidden motives on the part of the evaluator can interfere with accurate measurement. For example, private consultants, who must make a living by securing contracts from public agencies, may promise too much in writing their research design. Perhaps the most vivid example of this in recent years was provided by a program evaluation attempted by the Office of Economic Opportunity in 1972, in which 120 drug treatment centers in six cities were evaluated in a study involving interviews with 9,000 present and former drug abusers. The purpose of the study was to assess client characteristics and behavior, the delivery system, the relationship of the project to the communities themselves, and the program's cost-effectiveness. All of this was to be accomplished in thirteen months. After seven months of rather grotesque trial and error, the project was abandoned. During that time, the program evaluators (a private consulting firm) had collected data on nine treatment centers and 1,270 clients at a cost of more than $2 million.[63]

Avoiding such fiascoes can be enhanced by asking certain basic questions about the research design itself.[64] Is the research design explicit about important constraints in the study? Does it use standard evaluation procedures as much as possible? Have the evaluators adjusted expectations to known data reliability and availability? Does the evaluation rely on opinions as measures only if the program is intended to change opinions? Does it mandate a clear separation between the results of the data collection and analysis and the evaluators' judgments and beliefs? Does it specify at least one acceptable measure of accomplishment? Does it keep the questions relatively few in number? Does it establish priorities? And does the design require as few formal reports from the evaluators as possible, depending instead on frequent and informal contacts? While such questions may seem elementary, the sad fact is that they are rarely asked in many research designs.

ADMINISTRATIVE AND POLITICAL PROBLEMS IN EVALUATION RESEARCH

A second major problem in conducting evaluation research, apart from the scientific and technical ones, is the administrative and political difficulties to be surmounted in conducting an evaluation. Riecken observes that "in comparison with the vast amount of scholarly examination of the design and measurement features of evaluation, the matter of day-to-day execution of these tasks has received scant attention," and he notes further that political realities complicate evaluation management because evaluation "is always undertaken in a context of decisions about the use of resources and, accordingly, has implications for the acquisition, distribution and loss of social or political power."[65]

Who are the Evaluators?

To understand the administrative and political implications of evaluation research, we must first know who the evaluators are. Program evaluators play many social roles, and the roles they assume affect the ways they discharge their responsibilities. In his excellent study of policy analysts in the federal government, Arnold Meltsner identified four separate roles played by program evaluators: the *entrepreneur*, who has excellent analytical and political skills; the *politician*, who has reasonable political skills but who is less impressive in intellectual analysis; the *technician*, who has good analytical skills but is apolitical; and finally what Meltsner calls the *pretender*, who is weak both analytically and politically.[66] Similarly, K. A. Archebald has observed three roles: *academics*, or evaluation researchers who typically are funded by grant monies and conduct a study with minimal contact with the program's clients; *clinicians*, who respond only to their own interpersonal dynamic and who treat (quite patronizingly) the client as a patient who needs help to cure a sickness; and *strategizers*, who use the management consultant approach and who work with clients as if they were colleagues. Archebald contends that in an evaluation that blends all three evaluator roles, it is the program's clients who often have the ultimate responsibility for decisions regarding research and their consequences.[67]

Administrators against Evaluators?

Because of the social and political roles that program evaluators frequently play, tensions can develop between the evaluators and the line managers of an agency. As a result, it is unfortunately not unusual for conflict to erupt between the program managers and the program's evaluators, whom the managers may see as self- anointed prophets passing judgment on the managers' efforts to solve real and long-standing social problems. Mutual perceptions aside, evaluators often do have different perspectives, purposes, and values from the on-line practitioners. Conflict can occur if the practitioners feel themselves threatened—and objective analysis in and of itself, irrespective who is conducting it, often can be perceived as such a threat. Often, however, tensions between evaluators and managers result simply from the evaluators' failure to make a clear distinction between the administrative and personal qualities of the managers and the actual effectiveness of the treatment they happen to be using. In any event, there is an unusually rich empirical literature on the interplay of political and administrative forces extant among managers and evaluators.[68]

As a result of these problems, most experts in the field of evaluation agree that the evaluation of a program ought to be commissioned and sponsored by the highest level in an organization that has program responsibility and, on balance, evaluation that is conducted by an external agency or by a third- party consultant probably is preferable.[69] By commissioning an evaluation by the upper-most level of an organization and by using outside evaluators, some of the natural strains between practitioners and researchers are avoided. Notably such an approach can avoid those tensions that emanate from such diverse values as the following: specificity versus generality (researchers are more likely to be interested in long-term problem solving, while practitioners are more likely to be concerned with solving immediate problems); status quo versus change (practicing administrators, on the one hand, may attempt to conceal badly managed programs and to resist any change that they perceive as being potentially disruptive, while academic evaluators, on the other hand, often claim a superior knowledge of human affairs that predispose them to dramatize the inadequacy of the administrators); and, finally, academic knowledge versus practical experience (because the evaluator is, in fact, usually an academic, the practitioner views him or her as having no "real world" experience in or awareness of such practical problems as limited budgets and personnel resources).[70]

While the general thrust of the evaluation literature tends to favor the use of outside consultants, arguments can be made for either inside or outside evaluators. Contentions favoring the use of outside consultants include the perceptions that they are more objective; they are more likely to question the basic premises of the organization; they would be more effective mediators because of their objectivity; and they are more likely to devote their time more fully to the research problem at hand. Still, insiders have certain advantages, too, including a more detailed knowledge of the organization and the probability that they are in a better position to be able to do continuing, long-term program evaluation.[71]

A Note of Grace and a Case of Reality

In the field of public administration, ideology can become mixed with reality, and this is particularly true in the areas of program evaluation and productivity. An example of ideology being mistaken for reality is provided in the following synopsis of the final report of the President's Private Sector Survey on Cost Control (the Grace Commission). On the other hand, an example of public management being conducted effectively and without ideological bias is furnished by the subsequent case study conducted by the American Productivity Center on the City of Phoenix, Arizona.

The Grace Commission's report was publicly accepted in 1984 by President Reagan as his program for reducing the federal deficit. The Commission argued a commonly held ideology that by applying "solid business management" to the public sector, enormous savings could be realized. However, as the analysis that follows points out, there are anomalies in applying the unadapted techniques of business to the public interest.

Reality, rather than ideology, is more apparent in the case study of the City of Phoenix that follows the Grace Commission section. Phoenix is known as a "star" city among public administrators, and is one of the most effective and efficient urban governments in the country. The city has been able to attain this stature by constantly testing what management techniques work and what do not, and by monitoring the performance of the programs that it conducts. Empiricism replaces ideology.

The nominal predecessors of the Grace Commission (which, in many ways, were not at all its predecessors, since they were significantly smaller in both scope and number of participants), the Brownwell Commission, the Hoover Commissions, the Ash Council, and the Carter Reorganization Project were composed largely of analysts from many walks of life who were inside government or who knew a great deal about it. Not so with the Grace Commission. The Executive Committee of the President's Private Sector Survey on Cost Control consisted of 161 members and virtually all of them were executives in the business world. About a fourth headed firms listed in the Fortune 500, but also represented were about a third of the top fifty commercial banks in the country, the nation's three largest insurance firms, and other members of similar backgrounds. Only seven of the 161 members of the Executive Committee were from occupations that were not businesses, such as representatives from universities, labor, and the Heritage Foundation.

The reports themselves are unusually difficult to read. None is indexed; they are long; and the writing style is arid. Some parts of the reports are actually censored.

The analyses are of mixed quality. An example of a constructive analysis is a study of correspondence control in the Department of Health and Human Services, which found that it took fifty-eight days to answer a letter in the Office of the Secretary, compared to eighteen days at the Pentagon, and nine at a Prudential Insurance office. An example of a poor analysis is the report's criticism of the Department of Energy on the grounds that its span of control is considerably narrower than that of the federal government as a whole. What is not mentioned in this critique, however, is the fact that the department uses 90 percent of its budget allocations to contract out its programs, and greater control is often required.

Recommendations for achieving savings meet a similarly mixed fate. For example, the final report argues for cheaper packaging of ammunition for the military, but ignores prospective damage in shipping that would offset such savings. The report also urges that 7,000 small post offices and almost two-thirds of Social Security district and branch offices be closed in order to save money. No doubt savings would accrue, but at what cost in services? The question of government's obligation to provide services is not addressed in this instance, and is rarely addressed throughout the report.

The final report also contains some serious misrepresentations. First, the Commission grossly exaggerates the savings it claims would be achieved (nearly half a trillion dollars over three years) if its recommendations were followed. But as the Commission states in the fine print, its projected savings are of a "planning" quality and not of a "budget" quality, despite the fact that the proposed savings are presented in the context of the growing national debt. Similarly, the figures presented by the Commission refer not to mere savings but to revenue increases and accelerations in cash flow that the report contends will result if its recommendations were implemented; yet, faster revenue collections and slower disbursements are not true "savings," but merely bookkeeping artifices. Most important, however, the potential savings claimed by the Commission really are only estimates, and not well-grounded projections. Many of the recommendations by the Commission are of a sort that their financial implications simply are not measurable, even speculatively.

A second type of misrepresentation by the Grace Commission occurs in the context of its claim that its objective was not to change policy, but merely to improve efficiency in the federal government. Yet, as the General Accounting Office observed, "policy-oriented issues make up a large portion of the Commission's total estimated savings." For example, the report advocates repeal of the Davis-Bacon Act, the Walsh-Healey Act, and the Service Contracts Act; it urges the Environmental Protection Agency to propose new block grant programs to replace categorical grants for environmental assistance; it proposes that the sale or lease of public range lands in ten Western states be reevaluated; it supports increased production of plutonium and tritium in three nuclear facilities; it suggests that the Department of State push for a new voting system in the United Nations that is weighted for relative budgetary contributions to the UN; and it urges that the president be granted an item veto power. While such measures may result in greater savings by the federal government, they clearly are policy changes as well, and the Commission had a duty to say so that it did not fulfill.

Many of the proposals of the Grace Commission display a business-oriented prejudice that is not identified in the report for what it is. Most obvious in this regard is the Commission's commitment to a privatization philosophy. As in the report of the second Hoover Commission (reviewed in Chapter 11), it is urged that far more contracts be granted to the private sector to conduct and implement public programs.

Among other federal operations slated for privatization by the Grace Commission are the Military Commissary System, the Strategic Petroleum Reserve, hydroelectric power plants, space shuttle launching services, electronic data processing for the Social Security System, Coast Guard search and rescue operations, patient care in small military hospitals, operation of the army's personnel and payroll system, and municipal wastewater treatment. Many of these and other suggestions would result in extraordinary profits for certain industries.

A similar bias is found in the Grace Commission's clear preference for deregulation, including the deregulation of nuclear power plants. The Commission also recommends that more user charges be levied. However, user charges should be put on a *really* paying basis, not merely offsetting the full costs of providing a service, but charging what the market will bear and making a profit! Now *that* is private enterprise!

It appears that, in some ways, the President's Private Sector Survey on Cost Control may actually diminish rather than enhance the quality of government in the United States. For example, the Commission proposes than an Office of Federal Management be created that would centralize virtually all aspects of management in the federal government. It is unlikely that such an office would attain the alleged advantages of "business- like management," but certainly such an office would give unprecedented power to those in charge of it. It is at least debatable whether a highly centralized Office of Federal Management would be good for the quality or the responsiveness of government.

The Commission also made allegations and proposals that seem purposely designed to undermine morale in the federal service. J. Peter Grace, the Chair of the Commission, for example, continually insisted throughout the Commission's deliberations that "government is run horribly," despite the fact that many of the reports provided by his own Commission stated otherwise. In fact, the Commission admitted that top federal executives were inadequately paid

compared with their counterparts in the private sector, and suggested pay raises for them ranging from 20 to 30 percent. But at the lower levels of the federal bureaucracy, arguments were made by the Commission to significantly reduce pay; in making its case, no reference was made to the recommendation by the Advisory Committee on Federal Pay that overall federal salaries need to be raised by nearly 22 percent to catch up to private sector. The Commission also urged significant decreases in the size of the federal work force, but with little analysis to support such cuts.

Finally, many of the managerial innovations urged by the Grace Commission were not all that novel; in fact, the General Accounting Office has stated that about half of the proposals suggested by the Commission already had been recommended by the GAO, but had not been adopted. On the other hand, the Office of Management and Budget reported a year after the release of the Grace Commission's report that 879 (or 35 percent) of the Commission's 2,478 recommendations had been enacted by the Reagan administration, at a three-year cost savings of $111,882,000.

In sum, the President's Private Sector Survey on Cost Control has some pluses and it has some minuses. But unlike its predecessors, not only is the report of the Grace Commission far more sweeping in its scope and in its recommendations, but also its members were far less representative of people who understand government and who comprehend the obligation mandated by society for government to provide services.

Sources: Derived from: Charles T. Goodsell, "The Grace Commission," *Public Administration Review*; U.S. General Accounting Office, *Compendium of GAO's Views on the Cost Saving Proposals of the Grace Commission. Vol. I: Summary of Findings. Vol. II: Individual Issue Analyses*, GAO/OCG-85-I (Washington, D.C.: U.S. Government Printing Office, February 19, 1985); and Office of Management and Budget, *Management of the United States Government* (Washington, D.C.: U.S. Government Printing Office, 1985).

The City of Phoenix is the ninth largest city in the country and employs about 10,000 people.

It is one of the nation's fastest growing cities and, in part as a result of that growth, the city initiated a comprehensive plan to improve productivity in the early 1970s. At first, Phoenix tried a centralized approach that had an industrial engineering orientation, but this tack eventually proved to be so cumbersome that it was phased out. But the initiation of this system did begin what observers called a "cultural change" in the attitudes of both managers and their employees.

In 1977, another kind of approach was begun. A Citizens Productivity Advisory Committee was appointed to advise the city on how to improve municipal productivity, and as a result of its recommendations, a major effort was made to make departments more accountable and employees more participatory in decision making. Problem-solving work groups were established in every area of the city's business, and the results have been successful. An annual survey of city employees shows increased employee involvement in decision making for every year that the program has been in operation.

A similar effort was made to decentralize management—starkly in contrast to the recommendations of the Grace Commission. In 1980, the director of management and budget assigned twelve to fifteen of his staff members to operating departments to monitor productivity projects that departments undertake each year. By integrating these analysts into the operating departments, they become a part of the team of that department rather than being perceived as outside "graders."

The city also created a Value Management Resource Office, which combined the training and development staff with the operations analysis staff. This office functions as a team of internal consultants who use both industrial engineering and behavioral science methods to improve productivity. Included in its functions are surveys of employees and clients, workload distribution analyses, the development of work-output measures, the diagnosis of problems, work-group development, management consultation, conflict resolution, customized training, work flow and scheduling, productivity training, and decision-making assistance. The office provides some thirty formal training programs for city workers affecting about 800 employees each year.

Phoenix city government places a high value on training and education. It offers tuition reimbursement to any of its employees, provided that employees take courses that relate to their employment.

The city also has initiated a "pay for performance" compensation system that in effect is a modified Management by Objectives system. The system requires all departments to establish a plan for achieving their objectives and to list productivity improvement goals within a particular time frame. When these goals are achieved, salaries are adjusted with increases based on inflation rates plus merit increases that are closely tied to the attainment of objectives.

Among the most innovative approaches that Phoenix took was, beginning in 1978, the application of competitive bidding procedures not only for private companies but for its own city agencies as well. Thus, not only do private corporations bid for a city contract, but so do other city agencies, a process that has resulted in saving the city about $3 million a year. According to one city official, "We learn from losing a bid. We are more than willing to go after other departments…if their charges caused our bid to be too high! It's a team effort to cut costs. In theory, unless our city government is inherently inefficient, we should win the bids." Through this unusual process, in 1987 the city's trash collection department won back all its contracts by underbidding private trash collectors; prior to 1987, about half the city was serviced by private collectors because they had underbid the department.

Other innovations introduced by Phoenix include a computerized dispatch system for the fire department, rather than a radio dispatch system, which has greatly improved response rates and information available for units at the scene. The information displayed by computer includes such items as floor plans, the presence of handicapped or elderly residents, the location of dangerous substances, and a variety of other information.

The city also promotes the use of fees for service, or user charges, but without cutting into basic services. For example, there is a standard monthly fee for garbage pickups, but citizens may obtain more frequent service for an additional fee. The water department uses a similar plan by charging a higher fee per gallon as consumption increases beyond a baseline point. This emphasis on fee for services has forced all departments to contain costs.

The city's employee suggestion program also was significantly upgraded. As a result, program participation increased from 100 employees to 1,000, and documented productivity savings went up from $20,000 per year to more than $1,000,000 a year. The city has won a number of awards from the National Association of Suggestion Systems.

The city also uses management retreats in which city management personnel meet off site to share information and experiences twice a year, and the city has created a Citizens' Assistance Office to help residents resolve problems relating to city services.

Phoenix has one of the lowest tax bases in the nation and one of the highest service levels. So productive is the city that the Japanese government invited Phoenix's city manager to Tokyo to advise it on how to increase productivity. In an age when Americans are asking the Japanese how to manage, that is a kudo of no mean significance.

Sources: As derived from *Case Study 38*, American Productivity Center; Randy Fitzgerald, "We *Can* Lower Local Taxes," *Readers' Digest*; Michael DeCourcy Hines, "Cash-Strapped Cities Turn to Companies to Do What Government Once Did." *New York Times* (May 14, 1991) and personal conversations with Phoenix managers.

ETHICAL AND MORAL PROBLEMS IN EVALUATION RESEARCH

Finally, evaluators should be cognizant of some basic ethical and moral problems associated with the conduct of evaluation research. Principal among these are problems involving privacy, confidentiality, and informed consent.

The issues of privacy and confidentiality are not unique to evaluation research, but they do assume a somewhat different tenor in this context. In program evaluation projects, *privacy* refers to the state of the individual; *confidentiality* refers to a state of information. Thus, privacy becomes a matter between the evaluator and the respondent. It hinges on the degree to which the evaluator's questions, in and of themselves, are perceived by the respondent to be prying or embarrassing. Hence, privacy is not a matter of *who* knows the answer, but of whether certain kinds of knowledge are known to *anyone* other than the respondent. The test of an invasion of privacy is to ask if the respondent will voluntarily furnish answers under conditions that appear to appropriately restrict the use of those answers.

Confidentiality refers to the question of whether an investigator's promise of confidentiality to a respondent is sufficient or even necessary. The evaluator's promise, no matter how solemnly given, may not be sufficient because, under certain legal situations, the investigator must yield the information he or she has collected or go to jail. The legal fact of the matter is that social science research records are not protected under statutory law as a privileged communication, as are the records of lawyers and physicians.

Central to the ethical issues of privacy and confidentiality is the problem of *informed consent*, which refers to whether or not a respondent understands what he or she is consenting to. Such an understanding, of course, is particularly important in cases of human experimentation, but it also has a bearing on program evaluation studies. As Riecken observes,

...lawyers have questioned the legality as well as the ethicality of experimental design and random assignment of participants to treatment for purposes of program evaluation. The grounds for such questioning include the issues of informed consent, equal protection, and the statutory (or other) authority of the agency to conduct experimental evaluations.[72]

DOES EVALUATION MATTER?

We have reviewed a number of difficulties regarding program evaluation, but we have not asked what Republicans in the White House used to call the "big enchilada"—that is, is evaluation research used by anyone? Carol H. Weiss observes in this connection that

there is a pervasive sense that government officials do not pay much attention to the research their money is buying. The consensus seems to be that most research studies bounce off the policy process without making much of a dent in the course of events. Support for this notion surfaces in many quarters—among social scientists, executive branch officials, and members of Congress.[73]

Examples to support Weiss's assessment are plentiful, and perhaps the most notorious instance of program managers resisting program evaluation has occurred over the years in elementary and secondary education. Because the education establishment in the United States is a highly decentralized one, local educators have successfully resisted attempts to evaluate such basic programs as whether or not pupils are learning to read. Under Title I of the Elementary and Secondary Education Act of 1965, for example, the U.S. Office of Education (now the Department of Education) requested achievement test data from local school officials; the data were wanted both by Congress (which sought such data as a means of reforming education) and federal executives (who wanted the data as a management tool). Local school officials, however, thought these federal attempts at rather rudimentary program evaluation to be threatening and, although student scores on national tests had declined steadily since 1963 and had begun to rise again in 1982, local educators still have successfully resisted efforts by the federal government to find out more about student achievement in the nation.[74]

The example of public education indicates in broad strokes the basic problems to be overcome in getting governments to use program evaluations. At one level the reasons why program evaluations are used less frequently by policymakers than they might be are fairly straightforward. Often the research cannot produce results early enough to be employed in short-term policy decisions. The evaluator, is after all, often only an advisor, and policymakers are under no particular obligation to accept the evaluator's recommendations. Disagreements between evaluators and practitioners

contribute to the fact that the evaluation is not used; occasionally, for instance, administrators will claim that the "real goals" of the project were not accurately measured.[75]

At a deeper level, however, a lack of use of evaluation by policymakers stems from the different perceptions between practitioners and evaluators that were reviewed earlier. Evaluators generally tend to place the most importance on a study, and sometimes the demand for an evaluation is a signal that a program is in trouble. Adding to this problem is the fact that scarce staff may have to be reallocated to compile data (which may not be wanted by top administrators in the first place), leading to complaints by staff that they have less time, as a consequence, to carry out their assigned responsibilities. Thomas V. Bonoma suggests that the prior relationships between the evaluators and administrators whose program is being evaluated largely determines the nature of the evaluation that is subsequently conducted, the level of resistance to initiating changes recommended by the evaluation, and the strategies to be used by evaluators in overcoming bureaucratic resistance to their findings. Bonoma ranks these strategies for overcoming administrative resistance to organizational changes that are recommended by evaluation research along a continuum ranging from coercion and inducement, to rational persuasion, and finally to "consensual cooperation."[76]

Although the often-observed resistance of government executives to initiating recommended changes may be frustrating to the evaluators, it nonetheless should be recognized that the very act of program evaluation often serves a purpose that is both important and underrecognized by social scientists. Weiss calls this hidden purpose "the enlightenment function," citing as evidence for its existence three major studies on the uses of evaluation research that indicate, in Weiss's words, that "some other process is at work."[77] This process, according to Weiss, is not the conventional wisdom of the social researcher, which holds that

to the extent that he departs from the goals and assumptions adhered to by policymakers, his research will be irrelevant to the "real world" and will go unheeded. [Therefore, for maximum research utility,] the researcher should accept the fundamental goals, priorities, and political constraints of the key decision-making group. He should be sensitive to feasibilities and stay within the narrow range of low cost, low change policy alternatives.[78]

Weiss argues that this perception by the evaluation researcher is both cynical and naive. The real utility of evaluation research, according to Weiss, is that it is a form of social criticism and should be viewed by social scientists as such. "The enlightenment function" of evaluation research is based on assumptions that are quite at odds with the conventional wisdom of the social scientists. The enlightenment model

does not consider value consensus a prerequisite for useful research....it implies that research need not necessarily be geared to the operating feasibilities of today, but that research provides the intellectual background of concepts, orientations, and empirical generalizations that inform policy. As new concepts and data emerge, their gradual cumulative effect can be to change the conventions policymakers abide by and to reorder the goals and priorities of the practical policy world.[79]

The enlightenment model posited by Weiss is perhaps the most succinct and useful view of the role that program evaluation plays in modern public administration. Although not rigorously scientific, it does appeal to the basic precepts of how knowledge is used (i.e., information theory). In this view, evaluation research sensitizes policymakers. It opens new options that, over time, they are more likely to adopt because of the background data provided by an evaluation research project. Evaluation research may not be used as immediately and radically as the evaluation researcher might wish, but in the long run program evaluations are employed by policymakers, and perhaps on a broader plane than evaluation researchers realize.

Evaluation research is likely to reach the position that public administration has reached at the close of the twentieth century. In many ways, the current intellectual revival of evaluation research among public administrationists represents a return to the golden era of the 1930s when the "principles of public administration" paradigm was dominant. Fortunately, evaluation research has sidestepped the intellectual pitfalls of the "principles" period and has simultaneously pro-

vided the field of public administration with much of its long-needed scholarly focus. Like the "principles" of yore, evaluation research is a major means of demonstrating the legitimacy of government. Government has no profit margin by which it can demonstrate to the taxpayers a reason for existing. Instead, government must demonstrate more difficult concepts to justify itself, such as efficiency, effectiveness, and social worth in carrying out its programs. Evaluation research, in its sophisticated and deeply rooted appeal to Western beliefs in the scientific method, may provide one such means of demonstration and, as such, it is going to become an increasingly important aspect of public management in an age when government consumes more economic resources than ever before in history.

In its effort to demonstrate the efficient and effective use of public funds, evaluation research provides a graceful introduction to our next chapter on the public budget and how to use it.

NOTES

[1] Charles T. Goodsell, "The Grace Commission: Seeking Efficiency for the Whole People?" *Public Administration Review*, 44 (May/June 1984), p. 197.

[2] See, for example, Frederick W. Taylor, *Principles of Scientific Management* (New York: Harper & Row, 1911); and Fritz J. Roethlisberger and William J. Dickson, *Management and the Worker* (Cambridge, Mass.: Harvard University Press, 1939).

[3] F. Stuart Chapin, *Experimental Design in Sociological Research* (New York: Harper & Row, 1947).

[4] Theodore Newcomb, *Personality and Social Change* (New York: Holt, Rinehart & Winston, 1943).

[5] See, for example, Kurt Lewin, *Resolving Social Conflicts* (New York: Harper & Row, 1948); Ronald Lippitt, "Studies in Experimentally Created Autocratic and Democratic Groups," *University of Iowa Studies: Studies in Children's Welfare*, Vol. 16, No. 3 (1940), pp. 45–198; and Leon Festinger and Harold Kelley, *Changing Attitudes through Social Contact* (Ann Arbor, Mich.: University of Michigan Press, 1951).

[6] The best single synopsis of the state of the art in evaluation research through the mid-1960s is contained in: Edward Suchman, *Evaluative Research* (New York: Russell Sage, 1967).

[7] For a somewhat different review of public administration's experience with evaluative research, see: Harry P. Hatry, "Determining the Effectiveness of Government Services," in *Handbook of Public Administration*, James L. Perry, ed. (San Francisco: Jossey-Bass, 1989), pp. 469–473.

[8] Orville F. Poland, "Why Does Public Administration Ignore Evaluation?" *Public Administration Review*, 31(March/April 1971), p. 201.

[9] Nicholas Henry, *Public Administration and Public Affairs* (Englewood Cliffs, N.J.: Prentice-Hall, 1975), p. 222.

[10] Joseph S. Wholey, et al., *Federal Evaluation Policy: Analyzing the Effects of Public Programs* (Washington, D.C.: Urban Institute, 1970), p. 23.

[11] Richard E. Winnie, "Local Government Budgeting, Program Planning, and Evaluation," *Urban Data Services Report* 4, No. 5 (Washington, D.C.: International City Management Association, May 1972).

[12] Unpublished report conducted by the Council of State Governments and the Urban Institute, 1972, as cited in Harry P. Hatry, et al., *Practical Program Evaluation for State and Local Government Officials* (Washington, D.C.: Urban Institute, 1973), p. 17.

[13] For a description see: Susan Salasin and Laurence Kivens, "Fostering Federal Program Evaluation: Current OMB Initiatives," *Evaluation*, 2 (July/August 1975), pp. 37–41.

[14] For a description see: U.S. General Accounting Office, *Evaluation and Analysis to Support Decision-Making*, PAD-75-9 (September 1, 1976), pp. 1–2.

[15] U.S. General Accounting Office, *Federal Evaluation: Fewer Units, Reduced Resources, Different Studies From 1980*, GAO/PEMD-87-9 (Washington, D.C.: U.S. Government Printing Office, 1987), p. 1.

[16] U.S. General Accounting Office, *State and Local Productivity Improvement: What Is the Federal Role?* (Washington, D.C.: U.S. Government Publishing Office, 1978). The report said much the same for local governments, too.

[17] James E. Jarrett, "Productivity," *The Book of the States, 1982–83* (Lexington, Ky.: Council of State Governments, 1982), pp. 296–301.

[18] Judith R. Brown, "Legislative Program Evaluation: Refining A Legislative Service and a Profession," *Public Administration Review*, 44 (May/June 1984), p. 258.

[19] Theodore H. Poister, et al., "Centralized Productivity Improvement Efforts in State Government," *Public Productivity Review*, 9 (Spring 1985), p. 18.

[20] Rackham S. Fukuhara, "Productivity Improvement in Cities," *Municipal Year Book, 1977* (Washington, D.C.: International City Management Association, 1977), pp. 196–197. All cities between 25,000 and 1 million people were surveyed. The response rate was 43 percent.

[21] Theodore H. Poister and Gregory Streib, "Management Tools in Municipal Government: Trends Over the Past Decade," *Public Administration Review*, 49 (May/June 1989), pp. 242, 245. All cities with populations of 25,000 to 1 million were surveyed. The response rate was 42 percent.

[22] Theodore H. Poister and Robert P. McGowan, "The Contribution of Local Productivity Improvement Efforts in a Period of Fiscal Stress," *Public Productivity Review*, 8 (Winter 1984), pp. 386–394. All cities with populations of 25,000 to one million were surveyed in 1982. The response rate was 44 percent.

[23] Robert P. McGowan and Theodore H. Poister, "The Impact of Productivity Measurement Systems on Municipal Performance" (Paper prepared for delivery at the 1984 Annual Conference of the American Political Science Association in Washington, D.C., August/September 1984), pp. 12–13.

[24] David N. Ammons, "Common Barriers to Productivity Improvement in Local Government," *Public Productivity Review*, 9 (Winter 1985), pp. 293–310.

[25] David H. Foly and William Lyons, "The Measurement of Municipal Service Quality and Productivity," *Public Productivity Review*, 10 (Winter 1986), pp. 21–33.

[26] Jonathan P. West, "City Government Productivity and Civil Service Reforms," *Public Productivity Review*, 10 (Fall 1986), pp. 45–59.

[27] Francis G. Caro, "Evaluation Research: An Overview," in *Readings in Evaluation Research*, Francis G. Caro, ed. (New York: Russell Sage, 1971), p. 1.

[28] See, for example, Suchman, *Evaluative Research*, pp. 31–32; Michael Scriven, "The Methodology of Evaluation," *Perspectives on Curriculum Evaluation* (Chicago: Rand McNally, 1967), pp. 40–41; Michael Brooks, "The Community Action Program as a Setting for Applied Research," *Journal of Social Issues*, 21 (1965), p. 34.

[29] Eleanor Chelinsky, "Evaluating Public Programs," in *Handbook of Public Administration*, James L. Perry, ed. (San Francisco: Jossey-Bass, 1989), p. 259.

[30] Caro, "Evaluation Research," p. 2.

[31] See U.S. General Accounting Office, *Evaluation and Analysis to Support Decision-Making*, pp. 4–5.

[32] Henry W. Riecken, "Principal Components of the Evaluation Process," *Professional Psychology*, 8 (November 1977), p. 395.

[33] Scriven, "The Methodology of Evaluation," p. 43.

[34] See Wholey, et al., *Federal Evaluation Policy*, p. 62.

[35] *Ibid.*, pp. 24–26.

[36] R. A. Levine and A. T. Williams, Jr., *Making Evaluation Effective: A Guide*, R-788-HEW ICMUO (Santa Monica, Calif.: Rand Corp., 1971).

[37] Orville F. Poland, "Program Evaluation and Administrative Theory," *Public Administration Review*, 34 (July/August 1974), pp. 333–334.

[38] Evaluation Research Society Standards Committee, "Evaluation Research Society Standards for Program Evaluation," in *Standards for Evaluation Practice*, P. H. Rossi, ed. (San Francisco: Jossey-Bass, 1982).

[39] Much of the following discussion is based on Chelinsky, "Evaluating Public Programs," pp. 266–272.

[40] U.S. General Accounting Office, *Teenage Pregnancy: 500,000 Births a Year But Few Tested Programs*. GAO/PEMD-86-16BR. (Washington, D.C.: U.S. General Accounting Office, 1986).

[41] Bruce B. Buchanan, II, "The Senior Executive Service: How Can We Tell If it Works?" *Public Administration Review*, 41 (May/June 1981), pp. 349–358.

[42] See, for example, Robert K. Yin, "Life Histories of Innovations: How New Practices Become Routinized," *Public Administration Review*, 41 (January/February 1981), pp. 21–28.

[43] Chelinsky, "Evaluating Public Programs," p. 268.

[44] George Kelling, et al., *The Kansas City Preventive Patrol Experiment: Summary Report* (Washington, D.C.: The Police Foundation, 1974).

[45] U.S. General Accounting Office, *CETA Programs for Disadvantaged Adults—What Do We Know About Their Enrollees, Services, and Effectiveness?* GAO/IPE-82-2 (Washington, D.C.: U.S. General Accounting Office, 1982).

[46] U.S. General Accounting Office, *Drinking-Age Laws: An Evaluation Synthesis of Their Impact on Highway Safety*, GAO/PEMD-87-10 (Washington, D.C.: U.S. General Accounting Office, 1987).

[47] Chelinsky, "Evaluating Public Programs," p. 269.

[48] *Ibid.*

[49] U.S. General Accounting Office, *Evaluation and Analysis to Support Decision-Making*, p. 11.

[50] *Ibid.*, p. 13.

[51] *Ibid.*, p. 14.

[52] The section on conducting a program evaluation is drawn from *ibid.*, pp. 17–41.

[53] Roger B. Parks, "Technical Efficiency of Public Decision Making Units," *Policy Studies Journal*, 12 (December 1983), p. 337.

[54] A. Charnes, W. W. Cooper, and E. Rhodes, "Measuring the Efficiency of Decision Making Units," *European Journal of Operational Research*, 2 (September 1978), pp. 429–444.

[55] See, for example, Authella M. Bessent and E. Wailand Bessent, "Determining the Comparative Efficiency of Schools through Data Envelopment Analysis," *Educational Administration Quarterly*, 16 (Spring 1980), pp. 57–75; A. Charnes, W. W. Cooper, and E. Rhodes, "Evaluating Programs and Managerial Efficiency: An Application of Data Envelopment Analysis to Program Follow Through," *Management Science*, 27 (June 1981), pp. 668–697; Roger B. Parks, "Metropolitan Structure and Performance: Compositional and Relational Effects" (Paper prepared for the NATO Advanced Research Workshop on Analytical Models and Institutional Design in Federal and Unitary States, Erasmus University, Rotterdam, The Netherlands, June 1983); and Parks, "Technical Efficiency of Public Decision Making Units."

[56] Parks, "Technical Efficiency of Public Decision Making Units," p. 344.

[57] Riecken, "Principal Components of the Evaluation Process," p. 398.

[58] U.S. General Accounting Office, *Evaluation and Analysis to Support Decision-Making*, pp. 17–20.

[59] Edward Suchman, "A Model for Research and Evaluation on Rehabilitation," in *Sociology and Rehabilitation*, Marvin Sussman, ed. (Washington, D.C.: Vocational Rehabilitation Administration, 1965), pp. 64–65.

[60] Caro, "Evaluation Research," p. 22.

[61] Christopher Scanlan, "U.S. Measures Human Value, A Life-and-Death Calculation," *Philadelphia Inquirer* (September 2, 1990). Figures are for 1990.

[62] Caro, "Evaluation Research," p. 24. Much of this discussion is drawn from *ibid.*, pp. 23–27.

[63] H. Donald Messer, "Drug Abuse Treatment: An Evaluation That Wasn't," in *Program Evaluation at HEW: Research Versus Reality. Part 1: Health*, James G. Abert, ed. (New York: Marcel Dekker, 1979), pp. 113–168.

[64] The following paragraph is drawn from Donald R. Wideman, "Writing a Better RFP: Ten Hints for Obtaining More Successful Evaluation Studies," *Public Administration Review* 37 (November/December 1977), pp. 714–717.

[65] Riecken, "Principal Components of the Evaluation Process," pp. 401–402, 405.

[66] Arnold J. Meltsner, *Policy Analysis in the Bureaucracy* (Berkeley, Calif.: University of California Press, 1976), Chapter 2.

[67] K. A. Archebald, "Alternative Orientations to Social Science Utilization," *Social Science Informant*, 9 (April 1970), pp. 7–35.

[68] A good review of this literature, as well as some original research on the subject, is: John G. Heilman and David L. Martin, "On the Organizational Theory of Evaluation: Economic and Political Constraints and the Choice of an Evaluation Agent," *Administration and Society*, 18 (November 1986), pp. 315–333.

[69] Riecken, "Principal Components of the Evaluation Process," p. 405.

[70] Caro, "Evaluation Research," pp. 13–15.

[71] *Ibid.*, p. 17.

[72] Riecken, "Principal Components of the Evaluation Process," p. 408.

[73] Carol H. Weiss, "Research for Policy's Sake: The Enlightenment Function of Social Research," *Policy Analysis*, 3 (Fall 1977), p. 532.

[74] M. McLaughlin, *Evaluation and Reform: The Elementary and Secondary Education Act of 1965*, Title I, Report R-1292-RC (Santa Monica, Calif.: Rand Corporation, 1974).

[75] Caro, "Evaluation Research," pp. 12–13.

[76] Thomas V. Bonoma, "Overcoming Resistance to Change Recommended for Operating Programs," *Professional Psychology*, 8 (November 1977), pp. 451–463.

[77] Weiss, "Research for Policy's Sake," p. 535.

[78] *Ibid.*, p. 544.

[79] *Ibid.*

CHAPTER
8

THE BUDGET: CONCEPTS AND PROCESSES

Of the many variants of systems theory that have been applied to problems of public administration, budgetary concepts have had the longest and most pronounced impact on the field. Like the other techniques reviewed in the preceding chapters, the budget represents a technique of administrative control that has been extended conceptually from a negative to a positive (and increasingly political) function.

In this chapter, we shall trace the evolution of budgetary concepts in government. We shall also consider the impact, or lack of it, of budgeting concepts on various levels of American government, and the political significance of the budgetary process.

A HISTORY OF BUDGETARY CONCEPTS

Bertram Gross and Allen Schick have broken down, in slightly differing ways, the evolvement of budgetary thinking by public officials.[1] Briefly, the past development of the budget can be categorized into six periods: (1) traditional, or Line-Item Budgeting, with its control orientation; (2) Performance Budgeting (sometimes called Program Budgeting), with its management orientation; (3) Planning-Programming-Budgeting (PPB), sometimes called Planning-Programming-Budgeting System (PPBS), with its economic-planning orientation; (4) Management- by-Objective (MBO), with its emphasis on budgetary decentralization; (5) Zero-Base Budgeting (ZBB), with its stress on ranking program priorities; and (6) Budgeting-as-Political-Management, with its centralizing and legislative overtones.

In each of these thrusts, the idea of what a budget is, could be, or should be, has assumed a different cast. Nevertheless, the essential meaning of the word "budget" has remained unaltered. To borrow Aaron Wildavsky's definition, a *budget* is "a series of goals with price tags attached."[2] There are, of course, other and lengthier definitions of a budget, but Wildavsky's pithy one-liner has the blessed advantage of being unmysterious, accurate, and short, so we shall rely on it.

Line-Item Budgeting (1921–1939)

Most people know what a budget looks like. Each line on a sheet of paper has an item (for example, 112 pencils) on the left side followed by a cost ($5.00) on the right side; hence, the traditional budget acquired its descriptive title of "line-item," or "objects-of-expenditure."

Of course, governments have always had some form of line-item budget. In the ancient courts of Egypt, Babylon, and China, something was needed to keep track of expenses. But in American public administration, the refinement of the Line-Item Budget was a product of national political and reformist pressures. One such pressure was the drive to establish a consolidated "executive budget." The value behind this drive was one of ousting financial corruption in government, and the way to accomplish this goal was to consolidate public financial management bureaus under the chief executive.

This thrust related to a second pressure—the administrative integration movement. The proponents of administrative integration advocated the functional consolidation of agencies, the abandonment of various independent boards, the enhancement of the president's appointive and removal powers, and the short ballot, among similar reforms designed to assure efficiency and coordination in government.

The third pressure was the desire of political reformers to build in administrative honesty by restricting the discretionary powers held by public administrators. Thus, innovations such as competitive bidding for contracts, centralized purchasing, standardized accounting procedures, and expenditure audits emerged. All related directly to the notion that the budget was a useful device for controlling public administrators (if in a purely negative way) and for ensuring morality in government. Among other results of these forces, the Budget and Accounting Act of 1921 was enacted. This act centralized federal budget formation in the Bureau of the Budget (BOB), and established the General Accounting Office (GAO) as the congressional check on federal expenditures.

The Line-Item Budget rapidly became associated with governmental honesty, efficiency, and less propitiously, inflexibility. In 1923 Charles G. Dawes, as first director of the Bureau of the Budget (now the Office of Management and Budget), wrote: "The Bureau of the Budget is concerned only with the humbler and routine business of government....It is concerned with no question of policy, save that of economy and efficiency."[3] As a result of these very limited objectives, the Line-Item Budget emphasized such factors as skilled accountancy, the objects needed to run an office or program and their costs, incremental policymaking throughout government, dispersed responsibility for management and planning, and a fiduciary role for the budget agency. Technical definitions of items were stressed (for example, pencils, 112, with $1/2$- inch erasers, wood, No. 2 grade lead, 6" × $1/4$"), and the use of such phrases as "watch-dog of the treasury" and "balanced budget" were common, indicating the mentality of this control-oriented stage of budgetary thought.

Line-Item Budgeting will always be with us, and necessarily so; fundamentally, budgets must tell us how much each item costs, and the Line-Item Budget does this. But, as we shall see, the absence of abstraction inherent in, and the simplicity of, the Line-Item Budget do not render it suitable for larger purposes, and it is best used at the lower levels of the organization. Occasionally, this is not fully appreciated by executives, and when it is not, use of the Line-Item Budget can result "in micro-management at the macro level."[4]

Gross observes that the Line-Item Budget covered *inputs* only, meaning that it dealt only with what it took to make a project continue—typewriter ribbons, erasers, paper, and secretaries.[5] Consider two examples, paperclips and parks. Under a Line-Item Budget, the only policy-related questions that a public administrator would be channeled into asking are: (1) How many paperclips do we need and what will they cost? or (2) How many parks do we have and what will it cost to maintain them? We shall refer again to paperclips and parks as examples of how each successive concept of the budget changed the policy-related questions that pertained to them. The point is that the budget represents a way of thinking about, measuring, and evaluating public policy.

Performance Budgeting (1940–1960)

As early as 1913, budget officers displayed a recognition that the budget could be used for more than merely controlling the public's fiscal accounts. In that year, the Bureau of Municipal Research of New York City urged, in its officials' words, "a classification of costs in as many different ways as there are stories to be told." Practically speaking, the bureau developed a threefold scheme of classifying expenditures: by administrative units, by functions, and by items. Such an analysis was an extraordinarily farsighted concept of the uses of the budget, but it was ultimately rejected by the City of New York on the ground that inadequate accounting information was available.

Although lone voices were heard throughout the 1920s and 1930s advocating a budget attuned to government performance as well as to the objects of expenditure, the meaningful shift to this kind of thinking came with President Franklin D. Roosevelt's New Deal. A number of historical factors influenced this movement. One was the firm establishment of the control techniques advocated by the line-item budgeteers. With the setting up of accurate accounting, purchasing, and personnel practices, budgeting as a concept was released from many of its traditional watchdog duties. Second, the government was expanding enormously, and there emerged a corresponding need to centralize and coordinate managerial activities more effectively. The budget provided the obvious salient tool for systematically coordinating government management. Third, government was increasingly perceived as an institution that delivered benefits, and the budget in turn was seen as a means by which the appropriate managerial delivery systems could be measured.

With the New Deal, these factors congealed. Between 1932 and 1940 federal spending more than doubled. The President's Committee on Administrative Management recommended (in the form of Luther Gulick's and Lyndall Urwick's oft-mentioned report of 1937) that the Bureau of the Budget shed its control orientation in favor of a managerial emphasis, and that the BOB be used to coordinate federal administration under presidential leadership. In 1939, the BOB was transferred from the Treasury Department to the newly founded Executive Office of the President. The Bureau's staff was increased by a factor of ten, it developed new methods of statistical coordination and budgetary apportionment, and it increasingly drew its personnel from the ranks of public administration rather than from accounting. Executive Order 8248 officially expressed the new managerial role of the BOB.

...to keep the President informed of the progress of activities by agencies of the Government with respect to work proposed, work actually initiated, and work completed, together with the relative timing of work between the several agencies of the Government; all to the end that the work programs of the several agencies of the executive branch of Government may be coordinated and that the monies appropriated by the Congress may be expended in the most economical manner possible to prevent overlapping and duplication of effort.[6]

The managerial orientation of the budget was reified by the preeminence of administrative management in public administration and, to a degree, by scientific management in business administration. This general emphasis was known as "Operations and Management" (O & M), and government bureaucracies, particularly the BOB, became preoccupied with originating measures of work performance and performance standards. In 1949 the Hoover Commission's report gave this thrust the name by which we know it: Performance Budgeting. Prior to 1949 Performance Budgeting (which in some circles came to be known as Program Budgeting) was called "Functional" or "Activity Budgeting." Although the federal government had in fact been practicing Performance Budgeting, largely under the aegis of Harold D. Smith, director of the BOB (1939–1946), the Hoover Commission more or less clinched its worth by dramatizing the problems that the government faced under Line-Item Budgeting. The Commission observed that the federal budget for fiscal year (FY) 1949–1950 was 1625 pages long with approximately 1.5 million words, and the Commission questioned its utility as a document that was supposed to facilitate more coordinated and effective public management.[7] In 1950 President Harry S. Truman sent Congress the first full-fledged federal Performance Budget.

In sum, Performance Budgeting covered more administrative activities than had the traditional line-item budget. Now *outputs* as well as *inputs* were considered. Budget officers saw their mission not only as one of precise and controlled accounting, but also as one that would bring about the development of activity classifications, the description of an agency's program and its performance, and the exploration of various kinds of work/cost measurements. Administrative, as opposed to accounting, skills were stressed; activities of the agency were given precedence over the purchase of items required to run the office; and management responsibility became newly centralized. Although planning responsibility remained dispersed, policymaking remained incremental, and the role of the budget agency evolved from a fiduciary to an efficiency function.

What did this new role of the budget signify for our original examples of paperclips and parks? Under a Line-Item Budget, an administrator asked only input-related questions: How much will it cost next year to assure an adequate supply of paperclips for the office? How much will it cost next year to assume adequate maintenance of the parks for the public? Under a Performance Budget, an administrator was pushed into asking not only input- related questions, but output-related questions as well: How many papers will be clipped? How many people will be served by the parks? In other words, the *performance* of the objects of expenditure became important, and, as a result of output-related queries, we might anticipate administrative studies to be generated that would survey the average number of papers clipped per paperclip, or the average number of persons visiting each park. In short, how did paperclips and parks *perform*?

Planning-Programming-Budgeting (1961–1970)

While Performance Budgeting represented a step forward in budgetary theory, it did not delve into the deeper levels of government. Unquestionably, Performance Budgeting made a significant contribution in attempting to devise measurements of an agency's effectiveness, and this was to the public's good. But, as one New York state legisla-

tor exclaimed after looking over his state's performance budget, "Who the hell cares how much a pound of laundry costs?"[8] Such data represent needed knowledge, to be sure, but ultimately the more important issue is: How should funds be allocated among various programs? Which programs are the most important? After this issue is resolved, then we can begin evaluations of a program's performance.

There were other problems with Performance Budgeting. It was becoming increasingly subjective. The description of various programs that accompanied an agency's budget to the legislature were beginning to serve a justificatory function for each agency. Also, the management emphasis of Performance Budgeting was viewed increasingly as an impediment to effective public planning. Performance Budgeting (like Line-Item Budgeting) tended to increase the purview and costs of an agency's programs incrementally. This "keep-on-truckin'" attitude impaired the articulation of the single essential question of planning: Why? Why do we need this or that program? Instead, Performance Budgeting merely stated: We've got the program, so let's do it efficiently.

These concerns eventually led to the displacement of Performance Budgeting concepts in government by Planning-Programming-Budgeting (PPB). PPB-related notions had their origins in industry. As early as 1924 General Motors Corporation was using variants of PPB, and during World War II the Controlled Materials Plan of the War Production Board relied on PPB concepts. By the 1950s the U.S. Air Force's Rand Corporation began applying systems analysis to the evaluation of weapons systems and recommended the institution of "program packages" as budgeting units in Air Force planning. The Air Force rejected the idea, but later found it expeditious to retrench when Robert McNamara became Secretary of Defense in 1960.

McNamara had been trained as an executive in the confines of the Ford Motor Company. The defense establishment that he entered was beset by almost cut-throat competition between the services, each of which was vying for control of as many new weapons systems as it could acquire. Each service viewed its particular programs not only as vital to the defense of the nation, but also as essentially the nation's only defense. Hence, each service defined the country's defense problems in ways that suited their peculiar capabilities. Combined with the competitive milieu of the Pentagon, this viewpoint produced a situation in which the Air Force was preparing for a brief, nuclear war (which would be air-centered), and the Army was girding for a long, conventional war (which would be ground-centered). Thus, it was contended in 1961 before the Senate Subcommittee on National Security and International Operations that because the land and tactical air forces were being planned for different kinds of war, they were not ready to fight either.

McNamara and his "whiz kids" (a not entirely affectionate appellation given the McNamara team by the military) shook up the services. They felt the services were autonomous to a possibly dangerous point of inefficiency and uncoordination. McNamara's method for reestablishing central control of the military services was systems analysis, and the primary expression of this analysis was PPB. By 1964, PPB was standard operating procedure in the Defense Department. President Lyndon B. Johnson was sufficiently impressed by this development, and in 1965 he ordered PPB to be applied throughout the federal government. By 1967 the Bureau of the Budget had instructed the use of PPB in twenty-one agencies, with a final goal of thirty-six agencies.

What precisely is PPB? Taking its component concepts one by one, *planning* is the defining and choice of operational goals of the organization and the choice of methods and means to be used to achieve those goals over a specified time period. *Programming* is the scheduling and implementation of the particular projects designed to fulfill an organization's goals in the most favorable, efficient, and effective way possible. *Budgeting* is the price estimate attached to each goal, plan, program, and project. By way of example, one *official goal* of the U.S. government is the attainment of the people's welfare. When this goal is made operational, a variety of subgoals result. One such *operational goal* is the achievement of a certain minimum income level for every American family. One *plan* for achieving this operational goal is unemployment assistance. A *program* is the distribution of welfare checks. A *project* is the setting

up and managing of the various welfare bureaucracies in the United States.

Beyond simple definitions, however, PPB represents a systemization of political choice in the format of budget formulation. PPB is an effort to render decision making by public administrators as rational as possible. PPB represents a *rapprochement* between budgeting and planning. Its major characteristics are listed as follows:

1. PPB is an effort to integrate budgetary formulation with Keynesian economic concepts; that is, it attempts to consider the effects of government spending on the national economy.
2. PPB is an effort to develop and use new informational sources and technologies to bring more objective and quantitative analysis to public policymaking.
3. PPB is an effort to integrate systemswide planning with budgeting.

With the preceding characteristics defining its basic conceptual form, PPB also is associated with budget officers who have skills in economic analysis, as well as in accountancy and administration. The purposes of various programs become the chief concern, as opposed to their objects of expenditure or activities. Decision making becomes less incremental and more systemic throughout the bureaucracy. Management responsibility grows more supervisory in nature, while planning responsibility becomes increasingly centralized. Finally, the budgetary agency is seen more than ever before as a policymaking body—a far cry from Dawes's statement in 1923 about the Budget Bureau being concerned with the "humbler and routine business of government."

Another way of phrasing the preceding paragraph is to say that PPB is concerned not only with inputs and outputs, but also with *effects* and *alternatives*. How does this broadened conceptual scope of the budget affect the questions that we have been asking about our original examples of paperclips and parks? With inputs, you recall, we ask only: How much will a year's supply of paperclips or a year's program of park maintenance cost? With outputs, we must ask: How many papers will our paperclips clip, or how many people will visit the parks?

With effects and alternatives, however, our budget-related questions become considerably more sophisticated and penetrating. For example, in order to determine the effects of our paperclips, we must ask: What effect do the clipped papers have on the agency and its mission? Does paperclipping them facilitate the achievement of agency goals? Does the process expedite anything, or should paperclips be abandoned as an item on the budget? How do we measure the effects of the paperclips program on agency goals? After determining paperclips' effect on the accomplishment of the agency's mission, we then must ask about alternatives. Should we use staples instead? Is there an optimal paperclip/staple mix? Do other alternatives exist?

Parks present a similar dilemma. When we ask about the effects of parks, we also must ask: What are parks really meant to do? The answer, of course, is that the purpose of parks is to provide recreation to the public—to allow citizens to "recreate." Yet, we soon discover that recreation is not much of an answer, particularly when we try to measure the effects of the park program. It is no longer enough to count visitors per day to each park—that is, to measure the park's performance, or output. Now we must ascertain whether or not each visitor is "recreating" in the park—whether he or she is having fun. That chore is not only difficult, but it may be impossible. For instance, we may discover that after midnight the park is visited entirely by muggers, rapists, and their victims—not an entirely unwarranted assumption, given urban crime patterns. Under these conditions, we may assume that only half of the park's visitors from midnight to four in the morning—the muggers and rapists—are having fun—and it is not even good, clean fun. The other half of the park's 12:00- to-4:00 A.M. population—the victims—presumably are not.

This kind of thinking, which is enabled by PPB, also forces us to consider more systemic questions about parks. We may find out that the recreation function of a city affects other urban functions, such as crime control. If it is discovered that parks correlate positively with crime, we may wish to reconsider the utility of parks in light of the total urban system. At the very least, the role that parks play in the larger urban system will be clarified by asking questions about the effects of parks, and planning for public policy presumably will be made more precise, responsive, and rigorous.

Finally, we can consider alternatives to parks. Would public libraries provide more opportunities for recreating among the citizenry, and should monies allocated for parks be used instead for libraries? Might not many neighborhood miniparks provide more effective recreation than a few superparks? These and other alternatives would come up for evaluation under a PPB budget.

PPB was greeted with mixed feeling in various American governments. Despite President Johnson's executive order in 1965 that PPB be adopted by virtually all federal agencies, the *Rouse Report* of 1968 indicated that there was substantial resistance to its implementation in many agencies, including the Bureau of the Budget.[9] Much of this recalcitrance stemmed from the need for new information that the use of PPB required. A number of agencies simply had neither the information nor the ability to acquire it, and they fell back on generating largely useless reports as a means of bureaucratic compensation. This early emphasis by BOB on procedures fostered some resentment concerning PPB in the minds of many federal administrators, and the implementation of PPB concepts was not aided by the Johnson administration's premature insistence for unavailable data. Nevertheless, the *Rouse Report* did indicate some progress. Five of the sixteen agencies surveyed at that time were receiving substantial support from above in developing genuine PPB systems, and one was in the process of beginning development.

What ultimately buried Programming-Planning-Budgeting in most federal agencies, however, was its own tendency toward analytical overkill. Elmer Staats, then director of the Bureau of the Budget, reported a conversation with the secretary of agriculture (and the Department of Agriculture, ironically, was one of those five agencies that reported substantial progress in implementing PPB in the *Rouse Report*) that went as follows: "Elmer, I have a stack of PPBS papers on my desk about four feet high. What am I supposed to do with them?"[10]

State and local governments had mixed reactions regarding PPB. By 1968, twenty-eight states and sixty local governments reported that they were in the process of implementing PPB, and 155 additional localities were considering its adoption.[11] Once state and local officials decided that they liked PPB, however, other obstacles prevented its adoption. The principal hurdles were a lack of local resources or a lack of authority. Also in 1968, seventy-three local governments reported that they had decided against using PPB largely for those reasons.[12] New York and California, both early proponents of the notion, ultimately abandoned it.

Implementing PPB in American governments was unusually controversial. Nevertheless, its impact on public management has perhaps been more profound and ongoing than any other budgetary concept, so a review of its uses and misuses is appropriate.[13]

The Debate Over PPB. PPB's main advantage is to sharpen and clarify the policy options available to administrative decision makers. In this vein, PPB caused many agencies to reconsider their missions and how they had been defined, resulting in a broader range of policies being opened up. It also is felt that coordination is enhanced by the use of PPB because the hard analysis that it forces brings out the interrelationships among the various programs of the agency.

Most of PPB's liabilities revolve around its misuse or misinterpretation. One hazard is the question of values. PPB cannot make value choices; PPB can do no more than illuminate those choices, although some persons occasionally appear to argue that PPB somehow is actually making political decisions. This notion relates to the stress that PPB places on the use of quantification. Sometimes the quantification used by PPB is mindless; numbers are tacked onto issues purely for the sake of tacking on numbers, not because they in any way clarify the issues. This is particularly true for agencies with social welfare missions. Consider again our examples of parks. Assuming that we could quantify "fun" in some fashion, is it really necessary? Beyond that question, however, is it not actually dangerous? For example, are we willing to administratively define the park pastimes of muggers and rapists as "fun" in measuring the effects of our park program? Indeed, muggers and

rapists likely do consider their park activities fun, but is it in the public interest to include this kind of evidence as a justification for the park program?

This question, in turn, relates to what Anatol Rapoport has called "the seduction of technique."[14] Numbers, measurements, quantification, and sophisticated methodologies somehow make any program more politically saleable. By this rationale, PPB's use of quantification actually might becloud value issues. For example, in an effort to justify the city's park program to higher-level decision makers, an unscrupulous bureaucrat might argue that "50 percent of our 12:00-to-4:00 A.M. parkland users indicated a 100 percent fulfillment on the Likert-type Recreation/Fun Gratification Scale." While the statement sounds positive and "tough-minded," our bureaucrat would not mention that this 50 percent was composed wholly of muggers and rapists, nor indicate how muggers and rapists got their "recreation/fun gratifications," nor state that the other half of the park's users (the victims) were rated as having zero recreation/fun on the same scale.

For these reasons PPB often seems to be used most effectively in organizations centered around "hard" technology, such as the Department of Defense, which, in fact, has never discontinued the PPB systems introduced by McNamara. Measuring a new aircraft's costs and benefits is considerably easier and more accurate than measuring the costs and benefits of recreation, and those agencies that have missions centering on client-member technologies, such as the Department of Health and Human Services, are less likely to be able to use PPB with comparable efficacy. This is not to imply that PPB is not useful in the more humanistic agencies—any technique that facilitates the clarification of choice and responsive policymaking has utility, and PPB is such a technique. But its limitations— and potential perils—must also be recognized by public administrators.

Another hazard of PPB is its potentially "centralizing bias" and the corresponding diminution of legislative control over policymaking. PPB's stress on planning, goal clarification, and systematic and scientific decision making tends to force decisions "up" the hierarchy. Once decision choices are clear, the highest appropriate level of the bureaucracy is in a rational position to make a rational decision. The upper echelons are less likely to be "removed" from the problem with PPB than they are without it, and hence are more likely to make an optimal decision without relying as much on subordinates for input into the decision-making process; that input is provided by PPB. Moreover, because PPB emphasizes that a knowledge of the entire system is desirable before a decision should be made, it is increasingly evident that decision making should become centralized for the sake of systems analysis and comprehensive planning. As with the other techniques of management science, PPB assumes that it can help make the ideal, Weberian omniscient monocrat a reality.

It also is felt that a corresponding deemphasis of the legislature's role in policymaking could result from the use of PPB. It was noted in Senate hearings conducted in 1968 on the uses and abuses of PPB that agencies had not given Congress a full set of the internal PPB documents that agency bureaucrats had used in making their own policy choices, and this practice was seen as an undermining of congressional control over policymaking. Bureaucrats prefer to avoid embarrassing probes whenever possible. Although complete intraagency program-evaluation studies are available to a member of Congress on his or her specific request (except for national security documents), such requests are rare. But this possibly genuine diminution of legislative control over policymaking is not necessarily attributable to PPB. It is attributable to bureaucratic secrecy, which could be significantly cracked open by aggressive action on the part of Congress, if Congress so desired. Moreover, PPB presumably aided in clarifying the issues as they were presented in those intra-agency working papers that Congress seldom saw, and thus potentially PPB could have aided in increasing legislative policymaking control, if Congress had wished that to happen.

The Demise of PPB. In light of the kinds of policy questions engendered by PPB, it is of note that the Nixon administration decided to move steadily away from the policy-planning orientation of PPB. In the late 1960s, for example, then Secretary of Defense Melvin Laird spoke of instituting "participatory budgeting" in the Department of Defense. By this he meant that the admirals and generals would be able to participate more fully in budget formation, although participatory budgeting was seen by many outside critics as an attempt (ultimately unsuccessful) to dismantle the well-controlled and highly centralized PPB system established in the Pentagon by Robert McNamara.

Also during this period, President Nixon revamped (for virtually the first time since its founding in 1939) the Executive Office of the President in accordance with the recommendations of the President's Advisory Council on Executive Reorganization (the Ash Council). A Domestic Council was established as a new unit that in effect undercut the programmatic and planning responsibilities of the Bureau of the Budget. In 1970, the Bureau was retitled the Office of Management and Budget (OMB), indicating its new, managerial orientation. According to former President Nixon, "The Domestic Council will be primarily concerned with *what* we do"—that is, with policy and planning; "the Office of Management and Budget will be primarily concerned with *how* we do it and how *well* we do it"—that is, with management and effectiveness.[15] The effect of this shift has been to create additional layers of authority between budgeteers and policymakers, and to demote the function of the budget examiner.

In 1971 a memorandum to all federal agencies from the OMB concerning their budget preparations stated, "Agencies are no longer required to submit with their budget submissions the multiyear program and financing plans, program memoranda and special analytical studies...or the schedules...that require information classified according to their program and appropriation structures." Schick has written that "by these words, PPB became an unthing."[16]

Management-by-Objectives (1970–1976)

With the abandonment of Program-Planning-Budgeting by the federal government (with the notable exception of the Defense Department) and by many state and local governments in the late 1960s, budgeteers turned to a new concept of budgeting (or, more precisely, to a variant of budgeting): Management-by-Objectives. Management-by-Objectives got its start in the private sector, and in 1954, Peter Drucker wrote a book titled *The Practice of Management*, which generally is thought to be the first major expression of the MBO concept.[17]

Management-by-Objectives may be defined as "a process whereby organizational goals and objectives are set through the participation of organizational members in terms of results expected."[18] With this kind of definition, McGregor's Theory Y becomes an important component of the budgetary process. Management-by-Objectives encourages "self-management" and decentralization, advocates an integrated approach to total management, stresses the concept of communication and feedback, encourages organization development and change, and emphasizes policy research and the support of top management. MBO, in short, is an attempt to set objectives, track the progress of the appropriate program, and evaluate its results. Through this process, an organization decentralizes by operationalizing its objectives and by letting the individual managers most concerned with the appropriate aspects of the program achieve those objectives in the most effective fashion possible.

We have seen how PPB was concerned with inputs, outputs, effects, and alternatives as a budgetary posture. By contrast, MBO is in many ways a return to the world of Performance Budgeting. MBO is concerned with inputs, outputs, and effects, but not necessarily with alternatives. It deals primarily with agency performance and the effectiveness of governmental programs, but when it comes to forcing policymakers to ask what else—or what "other"—might government do to accomplish a particular social mission, then MBO appears to be at somewhat of a loss. MBO has a managerial orientation that stresses, in terms of personnel skills, something called "common sense." It is concerned paramountly with program effectiveness, and its policymaking style is decentralized. In terms of planning—and very much *unlike* PPB—MBO is comprehensive in one sense (*i.e.*, it sets operational goals centrally), but it allocates the implementation of that comprehensive planning responsibility to on-line managers. Thus, the budgetary agency becomes concerned chiefly with program effectiveness and efficiency, much in the style of the Program Budgeting of the 1950s.

In relating MBO to our previous examples of paperclips and parks, we do not ask what the alternatives to paperclips and parks might be in accomplishing the mission of the agency. Instead, we merely ask: How effective are paperclips in achieving the agency's mission? How effective are parks in achieving society's objectives? We do not ask, however, what alternatives there are to paperclips or to parks.

The advantages of an MBO system are obvious. It gives those people closest to the problem some latitude in dealing with that problem and simultaneously measures their performance according to criteria developed by policymakers at the highest level. An MBO system that works should permit individual initiative and innovation, but Management-by-Objectives is no administrative panacea, and, like any quantitatively based system, MBO can be used to obscure efficient and effective management as well as to enhance it.

Even so, MBO has been used in a number of governmental contexts, and it is perhaps somewhat surprising, given MBO's emphasis on decentralization and on the implementing of policy by subordinates that the federal government embraced Management-by-Objectives in a big way under the Nixon administration—an administration, as we noted in Chapter 1, not known for its trust of bureaucrats beyond the immediate confines of the White House. In explaining the introduction of MBO to the federal government by the Nixon White House, observers cannot avoid noting that "the attitude of the Nixon top management was one of low trust and contempt towards civil service."[19] It was, however, partly because of this distrust of civil servants that Nixon introduced MBO to government through the Office of Management and Budget, which he had staffed with officials who were closely associated with the business community.

Many federal administrators, as we noted, were becoming disillusioned with Program-Planning-Budgeting in the early 1970s, particularly because of what one observer called PPB's "unfortunate association with a passion for uniformity and detail,"[20] and MBO looked like a flexible alternative. In 1975 OMB issued Circular A-11, which required the submission of agency objectives with the fiscal year budget estimates. This, in effect, was a new budgetary format, and OMB was implementing an MBO concept. Soon afterwards, President Gerald Ford endorsed MBO, and the notion rapidly was adopted by a number of federal agencies.

As implemented in its short duration in the federal government, MBO emphasized productivity measurement, program evaluation, and the effort to establish social indicators of program effectiveness. As Jerry McCaffery points out,

MBO presents an interesting contrast to PPB. The latter is primarily a policy choice mechanism, operating periodically, with results in disaggregated down-the-line managerial decisions, while MBO could be classified as an administrative decision- making mechanism, operating continuously, which intermittently aggregates data for top level policy choices. In theory, the decision flow is opposite—PPB down and MBO up. The outstanding difference seems to lie in PPB's ability to compare programs across departmental lines. But PPB's weakness was its lack of flexibility, whereas MBO has great flexibility in system design and application.[21]

It was this flexibility, in contrast to PPB's alleged inflexibility, that made MBO attractive to many federal administrators under Nixon.

By 1976, MBO's last year of preeminence in the federal government, 41 percent of American cities were using it; six years later, 59 percent of these municipalities had adopted it, and its use has essentially leveled off since then. By 1984, two-thirds of 847 top- and mid-level state administrators responding to a survey conducted in ten representative states said that they were using Management-by-Objectives or that their units had been affected by it.[22] MBO's popularity among the grass-roots governments does not appear to be affected by its disfavor in Washington.

Zero-Base Budgeting (1976–1980)

Although President Ford had warmly embraced Management-by-Objectives, a new face in the White House brought in a new budgeting concept. The new face was Jimmy Carter, a nonestablishmentarian fresh from Georgia who had had a good experience with a concept called Zero-Base Budgeting (ZBB) when he was governor of that state. Indeed, Carter was the first elected executive to introduce ZBB to the public sector. Carter, as governor of Georgia, contended that ZBB was instrumental in making his government more cost-effective, noting that

The services provided by Georgia's state government are now greatly improved and every tax dollar is being stretched farther than ever before. There has not been a general statewide tax increase during my term. In fact there has been a substantial reduction in the ad valorem tax.[23]

Peter Pyhrr, perhaps the proponent most often associated with Zero-Base Budgeting, has stated that ZBB forced some major reallocations of resources in Georgia under the aegis of Jimmy Carter. Notably, as governor, Carter allegedly was able to reduce agency budget requests anywhere from 1 percent to 15 percent by using ZBB, whereas the corresponding program reduction within each agency ranged from no change whatever to the total elimination of the agency itself.[24]

Because of this thrust, ZBB is closely associated with "sunset legislation." A *sunset law* provides that, unless the legislature specifically acts otherwise, public programs or agencies are disbanded after a set period of time, for example, five to ten years. Programs and agencies are reviewed periodically by the legislature under this threat of termination, with the idea that overlapping jurisdictions and inefficient programs can be eliminated or possibly reworked.

The federal government has been considering such legislation since the mid-1970s, and Colorado became the first state to enact sunset legislation in 1976; by 1981, thirty-six states had passed sunset laws, although none have been adopted since then.

The results have been mixed. It has been learned that citizen participation in reviewing agencies and programs generally is sparse; sunset laws work most effectively when used in tandem with more orthodox oversight mechanisms, such as program evaluations; lobbyists can and do protect programs from being terminated. In addition, while peripheral boards and commissions are far more likely to be "sunsetted" than are entrenched agencies, it "appears that the termination component of Sunset has met with a modicum of success."[25] Sunset legislation has often led to the reorganization, splitting, and merger of state agencies and boards, and at least sixteen states have enacted "sunrise" regulations, which are designed to legislatively review proposals for the founding of new state agencies—at least some of which, it has been discovered, are "sunsetted" agencies trying to rise again.

It has not been demonstrated conclusively that sunset laws save money, and in 1983, Arkansas repealed its sunset law. Six other states followed, and another half-dozen states have suspended their laws, beginning in 1979. Twenty-three states retain sunset legislation on their books. Typically, the states most likely to "sunset" sunset laws are those with low levels of legislative professionalism (*i.e.*, their legislatures are composed of part-time legislators, have few staffers, etc.). However, "where legislators are committed and the legislative institution has sufficient capacity to manage the process effectively, Sunset continues to serve as a useful catalyst for oversight."[26]

Both sunset laws and Zero-Base Budgeting, in theory, mandate that the entire budget of an agency be reevaluated and that all programs be justified periodically. In practice, ZBB employs two steps. The first step is the development of "decision packages" for each agency, with each package containing a summary analysis of each program within the agency. These packages are ranked by the agency head in accordance with his or her perception of overall agency priorities. The second step requires that each decision package be evaluated by top management to determine whether it is justified for further funding. Programs that are considered ineffective or to have outgrown their usefulness are discarded, modified, or combined in other agencies. In short, Zero-Base Budgeting gets its name from the fact that each year's budget is computed from a hypothetical "zero base." It asks, what would we do with this agency's funds if they were not already committed? To determine such options, practitioners of ZBB identify each decision unit, analyze each decision unit within a decision package, evaluate and rank all decision packages to develop the appropriations request, and finally prepare a detailed operating budget that reflects those decision packages approved in the budget appropriations.

When President Carter came to Washington, Zero-Base Budgeting came with him; as one high-ranking officer in the Office of Management and Budget noted, "Never has any management fad so completely taken over this town."[27] By mid-1977, OMB had issued its Bulletin No. 77-9, stating that agencies had to rank their decision packages and submit the required documents in support of those packages. This bulletin was, in effect, the beginning of Zero-Base Budgeting in the federal government. Schick, an astute observer of the federal budgetary scene, noted that, with the introduction of ZBB to Washington, agency heads were notably speedy to adopt the concept. To quote Schick,

ZBB was introduced quickly and painlessly because it did not alter the rules of evidence for budgeting or the structure for budget choices. There is not a single bit of budgetary data unique to ZBB....Agency after agency accommodated ZBB to its existing budgetary framework. If an agency had a program budget, it selected programs as decision units; if its budget still was oriented to organizational lines, these became its ZBB categories.[28]

Schick points out that the key to the acceptance of ZBB by the bureaucrats in Washington rested with the notion of decision units and how to rank those decision units in terms of establishing priorities for budgetary choices. Because of this feature of ZBB, an agency head was given an unusual opportunity to define what a decision unit is, and, in effect, to fool around with how that decision unit is ranked with other units.

In 1981, the Office of Management and Budget officially terminated ZBB. But by that time, its popularity had extended to the grass-roots governments: as many as half the states are using it,[29] and about three-fourths of the nation's cities.[30]

Does Zero-Base Budgeting work? In a useful review of empirical research on the experiences of federal, state, and local governments with ZBB, Frank D. Draper and Bernard T. Pitsvada concluded that it works within narrow limits and certain circumstances.[31] Specifically, Draper and Pitsvada found the following:

• Zero-Base Budgeting is by no means as radical as its name implies; programs virtually never are cut to zero. Typically, government agencies submit their "cut-back" decision packages at levels ranging from 75 to 90 percent of the previous year's budgets.

- ZBB is useful for comparing programs and for assisting decision makers in deciding which ones they want to spend more on and which ones they want to spend less on. ZBB cannot (as was often touted in the 1970s) identify issues, set objectives, or determine alternative ways of conducting programs.

- ZBB can coexist on reasonably friendly terms with other budgetary concepts and processes. It adapts easily. In this sense, ZBB is a marginal and incremental budgetary tool, one not central to budgeting and management in the way that PPB is.

- With ZBB program managers clearly feel that they participate more in the budgetary process, and communication among all levels of the government bureaucracy is enhanced when ZBB is introduced. These are perhaps the most conclusive findings of the research.

- However, unless ZBB is introduced carefully, program managers can become parochial in their use of it and fail to see larger issues.

- Paperwork increases with ZBB, but its expansion appears to be controllable.

- Zero-Base Budgeting does not seem to reduce government spending by the federal and state governments, where expenditures are largely obligated by formula-based public programs, but most local administrators believe ZBB to be quite useful in holding down costs.

So what impact would Zero-Base Budgeting have on an agency's use of paperclips or a city's parks program? For one, a great many more public managers would be talking about both topics as the decision-making process progressed; ZBB pushes participation at all levels, and this is likely to the good. But the inputs, outputs, and effects of paperclips and parks would be incidental considerations; decision makers would be concentrating on alternatives. At the agency level, for example, the head of the "Office of Paper Fastening Technologies" would be deciding between paperclips, staples, tape, or glue, but at the top level a city manager might be choosing between purchasing more paperclips or closing more parks. These decisions would be formulated as decision packages and cast in terms of the agency's or government's broadly defined program or purpose. Ultimately paperclips and parks would be ranked and ordered

in terms of their relative usefulness to the government's overall mission.

Both MBO and ZBB represented reactions by public administrators to the relatively rigid, systemic, and centralized approaches that were attempted under PPB. They also were predicated on the assumption—as were their predecessors, Line-Item Budgeting and Performance Budgeting, as well as PPB—that the federal budget was determined each year by the president and Congress. But there was a growing and discomfiting realization among public officials that this was less and less the case.

The Emergence of the "Uncontrollables"

By 1981, when Ronald Reagan took office, the federal budgetary process no longer was driven by congressional or presidential initiatives, but by formulas, debt payments, and previous obligations. As one observer has noted, "The federal budget is driven by formulas. The figures for budgetary allocations still march across the pages of the budget document and each ranks by function and by agency, to all appearances the result of conscious annual decision. But in reality, a large proportion are derived from the operation of legislative formulas which automatically determine their amount."[32]

Some of these formulas are tied to the growth or shrinkage of a particular type of population, and government payments to individuals grow or shrink automatically as the number of recipients who are eligible increases or decreases; an example is unemployment insurance. Other formulas are based on the economy and are indexed for inflation; an example is the formula used to fund Social Security payments.

Irrespective of the formula used, these programs are called *entitlements* on the logic that a person meeting the qualifications of an entitlement program is "entitled" to its payments by right. Most entitlement programs are based on economic formulas and are linked to inflation. Of the federal government's sixteen major entitlement programs, eight are tied to the consumer price index and another three are partially indexed. Together, entitlements (or "payments to individuals") add up to massive transfers of federal revenues. About four in every ten American households receive some kind of cash benefit from the federal government, a figure that includes, in part, one-third of American households that receive some sort of in-kind benefit, such as health care, food stamps, and school lunches.[33]

The entitlement programs constitute the bulk—more than half—of a class of federal expenditures that federal policymakers call "relatively uncontrollable outlays," to use the official term. The "uncontrollables" constitute more than three quarters (over 76 percent) of *all* federal spending.[34] The term itself identifies what federal officials believe to be part of their problem: people no longer control the budget; uncontrollable obligations do.

Besides payments to individuals (the "entitlements" based on formulas), which amount to 42 percent of all federal budget outlays, uncontrollables also include interest on the national debt, which is a product of levels of deficit spending and current interest rates, farm price supports, contractual and similar obligations entered into by the government during the previous year, and a variety of open-ended programs and fixed costs. After payments to individuals and prior contractual obligations, interest on the debt constitutes the largest portion of all federal budget outlays: nearly 15 percent.

Federal administrators have ample reason to view the budget as increasingly uncontrollable and less subject to human policymaking. In 1970, uncontrollables accounted for less than 62 percent of total federal outlays. This is an impressive proportion. But by 1981, when President Reagan walked into the White House, impressive had ballooned to gigantic, and uncontrollables accounted for 70 percent of all federal spending.

Budgeting-as-Political-Management (1981–present)

Of course, Reagan failed to gain control of the uncontrollables, particularly the federal debt payments, and, as we have noted, by the time he departed the White House, uncontrollables accounted for not 70 percent of all federal budget outlays, as they did when he became president, but three-fourths; it appears that this proportion will grow higher under his successor. Nevertheless, the emergence of the uncontrollables, plus Reagan's determination to lower taxes, reduce entitlements, and increase defense spending, resulted in a phase of federal budgeting which we shall call "Budgeting-as-Political-Management." This phase has been continued by President George Bush with only slight alterations in the overall political goals: now new taxes are less resisted, and reductions in defense programs are included in the effort to reduce federal spending.

We use the term, budgeting "phase," because Budgeting-as-Political-Management is not really a budget system, as are Line-Item Budgeting, Performance Budgeting, PPB, MBO, and ZBB; it is, rather, an attempt to gain control over the federal bureaucracy and spending programs via the budget. As one observer put it, "There has not been a major drive to install a new [budget] system since President Carter promulgated the Zero-Base Budgeting system...." Nevertheless, although budgeting systems "no longer get much attention, each system has had a lasting effect. Their legacies continue to influence budget practices."[35]

In discussing Budgeting-as-Political-Management, we shall tease out some of these legacies left by budget systems of the past, and review some old budgeting techniques that have been revitalized as a result of Reagan's and Bush's efforts to reduce federal spending. We shall also examine their successes at using the budget as a means of gaining greater administrative control over their departments. Among the legacies of old budget systems are the new emphases on performance measurement (in the traditions of Performance Budgeting and MBO[36]), cutback management, and target budgeting. The techniques of cutback management have been developed over the years by many governments as a result of reduced revenues, especially at the state and local levels; target budgeting emerged incrementally at the federal level, beginning in the 1950s, although its advantages were seen more readily in the 1980s in the context of attempting to reduce federal expenditures.

Budgeting-as-Political-Management is composed of two components: the move toward "top-down" budgeting and the orientation toward budgeting for legislative advantage.[37]

Component 1: Top-Down Budgeting. Top-down budgeting refers to the fact that federal budget planning and decision making have become a continuous process, managed by the director of OMB and influenced by his or her political calculations of the moment. Top-down budgeting reflects the *joint* decisions of the director of the OMB and the White House staff.

Top-down budgeting is a complete reversal of the traditional budgeting system in the federal government, which was "bottom-up." In other words, agencies would send their spending requests upward toward the budget director and the president. These requests were filtered through a series of discussions and hearings, and planning ceilings for each agency were established under the general guidance of the director of the Office of Management and Budget. Ultimately the president approved or disapproved of the director's recommendations, and agency heads could appeal the recommendations of the director. While this system is still more or less in place, it is largely *pro forma*. The real system of budgeting now is from the top downwards.

Top-down budgeting was reinforced during the Reagan administration by the implementation of the OMB Director David Stockman's (who served as director from 1981 through 1985) drive to deal with the total budget (aside from defense, which President Reagan decreed was to be left virtually entirely to the Pentagon). In a radical departure from previous approaches to the budget, which amounted to incremental decisions on discretionary programs, Stockman succeeded in putting on the bargaining table the entire federal domestic budget including entitlements, indexed benefit programs, and all the other supposedly "uncontrollable" expenditures that had never been seriously questioned under the budget process.

A second phenomenon that reinforced top-down budgeting was the constant need to adjust the overwhelming problem of federal deficit spending, which was breaking all previous records and, in the view of some, endangering the international economy. In an effort to control the deficit, the director of the OMB was forced to look far beyond the prospects of "trimming fat" in government programs and to begin cutting out "muscle and bone." Because it would be highly unlikely for an agency director to take such an approach to his or her own programs, only the White House and its Office of Management and Budget could reasonably be expected to make such deep cuts. As one expert on the budget process has asked, "How does one convince administrators to collect information that might help others, but can only harm them?"[38]

Because of the problems inherent in this question, public administrators increasingly are using the technique of Target Budgeting as "a workable and useful supplement to, but not a substitute for, 'traditional budgeting.'"[39] *Target Budgeting* mitigates against the chances of unit heads "asking for the moon" in their budget requests (chances which are enhanced in "bottom up" budgetary systems) by assuring that top executives have an early opportunity to set tentative budget targets based on generalized estimates of budget needs, which are submitted by unit heads. These estimates are combined, and perhaps pared down, into a target budget for the larger unit (sometimes the entire government), and units are instructed to prepare detailed budgets based on a targeted total figure for their units that they cannot exceed. Often, agencies may submit second and third budgets, in which they list programs that they could undertake if they were granted a budget larger than the Target Budget mandated by topside.

Like Zero-Base Budgeting, Target Budgeting facilitates the setting of priorities, and it permits the chief executive to set goals prior to the submission of detailed budget requests, but in a far less arbitrary way; instead of requesting, for example, a fixed percentage of last year's budget, the chief executive can tailor his or her target budget for each unit based on the preliminary estimates made by those units, and his or her best judgment. Perhaps its greatest advantage, however, is that it provides a process for furnishing advance policy guidance to the agencies.

Component 2: Budgeting for Legislative Advantage. The second major component of Budgeting-as-Political-Management is that of budgeting for legislative advantage. Many of the authoritarian implications of top-down budgeting were mitigated against by the process of budgeting for legislative advantage, which required that the executive branch of the government deal more openly with Congress. In the past, administrations had left the defense of particular programs and the budget requests associated with them to the agency directors. With the advent of the Reagan administration, this was changed overnight. Now the OMB was accorded the responsibility of defending the administration's budget proposals at each congressional subcommittee and committee hearing. Ultimately this required that the OMB develop statements about what the president's desired budgetary outcome was for every committee and subcommittee, since it was only at these levels that decisions were really made about the ultimate shape of the federal budget.

To present a coherent budgetary document to Congress meant that the OMB had to reformat the budget into terms that Congress could comprehend as policy changes. On a technical level, this meant that the OMB budgetary proposals had to be transliterated from the traditional accounting categories used by the executive branch into statistical analyses that Congress (and other legislatures) uses to make budget decisions. Operationally, budgeting for legislative advantage meant that the top personnel of the Office of Management and Budget had to maintain a continuous presence in Congress at the subcommittee and committee levels. Politically, it meant that the director of the Office of Management and Budget and the director's top assistants had to be willing to argue against any changes proposed by Congress in the budget document submitted by the OMB, and to show how such changes would affect domestic spending.

Budgeting-as-Political-Management required the Office of Management and Budget to make some major internal changes. Among them was the development of a new budgeting document published by the OMB that was considerably more sophisticated as an advocacy paper than previous publications by the Office of Management and Budget had been.[40] Stockman also created a legislative liaison staff and appointed "bill trackers" whose primary function was to attend every hearing of a congressional committee or subcommittee and report on what occurs. Prior to 1981, no such staff had existed in OMB.

Most significantly, however, Stockman set up the Central Budget Management System as the focus of his management of the budget process.

The Central Budget Management System is a computer program that tracks budgetary decision making in Congress and projects the implications of alternative decisions along a wide range of dimensions. It allows the OMB to break down the president's budget into congressional committee and subcommittee allocations, into functional categories, into agency budgets, into comparisons with previous resolutions or the previous year's budget, and to calculate the cost of existing policy under a variety of definitions. It allows the OMB, on a daily basis, to keep track of all budget decisions being made at all levels. The Central Budget Management System allows the director to have a "rudder in his head showing him the general and detailed shape of the budget he wants."[41]

Stockman concluded that he needed something like the Central Budget Management System early in 1981 when he discovered that the ways that congressional analysts prepared budget estimates and the ways the OMB analysts prepared budget estimates resulted in billion dollar differences between the two estimates. Thus, television news stories were treating the nation to the spectacle of the director of the OMB appearing before congressional committees using a hand calculator to arrive at new budget estimates in an effort to reconcile the OMB figures with the congressional ones.

The Central Budget Management System was designed to change this, and it has. Increasingly, OMB is speaking the language of the congressional budget process, and the Central Budget Management System is at the heart of OMB's new-found ability to deal with Congress.

Some Consequences of Budgeting-as-Political-Management

What are the consequences of Budgeting-as-Political-Management? There are, as with any new and controversial approach to the budget, at least two different views. The traditionalists, at least many of them, believe that the old rules have disappeared and nothing has replaced them. The budgetary process itself is viewed as being on the edge of collapse. The old budgetary cycles are gone, budgets are based on estimates of income and expenditures that often have little bearing on reality, and the process itself has become heavily politicized, thus having a detrimental impact on the reputation of neutrality and integrity that federal budgeteers have long cultivated.

The other view is more upbeat. The Office of Management and Budget is once again central to policymaking in the executive branch. For the first time, the legislative and executive branches are discussing the budget in ways that are mutually comprehensible. Greater cohesion and control have been found in the budget figures themselves because they are more understandable and thus are more open to constructive debate.

Elements of both perspectives have merit, and the following discussion of the major consequences of Budgeting-as-Political-Management blends aspects of both views.[42] Although Budgeting-as-Political-Management had its initial impact at the federal level, increasingly it is having an effect on subnational governments, and we shall touch upon these effects as well.

1. Reinstatement of the chief executive in the budgetary process. Perhaps most important, the president has been reinstated in the budgetary (and policymaking) process in a major way. Between the new reconciliation process established by Congress in 1974 (to be discussed subsequently) and the transformation of the Office of Management and Budget under David Stockman, the president is in a better position than ever before to make policy for the whole of government.

2. Empowerment of the executive budget agency. The executive budget process, the budget's presentation to Congress, and ensuing negotiations over the budget between the two branches are now centralized as never before, and likely will remain so. It is now the Office of Management and Budget, particularly the top echelons of that office, that deal directly with the committees and subcommittees of Congress where the real budgetary decisions are made. As Hugh Heclo puts it, "No president or budget director is likely to want to go back to the days when the president's proposal was largely left to the tender mercies of the spending agencies and the committee system."[43]

This centralization of the executive budget process and the consequent empowerment of the executive budget agency may be the most endur-

ing change in the practice of government wrought by the Reagan administration. "The first Reagan year witnessed the striking and sudden emergence of OMB to the posture of principal executive leader, short of the president himself, in policymaking and politics."[44]

This posture has continued. Observers have noted how the four public administrators who hold "the unheralded title of associate director for programs in the Office of Management and Budget, a name worthy of a dutiful bean counter....[wield] power that outstrips that of most cabinet secretaries."[45] "Aside from cabinet officers and perhaps one or two people on the West Wing [of the White House] staff, they are arguably the most powerful people on the civilian side of the government."[46]

A similar phenomenon is happening in the states. A study of the state budget offices in three midwestern states concluded that "Budget offices and their staffs do indeed appear to exercise significant influence in state policy making," and that this influence was increasing over time.[47]

3. Development of a common language of the budget. Budgeting-as-Political-Management has provided both the executive branch and Congress with a new and more coherent way of looking at things. The OMB and Congress increasingly speak in the same language when it comes to the budget. Budget packages are now being voted on by members of Congress who have an improved knowledge over what the implications of their votes might be. This is by no means the result of actions only by David Stockman and the OMB; it is also a consequence of the impact that the Congressional Budget Office, established in 1974, has had upon members of Congress.

By the close of the Reagan era, it was clear that this common language was in place: "the Budget Summit Agreement of 1987 embodied a vocabulary and set of principles that would not just have been unacceptable in 1981, but more importantly, unrecognizable."[48]

4. A shift from allocative/incremental budgeting to economic forecasting. Economic assumptions and the formulas by which federal dollars are disbursed under certain entitlement programs have changed the budget process from one of annual allocations and incrementalism to one in which economic assumptions and entitlement formulas are emphasized. Increasingly, federal budgets are developed on the basis of economic projections. Yet who makes these projections and what assumptions they use in making them are often influenced by political factors.

Moreover, very small adjustments in the assumptions underlying economic projections can result in huge budgetary differences. "For example, $1 billion can be 'saved'...by lowering the forecasts of interest rates starting October 1...by less than one-half of one percentage point. No one can forecast interest rates with anything remotely resembling that degree of accuracy, and few would notice such a change. Faced with the choice of 'saving' $1 billion by cutting Social Security or by a minute change in economic assumptions, it is little wonder that the latter looks so tempting."[49] Estimates about economic growth yield even more dramatic differences than projections of interest rates, and an "increase of 1 percentage point in real growth [would lower] the deficit by $19 billion...according to a 'rule of thumb' by the Congressional Budget Office."[50]

5. Intensification of conflict. As a result of these dynamics, the budget process increasingly becomes a conflict over whose assumptions will be used in developing the budget. Analysts from the Congressional Budget Office use one set of assumptions in developing their economic projections, whereas analysts from the Office of Management and Budget use another set. These assumptions can be radically different; and even if not radically different, they can nonetheless result in radical differences in the ultimate budget figures. While the new era of Budgeting-as-Political-Management has brought about an increased ability of the executive and legislative branches to communicate with each other, it has not resulted in a system in which both branches are using the same basic assumptions about the future, and the differences in economic projections coming from the White House and Congress have been, on occasion, vast.[51]

Certainly under the Reagan administration, the prospect for conflict over these assumptions was magnified. The White House wanted to cut domestic spending while Congress, by and large, wished to protect it. Thus, as Naomi Caiden points out, the effort to cut budgets did not result in "decrementalism, an incrementalism in reverse with similar attributes. Rather it heightens conflict and destabilizes the budget process, placing strain on institutions, so that new rules begin to emerge, even though these may not be wholly satisfactory to participants. These rules relate to the base for cuts, veracity of the cuts, and a new vocabulary of budget cutting."[52]

Caiden's point leads us to the topic of cutback management, which deals directly with these "new rules" of budget cutting, and which have emerged, especially among local governments, in an effort to reduce conflict in the budget process. *Cutback management* is the collection of techniques that have been developed by practicing public administrators to reduce or eliminate public programs when confronted by fiscal constraints.[53] These techniques of cutback management include short-term and long-term approaches. Short-term cutback management includes hiring freezes, unilateral budget cuts, the reduction of the number of temporary employees, the deferring of maintenance, and the postponing of equipment purchases.

A hiring freeze simply means that no one new is hired, and relies on a process of natural attrition (*i.e.*, the natural process of employees retiring, or leaving the agency voluntarily for other jobs) to effect cost savings. There are a number of disadvantages to hiring freezes, notably that they are likely to hurt minorities and women first, since they often are disproportionately represented among the next groups in line to be hired by public agencies. Hiring freezes can also disadvantage some units of government more than others if, for whatever reason, they lose more employees to attrition than do other units, and yet, like those other units, are still not allowed to hire replacements. One remedy to these problems is to permit the hiring of one person for every three lost by attrition until an established level is reached.

"Across-the-board" budget cuts constitute another method of cutback management, and this approach has the advantage of relieving the senior public administrator of considerable stress, since it is, essentially, mindless: a 10 percent cut in the budgets of all units may be an easy decision for the chief executive to make, but it is insensitive to the varying needs and services of those units. Typically, unilateral budget cuts harm those agencies that have a high proportion of skilled workers providing sophisticated services, whereas they do not have a major impact on agencies which deliver a routine service that simply can be slowed down to accommodate a budget cut.

Reducing temporary employees, deferring maintenance, and postponing equipment purchases also are relatively stressless decisions for the senior public administrator to make when implementing cutbacks, and, like hiring freezes and unilateral budget cuts, they have the advantage of buying time for the longer haul. Ultimately, these techniques are short-term approaches. To actually reduce expenditures requires more thought.

Longer-term approaches to reducing expenditures can be accomplished by examining alternative delivery systems, achieving direct cost savings, and setting programmatic priorities and eliminating those programs that appear on the bottom of the priority list.

There are at least four ways of delivering public programs, often with the same level of service, but at a reduced level of cost. These include contracting with volunteer groups (as is done extensively by local governments and certain state and federal agencies, such as the U.S. Forest Service); using part-time and lower-cost personnel; privatizing services; and eliminating duplication of services through interagency agreements with other governments.

Using volunteers and part-time personnel are reasonably self-evident as cost-saving delivery systems for public programs. Privatization and intergovernmental agreements, however, are complex, and we devote Chapters 11 and 12 to discussions of these alternative systems of implementation.

Direct cost savings often can be achieved by reorganizing services to eliminate duplication. This can be done through intergovernmental agreements, as mentioned earlier, or by consolidating governments themselves. This latter approach, however, is rarely popular with the public; fewer than thirty city-county consolidations, for example, have taken place since the first one in 1805.[54] In addition, using a lower-cost employee, such as

student interns and temporary service personnel, who typically do not demand a high level of benefits, can result in direct cost savings as well.

Finally, priority setting can result in the elimination of low-priority programs and their expenses in an agency. Nevertheless, how those priorities, low and otherwise, are determined by agency administrators can be a painful process that requires sophistication and sensitivity to reduce the conflict that is inherent in making such choices. Practicing public administrators, particularly at the local level, seem to agree that the following steps should be taken in determining program priorities when faced with cutbacks:

- Be sure that all interested parties are informed of the need for cutbacks, and solicit their views on those cutbacks.
- Determine the criteria for how priorities should be set. While these criteria should be determined by the chief executive, the views of other employees in the agency should be carefully considered, and if possible, implemented.
- Establish a preliminary and tentative priority list based on the explicit criteria that have been developed for priority setting.
- Attempt to build some public consensus through various meetings and hearings to develop a final priority list.
- Insure that various elected officials and other pertinent decision makers approve of the priority list.
- Understand that there will never be complete agreement in the priority-setting process, but keep trying to explain to the public at large and to agency employees why the priorities have been set the way they have.
- Public executives faced with cutting public programs should remain calm, professional, honest, open, and unflappable in the process of setting priorities. Cutback management is, above all, a process of conflict reduction, and, as such, is the nuts and bolts of Budgeting-as-Political Management.

6. Emergence of a continuous and flexible budget cycle. Flexibility in the budget process and continuity of the budget cycle are now facts of federal life. The traditional budgetary timetable no longer holds, and the "continuing resolutions" on the budget and the special sessions of Congress called each year (in an effort to assure that federal employees are paid on time) are now the rule. The underlying reasons for these changes reflect the continuing need to adjust assumptions about the economy and the budget's impact on it as the fiscal year progresses.

7. Political power versus institutional strength at OMB.

It is probable that the OMB will continue to be a major factor in any new administration's relationship with Congress, and this may well be a lasting legacy of the Reagan administration. This increase in the OMB's political power in Congress may be offset by its declining institutional capacities as a policy developer.

Heclo phrases the irony well: "The problem of Stockman's way of doing business isn't its intent but its effect. It not simply depletes the stock of independent ideas from below, but undercuts any incentive to replenish the stock. The attenuated two-way communication between the larger political layers and career staff has the same effect of undermining institutional capacities. As career officials are less expected to understand the uses to which their information is put in the front office, so they become less able, and ultimately less interested, in understanding the larger picture. In this sense, OMB's political power may have increased while its institutional strength has diminished."[55]

8. Budgeting prevails over management and policy evaluation in OMB.

Finally, the Office of Management and Budget may be permanently changed as a partial consequence of Budgeting-as-Political-Management. Budget activities take up the time of about two-thirds of the OMB's staff, but other functions that Congress over the years has mandated the OMB to manage include the following: to study, coordinate, and recommend courses of action on organization and management problems; to review and coordinate the executive branch's legislative proposals; to review and negotiate proposed federal regulations and regulatory changes; to review and coordinate forms and other kinds of paperwork in an effort to reduce paperwork requirements for the public and for the government itself; to lead and coordinate the development of statistical standards throughout the government; to lead the coordination, standardiza-

tion, and improvement of management practices, particularly in financial areas; and to improve and direct procurement policies, regulations, procedures, and reforms.[56]

None of these nonbudgetary activities will be eliminated, but it appears that the budget will become even more of a central fact of agency life as a consequence of the patterns established under David Stockman. "The process" of getting the executive branch's budget through Congress will become more consuming than ever before, and this may occur at the expense of the OMB's management function.

It should be noted that the debate over the relations between management and budgeting at the OMB has been around for some time. It is a difficult argument to understand in some respects because the terms used in the debate have not been adequately defined. For instance, the federal government has yet to itemize what the term "management" actually encompasses; individual presidents have, in their turn, emphasized or deemphasized the role of management in their administrations; and oftentimes, particularly in recent years, the OMB has been cast into a competitive relationship with the White House staff over who will control federal management. In addition, the administrative capacities of individual agencies in the federal government have improved rather dramatically over the years, and the history of enthusiasm with which the Office of Management and Budget has imposed burdensome paperwork requirements on other federal agencies (notably through such budget systems as PPB, MBO, and ZBB), without producing notably lasting accomplishments in some instances, has reduced the OMB's credibility as a central management agency for the federal government.[57]

In the 1940s, the Office of Management and Budget (then the Bureau of the Budget) was admired more as a central management agency than as a budget agency, and this was particularly attributable to its large, astute, and active Division of Administrative Management.[58] However, the Eisenhower administration's acceptance in 1952 of the recommendations by the first Hoover Commission resulted in the elimination of the Division of Administrative Management, only to be replaced by a much smaller Office of Management and

Organization. A long decline in the management function of the OMB ensued, until the advent of the Nixon administration in 1968. But the new emphasis on management in the OMB by the Nixon administration entailed a critical redefinition of what "management" meant: "OMB's 'management' role was in effect redefined. The issue became the managerial *control* of government rather than managerial *effectiveness*."[59]

This emphasis on managerial control for political purposes declined during the Carter administration, and management as a concept was not given significant attention until the Reagan administration. And the Reagan administration gave the notion of management perhaps more attention than that of any other administration, with the possible exception of Franklin Delano Roosevelt's. Not only did President Reagan set up the President's Private Sector Survey on Cost Control (the Grace Commission), described in the previous chapter, but in 1982 he also established the President's Management Improvement Program—Reform 88, the President's Council on Integrity and Efficiency, the Cabinet Council on Management and Administration, and the President's Council on Management Improvement. All of these programs and organizations were notably active in their aggressive pursuit of more efficient governance, and none of them was particularly concerned with the role of the Office of Management and Budget in the management of the federal government. In fact, in the view of one observer, the OMB "lost much of its management policy leadership" to these initiatives.[60] By the closing years of the Reagan administration, there were at least five major proposals floating in federal executive circles and in Congress that dealt with radically upgrading the management capacity of the federal government, only one of which directly involved the OMB.[61]

Thus, it is not merely the introduction of Budgeting-as-Political-Management that has called into question the management capacities of the OMB; it has been a long-standing concern and debate which Budgeting-as-Political-Management has likely accelerated.

Politically managing paperclips and parks?

What about our ongoing examples of paperclips and parks? Budgeting-as-Political-Management would push budgeteers into taking a perspective that is highly political and goal-specific. In the Reagan administration that goal was to balance the budget by cutting (with the exception of defense) the volume of expenditures; so, for the moment, let us use that goal of cutting expenditures in discussing paperclips and parks.

Under Budgeting-as-Political-Management, budgeteers would ask: If paperclips and parks were deleted from the budget, whose ox would be gored? By how much would the total budget be reduced? Alternatives to paperclips and parks are not really considered, since the overriding objective is to cut spending. Similarly, outputs are incidental; it really does not matter what a public program is doing, since the budgeteers are prepared to cut whatever program that the legislature will allow. Inputs and effects, by contrast, are very much present. But only *goal-related* (in this case, economic) inputs and *goal-related* effects seriously interest the budgeteers. How much money are we spending on paperclips and parks? What will be the effect on the deficit if we eliminate them? Paperclips and parks are not differentiated in any way by budgeteers using Budgeting-as-Political-Management other than on the basis of the amount of money they consume—or, more broadly, how they affect the achievement of the overall goal. In all likelihood, these budgeteers would prefer to cut parks rather than paperclips from their budgets on the grounds that parks are more costly, and they would be quite pleased to eliminate both programs if the legislature would let them.

One fact emerges very clearly in Budgeting-as-Political-Management: Budgeteers and executive policymakers know their overriding goal and budget exclusively for that goal. As Budgeting-as-Political-Management is practiced in Washington, this goal is economic: cut the budget. But in theory, other goals are equally possible. For example, the goal of the executive branch might be to provide more and better parks. In this case, all other programs, such as paperclips, would be slashed by as much as the legislature would permit, and all savings and revenues would be redirected toward parks.

The point is that for the first time, budgeteers in a central budget office (such as the OMB) of a government can deal with the budget as a whole and use it to advance whatever goal they are pursuing. Budgeting-as-Political-Management appears to have succeeded, at least in relative terms, where Programming-Planning-Budgeting failed. The concept *really is* systemic and centralized; control by the top of the bureaucracy *really has* been achieved.

In summary, each budgetary form not only forces the bureaucrat to ask increasingly basic questions about the agency's programs, but each form connotes different patterns and functions for the whole of government as well. The principal features of and differences between the Line-Item, Performance, Planning-Programming- Budgeting, Management-by-Objective, Zero-Base Budgeting, and Budgeting-as-Political-Management concepts are summarized in Table 8.1.

THE BUDGETARY PROCESS

Regardless of what form of budgeting is used by a government, the methods through which an agency gets money remain essentially the same. Those methods, according to a critique by the National Urban Coalition, are characterized by secrecy, lack of a comprehensive review procedure, and inadequate decision criteria.[62]

Whether or not the National Urban Coalition is correct in its assessment, in 1974 Congress took the unprecedented step of revising substantially the budgetary process of the United States.[63] This revision was the Congressional Budget and Impoundment Control Act of 1974, which represented a unique effort by Congress to consider total federal expenditures and revenues together and to determine their effects on the economy. This meant that Congress was trying to focus directly on national budget priorities in the light of national goals and the performance of individual policy programs.

The act brought about budgetary reforms that were needed for a number of reasons. For example (and somewhat incredibly), neither the House of Representatives nor the Senate had committees that were charged with reviewing the president's annual budget proposals as a whole. Consequently, Congress voted only on individual

portions of the budget, and there was no process for reviewing what the total effects of such actions could do to the economy. Often individual appropriations bills were passed by Congress only after a considerable portion of the fiscal year to which the bills applied had already ended. Compounding this problem were the following factors: a one-year time frame for the execution of the budget process was unrealistic in terms of having any impact on the national economy; a number of spending patterns had developed over the years that were not subject to the normal appropriations process; the president could—and often did—impound funds that were appropriated on the basis of his own priorities; and Congress really did not have the analytical and staff capacities needed to properly analyze the president's budgetary requests and to develop worthwhile policy alternatives within the context of the federal budget.

The Budget and Impoundment Control Act of 1974 rectified these problems in several ways. First, it inaugurated a new institutional structure in Congress by establishing for each house a budget committee responsible for developing overall fiscal priorities among major programs.

Second, the Act coordinated decision making by requiring that, on two prescribed dates every year, Congress must vote explicitly on the budget as an entire package and on budget priorities; all subsequent decisions concerning the budget, in effect, must relate to these two votes. To facilitate this process, the entire fiscal calendar was changed from beginning on July 1st to starting on October 1st, beginning with fiscal year 1977.

Third, the Act established a timetable for scheduling different phases of action by Congress on the budget. In effect, the Act set up a PERT chart for the budgetary process; thus, appropriations bills, for example, cannot be considered by either house until authorizations have been passed and the first concurrent budget resolution has been adopted. Similarly, Congress is not allowed to adjourn under the Act until it has ironed out all differences on budgetary matters.

Fourth, the Congressional Budget and Impoundment Control Act improved budgetary control across the board. For example, those patterns of spending that had developed which were not

TABLE 8–1 Some Differences Between Budgetary Concepts

Feature	Line-Item (1921–1939)	Performance (1939–1959)	PPB (1960–1969)	MBO (1970–1976)	ZBB (1977–1980)	Political Management (1981–present)
Basic Orientation	Control	Management	Planning	Management	Decision making	Control and attainment of a single, systemwide goal
Scope	Inputs	Inputs and outputs	Inputs, outputs, effects, and alternatives	Inputs, outputs, and effects	Alternatives	Goal-specific inputs and goal-specific effects
Personnel skills	Accounting	Management	Economics and planning	Managerial "common sense"	Management and planning	Political, coordinative and knowledge relevant to the systemwide goal
Critical information	Objects of expenditures	Activities of agency	Purposes of agency	Program effectiveness	Purpose of program or agency	Does program or agency further the systemwide goal?
Policymaking style	Incremental	Incremental	Systemic	Decentralized	Incremental and participatory	Systemic and aggressive
Planning responsibility	Largely absent	Dispersed	Central	Comprehensive, but allocated	Decentralized	Centralized
Role of the budget agency	Fiscal propriety	Efficiency	Policy	Program effectiveness and efficiency	Policy prioritization	Attainment of a single systemwide goal

subject to the regular appropriations process (known as "backdoor spending") were largely wiped away and the president's capacity for impounding funds appropriated by Congress was stringently limited under the Act.

Finally, the Act established a Congressional Budget Office to improve Congress's analytical base and to require it to make five-year projections of the budget, thus assuring a greater degree of economic planning for the nation.

The Act has been considered a success by most observers, although in the view of some it has not accomplished all of the far-reaching reforms originally envisioned. Nevertheless, the House and Senate budget committees have been established and are working (sometimes smoothly), the Congressional Budget Office has proven to be quite successful, and overall fiscal targets have been developed (although they are rarely met). Figure 8.1 illustrates the structure of the new federal budgetary process as prescribed by the Congressional Budget and Impoundment Control Act of 1974.

Although understanding the process in its formal aspects is necessary, it is important to realize that the essence of the budgetary process is political. Aaron Wildavsky, Richard F. Fenno, Jr., and Jesse Burkhead, among others, have addressed what it means for a budgeteer to be a politician in securing an agency's funding, and a review of some of their thinking on the topic is worthwhile.[64] Although they broach the federal budgetary process almost exclusively, the same basic rules apply to state and local governments. Politics requires the use of strategies and the politics of the budgetary process is no exception. As Wildavsky observes in his classic essay on the topic:

What really counts in helping an agency get the appropriations it desires? Long service in Washington has convinced high agency officials that some things count a great deal and others only a little. Although they are well aware of the desirability of having technical data to support their requests, budget officials commonly derogate the importance of the formal aspects of their work as a means of securing appropriations.... But, as several informants put it in almost identical words, "It's not what's in your estimates but how good a politician you are that matters."[65]

STRATEGIES FOR BUDGETARY SUCCESS

To be a good budgetary politician requires the use of "ubiquitous" and "contingent" strategies.[66] Ubiquitous strategies are pervasive in nature and are required on a continuing basis by any agency. They are designed to build outside confidence in the agency and to add to its clientele. Contingent strategies are more particular, and depend on circumstances. They are designed to take advantage of unusual opportunities presented to the agency for the sake of defending or expanding its base. Budgetary strategies can be categorized as follows.

Ubiquitous Strategies

1. Find, serve, and use a clientele for the services you perform. The thought here is that an agency, when threatened, mobilizes its clientele. A case in point is the former Office of Economic Opportunity (OEO). When the OEO was budgetarily emasculated under the Nixon administration, various organizations representing the poor rose to its defense, fighting a remarkable rearguard action in the courts in an effort to preserve the OEO. Although the OEO can be faulted on other strategy counts, it unquestionably had found and used a clientele. A number of observers felt that the OEO had politicized and organized "the forgotten fifth" in this country to a point at which the poor could adequately fend for themselves when it came to passing and implementing federal legislation, with or without the OEO.

2. Establish confidence in the mind of the reviewer that you can carry out the complicated program (which he or she seldom understands) efficiently and effectively. Here, the key notion is that if legislators believe in your abilities, you can get just about anything you want. Exemplary in this regard is the National Science Foundation (NSF), founded in 1950. An early fear held by a number of citizens was that the NSF would become an all-powerful "science czar" of the United States. Through the strategic use of a low administrative profile, academic trappings, and by capitalizing on a popular romanticism concerning

FIGURE 8-1 The Federal Budgetary Process Prescribed by the Congressional Budget and Impoundment Control Act of 1974

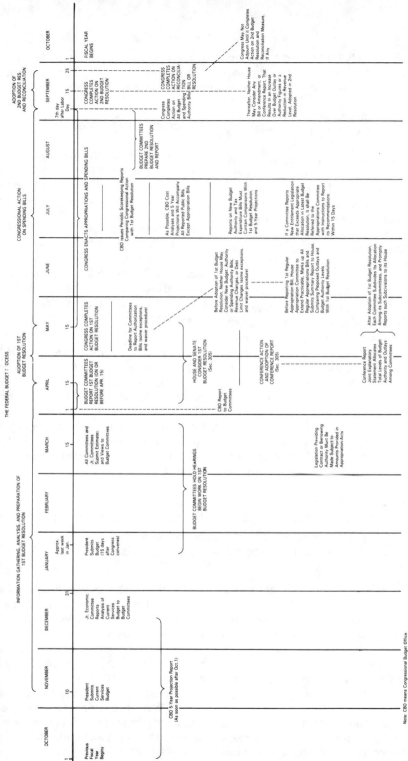

Note: CBO means Congressional Budget Office.

science, the NSF not only eliminated this worry but eventually was operating in a budgetary environment that permitted an awesome degree of latitude: science could (and should) be funded solely for the sake of science, and fellow scientists were deciding who among them should be awarded NSF grants.

The NSF's premise—that science should be funded according to what happened to interest scientists rather than for the achievement of larger social goals—ultimately (in the late 1960s) came under some hard questioning in Congress. But for many years the NSF enjoyed an impressive degree of budgetary success despite a virtual absence of accountability in terms of what it did with the money.

3. Attempt to Capitalize on the Fragmentary Budgetary Review Process. A notable example of this strategy is provided by the U.S. Air Force. Throughout most of the 1950s, the air force practiced "phased buying." This meant that the air force bought parts for a larger number of weapons than its appropriations request indicated it intended to purchase. As a result, Congress and the president were left with little choice but to authorize the purchase of the remaining parts if any of the weapons were to be useful. For many years, this questionable use of the fragmentary review process worked handsomely, but in 1957, after a public furor arose, Secretary of Defense Charles Wilson ended the practice.

Contingent Strategies

1. Guard Against Cuts in the Old Programs. There are a number of ways for an agency to do this; a favorite strategy is to cut the most popular program that the agency has, on the logic that citizen complaints will get back to members of Congress more speedily. Thus, the National Institutes of Health have been known to start a dental research program by cutting heart, cancer, and mental health research in its proposed budget. This resulted in constituent pressure, and because of this Congress restored these funds and approved the whole package.

2. Attempt to Inch Ahead with Old Programs. It is always easier to get new appropriations if they are made to look like old programs. A favored device for accomplishing this is the numbers game. The National Institutes of Health, for example, long have engaged in this strategy by reducing the number of its research grants ("Look! We're economizing!"), while increasing their size (thus inching ahead).

On the Financing of Government

In the following passage, a public administrator discussed how bureaucrats decide how to spend money. While satirical, his point is not entirely fictional.

In spite of evidence to the contrary, the System isn't free. There are dollars that are attached and because of this, many tyrocrats impede Program progress by their reluctance to spend the huge sums necessary to finalize a Program. So inhibiting, sometimes, is this feeling that by the time the money is requested, the Project for which it is intended is no longer required.

However, spending will come naturally and easily once it is understood that there are really two entirely different kinds of legal tender in use by the System! One counts; one doesn't.

The first type of money is the day-to-day or "real" kind that everybody uses to pay the bills. This type is rare, and always in short supply when needed most.

The other type is the tender used for bureaucratting; *i.e.,* Money of Unspecified Denomination, or MUD.

MUD is produced by a special process. Real Money is sent to governments in the form of taxes and is immediately machine processed to remove all the amount marks from both sides. Then when Bureaucracy wants to buy something, the proper number of blanks are selected and appropriate amount marks reinserted until there is enough to cover costs and still keep the pile to a manageable size. Since there are enormous amounts involved, the basic counting unit is the million, which Bureaucracy calls a *megabuck*. Below one megabuck, in the petty cash range, the unit is the thou or the K....

Once the money is put through the marks remover, any connection it had with its original owner is severed. With the last trace of value removed, and all pecuniary restraints with it, the Bureaucrat is free to function with maximum efficiency. That is, he can charge ahead to the extent that he is not delayed by a mispricked conscience or the tight-fistedness associated with "real" money.

For example, the head of a large government agency sent an aide to see to the printing of a sizable Report. In the interest of haste, it was taken to a private firm with the request that it be finished "by Friday morning. We need it for distribution." The printer pointed out some difficulties and a number of needed corrections, and told the aide that it couldn't be finished until the following Monday without spending a fortune for overtime. The aide, being totally uninhibited, replied, "To hell with the expense. The boss wants this on Friday, and money is no object!" Thanks to the aide's decision, the report—exploring the methods whereby the Agency could save money—was available for study on Friday as planned.

The advantages of effortless spending are clear and the MUD theory can be substantiated to promote it. A piece of hard evidence became available in the early 1960s when the United States wanted to borrow 500 megabucks from the International Monetary Fund to strengthen the dollar which was under heavy attack by foreign interests. The loan was approved, of course, since we are the heaviest contributor to the IMF. And were it not for the two different types of money, we would have been in the impossible position of borrowing our own money.

John Kidner, The Kidner Report: A Satirical Look at Bureaucracy at the Paper Clip and Stapler Level. Washington: Acropolis Books, Ltd., 1972.

---

3. Adding New Programs. The final contingent strategy used by budgetary officers is the incremental addition of new programs. Because the new and novel often are distrusted by those empowered to distribute money, every effort is made in the agency to make its new program look as old as possible. Variants of this strategy include the contention that the new program is only temporary, that it is exceedingly small and thus hardly worth examination, that it is merely a logical continuation of an old program, that it is an attempt to reduce some sort of backlog in the agency, and that it will save money.

On the other hand, an agency will occasionally try to make the program look as new and "with-it" as possible. This variant also has its uses. A favored strategy is christening the new program with an inspiring title—for example, the "War on Poverty," "Polaris," "Titan," and "Mission 66" (which was a park improvement program). Salesmanship is not neglected; members of Congress, on occasion, have been irritated by the use of the "Peter Rabbit" presentation—simple graphs, fancy brochures, and lots and lots of pictures. Salesmanship often is used in conjunction with the recognition of some new crisis. Witness the effects of such drama-ridden salesmanship on a member of one appropriations committee:

A week ago, Mr. Chairman, after this hearing about cancer, I went home and checked all the little skin flecks and felt for bumps and bruises. I lay awake that night and could have convinced myself I had cancer. And then more recently I lay awake listening to my heart after hearing the heart-trouble talk....And here I am listening to all this mental health talk...and I wonder what I am going to dream about tonight.[67]

If the foregoing strategy review sounds cynical, it is. To be cynical, however, is not necessarily to be scrofulous. Bureaucrats-as-politicians are capable of using cynical means for the sake of noble ends, and this phenomenon is well exemplified by the budgetary process.

An alternative always is possible, however. Cynical means can be used to attain cynical ends. As an administrative technique, the budget has its own combination of means and ends, methods and values. The ways in which these variables are interrelated by administrators are in essence political and they affect programs and people.

So it is, too, with another management technique, public personnel administration. Like budgeting, public personnel administration is draped with the trappings of professionalism, technology, and expertise, but it is also a system of values and politics. We consider this subject in the next chapter.

NOTES

[1] See: Bertram M. Gross, "The New Systems Budgeting," *Public Administration Review*, 29 (March/April 1969), pp. 113–137; and Allen Schick, "The Road to PPB: The Stages of Budget Reform," *Public Administration Review*, 26 (December 1966), pp. 243–258.

[2] Aaron Wildavsky, *The Politics of the Budgetary Process*, 2nd ed. (Boston: Little, Brown, 1974), p. 4.

[3] Charles G. Dawes, *The First Year of the Budget of the United States* (Washington, D.C.: U.S. Government Printing Office, 1923), p. ii, as cited in Schick, "The Road to PPB."

[4] Verne B. Lewis, "Reflections on Budget Systems," *Public Budgeting and Finance*, 8 (Spring 1988), p. 7

[5] Gross, "The New Systems Budgeting."

[6] Executive Order 8248, as quoted in Schick, "The Road to PPB."

[7] Commission on Organization of the Executive Branch of Government, *Budgeting and Accounting* (Washington, D.C.: U.S. Government Printing Office, 1949), p. 8.

[8] Quoted in Allen Schick, *Budget Innovation in the States* (Washington, D.C.: Brookings Institution, 1971), p. 127.

[9] Edwin L. Harper, Fred A. Kramer, and Andrew M. Rouse, *Implementation and Use of PPB in Sixteen Federal Agencies* (Washington, D.C.: U.S. Bureau of the Budget, April, 1969).

[10] Orville Freeman, quoted in Lewis, "Reflections on Budget Systems," p. 11.

[11] Harry P. Hatry, *Status of PPBS in Local and State Governments in the United States* (Washington, D.C.: Urban Institute, 1974).

[12] *Ibid.*

[13] Much of the following discussion is drawn from: U.S. Congress, Joint Economic Committee, Subcommittee on Economy in Government, *The Planning-Programming-Budgeting System: Process and Potentials*, 90th Congress, First Session (Washington, D.C.: U.S. Government Printing Office, 1967); and U.S. Congress, Senate, Committee on Government Opera-

tions, Subcommittee on National Security and International Operations, *Planning-Programming-Budgeting Inquiry of the Subcommittee on National Security and International Operations*, Parts I through IV, Hearings of August 23, September 20, October 18, 1967, and March 26, and July 11, 1968 (Washington, D.C.: U.S. Government Printing Office, 1970).

[14] Anatol Rapoport, *Fights, Games, and Debates* (Ann Arbor, Mich.: University of Michigan Press, 1960).

[15] Reorganization Message of President Richard M. Nixon to Congress, March 12, 1970, as quoted in Allen Schick, "A Death in the Bureaucracy: The Demise of Federal PPB," *Public Administration Review*, 33 (March/April 1973), p. 151.

[16] *Ibid.*, p. 146.

[17] Peter Drucker, *The Practice of Management* (New York: Harper & Row, 1954).

[18] Jong S. Jun, "Management by Objectives and the Public Sector, Introduction," *Public Administration Review*, 36 (January/February 1976), p. 3.

[19] Frank P. Sherwood and William J. Page, Jr., "MBO and Public Management," *Public Administration Review*, 36 (January/February 1976), p. 5.

[20] Chester A. Newland, "Policy/Program Objectives and Federal Management: The Search for Government Effectiveness," *Public Administration Review*, 36 (January/February 1976), p. 20.

[21] Jerry L. McCaffery, "MBO and the Budgetary Process," *Public Administration Review*, 36 (January/February 1976), p. 35.

[22] See: Rackham S. Fukuhara, "Productivity Improvement in Cities," *The Municipal Year Book, 1977* (Washington, D.C.: International City Management Association, 1977), pp. 193–200, for 1976 figure; Theodore H. Poister and Robert P. McGowan, "The Use of Management Tools in Municipal Government: A National Survey," *Public Administration Review*, 44 (May/June 1984), p. 218, for 1982 figure; Theodore H. Poister and Gregory Streib, "Management Tools in Municipal Government: Trends Over the Past Decade," *Public Administration Review*, 49 (May/June 1989), p. 242, for 1987 figure; in 1987, 62 percent used MBO; and Richard C. Elling, "Of Bandwagons and Bandaids: A Comparative Assessment of the Utilization and Efficacy of Management Techniques and Strategies in State Bureaucracies" (Paper presented at the 1984 Annual Meeting of the American Political Science Association, Washington, D.C.: August/September, 1984), for 1984 figure. The municipal surveys sampled all cities of 25,000 to one million people. Four hundred-four cities responded in 1976, 460 responded in 1982, and 451 in 1987. The state survey had a response rate of 40 percent (or 847 administrators) and included Arizona, California, Delaware, Indiana, Michigan, New York, South Dakota, Tennessee, Texas, and Vermont.

[23] Jimmy Carter, "Planning a Budget from Zero," *Innovations in State Government* (Washington, D.C.: National Governors Conference, 1974), p. 42.

[24] Peter A. Pyhrr, "The Zero Base Approach to Government Budgeting," *Public Administration Review*, 37 (January/February 1977), p. 7. It is probable, however, that Pyhrr is overstating the case, especially since Georgia was also undergoing a gov-

ernmental reorganization. See also: Thomas P. Lauth, "Zero-Base Budgeting in Georgia State Government: Myth and Reality," *Public Administration Review*, 38 (September/October 1978), pp. 420–430.

[25] Richard C. Kearney, "Sunset: A Survey and Analysis of the State Experience," *Public Administration Review*, 50 (January/February 1990), p. 53.

[26] *Ibid.*, p. 56.

[27] Quoted in: Donald F. Haider, "Zero Base: Federal Style," *Public Administration Review*, 37 (July/August 1977), p. 401.

[28] Allen Schick, "The Road from ZBB," *Public Administration Review*, 38 (March/April 1978), p. 178.

[29] Allen Schick, *Zero-Base 80: The Status of Zero-Base Budgeting in the States* (Washington, D.C.: National Association of State Budget Officers and The Urban Institute, 1979); and Elling, "Of Bandwagons and Bandaids," Table 7.

[30] About half of American municipalities of 25,000 to 1 million people were using "Program, Zero-Base, or Target-Base" budgeting in 1976, a proportion that has since leveled off at about three-fourths. See: Fukuhara, "Productivity Improvement in Cities," pp. 196–197; Poister and McGowan, "The Use of Management Tools in Municipal Government," pp. 217–218; Poister and Streib, "Management Tools in Municipal Government," p. 242; and Perry Moore, "Zero-Base Budgeting in American Cities," *Public Administration Review*, 40 (May/June 1980), pp. 253–258.

[31] Frank D. Draper and Bernard T. Pitsvada, "ZBB—Looking Back After Ten Years," *Public Administration Review*, 41 (January/February 1981), pp. 76–83. The principal studies of ZBB's use in the public sector are the following: Schick, *Zero-Base 80* (which focuses on state governments); Moore, "Zero-Base Budgeting in American Cities"; and, for the federal experience, Frank D. Draper and Bernard T. Pitsvada, *A First Year's Assessment of ZBB in the Federal Government—Another View* (Arlington, Va.: Association of Government Accountants, 1978); Frank D. Draper and Bernard T. Pitsvada, "Congress and Executive Branch Budget Reform: The House Appropriations Committee and Zero-Base Budgeting," *International Journal of Public Administration*, Vol. 2, No. 3 (1980), pp. 331–374; Comptroller General of the United States, *Streamlining Zero-Base Budgeting Will Benefit Decision-Making*, PAD 79-74 (Washington, D.C.: General Accounting Office, 1979); and Comptroller General of the United States, *Budget Formulation: Many Approaches But Some Improvements Are Needed*, PAD 80-31, Report to the House Committee on Government Operations (Washington, D.C.: General Accounting Office, 1980).

[32] Naomi Caiden, "The New Rules of the Federal Budget Game," *Public Administration Review*, 44 (March/April 1984), p. 110.

[33] Robert J. Lampman, "Secondary Consumer Income: Interfamily Transfer Flows, 1950–1978," Mimeograph (1983), Table 3.3.

[34] U.S. Bureau of the Census, *Statistical Abstract of the United States, 1990* (Washington, D.C.: U.S. Government Printing Office, 1990), Table 502, p. 313. Unless noted otherwise, the following discussion on uncontrollables is drawn from this source, and all figures are for Fiscal Year 1989.

[35] Lewis, "Reflections on Budget Systems," p. 4.

[36] For a good discussion of performance measurement and its resurrection in a budgeting context, see: Allen Schick, "Budgeting for Results: Recent Developments in Five Industrialized Countries," *Public Administration Review*, 50 (January/February 1990), pp. 26–34.

[37] The terms are drawn from Hugh Heclo, "Executive Budget Making" (Paper prepared for the Urban Institute Conference on the Federal Budget Policy in the 1980s, September 29–30, 1983), Mimeograph, pp. 14–25.

[38] Aaron Wildavsky, *Speaking Truth to Power* (Boston: Little Brown, 1979), p. 212. In light of the self-evident truth implicit in Wildavsky's question, it is odd how frequently public administrators engage in asking each other to recommend cuts in their own programs, and this practice seems to be particularly favored in state universities. For an intriguing case study of the perils of "bottom-up" budgeting, see: Edward Foster, "Planning at the University of Minnesota," *Planning for Higher Education*, 18, No. 2 (1989–1990), pp. 25–38.

[39] Lewis, "Reflections on Budget Systems," p. 15.

[40] Office of Management and Budget, *Major Themes* (Washington, D.C.: Office of Management and Budget, published annually).

[41] Unnamed official in the Central Budget Management System, Office of Management and Budget, as quoted by Heclo, "Executive Budget Making," p. 35.

[42] The primary sources for the following discussion are Caiden, "The New Rules of the Federal Budget Game," pp. 110–115; and Heclo, "Executive Budget Making," pp. 40–46.

[43] Heclo, "Executive Budget Making," p. 43.

[44] Frederick C. Mosher and Max O. Stephenson, Jr., "The Office of Management and Budget in a Changing Scene," *Public Budgeting and Finance*, 2 (Winter 1982), p. 28.

[45] Steven Mufson, "'PADs' Wise to Ways of Power," *Washington Post* (April 25, 1990).

[46] Fred Khedouri, quoted in *ibid.*

[47] James J. Gosling, "The State Budget Office and Policy Making," *Public Budgeting and Finance*, 7 (Spring 1987), pp. 67, 51. The three states were Iowa, Minnesota, and Wisconsin.

[48] David G. Mathiason, "The Evolution of the Office of Management and Budget Under President Reagan," *Policy Budgeting and Finance*, 8 (Autumn 1988), p. 14.

[49] Rudolph Penner, "Budget Assumptions and Budget Outcomes," *The AEI Economist* (August 1981), reprinted in the Committee for Responsible Federal Budget, *Symposium on the Congressional Budget Act and Process—How Can They be Improved?* (January 12–13, 1982), p. 4.

[50] Stephen E. Nordlinger, "U.S. Economic Seers Often Miss the Mark," *Baltimore Sun* (February 8, 1987).

[51] For summaries, see: *ibid.*; Paul Blustein, "The Outlook," *Wall Street Journal* (April 27, 1987); and Johnathan Rauch, "CBO's Wishful Thinking," *National Journal* (March 7, 1987), pp.1069–1078.

[52] Caiden, "The New Rules of the Federal Budget Game," p. 115.

[53] Much of this discussion is based on the chapter by Frank Sackton, "Financing Public Programs Under Fiscal Constraints," in *Managing Public Programs: Balancing Politics, Administration, and Public Needs*, Robert E. Cleary and Nicholas Henry, eds. (San Francisco: Jossey-Bass, 1989), pp. 147–166.

Among the better examples of the cutback management literature are: Charles H. Levine and Irene Rubin, eds., *Fiscal Stress and Public Policy* (Beverly Hills, Calif.: Sage, 1980); E. K. Kellar, ed., *Managing With Less* (Washington, D.C.: International City Management Association, 1979); G. W. Wynn, ed., *Learning from Abroad—Cutback Management: A Trinational Perspective* (New Brunswick, N.J.: Transaction Books, 1983); and Charles Levine, Irene S. Rubin, and G. Wolohojian, *The Politics of Retrenchment: How Local Governments Manage Fiscal Stress* (Beverly Hills, Calif.: Sage, 1981).

[54] National Association of Counties and International City-Management Association, "Consolidated County-Type Governments in the United States," Mimeograph, (1980); and Joel C. Miller and Richard L. Forstall, "Annexations and Corporate Changes: 1970—79 and 1980—83," *Municipal Year Book, 1984* (Washington, D.C.: International City Management Association, 1984), p. 101. By 1984, twenty-six city-county consolidations of any consequence had occurred.

[55] Heclo, "Executive Budget Making," p. 44.

[56] Mosher and Stephenson, "The Office of Management and Budget in a Changing Scene," pp. 25–26.

[57] Peter M. Benda and Charles H. Levine, "OMB and the Central Management Problem: Is Another Reorganization the Answer?" *Public Administration Review*, 46 (September/October 1986), p. 380.

[58] Frederick C. Mosher, *A Tale of Two Agencies: A Comparative Analysis of the General Accounting Office and the Office of Management and Budget* (Baton Rouge, La.: Louisiana State University Press, 1984), p. 107.

[59] Benda and Levine, "OMB and the Central Management Problem," p. 384.

[60] Chester A. Newland, "Executive Office Policy Apparatus: Enforcing the Reagan Agenda," in *The Reagan Administration and the Governing of America*, Lester M. Salamon and Michael S. Lund, eds. (Washington, D.C.: The Urban Institute Press, 1984), p. 166.

[61] Benda and Levine, "OMB and the Central Management Problem," pp. 387–388.

[62] National Urban Coalition, *Counterbudget: A Blueprint for Changing National Priorities, 1971–1976*, Robert S. Benson and Harold Wolman, eds. (New York: Praeger, 1971), p. xii.

[63] Most of the following discussion on the Congressional Budget and Impoundment Control Act of 1974 is drawn from Committee for Economic Development, *The New Congressional Budget Process and the Economy* (New York: Committee for Economic Development, 1975).

[64] Wildavsky, *The Politics of the Budgetary Process*; Richard F. Fenno, Jr., *The Power of the Purse: Appropriations Politics in Congress* (Boston: Little, Brown, 1966); and Jesse Burkhead, *Government Budgeting* (New York: John Wiley, 1956).

[65] Wildavsky, *The Politics of the Budgetary Process*, p. 64.

[66] The following discussion of budgetary strategy is drawn from *ibid.*, pp. 63–127.

[67] Quoted in *ibid.*, p. 120.

MANAGING HUMAN RESOURCES IN THE PUBLIC SECTOR

It is our purpose in this chapter to review four public personnel systems, to trace the development of the profession of human resource management in the public sector, to sketch the nuts and bolts of public personnel administration, and to consider some value dilemmas in the field. The traditional field of public personnel administration has expanded its conceptual boundaries and increasingly is called "human resource management"; it concerns the management of and policymaking for people and positions in the government bureaucracy. It long has been a mainstay in the field of public administration; its scholars traditionally have seen themselves as grappling with "people problems" and wrestling with the stuff of politics and the public interest. In recent years, however, human resource management has undergone some serious questioning in the public sector of its basic intellectual premises and has been buffeted by new developments in the public merit systems. Many public administrationists now favor dealing with "people problems" within the conceptual framework of organization theory, and the whole notion of "merit" has received new and bizarre meanings,

at least in the opinion of numerous human resource managers and academicians. While this chapter does not represent an attempt to "straighten things out" in the field, we shall consider some of the difficulties and challenges confronting public personnel administration.

PUBLIC PERSONNEL SYSTEMS

Frederick C. Mosher observed that there are at least four broad types of personnel systems functioning concurrently in American government: the political executive system, the general civil service, professional career systems, and the collective system.[1] Often, every one of these personnel systems can be found within the same agency.

The Political Executive System

"Political executives" are those public officials appointed to an office without tenure, who have significant policy-making powers, and who are outside the civil service system. They have been called "the true nexus between politics and administration."[2] There are about 3,000 political executive positions (*i.e.*, those that are presidentially appointed) in the federal government,[3] and uncounted thousands at the state and local levels. Contrast this number to the roughly 100 political appointees available to each of the prime ministers of Britain, France, and Germany.[4]

Expansion and Contraction. The number of political executives in the United States "is not fixed and varies depending on who does the counting and how positions are defined....What is important is the *trend* toward more political appointees for each presidential administration. The direction of this trend is not in dispute."[5] That direction, of course, is toward the appointment of greater numbers of public administrators who hold their positions, at least in the federal government, because presidents have put them there. Today's 3,000 presidential appointees are quite an increase from the 200 or so available to Franklin Delano Roosevelt, and the National Commission on the Public Service, a prestigious private group that was chaired by Paul Volcker, recommended that the number of presidential appointees be reduced from 3,000 to 2,000.[6]

It is less evident that the federal trend toward allowing greater numbers of political appointees is being emulated at the state and local levels. As we discuss later in this chapter, it appears that partisan gubernatorial appointments are in decline, and significantly larger proportions of career public administrators clearly are moving into the top agency positions in the states.[7] At the local level, the council–manager form of government and other reforms have resulted in fewer and fewer administrative positions being filled by locally elected chief executives.

In sum, the trends in the political appointee system appear to be a combination of expanding in the federal government and contracting at the state and local governments.

An Emphasis on Intellect. As a group of men and women in the public employ, political executives exhibit certain systemic tendencies. Most notably, perhaps, is the growing emphasis on intellect—partisan political experience seems to be of declining importance in the selection process. This

is not to imply that partisan sympathies and willingness to be a "team player" are not considerations in the appointment process, but it appears to be increasingly recognized that, in the words of the late President John F. Kennedy, "you can't beat brains." At the assistant secretary and deputy agency administrator level, Dean E. Mann and Jameson W. Doig found that 90 percent of this group in the Kennedy administration were college graduates, a figure that has risen with every administration since that of Franklin D. Roosevelt.[8] At the federal administrative level just below that of assistant secretary, a study by W. Lloyd Warner and others revealed that the political appointees in this group had more formal education than their counterparts in the military, civil service, and Foreign Service.[9] Education in the social sciences is increasingly represented among political executives, while the ratio of lawyers in this group (at least in the lower echelons) is only about 25 percent and declining. Of 108 assistant secretaries intensively studied by Mann and Doig, only 30 percent were appointed on the basis of a particular specialization, and the remainder because of "general experience."[10]

At the cabinet level, educations in law dominate. Nearly half of the secretarial and deputy secretarial appointments from 1952 to 1980 had law degrees; the next highest field of study represented at this level was economics.[11] Still, law in the longer view is declining as the predominantly represented field at the top of the federal hierarchy; during the nineteenth century, lawyers (a profession virtually synonymous with politics at that time) held around 90 percent of the cabinet-level appointments.[12]

A Decline in Traditional Partisanship. There also is a declining emphasis on partisanship in the political executive personnel system. One indication of this is that even when a presidential appointee is a member of the president's party, this common political loyalty appears to account for very little in securing the appointment. Mann and Doig concluded that a mere 10 percent of their sample of 108 assistant secretaries were appointed primarily by dint of "service to party."[13] A more recent study found that, between 1960 and 1978, the proportion of top-level presidential appointees who were affiliated with the president's party never exceeded 70 percent, and dipped as low as 56 percent.[14] Contrast this percentage with the 90 percent of the government's top-echelon appointees who were Democrats or closely affiliated with the president's party in Franklin Roosevelt's administration.[15] As we observed in Chapter 1, however, there has been a significant reemphasis on assuring the ideological loyalty of presidential appointees since 1981, although the correlations, if any, between these ideologically pure appointees and their partisan leanings has yet to be analyzed.

A Decline in Governmental Experience. If partisanship may be in decline in making presidential appointments, so is the practice of appointing people to top-level federal jobs who have had experience in government. Between 1933 and 1961, 80 percent of the cabinet and subcabinet political appointees had had some professional experience at the national level, and a third had devoted a major portion of their careers to the federal service.[16] Yet, studies of more recent presidential appointees indicate that these ratios are declining, and declining rather precipitously. About half of all cabinet secretaries appointed since 1953 have served only one to two years— hardly adequate time to begin comprehending the complexities of the federal system that they are supposed to manage.[17] Between 1953 and 1976, more than half of the eighty-seven people who served in the cabinet (forty-six of them) served less than half of a single presidential term. The four years of the Carter cabinet (1976–1980) were somewhat more stable, but not much, and Carter changed close to 40 percent of his original appointees to cabinet positions before his term was completed. Despite Ronald Reagan's early efforts to appoint loyalists, more than three quarters of his initial cabinet appointees were gone by the close of his first term, and only one remained by the end of his second.

At the subcabinet, policy-making levels of the federal governments, the lack of experience appears to be comparable, if not worse, and the situation is deteriorating. One study found that 69 percent of presidential appointees and 40 percent of noncareer supergrade appointees had had less than two years of government experience when in office.[18] Between 1960 and 1973, nearly two-thirds of the cabinet's undersecretaries and almost four-fifths of the assistant secretaries had worked less than two years for the same supervisor.[19] Less than half of the federal executives occupying these two echelons served for more than two years, and a fifth of them served for less than a year.[20] Research covering 1979 through 1985 found that, throughout the federal government, the average tenure of the political appointees in the Senior Executive Service (SES) was about eighteen months in one position, and even briefer in the higher positions: "Governmentwide, fully one-third of the political appointees in the SES change jobs or leave government every year."[21]

The Rise of the White House "Loyalty Tests." Both partisan fealty and governmental experience are qualifications of diminishing import in the political executive system. But loyalty to the occupant of the White House (including, it appears, loyalty to the president's ideology) is another matter, and it is clear that recent presidents have placed considerable stock in controlling the appointment of political executives.

This is new. When Mann and Doig conducted their study of assistant secretaries in 1965, they concluded that the appointment of these men and women was "a highly centralized and personalized process revolving around the respective department and agency heads," and when a rare difference of opinion arose between the secretary and the White House staff over a candidate, "the secretary generally won."[22]

This condition had begun to alter as early as the 1950s, but President Reagan culminated the reversal and rendered White House control over the political executive system complete. To quote the Director of the Presidential Personnel Office under Reagan: "We handled all the appointments: boards, commissions, Schedule C's, ambassadorships, judgeships....If you are going to run the government, you've got to control the people that come into it."[23]

This concern with control had its effects. From 1980 to 1986, according to an analysis by the Senate Committee of Governmental Affairs, the Reagan administration had reduced both the number of career civil service jobs available in most domestic agencies, and expanded the numbers of political appointees in the top ranks of these agencies. In these six years, the number of career administrators in the Senior Executive Service (or the top 7,000 federal managers) who were assigned to the twenty-four principal domestic agencies declined by 5 percent; the number of political, non-career appointees in the Senior Executive Service increased by 13 percent; and the number of Schedule C appointments (a fourth of which can be political appointments) grew by nearly 19 percent. These patterns were not consequences of growth, as the number of federal civilian employees working in domestic agencies decreased by almost 7 percent during this period. According to the chair of the Governmental Affairs Committee, Senator John Glenn, the Senior Executive Service had "become politicized by the Reagan administration at the expense of the career service."[24]

No one can dispute the desirability of a democratically elected chief executive establishing his or her control over the policy-making and policy-executing apparatus of the executive branch, and appointing loyalists in key positions is an important means of establishing this control. But there are problems. For one, establishing the kind of pervasive, centralized control over the political appointee system exemplified by the actions of the Reagan White House is simply very difficult to achieve. One former presidential personnel assistant, who was notorious for his belief in the necessity of the president controlling the appointment process, later admitted, "If you try to do everything, I'm not so sure you can succeed. It's an awfully difficult job just to handle the *presidential* appointees....if you try to do too much, you may be diluted to the point where you're not as effective."[25]

It is at least arguable that attempts to centralize all 3,000 presidential appointments in the White House, as was done in the Reagan administration, can result in some appointees of questionable quality. Because of some of Reagan's appointees, the "sleaze factor" in his administration became a recurrent target of the press, and perhaps with some reason. During Reagan's two terms as president (1981–1989), 7,462 federal officials were prosecuted—that is, they were indicted, convicted (3,226), or awaiting trial—for public corruption.

Compare this figure to the total number of prosecutions of federal officials for public corruption during the preceding eight years (1972–1980): 1,694. About four-and-a-half times more federal officials were prosecuted and convicted for corruption during the eight years of the Reagan administration than were prosecuted and convicted during the preceding eight years![26] Whether these prosecutions and convictions for corruption can be attributed to the way presidential appointments were made by the Reagan White House is impossible to judge (the argument could be advanced, after all, that more convictions for federal corruption in the Reagan administration is attributable to Reagan's prosecutorial zeal), but there did seem to be some substance to the press's charge of "sleaze" among some of Reagan's top administrators.

Perhaps more fundamentally, it is unclear that White House dominance of the Reagan stripe over the political executive system was needed to achieve competent bureaucratic responsiveness to presidential policy. A survey of all presidential appointees who served between 1964 and 1984 found that they believed strongly in both the competence and responsiveness of the career civil service; depending upon the administration, 92 percent to 77 percent of the presidential appointees stated that career federal employees were competent or very competent, and 89 percent to 78 percent said they were responsive or very responsive.[27] Similar views seem to be held by White House staffers, who typically are the most keen to establish presidential control over the standing bureaucracy, and the "evidence is overwhelming that experienced political appointees, regardless of administration, party, or ideology, believe that career executives are both competent and responsive."[28]

Political Executives at the Grassroots. In contrast to developments over the past three decades at the federal level, the political executive system of public personnel administration at the state level appears to be tilting more in favor of career administrators. But the state systems vary greatly in their pervasiveness; for example, the governor of Oregon controls fewer than a dozen patronage jobs, while the governors of Illinois and New York have the power to make thousands of such appointments. Importantly, however, the majority of these positions in such states as Illinois and New York are well below the executive level, typically with clerical and lower positions going to party loyalists. Moreover, research consistently indicates that the quality and professional career orientation of upper-echelon state administrators, including gubernatorial appointees, has been increasing steadily for at least the past twenty years.[29]

What is true for the states is even more in evidence among local governments. Close to four of every ten cities and towns (and over half of all cities with more than 25,000 people) use a council-manager form of government, in which *all* appointive powers rest not with the mayor, but with a professional city manager who reports directly to the city council.[30] But even in mayor-council cities (which account for 54 percent of all forms of municipal government[31]), the mayors are significantly restricted in their powers of appointment. Fifty-four percent of the mayors in mayor-council cities do not have the authority to appoint as many as four of the top urban managers (police chief, fire chief, city attorney, and chief personnel officer), and 13 percent of the mayors may not appoint even one of these executives.[32] And, as in the states, the professionalism of career public administrators in local governments clearly is on the rise—and it has been, in any case, traditionally quite high.[33]

Unlike the federal government, the grass-roots governments, it seems, are increasingly comfortable with a human resource management system that accords significant policy-making authority to career civil servants, and at the expense of political appointees.

The Civil Service System

The general civil service system comprises those white-collar, generally nonprofessional, career personnel who have tenure and who are administered according to traditional civil service practices. Its overriding characteristic is the emphasis that is placed on the *position*: the description of duties, responsibilities, requirements, qualifications, and so on, that go with the position. As a public personnel system, the civil service has been the historic locus of public administration and, of

course, public personnel administration as well. We shall concentrate more amply on the civil service later in this chapter; it is sufficient to observe for the moment that the civil service values the notions of "neutrality," "merit," and of being removed from "politics."

Professional Career Systems

The various career systems of the public service are made up of white-collar personnel, generally professionals and paraprofessionals, who are tenured in a *de facto* (*i.e.*, in actuality) if not always in a *de jure* (*i.e.*, in a legal) sense. The system's principal feature is the emphasis that is placed on the *person*, rather than on the position, as in the civil service system. In a career system an individual's career is administered in a planned manner; the individual is expected to advance upward through several hierarchical positions in which he or she can use professional expertise in increasingly responsible and effective ways. As with the civil service system, we shall examine career systems more fully in the following sections of this chapter. It is sufficient for now to note that career systems place high value on the concepts of "professionalism," "specialization," and "expertise," and that their rise in the public service has had a profound and disquieting impact on the more traditional civil service system.

The Collective System

The collective public personnel system refers to the arrangements and the problems caused by collective bargaining and the unionization of government employees. The system comprises primarily blue-collar workers (with a growing influx of white-collar workers from the civil service and career personnel systems) whose jobs are administered via agreements between management and workers. The collective "system" is as much an issue in public personnel administration as it is a system, so we shall treat it in more detail later in the chapter.

The four public personnel systems that have been described represent fundamental value differences in the practice of public personnel administration. What we shall do now, therefore, is trace briefly the evolution of public personnel administration in the United States, stressing the kinds of values represented by proponents of these systems. In this regard, we shall concentrate especially on the thinking underlying the civil service and career systems, since the concepts that they represent have historically had the greatest impact on public personnel administration.

THE DEVELOPMENT OF AMERICAN HUMAN RESOURCE ADMINISTRATION IN THE PUBLIC SECTOR

The evolution of American human resource administration can be divided into seven phases: the guardian period of a relatively high sense of administrative ethics; the period of unmitigated "spoils"; the reform period; the scientific management period with its concern for efficiency; the administrative management period with its emphasis on political executives versus career executives; the professional period that witnessed a huge influx in government of highly educated and socialized personnel from a wide spectrum of differing professional backgrounds; and our present period of professional public administration, which weds the values of professionalism and management in the public service. None of these periods, of course, is as discrete in time and as clear-cut in definition as the following review may imply.

Phase 1: The Guardian Period, 1789–1829

Mosher calls the guardian period "government by gentlemen,"[34] and it corresponds principally to George Washington's influential administration as president. Washington set the moral tone of the early federal bureaucracy by appointing men to office who were reputed to be persons of character as well as competence. Character was synonymous with merit, and merit during the administrations of Washington, John Adams, and Thomas Jefferson meant a respected family background, a high degree of formal education, and substantial loyalty to the president—in short, being a member of the establishment. Sidney H. Aronson's statistical analysis of the early public service in the United States shows that it was of a highly elitist nature, with roughly 65 percent of the highest-level appointees being drawn from the landed gentry, merchant, and professional classes.[35]

Moreover, the early public service was highly political. While ability and integrity were valued, it did not hurt to be a "team player." Aronson's analysis indicates that of the eighty-seven major political appointments made by Adams, sixty were new appointments. In other words, more than two-thirds of Washington's original appointments to top-level positions were tossed out by the new Adams administration. Similarly, of the ninety-two top appointments made by Jefferson, seventy-three were original appointments; stated another way, four-fifths of Jefferson's top administrators were team players.[36] So, while the guardian period may have been government by gentlemen, they were nonetheless political gentlemen. Nevertheless, the notions of character, ethical conduct, and public trust commanded considerable respect in making appointments to the public service during the first half-century of the American experiment.

Phase 2: The Spoils Period, 1829–1883

With the inauguration of Andrew Jackson as president in 1829, the United States government was put on a paying basis. That is, the government (and the taxpayers) paid the party that won. The period acquired its name from a remark made in 1832, attributed to Senator William L. Marcy of New York: American politicians "see nothing wrong in the rule that to the victor belong the spoils of the enemy."[37] The rationale underlying the spoils system was that if presidents were to emerge, like Jackson, from the class that earned its own living, then politics had to be made to pay. And history indicates that it did.

While Jackson symbolizes the ascension of the spoils system in the public bureaucracy, a more accurate assessment is that Jackson simply fostered the democratization of the public service. The percentage of top administrators appointed by his predecessor, John Quincy Adams, that Jackson removed so that he could appoint his own people to top posts was very similar to the percentage removed by Jefferson; for Jefferson, approximately 80 percent were original appointments, and for Jackson the figure was closer to 90 percent.[38] Nevertheless, Jackson likely started the process of making the public service a system redolent with bribery and graft. Power was transferred from one group (the gentry) to another (political parties), but never to the people as a whole.

Phase 3: The Reform Period, 1883–1906

The corrupt excesses of the spoils system during this period eventually resulted in a reform movement determined to rid government of those bureaucrats who owed their office to no more than party hack work. From 1865 to 1883, a small group of intellectual idealists agitated for thoroughgoing reform of the entire public personnel system. Notable in this respect were George William Curtis, Carl Schurz, Richard Henry Dana, and Thomas Jenckes. Largely as a result of their efforts, the New York Civil Service Reform Association, the nation's first, was founded in 1877. In 1881 thirteen associations modeled after the New York group merged to form the National Civil Service Reform League, now known as the National Civil Service League. British concepts of merit in the public service were of considerable interest to the civil service reform movement, and Dorman B. Eaton's report to President Rutherford B. Hayes (1877–1881) on the English civil service (published as a book in 1879) enhanced their influence.[39] The assassination of President James A. Garfield by a mentally ill, dissatisfied office seeker in 1881 effectively assured national legislation of civil service reform. In 1883 Congress passed the Civil Service Act (the Pendleton Act), which created a bipartisan Civil Service Commission (which was replaced in 1978 by the Office of Personnel Management and the Merit Systems Protection Board) responsible to the president and charged with the duty of filling government positions by a process of open, competitive examinations.

Although the Civil Service Act had been influenced by the British system of public service (notably by the British principles of competitive examinations and a "neutral" civil service free from partisan pressures), the Senate inserted some major provisos into the Act that were uniquely American in character. One such clause was that the Senators required civil service examinations to be "practical in character." While talented essayists of an academic sort might be nice to have floating around in the federal bureaucracy, it was far more important that the bureaucrat be able to do his or her job. This requisite provided the basis for a detailed system of position classification several years later; to be able to administer "practical" entrance tests, one first had to know what the job was all about.

Second, the Senate omitted the requirement that an applicant could enter the federal service only at the lowest grade. This permitted an "open" civil service with "lateral entry" as a possibility for all administrators (for example, a GS 13 level official in the Commerce Department could execute a "lateral arabesque" into a GS 13 position in the Transportation Department if he or she so desired).

Third, no special tracks were laid between the public service and the universities, unlike in Great Britain. Indeed, initially it was preferred that the service be as highly "democratic" in character as possible. Only in 1905 did the Civil Service Commission first observe that "the greatest defect in the Federal Service is the lack of opportunity for ambitious, well-educated young men," and only in the 1930s was a major effort begun to upgrade the educational level of the national bureaucracy.[40]

Finally, the Pendleton Act set up no special "administrative class," no "permanent undersecretaries," contrary to the practice in Britain and Western Europe generally. Thus, the idea of political neutrality was not upheld at the potential expense of social responsiveness; instead the top bureaucratic echelon was occupied by *political* executives.

The crusade for reform of the public service had three dominant characteristics. First, the reform movement had been negative. That is, the reformists wanted to do away with the spoils system and its attendant evils. Second, the movement had been highly moral in tone. In Mosher's words,

it associated what we now refer to as personnel administration with morality, with a connotation of "goodness" *vs.* "badness," quite apart from the purposes for which people were employed or the nature of the responsibilities they would carry.[41]

Third, and not too emphatically, the reform movement had been concerned with efficiency in government, and the reformers believed that the merit system would help assure "more efficient" (*i.e.*, less corrupt) practices. These characteristics, combined with the antielitist sympathies of the Civil Service Act itself, acted to create what Mosher has called a period of "government by the good"; ethics and egalitarianism were prized.[42] Managerial effectiveness, however, was an incidental consideration at best.

There were two lasting effects that this phase of moral rectitude had. The first was its influence on the study of public administration. Only four years after the passage of the Pendleton Act, Woodrow Wilson wrote his seminal essay on "The Study of Administration" (recall Chapter 2). The moral tone of Wilson's article reflected the mental set of the reform period, and it has been a continuing undercurrent in the study of public administration. Wilson, an ardent reformer and later a president of the Civil Service Reform League, facilitated the expansion of an ethical sense of public duty beyond the conceptual confines of the civil service and into the entire intellectual terrain of public administration. Relatedly, the old politics/administration dichotomy, long favored as an academic focus in the field of public administration, received much of its initial legitimacy and acceptance as a result of the thinking that dominated the reform period of public personnel administration. "Politics" was "bad" in the civil service, and "administration" was "good." Frank Goodnow's *Politics and Administration*, published in 1900, both reflected and strengthened the prevalent intellectual view that administration not only was "different" from politics, but also was somehow "better."

The second effect of the reform period related more to the practice of public administration: The continuing independence of the Civil Service Commission was fostered, and its use as a model in the reform of state and local governments was encouraged. The Commission evolved into a buffer against political pressure brought on by both Congress and the president. In this development during the reform period, not only was morality increasingly identified with public personnel administration, but also public personnel administration as a field gradually was disassociated from the substantive and managerial functions of government. To put it far too crassly, but clearly: The bureaucrats responsible for getting a job done and the bureaucrats responsible for keeping government moral became increasingly distinct entities.

Phase 4: The Scientific Management Period, 1906–1937

Increasingly, the academic field of public administration was being influenced by developments in business administration, which then was dominated by the time-motion, scientific management school represented by Frederick Taylor and by Frank and Lillian Gilbreth (recall Chapter 3). The ultimate value of this period was efficiency—in other words, doing the job with the least resources. The values, concepts, and structure of the civil service were most compatible with the notion of efficiency. During the reform period, efficiency had been associated with morality and lack of corruption. Efficiency also was "neutral," another traditional value of the civil service and public personnel administration. Thus, a somewhat inconsistent, but soothing, amalgam of beliefs emerged that packed goodness, merit, morality, neutrality, efficiency, and science into one conceptual lump. Of these values, efficiency came to represent the best of the rest, a value "more equal" than the others—what "good" public personnel administration was all about.

The drive for scientific management in government began at the local level, largely because American government was concentrated at this level at the beginning of the twentieth century. In 1902, aside from the national defense budget, nearly 75 percent of public expenditures were at the local level. Moreover, because the functions of local governments at that time were mostly to provide routine, physical services (*e.g.*, garbage collection, fire protection, water supplies, and so forth), local government tasks were often receptive to improved efficiency via the techniques of scientific management. Scientific management generated a concern in governments for such topics as planning, specialization, quantitative measurements, standardization, and the discovery of the "one best way" to perform a duty. Instrumental in inaugurating the scientific management period of public personnel administration was the founding in 1906 of the New York Bureau of Municipal Research. Mentioned in the preceding chapter for its advanced thinking on budgetary concepts, the Bureau was the prototype of numerous bureaus that later sprang up in cities throughout the country, most of them endowed with philanthropic funds and offering gratis their not-always- appreciated services to local officials.

The municipal bureaus provided the linkage between the techniques and values of scientific management and the public sector. Their staffs were enthusiastic developers of quantitatively oriented and detailed job descriptions, productivity measurements, training programs, examinations keyed to job-related abilities, and efficiency ratings. Science and technique were stressed, particularly in the field of testing applicants for employment qualifications.

There were some notable effects of the scientific management period in human resource management, both intellectual and practical. The intellectual effect was to strengthen the politics/administration dichotomy, already popular as a partial result of the reform period, in the study of public administration. Public personnel administration was where the quantitative action was in public administration, and "hard-nosed" public administration largely meant the application of scientific management for the sake of governmental efficiency.

The practical effects of the scientific management period were to widen the scope of the merit system in the federal government and to aid in the development of the city manager profession in the United States. Because of the considerable effort expended on the development of job descriptions, tests, and measurements, the informational basis for position classification was broadened significantly. Once a thoroughgoing system of position classification was capable of being implemented, it was only a matter of time before the civil service system would extend its control over the public personnel system. This it did. Although civil service regulations applied to less than 46 percent of the federal government's nonmilitary employees in 1900, by 1930 almost 80 percent of these employees were under its auspices. Much of this expansion can be attributed to the focus of the civil service system on the position as opposed to the

person, and the success of scientific management in rendering many public positions quantifiable, measurable, and susceptible to classification.

During the scientific management period, the city manager profession received its initial impetus. The justification of the city manager idea reflected the politics/administration dichotomy in public administration as it was enhanced by scientific management: that the city manager would administer the policy formed by the city council in an expert, scientific, and efficient fashion. The first genuine city manager plan was adopted in the United States in 1914, and the early literature on the topic almost exclusively related to the notion of the "professional manager," removed from, unresponsive to, and, indeed, contemptuous of local politics. Proposals were even made during this period to have for each state a manager, who would be an administrative counterweight to the political and policy-making governor. Indeed, although its stance has been modified substantially in recent years, the International City Management Association remains a relative bastion of the belief that public administration is separable from politics.

Phase 5: The Administrative Management Period, 1937–1955

The advent of the New Deal in 1932 brought with it a new view of the role of government: that the public sphere should be active, aggressive, and positive in the rectification of public problems. This attitude was reflected in public personnel administration. "Management" became the new goal of public personnel administration, and although it never displaced efficiency as a major value of the public service, the concept of management waxed and worked in tandem with efficiency.

The objective of management implied that there was something more to public personnel administration than mere efficiency. In reality—and more broadly—the traditional politics/administration dichotomy that had provided the essence of the field's focus was being questioned. Increasingly, people in the public service were perceived as having a political and policymaking role as well as an administrative function, and "management" served as a convenient code word with which to express this new dimension.

The benchmark for the advent of the administrative management period is the report of President Roosevelt's Committee on Administrative Management (known as the Brownlow Committee) in 1937.[43] The clear thrust of the Brownlow Committee's report was one of centralizing the powers and responsibilities of the president: agency functions should be consolidated, lines of authority and communication should be clarified, and the president's administrative authority should be enhanced. Although the committee favored extension of the civil service system "upward, outward, and downward," it nonetheless was critical of the Civil Service Commission's past attitudes as encouraging a narrow, specialized, and technically oriented breed of public bureaucrat. Generalism, too, was a clear value of the Brownlow Committee. Not only did the committee's predilection for generalist public administrators challenge the civil service system's long-standing emphasis on the position as the basis for personnel administration, but it blurred the distinction between politics and administration that dominated the whole of public administration as well. Although the committee rationalized the politics/administration dichotomy as valid, it hardly dwelled on it, and considered far more thoroughly those "positions which are actually policy-determining...." A series of executive orders beginning in 1938 on public personnel administration (notably Roosevelt's order of that year requiring the establishment of professionally staffed personnel offices in each major agency), the Social Security Act Amendments of 1939, the first Hoover Commission (1949), and the development of "little Hoover commissions" in the states extended and amplified the values of the administrative management period, as represented by the Brownlow Committee, throughout the federal and state structures: Public personnel administration was a part of the general managerial function (just like budgeting, planning, organizing, reporting, coordinating, and so forth), and the goal of human resource management in the public sector was to enhance the effectiveness of public management.

With Eisenhower's election as president in 1952, the comfortable separation between politics and administration that had served Democratic appointees to the federal service for so long as a rationalization of their personal policy preferences suddenly received a stark challenge. During the preceding twenty years of Democratic rule, the federal government had burgeoned to many times its size under Herbert Hoover. Few seasoned Republicans were available for duty in the new regime as a result of their long isolation from the federal bureaucracy, and many positions (and the Democrats in them) that entailed major policy-making powers were protected by civil service regulations (thus aggravating Republicans). At the same time, many New Deal public administrators felt themselves threatened by the rising tide of McCarthyism, which they associated with the Republican party. The problems of transition were severely exacerbated and highlighted the quintessential dilemma: how to render a theoretically neutral public service responsive to the political and policy preferences of a fundamentally new administration. As a result of this problem, a second Hoover Commission was created in 1953. Its report two years later included the first thorough analysis of the relations between political appointees and career administrators.[44]

The second Hoover Commission revitalized the faltering politics/administration dichotomy, which was by then under intellectual attack. It assumed that the distinction was valid, but that it should be made more operational, in terms of government personnel, than it was. Thus, the commission recommended that no more than 800 presidentially appointed political executives should fill top public positions and went on to propose a new upper-echelon administrative class of approximately 3,000 persons to be called the "senior civil service." These officials would be politically neutral career types and, significantly, transferrable from one post to another. For both groups, the abilities of the person would outweigh the requisites of the position. The proposal for a professional senior civil service *a la* the model of Western Europe died a quiet death in the late 1950s, but the idea that public administrators could and should be transferrable from agency to agency lived on and prospered by practice.

In terms of its overall impact, the administrative management period of public personnel administration integrated public personnel administration with other administrative functions under the value and rubric of "management."

Administrative management was perceived as an area of research and learning that was a needed profession for good government regardless of the specialty of any particular agency. Thus, the period witnessed the development of personnel directors in each agency who were responsible to (and a part of) the centralized managements of the agencies themselves. This intraagency personnel function was an effective agency counterforce to the quasi-autonomous Civil Service Commission; it proved especially useful as a means of hiring, promoting, demoting, and firing people on the basis of management's evaluation of their individual talents, but which personnel administrators were in no position to recognize or appreciate.

Phase 6: The Professional Period, 1955–1970

The idea of rendering public human resource more responsive and helpful to government managers did not fade away after the issuance of the report of the second Hoover Commission in 1955. Indeed, it strengthened over time. But another value was entering the milieu of public personnel administration by the mid-1950s: professionalism.

In a way, the stress that the second Hoover Commission placed on the differences and relationships between political executives and the career civil service signalled a recognition of the growing professionalism in government. The community of public personnel administration thought it knew who the political executives were—they were the principal administrative appointees of the elected chief executives—but who the career civil servants were was an increasingly problematic—and often frustrating—question. More and more, the career civil service was filling with highly-educated professionals in a wide variety of fields.

The public human resource management community was never terribly sensitive about the implications of the entry of lawyers, scientists, physicians, statisticians, and other professionals into the public bureaucracy. But their impact on public personnel administration was nonetheless real.

The Meaning of Professionalism and its Rise in Public Bureaucracies. A *profession* may be defined as an easily identifiable and specialized occupation, normally requiring at least four years of college education, which offers a lifetime career to the persons in it. Professionals are beset by status problems. They attempt to maintain their public visibility, yet they prefer accomplishing this task with dignity. (Surgeons, for example, seldom offer "cut-rate" prices to potential clients.) Professionals try to achieve status by refining their work content; the body of knowledge and expertise that must be learned (along with the manifold modes of acceptable behavior) in order to be "professional" grows with each passing year and becomes increasingly academic in character. Hence, professions and being professional are identified closely with the university and the professional association—institutions well removed from the usual circles of government. In this light, professionals also prefer autonomy, the right to do their own thing in their own way. Finally, and stemming fairly logically from the values of status, education, expertise, specialization, and autonomy already mentioned, professionals do not like politics. Nor, for that matter, do they like bureaucracy. This aversion is reasonable enough, given the historical struggles of many professions (*e.g.*, the city manager, the social worker, the librarian) to develop a corpus of knowledge and skill purged of detrimental influences from nonscientific, emotional, and ignorant outside sources. Put bluntly, however, professionals who choose the public service often must overcome their antipathy for its two major features: politics and administration.

The entrance of professionals into the public service is accelerating and its impact is deepening.[45] Nearly 40 percent of all "professional, technical, and kindred" (to borrow the Census Bureau's terminology) civilian workers in the United States are employed by a government, a figure that has remained stable since 1970.[46] Eighty percent of the federal work force is white collar (up from 70 percent in 1968) as opposed to blue collar, 55 percent of all federal civilian workers have some college training, at least 30 percent have a baccalaureate degree, and 16 percent have completed some postgraduate work.[47]

Not included in these figures are the engineers, scientists, and other professionals who are technically working for private industry, but whose salaries are paid by government contracts and grants. We do not know how many of these people there are, but it has been estimated that at least 3 million employees in the private sector are employed through contracts and grants let by the federal government alone.[48]

About a third of all government employees are engaged in some kind of professional or technical pursuit, a figure that is three times their proportion in the private sector. Professional, technical, and kindred public employees account for more than a fifth of all federal civilian employees, 39 percent of all state employees, and 42 percent of all local employees. More state and local personnel than federal workers are designated professional, technical, and kindred employees, primarily because more than half of state and local personnel are educators. But even when educators are deleted from these statistics, the percentage of professional, technical, and kindred personnel in government at all levels is still more than 21 percent, almost double the comparable percentage in the private sector.[49]

Who are these professionals? The federal government tends to favor the use of professionally trained military officers, Foreign Service officers, foresters, and scientists from virtually all the disciplines, while state and local governments employ social workers, psychiatrists, educators, and professors; all American governments hire engineers, public health physicians, lawyers, and computer specialists. Additionally, new, exclusively (or almost so) governmental professions are making an impact via vastly improved or totally new programs in higher education; examples of these include the following: police, tax assessors, penologists, employment security officers, public health paraprofessionals, park recreation specialists, purchasing experts, urban planners, librarians, environmental scientists, and, of course, graduates of public administration programs.

Although the Brownlow Committee report and the reports of the two Hoover Commissions barely considered professions other than that of administrative management, within ten years after publication of the second Hoover Commission's Report it was apparent that government managers were becoming concerned over the need for these other professions; the 1962 analysis by the Municipal Manpower Commission concentrated entirely on "APT" personnel, an acronym for administrative, professional, and technical personnel.[50] Similarly, studies of diplomatic personnel, public health personnel, and urban governance personnel all reflect an overriding awareness of the new role of the professional specialist in government. Yet, public personnel administration as a field has been curiously slow in recognizing the implications of professionalism. As Mosher has stated, few specialists "have recognized them—few even of the authors of books about public personnel administration."[51]

The Professional Paths to Power. While the growing importance of professionals in public administration seems clear, the precise channels of professionals' influence on government remains somewhat clouded. Mosher has identified some of these paths to power, and certainly the most obvious is that of being elected or appointed to high office. This route is, of course, dominated by the legal profession, which has "monopolized the judiciary, accounted for a majority of legislators above the local level, provided nearly two-thirds of American presidents and probably an equal proportion of state governors, and accounted for a plurality of top officials in the executive branches."[52] Professors, too, favor this road, with cabinets becoming increasingly dominated by academics since 1960.

Another route is the capture by individual professions of significant managerial positions in particular administrative agencies, such as the domination of the management of military units by career officers, the State Department by the Foreign Service professionals, the Office of Education by educators, and public works agencies by engineers. Mosher believes that "this pathway of professions to policy is probably the most important of all," since so many public policies of consequence are made in the bowels of these agencies.[53]

A third channel is the presence in all agencies of certain professions, which, while they do not control the agency, can influence its policies. For example, most bureaus have staff lawyers, human resource managers, budgeteers, planners, accountants, and so on; all of these and other agency professionals bring their own perspectives to bear on policy formation within the agency.

Professionals also can bring political pressure to bear from the outside, often working through their professional associations. Frequently, a "Mr. Inside"/"Mr. Outside" double play can be used to pressure public policy formulation—Pentagon brass working with veterans' organizations, for example, or lawyers teaming up with bankers.

Finally, professionals are able to use the very structure of federalism to further their power, largely by tinkering with the grants-in-aid system. Thus, state health professionals, for instance, may argue in tandem with federal health professionals for certain adjustments in intergovernmental funding formulas that subtly could accrue to the advantage of the health profession.

The Impact of Professionalism. While the effects of professionals on public personnel administration may be profound, precisely what those effects are and the patterns they may take are open to speculation. We have already considered the impact of professionals on organizations in Chapter 4, but the more general significance of professionalism on the public bureaucracy is worth some discussion in its own right.

Perhaps the most striking feature of professionals in the public service is the direct challenge that they pose to the traditional values of the civil service system, which focuses on the governmental job and its duties. Professionals make up the emergent and increasingly competitive career system (mentioned earlier in this chapter), which is characterized by its focus on the person rather than the position. These foci are fundamentally at odds. The civil service system is egalitarian by tradition, whereas the career system is elitist; what one does in a job is of paramount importance in the civil service system, whereas how one does it is of major significance in the career system; neutral and autonomous control of the entire public personnel system is valued by the civil service system, while planned and autonomous control of the individual professional is the concern of the career system. Although the merit system technically controls more than 90 percent of the federal employees in the public service, pressures from the various career systems throughout the government have, in fact, weakened the hold of the

traditional, position-centered system on the careers of many professionals. Indeed, the Office of Personnel Management has officially excepted approximately ninety different professions from its purview. What appears to be happening is the evolvement of new operational definitions of what "merit" means, and these definitions reflect the value differences between professionalism and traditional public personnel administration.

In addition to the rivalry that the career systems pose to the civil service system, there are at least three other effects that professionals have on the public service: the growing influence of professional elites inside government agencies, the growing influence of private professional associations on government, and the growing, but indirect, influence of universities on the personnel policies of public agencies.

Professional elitism appears to be an expanding source of conflict in some agencies. Research conducted among government agencies in California by Frederick Mosher and Keith Axtell indicates that the more established and recognized a profession is in society, and the scarcer the professionals available to a particular agency for hire, the more probable that the professional elite in question will exercise real and effective control over agency policies, standards, actions, and its entire personnel system, irrespective of the *de jure* control over personnel practices supposedly exercised by the civil service system. Mosher and Axtell found this to be the case regardless of governmental level—whether national, state, or local.[54]

A variation of the conflict that professionalism can bring to government is that of conflict between professional groups. City attorneys and city managers, for example, long have been at odds over their respective roles and responsibilities in municipal governance: Is the attorney a member of the "management team," or a "watchdog of the public trust" who happens to be paid a salary by the management team? Such conflicts can have a deleterious effect on governmental efficiency, effectiveness, and responsiveness.[55]

Professional societies are increasingly exercising considerable power in public affairs; the intimate connection between them and public personnel career systems enhances this power. Studies indicating this growing and discomfiting influence by the professions in government, mostly by political scientists, are too numerous to list, and the variations and subtleties that their influence can assume are limitless. It will suffice to note that the control professions possess over a particular sliver of knowledge enables these private professional associations to have considerable input vis-à-vis those public decisions made in their sphere of expertise. Studies of the decision process in regulatory agencies, the politics of professional licensing procedures in the states, the raw power and generously funded political activity of some "apolitical" professional societies, such as the American Medical Association, indicate the gravity of this problem not only for public personnel administration but for the public generally. For instance, Corinne Lathrop Gilb has questioned the special interest nature of the professions' impact on public decisions; Jethro K. Liebermann has scored licensing practices as monopolistic; and Guy Benveniste has warned public administrators of relying too heavily on the supposedly apolitical advice of professionals in making policies.[56]

Finally, the universities, those accreditors and sanctifiers of established and emerging professions, exercise an oblique influence on the dynamics of public personnel administration. Increasingly, academic standards (*e.g.*, university attended, grades, and faculty references) count more heavily in getting into the public service than does the traditional, position-centered entrance examination; more often than not, governments defer to universities the responsibilities for filtering applicants to administrative positions. The sheepskin is becoming the symbol of merit, and the more sheepskins the more meritorious the applicant.

The Dilemmas of Management and Professionalism

Professional, technical, and kindred employees attained their present share—almost 40 percent—of all public sector jobs in 1970, so we have selected that year as the closing date of the professional period in human resource management in the public sector. Yet, as with the field's administrative management phase (1932–1955), its impact on public personnel administration continues unabated. Together, Phases 5 and 6 pose grave dilemmas for the public human resource management community.

Mosher has pointed out that the two overriding values of public personnel administration for the future will be those of "professionalism" and "management." Together these two realities raise questions that have yet to be resolved by the American civil service: What is the relationship between the political executive service and the career service? What are the limits of loyalty that a public servant accords a leader, who is either elected by the people or appointed by elected officials of the people's government, when that public servant's superior issues directives that offend his or her interests or principles?[57]

We do not pretend to answer these eminently serious queries here, but clearly the rise of both the administrative management period and the professional period of public personnel administration has forced us to phrase these questions in tones more discomfiting than ever before. Both phases have contributed to the idea of the "professional public administrator," who blends the values of both "management" and "professionalism" in his or her public occupation.

Phase 7: Professional Public Administration, 1970–present

The emergence of public personnel administration's seventh and current phase is in many ways its most interesting. Its appearance implies a rejection of the entire civil service system, as one of the four public personnel systems that we described earlier. The concept of building a personnel system around the *position*—which is the rockbed of the civil service system—is simply not present; instead, the professional public administration period builds its edifice on the *person*.

In this sense, the professional public administration phase reflects the values of the professional career system, which is also predicated on developing the person in his or her career. But Phase 7 accepts few other elements of either the professional career system or the professional period of public personnel administration. Unlike the professional phase, the professional public administration phase accepts, indeed welcomes, both "politics" (as in *public*) and "bureaucracy" (as in *administration*) as the defining and entirely legitimate keystones of the *profession* of public administration. This is new.

The recognition by the field of public personnel administration of the role of the professional public administrator can be traced back to the Brownlow Committee of 1937. But at least an equally reasonable case can be made for a benchmark date of 1970 because it was in this year that the National Association of Schools of Public Affairs and Administration was founded, marking a critical point in the evolution of any profession—a commitment to it by the academic community—and it was also in 1970 that the National Civil Service League released its sixth Model Public Personnel Administration Law.

The Model Public Personnel Administration Law of 1970. The formulation of the Model Public Personnel Administration Law of 1970 by the National Civil Service League is important because it reflected the consensus in the community of scholars and practitioners involved in public personnel administration. By contrast, the Brownlow Committee was composed of scholars and practitioners who had their intellectual and professional roots largely in management and political science. The Model Public Personnel Administration Law of 1970 is significant, therefore, because it reflected "a sea change in the views of the cognoscenti about what the public service should be and how it should be governed."[58]

The Model Public Personnel Administration Law of 1970 replaced the League's previous model law of 1953, and it was a radically different document from all of its five predecessors. Rather than emphasizing the protection of the civil service against partisan patronage and similar transgressions, the 1970 law reflected the values of the Brownlow Committee of 1937: personnel directors should be appointed and removable by the executive; citizen advisory boards should replace the civil service commissions; a career civil service should be encouraged; and the interchange of public administrators among different departments should be facilitated. It went beyond the Brownlow Committee's report by advocating the recognition of public employee unions and collective bargaining, relaxing restrictions on political activities by civil servants, and advocating equality of opportunity. But the Model Law's basic thrust remained the same as that of the Brownlow Committee: "personnel administration must be regarded as a part of management, not a protector against it."[59]

The National Civil Service League's Model Public Personnel Administration Law of 1970 has not had a particularly noticeable impact on the federal government, but it has had a major effect on state and local governments. A survey of all state and local personnel systems taken in the mid-1970s found that 63 percent reported that they were greatly influenced by the model law in reformulating their personnel policies and regulations, and that between 1970 and 1975, 55 percent of state and local governments had taken steps to make their personnel directors more responsive to executive leadership.[60]

Watergate. But if the public personnel administration community in state and local jurisdictions was for the first time in the 1970s passionately embracing the importance of "public management," the nation was beginning to have quite a different reaction to the behavior of federal public managers. After an extended crucible that seared the nation, President Richard M. Nixon became, in 1975, the only president of the United States to resign from office. Nixon's resignation was the result of excesses and abuses of power that had been conducted almost entirely by elected officeholders and officers whom Nixon had appointed. Much of these excesses revolved around the Nixon White House's efforts to circumvent the federal civil service. Among the more notorious examples of this was the so-called Malek Manual, named after Fred Malek, a top White House official, who encouraged the appointing of high-level federal executives on the basis of partisan politics.[61]

Even though the line civil service was essentially uninvolved in Watergate, the public bureaucracy did not fare well in the public mind. As Mosher put it, "However justified or unjustified they may have been, the effects of Watergate unquestionably were to tarnish the reputation of the public service in general....It cannot be said that many leaders or other representatives of the career services were out blowing whistles or otherwise resisting the transgressions that were being pursued. And the U.S. Civil Service Commission, which had been set up in part as a watchdog of the integrity of the civil service system, did not attack, or growl, or even bark until the affair had ridden most of its course....Watergate generated doubts in the nation as a whole...about the public service as a whole, both career and noncareer."[62]

Watergate implied that human resource managers were not protecting the career civil service from presidential excesses. The "merit principle" was not being applied by those charged with applying it (*i.e.*, the Civil Service Commission) to promote and protect "good government" and all that phrase connoted for the traditional, merit-based values of public personnel administration.

The Civil Service Reform Act of 1978. But if public personnel administrators were notably weak-kneed when it came to protecting the merit principle from dilution by the White House, they seemed positively ferocious in using it to harass federal managers who were trying to administer their public programs. One survey of top-level civil servants found that half of the senior executives in the federal government and 60 percent of federal managers believed that they did not have enough authority to hire competent people when they were needed, and 40 percent of federal senior executives and 55 percent of federal managers did not believe that they had enough authority to promote people.[63] These public administrators appeared to attribute at least some of the reasons for their lack of managerial authority to the heavy hands of the personnel administrators and federal rules that were based on the values of the reform period of public personnel administration.

Because the Civil Service Commission seemed not to be doing its job when it should have been, and doing it all too avidly when it should not have been, pressures were generated for far-reaching changes in the personnel practices of the federal government. In his 1978 State of the Union Address, President Jimmy Carter said that reform of the civil service was "absolutely vital."[64] And the director of the U.S. Civil Service Commission backed him up with report after consterning report about the lack of control and authority held by federal administrators.[65]

As a consequence of these initiatives, there ensued a hugely ambitious and deep-reaching study of public personnel administration involving more than 1,500 practitioners, scholars, organizations, and other sundry experts. Ultimately the Civil Service Reform Act of 1978 was enacted, thus replacing the Pendleton Act, which had been civil service policy for the United States for ninety-five years.

The Civil Service Reform Act of 1978 replaced the Civil Service Commission with a three-member, bipartisan Merit Systems Protection Board, which is in charge of adjudications and employee appeals, and which has its own special counsel to investigate allegations that federal personnel and related laws have been violated. It also established an Office of Personnel Management, which advises the president on personnel matters and coordinates the government's personnel programs. The director of the Office of Personnel Management and his or her deputy are appointed and may be removed by the president. An independent Federal Labor Relations Authority was also established to oversee, investigate, promulgate, and enforce rules regarding federal labor relations programs.

The Act also was the first legislation to list merit system principles and prohibited personnel practices. It simplified and strengthened due process for employees, strengthened minority recruitment programs, and authorized the expenditure of funds for research and development in the field of human resource management.

Of importance, the Act states that authority and responsibility for managing people should be vested insofar as practicable in those supervisors who are responsible for programs, as opposed to centralized personnel agencies; decentralization is a clear value of the Civil Service Reform Act.

Federal administrators in the super grades and comparable pay levels are eligible under the legislation to join the Senior Executive Service. Out of the roughly 7,000 persons who were originally eligible, almost 99 percent have joined the Senior Executive Service and this level of participation has remained stable. Noncareer officials (*i.e.*, presidential appointments) may constitute no more than 10 percent of the Senior Executive Service, and 45 percent of the Service's positions must be reserved for career personnel.

The Senior Executive Service was designed to improve federal management by creating what amounted to a professional administrative class in the European tradition. Senior executives may be assigned, reassigned, or removed on the basis of their ability or performance. Contrary to traditional civil service concepts, rank in the Senior Executive Service is invested in the person as opposed to the position; members of the Service carry individual rank and therefore may be assigned to those areas in which their talents are most needed. Senior Executives are eligible for 20 percent bonuses each year for good performance; however, they also may be retired early and against their will.

Figure 9–1 illustrates the new organization of federal human resource management that resulted from the Civil Service Reform Act of 1978. Clearly, the essential idea of the Act was "management." As Mosher has stated, "The main thrust of the Carter reforms, repeated in virtually all the speeches and arguments of their supporters, was management....Here was the culminating event of 'government by managers,' espoused four decades earlier by the Brownlow Committee."[66] As a small but revealing indication of this change in perspective, the Office of Personnel Management (formerly the U.S. Civil Service Commission), in the year following the passage of the Act abandoned the name and content of its house organ, the *Civil Service Journal*, and retitled it *Management*.

A change in perspective is one matter; a change in practice, however, is another, and it is unclear that the Civil Service Reform Act has been effective in improving federal managerial

FIGURE 9–1 Federal Government-wide Organization for Personnel Management

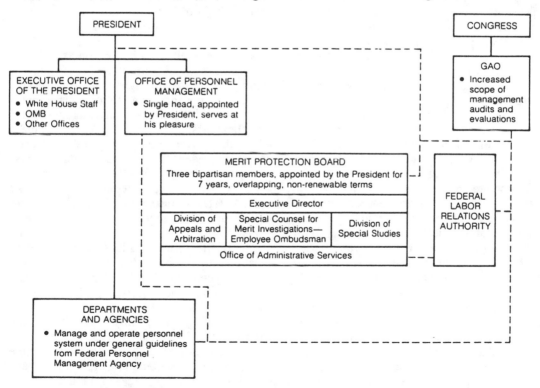

Source: Final Staff Report, Personnel Management Project, (Washington, D.C.: Government Printing Office, 1977), p. 244.

performance. A careful analysis of performance standards adopted for the Senior Executive Service in the U.S. Department of Labor, and conducted in 1980 and again in 1985, found "that with a single exception no significantly greater emphasis was placed on the 1978 Civil Service Reform Act (CSRA) goals in the fifth year of the program as compared to the first year....CSRA mandates appear to have had little direct impact on the performance standards of the Department's senior managers."[67]

Professional Public Administration at the Grassroots. The reforms in the federal civil service made their mark on subnational personnel systems. Within a year after the implementation of the Civil Service Reform Act, jurisdictions in thirty-two states had initiated changes that reflected the management-emphatic thinking underlying the new federal policies. By 1980, local governments in twenty states had begun experimenting with merit pay and performance appraisal systems. Perhaps as many as 30 percent of state and local governments have implemented new performance evaluation and innovation systems for their public employees since the Civil Service Reform Act was passed.[68]

State governments were, in some ways, well ahead of the federal government in recognizing the desirability of bringing personnel administration and public management closer together. In 1963, California became the first of fourteen states to create an executive personnel system, preceding the federal government's decision to found its Senior Executive Service by fifteen years. In fact, four states, all justly renowned for the professionalism of their administrative structures, had executive personnel systems in place before 1978, although federal initiatives clearly affected the decisions of many other state governments to establish their own executive personnel systems after that year. These state systems typically do not cover more than 1 percent of a state's employees, and, as with the federal experience, it is unclear how effective state executive personnel systems have been in both improving public management and in developing a cadre of talented top careerists in public administration.[69]

Quite aside, however, from the impact on state and local jurisdictions of the Model Public Personnel Administration Law of 1970, or the Civil Service Reform Act of 1978, or the independent initiatives of the states themselves, it is clear that these governments are encouraging the idea of professional public management. A careful study of state agency heads, which has been conducted periodically since 1964, indicates a deepening commitment to professional public management in the states.[70]

One indication is that their educational levels have gone steadily and dramatically up. In 1964, more than a third of state agency heads had not completed college, and 15 percent had not attended college. Forty percent held a graduate degree. By 1978, however, only 11 percent had not completed college, only 3 percent had not attended college, and 58 percent had earned their graduate degree, mostly in management and public administration.

A second indication of a deepening professionalism is that more state agency heads have chosen state public administration as a career. One measure of this commitment is the fact that state agency heads are entering the state service at an earlier age and pursuing long term careers in it. In 1964, 35 percent of state agency heads held their first position in state government before they were thirty years old, and their median age when they first entered state government was thirty-three. Fourteen years later, nearly half of the top state administrators had entered state public service before they were thirty, and their median age of entry had slipped to thirty.

Finally, there are indications that purely partisan appointments are in decline. The proportion of state agency heads whose job immediately prior to taking their present position was an elected office declined by half between 1964 and 1978, indicating that out-of-work politicians are being less cared for at the expense of state taxpayers than they once were. By contrast, the proportion of top state administrators who have moved up the agency ladder to the top spot has burgeoned from only 28 percent in 1964 to 41 percent in 1978. Table 9–1 indicates these trends among the state agency administrators.

Comparable data exist at the local level. Thirty-seven percent of all the nation's cities and towns use the council-manager plan,[71] which involves hiring a professional city manager who is hired and may be fired by the council. It is an increasingly popular form of local government, and forty-four of the country's 100 largest cities use it.[72] Over half of all American cities use the more traditional mayor-council plan, but at least 30 percent of these cities hire a chief administrative officer who is the functional equivalent of a city manager, except that he or she reports directly to the mayor instead of the city council.[73] Most of the nation's large mayor-council cities appoint a chief administrative officer. More than a fifth of the nation's more than 3,000 counties appoint an executive who is com-

TABLE 9–1 Personal and Background Characteristics of State Agency Heads (In Percentages, Unless Otherwise Indicated)

Characteristics	Compared Agencies				All Agencies 1978 (75 Agency Types)
	1964	1968 (27 Common Agencies)	1974	1978	
Age					
Under 40	13	14	17	22	26
40–49	28	29	31	33	31
50–59	35	38	33	31	31
60 and over	24	19	19	14	12
Mean age (years)	52	50	50	48	47
Median age (years)	53	51	50	49	48
Sex					
Male	98	95	96	93	92
Female	2	5	4	7	8
Ethnic Background					
White	98	97	96	92	93
Black	1	1	2	2	3
American Indian			0.1	1	1
Oriental	1	2	2	4	2
Spanish	NA	NA	NA	1	1
Educational Attainment					
High school or less	15	7	4	3	3
Some college	19	18	13	11	8
Bachelor's degree	25	15	18	15	15
Some graduate study		16	17	14	15
Graduate degree	40	45	47	56	58
Highest College Degree					
None	34	24	17	14	11
Bachelor's	25	31	36	29	31
MA or MS	8	10	13	18	24
Professional Master's	3	4	5	11	11
Doctorate (except JD)	9	13	12	13	12
Law (includes JD)	21	18	17	15	11
Major Areas of Specialization					
Accounting	15	21	23	21	18
Business	19	20	34	32	30
Legal	30	23	20	22	18
Management	NA	NA	46	53	52
Public Administration	14	19	46	45	44

Source: F. Ted Hebert and Deil S. Wright, "State Administrators: How Representative? How Professional?" *State Government*, 55, No. 1 (1982), p. 25.

parable in authority to the office of city manager used by council-manager cities.[74]

We recite these statistics to demonstrate that local governments are becoming increasingly sensitive to the need to manage their communities more professionally. Partisan politics are receding from many city halls, and professional management is being welcomed in the form of professional administrators entering more and more local governments.

These local public managers always have been a relatively well-educated lot. Even so, their educational attainments consistently are rising, and increasingly their educational goals reflect study in professional public management. In 1971, 27 percent of local public managers had a master's degree, but by 1980 this had increased to 51 percent. The proportion of local public managers who had not completed college shrank by more than half between 1971 and 1980; 26 percent of local public managers in 1971 had completed some college but had not received a degree, but by 1980 this proportion had declined to 12 percent.[75]

In addition, city and county managers and chief administrative officers show a growing preference for degrees in government and management as opposed to engineering. In 1971, one-third of the bachelors degrees held by local managers who had completed college were in engineering; by 1980 this proportion had been reduced to 13 percent. By contrast, less than a third of city managers who had completed college in 1971 held degrees in management or government, but by 1980 this ratio had increased to more than three-quarters.[76] The increasing commitment to higher education and to education in management, public administration, and government—along with its attendant and ongoing linkages with the universities—indicate a growing professionalism among America's local public managers that parallels what is occurring at the state level.

THE ORGANIZATION AND DYNAMICS OF PUBLIC PERSONNEL ADMINISTRATION

We have been discussing in rather broad strokes the underlying values and philosophies of public personnel administration that have emerged at various periods over the course of its evolution. These values and philosophies are critically important to understanding human resource management in the public sector. But what do public human resource managers actually do?

The Scope of "Merit"

The federal "merit system," which normally is taken to mean the general civil service system including general merit and special merit personnel systems (*e.g.*, the Public Health Service, Foreign Service, Federal Bureau of Investigation), encompasses almost 94 percent of all federal employees.[77] This is quite an increase from the merit system's coverage in 1884, after the passage of the Civil Service Act, when the merit system covered not much more than one in every ten federal employees.

Among the fifty states, thirty-six now have comprehensive merit systems, a trend that appears to be accelerating (in 1958 only twenty-three states could make this claim), and the remaining states have some form of a more limited merit system. The Social Security Act Amendments of 1939, which mandated the use of state merit systems in state agencies that managed federally assisted programs in health, welfare, employment security, and civil defense, and the Intergovernmental Personnel Act of 1970 (that was effectively curtailed in the early 1980s), which initiated a program of grants to inaugurate and improve merit systems in states and localities, were both instrumental in the development of merit-based personnel systems in state governments.

Merit systems are prevalent in American cities and towns as well. Excluding education, civil service protection covers an estimated 95 percent of municipal employees.[78] Only in county governments has the merit system been accepted with relative reluctance. It is estimated that it covers less than 10 percent of the nation's county employees, although some very populous states, notably California, New York, and New Jersey all require merit systems in their counties.

Although these figures are open to interpretation, and the various merit systems themselves are vulnerable to circumvention, the scope and expansion of the general civil service system in American government is impressive.

The Profession of Human Resource Management

The professional public personnel administrators who are hired to manage these merit systems focus their energies on several major activities: job analysis, human resource planning, performance appraisal, selection, employee development, discipline and dismissal, counseling, labor relations, communications, research and evaluation, wage and salary administration, benefits and services, and the political rights and constraints of public employees.[79] Some 272,000 people are employed in personnel work in both the public and private sectors in the United States, and of these 30 percent (about 81,000) work in the public sector. The number of employees in personnel has grown about 5 percent every year since 1970.[80]

Public personnel administrators are a reasonably well educated group.[81] Various studies indicate that 57 to 91 percent of public personnel administrators have a bachelors degree or higher, although the educational levels of public personnel managers appear to be slightly lower than those in the private sector (71 to 94 percent of private-sector personnel managers have a bachelors degree or higher).

Public personnel administrators exhibit greater differences from their private sector counterparts in terms of their college majors. Anywhere from 57 to 80 percent of personnel managers in the business world majored in areas that have a clear relevance to their jobs (*i.e.*, business, economics, industrial relations, or personnel management), in contrast to those in the public sector (11 to 34 percent of public personnel administrators majored in public administration, industrial relations, or personnel). Nevertheless, public personnel administrators appear to have a high job satisfaction, and most perceive their jobs as being a long-term professional career.

The Civil Service Structure: Classification, Pay, and Training

The Position Classification System. The basis of the civil service, irrespective of governmental level, is the position classification system. Public

personnel classification techniques received their impetus during the scientific management period of public personnel administration.

In 1923, as a result of increasingly vocal dissatisfaction over the lack of rigor in federal personnel classification policies and an ongoing belief in the "equal work for equal pay" ideology, Congress passed the Classification Act, which established the Personnel Classification Board to group public positions into rational classes on the basis of the comparable duties, responsibilities, and skills of each function. A new and more comprehensive Classification Act was enacted in 1949.

The Salary Structure. The Classification Acts provide the foundation for the salary structure of the federal government. At present there are four major pay systems in the federal government for civilian employees: the General Schedule (which applies to almost half of federal civilian personnel), the wage board system and the postal field service system (these two are the lowest paying systems), and various remaining pay systems of limited scope, such as that of the Foreign Service. The General Schedule (GS) has eighteen levels, each level having a number of steps within it.

The salaries of most top federal executives (*e.g.*, cabinet members, agency heads, undersecretaries, assistant secretaries, bureau chiefs, and members of independent commissions) are regulated under the procedures of the Federal Salary Reform Act of 1962 and the Federal Executive Salary Act of 1964. The Pay Comparability Act of 1970 delegated authority to the president to set salaries for General Schedule and Foreign Service employees; the president is assisted in this function by the director of the Office of Personnel Management, the director of the Office of Management and Budget, the Federal Employees Pay Council, and the president's Advisory Committee on Federal Pay. Their advice to the president is based on annual reports from the Bureau of Labor Statistics, which is charged with maintaining federal rates of pay that are comparable to those of private industry, a policy that was established by the Federal Salary Reform Act of 1962. The far-reaching Federal Employees

Comparability Act of 1990, the first significant reform of the federal salary structure in twenty years, is considered later in this discussion.

In an effort to attract executives for those top federal positions not covered by the Federal Salary Reform Act, in 1967 Congress established the Commission on Executive, Legislative, and Judicial Salaries, which recommends salary levels to the president for executive-level personnel in all three branches. The president has more discretionary authority in determining salary rates for these officials than he does for those administrators covered under the General Schedule and Foreign Service systems; thus far presidents have tended to resist recommendations by the Commission for substantial wage hikes in this group.

In part because of presidential recalcitrance, the salary situation for federal administrators was, by the early 1990s, reaching critical conditions. In 1987, the Commission on Executive, Legislative, and Judicial Salaries released an analysis showing that the purchasing power of the salaries earned by the top 3,037 federal officials (including judges and members of Congress, as well as cabinet secretaries and high-level administrators) had declined by 40 percent since 1969.[82] Another study conducted at the same time by the Twentieth Century Fund concluded that the purchasing power of the pay of the Senior Executive Service had declined by 30 percent between 1969 and 1985, whereas the purchasing power of executives' salaries in the corporate world had increased by nearly 69 percent during the same sixteen years.[83]

At the lower end of the scale, the story was much the same. Investigations conducted by the U.S. General Accounting Office in sixty-three metropolitan regions found that clerical and technical personnel in the private sector were paid more than were their counterparts in the federal government 90 percent of the time, and that the median advantage for the private sector positions was significant: 22 percent. By contrast, for the 10 percent of federal workers who were paid more than were their counterparts in the private sector, the median advantage was marginal: 5 percent.[84]

In light of the dramatically diminishing purchasing power of federal employees, it is perhaps not surprising that a survey conducted by the Merit Systems Protection Board found that the desire to make more money, the need to improve career opportunities, and poor pay were the three leading reasons (out of forty-six possible in the questionnaire) given by federal workers who had resigned from the federal government. Twenty-eight percent said that they had resigned from the federal government for reasons of inadequate compensation and poor prospects for advancement.[85]

To retain talented people in government, the Commission on Executive, Legislative, and Judicial Salaries recommended that the salaries of many officials, particularly administrators, be nearly doubled.[86] In keeping with presidential tradition, however, President Reagan discounted the Commission and Reagan recommended to Congress a pay raise for these officials that ranged from about 2 percent to 16 percent (the high figure being for members of Congress).[87] In fact, presidents seem rather churlish when it comes to recognizing their own people. A study instigated by Representative Patricia Schroeder of Colorado in 1986 found that in the six years since the creation of the Presidential Rank Awards Program, presidents had awarded only half of the bonuses for exceptional performance that they were entitled to grant top federal administrators.[88]

This situation did not pertain to the same degree in many state and local governments. As a respected British publication put it, "The secretaries of state and defense...are paid less than the city manager of Phoenix, Arizona, and the director of higher education in Georgia."[89]

In 1990, Congress took a significant step toward rectifying the problem of federal pay by enacting the Federal Employees Comparability Act. The Act represented a new federal pay system, and it implemented two major reforms: large pay hikes for top federal administrators, and the setting of federal salaries by locality.

As part of his agreement with Congress, President George Bush in 1990 increased the salaries of the Senior Executive Service by 22 percent, and the pay of the subcabinet officers by 29 percent. This dramatic increase was accomplished by an executive order, and brought the salaries of top federal executives closer to their counterparts in the private sector.

The Federal Employees Comparability Act also sets federal pay by a position's comparability with the private sector and by locality (*e.g.*, a federal worker in San Francisco is paid more than one employed in the same job in Statesboro, Georgia). In 1992 and 1993, federal employees are guaranteed an annual raise of up to 5 percent based on the Employment Cost Index, which measures the alterations in private local labor market salaries and wages. In 1994, the Act continues this procedure in modified form, but also guarantees that federal workers in high-cost cities will receive a locality-based raise of 20 percent of the total federal-private sector pay gap. From 1995 through 2005, the remaining differential will be closed by 10 percent in each of these ten years, although the president regains his broad authority to lower or raise salaries regardless of these benchmarks.

To accomplish this complex task, Congress established the Federal Salary Council, composed of three experts in labor relations and six representatives of employee organizations, all appointed by the president. The Council is charged with setting geographic boundaries for federal pay regions and, in cooperation with the Bureau of Labor Statistics, conducting pay surveys of nonfederal employers.

The Federal Employees Comparability Act of 1990 is breakthrough legislation that could reinvigorate the federal service.

Training Bureaucrats. A variety of in-service executive training programs are offered to public administrators, particularly at the federal level. In-service training is a relatively new development in public bureaucracies; most of it, in fact, emerged when the Government Employees Training Act was enacted in 1958. This Act required federal agencies to provide training for their personnel, using both public and private facilities. As a further stimulus, President Lyndon B. Johnson issued Executive Order 11348 in 1967, which encouraged the U.S. Civil Service Commission to work more actively with agency heads to develop in-service personnel training programs. Johnson's

Executive Order resulted in the creation of the Commission's Bureau of Training and Regional Training Centers nationwide, and, a year later, Johnson inaugurated the Federal Executive Institute in Charlottesville, Virginia. The Institute is designed for the enrichment of supergrade federal administrators, and similar centers have been established in California, Colorado, New York, and Tennessee for mid-range administrators, grades 13 through 15.

As the result of a presidential memorandum in 1969, a provision in the Equal Employment Opportunity Act of 1972, the Labor Department's Public Service Careers Program, and the activity of the Office of Training and Development of the Office of Personnel Management, all federal agencies have begun to develop in-service training programs designed to encourage the upward mobility of lower-echelon as well as mid-level personnel, with special emphasis on assuring the advancement opportunities of minority groups. About 200,000 federal managers participate in these programs each year. Nevertheless, when fiscal push comes to budgetary shove, it appears that federal administrators are prone to focus on agency training programs when they need to cut budgets, and to cut them back more than other programs.[90]

In-service training programs in the states and cities are less developed than in the federal bureaucracy. California is an exception, and has its own Executive Institute for state administrators; many large cities also have in-house training programs of high quality. Traditionally, however, most such programs are conducted by state or local universities, particularly those with institutes of government, institutes of public administration, or well-established continuing education programs that are well connected with the public administration faculty. About four-fifths of city and county managers and state executive and legislative officials report that they have used university-based institutes for training, research, technical assistance, analysis, and education, and they rank the services provided by these institutes as "moderately high" and comparable to services furnished by the private sector; state and local administrators gave their highest marks to university-based training programs, having ranked all types of services offered by universities.[91]

The Quiet Crisis

At critical points in the twentieth century, governments have been able to recruit prodigiously talented people. In the 1930s the "Depression virtuosos," who, in more prosperous times, would likely have been recruited by Wall Street, entered government service, especially at the federal level. They were followed by the "Baby Boomers" who came into the labor force in the 1960s—a large demographic balloon of well-educated, frequently idealistic young adults who entered the labor market during a period when governments were expanding and government service was hailed by the nation's leaders as a noble calling. President John F. Kennedy set the tone for those years when he said in 1963, "Let public service be a proud and lively career. And let every man and woman who works in any area of our national government, in any branch, at any level, be able to say with pride and honor in future years: 'I served the United States government in that hour of our nation's need.'"[92]

One does not hear rhetoric like Kennedy's anymore, and today conditions are different. Not only has the pay of public administrators slipped (at least in the federal government, although, as noted, there are auguries of improvement) in comparison to the private sector, but also the national labor pool is shrinking. Many elected officials are openly abusive of "the bureaucracy," and, certainly at the federal level, there is a widespread perception that the quality of newly hired public administrators is not what it once was.

The "Baby Boom" that made itself felt in the 1960s became, by the mid-1980s, a "Baby Bust," insofar as entrants into the work force were concerned. By 1995, the number of workers aged eighteen to twenty-four will have dropped by nearly six million people from 1984 levels, and will not begin to rebound until 2000.[93]

Add to this more competitive hiring situation the contempt often displayed for the public service by high public officials, and the prospects of government recruiting the best and the brightest dwindle further. Edwin Meese, Attorney General and adviser to Ronald Reagan, made headlines when he brought a "bureaucrat doll" to a cabinet meeting, explaining that it just sat and did nothing. As one observer noted, "If you hear that government

is the problem, not the solution, why would anyone want to be part of the problem?"[94]

As we noted in Chapter 3, there is evidence of a dissatisfied public service, perhaps more clearly so at the federal level, and one reason underlying this dissatisfaction is that federal employees believe the quality of new recruits to the federal work force is in steep decline. Extensive surveys of federal workers at all levels taken by the Merit Systems Protection Board have found that between 41 and 61 percent of all federal supervisors believed that the quality of all applicants had worsened, and that the decline was accelerating.[95]

The National Commission on the Public Service dubbed these conditions "the quiet crisis."

The Civil Service Dynamic

Getting a Job in Government. Between 1955 and 1974, the federal government gained most of its new recruits to the civil service through the Federal Service Entrance Examination, its first "universal" instrument for selecting college graduates for entry into the management positions of the federal government. The examination tested general verbal and quantitative skills, but in 1974, it was replaced with the Professional and Administrative Career Examination, which tested not only general competencies, but attempted to gauge the professional training of applicants. Blacks failed this examination in substantially greater numbers than did whites, and in 1981 the Office of Personnel Management signed a consent decree in which it agreed to eliminate its use.

Between 1981 and 1990, the finding of an entry-level administrative position in the federal government was, as the director of the Office of Personnel Management phrased it, "intellectually confusing, procedurally nightmarish, inaccessible to students, and very difficult to explain."[96] Applicants were hired at the individual agency level on the bases of college grade-point averages, references, interviews, or highly specialized written tests developed for specific jobs, such as "Tax Technician" and "Customs Inspector"; between 5,000 and 6,000 federal hires a year were made in these ways, including about 200 graduates per year of Master of Public Administration programs, who were brought into the federal government via the

Presidential Management Internship Program (begun in 1977), which channeled the top MPA graduates from campuses around the country into federal positions. Ironically, it was unclear at best that these methods were resulting in a more representative or talented federal service.[97]

In 1987, a U.S. district court judge demanded that the federal government develop a replacement examination, and in 1990, the Office of Personnel Management introduced a new "universal" test for selecting applicants for entry-level management positions in the federal government. Although its initial impact was modest (only 85,000 people took it when it was first introduced), it is anticipated that from 300,000 to 500,000 people will take the examination each year. Some 5,000 applicants are hired for positions in 118 different occupations via the new examination. The courts will monitor the results of these tests until the mid-1990s to determine whether they are nondiscriminatory.

The new federal examination for entry-level management positions was pre-tested in France and Spain, as well as in the United States. Although the test continues to assess language, reasoning, and quantitative abilities, it contains a new "biodata test" (a common examination in private industry), called "Individual Achievement Records," which focuses on determining experience, skills, achievements, and how applicants have played the hand that life has dealt them; blacks and whites score comparably on the Individual Achievement Records.

The federal experience with using (or not using) written tests has not been emulated at the state and local levels, where the courts have not really questioned the use of written examinations to determine entry into the public service.[98] We discuss this in greater detail later in the chapter.

Aside from scoring well on tests, how does one get a job in government? According to merit principles, all one should have to do is possess the proper educational and professional credentials and fill out an application. But more is involved, particularly when a personal interview is required. Employers in government (and presumably in private enterprise as well) often seem to prefer hiring someone who is professionally less able and personally more amiable. Consider the following passage from Frank J. Thompson's study of personnel politics in Oakland.

The attitudes of the statistical service officer show how important amiability can be. He would rather hire a mediocre programmer who is easygoing and pleasant, than a very able one who is abrasive—who "makes waves and stirs up trouble." On one occasion, he served on an oral board, which was interviewing a young lady. In terms of the applicant's computer knowledge, she was clearly superior to all the other applicants. But he and the other board members felt that she was too "aggressive and dynamic." There was too much "hostility" in her replies and, consequently, they flunked her.[99]

So much for merit principles in hiring. Some evidence suggests that the test-based merit system does not work even when judged by its own standards. In a 1970 study of the New York City civil service, which had roughly 250,000 out of a total of 400,000 employees who were considered "competitive class" employees (that is, they were hired and advanced on the basis of competitive tests), it was found that the "merit" system discriminated *against those applicants who are most qualified according to its own standards*. Candidates with low passing grades are actually *more* likely to be hired than those with high passing grades! Furthermore, this perverse result seems to hold true for all skill levels."[100] How so? The investigators found that the city had a lengthy waiting period between the date that an applicant took the examination and the date of hire—a median of seven months—and that, during this period, the best qualified were skimmed off by other employers. Conclusion: "New York City's civil service system functions as an inverse merit system (something the public at large has cynically assumed for years)."[101]

Being Promotable and Being Promoted. Once inside the civil service, many public administrators find that seniority counts when it comes to being promoted. In his analysis of the U.S. Civil Service Commission (now the Office of Personnel Management) Ivar Berg found that when "age and length of service are considered together, as a surrogate measure of experience [and as a genuine measure of seniority], the combination becomes the strongest factor in accounting for the promotion rates of the highest level, the GS 11-14 category...."[102]

The considerable advantages of seniority are a fact of life in virtually any organization, but the efforts made in the field of public personnel admin-istration to reward ability rather than more time-in-grade are worth a brief observance. The Office of Personnel Management first required formal pro-motion plans from federal agencies in 1959, and since 1969 the Office has been notably more aggres-sive in trying to minimize the detrimental effects of the seniority factor by emphasizing intraagency ranking procedures based on job-related standards and by broadening the scope of promotional searches within the agency. State and local govern-ments are more prone to rely on written tests as a basis for promotion than are federal agencies.

Being Demotable and Being Demoted. Ser-vice ratings are a device favored for determining not only promotions but also pay increases, de-creases, demotions, and dismissals. The first Hoo-ver Commission initially proposed the use of service ratings in government;[103] often they amount to little more than adjectival descriptions (*e.g.*, excellent, average, poor) by a supervisor of his or her employee. There are two principal kinds of service ratings, "trait rating" and "performance rating." Trait rating attempts to evaluate such per-sonality features as industry, intelligence, tact, and courtesy, while performance rating tries to judge how effectively the employee is fulfilling the du-ties of his or her position.

It is important to note that service ratings sym-bolize a fundamental aspect of administration that, though obvious, is often overlooked. Administra-tion affects people's lives. An administrative act can alter a person's self-concept, for good or ill, as well as influence the course of his or her occupa-tional future. Administration is power, and public administration can be very powerful indeed.

Getting Out of a Job in Government. The ways in which administration affects the lives of those in it are usually most dramatically visible when demotions and dismissals are being pro-cessed. Dismissal, of course, means being fired for cause. It does not refer to those employees who are (to use the current parlance) "riffed"—a derivative of the phrase "reductions in force"; these govern-ment workers often are the victims of economizing measures but who do not necessarily have low service ratings.[104]

Blowing Whistles. But this is not always the case, and talented administrators are occasionally fired for reasons other than "riffing" or low service ratings. An incident that dramatized this phenom-enon began in 1969 when A. Ernest Fitzgerald, a GS 17 Deputy for Management Systems in the Office of the Assistant Secretary of the U.S. Air Force, was effectively fired by the Air Force for his candid testimony before Congress on a $2 billion cost overrun incurred by the C-5A cargo transport plane development project—testimony that did not rest easily with the Pentagon brass.[105] Ultimately, it took thirteen years in court before Fitzgerald won full reinstatement in 1982.[106]

Fitzgerald is among the better known examples of a courageous (some would say crazy) class of public employees called "whistle blowers" be-cause they "blow the whistle" on their agencies for engaging in shoddy, incompetent, or corrupt prac-tices. At least 8,500 incidents of whistleblowing have been documented, and the practice appears to be growing.[107] Nevertheless, not all organizations appreciate being told (and having outsiders told) that they are abusing the public trust, and organi-zational vindictiveness in retaliating against whis-tle blowers is amply documented.

An unusual study of ninety whistle blowers (60 percent had been federal employees when they blew the whistle, and the rest had been in the private sector) found that 80 percent of the whistle blowers experienced a physical deterioration, such as loss of sleep or weight gain following their exposure of poor agency or corporate practices; 86 percent be-came emotionally depressed; 54 percent were har-assed by peers at work; 25 percent stated that a heavier financial burden was the worst consequence of their act; and 20 percent had no job. Eighty-two percent of the federal whistle blowers were hounded by their superiors, who used such techniques as reducing their responsibilities, closely monitoring their telephone calls and other activities, and giving them progressively worse performance ratings; and 51 percent of the federal whistle blowers reported that they had since transferred (or had been trans-ferred) to another agency.[108]

Another systematic study of 161 whistleblowers (80 percent of whom were public employees) found that the probability of losing one's job over the act of whistleblowing was less in the public sector than in the private sector, but it was still high: 59 percent of the public employees had lost their jobs, compared to 69 percent of their corporate counterparts. More than half became mired in personally expensive legal actions that lasted at least two years. Thirty-one percent sought psychiatric counseling, more than a fourth required medical consultation, and a majority reported significant disruptions of their family lives. Federal whistleblowers discovered to their dismay that the Merit Systems Protection Board, the Office of Special Counsel, and "all executive branch organizations of the United States government whose official responsibilities include handling complaints of waste, fraud, and abuse" were (in their opinion) the least helpful to them.[109]

Whistle blowers had best be prepared for a long, hard haul. But there is a bright side: most would do it again. In one survey, 81 percent said they would do it all over again, and 87 percent stated that they would blow the whistle again if presented with a similar situation in the future.[110] As one federal whistle blower put it, "Finding honesty within myself was more powerful than I expected."[111]

The "typical" whistleblower is a white, forty-seven year-old, well-educated family man who has been in his organization seven years.[112] About half are well-placed administrators or professionals who have considerable autonomy within the organization, although they do not appear to concentrate at any particular hierarchical level or share common career histories.[113] "The overwhelming majority of whistleblowers contacted are apparently uninterested in regulating their behavior to conform to particular situations....because they rely on their own attitudes and beliefs, which include a strong endorsement of universal moral standards as a guide."[114]

Does whistleblowing work? Yes, more or less. Although the after-the-fact rationalization of an act that brought immense personal pain likely enters into the respondents' replies in some fashion, 51 percent of the whistleblowers in one survey nonetheless reported that their actions resulted in some form of external investigation, and 62 percent stated that they saw evidence of change within their organizations.[115]

Dealing with incompetents. Whistle blowing, however, is one matter, and incompetence is another; rightly or wrongly, the procedures that must be followed to dismiss genuine incompetents can be time consuming and costly. The appeals procedure can be wearing for everyone involved, and due process of law must be observed so stringently that a class of lawyers that specializes in defending public employees fired from government has emerged.

Because firing a clearly incompetent public employee can take a notoriously long time, it is perhaps not too surprising that one of the major arguments that has emerged against civil service systems is that they provide a sinecure for life to public bureaucrats. Because their jobs cannot be threatened, they are responsible and responsive to no one. Nevertheless, it is unclear how firmly ensconced in their positions public bureaucrats really are. O. Glenn Stahl contends that, although it is difficult to compare the proportionate number of dismissals between the public and private sectors because of different databases, it nonetheless appears that

There is every reason to believe that the annual rate of removal, ranging from a little less than one to about one and a half percent of public jurisdictions in the United States as a whole, is exceeded, if at all, in certain categories of private employment, such as a few areas of manufacturing.[116]

In other words, according to Stahl, the proportionate numbers of people fired in both private enterprise and in government are about the same.

If these figures are accurate, then it is surprising that the rate of dismissal in the public sector is as high as it is, considering how inordinately difficult it is to fire a public employee. In California, for example, a teacher may demand a hearing upon receiving notice of dismissal and the school board, unless it rescinds its action, must file a complaint in Superior Court requesting the court to make an inquiry and to determine if the basis of dismissal is supportable. Then court-appointed referees hold hearings and report back to the court. A trial is held by the court itself, and a decision is made on whether the board may, in fact, dismiss the teacher. In effect, any contested dismissal of a California teacher brings the judiciary into the act. Stahl contends that this is "perhaps the most extreme instance of abridgement of executive power in American school administration."[117]

But even reaching the point of firing a public employee is difficult, and it is much more difficult to adjudge an employee's performance in some types of jobs than in others. Thompson has observed that the standards used in local government to evaluate performance can themselves be unclear, and the visibility of a subordinate to his or her supervisor can vary from agency to agency. For example, it is relatively clear whether or not a secretary is typing quickly and accurately, and a secretary is relatively visible to his or her supervisor. But in police departments, patrol officers are not very visible to their supervisors, nor is their standard of performance a particularly clear one.[118] Table 9–2 indicates the differences among public agencies in terms of a manager's ability to judge his or her subordinates' performance.

To compensate for these problems of assessing personnel in agencies where employees are relatively on their own, supervisors develop complicated performance forms and rating systems. Thompson contends that these forms seldom follow function, and to presume that the form is actually evaluating the performance of an employee is to likely be wrong. Nevertheless, bureaucrats are not spending their time ritualistically filling out useless pieces of paper. As Herbert Kaufman has pointed out in his classic study, *The Forest Ranger*, the forms actually are used to prevent problems from arising and to justify to outsiders a disciplinary action or decision to remove an employee. A record is kept by the forms, although the forms are seldom read by the supervisor when they are received.[119]

The employee, once dismissed or demoted, has extensive rights of appeal, and the example in California cited by Stahl is an excellent illustration of how far this appeal can go—and how precipitously. Employees who are fired often attempt to bring in outsiders and to apply public pressure to be reinstated. The ploy of expanding the scope of conflict between the employee and the employer, either in the courts or with the public, is a classic one in public employment circles. Thompson observed that in Oakland, while dismissals of the Oakland work force averaged less than 1 percent a year, almost two-thirds of those fired were on probation and therefore had no right of appeal to the city's civil service commission; however, at least one-third of those persons who were dismissed as regular, nonprobationary employees appealed their dismissal to the commission.[120] In short, a supervisor likely can expect problems if he or she fires someone in the public bureaucracy, but, if care is taken, the employee's basic rights are observed, and records are kept, then the dismissal of an incompetent worker can be done.

The "quit rate" dilemma. On the other hand, far more public administrators leave the bureaucracy on their own than are fired. At the federal level, the "quit rate"—that is, the voluntary turnover rate—among white-collar civil servants is 8.8 percent, when age of the federal workforce and agency-to-agency transfers are taken into account—factors that must be considered if a reasonable comparison to quit rates in industry is to be made. A quit rate of 8.8 percent is 2.1 percent higher than the comparable rate in industry, indicating greater dissatisfaction among white collar workers in the public sector than in the private one.[121]

TABLE 9–2 Evaluating On-the-Job Performance of Public Employees: Problems of Visibility and Standards

		Visibility of Employee Performance to Supervisor	
		Low	*High*
Standards of Performance	*Clear*	Building Inspectors	Secretaries Sanitation Workers
	Unclear	Police Patrol Officers Recreation Directors	City Planners

Source: Derived from Frank J. Thompson, *Personnel Policy in the City* (Berkeley, Calif.: University of California Press, 1975), p. 142.

The quit rate among personnel in local governments may even be significantly higher than in the federal civil service. Although relatively few of those who have made it to the top (such as city managers) voluntarily leave the public service, judging from the Oakland data considerably more of those at the lower levels leave. Young professionals in Oakland often found better options elsewhere; assistant planners had a turnover rate of 55 percent in a single year; junior accountant auditors, 19 percent; and recreation directors, 22 percent.[122]

Regardless of the internal dynamics of government personnel systems, it is clear that some very basic concepts of the "merit" system are being challenged by various social developments. These include the issues of affirmative action, unionism, and collective bargaining. We consider these issues in turn.

Riffed

Beginning in the early 1980s, the federal government began to "rif" public administrators. "Rif" is an abbreviation of "reduction in force." There are many ways to rif employees. Here is how it happened to one.

...Aside from the personal anguish he and his family are experiencing, the example of Burke Walsh illuminates a critical public question: the working of the federal government. It underscores one of the Reagan administration's blackest marks, the mindless wholesale destruction of the career public service, one I believe will cause damage to the country for years to come.

Two weeks before Christmas, Burke was informed he would be dismissed from his federal government job, effective New Year's Eve.

He was a victim of a sweeping government reduction in force—or RIF, in Washington parlance—sharply cutting back the Labor Department's Employment and Training Administration, the so-called CETA program. In particular, the information office in which he was working was being drastically reduced in size. He, and others, were out.

The dismissal meant more than the loss of his $50,000, Grade 15 government job, with all the obvious hardship for his family, the children's education, the mortgage payments, and the rest. It meant the end of a government career for which he had been recruited, and in which he had performed well.

And, Burke quickly found out, it also meant a severe problem he had not anticipated. Including his Army time, he has seventeen years of government service, three years shy of qualifying for a pension. Yet, under the present system, he will not be eligible for any pension payments for nine more years when he reaches the age of sixty-two.

What's more, he has found the government is singularly unconcerned about what happens to the career people it is dismissing, for no fault of their own.

"To my knowledge," he says, "there is absolutely no real assistance that you get once you are dismissed. No official representative of the government has ever contacted me. There has never been any official prescription of jobs or availabilities afforded me from the government for placement. There is no effort by the government to help me find jobs in private industry or in government. There's no government-wide policy to help someone in my circumstances, and that is the truth.

"As far as my department is concerned, there was no review of my situation taking into consideration the length and effectiveness of my service. No one ever really reviewed to see what kind of work I had done. I fitted into a slot that was official and I was dismissed. I had no recourse as far as that dismissal was concerned. There was no consideration of the fact that I was what in the government is called a five-point veteran. My wartime service in Korea did me no service at all. There was no panel that I could go to and say, 'Look, I've been here for seventeen years counting my service time. Maybe you'd like to take a look at this thing and ask whether you really intend to dismiss senior officials in their fifties.' But this was not done for me, and it was not done for anyone as far as I know....

"There's a perhaps unnecessary but pervading embarrassment that attends this situation," he says. "There's an embarrassment that you personally feel. There's an embarrassment that you feel with your peers and your family. You know they're feeling an embarrassment for you that you try to avoid as far as your dealings with them are concerned."

"You're embarrassed for yourself, and you're embarrassed for them. You can't avoid the feeling that the people around you have the feeling that there was some inadequacy on your part that led to your dismissal. You failed somehow. You failed them, and you failed yourself. All at a point in your career when you can't expect to have to come to grips with failure. You've done all the right things, made all the right moves. You've driven yourself to this point in a career— a career, not a job—and someone comes along and says you've done nothing wrong, but now you're out. And people look at you and they're embarrassed for you, and you are for yourself. It's a two-way street, and it's the damnedest two-way street you've ever been on.

"I've talked to people on the phone about this. I've talked to them face to face and, Haynes, this is the God's honest truth, I've had at least three or four people say to me, 'I could not take it.' They come just short of saying, 'Burke, I don't know how you haven't put a bullet in your head.'"

Burke is a proud man, and he remains proud of what the government has been and should be.

"I come from a family that's been in Washington for 135 years," he says. "They came here from Ireland, through Philadelphia. My great-grandfather was the maitre d' in the Willard Hotel during the Civil War. He was a Confederate, a friend of Jubal Early. Used to go out in the weeds and talk to him. That's the last time that we had a subversive in the family that I know of. All of our family have been—well, we've got our military heroes. My grandfather and his group of Emmett guardsmen charged up San Juan Hill with Teddy Roosevelt. Literally did. One of the

few people that actually got to shoot a Spaniard during the Spanish-American War. He went on to the Philippines. My father was in naval intelligence, so I have all kinds of Washington credentials, and rather honorable ones, I would think.

"I have a background that gives a sense of government. I didn't work for Ronald Reagan or Jimmy Carter or anyone else. From the day I came in, I felt that I had an obligation to the United States government. And if you want to know the truth, I feel the United States government has let me down, because I never broke faith with them. I was encouraged to come in. They asked me. I joined the government as a career station in life, not to get rich. I must confess, I joined it for the security of government, plus the fact I was told my talents would enhance government.

"As I've said to you before, there is waste in government. There's no question about it. But the way waste has been addressed is abysmal. It's ridiculous. Two administrations in a row have run against the government worker. What they've done is contribute to what they're trying to undo. The danger is that the kind of milieu we're developing now in the government could be translated into a much larger hurt for this nation.

"We've got to stop picking on the government. First of all, *we* created the government service. This nation created it. It's like the separation of church and state. It's an abiding thing there. It's part of the United States. It's like the Army and the Defense Department which are held in such reverence. It's there. It's part of what makes this whole thing go. Yet we've attacked it like it's a bastard child. If we don't stop this we'll be killing ourselves."

...A day will come, if it isn't already here, when the United States will need its most capable citizens to serve. How can the government possibly expect to attract such people when it, and its highest leaders, treat them so miserably?

To ask the question is to answer it.

Haynes Johnson, "Waste in Government: Wasting the Civil Servant," (*Washington Post,* March 28, 1982).

RACE, SEX, AND JOBS: THE CHALLENGE OF AFFIRMATIVE ACTION

One of the myths of American democracy is that jobs, especially public jobs, are open to all. They are not. Prejudice is still with us and working against both women and members of minority groups. Women, for example, often are disqualified from public jobs (such as fire fighting and police work) on the basis of physical "qualifications" that may not be necessary to do the work. Similarly, increasingly more rigorous requirements concerning formal education works against those minorities who already are disadvantaged in society, since, as a group, they are less likely to have attained as much formal education as whites; yet few people seriously argue that a high school diploma ever made its recipient intelligent or a quick learner. This argument is persuasive and as a result the public bureaucracy has witnessed the rise of "affirmative action." *Affirmative action* is a policy that argues for the hiring of members of disadvantaged groups on the grounds that government positions should be open to as many people as possible.

The Federal Impact

Affirmative action is a highly sensitive issue in public administration today. The federal government favors hiring members of deprived groups and consequently has implemented affirmative action policies that have had and are having a profound effect on the national employment picture. The major legislation in this area is the Civil Rights Act of 1964, which paved the way for the more specific efforts that followed. These included tougher executive orders by the president; prohibitions of discrimination in agencies and by private contractors on the federal payroll; more positive antidiscrimination policies by local, state, and federal civil service commissions; and some significant court decisions.

An especially important law, the Equal Employment Opportunity Act of 1972, has for the first time brought state and local governments under the provisions of the Civil Rights Act of 1964. The Act also provides the first statutory grounds for the

federal government's equal employment opportunity programs. The Act prohibits discrimination based on race, religion, sex, and national origin, and it directly affects some 3 million federal and 13 million state and local government employees. The U.S. Equal Employment Opportunity Commission (EEOC), which the Act established, may investigate charges of employment discrimination in state and local governments and, if no conciliation is achieved, the U.S. Department of Justice may bring suit against the alleged offender. On top of that, the person in question may also initiate his or her own private litigation.

In 1990, Congress enacted the Americans with Disabilities Act, which, for the first time, defined the disabled as a group entitled to basic civil rights. The law covers the physically impaired and people with learning disabilities, and prohibits discrimination against the disabled in employment and accommodations.

This kind of federal legislation, plus significant court cases, have made state and local governments and private employers extremely aware of the demands of minority groups, women, and the disabled.

The Quota Question

These realities in national policy bring us quickly to the question of quotas. *Quotas* in public personnel administration refer to the argument that the traditional entry and promotion qualifications of the civil service, such as high test scores, should be reduced or waived for the disadvantaged until the proportion of women and minority group members working in government at all ranks at least equals the proportion of women and minority group members in the population at large. In brief, each group, such as African-Americans, would have a quota, or a percentage, of the public jobs allotted to it which equals its percentage in the state's or city's population. If a city, for instance, had 10 percent blacks in its population, it would then follow that blacks should be allocated 10 percent of the jobs available in city hall.

Because of pressure generated for the establishment of quota systems, these systems in state and local governments have met with some success. In 1972, for example, a federal district court ordered that one black be hired for every newly hired white until the all-white Alabama State Police Force was 25 percent black, a figure corresponding to the percentage of blacks in Alabama according to the 1970 census. Again in 1972, while the federal court denied the legitimacy of an outright quota system, it nonetheless ordered the Minneapolis Fire Department to hire at least one minority applicant for every two whites in its next sixty openings.[123] In 1973, the federal court ordered the San Francisco Civil Service Department to establish two separate lists of candidates for entry-level positions and promotions, one for minorities and one for nonminorities, and to hire three minority candidates for every two nonminority candidates until the number of minority police patrolmen was brought up to at least 30 percent of the total. The court also ordered the department to promote one minority and one nonminority candidate until the total number of minority sergeants in the department reached at least 30 percent of the total number of sergeants. Similarly, openings in the Chicago police force were ordered to be filled in groups of two hundred, with one hundred positions to be filled by blacks and Spanish-surnamed males, thirty-three to be filled by women, and sixty-seven to be filled by other men.[124] Victor A. Thompson contends that the Chicago Police Department had more than six hundred vacancies in 1974 "as a result" of such court orders.[125]

Perhaps the most definitive early court ruling on quotas per se was given in the case of *Bratton* v. *Detroit*, although one must use "definitive" in this instance with circumspection. In the early 1970s, the Detroit police department originated an affirmative action plan mandating that black and white officers were to be promoted in equal numbers until 1990, or until half of the officer corps was black at every rank and level. Whites initiated a class action suit contending that such a quota violated their civil rights. The federal district court in 1980 denied this contention out of hand, but in 1983 the U.S. court of appeals did not; the appellate court had problems with the Detroit plan because it not only benefited officers who had suffered from illegal discrimination in the past (*i.e.*, blacks), but those who had *not* endured past discrimination (*i.e.*, whites), since the plan guaranteed that for every one black offi-

cer promoted, a white officer would be promoted as well. Hence, the appellate court remanded the plan back to the district court for further consideration. Even though the court of appeals had done this, the U.S. Justice Department petitioned the Supreme Court to hear the case, which the Court denied to do in 1984.

The upshot of this less-than-satisfying legal chronology is that the judiciary seems to have ruled that racially based quota systems are acceptable if prior discrimination has created a need for them, and whether the plan devised to implement quotas is "reasonable." Reasonableness is present if the plan does not stigmatize whites and sets specific goals. Factors to be considered in determining whether a plan to fill racial quotas is reasonable include: whether the affirmative action program is the only solution; whether it is temporary; whether it relates to its stated objective; and whether it avoids infringing unnecessarily on the interests of whites.[126]

In 1986, the U.S. Supreme Court did render some rulings on quotas in a series of three cases: *Wygant* v. *Jackson Board of Education, Local 93 of the International Association of Firefighters* v. *City of Cleveland,* and *Local 28 of the Sheet Metal Workers* v. *Equal Employment Opportunity Commission.* Although these decisions were characterized by close votes and numerous separately written opinions, the broadly sustained principle that appears to have been stated by the Court is that limited, carefully conceived plans designed to reduce the effects of prior discrimination may take race into account. Further, plans to implement quota systems that are meant to benefit minorities may also benefit persons who were not the actual victims of discrimination.[127]

While plans to implement quota systems may, as a side effect, benefit persons who were not actually victims of discrimination, they can also harm, inevitably, persons who were neither the victims nor the perpetuators of discrimination; this harm is, under certain circumstances, tolerable to the judiciary. In *United States* v. *Paradise*, the Supreme Court held in 1987 that quota plans that diffused the burden of implementation over many people were acceptable, although if the burden were to be borne by particular individuals, the quota plan might not be acceptable.

In *Paradise*, the federal district court had ruled that the Alabama Department of Public Safety had been unduly slow and discriminatory in promoting blacks, and ordered the department to implement a one-black-for-one-white promotion quota. The U.S. Department of Justice joined the State of Alabama in appealing the decision, claiming that the equal protection clause of the Fourteenth Amendment had been violated by the district court.

The Supreme Court upheld the district court, and did so unanimously in terms of finding the Alabama Department of Public Safety guilty of "pervasive, systematic, and obstinate discriminatory exclusion of blacks." But it upheld by only a five-to-four vote the district court's one-for-one quota plan, and much of the division centered on how intense the negative impact of the plan would be on innocent white officers applying for promotions. Justice Lewis Powell, Jr., wrote for the majority that "Unlike layoff requirements, the promotion requirement at issue in this case does not 'impose the entire burden of achieving racial equality on particular individuals,' and it does not disrupt seriously the lives of innocent individuals."

In sum, the *Paradise* decision reinforced the idea that "race-conscious relief" must be "narrowly tailored to the problem it is supposed to solve."[128]

Also in 1987, the Supreme Court added an interesting fillip to the concept of quotas. In *St. Francis College* v. *Al-Khazraji*, the Court held unanimously that Arabs, Jews, and other ethnic groups could no longer be counted as whites in discrimination suits. The Court cited a federal statute enacted in 1866 that banned racial discrimination in making its rulings, and, in so doing, instantly made into minorities people who were previously categorized as whites by the courts. Justice Byron R. White, in writing the full Court's opinion, said that the 1866 law was "intended to protect from discrimination identifiable classes of persons who are subjected to intentional discrimination solely because of their ancestry or ethnic characteristics," and not merely former slaves.

Perhaps the greatest beneficiaries of this decision, at least in terms of numbers, are the nation's 20 million Hispanics, who generally were classified as whites by the judiciary prior to the *St. Francis College* decision. But the decision potentially applies to any ethnic group—Russians, Iranians, Liberians, Chinese, Poles, Italians, Norwegians, and Anglo-Saxons, among many, many others.

In an important decision taken in 1989, the Supreme Court undercut a principal pillar of the judiciary's traditional if ambivalent support of quotas by holding that statistics alone cannot serve as adequate proof of discriminatory practices against women or minorities, if such practices are based on usual and reasonable business practices.

The case, *Ward's Cove Packing Company* v. *Antonio*, began in 1974 when minority workers in an Alaskan salmon cannery contended in court that minority workers were represented disproportionately in lower-paying jobs, that white workers were represented disproportionately in higher paying jobs, and that there was little promotion from within. These facts were never at issue, and under Title VII of the Civil Rights Act, these facts alone placed the burden of proof on the employer, Ward's Cove Packing Company, to show that it had not discriminated against minorities. The lower courts found that these conditions had a "disparate impact" on minorities, and, because of this impact, and whether or not Ward's Cove was intentionally engaging in discriminatory practices, it nevertheless was in violation of the Civil Rights Act.

The Supreme Court disagreed, and, in doing so, eliminated the "disparate impact" argument and the use of statistical bases alone in supporting claims of discrimination. In remanding the case back to the lower court, Justice Byron White, writing for the majority, stated that statistics must tie in closely with an employer's "specific employment practices" if they are to be used as evidence of racial or sexual imbalance. Legal observers believe that only new national legislation will be able to counter the effects of the Court's decision in *Ward's Cove*.

Tests: Problems of Validity and Bias

The Validity Question. A landmark court case that has had a major impact on public personnel practices was the 1971 U.S. Supreme Court case *Griggs* v. *Duke Power Company*. On the face of it, the *Griggs* decision had nothing whatever to do with governments. The Court ruled that the Civil Rights Act of 1964 banned discriminatory employment practices against blacks in a private company. Nevertheless, this decision has had considerable relevance for public personnel administration because it effectively bars those employment practices (notably intelligence tests and minimum education requirements) that operate to exclude members of disadvantaged groups when those practices cannot be shown to relate to job performance. The ruling did not demand the institution of flat quota systems in the employment of minority group members, nor did it preclude the use of tests in performance measurements. It did require that any such device must actually indicate levels of employee performance and individual potential objectively.

The Supreme Court's decision in *Griggs* lead us directly to the issue of test validity. *Test validity* is defined by answering this question: Do the several kinds of tests administered by the public bureaucracy for determining entry and promotion really indicate how well-qualified an employee is for a job? Test validity is determined by testing "successful" employees with tests that are thought to be job-related; presumably, their good job performance should correlate with high test scores, thereby validating the test used.

The Cultural Bias Question. The growing controversy over test validity relates to another problem of public personnel examinations, that of cultural bias in testing. *Cultural bias* refers to the tendency of those highly educated people of the dominant culture who write examinations to unwittingly slant the phrasing and nuances of their test questions in a way that reflects their own culture. Thus, people taking an examination who are not members of the dominant culture (*i.e.*, who are not white) are unfairly handicapped in their chances to score as well as those examinees who have been reared in the prevailing culture. After investigating the phenomenon of cultural bias in testing, the California State Personnel Board concluded that "written tests were more of a barrier to employment of minorities than any other phase of the selection process." Accordingly, the board instituted greater use of nonverbal aptitude tests, tried to root out culturally biased language in written examinations, and placed more members of minority groups on oral examination boards.[129]

Reflecting this concern over cultural bias in testing is a spate of recent court cases. In 1975, a federal court held (in *David* v. *Washington*) that the fact that black applicants failed a written test given to all applicants to a local police force at a rate more than four times that of white applicants was adequate evidence to prove that the examination had a "racially disproportionate" impact, and that blacks were therefore being discriminated against in police force hiring.

A second significant case is that of *Albemarle Paper Company* v. *Moody*, which was decided by the Supreme Court in 1975. In its decision, the Court stated that back pay could be awarded to an employee who had been denied a promotion as a consequence of discriminatory testing procedures, even though the employer was not intentionally discriminating. The decision also held that a promotion system based on supervisory ratings was questionable because subjective human judgments were involved. The case reified the importance of developing valid testing procedures for promotions and other personnel decisions.

In 1982, the Supreme Court again addressed the problem of cultural bias in testing in the public service in the case of *State of Connecticut, et al.* v. *Winnie Teal Adele*. Black state employees who had been serving as provisional welfare eligibility supervisors in Connecticut had failed a written examination. The passing rate for blacks was approximately two-thirds of that for white applicants. But the State of Connecticut argued that it had promoted more minorities than it had promoted whites, and so the "bottom line" of the states practices was not discriminatory against blacks or other minorities. Thus, the use of the test that had discriminatory effects was irrelevant, since more blacks nonetheless were being promoted than whites.

The Court disagreed with the state's arguments, and held that merely having a "bottom line" whereby more blacks were being promoted than whites was not satisfactory. The state still could not allow racial discrimination against those black employees who were failing a test that was itself discriminatory. The Court held quite clearly that cultural bias in testing is against the law.

The Bona Fide Occupational Qualification Question. A second area that relates to test validity concerns qualifications for jobs that are based on sex. For example, laws stating that women may not lift more than thirty pounds of weight on a job may prohibit perfectly qualified women from being considered for a position. These kinds of qualifications are referred to as "protective labor laws" on the logic that they are designed to "protect" women from being in jobs that are too strenuous for them.

In 1963 and 1964, federal legislation designed to eliminate sex discrimination was enacted and quickly came into conflict with a number of state protective laws. This legislation was the Equal Pay Act of 1963, and Title VII of the Civil Rights Act of 1964.

The Equal Pay Act was an amendment to the Fair Labor Standards Act of 1938 and was later extended in 1968. The Act was helpful in eliminating artificial qualifications that prevent women from being considered for certain jobs.

Title VII of the Civil Rights Act of 1964 made it unlawful to discriminate on the basis of sex as well as race. However, Title VII does allow an employer to discriminate on the basis of sex if such discrimination constitutes a "bona fide occupational qualification reasonably necessary to the formal operation of that particular business or enterprise."

Two major cases in 1968 and 1969 took issue with what a bona fide occupational qualification amounted to when applied to women. In 1968, the Supreme Court upheld in *Rosenfeld* v. *Southern Pacific Company* that certain weight lifting limitations for women established by California were not valid. In 1969, in *Weeks* v. *Southern Bell Telephone and Telegraph Company*, the court of appeals held that "an employer has the burden of proving that he had reasonable cause to believe…that all or substantially all women would be unable to perform safely and efficiently the duties of the job involved." This was the argument used to permit Weeks, a woman, to become a "switchman" thus voiding a thirty-pound weight-lifting limit for women established by the state. In effect, both cases held that certain state protective labor laws could not be used to deny women a job or promotion, and the burden of proof regarding the fairness of the bona fide occupational disqualification is on the employer, rather than on the employee.

Written Tests: Still in Extensive Use. The problems of validity, cultural bias, and bona fide occupational qualifications in personnel testing have cast doubt as to the use of tests to measure job-related ability as a means of controlling entry and promotion in public personnel administration. As we have noted, the federal government was barred by the courts for a decade from using a common written test for entry into the federal service because of problems of cultural bias. On the other hand, local governments continue to use written tests extensively; nearly 95 percent of the personnel departments of large cities (more than 100,000 people) report that they rely, at least in part, on a written examination for entry into certain kinds of positions.[130] Most examinations test performance skills and job knowledge, but aptitude tests are used in 44 percent of all cities and counties with populations greater than 50,000; 42 percent of these local governments test writing skills, and nearly a fifth administer intelligence tests[131]—examinations of a kind that would seem to require at least validation under the principles enumerated by the courts in the *Griggs* decision and in later cases. Nevertheless, only 35 percent of the cities report that they now offer fewer written tests than they did in 1972 (the year following the *Griggs* ruling), and 62 percent say they offer the same or more written examinations since 1972![132] Yet, when asked what are the principal obstacles that impede minorities from being hired by local governments, local managers identify "test results" as the single greatest disqualifier (38 percent), followed by educational requirements (20 percent).[133]

It appears that the grass-roots governments remain committed to the written entry examination, and that the judiciary has not seriously challenged these governments (in contrast to the federal government) in their continued reliance on written tests. Fortunately, state and local governments have taken the problem of cultural bias and sex discrimination in testing fairly seriously. A survey conducted by the National Civil Service League of every major state and local public personnel system (outside of education) in 1970 indicated that only 54 percent of them validated any tests in any way regardless of type—written, oral, or whatever.[134] But a second survey taken about five years later by the National Civil

Service League found that 87 percent had initiated test validation procedures.[135]

The Curious Question of "Comparable Worth"

A somewhat newer wrinkle in the fabric of affirmative action is that of comparable worth. *Comparable worth* means that employees should be paid the same rate of pay for performing tasks that involve roughly the same levels of importance, knowledge, stress, skills, and responsibilities, even though the tasks themselves may be quite different. For example, a secretary may be performing a task that compares favorably to that of a highway repair worker in terms of its importance to society, the knowledge and skills it requires, the mental demands it makes, the stress it induces, and its level of responsibility.

As a practical matter, comparable worth is being used to pressure employers to pay women as much as men, although, in theory at least, it could be used to pay minorities as much as whites. American women, on the average, earn about a third less than men, and minorities earn about a fifth less than whites.[136] Although these differentials are significantly narrower in the public sector, as we detail later, the differences nonetheless remain dramatic for public employees, too.

Women have potentially more to gain than minorities from the implementation of comparable worth for two reasons. One is that the average difference between women's salaries and men's salaries is significantly wider than the average difference between minorities' salaries and whites' salaries; thus, there is more to make up.

The other reason relates to the unit of analysis used in comparable worth, which is not individual positions, such as a secretary, but whole position classifications, such as all secretaries. Comparable worth as a concept relies on comparing different job classifications; when one job classification is judged to be of comparable worth to another job classification (for example, if secretaries are deemed to be comparable to highway repair workers), then both classifications must be paid at a comparable rate.

Questions of comparable worth are especially likely to rise when an entire position category is female-dominated, as secretarial and clerical categories usually are. These female-dominated classes are compared to job categories of comparable worth that are dominated by men, and if the female-dominated job class is found to be paid less than the male-dominated class, it is assumed that the pay differential is attributable to systematic discrimination against women, and all employees in that class (including men) must be paid at a rate comparable to that of the male-dominated class. Since female-dominated and male-dominated position classes are considerably more evident than are minority-dominated and white-dominated classes, women are favored in most efforts to attain comparable worth.

Comparable worth relies on the idea that the social value of occupations can be compared, and this can be a tricky business. Is, for example, a city's symphony conductor worth "more" to society than the head of the municipal waterworks? The contributions of the conductor may elevate and inspire our souls, but we need potable water. Because the theory of comparable worth leads to these kinds of questions, the chair of the U.S. Commission on Civil Rights (a black man) called the concept "the looniest idea since Looney Tunes came on the screen,"[137] and the Director of the U.S. Office of Personnel Management (a white woman), in testifying against comparable worth in Congress, stated that pressures for its adoption were "perplexing at best."[138] Women's rights groups immediately took sharp issue with both officials.

Perplexing or not, comparable worth is making headway among the grassroots governments. At least thirty states have established various kinds of commissions to study and make recommendations to their legislatures about adjusting state government salaries for purposes of achieving comparable worth between male- and female-dominated jobs.[139] Four states have gone farther. Minnesota, New Mexico, and Washington adopted comparable worth plans in 1983, and began the process of raising the salaries of numerous female-dominated job classes; Iowa initiated its comparable worth adjustments in 1984.

Much of the interest in comparable worth associates with the case of *American Federation of State, County, and Municipal Employees*

(AFSCME) v. *State of Washington.* A federal district court ruled in 1983 that Washington's state government had violated Title VII of the Civil Rights Act by discriminating against its employees on the basis of sex (despite the fact that the state already had initiated its own comparable worth plan), and ordered Washington to award back pay to 15,500 employees in female-dominated position classifications and to speed up the implementation of the state's comparable worth plan.

But the judiciary appears to be ambivalent on the issue of comparable worth. In 1984, the Ninth Circuit Court of Appeals upheld the decision of the lower court by ruling in *Spaulding* v. *University of Washington* that the university was not in violation of Title VII, even though it paid its nursing faculty (who are mostly women) less than faculty in male-dominated departments.

Most significant was the decision rendered in 1985 by the same court in the appeal by Washington State over the case it had lost in 1983, *American Federation of State, County, and Municipal Employees (AFSCME)* v. *State of Washington.* The Ninth Circuit Court of Appeals overruled the lower court and held that Washington did not have to award back pay to 15,500 employees in position classifications dominated by women. "Neither law nor logic deems the free market a suspect enterprise," said the court, adding that the Civil Rights Act did not obligate Washington "to eliminate an economic inequality which it did not create." Women's rights groups reacted to the decision immediately, vociferously, and hostilely.

Ultimately, the case was settled out of court, and Washington State agreed to set new pay levels for 62,000 state employees, at a cost of $400 million, in an effort to bring women's salaries in line with those of men. The effect of this decision was to provide "the nation's biggest test so far of paying women the same as men who have different but equally demanding jobs."[140]

What are the early test results? On the one hand, Washington State has been most successful in equalizing the pay of its male and female employees: from a 20 percent gap in 1986 to a 5 percent gap by 1990. On the other hand, problems abound. Four years following the settlement, job segregation by gender did not seem to have dissipated; because of the cost of the program, the pay for some state positions had slipped by as much as 30 percent in comparison with comparable positions in the private sector; as a result, recruiting had become much more difficult; pay compression (*i.e.*, the reduction of the difference between the wage levels of higher and lower ranks) had intensified; and men had left state government—male employment in Washington State government had declined from 50 percent of all employees to 47 percent over the four years.[141]

In light of these preliminary findings in Washington State's experience with comparable worth, it is perhaps not surprising that other states, like the courts, are approaching comparable worth with caution.

Although four states have taken the initiative in introducing comparable worth plans (and, in the case of Minnesota, extending the concept to its local governments as well), another four (Colorado, Florida, Missouri, and Nebraska) have explicitly rejected comparable worth. Yet, the people seem to be for it—perhaps by as much as three to one.[142]

Whether comparable worth is "looney," progressive, or merely "perplexing," it will be an issue for some time to come.

The "Reverse Discrimination" Dilemma

These ambivalent attitudes and public policies over not only comparable worth but also the whole spectrum of affirmative action, have resulted in the accusation of "reverse discrimination," a charge usually leveled by organizations composed largely of white males. White policemen in Dayton, Ohio, for example sued that city in 1973 charging racial discrimination in promotions.

The earliest well-known reverse discrimination case was that of *DeFunis* v. *Odegaard*, which involved a white male, DeFunis, who applied to the University of Washington Law School in 1971. His application was rejected by the law school and he filed a suit contending that the school's admission procedure had admitted minority applicants with test scores and grades lower than his. A trial court ordered him admitted in 1971, the decision was appealed by the University of Washington Law School, was overturned, and DeFunis then appealed his case to the U.S. Supreme Court, which adjudged his case moot in 1974.

The most famous reverse discrimination case, however, is *Regents of the University of California* v. *Bakke*, in which Allan Bakke, a white male, was denied admission to the University of California's Medical School at Davis because that institution had set aside a portion (16 percent) of each entering class for blacks and other "approved minorities." In 1977, the California Supreme Court upheld a lower court's ruling, and with it Bakke's position, by refusing to endorse racial quotas, arguing that doing so "would call for the sacrifice of principle for the sake of dubious expediency," going on to note that people should "be judged on the basis of individual merit alone." Both the lower court and the California Supreme Court, in deciding against the university, had ruled that the university had violated the Civil Rights Act of 1964 and, significantly, the Fourteenth Amendment of the Constitution, which forbids states to "deny to any person...the equal protection of the laws." The University of California appealed to the U.S. Supreme Court, which agreed to hear the case.

In 1978 the Supreme Court, in a five-to-four decision, ruled against the university, thus upholding the California Supreme Court. But the Court's ruling was not clear-cut. Justice Powell, writing the Court's main opinion, stated that the medical school had gone too far in considering race as a criterion for admission, but Powell also said (if rather vaguely) that affirmative action programs could properly be a factor in admitting students. Powell stated that, "Preferring members of any one group for no reason other than race or ethnic origin is discrimination for its own sake," holding that such discrimination, as expressed by rigid racial quotas, was in violation of the Fourteenth Amendment and was thus unconstitutional.

Equally important, each of the remaining four justices in the majority wrote their own separate opinions, and none of them took Powell's position that quotas were unconstitutional. Instead, they held that Bakke should have been admitted to the University of California medical school on the basis of the Civil Rights Act of 1964. Justice John Paul Stevens stated, in words reflecting this tack, that the act prohibited "in unmistakable terms...the exclusion of individuals from federally funded programs because of their race."

The distinction between ruling racial quotas unconstitutional (as Powell did) or illegal (as the other four justices did) is significant. If the majority had held that the University of California had violated the Constitution, then affirmative action programs across the country would likely have faced dismantling. Fortunately for these programs, however, all the nine justices agreed that affirmative action programs per se were neither unconstitutional nor illegal, and that being from a minority group could "be deemed a 'plus' in a particular applicant's file," to quote Justice Powell, although it would "not insulate the individual from comparison with all other candidates..."

Justice Thurgood Marshall, the Court's only black, wrote the dissenting opinion, stating that "If we are ever to become a fully integrated society, one in which the color of a person's skin will not determine the opportunities available to him or her, we must be willing to open those doors" that have been shut to blacks in the past.

The *Bakke* decision, although limited to education admissions policies, had obvious ramifications for affirmative action programs in all sectors and for that reason was greeted with demonstrations across the country calling for its overturn.

A year following the *Bakke* ruling, the Supreme Court heard a second case that came to be known as the "blue-collar Bakke" decision. In *Weber* v. *Kaiser Aluminum and Steel Corporation and United Steel Workers Union*, Brian Weber, a white lab technician, charged that both his employer and his union were discriminating against whites by mandating that a joint union and company training program for skilled craft jobs must have half of its available positions filled by whites and the other half filled by blacks. Weber had been denied entrance into the program, even though he had more seniority than two blacks who were admitted. The Court, in a five-to-two decision, held that Kaiser as well as other employers could consider race as one of many factors in hiring and promotion policies. The Court argued that Title VII of the Civil Rights Act of 1964 had been passed for the purpose of improving the economic status of blacks, and so a voluntary program in the private sector that gave special preferences to blacks was not in violation of the statute.

In 1984, the Supreme Court altered the direction of its moderately pro-affirmative action decisions in the area of reverse discrimination by overturning two lower courts and ruling in a six-to-three opinion that layoffs based on seniority did not violate Title VII of the Civil Rights Act. *Firefighters Local Union No. 1784, et al.* v. *Carl W. Stotts, et al.* involved the City of Memphis's decision in 1981 to lay off fire fighters on the basis of seniority (*i.e.*, last hired, first fired), a standard practice among unionized workers, and a resultant temporary restraining order by a federal district court forbidding the city to lay off any black fire fighters in the process. The reasoning of the district court in issuing its order was that Memphis had entered earlier into a consent decree, approved by the district court in 1980, which held in part that the city would try to attain a goal of a fire department that was 20 percent black. In the district court's view, to lay off fire fighters by seniority would not only violate the consent decree, but would disproportionately affect blacks, who had been hired later than whites. Thus, the city was ordered by the district court to lay off whites who had more seniority than blacks. This ruling was upheld by the U.S. court of appeals.

The Supreme Court took a different perspective, however, and stated that "there was no finding that any of the blacks protected from layoffs had been a victim of discrimination and no award of competitive seniority to any of them." Hence, the Civil Rights Act had not been violated by Memphis's decision to lay off its fire fighters on the basis of seniority because the intent of Congress in the Act is to "provide make-whole relief only to those who have been victims of illegal discrimination." In other words, black fire fighters in Memphis, according to the Court, had not been discriminated against in the past, and therefore a policy of last hired, first fired was an appropriate way to decide who was going to be laid off.

The likely effects of this decision is to make it more difficult for minorities and women to keep their jobs in unionized government agencies and industries because minorities and women tend to have less seniority than do white males. The Court's opinion—an important one for blue-collar public employees—was not greeted with favor by the nation's civil rights groups.

But in 1987, the Supreme Court made amends. In *Johnson* v. *Transportation Agency, Santa Clara County*, the Court held in a six-to-three decision that higher test scores, more job-related experience, and the judgment of a personnel examining board could be ignored in making a promotion on the basis of sex, even when there was no history of discrimination.

Diane Joyce and Paul Johnson were among seven qualified finalists who applied for the position of road dispatcher in the Transportation Agency of Santa Clara County, California. Johnson scored higher on the civil service test than Joyce (75 versus 73), and he had more experience and the recommendation of the examination board as the best qualified applicant. The agency's director nonetheless awarded the promotion to Joyce because all 238 of the agency's skilled crafts workers were men when the agency's affirmative action plan had been adopted nine years earlier by the Santa Clara Transit District Board of Supervisors, and the plan had targeted 36 percent of these positions for women. Johnson sued, contending that his rights had been violated under Title VII of the Civil Rights Act.

In deciding against Johnson, the Court cited the *Weber* case as precedent and noted, in its majority opinion written by Justice William J. Brennan, Jr., that the Transportation Agency had rightly based its decision to promote Joyce on "a multitude of practical, realistic factors," and that the agency "earmarks no positions for anyone; sex is but one of several factors that may be taken into account....the agency has no intention of establishing a work force whose permanent composition is dictated by rigid numerical standards."

Writing for the minority, Justice Antonin Scalia retorted that, with this decision, "Ever so subtly...we effectively replace the goal of a discrimination-free society with the quite incompatible goal of proportionate representation by race and sex in the workplace....Today's decision does more...than merely extend [*Weber*] to public actors....After today's decision the failure to engage in reverse discrimination is economic folly and arguably a breach of duty to shareholders or taxpayers....A statute [the Civil Rights Act] designed to establish a color-blind and gender-blind workplace has thus been converted into a powerful engine of racism and sexism....The only losers in the process are the Johnsons of the country....The irony is that these individuals—predominantly unknown, unaffluent, unorganized—suffer this injustice at the hands of a court fond of thinking itself the champion of the politically impotent."

Regardless of how reverse discrimination suits will be decided in the courtroom, it is clear that the problem is both real and divisive, not only for public administrators, but for the citizenry. A review of public opinion polls on the topic concluded that "Americans are sensitive to the distinction between *compensatory action* and *preferential treatment*" in the hiring and promotion of minorities and women.[143] In other words, vast majorities of whites, in various surveys conducted from 1972 until the present, respond that they approve of such actions as government job training programs for minorities, but draw the line in suspending normal merit standards as a means of hiring and promoting minorities. Indeed, blacks and women also respond in this way; in a Gallup poll, for example, blacks endorsed promoting minorities on the basis of "ability" over "preferential treatment" by 64 to 27 percent, and 71 percent of the women respondents favored the same distinction.[144]

Nevertheless, whose ox is getting gored remains a valid political principle, and the discrimination issue is no exception. College faculty members, for example, heavily favor using affirmative action criteria in deciding the admission of undergraduates to college (62 percent), but are not nearly so positively disposed toward the notion when it comes to deciding their own careers; less than 35 percent of the nation's professors favor giving preferential treatment to women and minority applicants for faculty positions.[145]

In responding to the dilemma of reverse discrimination, some state and local governments seem to have gone overboard—perhaps in part because of the wiliness of their employees.[146] For example, in 1977 fifty-three San Francisco police officers claiming that they were American Indians were hauled before the Equal Opportunity Commission, and all were officially reclassified as white.

In Los Angeles, a city long under federal pressure to desegregate its schools, both white and minority teachers began claiming they were of a different race in order to avoid being sent to another school district as part of the school board's efforts to attain faculties in each school that included at least 30 percent minorities. To counter this ploy Los Angeles established "ethnic review committees" that investigated "ethnic discrepancies" among teachers.

In New York, both teachers and pupils are "visually confirmed" by the board of education for racial identification purposes—and for subsequent assignment to a school.

If all this sounds a bit like "springtime in Hitler's Germany," it is. Racial certification, regardless of motivation, is unpalatable to most Americans. Nevertheless, racial review boards may be a standard component in the state and local governments of the future as public employees of all races try to "pass" for the sake of enhancing their work location and promotion prospects.

The Grass-roots Politics of Affirmative Action

Most jobs in government—some 13 million—are offered by the state and local levels, and it is at those levels where most of the political action is in terms of getting more minorities and women into public positions. But with time, the nature of this action has changed, and apparently for the better.

The Early Years: The Oakland Experience. How governments used to respond to the then ill-understood question of affirmative action has been detailed in Thompson's case study of Oakland.[147] In 1969, spokespersons for minority job hunters challenged Oakland's personnel director over his policies concerning affirmative action. The challenge came as the result of a report in 1969 issued by the U.S. Commission on Civil Rights, which observed that Oakland was the only major jurisdiction among seven metropolitan areas studied in which the three main minority groups were substantially underrepresented in the city's job rosters; with a minority population of almost 50 percent in Oakland, only 15.3 percent of city hall employees were black, 1.5 percent had Spanish surnames, and 1.6 percent were Asian-Americans.

Oakland's minority leaders focused on two strategies; they attempted to "bang Oakland officials over the head" with its own dismal record of minority employment, and they also tried to involve themselves in the recruitment structures of the city. A major target of the minorities was the police force; minority leaders felt that its written tests were culturally biased, and a suit was duly filed. Minorities also pressured for a Citizens' Advisory Committee for the force, which was resisted by the police chief and the personnel director, who saw it as a front for a community control board.

Oakland city officials were quick to construct their own version of a domino theory on affirmative action; that is, if one department "fell" to minority pressure, then all the departments would become more susceptible to affirmative action demands. Although Oakland officials had the legal and actual power to flatly deny the demands of minorities, they elected not to be so direct and thus avoid an image of unresponsiveness. Delay was a major tactic in this strategy. Because recruitment authority in Oakland's city hall was widely dispersed, officials had great deal of opportunity to pass the buck. One frustrated minority spokesman compared the bureaucracy of Oakland with a "monolithic multi-headed hydra—when we approach one head, it always tells us that the other head is responsible." Or, as another minority member stated, "In Oakland the buck never stops."[148]

City officials marshalled a variety of tactics designed to justify their own positions and throw the blame on the minorities. For example, the personnel director warned that "The city was responsible to the taxpayer and can't afford to hire people not capable of doing their jobs."

To be fair, not all of Oakland's officials were so recalcitrant on the issue. Some procedures were changed to encourage minority applicants, and the use of oral examinations was expanded to facilitate the entrance of minorities into city government. As Thompson observes, "Orals make favoritism feasible both in structuring the mechanism and scoring applicant responses. Furthermore, racial preference in the oral is not as visible within the bureaucracy as other adjustments aimed at helping minorities (for example, lowering credential requirements). Consequently, manipulation of the oral is less likely to precipitate organized opposition."[149] Thompson concluded that, in the face of demands from minorities to expand minority representation in the city, a personnel director would generally put more pressure on those city departments that have hired few minorities, have made little effort to recruit them, have jobs that require simple skills (at least in the opinion of the personnel director), and that have a substantial number of open slots. Despite these patterns, however, the lack of official enthusiasm for attracting minorities (not to mention women) to Oakland's municipal labor force seemed patent.

Auguries of Improvement. By the mid-1970s, there were signs that, rather than fighting a guerrilla action against minorities and women entering public service, the bureaucratic establishment was beginning to lead their charge, and this change of sides seemed particularly evident in local governments, including Oakland's. For example, a survey of more than 2,000 city managers conducted in 1974 found that only 46 percent of these cities had begun action plans for meeting affirmative action goals for women, but that in more than four-fifths of these cases the city manager had started the plan on his or her own initiative, and in only 52 percent of these initiatives did the manager have the support of the city council. For minorities, the figures were comparable: 55 percent of the cities had begun action plans for getting more minorities into local government, but the city manager had started 84 percent of these plans on his or her own initiative, and had the backing of the city council only 56 percent of the time. "While managers and chief administrators exhibit no strong personal commitment to [affirmative action] goals, they are *far and away* the principal initiators of affirmative action in their governments."[150]

By the 1980s, the use of affirmative action plans among local governments was considerably more universal and, if the research conducted in the early 1970s is any indication, this dramatically widening use was attributable more to the urban bureaucracy and less to the local political leadership. Ninety-three percent of all local governments have a formal affirmative action policy, 72 percent have integrated these policies into the personnel plans of each line department, and 52 percent have "numeric goals" (*i.e.*, quotas for minorities and women) as a written part of their policies (in 11 percent of the local governments, these quotas were imposed by court order).[151] Ninety-eight percent of local jurisdictions include minorities in their affirmative action plans (compared to 55 percent about a decade earlier), and 87 percent include women (up from a modest 46 percent approximately ten years earlier).[152] The larger the jurisdiction, the more likely it is to have higher scores on all measurements.

These numbers imply real public progress, and, as noted, this progress seems to be attributable to the public bureaucrats. More than 55 percent of city managers believe that government should intervene on behalf of women, more than 60 percent think that a woman should be hired if male applicants are only equally well qualified, and nearly four-fifths oppose expressions of sexism.[153] Only 6 percent of city personnel directors are opposed to quotas (a major point of controversy) for women and minorities.[154] Two-thirds of the states have adopted statewide policies against sexual harassment, and only eight have failed to address this issue in some important way.[155]

Even in the federal government, where, with the impact of the conservative administration of Ronald Reagan from 1981 to 1989, alarms were raised about a lack of continued federal commitment to equality of opportunity,[156] it appears that federal administrators did not lose their longstanding dedication to affirmative action. Even at the height of the Reagan administration, nearly half of the personnel directors in large cities perceived federal agencies to be supportive of aggressive affirmative action policies; more than 16 percent saw Washington as desirous of implementing additional steps to improve minority hiring; and only 9 percent reported "perceptions of federal activity in tune with well publicized Reagan administration policies, namely deemphasis on affirmative action...."[157]

The Effects of the Efforts

The Federal Effort: Progress. Attitudes and perceptions are one thing; accomplishment is another. At the federal level, the efforts to bring minorities and women into government have, by at least one measure, been largely successful. In 1967, not quite 19 percent of all federal full-time employees were from minority groups in a pop-

ulation in which less than 17 percent are minorities. By 1988, this figure had risen to 27 percent. Of these, 16 percent were blacks (whose proportion of the total American population is not quite 12 percent) and 5 percent were Hispanic (whose proportion is more than 6 percent of the total population). These are encouraging figures. But as Table 9–3 notes, minorities are far more fully represented on the bottom rungs of the federal career ladder than they are at the top. Forty-one percent of the bottom four rungs of the General Schedule and equivalent systems (federal pay systems that include some three-fourths of all federal full-time employees, both white collar and blue collar, excluding the U.S. Postal Service) are from minority groups. By contrast, less than 7 percent of the very top rungs of the same Schedule are occupied by minority groups.

A somewhat different configuration is evident for women in the federal employ. Women constitute 51 percent of the American population, 45 percent of its labor force, and 48 percent of the full-time white-collar employees who work in the federal government. In 1970, 33 percent of the federal white-collar work force were women. As Table 9–4 shows, the great bulk of women who work in the federal government are secretaries-clerks. Three quarters of women working for the federal government under the General Schedule and equivalent pay systems are found in the lowest grades, 1 through 6. Only 7 percent of the top federal executive force are women. However, women seem to be moving up the federal ladder. In 1970, only 1.4 percent of the two top grades in the federal pay system were occupied by women, and in 1980, 4 percent of these grades were held by women.

The State and Local Effort: Real Progress. Similar patterns can be found at the state and local levels. Table 9–5 displays some interesting data. A fourth of full-time state and local employees (excluding educators) are from minority groups, but as with the federal government, most minorities are found at the bottom rungs of the state and local employment ladders. However, it should be noted that state and local governments are substantially ahead of their federal counterpart in that significantly greater proportions of minorities are at the top of the state and local employment ladder.

TABLE 9–3 Full-Time Employment of Minorities in the Federal Executive Branch by Level and Pay System, 1980 and 1988

Pay System[1]	1980			1988		
	All Minority Groups[2]	Black	Hispanic	All Minority Groups[2]	Black	Hispanic
All Pay Systems, Total	24%	17%	4%	27%	16%	5%
General Schedule and Equivalent Systems, Total						
(77% of executive branch employees)	24	15	4	26	16	5
GS 1–4 ($10,213–$18–288)	33	24	5	41	15	7
GS 5–8 ($15,738–$28,070)	26	20	4	32	22	5
GS 9–12 ($23,846–$44,957)	15	9	3	20	11	4
GS 13–15 ($41,121–$74,303)	9	5	2	12	6	2
Executive Total	7	5	Fewer than 50	7	4	1
Wage Pay Systems (19% of executive branch employees)	30	21	6	33	19	7
Other Pay Systems (4% of executive branch employees)	15	9	2	18	6	3

[1] All data in this column are for 1988. In 1988 there were 2,125,100 full-time employees in the executive branch. Employees of federal corporations, such as the U.S. Postal Service, are not included.

[2] Includes American Indians, Alaska Natives, Asian Americans, and Pacific Islanders not shown separately.

Percentages have been rounded and may not total 100 percent.

Sources: Derived from: U.S. Bureau of the Census, *Statistical Abstract of the United States, 1990* (Washington, D.C.: U.S. Government Printing Office, 1990), p. 326, Table 528, and *1982–83*, p. 269, Table 460.

Thirteen percent of minorities, for example, are officials and administrators in state and local governments, and 20 percent are professionals of other kinds. These are the two most highly paid categories of the eight categories shown on the table.

Progress in minority hiring and promotion is relatively dramatic among the grass-roots governments. Although minorities still were paid, on the average, 7 percent less than whites in 1987, they were paid 14 percent less in 1980—a significant catching up. Only 9 percent of officials and administrators, and only 16 percent of professionals, were members of minority groups in 1980.[158]

Table 9–5 also displays data for women. As it shows, 42 percent of all state and local employees (again excluding educators) are women. As with the federal government, most women employees in state and local governments tend to be found on the lower rungs of the ladder, particularly in the paraprofessional and clerical categories. However, unlike the federal government, a significantly greater number of women are found in the upper rungs of the occupational ladder. Twenty-nine percent are officials or administrators in states and localities, and 48 percent are professionals, a percentage higher than the percentage of women working for state and local governments at all levels.

It is in the area of salaries that genuine disparities are evident. On the average, women earn 22 percent less than their male colleagues. As with minorities in state and local governments, however, progress is

TABLE 9–4 Full-Time White-Collar Civilian Employment of Women in the Federal Government, by Level and Pay System, 1970, 1980, and 1987

Pay System[1]	1970	1980	1987
Total Employment	33%	39%	48%
General Schedule and Equivalent Systems, Total (72% of full-time white-collar employees)	40	45	48
GS 1–6 ($10,213–$22,807)	72	74	75
GS 7–10 ($19,493–$34,136)	33	46	51
GS 11–12 ($28,852–$44,957)	10	19	30
GS 13–15 ($41,121–$74,303)	3	8	14
GS 16–18 ($67,038–$75,500)	1	4	7
Postal Pay System (27% of full-time white-collar employees)	N.A.	27	36
Other Pay Systems (2% of full-time white-collar employees)	46	36	40

[1]Pay ranges shown in this column are for 1988. In 1987, there were 2,203,000 full-time white-collar employees in the federal government.

Percentages have been rounded and may not total 100 percent.

Source: U.S. Bureau of the Census, *Statistical Abstract of the United States, 1990* (Washington, D.C.: U.S. Government Printing Office, 1990), p. 323, Table 520.

TABLE 9–5 Full-Time Employment and Occupation (Excluding Education) in State and Local Governments by Sex and Minority Groups, 1987

Percent Employed[1]	Total	Officials/ Administrators	Professionals	Technician	Protective Service	Para- professionals	Office/ Clerical	Skilled Craft	Service/ Maintenance
Women	42%	29%	48%	39%	11%	71%	88%	4%	20%
Minority Groups, Total[2]	25	13	20	22	20	38	28	21	42
Black	18	8	12	15	14	31	19	13	32
Hispanic	6	3	4	5	5	5	7	6	8

[1]In 1987, state and local governments employed 4,849,00 people full-time, excluding education.

[2]Includes other minority groups not shown separately.

Percentages have been rounded.

Source: As derived from U.S. Bureau of the Census, *Statistical Abstract of the United States, 1990* (Washington, D.C.: U.S. Government Printing Office, 1990), p. 300, Table 488.

evident—if somewhat less so. In 1980, women working in the grass-roots governments earned 25 percent less than men, and were less represented at the administrative (23 percent of officials and administrators were women) and professional levels (44 percent were women).[159]

Overall, state and local governments appear to be the institutional vanguard in giving minorities and women a better opportunity in American society. Not only are the grass-roots governments generally ahead of their federal counterpart in promoting women and minorities to the top rungs of the public career ladder, but they seem to be ahead of the private sector, too. An extensive analysis of data from the Equal Employment Opportunity Commission concluded that there were proportionately fewer white males, more women, and more blacks working at the technical, professional, and managerial echelons of state and local governments than there were in these positions in the corporate world. Only Hispanics were relatively disadvantaged in state and local governments on this dimension in comparison to the business sector.[160]

However, both African-American men and Hispanic men were paid more in high-level positions in state and local governments than they were in comparable positions in the private sector; in fact, black and Hispanic males in government were paid more than white males in government! Black women and Hispanic women working in government not only were paid more than their counterparts in the for-profit sector (although less than men of all races), but also, like minority men in government, minority women in government earned higher salaries than white women in comparable positions in the public sector. "In the aggregate, state and local governments are doing considerably better than the private sector in living up to the challenge of attaining sexual and racial-ethnic employment equity....by the relative standard of private sector performance, the record established by state and local governments has been quite impressive."[161]

A Demographic Solution? In light of the effort that has been expended by governments to provide more opportunities for minorities and women, it is ironic that the future looks far fairer

for these populations, but not entirely because of those efforts. Demographics may effect more "affirmative action" in the governmental (and corporate) workplace than affirmative action policies have yet done.

The number of jobs held by white males in the United States has been in steady decline since the mid-1970s. In 1976, nearly 49 percent of all jobs were held by white men, but, according to the U.S. Department of Labor, by 2000, only 39 percent of the nation's jobs will be held by white males.[162] Women, blacks, and Hispanics will take and are taking their place.

This loss of white males in the work force is due to the fact that the country's supply of young white men is shrinking by about 2 percent a year.[163] Young women, African-Americans, and Hispanics are replacing them; 68 percent of new workers in the 1990s are women and minorities.[164]

These demographic trends do not, of course, guarantee equality of opportunity to advance up the organizational ladder; but they do increase, and dramatically so, the entry of women and minorities into agencies and companies. Between these realities of the labor pool and continued efforts by governments and corporations to increase talent and representation at all levels of employment, equality of opportunity may be enhanced.

BLUE-COLLAR BUREAUCRATS: THE CHALLENGE OF PUBLIC UNIONISM

The unionization of public employees is a relatively new and occasionally discomfiting phenomenon in public administration. Nearly 17 percent of all union members are public employees; more than 6 percent of all union members work for the federal government, and more than 10 percent have jobs in state and local governments.[165] About 37 percent of all government workers belong to unions, a figure that has stayed roughly the same since 1980.[166]

Sixty percent of all federal employees are represented by about 100 unions or similar organizations, a figure that has remained constant since 1981.[167] The number of federal employees who actually are dues paying members of unions, however, is considerably lower. It is estimated that only about 30 to 35 percent of federal employees actually belong to unions.[168]

About 40 percent of all full-time state and local employees are members of unions: 31 percent of state employees, and 43 percent of local employees.[169] Table 9–6 breaks down the percentage of state and local full-time employees who are in labor unions by job function. Fire fighters have long led the list as the most heavily organized of public employees, followed by teachers and police. These and other occupational groups are represented by nearly 34,000 bargaining units.[170]

TABLE 9–6 Percentage of State and Local Employees (Full-Time) in Labor Unions by Job Function, 1980

Function	State and Local Governments
Fire fighters	77%
Teachers	70
Police	56
Sanitation workers	50
Highway employees	46
Public welfare employees	45
Hospital employees	42
All other functions	39

Percentages have been rounded.

Source: U.S. Bureau of the Census, *Labor Management Relations in State and Local Government, 1981* (Washington, D.C.: U.S. Government Printing Office, 1982).

The major unions of government workers are the National Education Association, with nearly 1.7 million members; the American Federation of State, County, and Municipal Employees (AFSCME), with more than 950,000 members; the American Federation of Teachers, with more than 450,000 members; the National Federation of Federal Employees, representing more than 150,000 federal workers (but only 45,000 pay dues); the National Treasury Employees Union, representing 120,000 federal employees (of whom only 65,000 pay dues); the American Federation of Government Employees, which is associated with the AFL-CIO and represents more than 700,000 fed-

eral workers (although only 180,000 are dues paying members); the Postal Workers union and the National Association of Letter Carriers, which represent more than 830,000 employers of the U.S. Postal Services (but which have only 213,000 and 201,000 members, respectively); the Fraternal Order of Police, with more than 150,000 members; and the International Association of Firefighters, with approximately 140,000 members.[171]

At the federal level, a number of unions more commonly associated with the private sector also bargain for public employees. For example, one third of the membership of the AFL-CIO's Service Employees International Union is composed of public workers, and it is the AFL-CIO, in effect, that is representing these workers to federal mediators.

Efforts to organize public employees are not new, and early attempts at organizing go back to the 1830s. In fact, the National Education Association was founded in 1857, roughly thirty years before the birth of the American Federation of Labor. And in the 1800s, public employees had good reason to organize. Police and fire fighters, for example, who are among the most heavily unionized public employees today, traditionally have tolerated among the worst working conditions. In 1907, the New York Health Department condemned thirty of the city's eighty-five police stations as uninhabitable, and the police worked from seventy-three to ninety-eight hours a week. Fire fighters, who commonly were paid low salaries, worked twenty-one hours *a day* and had only one day off in eight.[172]

Despite such conditions, there was considerable resistance to the unionization of public employees, mostly for ideological reasons, but also for economic ones. As merit systems developed in state and local governments, job security became more assured and working conditions did improve. There were (and are) also a spate of state and local laws forbidding or discouraging any kind of union activity by government workers (the constitutionality of these laws is at least questionable). White-collar workers, as a class, had never really identified with unionization and, finally, there was a considerable weight of public opinion against the notion of government workers being allowed to disrupt vital public services by resorting to the strike.

Securing the Right to Collective Bargaining

Although federal employees had secured the right to organize in 1912 with the passage of the Lloyd-La Follette Act, the rights to negotiate collectively and to strike were resisted until the 1960s, and the initial indications that attitudes were shifting on these issues came not from Washington but from state and local governments. In 1959, Wisconsin passed the first law requiring its local governments to bargain collectively.

State and local governments are only beginning to approach sophistication in their collective bargaining with organized employees. Generally, state and local policies on government negotiations with organized employees are of two types. The *collective bargaining* approach permits decisions on salaries, hours, and working conditions to be made jointly by employee and employer representatives. The *meet-and-confer* tack says only that both sides must meet and confer over these issues, but that management has the final decision.

Judging by their written policies, the great majority of states and localities prefer the collective bargaining approach. Forty-two states have a labor relations policy, and thirty-seven states use collective bargaining as their primary method of dealing with labor unions. Of the 13,342 local jurisdictions that have a labor relations policy (or 16 percent of all local governments), 88 percent use collective bargaining in dealing with employees.[173]

State and local governments are becoming increasingly innovative in bargaining with their employees. Englewood, Colorado, for example, has passed a city ordinance that stipulates that an impartial fact-finder's recommendations will be put on the ballot with the best offer of the union and management alongside it; then Englewood lets the voters decide the issues. Englewood reflects the increasing use of "goldfish-bowl bargaining," or "sunshine bargaining," in which the public is being brought increasingly into the negotiation process, a process that traditionally, particularly in the private sector, has gone on behind closed doors. In this way the public's right to know is protected, and the bargaining is opened up at a time when the public's knowledge can affect the outcome of the negotiation process.[174] About a dozen states have enacted sunshine bargaining statutes.[175]

Federal activity in the field of collective bargaining is marked by President John F. Kennedy's Executive Order 10988 of 1962. The order stated that certain conditions of employment could be bargained for collectively between agency management and employees; wages, hours, and fringe benefits, however, were excluded because these topics were subject to regulations of the various agencies and the Civil Service Commission.

Employee representatives found these limitations restrictive, and, in 1969, President Richard Nixon issued Executive Order 11491 in response to growing discontent. This order attempted to rectify a plethora of negotiating problems that had emerged since 1962: multiple labor representatives competing to bargain with management; the absence of third-party machinery; and the abuse of power by some agency heads in determining bargaining units, exclusive agents, and unfair employment practices. These latter decision-making areas were transferred from the agency heads to the assistant secretary of labor for Labor-Management Relations, and appeals from the assistant secretary's decision could be made to the Federal Labor Relations Council, a board composed of the chair of the Civil Service Commission, the secretary of labor, and a representative of the Office of the President. A Federal Service Impasse Panel also was created by the order, empowered to resolve bargaining impasses.

Within a few months of the issuance of Executive Order 11491, the first major strike by federal employees occurred. In March, 1970, about 200,000 postal workers staged an unprecedented walkout. For the first time, federal representatives bargained on salaries (subsequently ratified by Congress), and later Congress legislated the right of postal employees to bargain collectively for wages. This incident, in the eyes of many observers, rendered Executive Order 11491 obsolete, and as a result Executive Order 11616 appeared in 1971, amending minor portions of the previous order. Collective negotiations on salaries and fringe benefits remained off limits, however, and labor representatives did not consider Executive Order 11616 to be a substantial improvement.

In 1978, President Jimmy Carter's Reorganization Plan No. 2 created the Federal Labor Relations Authority as an independent agency. The new authority (whose functions were enacted into law later in 1978 with the passage of the Civil Service Reform Act) took over the responsibilities of the Federal Labor Relations Council, and its creation represented an attempt to clarify the role of organized labor in government. As formalized by the Civil Service Reform Act, federal employees had the right to join unions, but strikes and slowdowns were prohibited. Federal agencies which issue government-wide directives that affect all federal employees now must consult with labor representatives before major directives are issued.

Although the federal government has made some progressive moves in recognizing organized labor, it also has shown itself to be increasingly tough in dealing with unions. In the same year that the Civil Service Reform Act was enacted, President Carter signed Public Law 95-610, which prohibits union organization of the armed forces and punishes any member of the armed forces who might join a military labor organization. Existing unions that try to enlist soldiers and sailors for the purpose of organizing them into a collective bargaining unit also are subject to stiff penalties.

In 1981, the Federal Labor Relations Authority showed that it meant business when it was dealing with organized federal workers when it decertified the Professional Association of Air Traffic Controllers (PATCO)—that is, it no longer recognized the union as the official representative of its members. In effect, this act by the Federal Labor Relations Authority eliminated the union and deprived virtually all of its members of their jobs.

Collective Bargaining: The (Partial) Record in Dollars

Forty-three percent of all public employees are covered by collective bargaining agreements.[176] Unlike labor-management negotiations in the private sector, neither labor nor management in the public sector is bargaining about its own money. Public labor unions demand tax monies for wages that may or may not be in the public till, and public administrators negotiate with tax monies that likewise may not be in the public till. The person who pays is the taxpayer.

When we combine this reality with unions that have become increasingly sophisticated in their bargaining skills and financial research abilities (several public sector unions now have full-time professional staffs who do nothing but analyze state and local budgets[177]), it is not too surprising that public laborers have made considerable financial gains in their negotiations with public management, although the gains of public employee unions have been in decline in recent years. Currently, personnel costs account from 50 percent to 80 percent of a typical city budget, and much of this proportion stems from the gains that workers have made in collective bargaining. During the 1960s in particular, unionized public employees made dramatic gains in pay, with wage increases hitting more than 60 percent for some categories of employees during the decade.[178]

A major negotiating area between public employers and employees is that of pensions. In the case of police departments, for example, the national tendency has been to permit retirement at half-pay after twenty years of service. Such arrangements, of course, aggravate urban financial problems. New York City probably is the most outstanding example of what a pension plan can do to urban finances; city transit workers, police, fire fighters and other workers are allowed early retirement with generous benefits. The pension specialist of the American Federation of State, County, and Municipal Employees has stated that its "members are just beginning to realize that pensions can be negotiated." When queried where the money for higher pensions is coming from, the pension specialist for AFSCME replied, "That's the government's problem. Just because there is a pinch for money, it's no excuse to make the employees do without."[179]

Collective bargaining has given public employees a relatively good deal in comparison with workers in the private sector, and evidence of this is provided by a study conducted by the U.S. Bureau of Labor Statistics in twenty-two large and middle-sized representative cities. In a report that covered the eleven largest cities, it was found that in nine of them municipal workers in clerical jobs were paid more than their counterparts in both private industry and in the federal government. Most of these cities also showed higher pay scales for computer-related jobs and janitorial jobs. Employees in skilled and semiskilled blue-collar jobs earned more than their counterparts in industry, mainly because their jobs were steadier than those in the private sphere.[180] The Bureau of Labor Statistics did not address the issue of whether or not collective bargaining was a reason behind these kinds of increases relative to the private sector, but a study by the Institute of Labor Relations of twelve Michigan school districts concluded that collective bargaining appeared to have given teachers 10 to 20 percent more in wage increases than unilateral school board action would have furnished.[181] Another broader study of teachers' unions concluded that teachers' unions had succeeded in raising salaries from 5 to 20 percent across the country.[182]

It is important to realize, however, that most of these studies are fragmentary, and deal principally only with wages and pensions as opposed to other kinds of fringe benefits. Yet these other benefits could well loom even larger than wages and pensions in terms of their ultimate impact upon the taxpayer. One careful review of the literature found "no studies which have undertaken the detailed cost analysis of a large sample of contracts which would be necessary to calculate the impacts of working conditions, job security, and professional provisions on public budgets."[183] These nonwage areas include such items as the regulation of hours, caseload ceilings (for social workers and nurses, for example), arrangements for paraprofessionals, assignment and transfer provisions, standards for entry, promotions and reductions in force, professional development provisions, and other areas that have nothing to do with compensation but which are nonetheless expensive to conduct.[184]

The Public Strike: The Public Record

Because of the potential fiscal impact that collective bargaining can have on state and local governments, states and cities are often reluctant to "come across" to union demands. The result of such reluctance can be, and occasionally is, a strike.

It used to be that sanitation workers were the most frequent public employees to walk the picket lines, but more recently it has been teachers who are more inclined to strike. Table 9–7 indicates the number of work stoppages, employees involved, and days of idleness incurred among state and local government employees. Strikes by public employees peaked in 1979 at 593, and both the number of strikes and the length of their duration have been in remission since. The number of strikes by state and local employees is now around 300 per year.[185]

Strikes will always be with us, regardless of whether or not there are laws permitting or prohibiting strikes by public employees. Nonetheless, the emotional issue of the public employees' right to strike runs deep. One viewpoint holds that a strike by public employees amounts to an act of insurrection because such strikes are directed against the people themselves; the opposing view contends that the right of government workers to strike is a basic freedom protected under the Constitution. To deny public employees a right granted to workers in private corporations is to treat public personnel as second-class citizens. The courts thus far have held that there is no constitutional right of public workers to strike, but neither has the judiciary prohibited the enactment of laws permitting government employees to strike.

Unions versus "Merit": The Basic Differences

The future of collective bargaining, unionization, and the right to strike bode ill for the traditional merit standards of the civil service personnel system. At root, there are two differences between the "collective system" and the "civil service system." One difference concerns the notion of *sovereignty*. The civil service system holds that a public position is a privilege, not a right, and that each public servant is obliged to uphold the public trust accorded to him or her by a paternalistic government. Conversely, the collective system holds that employees are on an equal footing with employers, and that they have a right to use their collective powers as a means of improving their conditions of employment. The civil service system sees this contention as a threat to the sovereignty of the state. At the same time the collective

TABLE 9-7 Work Stoppages in State and Local Governments, 1980

Item	Total[1]	Education			Highways	Hospitals	Police and Fire Protection	Public Welfare
		Total	Instructional	Other				
Work stoppages (number)[2,3]								
Total	502	287	225	62	45	20	63	14
State	22	7	4	3	0	4	1	1
Local	480	280	221	59	45	16	62	13
Employees involved in work stoppages (1,000)[2]								
Total	233	126	99	27	3	7	10	3
State	16	4	2	2	0	1	Fewer than 500	Fewer than 500
Local	217	122	97	25	3	6	10	3
Days of idleness (1,000)[2]								
Total	2,407	1,534	1,235	298	26	32	92	23
State	90	37	18	20	0	2	Fewer than 500	Fewer than 500
Local	2,317	1,496	1,218	278	26	30	92	23

[1]Includes other functions, not shown separately.

[2]Represents period from October 16 of previous year to October 15 of year stated.

[3]Contains duplication; each work stoppage is counted separately for each function affected, but only once in total work stoppage.

Source: Derived from U.S. Bureau of the Census, *Statistical Abstract of the United States, 1985* (Washington, D.C.: U.S. Government Printing Office, 1984), p. 425, Table 711.

system views the traditions of the civil service as redolent of worker exploitation.

The second difference concerns the concept of *individualism.* The American civil service system long has valued the ideal that the individual worker be judged for a position on the basis of his or her unique merits for performing the duties of a particular job; the collective system argues that the identity of the individual should be absorbed in a collective effort to better the conditions of all workers. Hence, the relations of the individual with his or her government employer are replaced by a new set of relations that exists between the government employer and a collective "class" of employees. Among the conflicts that result from these fundamental differences between the two systems over the concepts of sovereignty and individualism are these: disputes over employee participation and rights (equal treatment versus the union shop); recruitment (competitive tests versus union membership); promotion (performance versus seniority); position classification and pay (objective analysis versus negotiation); working conditions (determination by legislatures and management versus settlement by negotiations); and grievances (determination by civil service commissioners versus union representation to third-party arbitrators).

DOES PUBLIC PERSONNEL ADMINISTRATION HAVE A FUTURE?

The problems reviewed here are complex and massive. Public personnel administration, like any other form of public administration, has large dollops of politics as part and parcel of it. The historic efforts of "good government" reformers to rid public personnel systems of "politics" have traditionally been based on the introduction of "merit principles" in the management of the public bureaucracy. Merit principles, as they normally have been understood, are now under considerable attack. The efforts to include more minorities and women in government, the drive to bring more professionals into government (who often do not identify with the public service in the same sense that traditional personnel specialists have related to it), the reality of strikes, unionism, and collective bargaining, and the

drive to overhaul the civil service, all lead one to wonder what "merit" in public human resource management really means.

Concerns such as these inevitably lead one to speculate on the continuing role of the personnel function in government. One of the unique aspects of the public sector is that important systemwide missions are sometimes superimposed upon the public bureaucracy that have nothing to do with the day-to-day implementation and management of programs and policies, but which do reflect strongly held social values. Not only are government bureaucracies supposed to administer legislatively enacted public policies for all the people, but they are also directed by legislatures to "clean up their own houses" in certain areas, such as kicking out the party hacks (*i.e.,* instating the "merit principle") or eliminating discrimination on the basis of race or sex (*i.e.,* the implementation of affirmative action). (It is of note that legislatures—certainly Congress—rarely if ever apply these same "house cleaning" rules to themselves. Congress, for example, has never permitted its personnel practices to be subject to the Office of Personnel Management or any other civil service agency, and it has never applied affirmative action standards or veterans' preference policies to its own treatment of employees.)

To achieve these social missions, the legislature, or the bureaucracy itself, typically creates a new agency to bring the other agencies into line. In 1883, the U.S. Civil Service Commission was set up to assure that incompetents were not hired by all the other federal agencies. Various agencies were established by Congress in 1964 and 1972, such as the U.S. Civil Rights Commission and the Equal Employment Opportunity Commission, and existing agencies gained new powers to assure that minorities, women, and the handicapped were fully represented in the government bureaucracy. In 1978, Congress established the Senior Executive Service and the Office of Personnel Management to disburse something called "management" throughout the federal structure.

These are all desirable objectives. But when they are met—or when they come into conflict with new social missions—perhaps it is time to reconsider the duties and activities of the various organizations that were created to implement them.

An example of this may be the "merit principle." The principle has been implemented. Party hacks seldom are found in the federal bureaucracy. Although there are some exceptions, the rampant spoils system of the last century is no longer with us. More important, the implementation of the "merit principle" has come into conflict with new social missions, notably affirmative action and management improvement in government.[186]

As a consequence, the traditional functions of human resource management in the public sector seem a little obsolete. Job classification and analysis—a basic tenet of public personnel administration—is an example. Agency administrators typically must bargain with personnel administrators about how high or low a position should be ranked in the agency hierarchy, and what kinds of qualifications prospective applicants should have. Often agency heads, who are interested in effective management, and personnel administrators, who want uniformity in the classification system, find themselves at odds. Moreover, human resource managers may not comprehend the wide-ranging professional and administrative needs of the more general public manager. An allegedly true example of this concerns the state agency administrator who asked the state personnel department to find job applicants who understood the management technique of "path analysis"; the personnel department responded that since the agency was not responsible for forestry programs, a knowledge of "path analysis" for the position would not be required.

We are not arguing for the abolition of government personnel departments. But we do suggest that their uses have changed. Perhaps such traditional activities of public personnel administration as job classification and analysis, human resource planning, performance appraisal, selection, discipline, and dismissal should be turned over to agency administrators. Placing the control of these functions directly in the hands of the agency heads should strengthen public management. It is still desirable, however, that other traditional activities of public personnel administration be retained in one or more separate staff units, such as personnel departments, on the grounds that they are less critical to the management function or can be handled more effectively by a central agency;

these activities include employee development, labor relations, research, and the administration of wages, salaries, benefits, and services. Of particular importance is employee development and training, an activity that government personnel departments have not emphasized in the past.

Public personnel administration does have a future. Nevertheless, it is a future that will require some adaptation.

NOTES

[1] The following discussion is drawn largely from Frederick C. Mosher, *Democracy and the Public Service*, 2nd ed. (New York: Oxford University Press, 1982), pp. 110–216.

[2] Frederick C. Mosher, *Democracy and the Public Service* (New York: Oxford University Press, 1968), p. 166. Unless noted otherwise, all references to this work are of the second edition (1982).

[3] In 1984, there were 523 presidential appointment positions (up from seventy-one in 1933) requiring Senate approval; 700 positions out of the 7,000 slots in the Senior Executive Service are available for appointment by a president; and, in 1985, there were 1,665 Schedule C (or policy-related positions at the GS 15 level and below) appointments (up from 911 in 1976), 25 percent of which are subject to appointment by the president. In 1984, there were 2,951 "noncareer employees" in the executive branch (up from 2,794 in 1979), excluding the White House staff, military, Foreign Service, and Public Health Service. See: James P. Pfiffner, "Political Appointees and Career Executives: The Democracy-Bureaucracy Nexus in the Third Century," *Public Administration Review*, 47 (January/February 1987), p. 58. See also: Patricia W. Ingraham, "Building Bridges or Burning Them? The President, the Appointees and the Bureaucracy," *Public Administration Review*, 47 (September/October 1987), p. 427.

[4] Pfiffner, "Political Appointees and Career Executives," p. 57.

[5] *Ibid.*, p. 58. Emphasis is original.

[6] Judith Havemann, "Panel on Public Service Leaves Unfinished Agenda," *Washington Post* (July 23, 1990).

[7] F. Ted Hebert and Deil S. Wright, "State Administrators: How Representative? How Professional?" *State Government*, 55, No. 1 (1982), pp. 23–25.

[8] Dean E. Mann and Jameson W. Doig, *The Assistant Secretaries: Problems and Processes of Appointment* (Washington, D.C.: Brookings Institution, 1965).

[9] Lloyd W. Warner, et al., *The American Federal Executive* (New Haven, Conn.: Yale University Press, 1963).

[10] Mann and Doig, *The Assistant Secretaries.* But see also: Thomas P. Murphy, Donald E. Nuechterlein, and Ronald J. Stupak, *Inside the Bureaucracy: The View from the Assistant Secretary's Desk* (Boulder, Colo.: Westview Press, 1978); and Hugh Heclo, *A Government of Strangers: Executive Politics in*

Washington (Washington, D.C.: Brookings Institution, 1977). Both of these more recent works tend to support the earlier study.

[11] Steven E. Rhoads, "Economists and Policy Analysis," *Public Administration Review*, 38 (January/February 1978), p. 113.

[12] Mosher, *Democracy and the Public Service*, p. 179.

[13] Mann and Doig, *The Assistant Secretaries*, p. 120.

[14] Roger G. Brown, "Party and Bureaucracy: The Presidents Since JFK" (Paper prepared for the 1981 Annual Meeting of the American Political Science Association, New York, September 3–6, 1981), Tables 1–10. This analysis included all cabinet, subcabinet, policymaking officials, judges, and ambassadors. The percentage of appointees who were members of the president's party that were appointed by Kennedy was 70 percent; Johnson, 56 percent; Nixon, 70 percent; Ford, 61 percent; and Carter, 61 percent. The Carter appointees cover only 1977 and 1978. After 1978 information on partisan affiliation became unavailable on a systemic basis.

[15] David T. Stanley, Dean E. Mann, and Jameson W. Doig, *Men Who Govern* (Washington, D.C.: Brookings Institution, 1967), p. 24.

[16] Mann and Doig, *The Assistant Secretaries*.

[17] Harold Seidman, ed., "A Mini-Symposium: President Nixon's Proposals for Executive Reorganization," *Public Administration Review*, 34 (September/October 1974), p. 490.

[18] Joel D. Aberbach, James D. Chesney, and Burt A. Rockman, "Exploring Elite Political Attitudes," *Political Methodology*, Vol. 2, No. 1 (1975), pp. 1–28. The survey was conducted in 1970.

[19] Arch Patton, "Government's Revolving Door," *Business Week* (September 22, 1973), p. 13.

[20] National Academy of Public Administration, *Watergate: Its Implications for Responsible Government* (New York: National Academy of Public Administration, 1974), p. 107.

[21] Ingraham, "Building Bridges or Burning Them?" p. 429.

[22] Mann and Doig, *The Assistant Secretaries*, pp. 99, 165.

[23] Pendleton James, quoted in Pfiffner, "Political Appointees and Career Executives," p. 59.

[24] Senator John Glenn, quoted in Judith Havemann, "Top Federal Jobs 'Politicized,'" *Washington Post* (August 6, 1987). For an explanation of the presidential role in the Senior Executive Service and Schedule C appointments, see Note 3.

[25] Fred Malek, Presidential Personnel Assistant in the Nixon Administration, quoted in *ibid.*, pp. 63–64.

[26] As derived from: U.S. Bureau of the Census, *Statistical Abstract of the United States, 1986* (Washington, D.C.: U.S. Government Printing Office, 1985), Table 301, p. 175; and U.S. Bureau of the Census, *Statistical Abstract of the United States, 1990* (Washington, D.C.: U.S. Government Printing Office, 1990), Table 318, p. 185.

[27] National Academy of Public Administration, *Leadership in Jeopardy: The Fraying of the Presidential Appointments System* (Washington, D.C.: National Academy of Public Administration, 1985), p. 67. The high figures in both categories were provided by presidential appointees in the Johnson admin-istration; the low figures were given by those in the Reagan administration. The response rate was 56 percent.

[28] Pfiffner, "Political Appointees and Career Executives," p. 61.

[29] See, for example, Hebert and Wright, "State Administrators," pp. 23–25, and Deborah D. Roberts, "A New Breed of Public Executive: Top Level Exempt Managers in State Government," *Review of Public Personnel Administration*, 8 (Spring 1988), pp. 20–36.

[30] As derived from Table 3, *Municipal Year Book, 1990* (Washington, D.C.: International City Management Association, 1990), p. xiv.

[31] *Ibid.*

[32] Heywood T. Sanders, "Governmental Structure in American Cities," *Municipal Year Book, 1979* (Washington, D.C.: International City Management Association, 1979), p. 104.

[33] Richard J. Stillman, II, "Local Public Management in Transition: A Report on the Current State of the Profession," *Municipal Year Book, 1982* (Washington, D.C.: International City Management Association, 1982), pp. 164–171.

[34] See Mosher, *Democracy and the Public Service*, p. 58.

[35] Sidney H. Aronson, *Status and Kinship in the Higher Civil Service* (Cambridge, Mass.: Harvard University Press, 1964), p. 61.

[36] *Ibid.*

[37] Quoted in Leonard D. White, *The Jacksonians* (New York: Macmillan, 1954), p. 320.

[38] Mosher, *Democracy and the Public Service*, pp. 66–72.

[39] *Ibid.*, p. 67.

[40] U.S. Civil Service Commission, 22nd Report (Washington, D.C.: U.S. Government Printing Office, 1905), quoted in *ibid.*, p. 69.

[41] *Ibid.*, p. 68.

[42] *Ibid.*, p. 66.

[43] Committee on Administrative Management, Louis Brownlow, Chair, *Personnel Administration in the Federal Service* (Washington, D.C.: U.S. Government Printing Office, 1937).

[44] Commission on Organization of the Executive Branch of the Government, *Personnel and Civil Service* (Washington, D.C.: U.S. Government Printing Office, 1955).

[45] The bulk of the following discussion is drawn from Frederick C. Mosher and Richard J. Stillman, II, "Introduction to Symposium on the Professions in Government," *Public Administration Review*, 37 (November/December 1977), pp. 631–632; and Mosher, *Democracy and the Public Service*, pp. 110–142.

[46] Mosher, *Democracy and the Public Service*, p. 113.

[47] Terry Newell, "The Future and Federal Training," *Public Personnel Management*, 17 (Fall 1988), p. 264, and Beverly A. Cigler, "Public Administration and the Paradox of Professionalism," *Public Administration Review*, 50 (November/December 1990), p. 637. Figures are for 1983 and 1985.

[48] Barbara Blumenthal, "Uncle Sam's Invisible Army of Employees," *National Journal* (May 5, 1979), p. 732.

[49] Frederick C. Mosher, "Professions in Public Service," *Public Administration Review*, 38 (March/April 1978), p. 147; and Mosher, *Democracy and the Public Service*, p. 113.

[50] Municipal Manpower Commission, *Governmental Manpower for Tomorrow's Cities* (New York: McGraw-Hill, 1962).

[51] Mosher, *Democracy and the Public Service*, 1st ed. (1968), p. 124.

[52] Mosher, "Professions in Public Service," p. 145.

[53] *Ibid.*

[54] Frederick C. Mosher and Keith Axtell, unpublished studies cited in Mosher, *Democracy and the Public Service*, pp. 136–137. But see also the first edition (1968), p. 127.

[55] Doyle W. Buckwalter and J. Ivan Legler, "City Managers and City Attorneys: Associates or Adversaries?" *Public Administration Review*, 47 (September/October 1987), pp. 393–403.

[56] See: Corinne Lathrop Gilb, *Hidden Hierarchies: The Professions and Government* (New York: Harper & Row, 1956); Jethro K. Lieberman, *The Tyranny of the Experts: How Professionals Are Closing the Open Society* (New York: Walker, 1970); and Guy Benveniste, *The Politics of Expertise*, 2nd ed. (San Francisco: Boyd & Fraser, 1977). See also: Stephen L. Esquith, "Toward a Theory of Professional Power" (Paper presented at the 1985 Annual Meeting of the American Political Science Association, New Orleans, August 29–September 1, 1985).

[57] Mosher, *Democracy and the Public Service*, pp. 104–105.

[58] *Ibid.*, p. 103.

[59] *Ibid.*

[60] Jean J. Couturier, "The Quiet Revolution in Public Personnel Laws," *Public Personnel Management* (May/June 1976), pp. 150–159. Three hundred thirty-eight public personnel systems responded to the survey.

[61] "The 'Malek Manual'" is published in *The Bureaucrat*, 4 (January 1976), pp. 429–508. One reviewer has said it "stands as the best guide as to how the federal civil service works, as well as a monument to concerted attempts to achieve political control over large sections of the federal bureaucracy." See: H. Brinton Milward, "Politics, Personnel, and Public Policy," *Public Administration Review*, 38 (July/August 1978), p. 395.

[62] Mosher, *Democracy and the Public Service*, pp. 104–105.

[63] Office of Personnel Management, *Federal Employee Attitudes, Phase I: Base Line Survey, 1979, Government-Wide Report* (Washington, D.C.: U.S. Government Printing Office, 1979), p. 25.

[64] Jimmy Carter, *State of the Union Address* (January 19, 1978).

[65] A good example is Alan K. Campbell, "Civil Service Reform: A New Commitment," *Public Administration Review*, 38 (March/April 1978), especially pages 101–102.

[66] Mosher, *Democracy and the Public Service*, p. 107.

[67] Frank A. Yeager, "Assessing the Civil Service Reform Act's Impact on Senior Manager Work Priorities," *Public Administration Review*, 47 (September/October 1987), pp. 417, 422.

[68] Office of Personnel Management, *Civil Service Reform: A Report on the First Year* (Washington, D.C.: U.S. Government Printing Office, 1980); Nolan J. Argyle, "Civil Service Reform: The State and Local Response," *Public Personnel Management* (Spring 1982), pp. 157–164; and Dennis L. Dresang, "Diffusion of Civil Service Reform," *Review of Public Personnel Administration*, 2 (Spring 1982), pp. 35–47.

[69] See, for example, Roberts, "A New Breed of Public Executive"; Frank P. Sherwood and Lee J. Breyer, "Executive Personnel Systems in the States," *Public Administration Review*, 47 (September/October 1987), pp. 410–416; H. O. Waldly and Annie Mary Hartsfield, "The Senior Management Service in the States," *Review of Public Personnel Administration*, 4 (Spring 1984), pp. 28–39; and A. Finkle, H. Hall, and S. Min, "Senior Executive Service: The State of the Art," *Public Personnel Management*, 10 (Fall 1981), pp. 299–312.

[70] The following paragraphs are drawn from Hebert and Wright, "State Administrators," pp. 24–25.

[71] As derived from Table 3, *Municipal Year Book, 1990*, p. xiv.

[72] Frank Turco, "Leadership of Most Big Cities Picked Through Some Type of Ward System," *The Arizona Republic* (November 27, 1982). Figures are for 1982.

[73] Sanders, "Governmental Structure of American Cities," p. 102.

[74] As derived from Table 4, *Municipal Year Book, 1990*, p. xvi.

[75] Allan Klevit, "City Councils and Their Function in Local Government," *Municipal Year Book, 1972* (Washington, D.C.: International City Management Association, 1972), pp. 15–19; Raymond Bancroft, *America's Mayors and Councilmen: Their Problems and Frustrations* (Washington, D.C.: National League of Cities, 1974); and Stillman, "Local Public Management in Transition," p. 163.

[76] Stillman, "Local Public Management in Transition," p. 163.

[77] O. Glenn Stahl, *Public Personnel Administration*, 8th ed. (New York: Harper & Row, 1983), p. 42. Figure is for 1980.

[78] *Ibid.*, p. 43; and Andrew W. Boessel, "Local Personnel Management," *Municipal Year Book, 1974* (Washington, D.C.: International City Management Association, 1974), pp. 92–93.

[79] Dennis L. Dresang, *Public Personnel Management and Public Policy* (Boston: Little, Brown, 1984), p. 4.

[80] Steven W. Hays and T. Zane Reeves, *Personnel Management in the Public Sector* (Boston: Allyn and Bacon, 1984), p. 87. Figures are for 1980. These figures are somewhat misleading in that perhaps 40 to 50 percent of cities and counties lack full-time personnel directors; typically, other functionaries, such as city and county managers or department heads add the duties of personnel director to those that they already have. See: Office of Personnel Management as cited in *ibid.*

[81] The following information was gleaned from Myron D. Fottler and Norman A. Townsend, "Characteristics of Public and Private Personnel Directors," *Public Personnel Management*, 6 (July/August 1977), p. 252; American Society of Personnel Administrators, *The Personnel Executive's Job* (Englewood Cliffs, N.J.: Prentice-Hall, 1977); and William A. Jones, "Occupational Perceptions of Federal Personnel Admin-

istrators in a Regional City," *Public Personnel Management*, 5 (January/February 1976), pp. 52–58.

[82] Commission on Executive, Legislative, and Judicial Salaries, *High Quality Leadership: Our Government's Most Precious Asset* (Washington, D.C.: Commission on Executive, Legislative, and Judicial Salaries, 1987).

[83] Task Force on the Senior Executive Service, Twentieth Century Fund, *The Government's Managers* (New York: Priority Press, 1987). See Also: Task Force on Pay and Compensation, *Report of the Task Force on Pay and Compensation to the National Commission on the Public Service* (Washington, D.C.: National Commission on the Public Service, 1989). The Task Force found (p. 206) that "From 1970 to 1987, the cost of living as measured by the Consumer Price Index increased by 183 percentage points; pay for white-collar workers in the private sector increased 165 points, and pay for federal white-collar work increased 124 points."

[84] U.S. General Accounting Office, as cited in Bennett Minton, "GAO Study Confirms Pay Gap," *Federal Times* (June 11, 1990). Most of the federal jobs compared were in the lowest ranges, GS 1 to GS 7, although some positions were as high as GS-13. Data available for 1988 were analyzed.

[85] Merit Systems Protection Board, as cited in J. Jennings Moss, "Higher Pay Cited as Top Lure by Civil Servants Who Quit," *Washington Times* (May 30, 1990). The reasons cited most frequently for resigning after pay and advancement concerns were organizational management concerns, with 17 percent—a distant second.

[86] Jeanne Saddler, "Panel Recommends Large Pay Increase for U.S. Officials," *Wall Street Journal* (December 16, 1986).

[87] "Even Bureaucrats Deserve a Raise," *Business Week* (January 26, 1987), p. 26.

[88] Judith Havemann, "Presidents Seem Bashful About Managers' Bonuses," *Washington Post* (May 7, 1986).

[89] "Federal Pay: Better at the Top," *The Economist* (January 10, 1987), p. 35.

[90] U.S. General Accounting Office, *Training Budgets: Agency Budget Reductions in Response to the Balanced Budget Act* (Washington, D.C.: U.S. General Accounting Office, 1986), p. 2. The GAO's analysis of fifty-six federal agencies in Fiscal Year 1986 found that forty-two of them cut training budgets in an effort to comply with the Deficit Control Act (*i.e.*, the Gramm-Rudman-Hollings Balanced Budget Act), and that thirty of the agencies cut their training budgets by 10 percent or more, even though the Act required a reduction of only 4.3 percent.

[91] Joseph W. Whorton, Jr., Frank K., Gibson, and Delmer D. Dunn, "The Culture of University Public Service: A National Survey of the Perspectives of Users and Providers," *Public Administration Review*, 46 (January/February 1986), pp. 39–40. Seventy-nine percent of local administrators and 80 percent of state administrators reported using universities for assistance of some sort at least once over the last three years. Two-hundred forty local executives responded (a 55 percent response rate), and 198 state officials in all states (a 66 percent response rate). See also: James D. Slack, "Information, Training, and Assistance Needs of Municipal Governments," *Public Administra-*

tion Review, 50 (July/August 1990), p. 453. Sixty-eight percent of 500 mayors and city managers who received Slack's questionnaire responded. Forty-nine percent of the respondents said that they had been contacted by universities regarding training services.

[92] John F. Kennedy, quoted in E. J. Dionne, Jr., "Can A Renaissance Pull Government Service Out of the Doldrums?" *Washington Post* (August 3, 1990).

[93] Human Technology, Inc., *The Future Environment for Federal Workforce Training and Development: An Analysis of Long-Term Trends and Their Impacts*. Report to the U.S. Office of Personnel Management. (McLean, Va.: Human Technology, 1986), p. 9.

[94] Steven Kelman, quoted in Dionne, "Can A Renaissance Pull Government Service Out of the Doldrums?"

[95] Merit Systems Protection Board, as cited in Judith Havemann, "Employer Survey Reports a Drain in Quality." *Washington Post* (June 26, 1990). The Merit Systems Protection Board surveyed 15,939 federal workers at all levels in 1990. A comparable survey by the Board conducted in 1986 also found large numbers of federal supervisors who believed that the quality of applicants had declined.

[96] Constance Horner, as quoted in Judith Havemann, "New Federal Job Exams Set for June," *Washington Post* (April 22, 1990).

[97] Carolyn Ban and Patricia W. Ingraham, "Retaining Quality Federal Employees: Life After PACE," *Public Administration Review*, 48 (May/June 1988), pp. 708–725.

[98] Lana Stein, "Merit Systems and Political Influence: The Case of Local Government," *Public Administration Review*, 47 (May/June, 1987), p. 267; and Couturier, "The Quiet Revolution in Public Personnel Laws."

[99] Frank J. Thompson, *Personnel Policy in the City: The Politics of Jobs in Oakland* (Berkeley: University of California Press, 1975), p. 106.

[100] E. S. Savas and Sigmund G. Ginsburg, "The Civil Service: A Meritless System?" *The Public Interest*, 32 (Summer 1973), p. 76. Emphasis is in original.

[101] *Ibid.*, p. 77. Emphasis is in original.

[102] Ivar Berg, with the assistance of Sherry Gorelick, *Education and Jobs: The Great Training Robbery* (Boston: Beacon Press, 1977), p. 107.

[103] Commission on Organization of the Executive Branch of the Government, *Personnel Management: A Report to the Congress* (Washington, D.C.: U.S. Government Printing Office, 1949).

[104] For a thoughtful statement on federal "riffing," see: U.S. Merit Systems Protection Board, *The RIF System in the Federal Government: Is It Working and What Can Be Done to Improve It?* (Washington, D.C.: U.S. Office of Merit Systems Reviews and Studies, 1983).

[105] For a description of the Fitzgerald episode, see Barbara Newman, "The Cost of Courage," and A. Ernest Fitzgerald, "Fitzgerald on Fitzhugh," in *Blowing the Whistle: Dissent in the Public Interest*, Charles Peters and Taylor Branch, eds. (New York: Praeger, 1972), pp. 195–206 and 207–221.

[106] N. R. Kleinfield, "The Whistle Blowers' Morning After," *New York Times* (January 19, 1986).

[107] *Ibid.*

[108] Unpublished study by Karen L. Soeken and Donald R. Soeken, "A Survey of Whistleblowers: Their Stressors and Coping Strategies," 1987, as reported in: Clyde H. Farnsworth, "Survey of Whistle Blowers Finds Retaliation but Few Regrets," *New York Times* (February 22, 1987). Soeken and Soeken sent questionnaires to 233 individuals and obtained a response rate of 40 percent. A comparable, though more anecdotal, survey of fifty-five whistle blowers was conducted by Myron Peretz Glazer and Penina Migdal Glazer, *The Whistleblowers: Exposing Corruption in Government and Industry* (New York: Basic Books, 1989).

[109] Philip H. Jos, Mark E. Tompkins, and Steven W. Hays, "In Praise of Difficult People: A Portrait of the Committed Whistleblower," *Public Administration Review*, 49 (November/December 1989), p. 554. Questionnaires were sent to 329 whistleblowers, and a response rate of 56 percent was obtained. A particularly thorough bibliography of whistleblowing appears on pp. 560–561 of the article.

[110] *Ibid.*, p. 555.

[111] Quoted in Farnsworth, "Survey of Whistle Blowers Finds Retaliation but Few Regrets."

[112] Soeken and Soeken, "A Survey of Whistleblowers." Other surveys show essentially the same personal characteristics.

[113] Jos, Tompkins, and Hays, "In Praise of Difficult People," p. 556.

[114] *Ibid.*, p. 557. See also: Marcia P. Miceli, Bonnie L. Roach, and Janet P. Near, "The Motivations of Anonymous Whistleblowers: The Case of Federal Employees," *Public Personnel Management*, 17 (Fall 1988), pp. 281–296.

[115] Jos, Tompkins, and Hays, "In Praise of Difficult People," p. 555.

[116] O. Glenn Stahl, *Public Personnel Administration*, 7th ed. (New York: Harper & Row, 1976), p. 309. All other references to Stahl are to the eighth edition (1983) of this work.

[117] Stahl, *Public Personnel Administration*, p. 158.

[118] Thompson, *Personnel Policy in the City*, pp. 142–143.

[119] Herbert Kaufman, *The Forest Ranger* (Baltimore, Md.: Johns Hopkins University Press, 1960), p. 158.

[120] Thompson, *Personnel Policy in the City*, p. 156.

[121] Congressional Budget Office study, as cited in Mike Causey, "What Is the Quit Rate?" *Washington Post* (March 12, 1986). The federal quit rate is a subject of hot political dispute in Washington's bureaucratic circles. For a description of it and why, see the third edition (1986) of this book, p. 241.

[122] Thompson, *Personnel Policy in the City*, p. 161.

[123] Charles S. Rhyne, "The Letter of the Law," *Public Management*, 57 (November 1975), pp. 9–11.

[124] *Ibid.*

[125] Victor A. Thompson, *Without Sympathy or Enthusiasm: The Problem of Administrative Compassion* (University, Ala.: The University of Alabama Press, 1975), p. 79.

[126] John M. Capozzola, "Affirmative Action Alive and Well Under Courts' Strict Scrutiny," *National Civic Review*, 75 (November/December 1986), pp. 355–357.

[127] *Ibid.*, p. 355.

[128] John Nalbandian, "The U.S. Supreme Court's 'Consensus' on Affirmative Action," *Public Administration Review*, 49 (January/February 1989), p. 39.

[129] Vernon R. Taylor, "Cultural Bias in Testing: An Action Program," *Public Personnel Review*, 29 (July 1968), p. 170.

[130] Stein, "Merit Systems and Political Influence," p. 267. Police positions are the highest scorer in this regard, with nearly 97 percent of large cities reporting that they use written tests for determining hires in the police field, followed by positions in fire departments and clerical jobs; the lowest use of written examinations (15 percent) is for positions as sanitation workers. About 45 percent of the cities use written tests for entry-level professional positions. Stein sent questionnaires to personnel departments in 172 cities with 100,000 people or more, and obtained a response rate of 86 percent. Data are for 1986.

[131] "Local Government Recruitment and Selection Practices," *Municipal Year Book, 1986* (Washington, D.C.: International Management Association, 1986), p. 47. Questionnaires were mailed to 850 cities and counties with 50,000 people or more. The response rate was 41 percent. Data are for 1984 and 1985.

[132] Stein, "Merit Systems and Political Influence," p. 267.

[133] Evelina R. Moulder, "Affirmative Action: The Role Local Governments Are Playing," *Municipal Year Book, 1986* (Washington, D.C: International Management Association, 1986), p. 26. Questionnaires were mailed to 850 cities and counties with more than 50,000 people. The response rate was 41 percent. Data are for 1984 and 1985.

[134] Jean Couturier, "Court Attacks on Testing: Death Knell or Salvation for the Civil Service System," *Good Government*, 88 (Winter 1971), p. 12.

[135] Couturier, "The Quiet Revolution in Public Personnel Laws."

[136] In 1984, the median weekly earnings of all full-time wage and salary workers who were blacks were 78 percent of the median weekly earnings of whites. These percentages are derived from data presented in: U.S. Bureau of the Census, *Statistical Abstract of the United States, 1986*, p. 419, Table 704. In 1987, full-time working women's earnings were about two-thirds of those of men, and men who had graduated only from high school earned almost $2,000 more per year than did women who had graduated from college. See: Women's Research and Education Institute, *The American Woman, 1990–91*, as cited in Spencer Rich, "Women's Pay Still Far Behind Men's, Group Reports," *Washington Post* (April 26, 1990).

[137] Clarence M. Pendleton, Jr., quoted in: Associated Press, "Rights Panel Chief Scoffs at Idea of Comparable Pay for Women," *New York Times* (November 17, 1984).

[138] Constance Horner, quoted in Mike Causey, "Comparable Worth Plans," *Washington Post* (April 22, 1987).

[139] The following discussion is drawn from: Keon S. Chi, "Comparable Worth: Implications of the Washington Case," *State Government*, 57 (No. 2, 1984), pp. 34–45; and Keon S.

Chi, "Comparable Worth in State Governments," *State Government News*, 27 (November 1984), pp. 4–6.

[140] Peter T. Kilborn, "Wage Gaps Between Sexes Is Cut In Test, but at a Price," *New York Times* (May 31, 1990).

[141] *Ibid.*

[142] James E. Campbell and Gregory B. Lewis, "Public Support for Comparable Worth in Georgia," *Public Administration Review*, 46 (September/October 1986), pp. 432–437; and Mark A. Emmert, "Public Opinion of Comparable Worth: Some Preliminary Findings," *Review of Public Personnel Administration*, 6 (Fall 1985), pp. 69–75.

[143] Seymour Martin Lipset and William Schneider, "An Emerging National Consensus," *The New Republic* (October 15, 1977), p. 8. Emphasis is in original.

[144] *Ibid.*, p. 9. See also Lindsey Gruson, "Survey Finds 73% Oppose Racial Quotas in Hiring," *New York Times* (September 25, 1983).

[145] Lipset and Schneider, "An Emerging National Consensus," p. 9. Figures are for 1975.

[146] The following examples of "reverse passing" are in: "Disadvantaged Groups, Individual Rights," *The New Republic* (October 15, 1977), p. 7; and Eliot Marshall, "Race Certification," in *ibid.*, p. 19.

[147] Thompson, *Personnel Policy in the City*, pp. 112–130.

[148] *Ibid.*, p. 120.

[149] *Ibid.*, p. 136.

[150] Robert J. Huntley and Robert J. McDonald, "Urban Managers: Organizational Preferences, Managerial Styles, and Social Policy Roles," *Municipal Year Book, 1975* (Washington, D.C.: International City Management Association, 1975), p. 157. Emphasis has been added. Data are for 1974.

[151] Moulder, "Affirmative Action," p. 25.

[152] *Ibid.*, p. 26, for 1984–1985 data; and Huntley and McDonald, "Urban Managers," p. 154, for 1974 data.

[153] James D. Slack, "Affirmative Action and City Managers: Attitudes Toward Recruitment of Women," *Public Administration Review*, 47 (March/April 1987) pp. 202–203. Two-hundred ninety city managers responded to the survey. Data are for 1985.

[154] Stein, "Merit Systems and Political Influence," p. 270.

[155] Cynthia S. Ross and Robert E. England, "State Governments' Sexual Harassment Policy Initiatives," *Public Administration Review*, 47 (May/June 1987), p. 261. Data are for 1985.

[156] See, for example, Slack, "Affirmative Action and City Managers," p. 204.

[157] Stein, "Merit Systems and Political Influence," p. 270. Data are for 1986.

[158] As derived from U.S. Bureau of the Census, *Statistical Abstract of the United States, 1990*, p. 300, Table 488, and U.S. Bureau of the Census, *Statistical Abstract of the United States, 1982–83* (Washington, D.C.: U.S. Government Printing Office, 1982), p. 305, Table 504.

[159] *Ibid.*

[160] Nelson C. Dometrius and Lee Sigelman, "Assessing Progress Toward Affirmative Action Goals in State and Local Governments: A New Benchmark," *Public Administration Review*, 44 (May/June 1984), pp. 241–246. Data are for 1980.

[161] *Ibid.*, pp. 244–245.

[162] U.S. Department of Labor, as cited in Robert A. Rankin, "Changing Demographics May Make Affirmative Action Moot in 1990s," *Philadelphia Inquirer* (July 1, 1990).

[163] Audrey Freedman, quoted in *ibid.*

[164] U.S. Department of Labor, as cited in *ibid.* See also: Hudson Institute, *Workforce 2000* (Indianapolis, Indiana: Hudson Institute, 1987).

[165] U.S. Bureau of the Census, *Statistical Abstract of the United States, 1982–83*, p. 410, Table 683. Figures are for 1978.

[166] U.S. Bureau of the Census, *Statistical Abstract of the United States, 1990*, p. 419, Table 689. Figure is for 1988.

[167] Judith Havemann, "Federal Relations Marred by Increasing Strife," *Washington Post* (May 31, 1987).

[168] James W. Singer, "The Limited Power of Federal Worker Unions," *National Journal*, 10 (September 30, 1978), pp. 1547–1551.

[169] U.S. Bureau of the Census, *Statistical Abstract of the United States, 1986*, p. 425, Table 714. Figures are for 1982.

[170] *Ibid.* Figure is for 1982.

[171] *Ibid.*, p. 423, Table 712; U.S. Bureau of the Census, *Statistical Abstract of the United States, 1990*, p. 418, Table 687; and Havemann, "Federal Labor Relations Marred by Increasing Strife." Data are for 1983, except data on federal unions, which are for 1987, and data on the U.S. Postal Service, which are for 1989.

[172] Hugh O'Neill, "The Growth of Municipal Employee Unions," in *Unionization of Municipal Employees*, Robert H. Connery and William V. Farr, eds. (New York: Academy of Political Science, 1970), p. 4.

[173] U.S. Bureau of the Census, *Statistical Abstract of the United States, 1986*, p. 298, Table 487. Figures are for 1982, except for the number of states that have collective bargaining policies, which is for 1985. See: John Thomas Delaney and Raymond D. Horton, "Managing Relations with Organized Employees," in *Handbook of Public Administration*, James L. Perry, ed., (San Francisco: Jossey-Bass, 1989), p. 439.

[174] Sam Zagoria, "Attitudes Harden in Governmental Labor Relations," *ASPA News and Views*, 26 (December, 1976), pp. 1, 21, and 22.

[175] Marvin J. Levine, "The Status of State 'Sunshine Bargaining' Laws," *Labor Law Journal* (November, 1980), p. 713.

[176] Delaney and Horton, "Managing Relations with Organized Employees," p. 439.

[177] Llewellyn M. Toulmin, "The Treasure Hunt: Budget Search Behavior by Public Employee Unions," *Public Administration Review*, 48 (March/April 1988), pp. 620–630.

[178] Sterling Spero and John M. Capozzola, *The Urban Community and Its Unionized Bureaucracy* (New York: Dunellen, 1973), p. 218.

[179] *Ibid.*, p. 219.

[180] Stephen H. Perloff, "Comparing Municipal Salaries with Industry and Federal Pay," *Monthly Labor Review*, 94 (October, 1971), pp. 46–50; and Spero and Capozzolla, *The Urban Community*, pp. 219–220. The study was conducted in 1971.

[181] Charles N. Rehmus and Evan Wilner, *The Economic Results of Teacher Bargaining: Michigan's First Two Years* (Ann Arbor, Mich.: Institute of Labor and Industrial Relations, 1958).

[182] R. W. Schmenner, "The Determination of Municipal Employee Wages," *The Review of Economics and Statistics* (February, 1973), as cited in Anthony H. Pascal, "The Hidden Costs of Collective Bargaining in Local Government," *Taxing and Spending*, 2 (Spring, 1980), as reprinted in Barry Bozeman and Jeffrey Straussman, eds., *New Directions in Public Administration* (Monterey, Calif.: Brooks/Cole, 1984), p. 258.

[183] Pascal, "The Hidden Costs of Collective Bargaining in Local Government," p. 259.

[184] *Ibid.*, pp. 260–261.

[185] "Now the Belt Tightens on Public Employees Too," *U.S. News and World Report* (July 26, 1982), pp. 59–60.

[186] An example of this conflict is provided by O. Glenn Stahl, a distinguished scholar and practitioner of public personnel administration who is as staunch a defender of the merit principle in American government as one is likely to find today. Stahl writes that a policy of affirmative action "discourages achievement and puts a premium on that attitude that effort is unnecessary to win a job—neither of which conditions bodes any good for the quality of American life....We cannot expect a miraculous transformation [of the civil service system] overnight." See: O. Glenn Stahl, "A Fair Look at Fair Employment," *Public Employment Practices Bulletin*, 1971. The *Bulletin* was published by the International Personnel Management Association.

PART FOUR: Implementation

CHAPTER

10

APPROACHES TO PUBLIC POLICY AND ITS IMPLEMENTATION

The area of public policy, like the field of public administration itself, has had an ambivalent intellectual evolution. Public policy exists in both political science and public administration, but in different guises. Whatever its form, however, public policy is what public administrators execute, and it provides a fitting introduction to this section on implementation.

THE EVOLUTION OF PUBLIC POLICY ANALYSIS: PUBLIC ADMINISTRATION VERSUS POLITICAL SCIENCE

Occurring concurrently with the evolution of "self-aware" public administration was the development of the subfield of "public policy" within political science departments. And the subfield emerged for many of the same reasons that motivated public administration to secede from political science, particularly the concern shared by some political scientists that their field was far more concerned with science than politics. One of the early contributors to the public policy subfield, Austin Ranney, put it well: "at

least since 1945 most American political scientists have focused their professional attention mainly on the *processes* by which public policies are made and have shown relatively little concern with their *contents*."[1] Ranney and his colleagues took issue with this emphasis, and believed that a more substantive approach was needed. From its beginnings, in short, public policy has been an effort to "apply" political science to public affairs; its inherent sympathies with the "practical" field of public administration are real, and many of those scholars who identify with the public policy subfield find themselves in a twilight zone between political science and public administration.

Perhaps the first formal recognition by political scientists of the importance of public policy was a small meeting held in 1965 under the auspices of the Committee on Governmental and Legal Processes of the Social Science Research Council. Out of this meeting emerged "a consensus that the most timely and urgent question...is: What professional expertise and obligations, if any, have political scientists to study, evaluate, and make recommendations about the contents of public policy?"[2] Two committee-sponsored conferences on the question followed in 1966 and 1967, and the papers presented at them were published in the following year.[3]

Also in 1967, the American Political Science Association's Annual Conference featured a panel on public policy under its "American Politics" section, and four papers on public policy were presented at the meeting. In 1970, the Association granted public policy its first section at its annual conference; by now the number of papers on the topic exceeded thirty. By 1982, 140 papers on public policy analysis were given at the annual meeting, involving thirty-six panels,[4] and now public policy presentations are routine in political science circles.

Public policy was even more popular among political scientists than the proliferating presentations of papers on the topic indicate. During this period the Policy Studies Organization was founded (in 1972), and it provided additional outlets for political scientists interested in public policy—within a decade of its creation, the organization had more than 2,000 members. The Policy Studies Organization publishes *Policy Studies Review*, which reflects a more public administration hue, and *Policy Studies Journal*, which casts a longer shadow in political science. But the organization's membership appears to be dominated by political scientists—more than two-thirds are political scientists.[5]

The Policy Studies Organization, of course, is not the only association of scholars with an interest in public policy. The Association for Public Policy Analysis and Management, the American Institute for Decision Sciences, and the Public Choice Society are examples of others, and there are more. But most of these groups have an intellectual cast that is distinctly economic or operations research in nature.

An important component of the public policy subfield is comparative, or cross-national, public policy. The specialization began to emerge in the early 1970s, and in 1975 a book on the topic received the Gladys M. Kammerer Award from the American Political Science Association.[6] More than a quarter of the public policy papers presented at the annual conferences of the American Political Science Association are in the comparative area.[7]

Public policy as a subfield can be viewed as bisecting along two, increasingly distinct, intellectual branches. One is the substantive branch. The dominant mode of public policy as a subfield of political science has always been and continues to be substantive issues—what Ranney called "contents," and what Herbert Simon, years earlier, called "prescribing for public policy" (recall Chapter 2). Roughly half of the papers presented at the American Political Science Association's annual conferences in any given year deal with substance, such as the environment, welfare, education, or energy. The journals and papers published by the Policy Studies Organization also reflect this substantive bias. Paramountly, the substantive branch of public policy means a paper, article, book, or course on "The Politics of" some current issue.

The other, less leafy but nonetheless supple branch of public policy, is the theoretical branch. Susan B. Hansen has usefully categorized the literature constituting this branch (which she calls "three promising theoretical trends") in terms of political economy, organization theory, and program evaluation and implementation.[8] There are, of course, other ways in which this literature may be categorized, and we use a different, more detailed system of categories in this chapter.

The "problem" of public policy as a subfield of political science is what it symbolizes for both political science and public administration.

First, political scientists and public administrationists seem to have different definitions of what they are doing in the subfield and why. Those public policy researchers who identify primarily with political science seem to be those who, by and large, work on the subfield's substantive branch ("The Politics of" something), whereas those who identify with public administration seem to be found more frequently on its theoretical branch, and are more concerned with problems of research design, public choice, strategic planning, implementation, organization, program evaluation, efficiency, effectiveness, productivity, and those kinds of public policy questions that are only incidentally related to matters of substance and content. The differences in these two approaches parallel the differences that the field of public administration has with political science: public administrationists have always preferred studying questions of public policy that relate to "knowledgeable action" as opposed to an "intellectualized understanding" of public issues.

Of these two approaches to the study of public policy, the future seems fairer for that preferred by public administrationists. While there will always be both room and need for each tack, the substantive one has a deadly deficiency in the longer haul: it is, by dint of its structure, essentially atheoretical. One cannot "build" theory on the basis of ultimately transitory public events. True, there will "always" be public policies for health, energy, environment, welfare, or whatever, but how does understanding these issues as discrete phenomena get us very far in understanding the process of public policy—its formulation, execution, and ongoing revision—so that we can develop ideas that enable us to make more responsive policies in all areas and deliver them more effectively? Individual studies of individual public issues often yield us an appreciation of the issues involved, and this is important and useful; but aside from their utility as case histories, these studies by themselves cannot really address the larger theoretical questions, the answers to which can, one hopes, be of use to public decision makers regardless of the policy arena in which they are making policies.

A more worrisome aspect of political science's preference for the substantive approach to policy studies is that its intellectual evolution will parallel the experience of comparative public administration in that it will try to do too much, and will end up, to requote Robert T. Golembiewski on the dilemma of comparative public administration, creating "a self-imposed failure experience...an unattainable goal."[9] Certainly this dreary prospect at least seems possible when we appreciate the number of public policies extant, all of them fairly panting to be analyzed, and the problem is especially evident in the area of comparative public policy. The literature of comparative public policy is heavily substantive,[10] but as Elliot J. Feldman points out, the specialty has yet to develop a "guiding theory" of its own to focus research.[11]

A second problem of public policy analysis in its political science mode is that it smacks of an effort by political scientists to fill the vacuum created by the departure of public administration—a last gasp, croaked in the general direction of "hands-on" political science and, of course, "relevance." In this fashion, political science, symbolically at least, retains public administration without admitting it. The fact that the explosive growth of the public policy subfield correlates remarkably in time (*i.e.*, the 1970s) with the secession of public administration lends some credence to this notion. Figure 10-1 illustrates some rough measures of this relationship.

There is nothing sinister in this effort to reestablish within political science a concern with what is "applied" and "relevant" under a new guise called public policy, but if this is the motivation, then it seems unlikely to succeed. Public policy in its substantive mode may not be, as we have noted, a vehicle ready for long journeys. It is no replacement for public administration. An understanding of education policy, for example, is no substitute for an understanding of human resource management, public budgeting and finance, organization theory, intergovernmental administration, program evaluation and the several other interrelated areas that compose the public administration field.

In this chapter we review the literature of public policy that relates to public administration because it provides a logical introduction to our section on implementation. We bisect the literature into two broad streams. The first is the attempt to analyze the *process* of public policy making and implementation; it endeavors to be descriptive rather than prescriptive in tone. In terms of models of public policy, the elite/mass, group, systems, institutionalist, neo-institutionalist, and "streams and windows" models would fall crudely under the rubric of processually oriented, descriptive literature on public policy making.

The second stream attempts to analyze the *outputs* and *effects* of public policy, and it is more prescriptive than descriptive. A related tangent is the effort to prescribe ways to improve the content of public policy by improving the way public policy is made. Using these schemata, the incremental, rational, and strategic planning models of public policymaking represent this thrust.

In reviewing briefly both the processual and the output-oriented thrusts of public policy analysis, our purpose is simply that: to review. One ought to be aware of public policy analysis as a literature. Public policy is a broad field whose principal utility is one of clarification about how the public policymaking and implementation process works.

FIGURE 10-1 Growth of Autonomous Public Affairs/Administration Academic Units,[*]
1973–85, and Public Policy Papers Presented, APSA Conferences, 1967–82, Selected Years

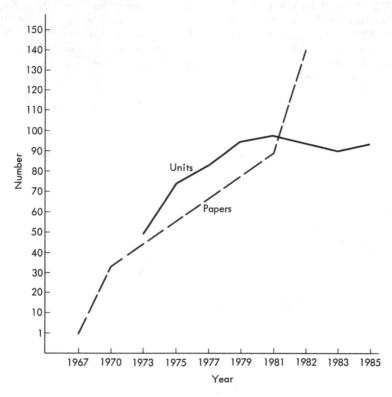

[*]*Note*: Autonomous academic units are those departments and schools of public affairs or public administration that report to a dean or vice-president in a university.

Source: For data on public affairs/administration units, *Directory: Programs in Public Affairs and Administration, 1973, 1975, 1977, 1979, 1981, 1983, and 1985* (Washington, D.C.: National Association of Schools of Public Affairs and Administration). For data on public policy papers presented at the annual conferences of the American Political Science Association, Susan B. Hansen, "Public Policy Analysis: Some Recent Developments and Current Problems," in Ada W. Finifter, ed., *Political Science: The State of the Discipline* (Washington, D.C.: The American Political Science Association, 1983), pp. 218–219.

MODELS OF PUBLIC POLICYMAKING AND IMPLEMENTATION AS A PROCESS

The Elite/Mass Model

Of the six emphases we shall consider under this heading (elite/mass, group, systems, institutionalist, neo-institutionalist, and "streams and windows"), the emphasis represented by the elite/mass model may be among the most germane to public administrators. Increasingly, public administrators appear

to be perceived less as "servants of the people" and more as "the establishment." In cursory form the elite/mass model contends that a policy-making/policy-executing elite is able to act in an environment characterized by apathy and information distortion and thereby govern a largely passive mass. Policy flows downward from the elite to the mass. Society is divided according to those who have power and those who do not. Elites share common values that differentiate them from the mass, and prevailing public policies reflect elite values, which may be summed up as: preserve the status quo. Finally, elites have higher incomes, more education, and more status than the mass. Perhaps the classic expression of elite theory can be found in C. Wright Mills's *The Power Elite*.[12]

A diagrammatic version of the elite/mass model that relates it to public administration is found in Figure 10-2.

The Group Model

A second model of public policy is the group model. In these days of questionable campaign contributions, powerful vested interests, and the "military-industrial complex," the notion of pressure groups and lobbies also has relevance. Another way of describing the group model is the "hydraulic thesis," in which the polity is conceived of as being a system of forces and pressures acting and reacting to one another in the formulation of public policy. An exemplary work that represents the group model is Arthur F. Bentley's *The Process of Government*.[13]

Normally, the group model is associated with the legislature rather than the bureaucracy, but it also has long been recognized by scholars that the "neutral" executive branch of government is buffeted by pressure groups, too. The numerous studies by political scientists on federal regulatory agencies, for example, all point to the same conclusion: The agency ultimately is "captured" by the group that it is meant to regulate, and its administrators grow increasingly unable to distinguish between policies that are beneficial to the interests of the public and policies that are beneficial to the interests of the groups being regulated. What is good for the group is good for the nation, in the eyes of the regulators. An excellent overview of this phenomenon is provided by Louis M. Kohlmeier's *The Regulators*,[14] and a superb theoretical explanation of why it works the way it does can be found in Murray Edelman's *The Symbolic Uses of Politics*.[15] Figure 10-3 illustrates the group model.

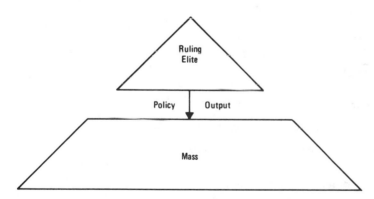

FIGURE 10-2 The Elite/Mass Model of Public Policy Making and Implementation

FIGURE 10-3 The Group Model of Public Policy Making and Implementation: I

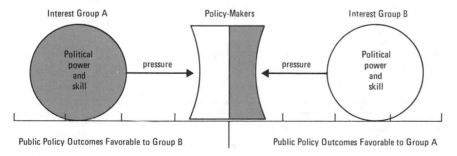

Bureaucracies, particularly in regulatory agencies, seldom encounter the countervailing pressures illustrated in Figure 10-3. In other words, Interest Group A might be the drug manufacturers, the Policy Makers might be the Food and Drug Administration, and Interest Group B might be the unorganized public. This situation might be diagrammed more accurately by Figure 10-4.

The Systems Model

A third emphasis in the processual public-policy literature is the systems model. The systems model relies on concepts of information theory (*e.g.*, feedback, input, output) and conceives of the process as being essentially cyclical.

The systems model is concerned with such questions as: What are the significant variables and patterns in the public policy-making system?

What constitutes the "black box" of the actual policymaking process? What are the inputs, "with inputs," outputs, and feedback of the process? A representative author of this literary stream is David Easton, particularly his *The Political System*.[16] The emphasis is diagrammed in Figure 10-5.

The Institutionalist Model

We include in the public-policymaking-as-a-process literature the traditional institutionalist model. The institutionalist model focuses on the organization chart of government; it describes the arrangements and official duties of bureaus and departments, but customarily it has ignored the linkages between them. Constitutional provisions, administrative and common law, and similar legalities are the objects of greatest interest; the behavioral connections between a department and the

FIGURE 10-4 The Group Model of Public Policy Making and Implementation: II

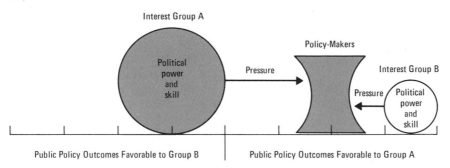

FIGURE 10-5 The Systems Model of Public Policy Making and Implementation

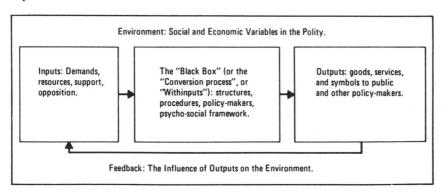

public policy emanating from it are of scant concern. Carl J. Friedrich's *Constitutional Government and Democracy* is a representative work.[17] Illustratively, an institutionalist model would look like the diagram in Figure 10-6.

With the onrush of the "behavioral revolution" in political science, institutional studies of the policy process were swept aside in favor of studies that relied more heavily on the group, systems, and elite/mass models, in about that order of emphasis. Yet the institutionalist model had a use, and it may experience a resurgence of favor in the future. The "new federalism" and executive reorganization plans, among the other actual and potential rearrangements of the government bureaucracy, necessitate a renewed understanding of how the structure of government works before the public policy-making process can be analyzed fully.

The Neo-Institutionalist Model

Despite a possible reemergence of institutionalist theory, however, a recent stream of public policy literature has surfaced that might best be described as neo-institutionalism, and it rests on a considerably more sophisticated analytical plane. Theodore J. Lowi, Randall B. Ripley, Grace Franklin, Robert Salisbury and John Heinz, Dean Schooler, Jr., and Michael Hayes, number among its major contributors, and they attempt to categorize public policies according to policy-making subsystems.[18] For example, Lowi classifies policies by four "arenas of power": redistributive, distributive, constituent, and regulative.

In a *redistributive* arena of power, for instance, power is "redistributed" throughout the polity on a fundamental scale. Redistributive policies tend to be highly ideological and emotionally charged for particular groups, involving a fight between the "haves" and "have-nots," but having low partisan visibility. Usually they are centered in the bureaucracy. Lowi, in fact, considers redistributive policies to be concerned with "not use of property but property itself, not equal treatment but equal possession, not behavior but being," and believes, because of the secrecy enshrouding the redistributive policy process, that the policy process which takes place primarily in the government bureaucracy has received the least study by social scientists.[19]

Lowi's remaining policy arenas are less far-reaching in scope. A *distributive policy* is one in which benefits are made directly to individuals, but there are really no particularly visible costs associated with the policy. For example, various policies conducted by such agencies as the Weather Bureau and the Corps of Engineers implement distributive policies.

Regulative policies differ from distributive policies in that they are far more likely to be identified with costs to particular groups. Such agencies as the Federal Communications Commission and the Federal Aviation Administration are empowered to punish the violators of federal regulations, and their sanctions are both apparent and real.

A *constituent policy* is one that affects the people as political actors directly, such as a reapportionment statute. But constituent policies do not single out individuals for either punishments or rewards, and tend to reallocate political and economic values through the social structure itself.

Figure 10-7 diagrams the neo-institutionalist approach to public policymaking. As it indicates, the neo-institutionalist approach is predicated on two dimensions: the probability of coercion and the target of coercion. The *probability of coercion* may be remote or immediate. In the regulative

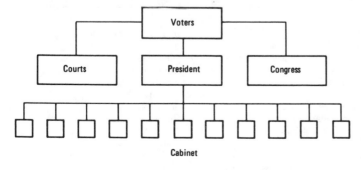

FIGURE 10-6 The Institutionalist Model of Public Policy Making and Implementation

policy arena, for example, the possibility of coercion is quite immediate because violators of federal regulations may be punished. Moreover, violators of federal regulations may be punished as individuals; a company violating the Sherman Antitrust Act, for example, will be punished as an individual company. Thus, we come to the *target of coercion*, which may be individual or systemic. In constituent and redistributive policy arenas, the government attempts to manipulate the conduct of the system itself through, for example, changes in the federal reserve discount rate, which can have a huge impact on the level of investments in the national economy. Yet these kinds of policies do not single out individuals as targets for coercion.

Lowi argues that from these policy arenas, which are determined by the target and probability of government coercion, emerge certain identifiable types of political behavior.[20] For example, distributive policies are more likely to combine electoral and decentralizing political tendencies, while, as we have noted, redistributive policies tend to have low

partisan visibility and to be highly centralized. Figure 10-7 also lists some of the political behaviors associated with each policy arena.

The neo-institutionalists, in sum, are concerned chiefly with political institutions, but with an eye toward generating theoretical predictions about how policy types relate to the branches of government, to the polity generally, and to the typologies of political behaviors associated with each policy arena.

The "Streams and Windows" Model

A final major model of public policymaking as a process is provided by John W. Kingdon.[21] Kingdon studied the agenda setting and policymaking process in two major fields, health and transportation, from 1976 through 1979. Over the four years, he conducted nearly 250 personal and detailed interviews. Kingdon applied to his empirical data the theoretical construct (with some slight variations) concerning "organized anarchies" developed by Michael Cohen, James

FIGURE 10-7 The Neo-Institutionalist Model of Public Policy Making and Implementation

		TARGET OF GOVERNMENT COERCION	
		Conduct of individual	*Conduct of system*
PROBABILITY OF GOVERNMENT COERCION	Remote	*Distributive* policy arena, e.g., agricultural subsidies *political behaviors and characteristics:* decentralized disaggregated local partisan/electoral logrolling legislatively centered	*Constituent* policy arena, e.g., reapportionment of legislature *political behaviors and characteristics:* centralized systemic national ideological partisan/electoral logrolling legislatively centered
	Immediate	*Regulative* policy arena, e.g., elimination of fraudulent advertising *political behaviors and characteristics:* decentralized disaggregated local special interests bargaining among groups bureaucratically centered	*Redistributive* policy arena, e.g., progressive income tax *political behaviors and characteristics:* centralized systemic national ideological special interests bargaining among groups bureaucratically centered

March, and Johan Olsen in 1972, and which was described in Chapter 4.

Kingdon observed three "streams" that, for the most part, flow independently of one another and which constituted the policy-making process. The first of these is the *problems stream*, which involves focusing the public's and policymakers' attention on a particular social problem, defining the problem, and either applying a new public policy to the resolution of the problem or letting the problem fade from sight. Getting attention for the problem may be accomplished by a number of processes: the routine monitoring of social data; the occurrence of certain "focusing events," such as a powerful symbol like Proposition 13 in California, which called national attention to the accelerating "tax revolt"; and the feedback from existing programs that can be obtained through such devices as congressional casework or the ongoing administration of public programs. Problems typically are defined in terms of *values*, such as conservative or liberal orientations; *comparisons*, such as the United States versus the Union of Soviet Socialist Republics; or *categories*—for example, is public transit for the handicapped a "transportation" problem or a "civil rights" problem? Categorizing the problem becomes quite significant in how the problem is resolved.

The second stream is the *political stream*. It is in the political stream that the *governmental agenda*—in other words, the list of issues or problems to be resolved—is formed. This formulation occurs as the result of the interaction of major forces: the "national mood"; the perspective and clout of organized interests; and the dynamics of government itself, including personnel turnover, the settling of jurisdictional disputes among agencies and branches, and so forth. The primary participants in the formulation of the governmental agenda are what Kingdon calls the "visible cluster," or those participants who are most readily seen on the public stage. They include the administration, including high-level political appointees and the president's staff; members of Congress; the media; interest groups; those actors associated with elections, parties, and campaigns; and general public opinion. A consensus is achieved by bargaining among these participants, and at some point a "bandwagon" or "tilt" effect occurs that is a consequence of an intensifying desire by the participants to be "dealt in" on the policy resolution and not to be excluded.

The third stream is the *policy stream*. It is in the policy stream that the *decision agenda* or "alternative specification" is formulated. The decision agenda is the list of alternatives from which a public policy may be selected by policymakers to resolve a problem. Here the major forces are not political, but intellectual and personal. Ideas and the role of the "policy entrepreneur," or the person who holds a deep and long-abiding commitment to a particular policy change, are paramount. The major participants in the formulation of the decision agenda are what Kingdon calls the "hidden cluster." These include career public administrators; academics; researchers and consultants; congressional staffers; the Office of Management and Budget; and interest groups (interest groups, in Kingdon's analysis, are significant actors in both the visible and hidden clusters).

The policy stream moves from the formulation of a decision agenda to a "softening-up phase" in which "trial balloons" are released and a variety of suggestions are made both publicly and privately about how to resolve a particular problem. These ideas survive according to the criteria of whether they are technically feasible; whether they are acceptable to broad social values; and what future constraints—such as budgetary limitations and the prospects of political acceptance and public acquiescence—are anticipated by the actors in the policy stream. Unlike the political stream, consensus (or the "short list" of policy alternatives) is developed not by a bargaining process, but by the use of persuasion and rational argumentation among the participants in the policy stream. As in the political stream, however, a "bandwagon" or "tilt" effect occurs, and this happens when problems can be connected with alternative solutions and the solutions themselves are not perceived as being "too new" or radical.

When these three streams—problem, political, and policy—meet, a public policy can result. Kingdon calls these occasions "windows." Windows open because of a change of administration, changes in Congress, a shift in the national mood, or when a pressing public problem emerges. When the window opens that results in a restructuring of the *governmental* agenda, it could be solely the result of occurrences in either the problem stream or the political stream. But for a window to open that results in a restructuring of the *decision* agenda, the joining of all three streams is required. In this latter case, the role of the policy entrepreneur is critical, and entrepreneurs must have legitimacy, connections, and persistence to be successful.

In many ways, Kingdon's analysis provides us with the single most satisfactory explanation of policymaking as a process. Although his analysis has limitations, it nonetheless is comprehensive, systemic, and empirical. This is a rare combination in the literature of public policy as a process, and it should not be dismissed lightly. Figure 10-8 is a simplified diagram of Kingdon's "streams and windows" model of public policymaking.

MODELS OF PUBLIC POLICYMAKING AND IMPLEMENTATION AS AN OUTPUT

Our second major thrust of public policy analysis tends to stress the policy itself. In this stream analysts appear to be more normative and prescriptive, and less "value-free" and descriptive. They are more concerned with how to improve the content of public policies themselves and how to improve the ways in which public policies are made, with the objective of forming better policies.

In the past there were only two models, incrementalism and rationalism. The former attempts to describe how the public policy-making process "really works" and what is good or bad about it; the latter explains how the process of incrementalism could or should work and offers suggestions toward this end. Thus, the incrementalist and rationalist models really are two poles of the same continuum; that is, they are both concerned with the "black box" of policymaking. More recently, "strategic planning" has emerged as an approach that occupies a place on the continuum midway between incrementalism and rationalism.

It is worth keeping in mind that neither the incrementalist nor the rationalist model of public policymaking is a particularly accurate description of the process of public policy formation. In his careful empirical analysis of the agenda-setting and policy-making process, Kingdon found that there were "as many nonincremental as incremental changes" in the policy processes that he studied.[22] What Kingdon meant by this, however, was

that some policies were changed or implemented very gradually and slowly over time, while others, after festering for years in the bowels of policymaking institutions, hit the public agenda virtually overnight and were rapidly put in place. But Kingdon's use of the term "nonincremental" does not mean that the policy-making process is rational. It merely means that the policy-making process can be quick. Hence, while public policy may not necessarily be made incrementally, neither is it necessarily made rationally.

The Incrementalist Model

In many ways, the incrementalist model of public policy already has been considered in Part Two on organization theory. "Satisficing," organizational "drift," "bounded rationality," and "limited cognition," among other terms of the literature of model synthesis in organization theory, reflect the basic idea of the incrementalist paradigm.

The various writings of Charles E. Lindblom are associated most closely with incrementalism and, in fact, it was he who is as responsible as anyone for the notion's name, *disjointed incrementalism*, as a description of the policy-making process.[23] *Disjointed*, in this context, means that analysis and evaluation of conditions and alternative responses to perceived conditions occur throughout society, while *incrementalism* means that only a limited selection of policy alternatives are provided to policymakers, and that each one of these alternatives represents only an infinitesimal change in the status quo.

Before Lindblom made the incrementalist idea more academically legitimate (and pompous) by dubbing it "disjointed incrementalism," he called the concept "muddling through."[24] Muddling through, as a term, not only is a more colorful description of the policy-making process, but is also clearer and self-explanatory.

Basically, the incrementalist model posits a conservative tendency in administrative decision making; new public policies are seen as being variations on the past. The public policymaker is perceived as a person who does not have the brains, time, and money to fashion truly different policies; he or she accepts the policies of the past as satisficing and legitimate. There are also certain "sunk

FIGURE 10-8 The Streams-and-Windows Model of Public Policy Making and Implementation

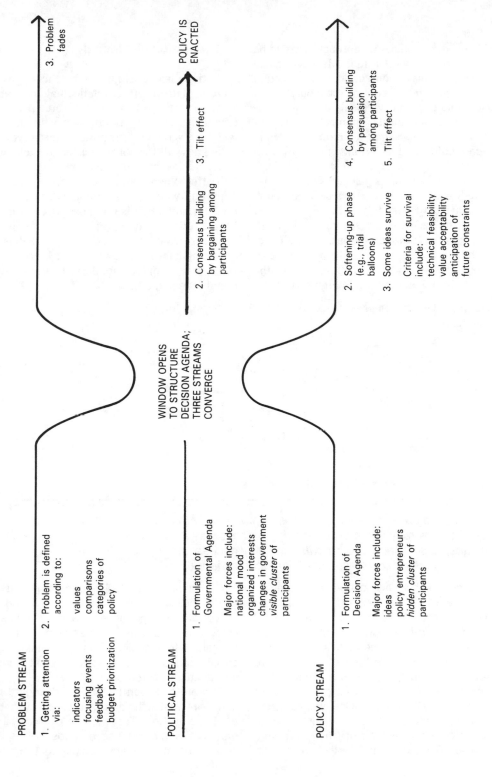

PROBLEM STREAM

1. Getting attention via:

   indicators
   focusing events
   feedback
   budget prioritization

2. Problem is defined according to:

   values
   comparisons
   categories of policy

3. Problem fades

WINDOW OPENS TO STRUCTURE DECISION AGENDA; THREE STREAMS CONVERGE

POLITICAL STREAM

1. Formulation of Governmental Agenda

   Major forces include:
   national mood
   organized interests
   changes in government
   visible cluster of participants

2. Consensus building by bargaining among participants

3. Tilt effect

POLICY IS ENACTED

POLICY STREAM

1. Formulation of Decision Agenda

   Major forces include:
   ideas
   policy entrepreneurs
   hidden cluster of participants

2. Softening-up phase (e.g., trial balloons)

3. Some ideas survive

   Criteria for survival include:
   technical feasibility
   value acceptability
   anticipation of future constraints

4. Consensus building by persuasion among participants

5. Tilt effect

costs" in existing policies that probably would be impossible to retrieve if a radically new course were taken, and this discourages innovative action from the standpoint of political economy. And because social goals are devilishly difficult to operationalize, an incremental approach is certainly an easier row to hoe than a rational, systemic approach would be. Finally, incrementalist policies are nearly always more politically expedient than are rationalist policies that necessitate fundamental redistributions of social values. As Ralph Huitt concluded in his study of political feasibility, "what is most feasible is incremental."[25] In short, there are reasons (*rational* reasons, given the nature of the political system) for the prevalence of the incrementalist model. An illustration of the incrementalist model is shown in Figure 10-9.

The Rationalist Model

Rationalism attempts to be the opposite of incrementalism. As an intellectual endeavor, rationalism tries to learn *all* the value preferences extant in a society, assign each value a relative weight, discover all the policy alternatives available, know all the consequences of each alternative, calculate how the selection of any one policy will affect the remaining alternatives in terms of opportunity costs, and ultimately select that policy alternative that is the most efficient in terms of the costs and benefits of social values. Whether or not these goals can be realized, the point is that the rational model works toward their achievement, and toward the reduction of non-rational incrementalism.

FIGURE 10-9 The Incrementalist Model of Public Policymaking and Implementation

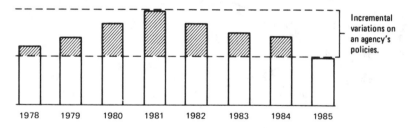

Public Administration and the Policy Process

The following passage attempts to "place" the role of the public bureaucracy in the policy-making process. As it indicates, to so "place" the bureaucracy may necessitate a basic reconsideration of traditional democratic theory.

It is remarkable how unappreciated the significance of the bureaucracy is among America's political thinkers. It is evident from reading *The Federalist* that the country's most original contributors to the world's political literature did not anticipate the rise of the public bureaucracy, much less its institutional dominance in the public policy-making process, nor the fact that by the middle of the twentieth century there would be more Americans earning their livelihoods by working for it than there were Americans living when the Constitution was writ-

ten. Less understandably, our current generation of political thinkers...also have failed to appreciate the importance of the public bureaucracy, despite its awesome magnitude, its growing administrative reliance on the techniques of social science, and its financial support of their own academic research,...

Is there a reason behind the disregard for and disinterest in the public bureaucracy that is exhibited by the bulk of modern political thinkers? One can conjure several possibilities, including that of rampant stupidity, but...I shall offer only one hypothesis. It is: The bureaucracy, as a public policy-making institution in a technological society, is antithetical to the pluralist paradigm of the democratic process originally conceived by James Madison and perpetrated by most of his intellectual progeny.... More pointedly, the Madisonian notion that the interests of the public will be best served in a democracy by the policy of compromise emerging from the contentions of interest groups (which "represent" those "publics" affected by the policy resolution) is of dubious validity in a techno-bureaucratic state. In brief, two overwhelming factors of modern culture—technology and bureaucracy—undermine what one political scientist has described as the "hydraulic theory" of the democratic process. The hydraulic thesis constitutes the basis of the pluralist paradigm shared by mainstream political scientists, and it is apparent, given the short shrift accorded the public bureaucracy, public administration, and technology assessment by political scientists as objects of study, that few scholars interested in politics are capable of denying interest-group pluralism as an apologia for how the public interest is achieved in a democracy.

Perhaps the hydraulic thesis still "works" (*i.e.*, interest group compromises are indeed in the public interest) in legislative and adjudicative policy settings, and perhaps its "provability" in these settings accounts for why political scientists much prefer studying voting behavior, legislative committees, lobbyists, and the judicial process in contrast to "bureaucratic politics." But in order to "work," the hydraulic thesis by necessity rests on at least three implicit assumptions concerning the political processes: that (1) all publics affected by a particular policy question are aware that its resolution will affect them, (2) all affected publics have a reasonable understanding of the policy question, and (3) if the affected publics are unaware of the policy question, it is only a matter of time before they find out about it and join in the policy-making fray in order to protect their interest.

These assumptions, combined with some strictly enforced rules of the game, such as freedom of the press, provided a rational foundation on which the hydraulic thesis could be constructed as an explanation of the policy-making process in a democracy—at least in the eighteenth century. Yet, in the twentieth century, the interlaced forces of bureaucracy and technology deny these assumptions. For its part, bureaucracy denies assumptions No. 1 and No. 3. The well-documented penchant of bureaucrats for secrecy, and the mounting evidence that neither bureaucrats nor the citizenry always act on their "most rational" self-interest, undercut the premises that people *know*, that people are *informed*, of what matters, and that they will act on what matters.

Technology denies assumption No. 2. Technology, or what is perceived by the people as being science "applied" for the rectification of their problems, is not simple. Technology is complicated, and it becomes more complicated when, as public bureaucrats are wont to do, technology is cast into the context of systems analysis in an effort to inhibit the proliferation of its socially dysfunctional side effects. Technology and its social assessment, by their very complexity, deny understanding to the people of what their problems are. Such concepts as "technocracy," "professionalism," "politics of expertise," "technipol," "systems politics," "noetic authority," and "participatory technology" represent intellectual efforts to address the enormous political problems of bureaucracy and technology not considered in the Madisonian pluralist paradigm—nor, for that matter, in the Constitution that Madison largely wrote. Yet, if democratic political processes are to be retained under the Constitution, bureaucracy and technology must be integrated into its framework, for the twin factors may be, in their essence, antithetical to democratic values.

Nicholas Henry, "Bureaucracy, Technology, and Knowledge Mangement," *Public Administration Review*, 35 (November/December, 1975), pp. 572-573. *Public Administration Review*

Much of the rationalist model deals with the construction of public policies that assure better public policies. Yehezkel Dror (as good a representative as any of the rationalist modelists) calls this concern "metapolicy," that is, policy for policy-making procedures.[26] In this emphasis the rationalist model dwells on the optimal organization of the government structure that will assure undistorted information flow, the accuracy of feedback data, and the proper weighing of social variables.

Diagrammed, the rationalist model renders public policy formation into a linear flow chart, reminiscent of Operations Research, Path Analysis, and the related computer-programming techniques of the systems approach and information theory, as Figure 10-10 demonstrates. While Figure 10-10 may remind one of the systems model (Figure 10-5), the rationalist model actually deals only with the "black box" of the systems model. (So, for that matter, does Figure 10-9, the incrementalist model.) That is, the rationalist model articulates how public policy should be formed within government, or how the elements of the conversion process that change environmental inputs into environmental outputs should be arranged optimally. This is what makes the rationalist model so useful to public administration because, in one sense at least, making policy better is what the field ultimately tries to do.

Public choice and political economy. A significant variation of the rationalist model is the literature dealing with public choice and political economy. The public choice literature has been of growing importance to public administration since at least 1963, when a small collection of scholars met to discuss, in their words, "developments in the 'no-name' field of public administration."[27] Since then, *public choice* and *political economy* are the terms most frequently used in describing this literature.

Public choice offers a variety of intellectual directions. Besides its overarching emphasis on the rationalist model as a policy-making tool, public choice is concerned with the nature of public goods and services (Otto Eckstein, Robert L. Bish, and L. L. Wade and R. L. Curry, Jr.[28] would be representative of this literary emphasis), the relationships between formal decision-making structures and human propensities for individual action (*e.g.*, Gordon Tullock, Anthony Downs[29]) and for collective action (*e.g.*, Mancur Olson[30]), the requisites of constitutional government and corresponding patterns of collective action (*e.g.*, James M. Buchanan and Gordon Tullock[31]), and the interstices between producers, performance, consumer interests, and the provision of public goods and services (*e.g.*, Garrett Hardin, Joseph J. Seneca[32]).

Using the concepts of political economy, we can assess public policy in new ways. Consider, for example, the problems of air pollution, the energy crisis, and the role of the automobile, which accounts for roughly 60 percent of the air pollutants in the United States and almost 40 percent of its fuel consumption. Rather than passing a flatly stated law that says little more than "Thou shalt not pollute nor use too much gas," a political economist would likely turn instead to the tax structure. He or she would reason that if a particular citizen chose to buy a Cadillac rather than a Honda, the general citizenry should not have to bear the common costs of that citizen's choice (*i.e.*, the extra pollutants emitted and fuel consumed by the Cadillac), but neither should all the other citizens be denied the Cadillacs if they really want them. Thus, a special tax should be established that taxes cars according to the pollutants they emit and the energy resources they consume; the more pollutants and gas, the higher the tax. In this method, the individual citizen still can buy a Cadillac, but the costs of the purchase to the general citizenry will be offset by the special tax that the owner is forced to pay and by using the receipts from that tax for pollution abatement and energy research programs. Such is the nature of assessment in the public choice literature.

On a more sophisticated plane, public choice is concerned with *Pareto optimality*, a concept originally developed by the economist Vilfredo Pareto. Or, more exactly (and because optimality is supremely difficult to achieve in any context), public choice concerns "Pareto improvements," and the notions of trade-offs and externalities. To borrow E. J. Mishan's definition, a *Pareto improvement* is "a change in economic organization that makes everyone better off—or, more precisely, that makes one or more members of society better off without making anyone worse off."[33]

FIGURE 10-10 The Rationalist Model of Public Policy Making and Implementation

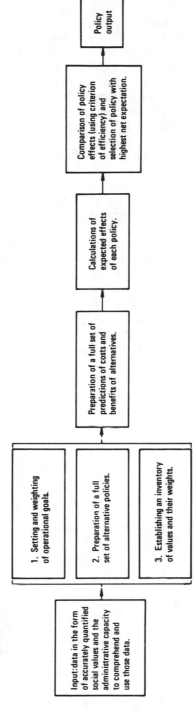

Pareto optimality may be illustrated with reference to public choice in graphic form. Figure 10-11 posits a hypothetical social value ("X") relative to the accomplishment of all other social values. The *indifference curve* refers to the combination of values about which society is indifferent (at least up to a point); the *value achievement curve* indicates the optimal combination of values that it is possible for government to encourage given limited resources. The point of optimal achievement of Value X and optimal achievement of all other social values constitutes the point of Pareto optimality. The closer that society gets to the point of Pareto optimality is considered a Pareto improvement.

Figure 10-11 also illustrates what the public choice writers mean by *trade-offs*. A trade-off refers to what value is being traded (and the social costs and benefits incurred in such a trade) for what other value. In other words, every time Value X is achieved more fully, all other values are correspondingly reduced in achievement; the benefits gained by increasing resource input into Value X must decrease resource input into all other values.

A related term common to the public choice literature is *externality*, or *spillover effect*. When a public policy in one sphere of social action affects other spheres of social action, the manner in which the other sphere is affected is called an *externality*; that is, the effects of a public policy in one sphere "spill over" into other spheres. Externalities may be positive or negative, intended or unintended. For example, a positive, intended spillover effect of reducing corporate taxes might be to raise employment levels. A negative, unintended externality of the same public policy might be to reduce the financial resources available to the government for welfare programs.

Public and private goods and services. Vincent Ostrom, Elinor Ostrom, and E. S. Savas, among others, have contributed yet another important variation of the rationalist model that stems largely from the public choice school.[34] This school of public choice theory deals with what kinds of goods and services should be delivered by government, and what kinds should be delivered by the private sector. To make this

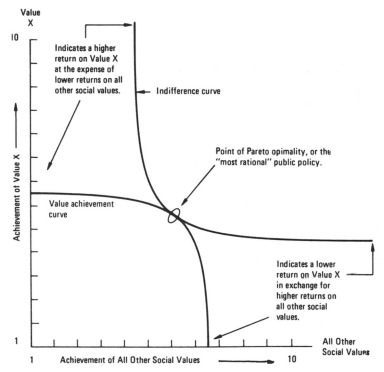

FIGURE 10-11 Pareto Optimality and Public Choice

distinction, two concepts are employed: exclusion and consumption.

Exclusion refers to the degree of control that both the buyer and seller have over a particular commodity; in other words, how easy is it to exclude users or owners from using or owning a particular good or service? Most goods are like a bag of groceries; for a buyer to walk out of a supermarket with a bag of groceries requires that both the buyer and seller agree to a price. In this case (which is the most common one in the real world), the seller exercises a high level of exclusionary control.

But other goods and services are not so easily controlled. For example, a lighthouse has a very low level of exclusivity. All ships within sight of the lighthouse can benefit from its service. Exclusion, in short, is a matter of economics rather than choice. Some goods and services can be excluded from the marketplace more readily than others.

The second major point used by public choice theorists in this stream of literature is that of *consumption*. Some goods and services may be consumed, or used, *jointly* (*i.e.*, simultaneously) by many consumers without being diminished in either quality or quantity, whereas other goods and services are available only for *individual* rather than joint consumption. An example of joint consumption would be a television broadcast. All viewers may "consume" a television program "jointly" without the program being diminished in either quality or quantity. A pizza and a haircut provide examples of individual consumption of a good and a service. Once they are consumed by an individual, no one else has access to them.

Using the notions of exclusion and consumption, we can begin to classify goods and services according to certain kinds of "pure forms." Savas lists these as being private goods, toll goods, common-pool goods, and collective goods.[35]

Private goods and services are pure, individually consumed goods and services for which exclusion is completely feasible. There is no problem of supply. The marketplace provides private goods readily, and this supply is based on consumer demand. Government's role in the supply of private goods and services is largely limited to assuring their safety (such as in building inspections),

honest reporting (such as in weights and measures), and so forth.

Toll goods and services are pure, jointly consumed goods and services for which exclusion is completely feasible. As with private goods, toll goods can be supplied easily by the marketplace, and excluding consumers from using them is entirely practicable. But unlike private goods, consumption of toll goods is joint rather than individual. This is because many toll goods are natural monopolies, which means that as the number of users increases, the cost per user decreases. Examples include cable television, electric power, and water supplies. In the case of toll goods, government action may be required to assure that monopolies are created and granted in the first place and then regulated so that proprietors do not exploit their monopolistic privileges unfairly.

Common-pool goods and services are pure, individually consumed goods and services for which exclusion is not feasible. In the case of common-pool goods we do have supply problems, and this differentiates common-pool goods from both private goods and toll goods. There is neither a requirement to pay for common-pool goods nor any means to prevent their consumption; they are, in the short term, "free."

Common-pool goods bring us to the problem of what Garrett Hardin called the "tragedy of the commons"—that which belongs to everyone belongs to no one, and the problem of common-pool goods is that they can be easily squandered to the point of exhaustion. An example would be the clean air supply. Until government imposed regulations on the emission of air pollutants, the air was a "free good," at least from the perspective of the industrialist who could use it as a vast dumping bin for pollutants. The air was, in this sense, a "commons." Government has a much larger role in the administration of common-pool goods than it does in private and toll goods because it makes sense for government to regulate common-pool goods so that they are not destroyed by overconsumption.

Finally, there are *collective, or public, goods and services*, which are pure, jointly consumed goods and services for which exclusion is not feasible. The marketplace cannot supply these goods because they are used simultaneously by many people, and no one can be excluded from consuming them. Individuals have an economic incentive to exploit collective goods without paying for them, and to thus become what public choice theorists call "free riders." National defense, broadcast television, and police protection provide examples of collective goods.

Collective goods differ from common-pool goods on the basis of consumption. Common-pool goods are individually consumed (and, because of this, may be completely consumed), while collective goods are jointly consumed without diminishing the quality or quantity of the goods and services themselves.

It is in the area of collective goods that government has the greatest responsibility for management regulation. When we realize that such basic services as police protection are considered a collective good in this construct, the importance of government intervention in the marketplace seems obvious.

Figure 10-12 provides examples of goods and services along the four typologies that we have discussed.

Savas argues that private goods "have been undergoing reclassification as common-pool goods, and toll goods have been subsidized or provided free so that they resemble collective goods," and he provides as evidence of his argument dramatic increases in federal expenditures for such public policy areas as health, education, income maintenance, and housing, all of which were predominantly private goods and toll goods until the government, in effect, reclassified them by entering the marketplace. He urges that we reconsider the role of government in providing

private and toll goods and services, and offers a variety of alternative institutional arrangements for the delivery of these goods and services. These include direct government service, intergovernmental agreements, contracts with the private sector, franchises (or the awarding of a monopoly to a private firm to supply a particular service, which usually entails the firm's regulation by a government agency), grants (or a subsidy given directly by the government to a producer, which can include tax subsidies), voucher systems (which, unlike grants, do not subsidize a producer, but instead subsidize the consumer and permit consumers to exercise a relatively free choice in the marketplace—food stamps are an example of the voucher system), marketplace mechanisms, voluntary service, and self-service. (The final three arrangements are self explanatory and do not involve the public sector.)

Table 10-1 lists these alternative arrangements for the delivery of goods and services and categorizes them by the most appropriate and efficient means for their delivery. As one can see, this construct (which has a certain theoretical elegance) would work to reduce government's role in the provision of a variety of goods and services that government presently provides. Beyond this aspect, however, understanding how means of delivery might match most logically with type of service could result in more sophisticated and effective delivery systems for public services.[36]

Technology assessment. A final variant of the rationalist model, like public goods and services,

FIGURE 10-12 Goods and Services According to the Criteria of Exclusion and Consumption

		Consumption/Use	
		Individual Use	*Joint Use*
	Feasible	Private Goods and Services (a bag of groceries, a haircut, a meal in a restaurant)	*Toll Goods and Services* (cable television, telephone service, theaters, libraries, electric power)
Exclusion			
		Common-Pool Goods and Services (water in a public well, fish in the ocean, air to breathe)	*Collective or Public Goods and Services* (peace and security, public safety, pollution control, weather forecasts, public television, and radio)
	Unfeasible		

TABLE 10-1 Types of Goods and Services and Institutional Arrangements for Their Delivery

Arrangement	Private Goods	Toll Goods	Collective Goods	Common-Pool Goods
Government service		x	x	x
Intergovern- mental agreement		x	x	x
Contract		x	x	x
Franchise		x		
Grant	x	x		x
Voucher	x	x		x
Market	x	x		
Voluntary		x	x	x
Self-Service	x			

Source: E. S. Savas, *Privatizing the Public Sector: How to Shrink Government* (Chatham, N.J.: Chatham House, 1982), p. 77.

technology assessment also relies on concepts developed in the public choice school, notably the idea of externalities. Technology assessment is an effort to evaluate new technologies in light of their spillover effects throughout society. Thus, public policies for new technologies become the objects of analysis. A variant of technology assessment is technological forecasting, which is the attempt to predict what effects very new technologies might have on society. For instance, medicine may be viewed as a technology that, in its success in extending the life span, has been more responsible than any other factor for the population explosion.

Consider another example, one perhaps more modest but also more germane to most readers: the photocopy machine. Photocopiers have lived up to all the original hopes that were held for them. As an information technology, photocopiers have facilitated research, record keeping, and decision making. They have probably reduced the inclination of patrons to vandalize volumes in libraries. They have eased the process of education throughout society and have made life far more convenient for innumerable people who handle paper as part of their jobs. They may even have contributed to more responsive policymaking in public organizations because they speed the information flow in the bureaucracy. They have made some people a lot of money. But the photocopier also has brought with it certain unintended externalities. Roughly 30 billion photocopies are made every year in the

United States, and empirical research indicates that approximately 60 percent of these copies may be of materials protected by copyright.

Some questions inevitably come to the fore: If photocopies were unavailable, would sales of copyrighted books and periodicals rise? Is popular use of photocopying technologies cutting into the royalty payments of authors and publishers? And if so, are royalties being reduced to a point sufficient to undermine the financial incentive of authors to write and of publishers to risk capital to publish? Ultimately, have these machines contributed to a less creative society? Or will they? Is the incentive to develop new ideas in science, social science, and literature decreased by the emerging photocopier/copyright relationship, or is there more incentive because of the added convenience provided by photocopiers in transmitting new ideas? Although there are many opinions, many of them heated, among authors, publishers, librarians, and educators, the impact of the technology of photocopying on society has yet to be adequately assessed.[37]

Presumably, a more rigorous system of technology assessment and technological forecasting by the government could aid in achieving a more rationally planned society. As a significant step in this direction, Congress passed a bill in 1973 establishing an Office of Technology Assessment with a mission of advising Congress on matters of technology assessment. The office is seen by some observers as representing a congressional effort to offset the almost total monopoly of scientific and technical information held by the executive branch.

Regardless of how the Office of Technology Assessment performs, the function of technology assessment remains a new and important aspect of public policy analysis generally, and of the rationalist model particularly. Many agencies of government can use it in evaluating their programs. Gabor Strasser has stated that technology assessment actually has a rather broad meaning:

A systematic planning and forecasting process that delineates options and costs, encompassing economics as well as environmental and social considerations that are both external and internal to the program and/or product in question, with special focus on technology-related "bad" as well as "good" effects.[38]

With this definition in mind, look at Figure 10-13, which illustrates the elements of technology assessment.

THE DEFICIENCIES OF INCREMENTALISM AND RATIONALISM

Both incrementalism and rationalism are attempts to improve the outputs of public policies, to make the contents of public policy "better." But in their efforts to do this, neither the incrementalists nor the rationalists have been particularly willing to work together.

Criticisms of the Rationalist Model

Incrementalists have criticized the rationalists on a variety of grounds. For example, they point out that there is often a wide gap between planning and implementation, and it is undeniable that many plans have been written only to collect dust on many shelves, even though these plans had cost considerable sums of time and money to develop.[39]

Another problem is that rationalists often ignore the role of the entrepreneur. To be implemented and to work, a plan must be more than computer runs

FIGURE 10-13 Technology Assessment in Public Administration

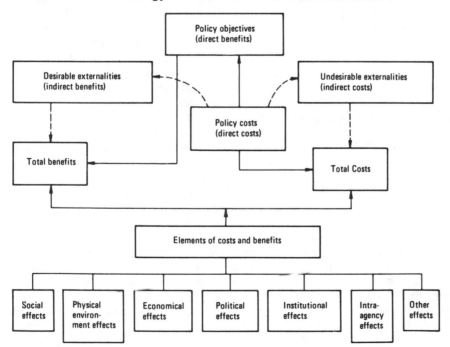

and printouts; a plan requires people and leadership to make ideas happen. Technical competence is not the same as leadership. Kingdon, for example, has shown how critical the "policy entrepreneur" is in both developing and implementing public policies in the federal government.[40]

A third criticism is that the rationalists are far too mechanical in their approach to what is in reality a complex form of life—the administrative organization. Organizations are less like machines and more like organisms, the criticism continues, and this fact has not been recognized by the rationalists. As a consequence, the rationalists typically ignore the "human factor," and this diminishes the utility of the plans that they develop. As one critic has noted, "This is an era of ecology...we can no longer profitably discuss our world and its future in simple linear terms...for the evidence all around us is of multidimensional, complex actions."[41]

A fourth criticism of the rationalists' approach is that the predictions it makes often are wrong, or that it fails to make predictions when there appears to be ample evidence warranting certain predictions. The rationalists have a less than terrific record as forecasters of future events.[42]

Finally, it has been alleged that the effort to "gin up" large scale comprehensive planning programs ends up spending more than the plans ultimately save their investors or the taxpayers. "In most states, it is very probable that the new costs of data manipulation have been met largely by reducing the support of the activities which are measured."[43] Planning in the comprehensive, rationalist mode, in short, costs more than it saves.

Criticism of the Incrementalist Model

These are not untoward criticisms of the rationalists' approach. However, the incrementalists also have their critics. "Muddling through" has been described as "a form of tiptoeing naked and buttocks-first into history"[44]; examples of such mindless and irrational incrementalism include the American experience in Vietnam.

A major criticism of the incrementalist model is that it is based on a bargaining concept. Unfortunately, bargaining tends to be far more successful in making policy when resources are relatively unlimited and there is something extra to divide up among the participants. In times of scarcity, however, other methods (usually rational methods) must be found to make hard choices.

A second criticism of incrementalism is what Harold Enarson has called "the beagle fallacy," or the fact that beagles have a superb sense of smell but very limited eyesight and often will miss a rabbit that is directly in front but downwind of them.[45] Incrementalists tend to downplay the use of models, including computer models, that provide clear information and delineate alternatives. Models, when well done, can provide precise knowledge about interrelationships and in a way that no other approach can do. Incrementalism often results in the obscuring of interrelationships because, as a bargaining concept, the real objectives of participants often are deliberately hidden by the participants themselves. In this criticism, incrementalists are viewed as skilled players in a poker game, but none of them has been told that the objective of the other players is to win money.

A third criticism of incrementalism is that the incrementalists are singularly deficient in imagination. They have no vision and dislike imagining alternative solutions. Only what is, is real to the incrementalists. As one critic has put it, "Like beautifully muscled illiterates, incrementalists...have overdeveloped powers of political calculation and underdeveloped powers of social imagination."[46] Related to this charge is the concern that incrementalists are so wrapped up in political gamesmanship, they actually become anti-intellectual in their approach to the solution of social problems.

Finally, incrementalism is an inherently conservative approach. Drastic and far-reaching changes are eschewed in favor of minor adjustments. As change becomes more rapid and more endemic in America's techno-bureaucracy, the innate conservatism of incrementalism becomes less responsive and more counterproductive.

These are the main criticisms that the incrementalists and the rationalists allege about each other. But criticisms, no matter how accurate, are not always constructive. As Amitai Etzioni put it, "What is needed…is a strategy that is less exacting than the rationalistic one, but not as constricting in its perspective as the incrementalist approach; not as utopian as rationalism, but not as conservative as incrementalism; not so unrealistic a model that it cannot be followed, but not one that legitimizes myopic self-oriented, noninnovative decision making."[47]

THE STRATEGIC PLANNING MODEL

This "third approach" suggested by Etzioni has since acquired the title of "strategic planning," or, less frequently, "strategic decision making" or "strategic management," and it is an eminently useful concept in that it attempts to combine the strongest features of incrementalism and rationalism, yet avoid their pitfalls. Strategic planning emerged largely in the world of business and, as George Keller has pointed out, its birthplace is not too surprising when we realize that corporations have grown more competitive, more oriented toward long-term growth, more politically regulated, and increasingly aware of the psycho-emotional needs of their employees. Yet they must also cope with fiscal reality, deficits, ecologists, religious groups, and other environmental pressures that force corporations into a bargaining mode.[48] Hence, strategic planning recognizes that "organizations have *both* localized, short-term, and bottom-line demands and all-organization, long-term, and investment-strategies-for-the-future demands. They must live with the familiar today, yet also must be forever looking out for how to live in a very different tomorrow."[49]

Strategic planning is an attempt to recognize this reality. Alfred Chandler, Jr., first called attention to the practical emergence of strategic planning in major American corporations in 1962.[50] Since that time, however, strategic planning has made an impact on public agencies, and there is, according to some scholars, "ample evidence of the practical importance of the strategic management function in public organizations," despite the unique problems of "external factors" with which strategic planners in the public sector must deal.[51]

Strategic planning is neither the personal vision of the chief executive officer nor a collection of unrelated plans drawn up by department heads. Strategic planning is done by the top line officers of the organization, from the chief executive officer through the upper levels of middle management. It is not done by planners. As one planning official wrote, "First we ask: who is leading the planning? If it is a planner…we are in trouble."[52]

As Keller observes, the strategic plan does not substitute numbers for important intangibles, such as human emotions, but it does use computers and quantification to illuminate choices. It attempts to go beyond a simple surrender by the organization to environmental conditions, and in this sense it is by no means a way of eliminating risks. What a strategic plan does is place line decision makers in an active rather than in a passive position about the future of their organization. It incorporates an outward-looking, proactive focus that is sensitive to environmental changes, but does not assume that the organization is necessarily a victim of changes in its task environment. As Richard Cyert has put it, "The aim of strategic planning is to place the unit in a distinctive position relative to its environment."[53]

Strategic planning concentrates on decisions rather than on extensive documentation, analyses, and forecasts. In this sense, it attempts to free itself of the constraints alleged by critics of the rationalist model to the effect that rationalist approaches cost more than they save, and have no particular bearing on decision making in an organization. Because it is decision oriented, strategic planning blends economic and rational analyses, political values, and the psychology of the participants in the organization. To do this requires that strategic planning be highly participatory and tolerant of controversy. This participatory aspect of strategic planning leads strategic planners to concentrate on the fate of the whole organization above all other concerns; the fate of subunits in the organization are clearly secondary to this overriding value.

In these ways, strategic planning is an attempt to reconcile the rationalist and incrementalist approaches to the problem of public policy formulation. Figure 10-14 represents an attempt to synthesize the main features of strategic planning.

FIGURE 10-14 The Strategic-Planning Model of Public Policy Making and Implementation

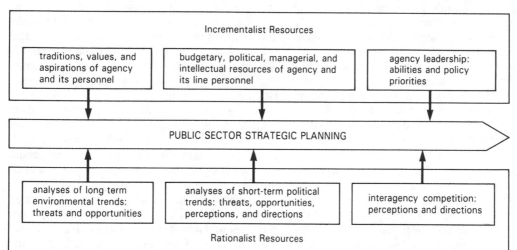

STRATEGIC PLANNING: THE PUBLIC EXPERIENCE

Although strategic planning has been described as "a hearty, public-sector perennial,"[54] there is relatively little empirical research about how strategic planning is used in the public sector.[55] Nevertheless, it is clear that strategic planning is of more limited use in the public sector than it is in the private one. The "pervasive vagueness" of agency missions; environmental constraints in the form of interest groups, media, and other forces that render "bold moves" by public sector executives "almost completely impossible"; the uniquely omnipresent need to be sensitive to how a policy will be perceived, not just what it will do; arbitrary time constraints, such as budget and election cycles, that can rush or delay strategic decisions in ways that they no longer are strategic; and coalitions which are usually prone to disintegrate prior to the complete implementation of a strategic plan—all these and more limit the use of strategic planning in the public sector.[56]

Some observers have gone so far as to suggest that public administrators are so boxed in by their task environments that it is legitimate to define public strategic planning in some agencies as a bunker mentality, which is, essentially, little more than an implicit agreement among public administrators to "hunker down" and protect their organization against external threats,[57] or, at best, a way of competing with other public organizations for resources.[58]

But if one is to define strategic planning as it is generally understood, that is, "a disciplined effort to produce fundamental decisions and actions that define what an organization…is, what it does, and why it does it," then, "whatever the merits of strategic planning in the abstract, normal expectations have to be that most efforts to produce fundamental decisions and actions in government through strategic planning will not succeed."[59] Of course, such a statement must be placed in context; any process that is meant to force basic change in any organization, whether public or private, is unlikely to succeed more frequently than it fails.

Nevertheless, the use of strategic planning in the public sector potentially can produce beneficial results on a routine basis, as well as wreak fundamental organizational change on an intermittent one. At the very least, public strategic planning articulates implicit organizational objectives and issues, ranks them by priority, and communicates these objectives and issues to members of the organization. At root, public strategic planning is a method of making the decision premises (which we discussed in Chapter 4) of public administrators more uniform, and, because of this, strategic planning enhances the likelihood of improved organizational coordination and effectiveness. This is wholly good, but there is a lurking peril in that, by openly identifying and legitimizing specific organizational goals, morale can suffer if the public organization fails to attain those goals—typically because of declining budgets. As we discussed in Part Two, the uniqueness of the public organization is its vulnerability to its task environment, and this vulnerability wars against the unilateral utility and use of strategic planning. In the context of the public sector, strategic planning tends to overpromise (or, at least, raise expectations), and, if promises are unkept, disappointment and malaise can seep through the organization.

As a consequence of this peril of public strategic planning, public administrators may not only approach it cautiously, but also, should they opt to take the plunge and attempt to channel the energies of their agency into developing a strategic plan, they appear to confront more obstacles than their counterparts in the private sector. An analysis of six local governments and two units of a county government in Minnesota found that a government or public agency is the most likely to succeed in initiating and completing a strategic plan if it has a "powerful process sponsor" (*i.e.*, one or [typically] more major figures who endorse the idea of strategic planning, even if tepidly); a strong "process champion" (a skilled administrator who knows what he or she is doing and believes in strategic planning); an agency-wide expectation of disruptions and delays; a willingness to be flexible about what, precisely, a strategic plan really is; an ability of administrators to derive satisfaction and a sense of progress at particular points in time during the plan's initiation; and a capacity to build and use different arguments in evaluating the plan.[60]

Initiating strategic planning seems to require considerable administrative effort in any context, but particularly so in public organizations. Moreover, its form in the public sector differs from its form in the private one. In the Minnesota research, it was concluded that "governmental strategic planning probably should be judged by different standards than private-sector, corporate strategic planning"; none of the governments and agencies "was able to follow the linear, sequential planning models of the business policy textbooks, and none was able to prepare a public-sector equivalent of the slick corporate strategic plan."[61]

While messy, however, public strategic planning is not necessarily ineffective. If a public organization can complete a strategic plan, then it has been able to identify issues, prioritize them, and formulate ways of—that is, strategies for—dealing with them. But just how effective public strategic plans are—that is, do they measurably facilitate public administrators in achieving their goals and resolving issues?—is not clear. One review of the literature concluded that "no careful study of the effectiveness of governmental strategic planning has been done", although it is known that those public administrators who develop and complete strategic plans believe that their efforts are worthwhile.[62]

Strategic planning is a means of implementing public policy, and, as such, is one of the "approaches to public policy and its implementation" that we have reviewed in this chapter. Implementation is the subject of the final section of this book, and concerns the question of how things get done, or, more specifically, how policies are delivered to the public. Aside from the techniques of public management themselves, which we explained in Part Three, public policies are implemented through grants and contracts with other governments and private firms. We consider these methods in the next two chapters.

NOTES

[1] Austin Ranney, "The Study of Policy Content: A Framework for Choice," *Political Science and Public Policy*, Austin Ranney, ed. (Chicago: Markham, 1968), p. 3. Emphases are original.

[2] Austin Ranney, "Preface," in *ibid.*, p. vii.

[3] *Ibid.*

[4] Susan B. Hansen, "Public Policy Analysis: Some Recent Developments and Current Problems," *Political Science: The State of the Discipline*, Ada W. Finifter, ed. (Washington, D.C.: American Political Science Association, 1983), pp. 217–245.

[5] *Ibid.*, p. 239. In 1979, 68 percent of the members of the Policy Studies Organization were political scientists, although this figure may include academics who identify with public administration as well.

[6] The book was Arnold J. Heidenheimer, Hugh Heclo, and Carolyn Teich Adams, *Comparative Public Policy: The Politics of Social Choice in Europe and America* (New York: St. Martin's Press, 1975).

[7] Hansen, "Public Policy Analysis," p. 219. In 1982, 27 percent of the public policy papers took a comparative approach.

[8] *Ibid.*, pp. 220–229. Some license has been taken with Hansen's categories. Hansen calls the literature of program evaluation and its attendant case studies "changing conceptions of policy failure," which strikes us as a somewhat idiosyncratic descriptor.

[9] Robert T. Golembiewski, *Public Administration as a Developing Discipline, Part I: Perspectives on Past and Present* (New York: Marcel Dekker, 1977), p. 147.

[10] Bibliographies dramatizing this point include: B. Guy Peters, "Comparative Public Policy (A Bibliography)," *Policy Studies Review*, 1 (August 1981), pp. 183–197; and Douglas E. Ashford, Peter J. Katzenstein, and T. J. Pempel, eds. *Comparative Public Policy: A Cross-National Bibliography* (Beverly Hills, Calif.: Sage, 1978).

[11] Elliot J. Feldman, "Comparative Public Policy: Field or Method?" *Comparative Politics*, 10 (1978), pp. 287–305.

[12] C. Wright Mills, *The Power Elite* (New York: Oxford University Press, 1956).

[13] Arthur F. Bentley, *The Process of Government* (Bloomington, Ind.: Principia Press, 1949). First published in 1908.

[14] Louis M. Kohlmeier, *The Regulators: Watchdog Agencies and the Public Interest* (New York: Harper & Row, 1969).

[15] Murray Edelman, *The Symbolic Uses of Politics* (Urbana, Ill.: University of Illinois Press, 1964).

[16] David Easton, *The Political System* (New York: Knopf, 1953).

[17] Carl J. Friedrich, *Constitutional Government and Democracy* (Boston: Little, Brown, 1941).

[18] See, for example, Theodore J. Lowi, "Decision-Making versus Policy-Making: Towards an Antidote for Technocracy," *Public Administration Review*, 30 (May/June 1970), pp. 134–139; Theodore J. Lowi, "Four Systems of Politics, Policy, and Choice," *Public Administration Review*, 32 (July/August 1972), pp. 298–310; Randall B. Ripley, "Introduction: The Politics of Public Policy," *Public Policies and their Politics: An Introduction to the Techniques of Government Control*, Randall B. Ripley, ed. (New York: Norton, 1966), pp. i–xv; Randall Ripley and Grace Franklin, *Congress, the Bureaucracy, and Public Policy*, 2nd ed. (Homewood, Ill.: Dorsey Press, 1980); Randall Ripley and Grace Franklin, *Bureaucracy and Policy Implementation* (Homewood, Ill.: Dorsey Press, 1982); Robert Salisbury and John Heinz, "A Theory of Policy Analysis and Some Preliminary Applications," *Policy Analysis in Political Science*, Ira Sharkansky, ed. (Chicago: Markham, 1970), pp. 39–60; Dean Schooler, Jr., *Science, Scientists, and Public Policy* (New York: The Free Press, 1971); and Michael Hayes, "The Semi-Sovereign Pressure Groups: A Critique Theory and an Alternative Typology," *Journal of Politics*, 40 (February 1978), pp. 134–161.

[19] Theodore J. Lowi, "American Business, Public Policy, Case Studies, and Political Science," *World Politics*, 16 (July 1964), p. 691. But see also: Theodore J. Lowi, "Population Policies and the American Political System," *Political Science and Population Studies*, Richard L. Clinton, William S. Flash, and R. Kenneth Godwin, eds. (Lexington, Mass.: D.C. Heath, 1972), pp. 25–53. For an attempt at integrating some of the contributors to this literature, see: Leonard Champney, "Public Goods and Policy Types," *Public Administration Review*, 48 (November/December 1988), pp. 988–994.

[20] Lowi, "Population Policies and the American Political System," pp. 29–33.

[21] John W. Kingdon, *Agendas, Alternatives, and Public Policies* (Boston: Little Brown, 1984).

[22] *Ibid.*, p. 85.

[23] Charles E. Lindblom, *The Policy Making Process* (Englewood Cliffs, N.J.: Prentice-Hall, 1968).

[24] Charles E. Lindblom, "The Science of Muddling Through," *Public Administration Review*, 19 (Spring 1959), pp. 79–88.

[25] Ralph K. Huitt, "Political Feasibility," in *Political Science and Public Policy*, Austin Ranney, ed. (Chicago: Markham, 1968), p. 274.

[26] Yehezkel Dror, *Public Policy Making Reexamined* (San Francisco: Chandler, 1968), p. 8.

[27] Vincent Ostrom and Elinor Ostrom, "Public Choice: A Different Approach to the Study of Public Administration," *Public Administration Review*, 31 (March/April 1971), p. 203.

[28] See: Otto Eckstein, *Public Finance*, 2nd ed. (Englewood Cliffs, N.J.: Prentice-Hall, 1967); Robert L. Bish, *The Public Economy of Metropolitan Areas* (Chicago: Markham, 1971); and L. L. Wade and R. L. Curry, Jr., *A Logic of Public Policy: Aspects of Political Economy* (Belmont, Calif.: Wadsworth, 1970).

[29] Gordon Tullock, *The Politics of Bureaucracy* (Washington, D.C.: Public Affairs Press, 1965); and Anthony Downs, *An Economic Theory of Democracy* (New York: Harper & Row, 1957).

[30] Mancur Olson, *The Logic of Collective Action* (Cambridge, Mass.: Harvard University Press, 1965).

[31] James M. Buchanan and Gordon Tullock, *The Calculus of Consent: Logical Foundations of Constitutional Democracy* (Ann Arbor, Mich.: University of Michigan Press, 1962).

[32] Garrett Hardin, "The Tragedy of the Commons," *Science*, 162 (December 13, 1968), pp. 1243–1248; and Joseph J. Seneca, "The Welfare Effects of Zero Pricing of Public Goods," *Public Choice*, 7 (Spring 1970), pp. 101–110.

[33] E. J. Mishan, *Economics for Social Decisions: Elements of Cost-Benefit Analysis* (New York: Praeger, 1972), p. 14.

[34] Vincent Ostrom and Elinor Ostrom, "Public Goods and Public Choices," in *Alternatives for Delivering Public Services*, E. S. Savas, ed. (Boulder, Colo.: Westview Press, 1977), p. 7–14; and E. S. Savas, *Privatizing the Public Sector: How to Shrink Government* (Chatham, N.J.: Chatham House, 1982). See also Hardin, "The Tragedy of the Commons" and Seneca, "The Welfare Effects of Zero Pricing of Public Goods."

[35] Savas, *Privatizing the Public Sector*, p. 33. Much of the following discussion is drawn from Savas, pp. 29–52.

[36] A good, practical case for this (and for Table 10-1) is made in: Harry P. Hatry, *A Review of Private Approaches for Delivery of Public Services* (Washington, D.C.: Urban Institute Press, 1983).

[37] For additional information on this complex topic that uses the perspective of technology assessment, see Nicholas Henry,

Copyright/Information Technology/Public Policy, Volumes I and II (New York: Marcel Dekker, 1975 and 1976); and Nicholas Henry, ed. *Copyright, Congress, and Technology: The Public Record, Volumes I, II, III, IV, and V* (Phoenix, Ariz.: Oryx Press, 1978, 1979, and 1980).

[38] Gabor Strasser, "Technology Assessment: A Fad or a New Way of Life?" *Science Policy Review*, 5, 1 (1971), p. 7.

[39] See, for example, David Clark, "In Consideration of Goal-Free Planning: The Failure of Traditional Planning Systems in Education," *Educational Administration Quarterly*, 17 (Summer 1981), pp. 42–60.

[40] Kingdon, *Agendas, Politics, and Public Policies*. But see also Joseph Schumpeter, "The Creative Response in Economic History," *The Journal of Economic History*, 7 (November 7, 1947), pp. 149–159.

[41] Derek Viray, *Planning and Education* (London: Routledge and Kegan Paul, 1972), p. 4.

[42] For examples of critiques of the forecasting weaknesses of the rationalists models, see Paul and Benjamin Ward, *What's Wrong with Economics?* (Basic Books, 1972); Seymour Martin Lipset, "The Limits to Futurology in Social Science Analysis," in *The Third Century: America as a Post Industrial Society*, Seymour Martin Lipset, ed. (Cooper Institution Press, 1979), pp. 3–18; and William Ascher, "Forecasting Potential of Complex Models," *Policy Sciences*, 13 (May 1981), pp. 247–267.

[43] Emerson Shuck, "The New Planning and the Old Fragmentism," *The Journal of Higher Education*, 48 (September/October 1977), pp. 494–602.

[44] George Keller, *Academic Strategy: The Management Revolution in Higher Education* (Baltimore, Md.: Johns Hopkins University Press, 1983), p. 111.

[45] Harold Enarson, "The Art of Planning," *Educational Record*, 56 (Summer 1975), p. 173.

[46] Keller, *Academic Strategy*, p. 113.

[47] Amitai Etzioni, *The Active Society* (The Free Press, 1968), p. 283. See also: Amitai Etzioni, "Mixed Scanning: A Third Approach to Decision Making," *Public Administration Review*, 27 (December 1967), pp. 385–392.

[48] Keller, *Academic Strategy*, p. 115.

[49] *Ibid.*, p. 116.

[50] Alfred Chandler, Jr., *Strategy and Structure: Chapters in the History of the Industrial Enterprise* (Cambridge, Mass.: MIT Press, 1962). Other seminal contributions to the literature of strategic planning include H. Igor Ansoff, *Corporate Strategy* (McGraw-Hill, 1965); Kenneth Andrews, *The Concept of Corporate Strategy*, rev. ed. (New York: Dow Jones-Irwin, 1980); Daniel Bell, "Twelve Modes of Prediction," *Daedalus*, 93 (Summer 1964), pp. 845–880; Henry Mintzberg, "Packets of Strategy Formulation," *Management Science*, 24 (May 1978), pp. 934–948; and James Bryan Quinn, "Strategic

Change: Logical Incrementalism," *Sloan Management Review*, 20 (Fall 1978), pp. 7–21.

[51] Barton Wechsler and Robert W. Backoff, "Policy Making and Administration in State Agencies: Strategic Management Approaches," *Public Administration Review*, 46 (July/August 1986), p. 326.

[52] Michael Aiken and Jerald Hage, "The Organic Organization and Innovation," *Sociology*, 5 (January 1971), p. 80.

[53] Richard Cyert, as quoted in Keller, *Academic Strategy*, p. 147.

[54] Gerald J. Miller, "Unique Public-Sector Strategies," *Public Productivity and Management Review*, 13 (Winter 1989), p. 133.

[55] *Ibid.*, p. 139. Among the more empirical attempts to analyze the use of strategic planning in the public sector are: Barry Bozeman, "Strategic Public Management and Productivity: A Fire House Theory," *State Government*, 61 (Winter 1983), pp. 2–7; John M. Bryson, *Strategic Planning for Public and Nonprofit Organizations: A Guide to Strengthening and Sustaining Organizational Achievement* (San Francisco: Jossey-Bass, 1988); John M. Bryson and William D. Roering, "Initiation of Strategic Planning by Governments," *Public Administration Review*, 48 (November/December 1988), pp. 995–1004. J. M. Stevens, "Strategic Public Management and Productivity Improvement: A Symposium," *Public Productivity Review*, 8 (Winter 1984), entire issue; J. M. Stevens and Robert P. McGowan, "Managerial Strategies in Municipal Government Organizations," *Academy of Management Journal*, 26 (September 1983), pp. 527–534; and Wechsler and Backoff, "Policy Making and Administration in State Agencies," pp. 321–327.

[56] Miller, "Unique Public-Sector Strategies," pp. 137–138.

[57] Wechsler and Backoff, "Policy/making and Administration in State Agencies," pp. 321–327.

[58] James E. Skok, "Toward a Definition of Strategic Management for the Public Sector," *American Review of Public Administration*, 19 (June 1989), pp. 133–147.

[59] Bryson and Roering, "Initiation of Strategic Planning by Governments," p. 995.

[60] *Ibid.*, pp. 321–327. See also: Wechsler and Backoff, "Policy/making and Administration of State Agencies," pp. 321–327. Wechsler and Backoff found a similar set of eight variables in their study of Ohio state agencies.

[61] Bryson and Roering, "Initiation of Strategic Planning by Governments," p. 1002. For another treatment of the limitations of strategic planning in the public sector, see: Arie Halachmi, "Strategic Planning and Management? Not Necessarily," *Public Productivity Review*, 10 (Winter 1986), pp. 35–50.

[62] Bryson and Roering, "Initiation of Strategic Planning by Governments," p. 1003.

CHAPTER
11
GOVERNMENT CONTRACTING AND THE PUBLIC AUTHORITY

In this chapter, we examine a facet of public administration that most books ignore: How and why governments implement public programs by hiring the private sector to do the work for them. As we detail later, this "privatization" of public policy is no small phenomenon. It includes government contracting with private enterprise and the incorporating of public authorities.

The heavy use by American governments of the private and quasi-private sectors to implement public policies is a phenomenon peculiar to this country. It relates to some deep, underlying belief-sets that may be unique to the American political culture. In the United States, there exists a pervasive myth that "business is better"—that private enterprise is more efficient and effective in getting the job done than is "the incredible bulk" of government. Although this is an unproven thesis, it nonetheless remains as a deeply held belief. One empirical analysis of contracting out by local governments, for example, concluded that "To the extent that cost reduction is a motivation [for contracting out services to be delivered by private companies], the decision makers I studied made the more costly choice [of contracting out], evi-

dently relying on the unexamined assumption of private sector efficiency."[1]

PUBLIC ADMINISTRATION AND AMERICAN ORTHODOXY

The myth that private enterprise can conduct public programs more efficiently and effectively than can government has supported the expansion of government contracting with private companies (especially at the federal level) and the rise of government corporations (almost entirely at the subnational level) as two of the three primary means of implementing public programs. (The third is the system of intergovernmental administration, considered in the next chapter.) The business administration literature reflects this popular belief-set.

Orthodox management theory strongly contends that the freer a manager is from public accountability, the more effective manager he or she will be. Thus, we hear arguments voiced for "privatizing" public agencies in order to make them more effective deliverers of public services; more often than not, for example, city garbage often is collected by private companies contracted by local governments. The principal points that proponents of standard administrative theory make in supporting their claims revolve around freedom from civil service systems, governmental pay scales, any kind of overview by a central budget administration, and governmental regulations on purchasing, contracting, and price-setting practices. While these same proponents often argue strongly for just these kind of controls on government agencies, they feel they are not appropriate, and indeed detrimental, to the effectiveness of private management and government corporations.[2]

These orthodoxies have had a profound affect at all levels of government. They have worked to encourage policymakers to abjure public administrators in favor of using private administrators to implement public programs. But the federal government and the state and local governments have faced very different constraints in accommodating the deeply ingrained cultural value of "business-like" government.

Coping at the Federal Level

The federal government, to cope with the exigencies of the Depression and later of World War II, had established a plentitude of federal government corporations. By 1945, there were sixty-three wholly owned federal corporations, thirty-eight partly owned ones, nineteen federal credit agencies, and hundreds of military-owned businesses. By 1953, Washington was "the largest electric power producer in the country, the largest insurer, the largest lender and the largest borrower, the largest landlord and the largest tenant, the largest holder of grazing land and timberland, the largest owner of grain, the largest warehouse operator, the largest shipowner, and the largest truck fleet operator."[3]

Such public enterprise did not rest easily with corporate America. The U.S. Chamber of Commerce, investor-owned utilities, and the National Association of Manufacturers, among other special interests launched a concerted lobbying drive to induce the feds to evict themselves out of "competition" with the private sector. This effort coincided with a conservative presi-

dency, McCarthyism, and the cold war—all of which served to keep "leftist" counterarguments muted. Moreover, the prestigious reports of the first and second Hoover Commissions in 1949 and 1955 on the management of the federal government were extremely useful to the foes of public enterprise. Former President Herbert Hoover, no friend of liberal thought, headed the commissions, which, with no evidence whatever, concluded that "the genius of the private enterprise system" led to its "initiative, ingenuity, inventiveness, and unparalleled productivity," whereas "the normal rigidities that are part of government, obviously" mitigated against the flowering of these attitudes in "government business enterprises."[4] These professions of conservative faith did not fly in Congress, but they soared in Eisenhower's White House. Through a series of executive orders, most of the federal government's public authorities were reorganized or dismantled; although estimates vary, there are by one count only eighteen government corporations owned entirely by the feds.[5] Examples include the Tennessee Valley Authority, the Communications Satellite Corporation, the Corporation for Public Broadcasting, and the Export-Import Bank.

The view that the private sector somehow "can do it better" still prevails. Consider the argument expressed by a conservative member of the House of Representatives: "I do not believe government has any business being in business. I see no reason why it should compete with the private sector in providing goods and services. In those instances where the costs to the government will be less when a good or service is obtained by contract, that ought to be the course followed."[6] Hence, if the special business interests loath government corporations, they nonetheless adore government money, and these same interests have pushed for the "privatization" of government on the grounds that "business can do it better." To accommodate this mind-set, the federal government began contracting out its programs with a vengeance, and federal contract costs now exceed the federal payroll.[7]

Today, especially at the federal level, an ideology of privatization prevails, and perhaps more strongly than at any time in history. As astute observers of federal management have noted,

The supply-side emphasis on "contracting out" to the private sector...is traditional doctrine for Republican administrations, and has acquired a respectable niche in public administration theory....What is novel about the supply-side approach is the belief that the multiplier ratio is larger than previously supposed—that few federal dollars can produce large effects and that the federal government's act of calling attention to a problem can stimulate useful action in society, sometimes even without federal funds. Here one must be careful to avoid illusion. The leverage of federal funds for good or ill is considerable and perhaps much greater than was supposed a decade ago. But there are limits to what can be accomplished through "cost sharing" devices....Also, to contract out effectively for services requires an alert, highly competent, and knowledgeable bureaucracy....But the realities of the American political system make it impossible for an executive branch agency to treat the expenditure of public funds in the same way a private company can manage its vendors.[8]

Coping at the Grassroots

State and local governments are faced with precisely the same conservative mind-set as Washington, but were forced to find a different tactic to steer around it. State and local officials found that they had to circumvent conservative mentalities by using the government corporation, because the privatization option was less available to them. Saddled with moribund constitutional limitations on public debt (only a third of the state constitutions were written in this century) and cumbersome financing procedures (for instance, in stark contrast to the situation at the federal level, only two states, Connecticut and Vermont, are not required by their constitutions to balance their budgets each year), yet whipped by demands for additional public services, state and local governments discovered (with federal encouragement) the manifold fiscal loopholes provided by the government corporation.

Moreover, unions of organized public employees are relatively stronger at the grassroots than in Washington; between 1960 and 1980, the membership of public employee unions more than tripled at the subnational levels, and currently more than a third of all state and local employees are organized. Organized labor can and does exert considerable pressure against state and local administrators not to "contract away"

the jobs of public employees to the private sector; often, such restrictions are written into state civil service statutes.

One survey of sanitation services in all cities in the United States with 10,000 people or more found that the presence of unionized municipal sanitation employees had a clear and adverse impact on the cities' decision to contract these services with the private sector. Privatized sanitation services were much less likely to be present in cities where sanitation workers were organized, although they were more likely to be found in unionized cities where the relations between unions and management had a history of tension and contention. While the study concluded that the opposition of unions to privatization is "rational," in that unionization declined in those cities where privatization was implemented, privatization "did not necessarily lead to high unemployment among displaced workers" for several reasons, not the least of which was that former municipal workers often were hired by the private firm winning the contract.[9]

As a result of these conditions, there are perhaps 18,000 government corporations chartered by subnational governments, the bulk of which were founded after 1950.[10]

In short, government administrators at the federal, state, and local levels have found two different maneuvers that they can use to steer their ways around conservative belief systems. At the federal level, this method is the government contract awarded to the private entrepreneur. At the state and local levels, it is the public authority chartered, but not managed, by the government.

THE POLITICS OF PRIVATIZATION

Government's choice to provide public services by contracting with private corporations can bring with it several advantages, most of which relate to political flexibility. Political debts can be paid off, the size of governments can, at least on paper, be reduced, and genuine and responsible political responsiveness can, on occasion, be attained by maneuvering around a cumbersome public bureaucracy. These motivations, it should be stressed, hold true for public administrators at all levels of government, not just federal administrators, although the federal government remains the public sector's primary "privatizer." Let us consider some of these incentives in turn.[11]

- Contracting out, as opposed to using government personnel, permits the government to experiment with policies and new delivery systems. The government can always terminate a contract if the experiment fails, with little or no objection by an affected public.

  The desirability of using the private sector, rather than their own agencies, to try out new policies and delivery mechanisms, appears to be highly valued among public administrators. One survey of sixteen cities across the United States that privatized, or were seriously considering privatizing, federally mandated improvements in wastewater treatment works, found that these cities did so, in part, because they had "innovative managerial and institutional strengths."[12]

- Privatizing permits the government to hire specialists and people of unusual talent, without paying as much attention to such "affirmative action" items as sex, ethnicity, or veteran's status that can affect government hiring.

- Contracting out permits government agencies to benefit from, and have their services enhanced by, the existence of voluntary or charitable organizations that already may be doing what the government wishes to do. As we discuss in Chapter 12, this arrangement is known as "co-production."

- Certain short-term savings often can be realized, for example, civil service rules on pay scales and fringe benefits may be skirted by using contractors who pay only minimum wages to their employees. Other short-term savings can be obtained by leasing rather than purchasing new buildings, since the resultant government budget will show only the annual cost of the rent, as opposed to the expense of a capital project.

  But the realization of long-term savings is considerably less clear. One analysis of financial data covering a nine-year period for 100 cities in Massachusetts that had contracted out their property tax assessments (a relatively popular function for local governments to privatize) found that "the private sector does not have a claim to cost savings in this instance....Policymakers may do well to view contracting out as a temporary solution to technical infeasibility and should reevaluate their positions at the termination of contracts."[13]

- The personnel working for government can be expanded through contracts, even though the official size of the civil service remains the same or is actually reduced. This final point is especially pertinent when we consider the burgeoning pension programs for government employees at all levels. The actual cost of the pension programs to taxpayers is not completely known, but it is known that these programs are unusually (and perhaps unrealistically) generous.

- Finally, more political risks often can be borne by government when privatization is used. The government becomes a less visible, less direct actor when public policies are privatized.

  Empirical studies indicate that risk avoidance, particularly the avoidance of political risks, is a major motivation in exercising the privatization option among public administrators. The survey of sixteen cities dealing with the implementation of improvements in wastewater treatment plants, mentioned earlier, found that overcoming "resistance to the attendant political and economic risks" was a large consideration in making the decision to privatize.[14]

The decision by policymakers to contract out the implementation of their policies to private entrepreneurs is, in short, at least as much a political decision as it is a managerial and financial one. As we discuss later in this chapter, political considerations also appear to play a prominent role in the decisions made by public officials to create government corporations for the delivery of public services.

THE PRIVATIZATION OF FEDERAL POLICY

Nearly a fifth of all federal expenditures—about $200 billion—flow to private interests through contracts. Nearly four-fifths of this amount goes to private businesses in the United States; most of the remainder involves purchases of goods and services by the Department of Defense in foreign countries; and a small amount, about 3 percent of these dollars, goes to American educational and nonprofit institutions.[15]

How these "de-federalized" funds are spent, and on what, is not easily ascertained. Slightly more than half of the government's contract dollars are expended on supplies and equipment; more than a third goes to construction and other services, such as leasing arrangements and management consultants; and 14 percent is allocated to research and development (R & D).[16] The federal government directly supports about half of the entire national R & D effort through a combination of grants and contracts.[17]

It has been estimated that there are some 3 million "indirect" federal employees in the private sector (more than the number of "direct" federal civilian employees) working for the government under contracts with corporations and other organizations.[18] The federal government lets, on the average, about 17 million contracts a year to private enterprise.[19]

Even in an age of an alleged "peace dividend," the Department of Defense remains Washington's biggest business. Three quarters of all the federal government's expenditures on procurement contracts go to the Defense Department. Eighty percent of the federal funds contracted to business and nearly 30 percent of the funds going to educational and nonprofit institutions are Defense dollars. The bulk of Defense Department contracts is spent on supplies and equipment.[20]

Contracts and Consultants

A significant portion of the total contract portion of the federal budget (perhaps $15 billion) may be contracted to consultants, an area of considerable bureaucratic murk.[21] The Office of Management and Budget has, variously, stated that the number of consultants hired by federal officials in the late 1970s ranged from a high of 33,926 per year to a low of 18,393.[22] Both figures are improbably low. So murky is consulting that in 1989, the General Accounting Office was unable to ascertain, after an extensive study, how much the federal government spent on consultants.[23]

Private consultants often are among the most ardent in their arguments that private management somehow is more efficient than public management. For example, consultants were called in to the state of Connecticut to analyze methods of solid waste disposal. Their report was notably ideological in its view that private business could handle the problems of solid waste disposal far more effectively and efficiently than could government. "The apparent assumption of the consul-

tants was that inefficiency is inevitable in government agencies, even when those agencies are headed by businessmen (and, conversely, that efficiency is standard in authorities, even when they are headed by politicians)."[24] Similarly, when the Arthur D. Little, Inc., consultants analyzed postal services for the U.S. government in 1968, its report concluded, with essentially no evidence whatever, that an independent postal service would be a more "businesslike" operation, and therefore could provide less costly service, than would a public agency. When the reorganization of the postal service was accomplished in 1971, converting it from a public agency to a public corporation, the effect was to "substitute business patronage for political patronage."[25]

Who are these consultants? No one has a definitive list, but they include economists, social scientists, education specialists, management consultants, operations researchers, transportation consultants, and urban affairs consultants. These operations range from the infinitesimal (the so-called boutiques that are highly specialized and come and go) to the very large (such as Westinghouse and General Electric). The Washington-based consultants (almost 20,000 of them, working in more than 1,300 firms, by one count[26]) are known as the "Beltway bandits" because many of them are located near the Beltway Road that circles through the suburbs of Washington, and they have their own lobby in the capitol, the Professional Services Council.

Among the more intriguing recipients of government contracts are the so-called nonprofits. Technically, a nonprofit consulting firm, voluntary community group, or research organization (such as a university), is legally not a profitmaking organization and is not taxed on the grounds that it cannot sell stock and therefore distribute profits to shareholders.

Perhaps the most fascinating aspect of the nonprofits is that, in many cases, the government itself established them as private think tanks that would provide independent research for federal agencies. The Defense Department has been the most active in establishing these organizations, known as Federal Contract Research Centers, and in the mid-1970s these were estimated as having federal contract incomes of more than

$1.7 billion.[27] Representative Federal Contract Research Centers include the Systems Development Corporation; Aerospace, Inc.; the Mitre Corporation; and a number of others.

Although the Federal Contract Research Centers are big operations, their legality is unclear. The Government Corporation Control Act of 1945 seems to prohibit, in rather firm phrases, the creation of government corporations (which these Centers are) without the approval of Congress. Nevertheless, neither Congress nor the Comptroller General have been especially enthusiastic in their enforcement of the Act as it applies to Federal Contract Research Centers, which have been established unilaterally by the executive branch.[28]

Other nonprofit research and consulting organizations are nominally the results of efforts by private industry, but often with substantial government encouragement, as opposed to outright creation by the government. One survey, conducted by the National Science Foundation, found 159 nonprofit research organizations of this kind. Nearly two-thirds of their research contracts came from the federal government, with the four largest of these organizations receiving a third of the total federal dollars contracted with the group; the eight largest took half of the federal contracts.[29] These organizations include Stanford Research Institute, founded in 1946 by Stanford University; Battelle, founded by Gordon Battelle in 1923; the Brookings Institution (founded in 1926); the National Bureau of Economic Research (founded in 1920 by private economists, who developed such concepts as the Gross National Product); the Committee for Economic Development; and a number of others.

Consultants to the federal government operate in somewhat of a nether world, and prefer it that way. It was only in 1990 that federal regulations appeared that required consultants who contracted or subcontracted with federal agencies to disclose their other public and private clients with whom they have worked over the past year. This requirement was issued because of a growing ethical problem: Consultants were promoting their other clients for government contracts with the federal agencies with which they were consulting. One member of Congress has estimated that 70 percent of all the information released by the federal government is tainted by dint of having been formulated by consultants who could have a conflict of interest.[30] Presumably, federal administrators, as a result of the regulations of 1990, will at least be in a position to know when the consultants whom they have hired are working "both sides of the street." The public, however, will not be in the same position to know, since the disclosure forms are not available to the public.

It is also unclear if these regulations will work. "Washington's army of consultants has generally accepted the new rules without much more than grumbling—an indication that the regulations are not expected to significantly affect the way consultants go about their business."[31] Nevertheless, the Beltway bandits are so ensconced in the Washington way of doing business that even their most fervent critics agree that the federal government would "stop" in the unlikely event that their services were suddenly and unilaterally terminated.[32]

The Structure of Federal Privatization

All federal agencies contract out work to private firms under the general policy stated by Office of Management and Budget Circular A-76, which traces its roots to Bureau of the Budget Bulletin Number 55-4 of 1955, and which voiced President Dwight Eisenhower's general policy of relying on private enterprise to supply federal needs. OMB Circular A-76 was issued in 1966 and expanded in 1979 and in 1983; it states that it is the government's policy "to rely on competitive private enterprise to supply the commercial and industrial products and services it needs," although as the directive reluctantly notes, the government should perform those duties that "are inherently governmental in nature, being...intimately related to the public interest."

Although OMB Circular A-76 stipulates that rigorous cost comparisons between in-house executions and contracting out should be done for any given project, such comparisons rarely are made, largely because there are virtually no resources for doing so. The Office of Management and Budget (OMB), located within the Office of the President, and the General Accounting Office (GAO), which reports directly to Congress, are the two major federal agencies charged with assuring contract compliance and the efficiency and effectiveness of government programs generally. Yet the OMB has only one understaffed unit within it, the Office of Federal Procurement Policy, created in 1974, that deals with contracting services. Relatedly, the GAO has found the management of contracting to be less than tight on a number of grounds, but it has not really taken a hard look at the overall problem.

The federal contracting system is one of inordinate complexity. In the procurement area alone, which accounts for the bulk of federal contracts, there are some 4,000 separate legislative provisions instructing bureaucrats how to contract. These laws are interpreted by 887 sets of regulations that the bureaucracy has imposed upon itself. These regulations add up to 64,600 pages, about a third of which are changed every year. Some 150,000 federal employees who handle contracts and who deal with tens of thousands of private businesses and 485 separate federal procurement offices in the process, must keep abreast of these changes.[33] In the Defense Department alone, there are 25,000 auditors and inspectors who check up on procurement regulations that exceed 30,000 pages. These regulations are issued by seventy-nine different Pentagon offices, which must report to fifty-five congressional subcommittees and twenty-nine congressional committees.[34]

The Process of Federal Privatization

The 150,000 federal contracting officers who must deal with the welter of regulations regarding privatization have an influence beyond their nominal station. Phillip J. Cooper notes that "the interaction of companies with federal contracting officers results in the adoption by firms of a set of prices and conditions for doing business with the federal government which are then applied to state and local activities. The negotiations with federal contracting officers…constitute de facto preemption of local negotiating efforts."[35]

Integration: Public Agency meets Private Organization. Cooper has described the contractual administrative process as an "integration-operation-separation model." The integration phase is, in Cooper's words, "politically overloaded…the concept that the contracting officer's primary pur-

pose is to acquire a contract that promises the highest quality at the lowest price is misleading if not false…the primary task of the contracting officer is to balance political demands and supports with budgetary restrictions and governmental needs."[36]

Accordingly, firms are sought by the federal government in one of two ways: the "contract negotiation process" or the "advertised bid process." Although advertised bidding for virtually all contracts is required under federal law, notably by the Armed Services Procurement Act of 1949, by "the calculations of most authors and government reports, approximately 85 percent of contract expenditures" are never let for bid.[37]

All government contracts, whether they already have been awarded or not, are listed in the official government publication, *Commerce Business Daily.* More than 30,000 copies are distributed every day, five days a week. Although two-thirds of these contracts already have been awarded (or virtually so) without competitive bidding, much of the remaining third appear to have been quietly let by federal officials under the table to favored contractors, and advertising them in *Commerce Business Daily* is strictly *pro forma.* The editor of the *Daily* has noted several "scams" that agencies use to avoid competitive bidding, such as miscoding a contract in the advertisement so that potential bidders can never find it ("That happens pretty often"); mentioning a particular firm in the ad itself ("That's a pretty clear tipoff that there's not going to be any competition"); and mandating absurdly brief deadlines for bids. In addition, billions of dollars worth of federal contracts are never advertised at all in *Commerce Business Daily*—perhaps $4 billion in research contracts alone in 1979, for example. More significantly, the Beltway bandits consider the process a joke; according to one, "Anybody who believes you read the [*Commerce Business Daily*] and get your contracts [from it], is out of it. You'd starve."[38]

Negotiated contracts, obviously, constitute the vast bulk of federal contracts, at least as measured by dollars expended. These are of two types. The first is the "negotiated competitive contract." In this version, a group of firms are involved in direct negotiations, or some advertising is actually indulged in and negotiations are initiated with the most interesting prospects. The other is the "sole source contract." In this contract, the contracting officer selects whatever firm or organization that he or she believes is capable of meeting the terms of the contract. Regardless of whether the contract was negotiated or bid upon, the contracting officer's decisions are virtually never overturned on appeals made by disappointed rivals. "Once integrated into the public sector, firms tend to remain there."[39]

Operation: A New Intimacy Between Agency and Organization. The "operation phase" follows integration, in which the contractor is legally bound to the government, and this phase often involves an interesting intimacy between contractor and agency. Both sides "play games." Private companies tend to deflate their cost estimates to secure the contract. But it is a practice in which public agencies are complicit: "one of the things that we have got to stop doing in our contracting is playing games—the government and the contractor....We know that if we tell the [Department of Defense]...how much something is really going to cost, they may scrub it. And they know that if they tell the Congress how much it's really going to cost, the Congress may scrub it. So you start in with both sides knowing that it is going to cost more."[40]

Another aspect of the problem is the well-publicized "revolving door." When federal officials retire or resign from government, especially if they were in jobs that involve agency contracts with the private sector, they frequently end up as high-salaried executives in the company with which they dealt as a federal administrator. One investigation by the Federal Pay Commission found that when top federal employees left government for private industry, their salaries went up, on the average, by almost 75 to 100 percent. The longer one was in government service, the more lucrative one's opportunities outside of it.[41]

About a quarter of all military officers who retire at the rank of major or above go to work for Defense Department contractors.[42] One study found that, of those military retirees who did go to work for defense firms, 28 percent had taken jobs that related directly to work that they had been doing while in active service.[43] The country's top eight defense contractors alone hired 1,455 military officers who retired in the 1970s. These "retirees" appear to do very well in their second careers. A minimum retainer for services in the defense industry is $30,000 a year, plus expenses, and consultants who once held important positions in the Pentagon commonly commanded $100,000 a year from each company that purchased their services.[44]

Moreover, it is not uncommon for public officials to start careers in government, leave for industry, return to government, and so on and so forth. This is the "revolving door" phenomenon so often decried by the press. As one former contract officer at the Department of Energy, which spends nearly nine-tenths of its budget (about $11 billion) on contracts with private companies, has noted, "People at DOE bounce back and forth between government and industry just like Ping-Pong balls."[45] There have been cases recorded of old friends monitoring the contract compliance of each other. First, one works for the agency letting the contract, and the other works for the company receiving it; later, the roles are reversed, as one leaves the agency to work in the same company, and the other returns as a consultant to the agency to monitor the contracts that the agency awards to the company! And so the revolving door goes.[46]

It is not surprising that many public officials who administer contractual relationships with private companies see these contractors as prospective employers; objectivity, consequently, can become blurred. One major general in the air force, for example, accepted a job with a consultant firm that had just been awarded a $97,303 noncompetitive bid by *him.* He was then directed by the firm to manage the contract that he had just awarded it. He did, and a year later the contract was renewed by the air force for another $99,774.[47]

This kind of relationship between government and business is not isolated. A report on contracting practices in the Pentagon issued by the General Accounting Office found not only that more than four-fifths of its contracts had been awarded without competitive bidding, but also that more than half of these went to former high-level Pentagon executives. Almost three quarters of the contracts awarded to former Defense Department officials were awarded without competition. Indeed, more than half of all contracts awarded by the Pentagon, competitive or otherwise, went to former Pentagon employees. Significantly, 40 percent of the contracts awarded by the Defense Department were originally suggested by the contractor instead of by the department, a figure which appears to be about double that of civilian agencies.[48]

Even more disturbing, another investigation by the General Accounting Office concluded that a proportion of 5,100 former high- and mid-level Pentagon employees, who had retired three to four years earlier, had gone to work for contractors with whom they had dealt as federal officials (26 percent). Some of these Pentagon employees had worked with these contractors on the same project in both their federal and postfederal careers (21 percent). Some had been responsible in the Pentagon for Defense Department contracts that subsequently supported their private employment (7 percent). An estimated 32 percent of these former Pentagon employees fell into one or more of these categories. "The public could perceive," reported the GAO, that these former public administrators "may not have acted in the best interest of the government because they viewed a defense contractor as a potential employer."[49]

Although there are numerous federal statutes banning conflicts of interest between former federal employees and private companies, few, if any, work. Former public officials, depending on the circumstances, can be prohibited from representing private interests to their former agencies from anywhere from a year after their departure to a lifetime, and penalties for violating these laws can be as much as two years in jail and $10,000 in fines. The Ethics Reform Act of 1989 actually prohibits former federal executives from lobbying not only their former agencies but also in their area of expertise for a year following their departure from the government. But failure to enforce these statutes generally relates to what "representation" in such instances really means, and to the concomitant difficulties in proving representation.

Separation: The Unfulfilled Act. The final phase in the contracting cycle is that of separation, or how the government terminates contractors and resolves disputes.

Neither termination nor dispute resolution are simple acts, since agencies typically accept goods and services from contractors over a prolonged period of time. Moreover, terminating a contract often has adverse implications for the public contracting officer as well as for the contractor: often, a contract cancellation "drastically disrupts careers of those associated with it, including government administrators, private contractors, and scientists and engineers....[It] hurts regional economies. What causes pain locally triggers congressional rescue activity."[50]

Bringing Congress into the act is in the interest of neither the agency nor the firm, but especially not of the agency. Thus, "government contractual relationships may be more like treaties than contracts in that often no real separation occurs. Certain obligations, which are in most cases politically rather than legally enforced, remain."[51]

Two Models of Contracting

The treaty-like nature of federal contracting and procurement procedures relates to two very different perspectives on government's relationship with industry. These opposing world views have been called the *formal model* of contracting and procurement and the *joint management model*.[52]

The formal model envisions the relationships within the Federal Contract Procurement System and, for that matter, within the military-industrial complex itself, as discrete, highly task-specific arrangements among parties that are entirely independent of one another. Buyers are wholly separate from sellers. As Raymond G. Hunt observes, "The steam behind the...[formal model] comes from a number of sources: ideologies about the American free enterprise economy and anxieties about creeping socialism; desires to contract fairly; apprehensions about a nefarious military-industrial complex; fears of the political-moral dangers of anything other than arms-length government-industrial dealings; pragmatic hopes for market-compelled efficiencies and economy; and optimistic expectations that, bolstered by sophisticated systems analysis and management science devices, market-based fixed price arrangements can be contrived that will solve many vexing procedural and managerial problems in the [Federal Contract Procurement System]...simply by making them go away."[53]

By contrast, the joint management model emphasizes cooperative problem solving between the public and private sectors and shared managerial tasks. The joint management model assumes that no mechanistic formal model strategy "can be competent to dynamic undertakings such as [research and development] or modern complex system acquisition....in sharp contrast with the [formal model], the basic feature of the cooperative [joint management model] is a more or less even, although perhaps fluctuating, distribution of power between the participating actors and organizations"—in other words, the government buyer and the private seller.[54]

The Formal Model: Major Contractual Types. Among the contractual forms that are used under the formal model are *fixed-price contracts*, which state that a private company will deliver whatever service or product is written into the contract on a predetermined date for a price that will not vary, regardless of unanticipated circumstances that may or may not arise prior to the delivery date.[55]

Another form of contract that falls under the category of the formal model is called *total package procurement*. Total package procurement amounts to a set of somewhat artificial devices designed to simulate a competitive market situation. Under total package procurement, contractors are invited to bid on a single package that runs from development, through production, to eventual operational support of a project. The idea was to encourage competition, reduce the length of contract negotiations, and to enhance the possibility of more frequent fixed price contracting. Total package procurement was abolished in the early 1970s after it was attempted on such fiascoes as the production of the C-5A cargo plane and several other projects that ended in gross cost overruns.

A third version of the formal model is the *incentive contract*. Incentive contracts attempt to encourage contractors to increase the quality of their performance by permitting them to share in any monetary gains that may derive from improvements that they are able to attain in a particular project. For example, if a project is delivered ahead of schedule, the incentive contract would provide a bonus to the contractor on the logic that, by being ahead of schedule, the contractor saved the government money. In practice, incentive contracts rarely work because it is so difficult to project in any reasonable amount of detail what it will take to effect a contractor's day-to-day decisions and what specific improvements must be obtained. According to some citizens, the assumptions implicit in an incentive contract are, in fact, so complex that they have essentially failed as a method of implementing the formal model, the essence of which is the fixed-price contract.[56]

Fixed-price contracts, total package procurement, and incentive contracts are the major forms of contracting reflecting the values of the formal model, but the kinds of contracts used under the joint management model display an entirely different belief system, one, as we stated earlier, that assumes a close working relationship between the contractor and the government.

The Joint Management Model: Major Contractual Types. The major type of contract used by the joint management model is the *cost-plus contract*. A cost-plus contract underwrites the contractor's risks by assuring that the government will cover all costs accrued by the contractor in developing a project and then adds an additional amount as the contractor's profit.[57]

There are at least two kinds of cost-plus contracts. One is the *cost-plus-fixed-fee contract*, which provides for reimbursement of the contractor along with payment of a fee negotiated as a percentage of estimated costs of performance that has been established prior to undertaking the work. The cost-plus-fixed-fee contract succeeded the now illegal *cost plus percentage of cost contract*, which based fees charged by the contractor on actual costs. This type of contract was eliminated because it encouraged contractors to be as costly as possible, since their profits were based on the costs they incurred. A second type of cost-plus contract is the *cost-plus-award-fee contract*. Cost-plus-award-fee contracts permit payments of a fee to a contractor on the basis of after-the-fact evaluations of performance by government officials. Both cost-plus-fixed-fee contracts and cost-plus-award-fee contracts have been criticized on the grounds that they lead to cost overruns or are highly subjective because awards are determined by government administrators.[58]

Contracting and Weltanschauungen. The world views of the formal and joint management models of procurement and contracting are polar opposites. The formal model sees the public and private sectors as separate, perhaps adversarial, entities. It also assumes that everyone understands what the job is, and how it is to be done. The joint management model does not distinguish between the public and private sectors; "a buyer actively participates in a seller's operational decisions and one can hardly tell the players except from the logo on their coveralls."[59] Also in contrast to the formal model, the joint management model often assumes—at least in R & D contracting—that no one really understands what the job is and how it is to be done. This is sensible. Research and development projects are, by definition, projects that explore the unexplored, so much of "the job" to be done always is unknown. And R & D projects are an important component in federal contracting: more than 70 percent of all federal R & D spending is contracted out to private enterprise, and Washington supports more than half of all research and development in the nation.[60]

The joint management model is less acceptable politically than the formal model. It assumes that the world, including the federal government and private corporations, is interdependent, while the formal model does not recognize interdependency.

Both models have relevance. Government hostility to the private sector implied by the formal model may be justified when we learn of inordinately lax cost controls exercised by the government over private contractors, and what appears to be extraordinary avarice evidenced by contractors. The hammer, for example, falls somewhat short of what we think of as cutting-edge technology. Yet the Pentagon has been charged by its contractors and has paid them more than $350 for a hammer that can be purchased in a hardware store for seven dollars. Incidents such as these are not isolated. Can we really accept the trusting premises of the joint management model in light of these occurrences?

It is also apparent, however, that we often do not know what is entailed in fulfilling a contract, and in this sense the assumptions of the joint management model are accurate. The space shuttle and the stealth aircraft, for example, represent R & D contracts that could never be conducted (at least not honestly) on the basis of a fixed-price contract. How does one fix the price of making an idea into a reality? But one can fix the price of a reality that is known, common, and routine, such as collecting garbage, manufacturing bullets, or buying hammers, and these more mundane kinds of government contracting often seem to be overlooked by critics of the formal model, who tend to stress the complexities of the world of research and development in their arguments.

FEDERAL CONTRACTING: A CRITIQUE

Irrespective of the contracting model employed, it may be that neither the manpower nor the will to assure compliance by outside contractors exists at the federal level. Hence, we witness an absence of any kind of central record keeping by governments concerning their contractors; a lack of program integration; no kind of central control over service quality, prices charged to clients, and cost overruns; a rather insidious irresponsibility developing among government bureaucrats who are charged with monitoring and arranging contracts; and units charged with controlling compliance, but which cannot, because they already have overloaded working schedules.[61] The Department of Defense, the largest single contractor in government, has itself observed that "accurate information on the nature and extent of contract studies within the Department is difficult and often impossible to obtain....there is no effective control of contract studies within the Department."[62]

Conspiracy or Chaos?

Statements by federal contract officers in other departments on research and consulting contractors perhaps are more colorful.[63] "The bottom line on contracts—pure paper studies....The public gets ...maybe 10 percent of their money's worth," said one officer. And, of one $250,000 study, described as "an unintelligible pile of papers," a federal administrator said,

"Nothing was received and we paid thousands for it. It really is a lot of gobbledygook....As a taxpayer, I'm sick." Another said, "We're so busy trying to shovel money out the door, we don't have time to see what happens to it after it leaves. All the money could be stolen and I wouldn't know it....The place is a madhouse."

The waste, and the opportunities, are also recognized by the more enlightened contractors. A board member of the Institute of Management Consultants observes: "It's a game....Government comes to us and wants help in identifying their problems, but they don't seem to be able to use the material. They could spend much less and get more for it."[64]

"It looks like a conspiracy, but really it's chaos."[65] So stated one of the nation's leading experts on governing-by-contracting, and likely he is accurate. Nevertheless, conspiracy can capitalize on chaos more readily than on order, and the milieu of federal contracting smacks more of the former than the latter.

Government and Business: Four Cases

The examples are almost endless, but consider four instances of the relationships between government and business as they pertained to working together in the public interest.

Contracting in conflicts of interest. Monsanto Research Corporation, an arm of Monsanto Chemical Company, was awarded a $5.8 million contract by the Environmental Protection Agency (EPA) to measure the environmental dangers of various chemicals, including acrylonitrile. Monsanto is the nation's fourth largest producer of chemicals, and the world's largest manufacturer of acrylonitrile, a chemical used extensively in industry. Its wholly owned subsidiary, Monsanto Research, reported to the EPA that acrylonitrile was not hazardous to the environment, although an EPA official stated, "Quite frankly, I don't see how they reached that conclusion....It was not reasonable based on the data we have....Our conclusion is that acrylonitrile is one of the biggest sources of hydrocarbons in the petrochemical industry. It is a major polluter."[66]

Similarly, Exxon Research and Engineering Corporation, a branch of Exxon Oil Company, the world's largest oil producer, was hired by EPA to write the agency's environmental regulations for off-shore oil drilling. On the very day the EPA signed the $965,000 contract with Exxon (June 25, 1975), the Company discharged almost half a million gallons of polluted water into the sea near Alaska's Prudhoe Bay—a gross violation of EPA standards for which Exxon was later fined $100,000. When Exxon Research and Engineering Corporation sent its report to the Environmental Protection Agency, the agency's contract officers labeled it "shallow" and self-serving. Exxon had concluded that off-shore oil drilling did not pose any serious pollution problems. According to one EPA official, "There was a lot of p. r. [public relations] nonsense in a technical report extolling their environmental awareness."[67]

Contracting in corporate incompetence. Conflicts of interest are one thing, incompetence another. Consider two additional cases. One occurred between 1969 and 1973 when the Stanford Research Institute (SRI) was hired by the U.S. Office of Education (now the Department of Education) to evaluate the progress of children enrolled in its Headstart Program. When the report from Stanford Research Institute finally arrived, six months late, at the Office of Education, it was judged, with considerable reason, to be unacceptable. The director of the Headstart Evaluation Branch of the Office of Education "found not only that the work was poor, but that SRI had plagiarized, from among all possible sources, her own work."[68] She went on to note that one section of the report was "lifted almost word for word from my 1969 paper....can't your staff think for itself?"[69]

Despite what amounted to unequivocal proof that the Stanford Research Institute had no personnel qualified to undertake an evaluation of the Headstart and, later, the Followthrough Programs for the Office of Education, SRI's contracts were continued. Ultimately, the Stanford Research Institute was involved in an Office of Education contract amounting to more than $13 million; the Institute's "fee," by which was meant profit, for this project was $857,000.

Consider another example, the experience of the federal government when it undertook the largest job evaluation project ever attempted through a private contractor. When Congress created the U.S. Postal Corporation out of the old Postal Service in 1969, a remaining problem was the job status of the Postal Corporation's 750,000 employees. Reviewing and recategorizing the work of these employees amounted to a huge project in public personnel administration, yet the decision to let the contract in 1970 ultimately devolved to one man, whose background largely was in private business. He contacted a small number of corporations, but eventually awarded the contract to Westinghouse Corporation, which had bid $3 million—a bid that was $300,000 more than the next highest bid, and a million dollars more than the average bid of the four other bidders.

Cost and quality do not always correlate, and Washington's experience with Westinghouse shows that incompetence can come highly priced. By way of indication, the team of fifty self-designated experts that Westinghouse assembled to conduct a sophisticated study of personnel management included a sales manager of a soft drink vending equipment company, and a nuclear safety engineer.[70] According to Congress, not one member of this team had "specific and direct job evaluation experience."[71] In fact, so uncertain was Westinghouse over its own abilities in this area that it hired Fry Consultants to actually train its own people so that they could conduct the study!

Westinghouse was so grossly unqualified to conduct a personnel study that its ineptness eventually resulted in the most detailed congressional investigation into a consultant contract ever undertaken. Among other problems, the House Post Office and Civil Service Committee concluded that not only had the contract been awarded to a firm that had absolutely no experience or ability in the field for which it was hired, and had made by far the highest bid to conduct the study, but also that there were no criteria in existence by which *any* contractors were selected! This lack of criteria applied not only to the Postal Corporation study, but apparently to the whole of the federal government as well with regard to the letting of contracts.[72]

To Privatize or Not to Privatize? Questions of Efficiency, Policy, and Corruption

Should government privatize or not? Was the Office of Education less or more efficient than the Stanford Research Institute in managing the Headstart and Followthrough evaluations? True, Stanford Research Institute did not chalk up an admirable record in the process but, on the other hand, neither did the Office of Education by letting the contracts in the first place and, further, by not terminating them when its administrators found that the evaluations were being conducted with inordinate slovenliness. Was the Westinghouse Electric Corporation less or more efficient than the Postal Corporation in conducting the personnel reclassification study? Competency is difficult to ascribe to either party.

Although we have deliberately steered shy of arguing the obverse of the conventional wisdom (*i.e.*, that business is more efficient than government) by contending that government is innately more efficient than private enterprise, it does appear that government agencies may be able to execute some of their policies less expensively than private contractors are doing. One estimate, for example, placed the cost of personnel working under federal grants and contracts at *seven times* the cost of full-time federal personnel.[73] On the other hand, it also appears that government employees are doing jobs that may be best left to the private sector. The federal government, according to the Office of Management and Budget, pays some 400,000 of its employees to operate nearly 12,000 commercial or industrial activities that could be provided by private sources, at an annual cost of at least $18.5 billion.[74]

The efficiency question. It has been only comparatively recently that the federal government has taken any sort of genuine interest in empirically determining, rather than ideologically justifying, the assumption that "business is better." Consider the fate, for example, of OMB Circular A-49, which was issued by the then Bureau of the Budget in 1959. It urges government agencies to evaluate and maintain evaluations of the work of consulting contractors. The Circular has been virtually forgotten by federal officials, although it is still on the OMB's list of active regulations. One study found that OMB had assigned not one of its employees to be responsible for its administration; "OMB Circular A-49 washes out in the files after 1962."[75] Although there are signs of improvement, so lax has the federal government been in following up on the performance of contractors that even debarred and suspended firms can still receive federal contracts. One investigation by the Senate uncovered instances where companies that had been suspended by certain federal agencies for fraud were nonetheless acquiring contracts from other federal agencies.[76]

Beginning in the late 1970s, Congress and federal administrators began to take a renewed interest in the question of whether private companies really could supply federal needs more efficiently than public agencies. The first indication of this questioning was a congressional exempting of certain governmental functions from the provisions of OMB Circular A-76 during the 1970s. In 1979, Circular A-76 was altered, for the first time, so that detailed work statements would be used to evaluate just how well federal work was done by private contractors; a second major change was introduced in 1983, and agencies were directed to determine the most efficient way to complete a project in-house before comparing costs to have it done in the private sector.

In 1987, two new policies were introduced that indicated a further federal effort to get a handle on whether cost savings were actually being realized under OMB Circular A-76. One policy was Executive Order 12615, which essentially directed the Office of Management and Budget to conduct more rigorous and regular analyses of the savings acquired by contracting out under the provisions of OMB Circular A-76, with OMB picking up those savings at the agencies' expense. The other policy was the Commercial Activities Contracting Act of 1987, which focused on assuring the reliability and accuracy of reported savings accrued via contracting out.

Despite these and other efforts, however, the assessment of whether privatizing federal projects actually saves money is still undone. The cost studies ordered by Executive Order 12615 have been barely undertaken at all; methodological disputes abound, and so "a hard accounting of money saved and where it went is lacking";[77] and nineteen of twenty-one federal agencies surveyed believed that the goals of OMB Circular A-76 were unrealistic.[78] The chair of the Senate Budget Committee wrote the director of the Office of Management and Budget in 1990 that "The pursuit of the [federal privatization] program by the Reagan administration seems to have been built around the dubious ideological objective of 'privatization' without serious regard for efficiencies achieved or money wasted."[79]

The policy question. Compounding the already extraordinary difficulties involved in determining "privatized" governmental efficiency are the problems unique to managing public programs in a political world. Paramountly, these problems occur when "advice" from private interests waxes into policy executed by public administrators. The General Accounting Office has called Congress' attention to this fundamental dilemma in formal reports dating from 1961. As one of them put it, "Federal agencies have used contractors...to perform work that should be done by Federal employees because it involves basic management decisions. Although contractors may not be making final decisions, we are concerned about the extent to which contractors are influencing agencies' control of Federal policies and programs....it is sometimes difficult to tell where 'advice' stops and 'performance' begins."[80] Or, as a top official of GAO put it more pithily, "We've seen situations where an agency contracts out so much of its data gathering and policy analysis that it thinks it has control, but the consultant is, in effect, making the decision."[81]

The power that private interests have over public policy "makers" in the bureaucracy can be traced to their control of information. For example, the Institute for Government Research, founded in the early part of the century (in 1926 it merged with the Robert Brookings Graduate School and the Institute for Economics to form the Brookings Institution), was instrumental in drafting the Budget and Accounting Act of 1921, which provided not only the first guidelines for writing an annual, coherent budget for the federal government, but also created the Bureau of the Budget (now called the Office of Management and Budget) and the General Accounting Office—the two most important fiscal agencies in Washington. In fact, President Warren G. Harding in 1921 asked the Institute for Government Research to actually *write* the federal budget! This was a rather incredible delegation of power by a government to a private body. "If there is any task that is supposed to be an official and nondelegable executive function, it is the preparation of the budget."[82]

Nevertheless, comparable activities occur today. In the 1970s, for example, the Federal Power Commission and the Department of the Interior requested the American Gas Association to make the official estimates on national gas reserves. So sensitive was this information that the government permitted the natural gas industry to withhold data from the public in making its official estimates.[83] This kind of policy dominance by the private sector seems to prevail in the energy field, although, according to the General Accounting Office, it is by no means exclusive to it: Education, Health and Human Services, and Defense, for example, are hardly immune from it.[84]

All too frequently, the complexities that emerge from the interface between contractor and government make worthwhile public programs distressingly vulnerable. One of the sadder examples of the public's loss, resulting from an arrogant press, understandably frustrated contractors, an ignorant Congress, and timid bureaucrats, concerns a $3.4 million, five-year contract awarded in 1975 by the National Institute on Drug Abuse to Medical Research Applications, Inc. The firm was to collect clinical data on LAAM, a German drug reputed to be more effective than methadone for treating heroin addicts, and to develop it for widespread use. By 1979, the research (involving 6,000 addicts) was essentially completed, "and the work was found to be very good."[85] But columnist Jack Anderson was attacking the Institute (and Congress) as a wanton wastrel of taxpayers' dollars, citing the LAAM research contract as but one example. Consequently, the House Subcommittee on Health and the Environment questioned the Institute's management of the contract. Soon, according to the federal project officer in charge of the contract, Institute "people were saying, 'If we do this

wrong, Anderson will write an article about us'....Everybody was afraid."[86] When the nearly completed research project came up for renewal of its contract, the Institute withdrew its funding. Because of this termination, Medical Research Applications boxed up some 400,000 pages of first rate data that it had amassed, and stored them—as was its legal right under its contract with the Institute.

The research, a critical part of a larger, $10 million research effort on LAAM sponsored by the Institute, has never been used, either by the government or the contractor; both sides need the other's data if LAAM is to be used in the United States to relieve heroin addiction. Both sides agree on one thing, however; misguided politics prevailed: A federal official familiar with the episode stated, "It was the government bureaucracy that botched it up. It was politics. The thing is, the contractor did a very good job."[87]

In short, effectiveness, efficiency, and the proper role of the private sector in the public's business are difficult to demonstrate empirically one way or the other.

The corruption question. All to frequently, honesty is difficult to demonstrate empirically in the federal contracting culture. The examples of fraud and corruption, particularly in the area of defense contracting, are becoming almost legion. Between 1983 and 1990, twenty-five of the 100 largest contractors for the Pentagon were found guilty of procurement fraud, some of them more than once.[88] "Operation Ill Wind," begun covertly in the mid-1980s by the U.S. Justice Department (it became public only in 1988), had, by 1990, convicted for procurement fraud thirty-nine corporate executives, government officials, corporations, and consultants who had contracts with the Defense Department, with a total of 100 convictions ultimately anticipated.[89]

"Fraud," it should be noted, does not mean the inadvertent failure to dot the proverbial "i" in a procurement contract. In the case of Operation Ill Wind, for example, it meant that the thirty-nine convictions (as of 1990) had led to the recovery of more than $24 million in fines and forfeitures. Fraud means practices such as bribing public administrators to obtain inside, often secret, information for purposes of bid-rigging; falsifying weapons test results; failing to conduct specifically contracted tests, and then lying about it; grossly overcharging the government with padded accounts; and hiding the bad news about grotesque cost overruns long after such overruns should have been reported.

Why does fraud continue unabated? Because, with few exceptions, the federal government keeps coming back for more.[90] Not one of the twenty-five major corporations convicted of procurement fraud between 1983 and 1990 was barred from further contract work with the federal government. For example, Northrup Corporation in 1990 pleaded guilty to falsifying test results on missile and aircraft components; the Pentagon "debarred" (that is, suspended) the division of Northrup which had been responsible for falsifying the results, but the other divisions of Northrup, notably one that supplied a component for the U.S. Marine Corps' Harrier jet, were permitted to continue their defense contracts and bid for new ones. Some companies are not even as inconvenienced as Northrup was. In 1990, Emerson Electric Company pleaded guilty to no fewer than four felony counts for overcharging the government for electronics components, but it remained on the government's approved list of contractors. The list goes on.

The reason why the federal government keeps contracting with proven felons relates, in the view of some, to a contracting culture in the federal bureaucracy, particularly in the Pentagon, that places scant value on acquiring one's money's worth. As a former procurement officer for the U.S. Air Force put it, "It doesn't matter if you screw everything up, as long as you keep the dollars flowing."[91] When this entrenched bureaucratic culture (which places a premium on hiding the bad news, whether it is corruption or cost overruns, for the sake of assuring an unimpeded flow of federal allocations from Congress) is combined with the daunting political difficulties of separating, even in the face of criminal convictions, contractor from agency (which, as we discussed earlier, are conjoined more by "treaty" than by contract), then the vast dimensions of the problem become clearer. Corruption in contracting will never be controlled as long as careers depend more on maintaining that flow of federal dollars than on managing it.

Just how deeply this culture penetrates can be judged by the brief history of the Pentagon's position of under secretary of defense for acquisition—a position created as a civilian "procurement czar" by Congress in 1986 as a means of cleaning up the contracting situation in the Department of Defense. Within the space of its first four years of existence, the position's first three occupants failed to bring any control to procurement, and each had resigned under pressure.[92]

We stated earlier that effectiveness, efficiency, and the proper role of the private sector in the public's business are difficult to demonstrate empirically one way or the other. But this empirical difficulty does not extend to demonstrating the existence of widespread corruption, which can be and has been proven in court, nor to showing the federal government's lethargy in responding to that corruption.

CONTRACTING AT THE GRASSROOTS

Although contracting out at the state and local levels has never attained the proportions achieved by the federal government, it nonetheless represents a significant way that state and local governments implement their public programs. Table 11-1 lists the major categories of public services that are privatized by cities and counties.

The kinds of services that local governments contract out to private corporations are surprisingly broad. Contracts are let for construction; the purchasing of equipment, supplies, concessions, and franchises; and the supplying of services, such as solid waste collection and disposal. Research indicates that local governments, in particular, privatize services; significant numbers of local governments contract out architectural and engineering services, street maintenance, building repair, and (depending upon the study) garbage collection.[93]

Governments versus Corporations

Governments are not relegated to contracting only with the private sector; they may also contract with the public sector in the form of other governments. This phenomenon, usually called "intergovernmental service agreements," does

TABLE 11-1 Local Services Contracted with the Private Sector

Frequency Contracted (Percent)	Type of service		
	Professional	Housekeeping	Direct citizen delivery
50% or more	Architectural services	Street construction	
	Engineering services	Building repair	
33-49	Legal counsel	Equipment maintenance	Solid waste collection Ambulance Services
15-32	Land use/ planning	Building maintenance	Nursing for the elderly Child day care Halfway houses Snow removal
	Vehicle maintenance		
	Administrative support		
	Food service for employees		
	Street maintenance		
5-11	Grounds maintenance		Recreation for the elderly Leaf collection Public recreation
	First aid for employees		
	Police communication		

Source: Patricia S. Florestano and Stephen B. Gordon, "A survey of City and County Use of Private Contracting," *The Urban Interest,* 3 (Spring 1981), p. 25. The data in the table represent 225 responses to a survey of 803 member agencies of the National Institute of Governmental Purchasing.

not boast a snappy moniker like "privatization"; if it did, presumably it would be called "publicization." We consider intergovernmental arrangements for implementing public policy more extensively in Chapter 12.

Table 11-2 lists the major services that cities contract out to private firms as a percentage of all the contracts they let, that is, contracts let to other governments and private firms combined. Of the twenty-three services listed, contracting to pri-

vate companies increased in all but four from 1972 to 1982. These increases occurred primarily at the expense of intergovernmental service contracting by cities.[94]

The data in Table 11-2 are supported by other measures of the growth in privatization at the grassroots. State and local spending for services provided by the private sector nearly tripled between 1975 and 1982, when it hit $81 billion, and in some city governments a third of the budget is

TABLE 11-2 Cities' Use of Private Contracting as Percentage of Their Use of All (Public Plus Private) Contracting

	1972 survey (2,375 cities responding)	1982 survey (1,439 cities responding)
Services with similar names in both surveys		
Solid waste disposal	44%	46%
Street lighting	80	66
Utility billing	56	61
Ambulance services	57	60
Animal control	31	26
Housing	5	23
Hospitals	38	61
Recreational facilities	4	33
Parks	3	68
Museums	20	20
Legal services	84	90
Payroll	56	85
Tax assessing	14	15
Personnel services	8	73
Public relations	67	89
Services with slightly different names in both surveys		
Snow plowing	30	85
Crime prevention/patrol	2	42
Traffic control	4	20
Insect control	8	33
Public health	2	19
Drug/alcohol treatment	7	15
Mental health	18	14

Source: Lori M. Henderson, "Intergovernmental Service Arrangements and Transfer of Functions," *Municipal Year Book, 1985* (Washington, D.C.: International City Management Association, 1985), p. 201.

spent via contracts.[95] The privatization option is clearly an increasingly popular one among state and local officials.

Contracting and Co-production: Public Sector, Private Sector, and Third Sector

We should note that our use of the term "private sector" in our discussion of government contracting includes not only for-profit corporations but nonprofit organizations as well—organizations such as social service agencies, cultural groups, neighborhood associations, health organizations, and so forth, that are not government agencies. Tables 11-1 and 11-2 include nonprofit organizations but do not distinguish between them and for-profit companies. Those services that are identified in Tables 11-1 and 11-2 as "Nursing for the Elderly," "Child Day Care," "Halfway Houses," "Recreation for the Elderly," "Public Recreation," "Housing," "Hospitals," "Recreational Facilities," "Public Health," "Drug/Alcohol Treatment," and "Mental Health" often are provided by nonprofit organizations under contracts with local government agencies.

We are only beginning to learn about the contractual and fiscal connections between the public sector and the "third sector" as nonprofit, charitable, and voluntary organizations are sometimes called. Third sector organizations are major players in what has come to be known as *co-production*, or the cooperative relationship established between governments and third-sector organizations for the delivery of public services. Sometimes these co-productive relationships are informal, and do not involve monetary transfers or contracts, but, as often as not, they are contracted.

The Urban Institute has made some important contributions to our understanding of these co-productive relationships. In a careful empirical examination of 3,411 local nonprofit human service organizations in twelve representative metropolitan areas and four rural areas, the Urban Institute discovered that governments are unusually and surprisingly hefty supporters of supposedly independent, nonprofit human service organizations. More than 38 percent of the revenues of these organizations comes from governments![96]

Because of "pass through" arrangements (*e.g.*, federal monies to subnational governments that ultimately are used to fund contracts with nonprofit service organizations), identifying the level of government (*i.e.*, federal, state, or local), and each level's proportionate contribution via contracts to these agencies can be extremely difficult to ascertain. However, it appears that most of the funds that are used to support contracts with nonprofit human services organizations are federal funds that Washington has transferred as grants-in-aid to state and local governments, while almost all of the contracting agents who negotiate contracts with these organizations, so they may provide human services, are state and local officials. In any event, the point stands that governments are major actors in the supposedly "private" provision of public services.

In fact, governments are *the* major actors; the next largest source of revenues for nonprofit human services organizations is from the collection of fees, dues, and charges to clients and members of the organizations themselves (less than 30 percent). These sources are followed by others: private and direct giving by individuals (nearly 12 percent), funds from miscellaneous projects such as bake sales (6 percent), United Way fund (more than 5 percent), income from endowments and investments (less than 5 percent), foundation grants (less than 4 percent), corporate gifts (3 percent), and other sources contributing less than 2 percent. Total private giving to nonprofit human services organizations (which Americans typically perceive to be private charities) amounts to only 21 percent of their revenues, compared to the 38 percent of their income that is obtained from government contracts![97]

Just as governments support nonprofit organizations, so do nonprofit organizations support governments. Forty-two percent of *all* public spending for health care (excluding that provided by hospitals), social services, housing and community development, employment and training programs, and art and cultural programs goes to support the delivery of these programs *not* by government agencies, but by private, nonprofit groups![98]

Another 19 percent of government's human service delivery dollars is spent by means of contracts with private, for-profit organizations. In other words, an impressive 61 percent of public expenditures for human services is channelled to private-sector organizations, both nonprofit and for-profit, that are responsible for implementing these programs! The remaining 39 percent is delivered directly by government agencies. The largest single deliverer of publicly financed human services, however, remains the nonprofit sector: "It is this government-nonprofit partnership that forms the core of human service delivery systems in the United States."[99]

Public welfare in the United States, in sum, is mostly a private enterprise.

A More Manageable Task?

State and local governments appear to have a reasonably firm, if occasionally tenuous, grip on their private contractors. First, despite its growing popularity among the grass-roots governments, privatization nonetheless remains relatively restricted in its use at these levels, and so the supervisory chore is more manageable than at the federal level. A review of the literature on the topic concluded that subnational contracting of all types with private firms was "limited,"[100] and that privatizing public services by local governments ran a distant third to governments providing the services themselves or via intergovernment agreements. "Even in the case of the two governmental services most frequently contracted to private firms, refuse collection and engineering tasks, many more jurisdictions provide these two services themselves than contract with private firms or other governments."[101]

Second, public controls over certain categories of contracting are relatively thorough at the subnational levels. Virtually all state and local governments have detailed regulations governing construction contracts with private builders; they maintain sizeable building inspection operations and central purchasing units, which are normally responsible and well-run. Moreover, state and local governments have considerable experience in using the contract (in the form of letting franchises, leases, concessions, and arranging sales) as a device that actually makes money for governments rather than as a mechanism for spending it.

Third, competitive bidding, while not as common a practice as it perhaps should be, seems to be used frequently by subnational governments. One national study found that the proportion of local contracts let to the private sector on a competitive basis was about equal to the proportion that were negotiated,[102] in contrast to the estimated 85 percent of all contracts that are negotiated by federal agencies without competitive bidding.

Finally, oversight of a company's performance by state and local officials, while less than systematic, at least seems to be a matter of concern. One survey found a surprising propensity among these officials to take "the fairly dramatic step" of changing from private supplier to public provider, or vice versa, indicating an interest by state and local governments in determining whether the private sphere or the public one was the more efficient deliverer of services.[103]

Privatization: Official Opinion and Public Opinion

What do local officials themselves think about the contracting option? Table 11-3 indicates these opinions. By and large, local officials think that they get both efficient and effective service by privatization, although there are some substantial minority opinions to the contrary. But it should be noted that local officials have approached the contracting alternative with some caution. One study found that local governments contracted out no fewer than thirty-three services to private contractors, but that the average number of services contracted out by cities and counties averaged fewer than eight. "With such a large number of possible

services, an average of less than eight does not indicate a substantial movement from public to private service delivery."[104]

It is entirely possible that local government officials would be more enthusiastic about privatization than they are if their citizens were more trusting of the privatization option. However, the people are notably leery about turning over the delivery of public services to private corporations. Asked in a national survey whether they thought local government or private enterprise could deliver six selected services more efficiently, only one (hospital health care) was identified by Americans as a service that private vendors could provide more efficiently than local government—and then by the notably slender margin of 1 percent. Although more highly educated respondents evidenced a greater faith in corporate America as an efficient deliverer of local services (college graduates picked private enterprise as a superior provider of three of the six services), the point nonetheless stands that, in one of the globe's major bastions of capitalism, government generally is more trusted than corporations to deliver public programs efficiently. Table 11-4 provides details of the survey.

TABLE 11-3 Local Public Administrators' Opinions on Contracting Out Local Services

Statement	Responses (N = 225)
Contracting out costs *less* than government provision	43%
Contracting out costs *the same* as government provision	13
Contracting out costs *more* than government provision	27
No answer	17
Total	100
Contracting out results in quality *poorer* than government provision	7
Contracting out results in quality *the same* as government provision	32
Contracting out results in quality *better* than government provision	32
No answer	29
Total	100

Source: Patricia S. Florestano and Stephen B. Gordon, "A Survey of City and County Use of Private Contracting," *The Urban Interest*, 3 (Spring 1981), p. 25.

GOVERNMENT CONTRACTING: WHAT MUST BE DONE?

The relatively high concern displayed by local administrators in measuring and comparing the costs of services provided by the public and private sectors points to the fundamental dilemma of government contracting: American governments have no instrument and no established procedures for assuring that the public's business is conducted efficiently, effectively, and without undue influence by private interests. We are not arguing that government can be conducted more efficiently through public agencies, or through government corporations (considered next), or through private business. What we are suggesting is that improved means be established to determine which of these systems, and possibly other devices, would conduct particular projects most effectively and efficiently.

How can we make these determinations? At least three steps seem warranted. One is to estab-

TABLE 11-4 Popular Preferences about Local Service Deliverers, Private or Public, for Selected Services, 1985

	Parking Facilities			Street Maintenance			Hospitals		
	Private Companies	Local Government	Don't Know	Private Companies	Local Government	Don't Know	Private Companies	Local Government	Don't Know
Total Public	42%	48%	10%	21%	73%	6%	46%	45%	9%
Under 35 Years of Age	45	47	8	22	73	5	45	48	7
Over 65	34	50	16	17	71	12	47	36	17
High School Incomplete	37	50	13	16	74	10	34	54	12
College Graduate	50	45	5	29	69	2	67	28	5
Household Income									
Under $15,000	40	44	16	21	69	10	39	48	13
$40,000+	47	49	4	25	73	2	60	35	5
White	42	48	10	21	74	5	49	43	8
Nonwhite	45	43	12	19	70	11	29	58	13
Nonmetro	40	49	11	23	71	6	47	44	9
Metro—50,000 and over									
Fringe	41	50	9	19	76	5	47	44	9
Central City	47	43	10	21	71	8	46	46	8

Source: Advisory Commission in Intergovernmental Relations, *Changing Public Attitudes on Governments and Taxes, 1985* (Washington, D.C.: U.S. Government Printing Office, 1985), pp. 25-29.

TABLE 11-4 Popular Preferences about Local Service Deliverers, Private or Public, for Selected Services, 1985 *(Continued)*

	Parks and Swimming Pools			Garbage Collection			Ambulance Service		
	Private Companies	Local Government	Don't Know	Private Companies	Local Government	Don't Know	Private Companies	Local Government	Don't Know
Total Public	25%	68%	7%	41%	53%	6%	41%	52%	7%
Under 35 Years of Age	28	66	6	43	52	5	42	52	6
Over 65	22	64	14	36	52	12	37	49	14
High School Incomplete	24	65	11	33	59	8	32	58	10
College Graduate	26	70	4	48	50	2	55	42	3
Household Income									
Under $15,000	26	61	13	39	51	10	38	52	10
$40,000+	25	73	2	46	52	2	44	52	4
White	24	69	7	43	52	5	43	51	6
Nonwhite	27	63	10	26	65	9	26	60	14
Nonmetro	27	63	10	52	42	6	45	48	7
Metro—50,000 and over									
Fringe	22	74	4	41	55	4	39	54	7
Central City	25	68	7	27	66	7	38	53	9

lish within the chief executive offices at all levels of government (*i.e.*, the offices of the president, the governors, the mayors, and other local chief executives) an authority for government contractors that would have the power of advising the chief executives on matters concerning government contracting. This authority would categorize government contractors according to function and performance, establish performance auditing criteria, assist government contractors in efficiently conducting their business, establish annual reports on the activities of contractors, verify the reports that are made to governments by contractors, have the authority to establish and terminate government contracts as well as to settle disputes, and have the authority to work with the public prosecutors.[105] Some central authority that has access to the chief executives of American governments is needed to adequately control the public's business.

A second step that must be taken is the reeducation and intellectual upgrading of the more than 150,000 federal bureaucrats, and the uncounted state and local administrators, who manage the vast and complex contracts and grants processes of American governments. An indication of the low levels of education held by these federal officials is the fact that an individual in the federal procurement and contracting work force has, on the average, a high school diploma plus three months of college education. One-third of the contract officers who work for the Department of Education have not even completed their mandatory training on contracting and procurement procedures.[106]

Currently, a rare "window" exists to upgrade the educational level of this work force. One-half of the federal contracting-and-grants officers were eligible to retire in 1980,[107] and there is a unique opportunity to recruit new, highly educated personnel who are adequately educated and confident to manage the huge public contracting system. It is important that these recruits be not only well educated but also well socialized into the values of efficient and honest government. The current federal contracting work force, which has not much more than a high school diploma, is nonetheless responsible for expending some $200 billion a year in procurement contracts. Education becomes a major means in bringing the margins of the state under some degree of control for purposes of knowledgeable action.

Finally, it is important to professionalize contract management as a field, and the need for this professionalization seems particularly acute at the federal level. In addition to infusing more formally educated administrators into the practice of contract management, steps should be taken to assure that contract managers can be promoted to higher ranks as contract managers, and that, in a field where one is expected to deal as a peer with executives who travel in their own Gulfstream jets—executives who, moreover, may be tempted to attempt bribery as a cost-cutting ploy—contract managers be paid more than they currently are.

The lack of a professional corps of contract managers is indicated by the brief spells that federal contract managers are assigned to crucial projects. Despite the fact that no fewer than six special commissions since World War II have recommended that the tenure of program managers assigned to major weapons projects be lengthened, and despite legislation which was enacted in 1984 requiring that such administrators remain at their posts for at least four years, the average time that these contract managers spend on a weapons acquisition project actually decreased from twenty-five months in 1984 to twenty-one months in 1990![108] According to one observer, "the services broke the law 89 percent of the time."[109]

Why? In part because it does not pay a military careerist to devote a lot of time to contract management, beyond getting one's "ticket punched" as quickly as possible in the field, and moving on. In 1990, the Pentagon initiated a new policy that established a separate career path for acquisition specialists designed to offset this pattern. It is a step in the right direction of working against the Pentagon's contracting culture, which gives little credence to supervising private contractors.

THE GOVERNMENT CORPORATION

As we observed at the beginning of this chapter, the reluctance of local officials, in contrast to federal administrators, to privatize extensively is rooted in certain political realities, notably in the relatively vibrant unions of state and local employees that do not want to see their jobs "contracted away," and in the antiquated fiscal requirements that are often cemented into state constitutions. Nevertheless, state and local governments have borne the brunt of public demands for greater services over the last few decades and have, as a result, been forced to find ways to accommodate those demands. The answer that most states and local jurisdictions have found is the creation of the public corporation, a mysterious, veiled, and secretive entity that functions on the fringes of the public domain.

The government corporation, also known as the special authority or public authority, is an independent, legislatively created monopoly empowered to build, maintain, and manage public services and facilities, such as hospitals, bridges, university dormitories, tunnels, roads, senior citizen centers, public housing, seaports, mental health facilities, airports, pollution control programs, water and sewage plants, electrical power utilities, and a variety of other projects and equipment. Occasionally, special authorities have been established by governments to conduct relatively exotic public policies and facilities, such as thoroughbred horse breeding, foreign trade, radio stations, television networks, and railroads.

These special authorities have been created by all levels of government, but especially by state and local governments, and only until comparatively recently have they really been scrutinized as a species of quasi-government that flourishes on the margin of the state. The building public skepticism about public authorities stems from a plethora of new perceptions about their (heretofore) vaunted effectiveness and efficiency as implementers of public policy, their expanding numbers, and their burgeoning debts—for which the taxpayer ultimately is responsible.

FISCAL POWER

The developing economic power of government corporations is both impressive and often overlooked. Public authorities employ 3 percent of the national labor force and account for 15 percent of the nation's fixed investment. They control four-fifths of the local public transportation systems, three quarters of the country's water

systems, and a fourth of its electrical plants and railways. The Port Authority of New York and New Jersey, one of the larger government corporations, has more debt than thirty-nine states combined, and more operating revenues than all but nine of the nation's biggest cities![110] They spend more than $14 billion a year on operations and invest more dollars (about $10 billion annually) in new capital facilities than all state and municipal governments combined![111]

There are perhaps 18,000 government corporations; of these, perhaps sixty, and possibly closer to twenty (depending on one's definition), are federal corporations.[112] Although there are relatively few federal corporations, compared with the thousands of state and local ones, many of them, such as the U.S. Postal Service, with more than 800,000 employees and an annual budget approaching $40 billion,[113] have a huge fiscal impact on the nation. One class of federal corporation, the "government-sponsored enterprise," which boasts a total of only seven organizations, nonetheless controls more than $1 trillion in obligations and mortgage-backed securities, an amount that is growing rapidly![114]

Despite such heavy-hitting federal corporations, the vast bulk of government corporations function at the state and local levels. New York and Pennsylvania are the major states that use the public authority and, between them, have developed the two basic models for setting them up. In New York, public authorities are individually chartered by the state legislature. In Pennsylvania, however, local governments (cities, counties, towns, and special districts) can create government corporations through a number of different devices, and with little or no interference from the state. Most states, more than two-thirds, use the Pennsylvanian approach; in fact, only New York and Maine require that the state legislature enact specific legislation to establish each government corporation.

Public authorities support themselves by borrowing money in the nation's money markets, by grants from their sponsoring governments, and by charging user fees to customers who use the facilities they build—such as toll charges levied on drivers on toll roads. Most of their budgets, however, are borrowed, and special authorities have been consuming increasingly vast amounts of borrowed money.

Most of us have heard about these public authorities in the context of "tax-exempt municipal bonds." In fact, government corporations are able to raise more money for investment than either all-state or all-municipal governments precisely because bond buyers do not have to pay income taxes on the interest that these bonds generate. Public authorities are the largest single category of borrowers in the tax-exempt municipal bond market and borrow more money than all state and local governments combined! "This corporate investment exerts a massive influence on the patterns of development in the nation, an influence that is largely insulated from public debate."[115]

The rapid growth of the government corporation's fiscal role in the national economy is beginning to dwarf the very state and local governments that gave them birth. By 1979, fully half of all the long-term debts (which make up about 95 percent of all state and local debts) incurred by state and local governments had been incurred by public authorities (up from 28 percent in 1955).[116] Currently, public authorities are nearing 60 percent in terms of their annual share of all state and local long-term debt.[117]

This debt is "nonguaranteed" by state and local governments. That is, they are not technically obligated to pay off creditors in the event that the enterprises to which those creditors loaned money default. Nonguaranteed debts occur because most state and local governments are saddled with archaic constitutional clauses and statutes that place artificially low ceilings on how much debt a state or locality may incur, or that require inordinately cumbersome procedures to borrow funds, and because these governments genuinely need the money to meet fundamental public needs, such as public health and safety. To raise this money, and to circumvent their own policy restrictions on borrowing (which, in many instances, have remained unchanged since the last century), subnational governments have resorted to creating public authorities.

But these governments have additional fiscal motivations, too, when they create public authorities, and these relate largely to those financial and political motives underlying the decisions by public officials to privatize public policy via contracting with private companies. One study of 133 cities in Illinois with populations of 5,000 or more found that "very little shows that officials use enterprises [*i.e.*, municipal corporations] to get around high tax levels. The data are clear that these cities do not use enterprise funds to offer additional services when tax revenues decline....Most Illinois cities do not create enterprise funds to expand services at all, but they use them to deliver traditional services."[118] Another analysis of twenty-one cities in South Carolina that had created municipal electric corporations concluded that these enterprises not only raised revenues for these cities, but were used to subsidize local property taxes; "public avoidance" of resolving hard fiscal questions, and "fiscal illusion" in hiding the realities of municipal finance were cornerstone concepts in the creation of these municipal authorities.[119]

So it is fairly apparent that subnational governments have formed government corporations as their chief means not of expanding public services, but merely of coping with a citizenry that is, at one and the same time, both demanding more services and resisting the payment of more taxes. Since the debts of government corporations, however, are nominally not backed by the governments that established them, they can legally borrow as much as they like. As a result, much of the nonguaranteed debt of state and local governments has been incurred by the government corporations that they have founded.

Precisely how free of the mounting debts that are being incurred by special authorities these governments really are is debatable. Should a public authority default, the courts could well find that the government which created it nonetheless owes its creditors—and, in fact, the courts have so ruled in such cases.[120] Moreover, many government corporations are empowered by their creators to issue "moral obligation bonds," which means that, although a state or locality may not technically be responsible for an authority's debts, it nonetheless has a legally recognized "moral obligation" to back them. In short, it appears that if the typical government corporation goes bust, it is the taxpayer who may ultimately pay its "nonguaranteed" debt.

"Whoops!"

A recent incident illuminates the growing economic role that government corporations are playing in the nation.

The Washington Public Power Supply System (WPPSS), known as "Whoops!" to some critics, is a consortium of twenty-three public utilities in Washington State and eighty-eight additional public utilities in the Northwest. Created in 1957 by nineteen public utility districts and four Washington cities to construct a small hydroelectric project, WPPSS bumped along for years as a typical government corporation, thriving with ease in a monopolistic market. Then, in the early 1970s, after reading that the demand for electricity in the Northwest was expected to increase by 7 percent a year for the foreseeable future, the directors of WPPSS decided to build three nuclear power generators, and they later expanded the project to five.

By 1983, as a result of borrowing to finance the five plants, "Whoops" was more than $8.3 billion in debt. Like governments, government corporations such as WPPSS are free to raise revenues by selling "municipal" bonds in the bond market (even though they are not really municipalities). Investors in municipal bonds—nearly 90 percent of whom are private citizens—find municipal bonds attractive because the interest that the bonds earn is not subject to the income tax; they are tax free. And, at a 12.5 percent interest rate for some of its bond issues, the WPPSS consortium was selling a lot of bonds. In fact, WPPSS was the largest issuer of tax-exempt municipal bonds ever!

WPPSS was issuing a particular type of long-term municipal bond, the revenue bond, to underwrite its nuclear plants. Revenue bonds repay their buyers through fees collected from users of the project that they finance; in the case of "Whoops," for example, the bonds' purchasers would be paid back in the form of tax-exempt interest with the profits WPPSS made on selling electricity generated by its new nuclear facilities.

The other kind of municipal bond is the general obligation bond. General obligation bonds are backed by the full faith and credit of the government that issues them. In other words, a government is legally compelled to raise taxes, if

necessary, to meet its "general obligations." For this reason, all issues of general obligation bonds must be first approved in a referendum by the voters. Not so, however, with revenue bonds, and that is why governments (and government corporations) increasingly like them. In the face of tax revolts at the grassroots, state and local governments have been squeezed into issuing more and more revenue bonds. In 1970, 34 percent of all long-term tax-exempt bonds were revenue bonds; by 1983, 75 percent of these issues were revenue bonds, a percentage that has remained constant since that year.

Governments feel constrained not only to issue revenue bonds to meet basic service demands, but also to finance projects that may not be so basic. State and localities now issue revenue bonds to underwrite all kinds of "private uses," such as building factories and housing, and buying pollution control equipment that would not have been contemplated before the tax revolt. The reasoning behind this maneuver is that the government is enhancing the public interest by making more jobs available, "leveraging in" private-sector dollars to strengthen the tax base, assuring public health, or whatever. But while revenue bonds may be in the best interest of a local jurisdiction's citizenry, they may not be in the best interest of their investors, who can lose their investments if the jurisdiction defaults.

In 1983, WPPSS defaulted. It was not a small default. In fact, it was an all-time national record: $2.25 billion was defaulted on revenue bonds that had been issued for plants 4 and 5, a sum that amounted to 2.4 percent of all municipal debt in the United States at the time.

What happens when a public authority, or a government, defaults? It does not necessarily declare bankruptcy and go out of business (as WPPSS did not); it merely declines to pay its investors—about 100,000 individual investors in the case of the "Whoops" default, such as the retired Tulsa policeman who had invested $45,000 in plants 4 and 5. In fact, more than half of the investors in plants 4 and 5 were retirees, and nearly nine out of ten of these retirees were counting on their investments in WPPSS for a significant portion of their retirement income. Although, upon default, the bond issuer must sell the holdings it has acquired under the bond issue and turn over the proceeds to its investors, these returns typically amount to pennies on the dollar. Who, for example, would be in the market for two partially constructed nuclear plants and the roads leading to them?

Another effect of default (and especially the largest municipal bond default in the nation's history), is that it hurts others besides the investors. The governor of Washington released a study concluding that the WPPSS default would cost the state 20,000 jobs.

Finally, the viability, competence, and ethics of the bond market, Wall Street, and government come under question. In the case of WPPSS, perhaps with reason. Even after the board of WPPSS was well aware that the Northwest's projected electricity consumption rate was never likely to attain a growth rate of 7 percent a year, and, in fact, was increasing by closer to 1 percent annually, plants 4 and 5 were begun anyway. Because "Whoops" wanted to spread the wealth (and reap the resultant political support), forty-five to sixty-five contractors were employed on each job site, where nine to ten would have been the norm, resulting in a sixfold hike in the system's original cost estimates.

"Wall Street was intimately involved every step of the way, and kept the spigot wide open until belated investor skepticism forced it closed,"

according to *Business Week* magazine. An open fiscal spigot apparently was irresistible to the small-town businessmen who largely made up the WPPSS board. According to their own chairman of the board, the WPPSS directors "had unlimited money. That was the worst of it." As one director put it, "Whenever cash was low, we'd just toddle down to Wall Street."

Wall Street was so pleased to sell the increasingly questionable "Whoops" bonds (pleased, possibly, to the point of "bond dumping" WPPSS issues on unsuspecting investors), that the Securities and Exchange Commission (SEC) launched an investigation similar to the one that it conducted in 1977 of New York banks, after New York City had nearly defaulted in 1975. The SEC's 1,000-page report in that case alleged that in 1975 the six banks sold $4 billion in city bonds when they knew a possible default was imminent, while simultaneously dumping their own New York City bonds before the roof fell in.

The Washington Public Power Supply System expresses many of the dilemmas of government corporations. They are controlled neither by public institutions nor economic competition, yet they are increasingly important political and fiscal forces. *Caveat emptor.*

The preceding discussion is drawn from: "The Fallout from 'Whoops,'" *Business Week* (July 11, 1983), pp. 80–87; James Bennett and Thomas DiLorenzo, "Utility Bond's Default: Iceberg's Tip?" *Washington Times* (October 26, 1983); "Learning from Whoops," *Wall Street Journal* (July 27, 1983); "WPPSS Default Investigated," *Washington Post* (November 30, 1983); Andy Logan, "Around City Hall," *The New Yorker* (January 23, 1978), pp. 98–103; and Carrie Dolan, "Several WPPSS Issues Still Unresolved," *The Wall Street Journal* (October 24, 1985).

The Evolution of the Government Corporation

Fiscally speaking (and, for that matter, politically speaking, too), the relationship of government corporations to the subnational governments is not merely one of the tail wagging the proverbial dog, but of figuring out which end of this moving and shaking mass is the tail and which is the dog!

This disturbing situation is in part the result of fiscal experimentation by the federal, state, and local governments over the past two centuries.

The first government corporations were banks chartered by the states; the federal government often held significant portions of the stock of these banks. Later in the nineteenth century, when all companies in nearly all the states were required to have a special state charter to set up business, a relationship frequently would develop between individual legislators and corporate interests to expedite the applications of business charters. Over time, these relationships reached such an intimacy that major scandals erupted in many states, and both states and municipalities would often default on their debts because their governments had invested in questionable business projects that had gone under. These defaults occurred well into the 1920s, and often involved investments of public funds in real estate developments.

As a consequence of these statewide and local defaults on debt, and also as a result of the public administration reform movement that was sweeping the nation around the turn of the century, virtually all state constitutions still have archaic prohibitions not only on debt, but also against lending or granting state or local money or credit to individuals or firms, and these clauses have inhibited the development of public ownership and investment in private corporations. As an alternative, state and local constitutions and statutes have encouraged the development of the publicly chartered, quasi-governmental public authority because its revenue bond method of financing allows states and localities to at least indirectly fund capital projects that are sometimes desperately needed.

The federal government is the single entity most responsible for the proliferation of subnational special authorities and their deepening debt. More than any other single factor, federal tax laws have shaped the evolution of the public corporation at the state and local levels, although there is no constitutional reason why, for example, state and municipal bonds should be exempt from the federal income tax. In 1913 the Sixteenth Amendment permitted Congress to collect taxes on incomes, and it specified that Congress may do so "from whatever source derived"—including, obviously, income from municipal bonds. In addition to its tax-exempt status, the municipal bond market is, remarkably, the only major securities market that is free from oversight by the federal Securities and Exchange Commission, thus permitting it greater flexibility in competing for investors.

Federal involvement in the development of public authorities can be traced to the federal government's purchase of the Panama Railroad Company in 1904. Its involvement intensified

during World War I, when Washington set up a number of federal corporations to assist in the war effort: shipping, housing, sugar and grain marketing, and finance were the major areas of federal corporation involvement during this period. Most of these special authorities were disbanded after the Armistice, but, with the Depression, Washington took a renewed interest in the concept. One of Herbert Hoover's last acts as president was the creation of the Reconstruction Finance Corporation in 1932, a federal authority that financed the establishment of numerous state and local government corporations designed to put men and women back to work on capital improvement projects.

It was Franklin Delano Roosevelt, however, who saw in the government corporation a unique opportunity to circumvent antiquated state limitations on debt while still funneling obviously needed capital into the economy, and it was the Roosevelt administration that set up the system we have today of "nonguaranteed" public authority debt. Roosevelt's approach was twofold: He encouraged the use of nonguaranteed debt, and he promoted the creation of public authorities by states and communities.

Roosevelt's Public Works Administration strongly encouraged the use of nonguaranteed debt by state and local governments, and its effectiveness was striking. Between 1931 and 1936, the number of states permitting nonguaranteed debt rose from thirty-one to forty. Today, all states allow its use, and more than half of all municipal long-term debt is nonguaranteed.[121]

Roosevelt's successes in the area of government corporations, however, were even more dramatic. FDR drafted "model legislation" for state and local governments to follow in creating government corporations; wrote a personal letter to all the nation's governors in 1934, urging that they back his model code and modify their states' laws on debt; and channeled large slices of the federal budget into the Reconstruction Finance Corporation (in 1933, this single government corporation alone accounted for more than half of *all* federal outlays) and Roosevelt's own Public Works Administration, the two principal federal corporations that bought the revenue bonds of the state and local government corporations that flourished under Washington's guidance.[122]

These policies brought quick results. By 1948, forty-one of the forty-eight states had adopted variants of FDR's model legislation, and twenty-five states had authorized their local governments to set up government corporations entirely by local initiative. Continuing federal encouragement (such as that provided by various grant programs) and federal tax shelters for certain kinds of investments (such as housing projects) have resulted in more subnational government corporations, although more recent direct federal involvement in their development has not matched that of the 1930s and 1940s.[123]

By the end of World War II, public authorities across the country stood at a number of crossroads. The public authorities created during the 1930s, were for the most part, intended by the federal agencies that funded their creation to be "self-liquidating" corporations; that is, once their capital costs were paid off through the use of user charges (such as bridge tolls), the authorities themselves could go out of business and turn their functions over to state or local governments. Such, at least, was one option that the authorities had. Another alternative was that user charges could be continued, and the revenues could be deposited in state and local general funds. Finally, government corporations could keep the user charges flowing into their corporate treasuries and use those revenues to finance new projects. If they took this final route, public authorities would no longer be required to ask governments for tax funds.

The managers of special authorities, for the most part, chose the final route. Even though FDR's bureaucracy for financing subnational government corporations was dismantled during the 1950s (the federal Reconstruction Finance Corporation, created in 1932, was perhaps the major backer of state and local special authorities throughout the 1930s, and it was abolished in 1954), state and local corporations that the feds had originally underwritten lived on and prospered in their monopolistic marketplaces.

Political Power

Political control over a public authority is a supremely difficult achievement. The government corporation is, in theory, responsible to those who appoint its board members, and normally this is the governor. Although political patronage often dominates the initial appointments of members of the boards of directors of public authorities, the staggered terms of board membership inhibit any kind of effective political control by the governor.

The supervision of government corporations is typically assigned to an executive agency or several executive agencies of the government. But very few states and localities have emulated the kinds of relatively rigorous controls exercised over federal public corporations, principally through the Government Corporation Control Act of 1945. In most state governments, no single department even maintains an accurate listing of active public corporations, who their officers are, or even what their addresses are. In fact, the Securities Industries Association has no more information than do state governments on the financial transactions of government corporations.[124]

State legislatures and city councils also have very limited control, if any, over their own public authorities. Although the statutes that establish public authorities can be and frequently are very specific and detailed, once the authority is established, legislative control often becomes a mockery. Legislators ritualistically carp that they have very little control over their own bureaucracies, much less the independent public authority, and even "sunset legislation," which we described in Chapter 8, has not been effective in implementing any kind of thorough legislative review of the government corporations. Thus, while elected bodies may have a rather impressive array of sanctions with which to threaten public corporations, they do not have any realistic means of enforcing those sanctions.

This problem is compounded by the intergovernmental system that exists in almost all states for establishing public authorities, and which permits counties and municipalities to create public corporations essentially on their own, and often these local charters are vague and unstandardized.[125]

Suing government corporations in court has not provided consistent public control over government corporations. Although the courts have chipped away, on occasion, at the more arbitrary actions of certain public corporations, this process has been piecemeal at best, and the judiciary has not produced any guidelines of consequence for the control of public authorities.

An Absence of Control

These realities have contributed to an independence of economic and political action that any company executive or elected politician would envy. Public authorities, although chartered by governments, are rarely controlled by them. The career-oriented professional managers of government corporations are casually supervised by politically appointed boards that do not spend an inordinate amount of time at such chores. Tax-exempt bond holders have less interest in scrutinizing the day-to-day activities of the government corporation than, perhaps, do the stockholders of private corporations. As long as the public corporation meets the minimum revenue-producing requirements, its management does not have to show increasing profits, dividends, or stock prices. Marketplace competition for most public corporations is minimal because they operate in monopolistic economic conditions, and revenues, as a consequence, rarely decrease. Moreover, management of public corporations can operate at a much higher level of secrecy than can private firms, which must report their finances to the Securities and Exchange Commission. In short, the managers of the public corporations have all the powers and autonomy of management that are shared by their counterparts in the private corporation, and that the on-line, government bureaucrat does not have; yet, the manager of a public corporation does not have to be responsive or responsible to the stockholders, bondholders, board of directors, or even the public. As a result of this uniquely independent position in the marketplaces of both commerce and politics, public authorities have waxed more powerful at the expense of the subnational governments that chartered them, especially local governments.

Inadequate political controls over public authorities have contributed to their narrowness of view in formulating policy—an approach that "defines out" the less lucrative, people-oriented projects and "defines in" capital projects that often can disrupt the polities in which they reside, or, at the very least, not attempt to alleviate the more pressing and interrelated public problems of the area.

A relative absence of political accountability has led to certain behavioral commonalities among special authorities, such as to build (and to borrow to build) with minimum delay; to choose projects that are more conducive to garnering profits than providing public service; to rarely innovate in their approaches to alleviating public problems; and to stress physical rather than social objectives.[126]

These corporate tendencies, which are shared by public authorities across the country, tend to reinforce one another, and constitute the ultimate policy biases of government corporations. For example, public authorities are often the targets of environmental groups, in part, because of their emphasis on the speed of a construction project's completion with scant concern about possibly detrimental environmental impacts. Public authorities frequently are responsible for highway and airport construction and, in many instances, such projects have destroyed neighborhoods and promoted the energy crisis by implicitly assuming, as an integral part of their plan, that the automobile's use will continue unabated. Such policy biases may have resulted from a lack of control by government and from an absence of public participation. As Annmarie Hauk Walsh observes, "the successes of public authorities have, in fact, motivated much of the criticism of them. Critics on the left seek a more purposeful, dynamic, and democratically controlled public sector. Those on the right seek to reduce the scope of government enterprise, or at least check its growth, and to limit its activities to those that aid private endeavors,...public authorities have withstood such assaults practically unscathed and continue to claim rights of independent management."[127]

If government corporations are "practically unscathed," it does not bother all observers. Not everyone agrees that government corporations are unaccountable, loose cannons, rolling on the fiscal and political decks of the nation. Indeed, they are extraordinarily useful. Jameson W. Doig, for example, suggests that public authorities are precisely what Woodrow Wilson had in mind when he wrote his essay on administration a century ago.[128] Government corporations, because they do possess what Wilson called "large powers," and because they do separate "politics" from "administration" more than most public entities, attract large people to their employ—the David Lilienthals and the Robert Moses of the world. Additionally, they attract and retain more specialized but talented professionals, such as planners and engineers, because they are insulated from the tides of electoral politics. Such drawing power by governments, even by quasi-governments, is not to be dismissed lightly.

Moreover, unlike government agencies, special authorities possess a distinctive ability to conduct long-term planning that often is absent in the public sector, and in part because of this ability, accountability for the actions of public authorities is not all that absent. In one sense, for example, those government corporations that span several local jurisdictions constitute a far more visible and coherent focus for concerned citizens than do a batch of "mini-govs," all trying to deal with the same problem in their separate, fragmented ways. The concept of "professionalism" itself, which is a deeply imbued value among personnel in public authorities, also provides a brake on the emergence of projects that would seriously violate the public interest as well as professional standards. But, as Doig points out, when all is said and done, problems of accountability persist. Nevertheless, these problems must be balanced with the public's need to get things done.

If the states and localities seem to have avoided the worst excesses of Washington in privatizing public policies by contracting them out, it is equally possible that they, as an alternative, may have created some excesses of their own in the form of government corporations. These man-made organisms, originally developed as the corporate progeny of their parent governments, clearly have a political life—and a will—of their own.

THE NEW YORK EXPERIENCE: MOSES VERSUS ROCKY

Consider, in this regard, the experience of New York, both city and state. Nowhere have the potentialities and pitfalls of the government corporation—and its high political drama—been illustrated more vividly than in New York, particularly [in the] the rise of Robert Moses and his Triborough "empire," and Moses's ultimate conquest by the late Governor Nelson A. Rockefeller, who was unique in his own use (and abuse)

of the government corporation. Few, if any, examples can furnish as rich a study of what the special authority means in American politics than New York's experiences with it.

Moses: Master Builder or Massive Destroyer?

The late Robert Moses held an unbelievable quantum of power in New York State for forty-four years (1924–1968) and in New York City for thirty-four years (1934–1968). It is not hyperbolic to dub him America's greatest builder. He changed the face of New York by raising and spending $27 billion (in 1968 dollars) for public works.

Through shore line projects, he added 15,000 acres to the city and changed its physical configuration. With one exception (East River Drive), Moses built every major expressway in the metropolitan region. Nine enormous bridges link the island city of New York; Moses built seven of them. Lincoln Center, the New York Coliseum; the campuses of Pratt Institute and Fordham and Long Island universities; the headquarters of the United Nations; 416 miles of landscaped parkways; Jones Beach; more than 1,000 apartment buildings housing more people than live in Minneapolis; 658 playgrounds; 673 baseball diamonds; 288 tennis courts—all these and more are his. Beyond the city, Moses built huge power dams on the St. Lawrence and at Niagara, Massens, and elsewhere; he also built more parkways, public beaches; and parks. Especially parks. By the time Moses had finished, New York owned 45 percent of all the nation's acreage devoted to state parks![129]

To build, Moses destroyed. A quarter million people—the equivalent population of Chattanooga—were dispossessed for his highways. Perhaps another quarter million saw their homes razed for other kinds of projects. His apartment buildings, parks, and playgrounds, with few exceptions, were built for the white and the wealthy. His expressways slash through a region of 14 million people, carving the metropolis into separate and often mutually hostile enclaves of rich, poor, white, and black.[130]

Moses entered the New York scene in 1924, when Governor Alfred E. Smith asked him to design the State Council on Parks, and he quickly assigned himself as chair with a tenure that extended beyond that of the governor's term. He also exempted the new State Council on Parks from the state civil system, granted it independent bonding and land acquisition powers, and used the Council to further his own ambitions. When Franklin D. Roosevelt succeeded Smith as governor of New York in 1929, Moses's power in state government began to wane. Nevertheless, he was able to keep his position in the State Council on Parks and began seeking bureaucratic allies in the federal government.

In 1932, FDR was elected president, and in the same year Moses made his alliance with Jesse Jones, who had been appointed by Herbert Hoover as head of the newly created federal Reconstruction Finance Corporation (RFC). Both staunch Republicans, Jones and Moses disliked the Democrat Roosevelt, an antipathy that likely cemented their bond. With Jones and his Reconstruction Finance Corporation as his new-found ally in Washington, Moses worked himself into the position of heading up New York State's efforts to put Depression-wracked New Yorkers back to work through the creation of capital projects that were financed with federal funds provided by Jones's RFC; and Moses immediately began building the Triborough Bridge with RFC grants.

In 1936, Moses was appointed by the mayor of New York City as chair of the Triborough Bridge Authority, and he served in that capacity until 1966. Using as his power base his position as the state's liaison with the federal public works funding programs, Moses moved forcefully to enhance his chairmanship of the Triborough Bridge Authority by setting up two additional authorities that were approved for federal funding, the Henry Hudson Parkway Authority and the Marine Parkway Authority. To solidify his position, Moses created a board for each authority, but appointed himself as the only board member. In 1938, both authorities were absorbed in the newly created New York City Parkway Authority, and, once again, Moses wrote himself in as the only member of the board.

During this period, Moses was consolidating his power with considerable speed. In 1934 alone, he became president of the Long Island Parkways Commission, commissioner of the New York City Parks System (which he remained until 1960), and

chair of the New York State Council on Parks (a position he held until 1963), and he established the Beth Page and Jones Beach park authorities.

Moses was capitalizing on national trends of the time. As one analyst points out, "Moses used building blocks typical of public authority structures: independent financial power, corporate leadership, business patronage, civic reputation, and freedom from the encumbrances of democracy."[131] Thus, Moses consolidated his power position and political independence by drafting legislation, graciously enacted by the New York State legislature in 1946, that merged the Triborough Bridge Authority, the New York City Parkway Authority (which only eight years earlier had merged the Henry Hudson Parkway Authority and the Marine Parkway Authority under its auspices), and the New York City Tunnel Authority (which had been created in 1945 with Moses as its chief executive officer) into the Triborough Bridge and Tunnel Authority (TBTA). The effect of this exercise in bureaucratic imperialism was to enhance Moses's already considerable influence in New York; ultimately, Moses headed fourteen state and city agencies at the same time.

Significantly, the legislation that Moses had drafted gave TBTA the right to refinance any of its outstanding debt at any time, thus granting Moses an extraordinarily solid power base; as soon as profits were amassed, but just before debts were about to be paid off, Moses could issue new bonds and start a new project. This, in fact, was precisely what Moses did since new projects could be financed with ease in the tax-exempt and laxly regulated municipal bond market.

Triborough's (TBTA's) regulations and bonding powers cannot be changed by federal, state, or local governments; its army of bridge and tunnel officers and parkway police reported only to Moses; and its toll booths provide a cornucopia of self-renewing treasure. At its peak (attained in 1960), Triborough controlled a land mass half the size of New York City itself, and annual revenues had neared a quarter of a billion dollars.

Those who believe that men and women who dedicate their careers to public service face a life of genteel economic modesty should explore the world of government corporations. Moses maintained a yacht for his personal use that was skippered by three captains. Four dining rooms scattered around the city, each with its own full-time staff and chefs, served only Moses and his guests. Triborough secretaries not only were paid higher salaries than were New York City commissioners, but they were also given bigger cars and their own chauffeurs, who were on call twenty-four hours a day. The group of Triborough managers known as "Moses Men"—his closest allies—were made millionaires and multimillionaires by Moses.

Moses's period of greatest power and building occurred from 1946 through 1953. During this period, essentially no construction of consequence was even attempted in Gotham without his approval. As we noted in Chapter 4, for thirty-four years, Moses played an important role in establishing the city's priorities, and for seven years, he established all the city's priorities.[132]

Moses was powerful far beyond the boundaries of the country's most important city. He changed the nation, too. In the fields of parks, highways, and urban renewal, Moses was a formative force in the country.

In parks, it was Moses who conceived the notion of state and urban recreational complexes linked by landscaped parkways. Prior to Moses, twenty-nine states did not even have a single park, and six had only one. The parks system he bulldozed in New York was widely copied across the nation.

In highways, Moses had completed half a dozen urban expressways in metropolitan New York City before Congress passed the Interstate Highway Act of 1956, which funneled federal money into the construction of urban freeways across the country. Prior to the Act—which Moses was instrumental in drafting—metropolitan highways were virtually nonexistent except in New York.

Moses also was critical in drafting the Housing Act of 1949, which inaugurated the nation's controversial Urban Renewal program, and Moses was quick to use the federal program that he himself had helped form. Eight years after the passage of the Housing Act, Moses, who controlled all Urban Renewal projects in New York, had spent more than twice the amount of federal urban renewal dollars than all the other American cities combined! His contracts were used as models for Urban Renewal administrators across the country.

There was a fourth field in which Moses shaped America: urban planning. He was against it. Although he served on the New York City Planning Commission for eighteen years (1942–1960), he blocked all attempts to establish a rational, comprehensive plan for the city at every turn. The lack of effective urban planning in all major American cities reflects the policy biases of the special authorities that Moses directed. As the urban scholar Lewis Mumford, one of Moses's most tenacious foes, has written, "In the twentieth century, the influence of Robert Moses on the cities of America was greater than that of any other person."[133]

Was his influence good or ill for New York and the nation? Moses's special authorities built needed public works that, in all probability, would never have been built without the bold concepts he originated. But the human costs of his Herculean projects, and the physical devastation that highways and Urban Renewal have wrought in America's cities in the absence of local planning, may not have been worth the price.

How did a man, initially dismissed as a "Goo Goo" (for "Good Government" reformer) by New York's Tammany Hall, come to wield such power? Moses built his power on an adoring media, the greed of others, tight secrecy (few have ever seen Triborough's detailed financial records), and political savvy that occasionally degenerated into personal vindictiveness. Much of his empire was built on deceptions, the most notable being that the government corporation was "above politics" (an assertion bought with slathering eagerness by the press) and was economically efficient. Through the nickels and dimes collected at his tollbooths, Moses bankrolled huge economic interests in New York and paid off individuals (perfectly legally) who were important to him. The retainers that Triborough granted to public relations firms alone hit about $250,000 a year; legal fees amounted to another quarter of a million dollars, and insurance commissions were half a million dollars annually. Moses was giving out a million dollars a year to those who played ball in a game he umpired in a modern-day equivalent of Tammany Hall's Christmas turkey baskets.[134]

But a million dollars a year in Tammany Hall turkeys does not compare to the real plums Moses could distribute. Because Moses did not have to be particularly cost conscious, he could let very fat contracts to banks, labor unions, and the private sector. As a consequence, his union and business support was almost unprecedented in the New York City metropolitan area. They, like the media, could always be depended upon for support when summoned—a loyalty that was enhanced considerably by the fact that, for twenty years (1948–1968), Moses maintained a secret agreement with the State Department of Public Works that gave him a personal veto over all contracts awarded by the department in metropolitan New York.[135]

Moses gave a new meaning to political pressure, boasting that "nothing I have ever done has been tinged with legality."[136] Moreover, he could use political pressure with a savagery that made old-time pols look like Goldilocks. Moses kept on his payroll men whom he called "bloodhounds." Moses's bloodhounds were charged with, among other unpleasantries, building embarrassing dossiers on persons of influence. If a man's past was inadequately juicy, Moses would cause the sins of the fathers to be visted upon the children. A well-known and esteemed financier once rose during a City Planning Commission hearing to oppose a zoning change sponsored by Moses, only to hear Moses reply by reading into the hearing transcript newspaper accounts of a scandal, which had no connection whatever with the zoning change, in which the financier's father had been implicated forty years earlier, when the financier was a child.[137] Moses ruined the careers of at least a dozen public officials with these tactics.

If all else failed, Moses would innovate. Although municipal-level communism is ludicrous on the face of it, two "Red Scares" and ensuing witch hunts erupted in New York City in 1938 and 1958; both were largely fueled by gossip and misinformation leaked to the press by Moses. For example, when New York City Council member Stanley Isaacs opposed Moses on the grounds that he was razing, on a vast scale, low-income housing in the city, Moses was vicious in his counterattack. Isaacs wanted to reduce the demolition of old housing and add antidiscrimination clauses for new public housing that was being built. Moses steamrollered Isaacs, citing, among other points, that "Isaacs runs as a Republican among conservatives and is a pinko among radicals."[138] Similarly the Tuscarora Indi-

ans objected to the prospective flooding of their land by the construction of Niagara Dam, a pet Moses project. Moses subsequently described the tribal leaders as "utterly incredible and clownish"[139] Another opponent was described by Moses as being "the infant prodigy who continued to be an infant long after he had finished being a prodigy."[140] As one observer has noted, "Moses was probably ruder, more manipulative, and more powerful than other authority managers...but regardless of the merits of the results, Moses spoke and acted as can only an authority manager—who will never face election himself or require direct support from community groups and other politicians, and who is not accountable to stockholders, competitors, or questioning board members."[141]

As noted, efficient management, while hardly a watchword in the Triborough empire, nonetheless was a widely accepted Moses myth that was critical to his political success. But the extent of the mismanagement, quite aside from the personal luxury that the unending flow of silver from the tollbooths provided the Triborough's administrators, is nonetheless startling; for example, Moses, on a single bridge, paid $40 million in interest that he did not need to pay, and the state secretly underwrote Triborough to the tune of hundreds of millions of dollars. The city purchased much of the land on which Moses's projects were built; by turning the property over to Moses, Gotham also exempted this valuable land from its own tax rolls.[142]

Although Moses touted the supremacy of business efficiency, his first real venture into the free enterprise marketplace was a total failure. In 1962, Moses took over the second New York World's Fair project and raised funds by promising investors that he could turn the World's Fair into a profit-making event. In fact, Moses was so keen on turning a profit, that he initially opposed cut-rate tickets for schoolchildren. Nevertheless, when the project was completed, Moses defaulted on almost two-thirds of the fair's debts. Moses failed his first real test in the marketplace.[143]

The myth of the government corporation as being just another competitor in the marketplace and the unwarranted image of its managerial efficiency were beginning to fade in the 1960s, and this change in public attitude toward government corporations may have been encouraged by the behavior of Moses. In 1965, a number of bankers (after discovering that Moses, as president of the New York World's Fair, had guaranteed himself $100,000 in salary and annual expenses) resigned from the World's Fair Finance Committee on the grounds that Moses would not give them adequate financial information on how he was running the fair's operations.

A Rocky Conquest: Rockefeller and His Follies

Robert Moses continued his remarkable successes throughout the 1950s. But in 1958, Nelson A. Rockefeller was elected governor of New York, and he began to challenge Moses's heretofore undisputed preeminence over the region's public corporations.

Rockefeller's challenge was made easier when in 1959, Moses received his first "bad press" as a result of his chairmanship of New York City's Slum Clearance Committee. Scandals erupted in the program that were widely publicized, and since slum clearance contract records were open to the public (unlike most financial records of the enterprises that Moses headed), the opportunities for media criticism of Moses were relatively ample.

The essence of Rockefeller's attack on Moses was his aggressive development of his own public authorities at the state level; by so doing, he was creating competition for Moses. In 1963, Rockefeller asked Moses to retire as head of the State Council on Parks, a position Moses had held since 1934. Rockefeller wished to appoint his brother Lawrence to the position, and Moses objected. Characteristically, Moses relied on a political device that had served him well in the past; he threatened to resign, not only from the State Council on Parks, but from the chairmanship of the New York Power Authority and several other state posts as well. His decision to escalate the conflict was ill-advised. Rockefeller happily accepted Moses's departures from all the state posts for which he had tendered resignations!

While Rockefeller had won a battle, his real objective was to reduce Moses's power in the transportation field. To do this, Rockefeller had to gain control over transit finance in the state, and in 1967 he successfully pushed a huge, $2.5 billion,

general obligation bond issue to support transportation. Rockefeller was accorded this bond issue by a statewide referendum, and it gave him the freedom to build transportation facilities that formerly had been controlled almost exclusively by Moses. Rockefeller then went to the state legislature and broadly reorganized New York's transportation policy machinery by creating the Metropolitan Transportation Authority. Central to this reorganization was the inclusion of Moses's Triborough Bridge and Tunnel Authority into Rockefeller's new Metropolitan Transportation Authority. Moses fought this merger on every front, including the courts, and lost on all of them. In 1968, the merger was achieved, and Moses was edged out of regional transportation policymaking. The merger also marked the downfall of the world's greatest builder.

The experiences of Robert Moses illustrate (if on a somewhat larger than life scale) the problems inherent in the operation of government corporations in a democracy: their freedom from accountability, both political and financial. The decline of Moses's prestige and power was at least the partial result of a series of direct challenges to Robert Moses by Governor Nelson Rockefeller. The bitter war waged between Rockefeller and Moses illuminates how public authorities can weaken not only the powers of local governments but of state governments as well. As with government corporations at the local level, public authorities at the state level also function in a political atmosphere of scant accountability to the public and its elected and appointed representatives. But Rockefeller's experience with public corporations deviated from this pattern. Although the device of the state government corporation is used more extensively in New York than in any other state, public authorities created by Rockefeller were unique in that he, as governor, controlled them absolutely. While this is not to say that these corporations were publicly accountable, at least an elected governor actually governed them—and with a rare thoroughness.

Nelson A. Rockefeller served as governor of New York from 1958 through 1974, and his ambitions to redevelop the physical plant and appearance of the state were rivaled only by Robert Moses and possibly the pharaohs of ancient Egypt. Included in Rockefeller's plans were the redevelopment of

Manhattan, for which he committed more than $6 billion. Rockefeller hoped to build, among other edifices, the World Trade Center. He wanted to renovate docks and renew the face of the city. His plans included the creation, virtually out of whole cloth, of a major state university system, which ultimately became the second largest in the country; the construction of massive public housing and public health facilities; and the reconstruction and redesign of the capital city of Albany, rendering it, in the words of one observer, "architecturally respectable."[144] (Those who have seen Albany before and after the Rockefeller regime could reasonably conclude that what Rockefeller accomplished there is analogous to building the Great Pyramid in the middle of Altoona, Pennsylvania.) For fillers, Rockefeller built new mental health facilities, established a thoroughbred horse breeding program for the state, and raised private capital for the construction of new nursing homes, colleges, dormitories, hospitals, prisons, and a variety of other projects. All these enormous undertakings were accomplished through public authorities.

Why did Rockefeller rely so extensively on the government corporation to achieve his ends? The reasons are typical explanations of why public authorities have proliferated in recent years. One is that Rockefeller had little regard for the desultory pace of his own state bureaucracy, particularly the hide-bound Department of Public Works. Nor, as an art connoisseur of considerable note, did he care for the kind of architectural design that all too frequently emanated from that department. So Rockefeller turned to the public corporation as a means of building both faster and better, since his public authorities could pay higher architectural fees and avoid reams of red tape.

The government corporation also enabled Rockefeller to bypass voter disapproval of many of his projects. Just two years prior to Rockefeller's taking office, the voters, for example, had voted for a third time to limit a housing bond issue. When Rockefeller became governor in 1958, he quickly created a Housing Finance Agency as a government corporation that built low-income housing. In 1961, New Yorkers defeated for a fourth time a major bond issue for higher education, so Rockefeller created the State University Construction Fund as a public authority

designed to raise money for the same purpose that the voters had denied in their defeat of the bond issue. In 1965, voters rejected for a fifth time a low-income housing bond proposal, which Rockefeller answered with his creation of the Urban Development Corporation. Through these and other authorities, Rocky could borrow, veil his borrowing from the public eye, and make the legislature pay later.

Finally, Rockefeller found that, in an accounting sense, he could at least convey the appearance of balancing his state budget by creating public authorities, and this had political benefits. In 1962 Rockefeller pushed through a law that changed state accounting methods by striking the requirement that money granted by the state to public authorities be listed in the state budget. The effect of this change was to grant Rockefeller a major political boon, since his budgets now looked considerably leaner by not listing the costs of his public corporations in them. And such "fiscal responsibility" was in harmony with his "pay as you go" motto that characterized his four gubernatorial campaigns.

We have noted that Rockefeller was unique in that he was a governor who really controlled his own government corporations. How did he accomplish this?

One method was Rockefeller's connections with the New York financial community. Few governors have the fiscal background of a Rockefeller, and, as governor, Rocky capitalized on his network within the exclusive world of high finance. Rockefeller was able to raise more than $6 billion from Wall Street simply because the bankers trusted him.

Rockefeller also freed his public authorities from the fetters of the state. Although the state of New York was legally responsible for paying off the vast public debt that Rockefeller's government corporations incurred, Rocky was adroit in assuring that the legislature and bureaucracy had virtually no control over these government corporations' policies and operations. Of the twenty-two state corporations that Rockefeller created during his administration, fourteen (including such major ones as the Urban Development Corporation) were completely beyond the scope of New York's public authorities law. This meant that almost two-thirds of the public authorities Rockefeller founded had boards appointed exclusively by Rockefeller. In addition, they were exempt from state budgetary controls and did not have to submit their policy decisions to the governor for approval. And, in the case of the Urban Development Corporation, not even its own board of directors could review its budget! Moreover, those remaining government corporations created by Rockefeller that did fall under the state's public authorities law were often able to avoid any close supervision. For example, the Metropolitan Transportation Authority (MTA), a Rockefeller creation, submitted such jurisdictionally complex and fiscally convoluted budget reports to the legislature that the legislative staff became understandably confused and effectively gave up trying to conduct responsible oversight of the agency.

Rockefeller used his personal administrative appointments to control his public authorities in a spectacular way. Unlike other governors in other states, Rockefeller, using his almost unlimited wealth and a rare political ruthlessness, appointed directors of his various government corporations who were personally committed and loyal only to him. For example, Rockefeller hired Edward J. Logue to head his Urban Development Corporation (UDC), and he went to extraordinary lengths to protect Logue politically, including threatening legislators, saying that he would "take away their judgeships" if they failed to support Logue. Logue was appointed directly by the governor; in fact, not only did the board of directors of the Urban Development Corporation have no legal voice in the hiring of its own executive director, but also the chair of the UDC board of directors had no managerial control whatever over its own executive director, who reported directly to Rockefeller. Similarly, Rockefeller appointed his long-time executive secretary, Alton Marshall, to positions on the boards of the Urban Development Corporation Board and the New York Sports Authority.

While there are many examples of appointees to the board of public corporations who had a total loyalty to Rockefeller, perhaps the most remarkable is William J. Ronan, who, under Rockefeller, was both chair of the board and chief executive officer of the Metropolitan Transportation Authority, and later he served on the boards of the New

York Port Authority (as chair) and the New York Power Authority. So extensive was Ronan's influence, thanks to Rockefeller's unstinting support, that he became known as the "Holy Ronan Empire." Ronan paralleled Robert Moses in that he had been a student of public administration and had conducted some outstanding research on the concept of the public authority; in fact, prior to his first appointment in the state government in 1959, Ronan had been dean of the Graduate School of Public Administration at New York University.

One of the major reasons that Rockefeller was able to retain the loyalty of people like Logue, Marshall, and Ronan was his generosity. Rocky made them all rich. Ronan received his first gift of $75,000 from Governor Rockefeller in 1958, and it was estimated that, during his sixteen years as governor, Rockefeller eventually gave Ronan as much as $650,000. Logue, as chair of the UDC, received gifts and loans from Rockefeller that totaled more than $175,000, while Marshall was loaned more than $300,000 in 1970 alone.[145] There are many other examples of Rockefeller's largess.

Perhaps because Rockefeller's chief appointees were not working in a world of personal fiscal reality, none of them was terribly skilled in financial management and cost control. When Rockefeller turned the state house over to the Democrats in 1974, many of his public corporations were in deep financial trouble. For example, very soon after Ronan left as chair of the board of the MTA in 1973, virtually all projects under construction (including partially dug tunnels) had to be halted by his successor because there were no funds left to complete them. The Urban Development Corporation, headed by Logue, was spending $1 million a day in 1974,[146] and it was in such serious financial difficulty that Logue was forced to resign in 1975, shortly after a new governor assumed office.

Rockefeller's government corporations had, among other things, overestimated student housing needs, set up a situation in which private developers could manipulate mental health facilities for their own profit, and imposed a highly questionable financial system for state transportation. In sixteen years, Rockefeller had created so many public authorities of such enormous scope that they currently account for more than a third of all revenue bonds that have been issued across the country! Public authorities are still the single most important sector of public finance in the state of New York. When a Democratic governor took over in 1975, he was confronted with a debt incurred by the state's public authorities of more than $12 billion (in 1962, the outstanding debt of New York's public authorities was only $129 million), or almost four times the amount of debt incurred by the state government itself! Moreover, the state had been obligated to pay off two-thirds of this $12 billion, and the state's public authorities still were planning to embark on projects that would involve legislative appropriations of an additional $1.9 billion during the next five years.[147]

For better or worse, New York symbolizes and epitomizes the rise of the public corporation and its relationships with state and local governments. Public authorities, which are beginning to dominate the financial structures of subnational governments, now largely control critical public programs, particularly in energy, water, communication, and transportation; as some observers have put it, the American experience with government authorities has been one of extending "the public's credit, rather than the public's control"[148] in these and in a wide spectrum of other policy areas.

NOTES

[1] Robert H. Carver, "Examining the Premises of Contracting Out," *Public Productivity and Management Review*, 13 (Fall 1989), p. 38.

[2] Annmarie Hauk Walsh, *The Public's Business: The Politics and Practices of Government Corporations* (Cambridge, Mass.: MIT Press, 1978), p. 40.

[3] *Ibid.*, p. 29.

[4] U.S. Commission on the Organization of the Executive Branch of the Government, *Business Enterprises: A Report to the Congress* (Washington, D.C.: U.S. Government Printing Office, 1955), p. xi.

[5] Harold Seidman, *Politics, Position, and Power: The Dynamics of Federal Organization*, 3rd ed. (New York: Oxford University Press, 1980), p. 238. Other attempts to count the number of federal corporations include: Walsh, *The Public's Business*; U.S. General Accounting Office, *Congress Should Consider Revising Basic Corporate Control Laws*, GAO/PAD-83-3 (Washington, D.C.: U.S. General Accounting Office, 1983); National Academy of Public Administration, *Report on Government Corporations* (Washington, D.C.: National Academy of Public Administration, 1981); U.S. Congressional Research Service, *Administering Public Functions at the Margin*

of Government: The Case of Federal Corporations, CRS Report 83-236 (Washington, D.C.: U.S. Congressional Research Service, 1983); and Michael Denning and David J. Olson, "Public Enterprise and the Emerging Character of State Service Provisions" (Paper presented at the 1981 Annual Meeting of the American Political Science Association, New York, September 3–6, 1981). Walsh lists nineteen federal corporations; the GAO concluded that there were forty-seven federal government corporations; the National Academy of Public Administration found thirty-five; the Congressional Research Service located thirty-one; and Denning and Olson unearthed fifty-eight. The varying statements by scholars and federal agencies on how many federal corporations exist indicates little is known about them, but we know far more about federal corporations than we know about government corporations at the subnational levels.

[6] Jack R. Kemp, "Statement," Committee on Post Office and Civil Service, U.S. House of Representatives, *Contracting Out of Jobs and Services* (Washington, D.C.: U.S. Government Printing Office, 1977), p. 43.

[7] Walsh, *The Public's Business*, p. 33.

[8] James D. Carroll, A. Lee Fritschler, and Bruce L. R. Smith, "Supply Side Management in the Reagan Administration," *Public Administration Review*, 45 (November/December 1985), p. 812.

[9] Timothy Chandler and Peter Ferrille, "Municipal Unions and Privatization," *Public Administration Review*, 51 (January/February 1991), p. 15. The authors mailed questionnaires to 2,758 public works directors in 1989; 1,541 usable responses were obtained, for a response rate of 56 percent.

[10] Paralleling the federal situation, but more strikingly, an indication of the dismal state of our knowledge about government corporations at the subnational levels can be inferred from the widely varying estimates about such a basic datum as how many of them there are. Annmarie Hauk Walsh concludes that there are from 5,000 to 7,000 public authorities, a number which excludes authorities that are not organizationally independent of government agencies. But Charles E. Lindblom contends that if these public corporations are counted (which are authorized to issue general obligation bonds), the number jumps to 18,000. See: Walsh, *The Public's Business*, p. 5; and Charles E. Lindblom, *Politics and Markets: The World's Political Economic Systems* (New York: Basic Books, 1977), p. 114.

[11] Unless noted otherwise, the following discussion is drawn from: Ira Sharkansky, "Government Contracting," *State Government*, 53 (Winter 1980), pp. 23–24; and Donna Wilson Kirchheimer, "Entrepreneurial Implementation in the U.S. Welfare State" (Paper presented at the 1986 Annual Meeting of the American Political Science Association, Washington, D.C., August 28–31, 1986).

[12] Gerald W. Johnson and John G. Heilman, "Metapolicy Transition and Policy Implementation: New Federalism and Privatization," *Public Administration Review*, 47 (November/December 1987), p. 468.

[13] Carver, "Examining the Premises of Contracting Out," p. 38.

[14] Johnson and Heilman, "Metapolicy Transition and Policy Implementation," p. 468.

[15] Federal Procurement Data System, *Special Analysis 1: Federal Contract Awards over $10,000 by Type Preliminary Data of Contractor*, Fourth Quarter Fiscal Year 1979 (Washington, D.C.: Federal Procurement Data Center, 1979), p. 3. In Fiscal Year 1986, more than $183 billion was spent by the federal government for goods and services. See: Federal Procurement Data Center, U.S. General Services Administration, *Federal Procurement Data System Standard Report, Fiscal Year 1987 First Quarter (October 1, 1986 through December 31, 1986)* (Washington, D.C.: Federal Procurement Data Center, 1987), p. 7.

[16] *Ibid.*

[17] National Science Foundation, as cited in "National R & D Spending to Exceed $57 Billion in 1980," *Research Management*, 22 (July 1979), p. 3.

[18] Barbara Blumenthal, "Uncle Sam's Invisible Army of Employees," *National Journal* (May 5, 1979), p. 732.

[19] U.S. House of Representatives, Committee on Post Office and Civil Service, *Contracting Out of Jobs and Services* (Washington, D.C.: U.S. Government Printing Office, 1977), p. 31.

[20] Federal Procurement Data System, *Special Analysis 1*, p. 11; and U.S. Census Bureau study, as cited in Spencer Rich, "California Cashes In On Federal Contracts," *Washington Post* (March 27, 1987).

[21] According to CBS's program "60 Minutes" of November 30, 1980, estimates about the annual amount spent by Washington on consultants range from $400 million to $15 billion. Figures vary widely. In 1977, the OMB toted up $1.8 billion in federal consulting contracts after an incomplete survey of sixty-four agencies. In 1978, using a narrower definition of "consultant" (a rigor apparently encouraged by growing congressional concern over the bureaucracy's penchant for hiring consultants), the OMB was able to reduce this figure to $454 million. See James W. Singer, "It Seems to Be a Bureaucratic Rule—When In Doubt, Hire a Consultant," *National Journal* (November 17, 1979), p. 1932. In 1981, the president, in effect, stated that his own Office of Management and Budget was grossly understating the extent of the use of consultants by the feds when he ordered that the government must cut $500 million from its annual consulting costs—a sum higher than the government's total expenditures on consultants, according to the OMB. In so doing, the White House implicitly accepted the estimates of the General Accounting Office, which contended that the federal government spent $3.8 billion on consultants in fiscal 1980. See: Sarah Griffith, "While Hardly Anyone Was Looking, The Budget Ax Fell on Consultants," *National Journal* (November 7, 1981), pp. 1990–1992.

[22] Singer, "It Seems to Be a Bureaucratic Rule," p. 1932. The use of consultants by the federal government is guided by Office of Management and Budget Circular A-120, issued in 1980. OMB Circular A-120 provides a very broad definition of consultants and what they do. Consulting is defined as advisory services on managerial concerns, and consultants may be hired via a procurement contract, appointed to an advisory committee, or even appointed to the Civil Service itself.

[23] Stuart Auerbach, "Disclosure Rules on Consultants Held Insufficient," *Washington Post* (November 2, 1990).

[24] Walsh, *The Public's Business*, p. 49.

[25] *Ibid.*, p. 50.

[26] In 1979, there were 19,212 management, public relations, and general consulting services employees working for 1,311 firms. These figures represented an increase of almost 30 percent each in the number of consultants and in the number of firms from five years earlier. See: "Consultants: New Target for Budget Trimmers," *U.S. News & World Report* (December 21, 1981), p. 39.

[27] Daniel Guttman and Barry Willner, *The Shadow Government* (New York: Pantheon, 1976), p. 21.

[28] Harold Seidman, *Politics, Position, and Power*, pp. 268–269.

[29] National Science Foundation, *Scientific Activities of Independent Nonprofit Institutions* (Washington, D.C.: U.S. Government Printing Office, 1971).

[30] As appearing on the program, "60 Minutes," CBS Television Network, November 30, 1980.

[31] Auerbach, "Disclosure Rules on Consultants Held Insufficient."

[32] Daniel Guttman, "60 Minutes."

[33] Federal Procurement Data System, as cited in T. R. Reid, "Protection for Nation's Largest Consumer," *Washington Post* (October 30, 1981); and "Federal Procurement Institute Gets Going," *Contract Management*, 17 (November, 1977), p. 10.

[34] Study conducted by the Center for Strategic and International Studies, as cited in George Melloan, "Even Generals Get the Arms-Procurement Blues," *Wall Street Journal* (June 23, 1987).

[35] Phillip J. Cooper, "Government Contracts in Public Administration: The Role and Environment of the Contracting Officer," *Public Administration Review*, 40 (September/October 1980), pp. 460–461.

[36] *Ibid.*, p. 462.

[37] *Ibid.*, p. 463.

[38] John O'Mally, editor of *Commerce Business Daily*, and Vince Villa, Washington consultant, as quoted in "Most Ads for Contractors Meaningless," *Washington Post* (June 25, 1980).

[39] Cooper, "Government Contracts in Public Administration," p. 462. See also: Richard E. Speidell, "The Judicial and Administrative Review of Government Contract Awards," *Law and Contemporary Problems* (Winter 1972), p. 63; and William J. Spriggs, "The Judicial Role of the Contracting Officer in U.S. Government Contracting," *Washburn Law Journal* (Fall 1971), p. 213. It is possible (although, in our view, doubtful) that this pattern may change as a result of the Competition in Contracting Act of 1984, which permits the GAO to hold up work awarded to one contractor if another bidder has filed a legitimate protest. However, the U.S. Assistant Attorney General has stated that he considers the Act to be unconstitutional. See: Myron Struck, "Clash Looms on New Contracting Act," *Washington Post* (October 31, 1984).

[40] Gordon Rule, quoted in William Proxmire, *Report from the Wasteland: America's Military Industrial Complex* (New York: Praeger, 1970), p. 83. Rule was a civilian cost containment expert for the navy.

[41] Former federal administrators averaged a 72 percent increase in wages when they entered industry; former members of Congress increased their salaries by 100 percent; former judges were in between. See: Federal Pay Commission Study, as cited in United Press International, "Private Firms Prize Ex-Officials," *The Arizona Republic* (November 17, 1976).

[42] Knight News Service, "Pentagon Retirees' Expertise Eagerly Snapped Up by Defense Firms," *Baltimore Sun* (December 5, 1982). The study analyzed retirees' records from 1980 through 1982.

[43] As derived from figures reported in a Knight-Ridder survey of 500 military retirees' files, cited in *ibid.*

[44] Figures are for 1970 through 1979. See Gordon Adams, Council on Economic Priorities, as cited in *ibid.*

[45] Newchy Mignone, as cited in: Jonathan Neumann and Ted Gup, "The Revolving Door: Industry Plums Await Retired U.S. Officials," *The Washington Post* (June 25, 1980).

[46] *Ibid.* The case involved the Navy and ManTech, Inc.

[47] *Ibid.*

[48] General Accounting Office, as cited in Associated Press, "Pentagon Management Pacts Awarded Without Competition, Probe Finds," *The Arizona Republic* (April 8, 1981). The GAO reviewed 256 contracts for management support services valued at $175 million.

[49] General Accounting Office study, as quoted in Mary Beth Franklin, "Pentagon-Industry Job Door Still Revolving, GAO Finds," *Washington Post* (May 8, 1987).

[50] W. Henry Lambright, *Governing Science and Technology* (New York: Oxford University Press, 1976), p. 123.

[51] Cooper, "Government Contracts in Public Administration," pp. 462–463.

[52] The source for much of this discussion is Raymond G. Hunt, "Cross-purposes in the Federal Contract Procurement System: Military R & D and Beyond," *Public Administration Review*, 44 (May/June 1984), pp. 247–256. Hunt calls the formal model the "F Model" and the joint management model the "J Model."

[53] *Ibid.*, pp. 248–249.

[54] *Ibid.*, pp. 250–251.

[55] R. H. Charles, "The Short Misunderstood Life of Total Package Procurement," *Innovation* (Winter 1971), p. 10.

[56] See, for example, Raymond G. Hunt, Irene S. Rubin, and Franklin S. Perry, *The Use of Incentives in R & D Contracting: A Critical Evaluation of Theory and Method* (Buffalo, N.Y.: State University of New York at Buffalo, Final Report of National Aeronautic and Space Association Grant NGR33-015-061, 1971).

[57] Hunt, "Military R & D and Beyond," p. 251.

[58] J. Ronald Fox, *Arming America: How the U.S. Buys Weapons* (Boston: Harvard University Press, 1974), p. 237; and Raymond G. Hunt, "R & D Management and Award Fee Contracting," *Journal of the Society of Research Administrators*, 6 (Summer 1974), p. 333.

[59] Hunt, "Military R & D and Beyond," p. 252.

[60] Henry Lambright and Albert H. Teich, "The Organizational Context of Scientific Research," in *Handbook of Organizational Design*, Vol. II, Paul C. Nystrom and William H. Starbuck, eds. (New York: Oxford University Press, 1981), pp. 305–379.

[61] Sharkansky, "Government Contracting," pp. 23–24.

[62] Blue Ribbon Defense Panel, *Report to the President and the Secretary of Defense* (Washington, D.C.: U.S. Government Printing Office, 1970), pp. 158–159.

[63] The federal contract administrators, in order of quotation, are: Roy Higdon, Environmental Protection Agency; David Webb, Health, Education and Welfare; and William Stevenson, Department of Energy. All are cited in: Jonathan Neumann and Ted Gup "An Epidemic of Waste in U.S. Consulting, Research," *Washington Post* (July 22, 1980).

[64] William Farris, cited in *ibid.*

[65] Guttman, "60 Minutes."

[66] David Muscone, quoted in Neumann and Gup, "An Epidemic of Waste in U.S. Consulting, Research."

[67] Steve Dorrler, as quoted in *ibid.*

[68] Guttman and Willner, *The Shadow Government*, p. 167.

[69] Response of Dr. Lois Ellen Datta, Chief, Headstart Evaluation Branch, Office of Education, 1970 letter to the Stanford Research Institute, as quoted in *ibid.*, p. 167.

[70] *Ibid.*, p. 38.

[71] *Ibid.*, p. 16.

[72] Subcomittee on Investigations, Committee on Post Office and Civil Service, House of Representatives, *Report on the Investigation of the Contract Between Westinghouse Electric Corporation and the U.S. Postal Service* (Washington, D.C.: U.S. Government Printing Office, October 19, 1971).

[73] The estimate applied only to what are now the Department of Education and the Department of Health and Human Services. See: Surveys and Investigation Staff, Committee on Appropriations, House of Representatives, *Report on the Manpower Policies and Practices of the Department of Health, Education, and Welfare* (Washington, D.C.: U.S. Government Printing Office, April, 1971), as reprinted in: Committee on Appropriations, U.S. House of Representatives, *Department of Labor and Department of Health, Education and Welfare Appropriations for Fiscal Year 1972. Hearing before a Subcommittee of the Committee on Appropriations, Part IV* (Washington, D.C.: U.S. Government Printing Office, 1971), pp. 1061–1066.

[74] As cited in: Comptroller General of the United States, *Civil Servants and Contract Employees: Who Should Do What for the Federal Government?* (Washington, D.C.: General Accounting Office, 1981), p. 18. In 1981, there were 11,637 such activities, and annual costs may have been as high as $30 billion.

[75] Guttman and Willner, *The Shadow Government*, pp. 45–46.

[76] As cited in United Press International, "Suspended Firms Still Get Contracts, Senate Panel Says," *Washington Post* (July 5, 1981). However, on-site inspections by Pentagon officials doubled from 40,000 in 1984 to more than 80,000 in 1985. See: Melloan, "Even Generals Get the Arms-Procurement Blues."

[77] Larkin Dudley, "Managing Efficiency: Examples from Contract Administration," *Public Administration Review*, 50 (July/August 1990), p. 487.

[78] U.S. House of Representatives Subcommittee on Human Resources of the Committee on Post Office and Civil Service, *Contracting Out and Its Impact on Federal Personnel and Operations* (Washington: U.S. Government Printing Office, 1990), forthcoming, as cited in *ibid.*

[79] Senator Jim Sasser, as quoted in John E. Yang, "Reagan-Era Efficiency Program Called Wasteful," *Washington Post* (April 28, 1990).

[80] Comptroller General of the United States, *Civil Servants and Contract Employees*, p. 6.

[81] Al Stapleton, as quoted in "Consultants: New Target for Budget Trimmers," p. 40.

[82] Guttman and Willner, *The Shadow Government*, p. 113.

[83] *Ibid.*, p. 119.

[84] Comptroller General of the United States, *Civil Servants and Contract Employees*, pp. 6–14.

[85] Ted Gup and Jonathan Neumann, "Federal Contracts: A Litany of Frivolity, Waste," *Washington Post* (June 23, 1980).

[86] Jack Blaine, as quoted in *ibid.*

[87] Quoted in *ibid.*

[88] Richard W. Stevenson, "Many Caught but Few Are Hurt For Arms Contract Fraud in U.S.," *Washington Post* (November 12, 1990).

[89] Ronald J. Ostrow and John M. Broder, "New Indictments a Possibility in Pentagon Probe," *Philadelphia Inquirer* (November 26, 1990).

[90] The following information in this paragraph is drawn from: Stevenson, "Many Caught but Few Are Hurt For Arms Contract Fraud in U.S."

[91] Quoted in: Russell Mitchell, "It Was Mr. Fixit Vs. The Pentagon—and the Pentagon Won," *Business Week* (December 24, 1990), p. 52.

[92] *Ibid.*

[93] See, for example, Patricia S. Florestano and Stephen B. Gordon, "A Survey of City and County Use of Private Contracting," *The Urban Interest*, 3 (Spring 1981), p. 25; and E. S. Savas, *Evaluating the Organization of Service Delivery: Solid Waste Collection and Disposal* (New York: Center for Government Studies, Graduate School of Business, Columbia University, 1976).

[94] Lori M. Henderson, "Intergovernmental Service Arrangements and Transfer of Functions," *Municipal Year Book, 1985* (Washington, D.C.: International City Management Association, 1985), p. 201.

[95] Keon S. Chi, "Privatization: A Public Option?" *State Government News* (June 1985), p. 6; and Annmarie Hauk Walsh and James Leigland, "Designing and Managing the Procurement Process," in *Handbook of Public Administration*, James L. Perry, ed. (San Francisco: Jossey-Bass, 1989), p. 483.

[96] Annie Millar, Carol De Vita, and Lester M. Salamon, *The Phoenix Nonprofit Sector in a Time of Government Retrenchment* (Washington, D.C.: The Urban Institute, 1986), p. 41. Figure is for 1982.

[97] *Ibid.* Figures are for 1982.

[98] Lester M. Salamon, "Government and the Voluntary Sector in an Era of Retrenchment: The American Experience," *Journal of Public Policy*, 6 (January/March, 1986), p. 7. But see also: John Stuart Hall, et al., *Government Spending and the Nonprofit Sector in Two Arizona Communities: Phoenix/Maricopa County and Pinal County* (Washington, D.C.: The Urban Institute, 1985), p. 47. Figure is for 1982.

[99] Salamon, "Government and the Voluntary Sector in an Era of Retrenchment," p. 7. Figures in the paragraph are for 1982.

[100] In 1975, 24 percent, or $36 billion, of state and local expenditures went to purchases of goods and services. See Donald Fisk, Herbert Kiesling, and Thomas Muller, *Private Provision of Public Services: An Overview* (Washington, D.C.: The Urban Institute, 1978), p. 87.

[101] *Ibid.*, p. 89.

[102] *Ibid.* Another survey found that more than 97 percent of American cities (1,350 cities responded) required sealed bids on purchasing contracts. On the other hand, nearly 87 percent of these same cities permitted bidding to be waived under certain circumstances. See Dan H. Davidson and Solon G. Bennett, "Municipal Purchasing Practices," *Municipal Year Book, 1980* (Washington, D.C.: International City Management Association, 1980), pp. 236–237, Tables 3/10 and 3/12.

[103] Fisk, et al, *Private Provision of Public Services*, p. 92.

[104] Florestano and Gordon, "A Survey of City and County Use of Private Contracting," p. 27. For an excellent analysis of how public administrators decide to use the public or private sector to deliver services, see: James Ferris and Elizabeth Graddy, "Contracting Out: For What? With Whom?" *Public Administration Review*, 46 (July/August 1986), pp. 332–344. This analysis was based on the data shown in Table 11-2.

[105] Based on Sharkansky, "Government Contracting," p. 25. See also: Ruth Hoogland De Hoog, *Contracting Out for Human Services: Economic, Political, and Organizational Perspectives* (Albany, N.Y.: State University of New York Press, 1984), especially pp. 1–33.

[106] "Federal Procurement Institute Gets Going," p. 10.

[107] *Ibid.*

[108] U.S. House of Representatives Armed Services Committee, Investigations Subcommittee, *Life Is Too Short: A Review of the Brief Periods Managers of Major Defense Acquisition Programs Stay on the Job* (Washington, D.C.: U.S. Government Printing Office, 1990), as cited in Molly Moore, "Military Revolving Door Quickens," *Washington Post* (July 3, 1990).

[109] Representative Nicholas Mavroules, as quoted in Moore, "Military Revolving Door Quickens."

[110] Denning and Olson, "Public Enterprise and the Emerging Character of State Service Provisions," pp. 6, 9.

[111] Walsh, *The Public's Business*, p. 6.

[112] See notes 5 and 10.

[113] U.S. Bureau of the Census, *Statistical Abstract of the United States, 1990* (Washington, D.C.: U.S. Government Printing Office, 1990), p. 548, Table 910. In 1988, the U.S. Postal Service employed 824,000 people, and had revenues of almost $36 billion.

[114] Ronald C. Moe and Thomas H. Stanton, "Government-Sponsored Enterprises as Federal Instrumentalities: Reconciling Private Management with Public Accountability," *Public Administration Review*, 49 (July/August 1989), p. 322. The U.S. Office of Management and Budget defines government-sponsored enterprises as "financial intermediaries directing capital to particular sectors of the economy." See: U.S. Office of Management and Budget, *Special Analyses: Budget of the United States Government, Fiscal Year 1990* (Washington, D.C.: U.S. Government Printing Office, 1988), p. F-21. A more rigorous definition of a government-sponsored enterprise is as follows: a privately owned, federally chartered financial institution with nationwide scope and limited lending powers that benefits from an implicit federal guarantee to enhance its ability to borrow money. See: Thomas H. Stanton, *Government-Sponsored Enterprises: Their Benefits and Costs as Instruments of Federal Policy* (Washington, D.C.: Association of Reserve City Bankers, 1988), p. iv. Using this definition, the seven government-sponsored enterprises in the United States are the following: the banks of the Farm Credit System (FCS), the Federal National Mortgage Association (Fannie Mae), the Federal Home Loan Mortgage Corporation (Freddie Mac), the Federal Home Loan Banks (FHLB), the Student Loan Marketing Association (Sallie Mae), the Financing Corporation (FICO) of the Federal Home Loan Bank System, and the Federal Agricultural Mortgage Corporation (Farmer Mac). Additional government-sponsored enterprises are under consideration.

[115] Walsh, *The Public's Business*, p. 6.

[116] Denning and Olson, "Public Enterprise and the Emerging Character of State Service Provisions," pp. 10, 42.

[117] U.S. Bureau of the Census, *Statistical Abstract of the United States, 1990*, p. 279, Table 464. In 1988, special districts and statutory authorities accounted for 59 percent of all long-term state and local debt.

[118] Irene S. Rubin, "Municipal Enterprises: Exploring Budgetary and Political Implications," *Public Administration Review*, 48 (January/February 1988), p. 548.

[119] Charlie B. Tyer, "Municipal Enterprises and Taxing and Spending Policies: Public Avoidance and Fiscal Illusions," *Public Administration Review*, 49 (May/June 1989), p. 255.

[120] For example, *Williamsburg Savings Bank* v. *State of New York* (1928), and *Robertson* v. *Zimmerman* (1935).

[121] Kathryn E. Newcomer, Deborah L. Trent, and Natalie Flores-Kelly, "Municipal Debt and the Impact of Sound Fiscal Decision Making," *Municipal Year Book, 1983* (Washington,

D.C.: International City Management Association, 1983), pp. 218–219.

[122] Ann Crittenden, "The Hoover Way to Help Sick Companies," *New York Times* (January 24, 1982).

[123] This discussion is drawn from Walsh, *The Public's Business*, pp. 27–29.

[124] *Ibid.*, p. 289.

[125] Nathanial S. Preston, "The Use and Control of Public Authorities in American State and Local Government." Ph.D. dissertation, Princeton University, 1960.

[126] Walsh, *The Public's Business*, p. 237.

[127] *Ibid.*, p. 4.

[128] Jameson W. Doig, "'If I See A Murderous Fellow Sharpening a Knife Cleverly...': The Wilsonian Dichotomy and the Public Authority Tradition," *Public Administration Review*, 44 (July/August 1983), pp. 292–303.

[129] Robert A. Caro, *The Power Broker: Robert Moses and the Fall of New York* (New York: Knopf, 1974), pp. 5–10.

[130] *Ibid.*, pp. 19–20.

[131] Walsh, *The Public's Business*, p. 213.

[132] Caro, *The Power Broker*, p. 38.

[133] Quoted in *ibid.*, p. 12.

[134] *Ibid.*, p. 18.

[135] *Ibid.*, p. 15.

[136] United Press International, "'Master Builder' Robert Moses, 92, Dies," *The Arizona Republic* (July 30, 1981).

[137] Caro, *The Power Broker*, p. 15.

[138] Robert Moses, *Public Works: A Dangerous Trade* (New York: McGraw-Hill, 1970), p. 438.

[139] *Ibid.*, p. 394.

[140] United Press International, "'Master Builder.'"

[141] Walsh, *The Public's Business*, p. 220.

[142] Caro, *The Power Broker*, p. 17.

[143] Walsh, *The Public's Business*, p. 220.

[144] *Ibid.*, p. 265.

[145] *Ibid.*, p. 271–272.

[146] *Ibid.*, p. 275.

[147] *Ibid.*, pp. 263–264, and 276.

[148] Denning and Olson, "Public Enterprise," p. 6.

CHAPTER

12

INTERGOVERNMENTAL ADMINISTRATION

Domestic public policy is implemented not merely by government, but by governments. The administration of a "single" public policy involves a pastiche of funding sources and public administrators interacting through all three levels of government, and the field of public administration calls this pastiche *intergovernmental relations*, or the series of financial, legal, political, and administrative relationships established among all units of government, which possess varying degrees of authority and jurisdictional autonomy. These relationships are called *federalism* when applied more narrowly to the federal government's relations with state governments, and the states' relationships with each other, although, in this book, we usually use "intergovernmental relations" and "federalism" interchangeably. *Intergovernmental administration*, sometimes called *intergovernmental management*, is the management and coordination of intergovernmental relationships for the purpose of achieving specific policy goals.[1]

FEDERALISM IN TURMOIL

The concept, structure, and practice of federal relations in the United States have been in turmoil since at least 1960. Authorities differ on the effects of new forms of federalism on the public and its interests. Theodore J. Lowi has attacked new variations of federalism, particularly those of the Johnson administration, as overly decentralized, inducing a "crisis of public authority" antithetical to the national interest, and indicative of "the end of liberalism."[2] On the other hand, Vincent Ostrom has applauded the decentralizing overtones of new ventures in federal relations as beneficial to the assurance of a "compound republic"—that is, one where multiple and jurisdictionally overlapping administrative units are most responsive to the needs of the individual citizen.[3]

Considering how opinions differ among scholars on the nature of intergovernmental relations, it is not surprising to learn that we are dealing with an extraordinarily complex system. These complexities are administrative, jurisdictional, political, and financial—a list that is hardly surprising when we consider the enormous number of governments thriving in the United States. Table 12-1 identifies the 83,237 governments in the United States by type, and indicates their fluctuations between 1942, 1962, and 1987.

Much of the proliferation of units of local government occurred in the years following World War II, particularly around the fringes of big cities. It was largely due to "white flight" from the inner cities and unplanned metropolitan growth. The lack of prior planning for urban regions is particularly noticeable when we consider these examples of growth: Forty-four new suburban governments were created between 1945 and 1950 around St. Louis by builders desirous of escaping strict municipal building codes. New towns were formed around Minneapolis solely as a means of taxing a newly arrived industry, and one village was incorporated for the single purpose of issuing a liquor license. Bryan City, California, was created so that a circus owner could zone for animal populations as he saw fit. The town of New Squier, New York, was established so that a kosher slaughterhouse could be operated. Gardenia, California, was incorporated so that its residents might play poker legally.[4] Yet, eager as Americans appear to be to set up small towns, they are wary of creating large ones. Community efforts to merge urban and suburban governments have generally failed, despite frequently intensive efforts by urban political elites. With the exceptions of school districts,

which have been diminishing in number since the 1930s, and special districts, which have been steadily multiplying, the numbers of governmental units in all categories have remained more or less the same since 1960.

THE CONSTITUTION AND COURTS

The federal government interacts in major ways with both state and local governments. We shall consider federal interaction first with states, then with localities.

Much of the federal government's cooperation with state governments is specified by the Constitution, which organized the federal system around three basic ideas: (1) the drawing of boundaries between the governmental activities of the states and the nation; (2) the establishing and maintaining of the identity of the state and the national governments; and (3) the political integrating of the nation and the states.[5]

Section 8 of Article I of the Constitution was instrumental in making distinctions between state and national functions. It delegated seventeen specific powers to the national government, including defense, general welfare, and commerce, and it left the remaining powers to the states. These remaining powers are now known as "reserved powers," a phrase taken from the Tenth Amendment, which was added rather hastily by the founders in response to such populist rabble-rousers as Patrick

TABLE 12-1 Number of Governments in the United States by Level of Government, 1942, 1962, and 1987

Level of government	1942	1962	1987
Total	155,116	91,237	83,217
U.S. government	1	1	1
State governments	48	50	50
Local governments	155,067	91,186	83,166
Counties	3,050	3,043	3,042
Municipalities	16,220	18,000	19,205
Townships and towns	18,919	17,142	16,691
School districts	108,579	34,678	14,741
Special districts	8,299	18,323	29,487

Source: U.S. Bureau of the Census, *Statistical Abstract of the United States, 1985* (Washington, D.C.: U.S. Government Printing Office, 1984), p. 261, Table 433; and U.S. Bureau of the Census, *Government Units in 1987: Preliminary Report, GL87-7(P)* (Washington, D.C.: U.S. Government Printing Office, 1987), p.1.

Henry. The Tenth Amendment was designed to grant the states a more visible and defined territory for exercising their powers. Section 9 of Article I also dealt with states' boundaries by preventing the national government from doing certain things, such as suspending the writ of *habeas corpus*, and also by forbidding the states from doing certain things, such as entering into treaties with foreign nations and coining money.

The second area of constitutional federalism deals with establishing and maintaining the identities between state and nation. The most important clause here is Section 2, Article IV, which stipulates that "no new States shall be Formed or Erected within the jurisdiction of any other State; nor any State be formed by the junction of two or more States, or Parts of States, without the Consent of the Legislature of the States concerned."

Finally, the Constitution dealt with the integration of national and state governments, primarily by providing for cooperation among them in the performance of certain functions. For example, the states and the nation cooperate in amending the Constitution and electing a president. As Kenneth Vines observes, "Perhaps the most important factor in making possible political integration between the two levels is the scarcity of officials with a clearly defined identification with the states, resulting in the creation of a group of national officeholders who also have links to the states."[6] This arrangement, of course, was designed by the Founding Fathers. As James Madison noted in the *Federalist* papers, "a local spirit will infallibly prevail much more in the members of Congress than a national spirit will prevail in the Legislatures of the particular states."[7]

These three major features of the relations between the state governments and the national government—boundary settlement, separate identities, and national and state integration—were refined by the courts over time. Without question, the most influential single case in this process of refinement was *McCulloch* v. *Maryland*, which was settled by the Supreme Court under Chief Justice John Marshall in 1819. Marshall and his colleagues supported the expansion of national powers under the commerce clause of the Constitution, which gave the national government a powerful ability to interpret what was necessary and

proper in the way of policy under the Constitution. The case involved the state of Maryland's attempt to tax the second United States Bank, which was located in Maryland. Alexander Hamilton, as secretary of the treasury, had proposed a national bank and argued that it could be established under a strong national government, which could and should adopt such measures because they were "implied powers" under the Constitution, even though the Constitution did not specifically authorize such policies as the establishment of the bank. The Marshall Court agreed with Hamilton's argument, stating that, although a bank was not explicitly authorized as a power granted to Congress under the Constitution, it nonetheless was implied under Congress' abilities to establish and collect taxes, regulate commerce, raise and support armies, and so on. Hence, Congress had the ability to adopt appropriate measures for the realization of the powers granted to it by the Constitution, that is, to do whatever is "necessary and proper to implement its specified functions." This notion of implied powers as an interpretation of the "necessary and proper" clause of the Constitution is with us today, and (with the exception of the Civil War) remains the strongest statement of national power as opposed to state power. Table 12-2 lists the principal powers of the federal government and the implied powers of the states.

THE EVOLUTION OF INTERGOVERNMENTAL ADMINISTRATION

Operating within the formal rules of the game established by the Constitution and by subsequent judicial interpretation, localities, states, and the federal government have gone through a number of phases in their administrative relationships. During the twentieth century, we can discern at least seven such phases, often overlapping in time, but each possessing its own set of unique characteristics.[8]

Layer Cake Federalism, 1890–1930

The first of these phases occurred from the late nineteenth century to 1930, and was characterized by the conflict between states, localities, and

TABLE 12-2 The Constitution's Federal Divisions of Powers

Major powers of the federal government:

Tax for federal purposes.
Borrow on the nation's credit.
Regulate foreign and interstate commerce.
Provide currency and coinage.
Conduct foreign relations and make treaties.
Provide an army and navy.
Establish and maintain a postal service.
Protect patents and copyrights.
Regulate weights and measures.
Admit new states.
"Make all laws which shall be necessary and proper" for the execution of all powers vested in the U.S. government.

Major implied powers of the states:

Tax for local purposes.
Borrow on the state's credit.
Regulate trade within the state.
Make and enforce civil and criminal law.
Maintain a police force.
Furnish public education.
Control local government.
Regulate charities.
Establish voting and election laws.
"Powers not delegated to the United States by the Constitution, nor prohibited by it to the states are reserved to the states respectively, or to the people."

Washington. The major problems centered around defining the boundaries and proper spheres of influence among various governmental jurisdictions, and intergovernmental actors (*i.e.*, relevant public officials at all governmental levels) saw themselves in an adversarial and antagonistic relationship with each other. The mechanisms of intergovernmental relationships prior to 1930 were relatively simple and relied largely on legislative statutes, judicial rulings, and federal regulations. Intergovernmental relations were perceived and described in metaphorical terms during this period. This "Federalism metaphor," as Dell S. Wright called it, pictured governmental relations as "Layer Cake Federalism." In other words, people saw the relationships between governments as a series of layers: localities on the bottom, states in the middle, and the federal government on top. There was little, if any, interaction among the layers other than each governmental level defending its autonomy from encroachment by the other higher and lower levels.

Marble Cake Federalism, 1930–1960

The next federal phase occurred during the 1930s and the 1950s and represented quite a different composite of relationships than those of the previous period of intergovernmental conflict. The 1930s, 1940s, and 1950s were decades of "Cooperative Federalism" in which everyone faced up, essentially as an intergovernmental team, to the common problems of the Depression, World War II, and the rise of international communism. In stark contrast to the pre-1930s, officials involved in intergovernmental relations stressed collaboration and supportive relationships. The mechanisms of working relationships among governments moved from simple statutes and court orders to a national planning mode involving the introduction of formula grants and more sophisticated versions of intergovernmental tax credits. The federalism metaphor changed from "Layer Cake Federalism" to "Marble Cake Federalism"; increasingly, it was difficult to separate the governmental activities of localities, the states, and the nation.

Water Tap Federalism, 1940–1970

The next phase, which occurred during the 1940s through the 1960s, has been called "Concentrated Federalism." During this period, the shape of intergovernmental relations was increasingly functional, focused, and specific. The federal government attempted more aggressively to meet the public service obligations and the physical development needs of states and communities. In terms of the working styles of officials who participated in intergovernmental relations during this period, "politics" were largely "out" and "professionalism" was largely "in"; a kind of engineering mentality predominated. The new mechanisms of intergovernmental relations evolved from a national planning format to an emphasis on detailed and targeted categorical grants and the monitoring of certain service standards. The federalism metaphor changed from a "marble cake" to "water taps," stressing the focused and channeled nature of the concentrated federalism phase; that is, federal grants, released by Congress from the federal spigot, flowed from Washington to the states, and from the states to the localities.

Federalism in Flower, 1950–1970

The 1950s and 1960s saw the emergence of "Creative Federalism." Here the emphasis was on meeting the problems of urban America, the poor, the dispossessed, and minorities. The apolitical, engineering mentality held by officials who were involved in intergovernmental relationships during the concentrated period of federalism gave way to a more political view, focusing on the achievement of national goals as they pertained to President Lyndon Johnson's Great Society programs. The mechanisms for achieving all this were largely those of participation by the citizenry, program planning, and an increasing emphasis on project grants—that is, aid given by the federal government to states and localities for the completion of specific projects. The federal metaphor that had relied on plumbing ("water taps") was replaced with one that focused on botany; suddenly there was a "flowering" of federalism, a metaphor that emphasized the verdant proliferation of various intergovernmental programs.

Picket Fence Federalism, 1960–1980

The 1960s and 1970s saw the emergence of a new phase of federalism that stressed competition among subnational jurisdictions. After federalism's flowering phase, new problems emerged involving coordination, program effectiveness, the competency of delivery systems, and the accessibility of citizens to the policy-making process. As in the conflictually oriented phase of intergovernmental relations, a renewed emphasis was seen on disagreement, tension, and rivalry among competitors for federal grants. The mechanisms of intergovernmental relations shifted from project grants and participation to the consolidation of federal grants through such devices as block grants, revenue sharing, and the reorganization of categorical grants. The operative meta-

phor of federalism's competitive phase became "Picket Fence Federalism," which stressed the fragmented, discrete nature of the hundreds of different kinds of categorical and project grants that developed during this phase.

Federalism as Facade, 1970–1980

The 1970s saw the emergence of "Calculative Federalism." Calculative federalism amounted to the intergovernmental system's way of coping with new regulatory constraints. The main problems were ones of accountability, fiscal dependency, and diminishing public confidence in the institutions of government. The state and local officials who participated in intergovernmental relations perceived the shape of federalism to be one of gamesmanship, and concentrated their energies on such endeavors as using federal grants for the attainment of local goals that were not necessarily envisioned by federal policymakers. They also had to cope with an overload of demands for governmental services, while often functioning under budgetary constraints. Increasingly, the mechanisms of dealing with the relationships between governments stressed loans, entitlements, Washington's bypassing of state governments and its working directly with localities, and a variety of crosscutting regulations.

The metaphor of intergovernmental administration during this period was "facade." In other words, intergovernmental management and relations, as they had been traditionally understood, no longer existed; so powerful and dominant had the federal government become that the powers of states and localities, at least in relative terms, were no longer of consequence.

Fend-for-Yourself Federalism, 1980–Present

Finally, the 1980s and 1990s have witnessed the emergence of "Competitive Federalism," or "Fend-for-Yourself Federalism."[9] The federal government's intergovernmental preeminence of the 1970s began to dissipate after 1978, when (as we later detail) the federal government's contribution to the finances of state and local governments peaked as a share of their budgets, and began a decline that has yet to be arrested, and when the spending power of federal assistance to states and communities similarly topped out and began its uninterrupted downward spiral. Later in the 1980s, the federal government became increasingly mired by "the uncontrollables" (described in Chapter 8), and crushed by its own staggering deficit. In Fiscal Year 1981, the annual federal deficit exceeded $100 billion for the first time, in 1986 it topped $200 billion, and it continues to burgeon unabated.[10]

The effects of the feds' withdrawal of their fiscal support of subnational governments, combined with the federal deficit, have resulted in a situation in which all governments have had to become more innovative and more competitive to deliver services. But "competition" no longer refers to state and local governments competing among themselves for federal grants, as it did during the phase of Picket Fence Federalism. Today, competition means that all governments including the federal government, are competing with each other for revenues. "The essence of [Fend-for-Yourself Federalism] is that now Washington policymakers as well as state and local officials must go back, hat-in-hand, to a common source—the nation's taxpayers—when additional revenue is needed....there is growing evidence to suggest that absent a national crisis, Washington does not have the inside track in the emerging intergovernmental race for taxpayer support."[11]

Indeed not. Public opinion polls taken since 1972 show that the federal government has steadily slipped in the public's perception as the most efficient and effective level of government, relative to state and local governments. As Figure 12-1 shows, local governments first surpassed the federal government on this dimension in 1979, and state governments, long the butt of American po-

litical humor, now are almost at a par with the federal government when Americans are asked which level of government gives them the most for their money.

Over time, Americans have grown to view the federal, state, and local governments as increasingly alike in terms of their abilities to deliver services efficiently and effectively. This developing popular perspective has evolved at the expense of the federal government and to the great benefit of the state governments in particular. The principal point, however, is that the competence of each level of government is perceived by the people to be increasingly comparable in an age of reduced governmental revenues. As a consequence, federal, state, and local public administrators must compete with one another as never before to earn the respect and trust of their taxpayers if they are to increase their government's revenues. Fend for yourself.

In describing these phases of federalism, we have relied on hyperbole and caricature as methods of getting the main points across. This point should be kept in mind, particularly as it applies to our description of our present federal phase, "Fend-for-Yourself Federalism," because exaggeration can be misleading, and it is not our intention to promote what one wag has called, "the Henny Penny school of federalism"—that is, the notion that the sky of the intergovernmental system is falling, either because of too much or too little federal activity.[12]

Nevertheless, characterizing federalism along these seven phases is useful as a background in gaining a more complete understanding of the relations among America's governments—especially their fiscal relations, which typically have been the dominant, though by no means only, factor in each of these phases of federalism.

Back to Basics: A Founder on Federalism

The following excerpt is taken from Federalist Paper 51, written in 1788. In this brief condensation, the writer explores the nature of governmental relationships.

In order to lay a due foundation for that separate and distinct exercise of the different powers of government, which to a certain extent is admitted on all hands to be essential to the

preservation of liberty, it is evident that each department should have a will of its own; and consequently should be so constituted that the members of each should have as little agency

**FIGURE 12-1 Comparison of Opinions about the Level of
Government that Provides "The Most for Your Money," 1972–1988**

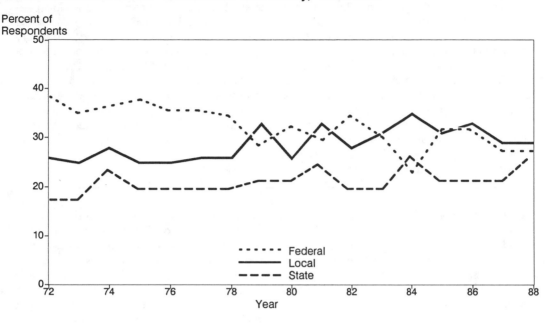

Source: Debra L. Dean, "Closing the Opinion Gap: State and Local Governments
Fare Well in ACIR Poll," *Intergovernmental Perspective*, 14 (Fall 1988), p. 24.

as possible in the appointment of the members of the others. Were this principle rigorously adhered to, it would require that all the appointments for the supreme executive, legislative, and judiciary magistracies should be drawn from the same fountain of authority, the people, through channels having no communication whatever with one another. Perhaps such a plan of constructing the several departments would be less difficult in practice than it may in contemplation appear....

But what is government itself but the greatest of all reflections on human nature? If men were angels, no government would be necessary. If angels were to govern men, neither external nor internal controls on government would be necessary. In framing a government which is to be administered by men over men, the great difficulty lies in this: you must first enable the government to control the governed, and in the next place oblige it to control itself. A dependence

on the people is, no doubt, the primary control on the government, but experience has taught mankind the necessity of auxiliary precautions....

In the compound republic of America, the power surrendered by the people is first divided between two distinct governments, and then the portion allotted to each subdivided among distinct and separate departments. Hence a double security arises to the rights of the people. The different governments will control each other at the same time that each will be controlled by itself....

It is of great importance in a republic not only to guard the society against the oppression of its rulers, but to guard one part of the society against the injustice of the other part. Whilst all authority in it will be derived from and dependent on the society, the society itself will be broken into so many parts, interests, and classes of citizens that the rights of individuals or of the minority, will be in little danger from interested combinations of the majority....

Justice is the end of government. It is the end of civil society. It ever has been and ever will be pursued until it be obtained, or until liberty be lost in the pursuit....

In the extended republic of the United States, and among the great variety of interests, parties, and sects which it embraces, a coalition of a majority of the whole society could seldom take place on any other principles than those of justice and the general good; whilst there being thus less danger to a minor from the will of a major party, there must be less pretext also to provide for the security of the former by introducing into the government a will not dependent on the latter, or, in other words, a will independent of the society itself. It is no less certain than it is important, notwithstanding the contrary opinions which have been entertained, that the larger the society, provided it lie within a practical sphere, the more duly capable it will be of self-government. And happily for the *republican cause*, the practical sphere may be carried to a very great extent by a judicious modification and mixture of the *federal principle*.

James Madison

FISCAL FEDERALISM

The old question in politics of who gets what, when, where, and how is nowhere more evident than in the intergovernmental money game. During the twentieth century, these political patterns have changed radically.

A World Turned Upside Down: A Century of Fiscal Change

The fiscal scene throughout the intergovernmental system has undergone some dramatic alterations during this century. In 1913, state government expenditures accounted for less than 1 percent of the Gross National Product, but by 1987 expenditures by state governments derived from their own tax bases (*i.e.*, not counting federal aid to states) amounted to 5.5 percent of the Gross National Product.[13] State government spending increased its proportion of total public expenditures (again excluding federal assistance) from not quite 12 percent in 1913 to more than 19 percent in 1987.[14] State fiscal assistance to their local governments also grew enormously during the century, from less than $100 *million* in 1913 to nearly $140 *billion* in 1987 (not counting federal grants passed on to local governments by the states).[15] State aid to local governments now accounts for a third of local revenues.[16]

The enormous monetary growth of the state and national governments had to come at someone's expense, and that "someone" was the local governments. In 1929, local governments expended nearly 60 percent of all public outlays, virtually all of it from their own sources of revenues, and these expenditures accounted for almost 5 percent of the Gross National Product; they were the dominant governmental actors in the American economy until the Depression. But by 1987, and in spite of the fact that the expenditure rates of local governments had expanded more rapidly than did the national economy, spending by local governments from their own revenue sources fell to slightly more than 9 percent of total public outlays[17] and to 3.5 percent of the GNP.[18]

The reasons why the federal government in particular expanded at the expense of both the state and the local governments, but especially the local governments, was the introduction in 1913 of the federal tax on income. Figure 12-2 shows the incredible productivity of the income tax by all levels of government and explains, at least in part, why the federal government became the dominant tax collector over the century. Prior to 1913, the income tax was the least productive tax, while the property tax was the most productive. But well before mid-century, the property tax had slipped to third place, and had been far outstripped by both the income and sales taxes as a source of governmental revenues.

The productivity of the income tax as a generator of government revenues had, of course, its effect on governments as revenue collectors. Figure 12-3 illustrates these effects. As it shows, local and state governments were displaced by the federal government as the major tax collectors.

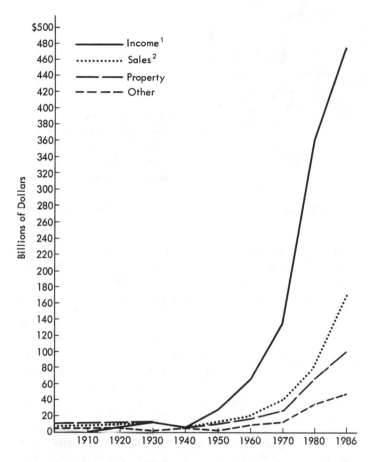

FIGURE 12-2 Tax Collections by Type of Tax, All Levels of Government, 1910–1986

Source: Advisory Commission on Intergovernmental Relations, *Significant Features of Fiscal Federalism, 1987* (Washington, D.C.: U.S. Government Printing Office, 1987), pp. 38–39

It is this central reality of intergovernmental finance that made much of fiscal federalism possible during this century. But within the milieu of a fiscally dominant federal government, Washington has waxed and waned as an intergovernmental actor.

The Rise of the Feds: 1913–1978

Until the Depression struck, local governments were the dominant tax collectors in the country, but now the nation's 83,166 local governments collect fewer taxes than either the fifty state governments or the federal government. In 1913, the year that the Sixteenth Amendment, which initiated a tax on income, was enacted, the federal government accounted for about 30 percent of all governmental outlays at all levels; federal aid to state and local governments was essentially nonexistent. In a federal budget of not quite $1 billion in 1913, only $12 million (a bit more than 1 percent) went to state and local governments.

Thirty-five years later (1948) these relationships had radically altered. By mid-century the national government was spending nearly two-thirds of all government outlays—a percentage that essentially holds to this day. Nevertheless,

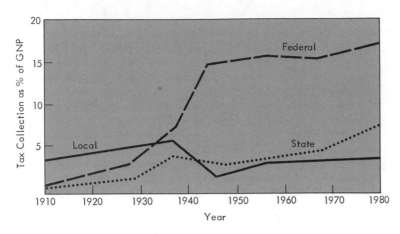

FIGURE 12-3 Tax Collections by Level of Government, as a Percentage of GNP, Selected Years

Source: As derived from U.S. Bureau of the Census, *Historical Statistics* (Washington, D.C.: Government Printing Office, 1977).

federal aid to state and local governments as a proportion of federal outlays still had not increased by very much; in 1948, federal aid to state and local governments accounted for less than 3 percent of the federal budget.

From 1948 to 1978, these relationships again altered radically. The role of the federal government in relation to the total economy grew by a third—from less than 14 percent to more than 22 percent of the Gross National Product.[19] Equally significant is that federal aid to subnational governments grew from less than $2 billion to almost $78 billion during that twenty year period. In 1978, federal grants-in-aid to state and local governments accounted for 3.6 percent of the Gross National Product, 17 percent of all federal outlays, and 26.5 percent of all outlays by state and local governments.[20] These were historic figures. Never before, and never again, would they be equalled or surpassed; 1978 was the year of greatest fiscal dominance by the federal government in the intergovernmental system.

The Fall of the Feds: 1978–Present

By the end of the 1980s, Washington's role in fiscal federalism was withering, as Figure 12-4 makes clear. Over the course of the next ten years (*i.e.*, by 1988), federal grants would slump by about a third from their 1978 levels to 2.4 percent of the Gross National Product, 10.8 percent of total

federal outlays, and 18.2 percent of all state and local outlays.[21] Projections, as Figure 12-4 indicates, anticipate even lower figures over time.

What, if anything, has filled the fiscal vacuum left by Washington's departure? Clearly, the states are the governments most willing to assume the responsibilities placed by the feds on the doorstep of the subnational jurisdictions. As two analysts have concluded, "we find that the most important developments [of the 1980s on intergovernmental relations] are twofold—the relative decline in the federal role and the rising role of the state governments. In part, the latter trend was a response to [President Ronald] Reagan's policies. His theory of federalism... has consistently favored the role of state governments."[22]

State spending levels, held constant for inflation, support this assessment; state spending from their own sources of revenues began a sharp upward swing in 1981 that still continues. Figure 12-5 illustrates this quite proactive fiscal posture that the states started to assume as the federal government withdrew from their affairs in the 1980s. Although the decline in federal grants to the states was not as dramatic as was the decline in federal aid to local governments during the 1980s (as we discuss shortly), the federal contribution to state revenues nonetheless sank from more than 26 percent of state general revenues in 1980 to less than 23 percent in 1987.[23]

FIGURE 12-4 The Rise and Decline of Federal Aid, 1958–1988—and 1998? (as a percentage of state-local outlays)

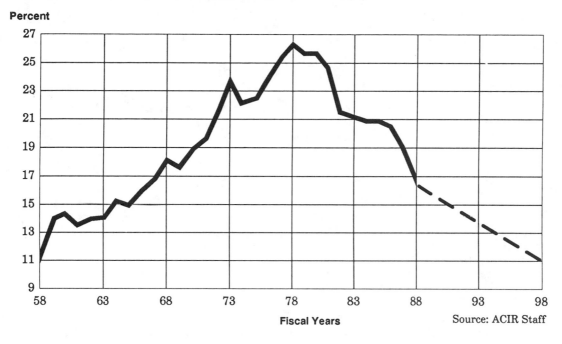

Percent

Fiscal Years

Source: ACIR Staff

Source: Robert Gleason, "Federalism 1986–87: Signals of a New Era," *Intergovernmental Perspective*, 14 (Winter 1988), p. 13.

The Politics of Grants-in-Aid: Categorical Grants, Block Grants, and the Brief but Edifying Life of General Revenue Sharing

Even though Washington's clout in the intergovernmental fiscal system is in decline, the federal government nonetheless remains dominant. As its dominance began to grow, Washington increasingly relied on grants-in-aid—that is, transfers of federal funds to state and local governments—to, at first, help them, and, later, to help itself.

Prior to 1960, federal grants were used to help state and local governments to achieve their own policy objectives, but following that year the increasing tendency was evident for the federal government to use the intergovernmental grants system to, in effect, bribe state and local governments to accomplish national objectives.[24] Between 1960 and 1981, the number of federal grants programs quadrupled from 132 to 538, indicating the new reliance that the federal government was placing on the grants system to achieve its ends.[25]

Categorical grants. Washington uses two major types of grants to pass money to the state and local governments: categorical grants and block grants. *Categorical grants* are highly specific and rather rigid programs that address narrow policy issues. The typical categorical grant has a number of strings attached, and each qualification must be met by the recipient in order to receive the grant. Categorical grants account for approximately 85 percent of the money that the state and local governments receive from the federal government. Washington obviously favors these categorical grants since they offer the most opportunity for retaining control over the expenditures of its money on the policy objectives for which federal dollars are spent.

FIGURE 12-5 State Direct General Expenditures in Constant (1986) Dollars

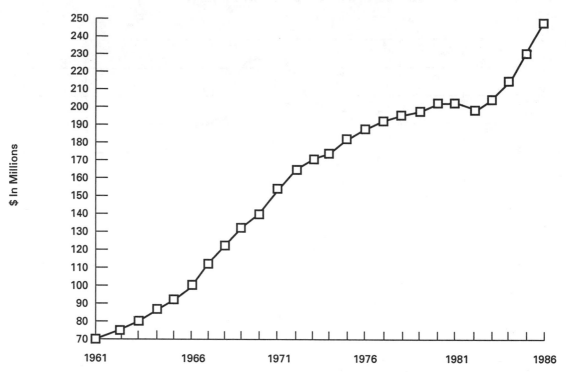

Source Richard P. Nathan and John R. Lago, "Intergovernmental Relations in the Reagan Era," *Public Budgeting and Finance*, 8 (Autumn 1988), p. 28.

Block grants. Block grants account for less than 15 percent of the money that Washington expends. A *block grant* is more general than a categorical grant, but still attaches some strings. Its major characteristic is that it allows the recipient to exercise more discretion in the ways that the federal dollars granted to it are expended.

Block grants generate substantial political heat. At the center of the argument is the level of trust that one has in state and local officials, as opposed to national officials, and the kinds of programs that each level of government would fund with block grant money. Those who favor focusing federal dollars toward the needs of the poor and the deprived tend to favor the use of categorical grants to achieve these ends, while those who favor letting state and local governments—or those governments that are somehow "closer to the needs of the people"—decide how and where money should be spent tend to favor the use of block grants.

Investigations do indicate that when state and local governments receive block grants, they tend to use the money for programs other than those related to the impoverished. For example, when Congress, at President Richard Nixon's urging, consolidated seven basic national programs under the Housing and Community Development Act of 1974, essentially converting them from categorical to block grants, and thereby giving local leaders more control over how the funds underwriting these programs were to be used, the Brookings Institution found that poverty programs had fared better under the old Model Cities program initiated during the 1960s than under the new Housing and Community Development programs. (Model Cities was one of those programs that was subsumed by the Housing and Community Development Act.) There had been a shift, both in funding and decision making, away from the poorest people in the neighborhoods to more mixed patterns, and programs had changed from an emphasis on social services, such as health and education, to short-term capital spending for projects such as parking lots and downtown renewal. Social services spending was found to be low under the Community Development programs.[26]

Nixon's halting steps toward decentralization of the intergovernmental grants system, which he took by increasing the stature of block grants, were accelerated by the Reagan administration. In 1981, Congress enacted the Omnibus Budget Reconciliation Act, which consolidated seventy-seven categorical grants and two block grants, with authority to spend $7.5 billion, into nine new or modified block grants. In addition, sixty-two categorical grant programs were eliminated altogether.

The effects of these consolidations and eliminations were dramatic, at least if we use the number of federal assistance programs as a measure. In 1981, Congress had funded 534 categorical grant programs and four block grants; in 1984, 394 categorical grants and eleven block grants were funded.[27] But Washington's propensity to use the categorical grant, despite Ronald Reagan's efforts to alter the federal government's reliance on the form, seems undiminished. By 1987, the number of categorical grants had rebounded to 422, and block grant programs had increased by a modest two, to a total of thirteen.[28] Moreover, when we use money as a measure, in contrast to numbers of grant types, the effects of Reagan's reforms are even less visible; block grants still account for less than 15 percent of the federal funds granted to states and localities.

Nevertheless, the still-marginal use of block grants as opposed to categorical grants by Washington has been accompanied by important changes in the system of fiscal federalism. First, states rather than local governments are now the prime recipients of federal block grants; the states, particularly during the 1960s and 1970s, often had been bypassed in the federal grant system. A second difference is that the states have even broader discretion in terms of how money channeled to them through block grants might be spent than they did under the block grant programs of the 1960s

and 1970s. Finally, and of greatest significance insofar as the recipients of grants from Washington are concerned, the total funding for the new block grant programs amounts to a large and overall reduction in funds for the programs that they are designed to implement. Unlike the Nixon block grant programs of the early 1970s, there was no "sweetened pot" to make the displacement of categorical grants by block grants more palatable to the more liberal members of Congress.

General Revenue Sharing. A third major form of intergovernmental assistance from Washington, which now no longer exists, was known as *General Revenue Sharing*, and it accounted for about 7 percent of the federal aid package. General Revenue Sharing was enacted by Congress in 1972 when it passed the State and Local Fiscal Assistance Act, and it was renewed by Congress for intervals of three to four years until late 1986, when Congress declined to reauthorize it. As a form of federal assistance to states and localities, Revenue Sharing had, by far, the fewest strings attached and disbursed funds to subnational governments by formula. Revenue Sharing was the most direct kind of federal aid insofar as local governments were concerned; Revenue Sharing funds went to 39,000 state governments, special districts, counties, cities, towns, townships, and Indian tribes; between 1972 and 1986, more than $83.5 billion in federal funds were distributed to these governments in the form of Revenue Sharing.

Revenue Sharing funds were distributed according to the proportion of federal personal income tax funds provided by state and local units of government; thus, the richer units of governments as defined by their tax bases, tended to be favored. About a third of the Revenue Sharing funds went to the states; the other two-thirds went to local governments.

Analyses of Revenue Sharing that were conducted since 1972 conclude that, while small cities and towns used about three quarters of their Revenue Sharing funds for new spending programs (mostly for capital projects), bigger urban areas with 100,000 people or more used only half of the money for new spending programs; the remaining half went to keep taxes down or to avoid borrowing. Among the states, only a third of shared revenues were used for new programs, and the tendency of both state and local governments to use Revenue Sharing funds for keeping a muzzle on the tax bite rather than for initiating new spending programs was the norm.

The parallels between how state and local governments used Revenue Sharing funds, and how they continue to use the government corporation and privatization, described in Chapter 11, are striking. State and larger local governments used shared revenues mainly to keep their fiscal heads above water by maintaining existing services without raising taxes. They merged Revenue Sharing funds with other revenue sources, thus reducing the political visibility of Revenue Sharing; retained traditional patterns of political power and enhanced the clout of entrenched special interests; and, contrary to widespread speculation (and hope), reinforced the existing inefficiencies of public management systems.[29]

A Regional Rivalry

One of the major effects of the dramatic growth of fiscal federalism during the 1960s and 1970s was the fostering of an increasingly cutthroat competitiveness among state and local governments for federal dollars. Although this competitiveness has abated with the advent of Fend-for-Yourself Federalism, it exacerbated a regional rivalry that continues at present. Despite the fact that they are among the wealthiest of the nation's regions, the Northeast and Midwest, beginning in the 1970s, have complained that they are losing industry and jobs to other sections of the country, especially to the Western and Sunbelt states. These regions argue that, since they have supported other regions in the country over the years through a variety of federal grants programs that have favored those regions that historically have been less wealthy, it is now time for the federal government to tilt its grants programs toward the Northeast and Midwest.

The contention that certain regions are favored by the federal grants system more than others is a controversial one. One reason why this is so is that it is difficult to determine what kinds of federal payments to regions are in the mix, for there are more transfers of federal funds to regions than merely grants to governments.

Table 12-3 is a set of indices that measure per capita federal payments to regions by type of payment. It shows that, in 1988, Washington transferred almost $3,500 in federal revenues, on the average, to every man, woman, and child in the nation. These transfers included grants to states and localities (such as Medicaid and Aid to Families with Dependent Children); salaries and wages that were paid to federal employees; payments to individuals (such as Social Security, Medicare, and food stamps); procurement contracts (more than three quarters of which were let by the Defense Department); and other payments (mainly agricultural supports and research grants awarded by the National Science Foundation).

Overall, the Southeast got the most federal dollars, but on a per capita basis the winner was the Southwest, followed closely by the Plains states. When we compare the forms in which those federal dollars were transferred, however, variations emerge. For example, when only federal grants to states and localities are considered (which make up 13 percent of all federal expenditures listed in Table 12-3), the Rocky Mountain states are clearly dominant; the Southwest leads in terms of salaries paid to federal employees (16 percent of the total); the Mideast surfaces as the top recipient of federal public assistance and social insurance dollars (48 percent of the total); the Southwest does astonishingly well in securing federal procurement contracts (19 percent of the total); and the Plains states are the clear leaders in garnering federal support dollars for farmers, research grants, and other miscellaneous payments (4 percent of the total).

For overall federal spending, there has been a dramatic narrowing of regional gaps since midcentury in terms of the tax revenue/federal grant ratio. As Figure 12-6 shows, the Southwest and Rocky Mountain states generally gain more federal disbursements than they pay in taxes, while states around the Great Lakes and in the Midwest generally pay more in taxes than they gain in federal funds, but these differences are diminishing. More recent analyses substantiate that the diversion of federal funds from the Frostbelt to the Sunbelt as a consequence of tax and spending policies continues to equalize, although "any lessening of the inequalities has been almost entirely accidental," and the federal government "has not

TABLE 12-3 Per Capita Federal Expenditures by Type and Region, 1988

Region	Index of Federal Expenditures (U.S. Average: 100)	Total (in millions)	Total Per Capita	Grants to State and Local Gov'ts	Salaries and Wages	Direct Payments to Individuals	Procurement Contract Awards	Other
United States	100	$849,492 (100%)*	$3,490 (100%)*	$451 (16%)*	$548 (16%)*	$1,661 (48%)*	$676 (19%)*	$153 (4%)*
New England	102	51,189	3,572	538	433	1,686	804	111
Mideast	105	165,320	3,665	511	571	1,781	660	141
Great Lakes	79	117,068	2,769	423	287	1,604	310	145
Plains	108	65,598	3,764	488	495	1,657	457	666
Southeast	98	02,491	3,417	430	595	1,706	594	92
Southwest	112	81,180	3,911	410	629	1,614	1,135	123
Rocky Mountain	101	26,685	3,542	575	617	1,429	669	254
Far West	101	132,338	3,541	430	557	1,661	785	108

* Percentages in parentheses are the percentages of total federal dollars expended in the category; percentages have been rounded.

Note: Alaska, Hawaii, and Washington, D.C., are not included in the table.

Source: Advisory Commission on Intergovernmental Relations, *Significant Features of Fiscal Federalism, 1989*, Volume II, M-163-II (Washington, D.C.: U.S. Government Printing Office, 1989), p. 44.

intentionally adjusted spending and tax policies to help one region or punish another."[30]

This "accidental" redistribution of regional treasure seems likely to accelerate. The unprecedented savings-and-loan debacle (reviewed in Chapter 1) will, in all probability, transfer huge amounts of federal insurance payments from thirty-seven states in the Far West, Plains, Southeast, and Northeast to thirteen states in the Rocky Mountains, Southwest, Southeast, and Plains, where the more spectacular savings-and-loans bankruptcies occurred. One analyst concluded that every man, woman, and child in Texas alone would receive more than $3,500 to $10,500 (depending on the final tab of the bankruptcies) over the next thirty years from federal taxpayers in other states because of the savings-and-loans failures.[31]

It is small wonder, perhaps, that these regional equalizing trends, however unplanned, have failed to reduce the growing tension among regions of the country and, increasingly, a variety of regional organizations have cropped up for this reason. For example, in 1977 the thirteen Western states formed the Western Governors' Policy Office (WESTPO) with a fully staffed office in Denver to conduct regional analyses of sensitive issues, but primarily WESTPO focused on energy policy. Similarly, in 1976 seven states in the Northeast (Connecticut, Massachusetts, New Jersey, New York, Pennsylvania, Rhode Island, and Vermont) formed a Coalition of Northeastern Governors and stated as one of its principal objectives the presentation of "a united front before the Congress and the national administration in an effort to redress the current federal expenditure imbalances."[32] The founding of WESTPO and the Coalition of Northeastern Governors was in part a reaction to the founding in 1972 of the Southern Growth Policies Board, a thirteen state organization that conducts research on economic growth management in the South and has a well-staffed office in Washington. In Congress, regions have banded together in a variety of formats including the New England Congressional Caucus, the Northeast-Midwest

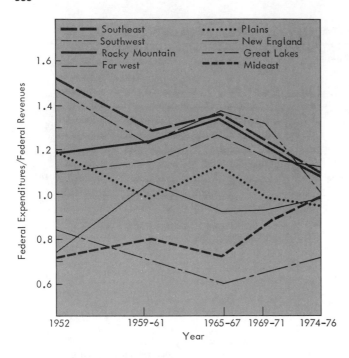

FIGURE 12-6 Ratio of Federal Expenditures to Federal Revenues by Region, 1952–1976

Source: Advisory Commission of Intergovernmental Relations, *Regional Growth: Flows of Federal Funds, 1952–1976* (Washington, D.C.: Government Printing Office, 1980), p. 55.

Economic Advancement Coalition, the Great Lakes Conference, the Sunbelt Conference, and the Western States Coalition (not to mention a Suburban Caucus, a Rural Caucus, and a Metropolitan Area Caucus), all of which symbolize a growing regional rivalry that has been promoted at least in part by the intergovernmental grants system, and, more recently, by "accidental" redistributions of federal dollars among the regions.[33]

A NEW APPROACH TO FEDERALISM

It was these conditions—the growing fiscal (and political) dominance of the federal government over state and local governments and the increasingly hot "grants war" fought between subnational jurisdictions competing for Washington's dollars—that led to the far-reaching proposals of President Ronald Reagan in 1982, calling for the reform of the federal structure. Although the implementation of these proposals was largely frustrated, Reagan's proposals for a "New Feder-

alism" symbolized his less-publicized successes in altering the role of the federal government in the intergovernmental system. These successes included a federal withdrawal from regional coordination and planning, a deregulation of intergovernmental administration, and, most important, a radical reduction in the fiscal support provided by Washington to states and communities. But Reagan's attempt to "sort out" the intergovernmental structure had merit simply because it illuminated the competing political values buried within that structure, and therefore we review it here.

A Not-so-Modest Proposal

At the heart of Reagan's reforms, as expressed in his proposal for a "New Federalism," was the notion that the federal government should not be involved in the business of state and local governments. This differed from the assumptions that have been held by federal policymakers since at least 1960, which held that the federal government should pay the governments of states and communities to implement national policies and federal goals.

To be fair, federal policymakers were beginning to question the role of Washington in the intergovernmental system before the advent of the Reagan presidency. President Jimmy Carter's Commission for a National Agenda for the Eighties had displayed a growing disinclination by a Democratic administration to further its involvement in state and local matters. In its *Report on Urban America*, the Commission advocated that a number of state and local issues be removed as matters of national concern: "The purpose and orientation of a 'national urban policy' should be reconsidered. There are no 'national urban problems,' only an endless variety of local ones. Consequently, a centrally administered national urban policy that legitimizes activities inconsistent with a revitalization of the larger national economy may be ill-advised."[34]

Nevertheless, Reagan's proposals were unprecedented. In his 1982 "State of the Union" address, President Reagan proposed his own version of "New Federalism." Under the first phase of this proposal, Washington would take over the Medicaid program in its entirety; Medicaid is a joint federal-state program that provides medical assistance to the indigent. In return, states and communities would absorb two significant welfare programs that are also run jointly by the state and federal governments: Aid to Families with Dependent Children (AFDC) and food stamps. Moreover, Washington would "turn back" to the states from sixty to seventy categorical grant and block grant programs in education, Revenue Sharing, transportation, community development, and social services; it would be up to the states if they wanted to accept any or all of these programs. But the states would not be required by Washington or anyone else to provide these and any other programs that had been returned to them.

Objections to President Reagan's proposals came from two very different sources. One was a national source and was related to the level of trust that national policymakers have in the motivations and capabilities of state and local administrators and legislators. Liberal members of Congress in particular were suspicious that the states would not favor the continuance of federal programs aimed at the poor, but instead would use the money received from the federal government to finance programs more acceptable to the middle class, such as tax reductions or road improvements.

A similar concern held by national policymakers related to the level of competency found in subnational governments. Some federal officials were openly worried about the abilities of state and local administrators to administer welfare programs.

The other source of objections to the Reagan proposals came from state and local officials themselves, and, unsurprisingly, did not relate to self-doubts about their own competence. Here, the issues dealt with fiscal equalization and balance. Could Washington turn back more and more responsibility to the states, while ignoring the fact that some states were rich and others poor? Would Washington, in a period of increasing fiscal limitations, still accept the notion that the federal government was obliged to distribute a monetary dividend to states and localities in the form of intergovernmental assistance? As a consequence of these concerns, state and local government lobbies also resisted the Reagan proposals. Ultimately, Reagan's efforts at "sorting out" intergovernmental relations went nowhere.

Regional Coordination and Planning: Washington Walks Out

Consequently, the Reagan administration tried less dramatic but significant ways to change the nature of federalism. In 1982, Washington began to get out of the business of encouraging regional intergovernmental coordination and planning.

Elimination of the "701" Planning Program. First, Congress began withdrawing funds that it had long allocated in support of various kinds of substate regional coordinating councils, such as Councils of Governments, which are voluntary associations of governments within the states that coordinate intergovernmental planning. Among the more important aspects of this cutting back by Washington was the elimination of "701" funding in 1982. The "701" program was established under Section 701 of the Urban Planning Assistance Act of 1954, and over the twenty-eight years of its existence it disbursed more than $200 million to state, regional, and local planning agencies for purposes of improving coordinated planning.

Largely as a result of federal requirements or financial incentives that can be traced back to at least the early 1950s, state and local governments have created over the years a vast network of substate intergovernmental and interagency coordinating bodies. There are roughly 2,000 of them. Some 600 of these are regional councils. About 70 percent of the regional councils are various kinds of policy councils. Some of these are controlled by the federal government, such as the Economic Development Districts (administered through the Department of Commerce) and the Rural Area Development Committees (managed by the Department of Agriculture). But almost half of the regional policy councils are planning councils, usually established by state legislation, and another 30 percent are voluntary councils of governments.[35] Many of these associations could not survive severe cutbacks in federal aid, and an estimated 10 percent of them closed their doors within a year after the reductions of "701" funding began.[36]

Elimination of the "A-95" Process. Second, and even more significant, the "A-95" process was eliminated in 1982 by Executive Order 12372. The "A-95" process had been established in 1969 by the Office of Management and Budget (OMB) Circular A-95. OMB Circular A-95 drew together federal mandates for state and local planning that were found in several federal statutes, particularly the Demonstration Cities and Metropolitan Development Act of 1966 (Model Cities), the Intergovernmental Cooperation Act of 1968, and the National Environmental Policy Act of 1969. It effectively required states and localities to set up OMB-recognized "clearinghouses" empowered to approve state and local grant requests if states and localities were to receive federal grants in a wide variety of fields. Although subnational jurisdictions formed these clearinghouses in various ways, most set up voluntary councils of governments.

Reagan's Executive Order 12372 replaced OMB Circular A-95 (which had, in many ways, permanently altered the face of intergovernmental administration) and permitted state and local governments to create their own review and planning procedures and to reduce federal regulations. Previously, review and planning procedures under "A-95" had been stipulated by the Office of Management and Budget.[37]

Elimination of the Federal Regional Councils. In 1983, the Reagan administration initiated a third tack in leaving problems of intergovernmental coordination to the locals—it eliminated the ten Federal Regional Councils. In 1969, Richard Nixon, resurrecting a presidential commission's report that had been buried by his predecessor in 1967, established ten Federal Regions designed to decentralize operational program decision making. These regions were a good idea. But in 1972, Nixon issued Executive Order 11647, which established a Federal Regional Council for each Federal Region. The councils were composed initially of the top administrators of seven major federal departments and agencies that had particular concerns in state and local affairs. Ultimately, the councils' scope was expanded to sixteen major agencies. The Office of Management and Budget had, for a number of years, pushed for the creation of these councils (or something like them) as a means of coordinating the management of federal domestic programs.[38]

It is less clear that the Federal Regional Councils were as good an idea as the federal regions themselves (which, unlike the councils, are still with us). Analysis after analysis concluded that the councils were either irrelevant or bothersome in the management of federal domestic programs.[39]

In 1982, Reagan radically reduced both the number of federal grants programs that the Federal Regional Councils were empowered to review, and the number of federal agencies that had membership on the councils. He redefined the councils' mission from one of managerial concern to a mission that was informational and deregulatory. In 1983, he abolished the councils altogether.

Robert W. Gage argues that Reagan understood the truly useful functions of the Federal Regional Councils better than either OMB or his predecessors. In Gage's view, the councils could have been most beneficial as facilitators of political networking, but not as managers of public programs.[40] But if Gage's assessment is correct (and it likely is), then Reagan's abolition of Federal Regional Councils can, in theory, be mitigated merely by encouraging federal regional administrators to get together for an occasional lunch.

The withdrawal of the federal government from the state and local structure of planning and program coordination amounts to a major, if not well heralded, change in the nation's intergovernmental relations. But the Reagan administration initiated (or, more accurately, accelerated the initiatives of its predecessors) two additional approaches as well: a concerted effort to deregulate intergovernmental relations (an effort reflected in Washington's withdrawal from the subnational planning and coordinative structure), and the reduction of both federal grants and the dollars in those grants to states and localities.

Deregulating Federalism

A primary component of the Reagan administration's drive to deregulate the federal grants system was the consolidation in 1982 of a number of categorical grants into larger block grants, which we reviewed earlier; these less specific larger block grants permitted more latitude by state and local officials in managing federally aided programs. But there remained the issue of a welter of federal regulations that characterize federal assistance packages.

State officials (and, as we discuss later, local officials, too) have had to devote increasing blocks of their time to administer federal dollars (and their accompanying rules and regulations) within their states. Governors in the 1960s devoted less of their time to state-federal business than did governors in the 1970s, and today the typical governor spends almost a full working day in a six-day working week to these concerns.[41] The impact of Washington on the states is clearly apparent, and only 3 percent of more than 100 former governors responding to one survey stated that they would advise new governors to spend less time than they did on state-federal relations.[42]

Despite the demands on their time that relations with Washington require, the governors believe that the time is worth it. Only 6 percent of the governors in the poll just mentioned believed that state-federal relationships were not significant to their overall programs to improve the quality of life for their states' citizens.[43]

Yet, there were frustrations. Washington had grown (at least until 1981, with the advent of the administration of Ronald Reagan) more intrusive in the affairs of state and local governments, and federal regulations over how states (and localities) must conduct their intergovernmental programs have proliferated. One study found that Washington imposed nearly 1,300 mandates on subnational governments in its intergovernmental programs; the average number of federal regulations affecting the jurisdictions examined was 570 regulations per subnational government![44]

Federal intergovernmental regulations come in four types:[45] crosscutting requirements, partial preemptions, crossover sanctions, direct orders. These are explained subsequently.

Crosscutting Requirements. These are the most numerous and have been around the longest; they apply to virtually all federal assistance programs and are used to further national objectives. For example, nondiscrimination clauses are in all federal intergovernmental programs, and if a state violates the clause, Washington can withdraw the program—or never grant it.

Partial Preemptions. The subnational governments are partially preempted from their traditional prerogatives in this kind of regulation because, if the states want federal aid, the federal government demands that the states adopt and administer program standards set by Washington, rather than by the states.

Crossover Sanctions. These permit the federal government to punish a state by reducing or withdrawing federal aid in one or more programs if its standards are not being satisfied in another program.

Direct Orders. An eyeball-to-eyeball standoff between a state capitol and the national capitol is the last occurrence federal officials want, so these are the least used; to pit Congress against the states raises serious constitutional questions. Nevertheless, Congress began mandating direct orders to subnational governments in the 1970s, such as its direct order in 1977 prohibiting cities from dumping sewage at sea.

Figure 12-7 shows the dramatic proliferation of all four types of regulations in federal intergovernmental programs since the 1930s. This expansion was felt by the states. Governors who served their states in the 1960s and 1970s believe strongly that these kinds of regulations have encroached on states' rights and responsibilities. More than 88 percent said that the federal government has assumed many of the responsibilities that appropriately belong to the states, and more than 86 percent thought that the intergovernmental system needed a "major overhaul."[46]

State administrators share these views, and go a step farther: they believe that federal governmental programs have distorted policymaking itself in their states. Surveys indicate that some three quarters of state agency heads believe that federal aid has led to national interference in state affairs. Eighty-three percent believed that there should be more decentralization of authority from the national government to the state. Even more significantly, 70 percent of state administrators in 1978 (up from 52 percent in 1964) felt that they would use federal assistance grants for different purposes if the "strings" attached to those grants were relaxed, indicating the distorting effect that federal aid may have on state priorities.[47]

There is a more subtle, but potentially equally harmful, impact of federal assistance on state governments. Because federal aid flows directly to state agency heads—federal intergovernmental funds for environmental improvements, for example, go directly from Washington to state environmental protection agencies—rather than to the states' chief executive officers, the governors, it has been suggested that those state agencies that

FIGURE 12-7 The Growth of Major Programs of Intergovernmental Regulation, by Type of Instrument, by Decade, 1930–1980.

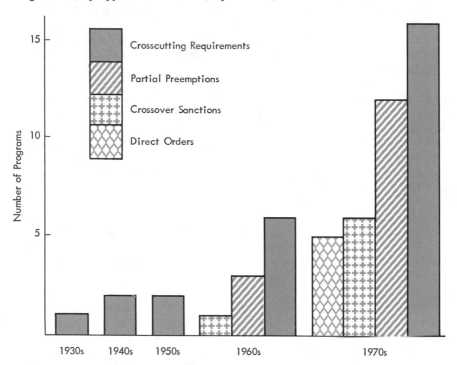

Source: Advisory Commission on Intergovernmental Relations, *Regulatory Federalism: Policy, Process, Impact and Reform*, A-95 (Washington, D.C.: U.S. Government Printing Office, 1984), p. 97.

are heavily funded by Washington are also more autonomous because they are less dependent upon their governors and legislatures for their budgets. Hence, Washington, through its intergovernmental programs, has made the governors' management task more difficult. And, despite the fact that virtually all governors believe that Washington's dollars helped them implement their programs for their states, there is some reason to believe that this conjecture is valid. Surveys of state administrators taken since 1964 have found that from 44 percent to 48 percent of state administrators admit they are less subject to supervision by the governors and the legislatures because of federal aid.[48]

Despite pledges made by the past four presidents to reduce federal mandates by "regulatory reform," the regulations stay and, indeed, multiply. The Nixon administration began this effort when it initiated a procedure by which the Office of Management and Budget reviewed regulations proposed by executive branch agencies prior to their required publication in the *Federal Register*. President Gerald Ford carried this process further and gave increased oversight authority to OMB specifically to determine the "cost effectiveness" of proposed rules.[49] President Jimmy Carter continued to pursue goals of further deregulation, and instituted procedures to limit government paperwork, and to expand citizen decision making in the rule-making process.

However, no president had been so concerned with regulatory reform as Ronald Reagan. As one of his first acts of office, President Reagan established a Task Force on Regulatory Relief, chaired by then Vice President George Bush (the Bush Commission). This high-level commission was composed of cabinet members and staffed by OMB. In addition, a number of the groups representing state and local officials were invited to nominate "burdensome, unnecessary, and counterproductive federal regulations" to be reviewed and eventually modified or eliminated by the Commission. More than 2,500 suggestions were received from approximately 300 individuals and groups including the National League of Cities, the National Association of Counties, the U.S. Conference of Mayors, and the National Governors Association.[50]

In 1981, the Bush Commission chose 100 of these regulations for review. After a year's analy-sis, the Commission issued proposed or final changes affecting thirty-eight of the 100 existing regulations. Twenty-five of these regulations have a primary impact on state and local governments. Of these twenty-five, six were actually acted upon.

If this seems like slow work, it was. From more than 2,500 nominations for change, the Commission changed only a handful after a full year of trying; many of these changes were not easy and raised substantial political opposition.

Cutting Back Fiscal Federalism

Finally and most important, not only did Reagan reduce the federal managerial presence among the grass-roots governments, but he reduced the federal fiscal presence as well. As Figure 12-4 shows, Washington's dollars to state and local jurisdictions were slashed, as a percentage of their total outlays, by a third. By the late 1990s, Washington's contribution to state and local expenditures will likely reach proportions last seen in the 1950s, or about a dime of every dollar spent by states and communities (down from more than a quarter in 1978). Yet, the cutbacks in federal aid are occurring precisely when states, localities, and communities are dealing with unprecedented tax revolts.

In sum, Ronald Reagan's impact on federalism was real. He proposed a massive overhaul and "sorting out" of fiscal federalism that would return intergovernmental relations to their condition before 1960; he withdrew the federal government from its longstanding role as a coordinator and planner of regional intergovernmental relations; he attempted to reduce (and to some degree succeeded) the number of federal regulations imposed on state and local officials administering federal grants; and, of paramount importance, he significantly cut federal assistance to states and localities. These were not minor acts.

INTERGOVERNMENTAL ADMINISTRATION: THE STATE AND LOCAL PERSPECTIVE

So far we have been discussing federalism largely from the viewpoint of the government in Washington. But the states and localities also

have active governments. In this section we review the states' relations with each other and
their involvement (or lack of it) in the business
of their cities, counties, towns, and other local
jurisdictions.

Interstate Cooperation—and Conflict

States have been known to cooperate and not
cooperate with each other, although the Constitution requires that "full faith and credit shall be
given in each state to the public acts, records, and
judicial proceedings of every state." Since the
clause applies only to civil matters and not necessarily to criminal violations, we occasionally witness states harboring fugitives from other states if
public officials feel that the fugitive has been
treated unjustly in the state from which he or she
has fled. States also cooperate to create interstate
compacts and interstate agencies.

There are 179 interstate compacts in operation,
the great majority of which have been entered into
during the past three decades. Only fifty-seven
interstate compacts were agreed to between 1789
and 1940, but during the next four decades, an
additional 122 of these agreements emerged.

Interstate compacts normally require congressional approval to be set into motion, and many
have evolved into ongoing interstate agencies.
There are more than sixty such agencies dealing
with educational concerns, river basin management, transportation, water fronts, fisheries, and
energy. Perhaps the most notable example of an
interstate agency is the Port Authority of New
York and New Jersey. Established in 1921 and
headed by six commissioners appointed by the
governor of each member state, the Port Authority
is in charge of virtually all transportation in the
New York and New Jersey areas. It has 8,000
employees, more employees than any other interstate agency (few interstate agencies exceed fifty
employees and a number have none).

Although most analysts delineate the kinds of
cooperative activity between states, few discuss
the kinds of conflict in which states engage. The
most obvious example occurred in 1861 when the
nation went to war with itself.

A more recent example concerns the gradually
developing shortage of water in the nation.[51] Although this shortage is more pronounced in the
West than in other parts of the country, some
researchers have estimated that by the year 2000
only three of the nation's nineteen water regions
will be able to live even close to comfortably
within the limits of their water supplies. (The three
exceptions are New England, the Ohio Basin, and
the South Atlantic-Eastern Gulf areas.)

This possible serious shortage in the nation's
water is already straining relationships among
states. Montana and Idaho threatened to sue the
state of Washington if that state seeded clouds over
the Pacific Ocean, thereby "stealing" water that
might have fallen as rain farther inland. Oregon
and Washington have resisted attempts to divert
water to areas in the western Sunbelt states. When
Boston embarked on a program to divert water
from the Connecticut River, Connecticut objected
because it did not wish to give up water rights that
it might need in the future. The eight states and
two Canadian provinces that surround the Great
Lakes—the world's largest reservoir of fresh
water—agreed in 1982 to block attempts to divert
their water unless all ten governments agreed.
Iowa, Nebraska, and Missouri filed suit opposing
South Dakota's efforts to divert part of the Missouri River to Wyoming; and El Paso, Texas, challenged New Mexico's law that forbids all
out-of-staters from using its groundwater.

Although water wars long have erupted among
the states, and will continue to do so as long as
water supplies deplete, hydraulic technology inno-
vates, and rivers meander, interstate antagonism is
surfacing in other fields as well. Thirty-three states
use some sort of severance tax—that is, a tariff on
natural resources exported to other states—and
some states have been using the device, according
to some regional analysts, as a weapon against
other states to recruit new industry by lowering
taxes. One estimate contends that the dozen states
that export energy to other states (such as Montana,
which has a 30 percent severance tax on coal) will
gain close to $200 billion over ten years through
their severance taxes on their energy supplies.[52]
Some states have threatened reciprocity; for example, the governor of Iowa floated the notion of
introducing a severance tax on corn.

Other statewide "exports" are free of severance
taxes, such as pollution spawned in one state but

which ends up in another states. Northeastern states long have argued that they are the primary recipients of the Midwestern air pollutants that produce acid rain. Other states export other kinds of undesirable items. Between 1978 and 1982, South Dakota gave ninety-three people charged with burglary, forgery, theft, and other felonies the choice of facing prosecution or moving to California; all ninety-three moved to the Golden State, whose officials promptly dubbed South Dakota's actions as outrageous. In 1984, Oregon hiked by up to $400 the income tax that it levies on some 40,000 Washington State residents who work in Oregon; Washington retaliated with a $30-a-month tax on Oregonians who work in Washington. Texan welfare officials take pains to inform their clients that benefits are higher in every other state except Mississippi and that welfare payments in Texas show no prospects of rising, while Florida officials have carefully explained to their Haitian refugees that ten other states might offer better relief aid.

All is not happy in the realm of the American states.

The States Tame Their "Creatures"

The states can cooperate with each other as equals, but their relationships with their own local governments are quite different. The phrase, "creatures of the states," describes the place of local governments relative to their state governments more than adequately. It is drawn from a statement made by Judge John F. Dillon in 1868 that is now known as "Dillon's rule." "Creatures of the state," a concept upheld by the U.S. Supreme Court in 1923, simply means that such units of government as counties, towns, townships, school districts, special districts, multipurpose districts, cities, and villages have no independence beyond what the state grants them. The state government determines the area of political and administrative discretion its subunits of government may or may not have. "This means that a city cannot operate a peanut stand at the city zoo without first getting the state legislature to pass an enabling law, unless, perchance, the city's charter or some previously enacted law unmistakably covers the sale of peanuts."[53]

State legislatures achieve this kind of control through the type of charter that they grant a city. Most city charters are quite long (New York City's, for example, fills several hundred pages) because the states often want to retain minute degrees of control. There are four general types of charters: special act charters, general act charters, optional charter laws, and home rule charters.

The *special act charters* are charters that have been drawn specifically for a particular city. Such cities remain completely under state legislative control; often these charters help state legislatures to pass laws that are written specifically for a particular city. Edward Banfield and James Q. Wilson quote by way of example an ordinance stating that "Fall River be authorized to appropriate money for the purchase of uniforms for the park police and watershed guards of said city."[54]

General act charters tend to categorize cities by population and then apply state legislation to all cities in each size category. Usual divisions are cities with less than 10,000 people, with 10,000 to 25,000 people, and so on.

Optional charter laws give city governments relatively more free choice. They offer optional forms of government that a city may wish to adopt, such as council-manager, commission, or whatever.

Finally, *home rule charters* provide cities with the greatest degree of self-governance. Still, home rule charters are furnished by the state legislature or the state constitution and may be taken away as easily as they are granted. Home rule got its start in 1875 in Missouri; today more than half of the states have constitutional clauses that provide for home rule charters. Roughly two-thirds of the cities in this country with populations of more than 200,000 people have some form of home rule. Political battles over acquiring urban home rule often are bloody, with good government groups, city mayors, and city managers usually pitted against rural legislators and large municipal taxpayer groups.

Regardless of the type of charter a city may have, the point remains that these charters are granted according to the discretion of the state polity; Judge Dillon's rule stands in that all cities and other units of government remain the creatures of the state.

State Urban Policy: A New Responsiveness

As the foregoing review of city charters implies, states can treat their creatures with severity or laxity. Joseph Zimmerman has observed that states may play the roles of inhibitor, facilitator, or initiator in their relations with their own local governments, and the role most frequently played in Zimmerman's view is, unfortunately, the first.[55] Nonetheless, the states have made strides in contributing constructively to urban government.

Nationally, counties tend to have less freedom than do cities; cities enjoy their greatest freedoms from state controls in functional areas, such as sanitation, and have the least liberty in the area of finance; and counties have the most freedom in personnel matters but, like municipalities, are most restricted by their states in the finance area. States clearly seem concerned with the fiscal health of their local governments.[56]

All states have established offices specifically endowed with responsibilities pertaining to local affairs, although only five existed prior to 1966.[57] These offices provide advisory services and assist the state in coordinating local administrative functions. Most are concerned primarily with regional planning; relatively few have responsibility for specific programs such as urban renewal, housing, and poverty.

The states have taken a variety of managerial and policy steps in dealing with their local governments. Ten states have created their own advisory commissions on intergovernmental relations patterned after the federal model, and another twenty-one have created similar advisory panels of local officials. Forty-three states have commissions on intergovernmental cooperation, and all states have departments of community affairs.[58]

Research indicates that those state commissions that focus on local governments tend to stress the desirability of fiscal reforms, of reducing functional fragmentation among local governments, and of providing greater authority and more home rule for local jurisdictions.[59] In a few states, these and related bodies are beginning to take on a genuine policy-making role for their urban and local governments. Texas, for example, has been active in discouraging the separate incorporation of satellite cities, as have Indiana and Minnesota, although to lesser degrees. In 1968 Connecticut abolished counties as a unit of government and, as a result, "state government may in effect become the metropolitan government unit in Connecticut, since Connecticut transferred county functions to the state."[60]

What of the larger panorama of the relationships between the states and their local governments? Is the role of the states declining, or is it actually increasing?

The typical answer to these questions, at least in the past, has been that the states have often proven to be more of a hindrance than a facilitator in resolving the problems of local governments. Consider, in this regard, the following conclusions from several studies: "Despite the increasing amount of effort that they have devoted to urban affairs, the states have continued to evidence little desire to intervene in metropolitan governmental reorganization—with the important exception of school districts."[61] Or, "Although states have increased their aid to local governments, such aid generally has not gone to the areas of greatest need."[62] Or, "If one were to use the past as the basis of forecasting the future role of the state and local government reorganization, the prospects for a new, affirmative role would be exceedingly dim."[63]

By the 1970s, however, such views were beginning to change. In part, this change resulted from the simple fact that more empirical and systematic investigations were being conducted on the relationships between states and their local governments. Studies indicate that the states tend to emphasize four policy areas when they deal with local governments: physical development, such as upgrading industrial and residential infrastructures; the enhancement of cooperation between the public and private sectors; fiscal incentives to help local development patterns; and citizen participation in the development of local objectives.[64]

Related research has concluded that states are really rather sensitive to the needs of their more depressed cities, at least when this sensitivity is measured by the amounts of money that states transfer to their needier urban areas. Localities receive grants from other governments in three forms: direct aid from their states, direct aid from the federal government, and aid from state governments that combine state funds with federal funds received by the states (or what are known as "passthrough" funds, since federal money is being "passed through" state governments to local governments). One analysis found that depressed cities benefited most favorably when they received intergovernmental grants through this final method, passthrough funding indicating an awareness by states of their more pressing urban problems. In fact, the state capitols may be more concerned with these issues than is Washington:

...a state-federal partnership in allocating aid to local jurisdictions has produced greater responsiveness to distressed cities than has federal aid alone. Among plausible explanations for this finding are the substantial management difficulties inherent in the federal attempt to deal directly with local governments, the perceived need for direct federal aid programs to include a sufficient number of local jurisdictions to assure majority votes in the Congress, and the inability of federal grant programs to take account of differing fiscal relationships among levels of government.... In contrast, individual states deal with smaller numbers of local governments, have a clearer understanding of their problems, and therefore can deal with those problems in a more responsive and flexible manner.[65]

Just as research has indicated the deepening and increasingly sensitive state interest in local problems, the apparent withdrawal of federal interest in the affairs of subnational governments has led some observers to conclude that the states will, by necessity, assume a new and more aggressive posture relative to their local communities.

As a consequence of these shifts at the national level, plus a growing body of information about state and local governmental relationships, the overall scholarly assessment of the states' role in local affairs is showing indications of change. As a leading scholar of intergovernmental relations has observed, "The states have been roundly and soundly chastised for their neglect of urban distress and decline. The criticisms are not without foundation. Yet a balanced view...shows the states on record as taking numerous and varied urban-oriented policy initiatives."[66]

Managing Intergovernmental Programs in the States

State governments have their own sets of intergovernmental relationships, but they conduct them quite differently from the feds. In fact, there is a radical difference in philosophy, and control over intergovernmental programs seems, on the whole, tighter at the state levels than at the national one. Rather than establishing "conditions" that a prospective recipient must meet to be eligible to receive federal assistance, states simply order their recipients (virtually always a local government) to implement programs on the basis of clear directives given by the state agencies; "bargaining" with recipients is rare in the states.[67]

This approach is quite different from controlling the implementation of a program through the conditions that are put on the government's aid program in the first place, such as is done almost exclusively by Washington. The relatively substantial authority that the states have is made possible largely because, from a legal perspective, localities are "creatures of the state" and subservient to it.

Another aspect of the different implementation styles between state governments and the federal government is the apparent fact that state agencies tend to be far more "nuts-and-bolts" and practically oriented in their implementation of intergovernmental programs. At the state level, the objective is one of getting a program accomplished, generally through direct mandates, and being done with it. Federal policymakers, however, see as a major aspect of their mission to be the inculcation of new social values and management techniques by the recipients of their funding. Thus, we see the proliferation of federal mandates over a wide variety of federal assistance programs. These kinds of extraneous (in the sense that they do not directly apply to the purpose of a specific program) requirements and conditions set by the federal government for states and localities are virtually nonexistent in state programs for local governments.

One of the local benefits of the states being a "simpler" source of local funding than the federal government is that local administrative costs can be held down. An analysis of public school districts across the United States found that, because federal education grants were much more complex, fragmented, and formal than were state fiscal transfers to school districts, those districts that had to rely more on federal funds than they did on state funds generated significantly more administrative positions. Interestingly, even locally funded school districts produced more administrative positions than did those that were more dependent on state funds (though still fewer positions than did districts which relied on federal grants), because local funding politics and procedures were more complex than were those of the states.[68]

Another difference between the state style of implementation and the federal style is that the legislature is directly involved in how state assistance to local governments is to be implemented. This implies, among other things, that the state legislators give their bureaucrats far less leeway than do their federal counterparts. It also implies, however, that state legislators are able to take a more responsible and detailed interest in state assistance to local governments, and that they have developed their assistance programs with the advice and input of officials from the local levels of government.[69]

How much of an impact local governments have in determining implementation procedures and processes that are mandated by state government tends to be a function of statewide wealth, urbanism, and high levels of population. The Advisory Commission on Intergovernmental Relations found, for example, that some statewide intergovernmental assistance systems are dominated by state government (in these states, the state government provides local assistance directly), whereas in others they are dominated by local governments (in these states, a federal-style grants system is used). State government dominance of the statewide intergovernmental assistance system seems to associate with the more populous, urbanized, and wealthy states.[70]

Another study, this one focusing more specifically on the states' use of mandates in dealing with their local governments, also found a strong correlation between a state's high affluence and a high tendency to issue mandates to its localities. The competitiveness of a state's political parties and a high quality of state public administration also associated with a state's propensity to issue mandates to local governments.[71]

Direct Federalism: The Feds and Cities

If anything, the federal government has a greater political impact on localities than on states. The formal linkage between local and national government often has been called "direct federalism," indicating that state governments are frequently bypassed. Nevertheless, the major impact of the federal government on local governments is more accidental than planned. For example, Rand Corporation studies have shown that federal officials may often have more control than local officeholders over the shape of the economy in a particular locality. The Rand studies indicated the following: in St. Louis, federal housing and highway policies attracted many central-city residents to the suburbs; in San Jose, federal military procurement procedures accelerated the local growth rate; in Seattle, federal civil aviation policies were probably detrimental to the area's major employer.[72] There is, in fact, substantial evidence to warrant the conclusion that "federal stimulation produced independent housing authorities, a type of special district, and federal encouragement of the growth of suburbia through underwriting liberal mortgage arrangements indirectly led to the creation of many new suburban governments," and that the creation of the federal Department of Housing and Urban Development and the Department of Transportation are "both institutional examples of recognition by the national government of its deep involvement in metropolitan affairs."[73]

From 1960 to 1980, this "deep involvement" by the federal government in local affairs increased. Although local governments received only 10 percent of the total federal aid package in 1965, by 1980 that figure had hit 30 percent.[74] Federal regulations on the conduct of local governments accompanied these and other federal grants programs with a vengeance. Of the nearly 1,300 federal mandates built into the intergovernmental grant system, a surprising number, 911, apply only to local governments or directly affect local governments through the states.[75]

It is predictable, perhaps, that local officials have developed a less than trusting attitude concerning the federal government. A national study of cities found that pluralities or majorities of local officeholders believed in most cases that federal regulations on local governments resulted from Washington playing an inappropriate role in urban affairs (40 percent); that their cities did not have the resources to comply with federal regulations (39 percent); that inefficient federal management made compliance difficult (65 percent); that Washington went too far in stipulating how its requirements should be met (51 percent); and that the mandates themselves were unrealistic (50 percent).[76]

One examination of the economic impact of federal regulations on seven localities in only five grant programs concluded that the cost borne by these local governments in complying with them was about $25 per citizen! Compliance costs in these five programs alone equaled 19 percent of the total federal aid received by the seven local governments, effectively canceling out what they had received from Washington under General Revenue Sharing![77]

Quite aside from concerns about management and money, federal intergovernmental programs may, in the view of local officials, also distort local policy. A survey of local administrators in all cities and counties that had received federal aid during the past year found that officials in about two-thirds of these cities and in roughly 80 percent of the counties stated that they would have made different budgetary allocations had they been permitted to do so. Seventy-five percent of both city and county administrators would have made moderate to substantial changes. More than two-thirds of the city administrators, and more than three quarters of the county administrators believed that their governments would shift their local funds to other efforts if their federal grants were cut off. Such a finding implies that local officials are making policy decisions to a large extent based on what federal money is available rather than on the basis of what their genuine local needs are.[78]

In an era of Fend-for-Yourself Federalism, however, it is likely that the hostility of local officials toward federal interference in local management has followed the decline of federal dollars to local governments. Federal contributions to the general revenues of local governments plummeted by almost half in considerably less than a decade—from more than 9 percent of local revenues in 1980 to 4.8 percent in 1987.[79] The termination of General Revenue Sharing (which was far and away the single federal assistance program most cherished by local officials) by Congress in 1986 had a disproportionately adverse impact on local governments, and this was particularly true for smaller and poorer local governments, some of which had relied on Revenue Sharing for nearly two-thirds of their total revenues. The National Association of Towns and Townships reports that 78 percent of the nation's 36,000 local governments with 25,000 people or fewer are receiving *no* federal assistance after the cancellation of General Revenue Sharing.[80] The thirty-nine federal grants-in-aid programs that dealt directly and exclusively with local administrators in 1980[81] had been slashed to sixteen programs by 1987.[82]

The pain accompanying this wrenching of the feds' fiscal hook from the financial flesh of local governments has been acute. Although the states relieved their local governments of some of their traditional functions by assuming responsibility for them, the states' contributions to the general revenues of local governments slipped only marginally throughout the 1980s, and remained more or less constant at about a third of local revenues.[83] Caught between falling federal contributions to their budgets, and steady-state contributions to their budgets from their state governments, communities have had to go to some extraordinary lengths to maintain local services. A 1990 survey of 576 cities with populations of 10,000 or more found that over three quarters (76 percent) had increased user fees over the course of the past year, and 41 percent had raised property taxes, the traditional main source of local revenues; yet, two-thirds of these municipalities reported that they were less able to balance their budgets than they had been a year earlier![84] It is among the local governments, apparently, where Fend-for-Yourself Federalism functions at its most meaningful level.

As federal dollars have departed local governments, however, so, in effect, have federal administrators. A survey taken in 1988 of mayors and city managers in Colorado found that more than 39 percent of them perceived their contacts with federal officials to be less frequent than they had been in 1980 (less than 12 percent thought that these contacts had increased); nearly 53 percent believed that their contacts with state officials had increased (less than 6 percent felt that these contacts had decreased in frequency); and almost 70 percent reported that their contacts with other local officials had increased since 1980 (compared to less than 2 percent who believed that these contacts were less frequent).[85] The federal administration of intergovernmental relations appears to be declining in proportion to the funds that it commits to those relations.

"Micro-Federalism": Neighborhoods and Cities

One of the more intriguing expressions of the many permutations surrounding the uniquely public question of reconciling area with power in ways that maximize efficiency, effectiveness, responsiveness, and democratic control can be found in the local movement toward "neighborhood governance." It began in the mid-1960s, and at least some of its origins can be traced to a reaction against what was (and often still is) perceived as the condescension of "professional managers" in the urban bureaucracy. Neighborhood governance advocates a limited disannexation of neighborhood communities rather than outright secession from city hall.[86] Three practical consequences of the neighborhood governance movement have been the rise of neighborhood corporations, neighborhood associations, and residential community associations.

Neighborhood corporations are nonprofit organizations, chartered by the state, and managed for the public benefit of specialized urban areas by area residents. Many received their initial funding in 1966 under the provisions of the Economic Opportunity Act of 1964, and later under the Model Cities program. An analysis of these groups concluded that, although their record of success had been spotty, neighborhood corporations had established a genuine rapport with residents. Nevertheless, just how representative the corporations are is open to question when it is realized that resident turnout to elect the directors of these organizations has been less than 5 percent of the eligible voters,[87] and it appears that more informal neighborhood associations have filled this role in recent years.

Like neighborhood corporations, neighborhood associations, or community action groups, received at least some of their initial impetus from the federal government: there are, in fact, 155 specific provisos in federal grants programs mandating citizen participation.[88] Probably the most significant of these is Congress' 1976 extension of General Revenue Sharing, which required citizen participation in the budgetary processes of the 39,000 local governments that received shared revenues; despite the demise of General Revenue Sharing a decade later, the impact of this mandate lives on.

Neighborhood associations are voluntary groups of citizens who work toward what they perceive to be the betterment of their communities; unlike neighborhood corporations, they have no state charter. There are an estimated 200 major neighborhood associations in the United States, ranging from the Bois d'Arc Patriots in Dallas to the Citizens to Bring Broadway Back in Cleveland.[89] Most neighborhood associations concern themselves with issues of planning and development, housing, freeway construction, race relations, taxes, and education, and they are estimated to comprise from 6 to 19 percent of a community's adult population.[90]

Finally, *residential community associations* are private organizations of home owners, condominium owners, and members of residential cooperatives that are governed under local real estate contract laws; their members typically elect a policy-making council from their ranks, impose mandatory fees on their members, and conduct certain kinds of public business, such as land management. They have been called "private governments," and they are growing; in 1960, there were fewer than 5,000 residential community associations, but today there are around 130,000 and they have some 12 to 15 percent of the American population as members.

Most residential community associations are in the Sunbelt and Mideastern states, and they bring with them new concepts of governance.[91] Their members in effect, pay dual taxes, with some going to local governments and some going to the association as the price of a level of service that is superior to the base level provided by the local government. They often exclude local officials from providing local services in their communities. Some have argued that the members of residential community associations exercise rights of dual citizenship.

Certainly residential community associations seem to exercise the rights of sovereign governments, and their administrators deal directly with local officials as peers on such questions as traffic, water, sewerage, parks, zoning, animal control, pollution, taxes, and a host of other public issues. Fifty-six percent of the officers of residential community associations responding to a national survey said that the level of cooperation between their associations and the local government was good, and 71 percent stated that they had been treated fairly by local officials.[92]

Neighborhood corporations, neighborhood associations, and residential community associations (and, we must note, these distinctions are not neat ones) are working within local jurisdictions as both a lobby and a government, and they are effective in both capacities. A study of 115 city councilmembers in California found that 94 percent of the councilmembers perceived these groups as a welcomed civic association phenomenon; only 28 percent identified organized economic interests as major political actors in their cities.[93] Only 16 percent of the councilmembers did not view any group as being influential in the formation of urban policy, and more than two-thirds identified two or more groups as influential.[94] This appears to be a recognition rate that is twice that of state legislators' perceptions of the power of civic associations and economic interest groups.[95]

More significantly, however, participation by these neighborhood associations in the local policy process brings results. More than four out of every ten local officials believe that the participation by these groups and other members of the public in their counties' and cities' budget processes has a measurable effect on the setting of local priorities; more than 60 percent of local officials have developed new federal grant proposals and sent them to Washington solely because of citizen participation.[96] As an assistant secretary in the Department of Housing and Urban Development put it, "Twenty neighborhood groups have accomplished more...than all of the federal programs."[97]

Interlocal Agreements

If there is tension between states and local governments, and Washington and local governments, and neighborhoods and local governments, local governments themselves seem to be getting on

famously with each other. Cities and counties have devised a number of ways of working together as a means of providing more, better, and cheaper services to their citizens, and they are cooperating with each other enthusiastically.[98] One method is the *intergovernmental service contract*, as when one jurisdiction pays another to deliver certain services to its residents. More than half—52 percent—of cities and counties have entered into intergovernmental service contracts. Cities and counties contract most frequently with each other for jails, sewage disposal, animal control, and tax assessing.

Another form of interlocal agreement is the *joint service agreement*, or an agreement between two or more governments for the joint planning, financing, and delivering of certain services to the residents of all participating jurisdictions. Sixty percent of cities and 54 percent of counties have entered into joint service agreements. The services most frequently provided under these agreements are libraries, communications among police and fire departments, fire control, and sewage disposal.

Cities have moved away (albeit marginally) from entering to intergovernmental service contracts since 1972 (when the first national survey on the practice was conducted), and they have shown an increasing preference for contracting with private firms and for negotiating joint service agreements with other local governments. Joint service agreements in particular are experiencing an upsurge in popularity: 35 percent of cities were involved in them in 1972, 55 percent in 1983.[99]

A third type of interlocal agreement is the *intergovernmental service transfer*, or the permanent transfer of a responsibility from a jurisdiction to another entity, another government, a private corporation, or a nonprofit agency. Transferring a responsibility permanently is a serious matter for any government because it is a sacrifice of authority and power, so it is perhaps surprising that 40 percent of cities and counties executed such transfers between 1976 and 1983. Favored areas of transfer were public works and utilities, health and welfare, and general government and finance.[100]

Regardless of the type of interlocal agreement, patterns emerge. Larger jurisdictions are far more willing to enter into them than are smaller ones. Council-manager cities and counties with a county administrator tend to favor them, as do inner cities over suburbs, and metropolitan counties more than nonmetropolitan ones. The motivation of local officials to enter into interlocal agreements is usually "economies of scale"—they believe that some services can be delivered more effectively and efficiently over larger tracts of territory, or by larger jurisdictions.[101]

FEDERALISM AND THE PYRAMIDING OF POWER

A final summing up on the nature of relations between governments in the United States points to one conclusion: that governmental power is centralizing despite Americans' ultralocalist leanings.

Perhaps the clearest indication of this can be seen by examining measures of financial resources, services, and worker availability. The nation's 19,000 municipalities raise less money today than do the nation's fifty state governments, and considerably fewer dollars than does the national government. Although money is paid to the national government and part of these revenues are sent back to the state and local governments through grants, this practice connotes, at least in the view of some, a centralization of governmental power at the national level.

But such centralization also may be happening at the state level. By ranking the local proportions of financial resources, services, and worker availability by state, G. Ross Stephens found that certain states were quite centralized in relation to their local governments, while others were relatively decentralized. Stephens concluded that larger states tend to be decentralized governmentally, whereas smaller states are more centralized.[102] Other studies by and large confirm Stephens's findings.[103]

There is additional evidence that governments are centralizing. Not only is centralization occurring at the state level, but at the local level, too. In national studies conducted since 1972, it has been found that, generally speaking, larger local governments are taking over the responsibilities of smaller ones.[104] Fifty-six percent of the intergovernmental service contracts let by cities, for example, are given to counties.[105] A plurality (48 percent) of all joint service agreements are entered into with counties, and counties are the principal service providers for more than half of all services provided through these agreements.[106] Most significantly, however, counties and regional organizations receive most of the intergovernmental service transfers; in other words, these relatively large units of local government are *permanently* taking over the traditional duties of cities and towns, *and at the request* of those cities and towns. Fifty-four percent of all intergovernmental service transfers go to counties, and 14 percent (the next highest percentage) to regional organizations, such as councils of governments.[107]

Whatever the cause and whatever the outcome, it appears that subnational governments are moving power not only *up* the intergovernmental pyramid, to higher levels of government, but *out* of smaller jurisdictions and into larger ones. If, it seems, the American people like ultralocalist government, the people whom Americans elect and appoint to run their governments do not. State and local officials have been engaged in a slow but steady process of centralizing and shifting responsibilities for service deliveries both upward and outward for many years in an effort to meet the needs of their citizens more effectively and efficiently. It is a process that shows no signs of reversing.

If this assessment is accurate, then it is a tribute to the professionalism and inventiveness of America's grassroots bureaucrats, because they have gradually centralized and consolidated major governmental functions over the years, while working within the confines of a national political culture that places an unusually high value on maintaining ultralocalist "responsiveness," and often at the price of impairing governmental efficiency and effectiveness.

In Part Four, we have been reviewing the ways that public administrators implement public policies. But implementation rests on decision making, and decision making in the public sector, in turn, is based on underlying moral and ethical assumptions held by individual decision makers about how the world works and what is right or wrong about how the world works. We consider this final, and perhaps most important, aspect of public administration next.

NOTES

[1] Two good discussions of the definitional differences among the terms used in this paragraph are: Deil S. Wright, "Federalism, Intergovernmental Relations, and Intergovernmental Management: Historical Reflections and Conceptual Comparisons," *Public Administration Review*, 50 (March/April 1990), pp. 168–178; and Vincent L. Marando and Patricia S. Florestano, "Intergovernmental Management: This State of the Discipline," in *Public Administration: The State of the Discipline*, Naomi B. Lynn and Aaron Wildavsky, eds., (Chatham: N. J.: Chatham House, 1990), pp. 287–317.

[2] Theodore J. Lowi, *The End of Liberalism* (New York: Norton, 1969), pp. 250–266.

[3] Vincent Ostrom, *The Intellectual Crisis in American Public Administration* (University, Ala.: University of Alabama Press, 1973), pp. 10–11.

[4] Henry S. Reuss, *Revenue Sharing: Crutch or Catalyst for State and Local Governments?* (New York: Praeger, 1970), pp. 53–56.

[5] This discussion is drawn largely from: Kenneth N. Vines, "The Federal Setting of State Politics," in *Politics in the American States*, 3rd ed., Herbert Jacob and Kenneth N. Vines, eds., (Boston: Little, Brown, 1976), p. 4.

[6] *Ibid.*, p. 7.

[7] Alexander Hamilton, John Jay, and James Madison, *The Federalist* (New York: Random House, 1937), p. 347.

[8] Unless noted otherwise, the following discussion is drawn from: Deil S. Wright, *Understanding Intergovernmental Relations*, 2nd ed. (Monterey, Calif.: Brooks/Cole, 1982), pp. 43–82.

[9] The following discussion is drawn from: John Shannon, "The Return to Fend-For-Yourself Federalism: The Reagan Mark," in Advisory Commission on Intergovernmental Relations, *Readings in Federalism: Perspectives on a Decade of Change*, SR-11 (Washington, D.C.: U.S. Government Printing Office, 1989), pp. 119–122; John Shannon, "Competitive Federalism—Three Driving Forces," *Intergovernmental Perspective*, 15 (Fall 1989), pp. 17–18; and John Shannon and James Edwin Kee, "The Rise of Competitive Federalism," *Public Budgeting and Finance*, 9 (Winter 1989), pp. 3–20.

[10] Advisory Commission on Intergovernmental Relations, *Significant Features of Fiscal Federalism, 1989*, Vol. I, M-163 (Washington, D.C.: U.S. Government Printing Office, 1989), p. 14.

[11] Shannon and Kee, "The Rise of Competitive Federalism," p. 11.

[12] Donna Wilson Kirchheimer, "Entrepreneurial Implementation of the U.S. Welfare State" (Paper presented at the 1986 Annual Meeting of the American Political Science Association, Washington, D.C., August 28–31, 1986), p. 1.

[13] Advisory Commission on Intergovernmental Relations, *Significant Features of Fiscal Federalism, 1989*, Vol. II, M-163-II (Washington, D.C.: U.S. Government Printing Office, 1989), p. 35.

[14] *Ibid.*, p. 41.

[15] *Ibid.*, p. 20.

[16] *Ibid.*, p. 66.

[17] *Ibid.*, p. 41.

[18] *Ibid.*, p. 35.

[19] Advisory Council on Intergovernmental Relations, *Significant Features of Fiscal Federalism, 1984*, M-141 (Washington, D.C: U.S. Government Printing Office, 1985), p. 8.

[20] Advisory Commission on Intergovernmental Relations, *Significant Features of Fiscal Federalism, 1989*, Vol. II, p. 18.

[21] *Ibid.*

[22] Richard P. Nathan and John R. Lago, "Intergovernmental Relations in the Reagan Era," *Public Budgeting and Finance*, 8 (Autumn 1988), p. 27.

[23] U.S. Bureau of the Census, *Statistical Abstract of the United States 1990* (Washington, D.C.: U.S. Government Printing Office, 1990), p. 282, Table 467.

[24] James L. Sundquist and David W. Davis, *Making Federalism Work* (Washington, D.C: Brookings Institution, 1969).

[25] Advisory Commission on Intergovernmental Relations, *Significant Features of Fiscal Federalism, 1989*, Vol. II, p. 21. If General Revenue Sharing is included, the 1981 figure would be 539 grants programs.

[26] Paul R. Dommel, et al., *Decentralizing Community Development: Second Report of the Brookings Institution Monitoring Study of the Community Development Block Grant Program* (Washington, D.C.: Brookings Institution, 1978).

[27] "Dimensions of the Federal Grant-in-Aid System: 1981–84," *Intergovernmental Perspective*, 11 (Winter 1985), p. 13. General Revenue Sharing is not included in these figures.

[28] Advisory Commission on Intergovernmental Relations, *Significant Features of Fiscal Federalism, 1989*, Vol. II, p. 21.

[29] Richard P. Nathan, et al., *Monitoring Revenue Sharing* (Washington, D.C.: Brookings Institution, 1975), and Richard P. Nathan and Charles F. Adams, Jr., *Revenue Sharing: The Second Round* (Washington, D.C.: Brookings Institution, 1977).

[30] Joel Havemann and Rochelle L. Stanfield, "'Neutral' Federal Policies are Reducing Frostbelt-Sunbelt Spending Imbalances," *National Journal* (February 7, 1981), p. 233. This analysis covered the years 1975 and 1979.

[31] Edward W. Hill, cited in Jerry Knight and John M. Berry, "States Take Sides on S & L Cleanup: 'Winners' and 'Losers,'" *Washington Post* (July 1, 1990).

[32] Representative of the Coalition of Northeastern Governors, as quoted in Bernard L. Weinstein and John Rees, "Sunbelt/Frostbelt Confrontation?" *Transaction* (May/June 1980), p. 17.

[33] David P. Mullhollan, Susan Webb Hammond, and Arthur G. Stevens, Jr., "Informal Groups and Agenda Setting" (Paper delivered at the Annual Meeting of Midwest Political Science Association, Cincinnati, Ohio, April 16–18, 1980).

[34] President's Commission for a National Agenda for the Eighties, *Urban America in the Eighties: Perspectives and Prospects* (Washington, D.C.: U.S. Government Printing Office, 1980), p. 99.

[35] David B. Walker and Albert J. Richter, "Regionalism and the Counties," *County Year Book, 1975* (Washington, D.C.: National Association of Counties and International City Management Association, 1975), p. 15.

[36] John F. Shirey, "National Actions Affecting Local Government: Cutbacks and Lowered Expectations," *Municipal Year Book, 1982* (Washington, D.C.: International City Management Association, 1982), p. 47.

[37] "Intergovernmental Focus," *Intergovernmental Perspective*, 8 (Summer 1982), p. 5.

[38] Martha Derthick, *Between State and Nation* (Washington, D.C.: Brookings Institution, 1974), pp. 163, 165.

[39] See: Advisory Commission on Intergovernmental Relations, *The Intergovernmental Grant System As Seen by Local, State, and Federal Officials*, A-54 (Washington, D.C.: U.S. Government Printing Office, 1977), pp. 212–214; Melvin B. Mogulof, *Federal Regional Councils: Their Current Experience and Recommendations for Further Development* (Washington, D.C.: Urban Institute, 1970); U.S. General Accounting Office, *Assessment of Federal Regional Councils* (Washington, D.C.: U.S. Government Printing Office, 1974); Derthick, *Between State and Nation*; and Rochelle L. Stanfield, "Federal Regional Councils—Can Carter Make them Work?" *National Journal*, 1 (June 28, 1977), p. 949.

[40] Robert W. Gage, "Federal Regional Councils: Networking Organizations for Policy Management in the Intergovernmental System," *Public Administration Review*, 44 (March/April 1984), pp. 135–135.

[41] Dennis O. Grady, "American Governors and State-Federal Relations: Attitudes and Activities, 1960–1980," *State Government*, 57, No. 3 (1984), pp. 110–111.

[42] *Ibid.*, p. 109.

[43] *Ibid.*

[44] Catherine H. Lovell, et al., *Federal and State Mandating on Local Governments: An Exploration of Issues and Impacts* (Riverside, Calif.: Graduate School of Administration, University of California, 1979), p. 82. Lovell and her colleagues found 1,259 federal mandates affecting state and local governments. See also: Catherine Lovell and Charles Tobin, "The Mandate Issue," *Public Administration Review*, 41 (May/June 1981), pp. 318–339.

[45] The following typology is described more fully in Advisory Commission on Intergovernmental Relations, *Regulatory Federalism: Policy, Process, Impact and Reform*, A-95 (Washington, D.C.: U.S. Government Printing Office, 1984), pp. 7–10. For another good treatment of this problem, see: Academy for State and Local Government, *Preemption: Drawing the Line* (Washington, D.C.: Academy for State and Local Government, 1986).

[46] Grady, "American Governors and State-Federal Relations," p. 107.

[47] Advisory Commission on Intergovernmental Relations, *State Administrators' Opinions on Administrative Change, Federal Aid, Federal Relationships*, M-120 (Washington, D.C.: U.S. Government Printing Office, 1980), pp. 39–59.

[48] *Ibid.*, p. 51.

[49] George C. Eads and Michael Fix, "Regulatory Policy," in *The Reagan Experiment*, George E. Palmer and Isabel V. Sawhill, eds. (Washington, D.C.: Urban Institute Press, 1982), pp. 134–136.

[50] Catherine Lovell, "Federal Deregulation and the State and Local Governments," in *Reductions in U.S. Domestic Spending*, John William Elwood, ed., (New Brunswick, N.J.: Transaction Books, 1982), p. 122.

[51] Much of the following discussion on interstate conflict is drawn from: Joanne Omang, "In This Economic Slump, It's a State-Eat-State Nation," *Washington Post* (June 14, 1982); and Richard Benedetto, "States Skirmish in 'Border War,'" *USA Today* (February 24, 1984).

[52] The twelve energy exporting states were projected to reap $193 billion in severance taxes between 1982 and 1992 by the Northeast-Midwest Economic Advancement Coalition, as cited in Omang, "In This Economic Slump."

[53] Edward C. Banfield and James Q. Wilson, *City Politics* (Cambridge, Mass.: Harvard University Press, 1963), p. 65.

[54] *Ibid.*, p. 66.

[55] Joseph F. Zimmerman, "The Role of the States in Metropolitan Governance" (Paper presented at Conference at Temple University, Philadelphia, August 17, 1973). Cited in John C. Bollens and Henry J. Schmandt, *The Metropolis*, 3rd ed. (New York: Harper & Row, 1975), p. 58.

[56] Carl W. Stenberg, "The New Federalism: Early Readings," *Public Management* (March 1982), p. 5; and Joseph E. Zimmerman, *The Discretionary Authority of Local Governments*, Urban Data Service Reports, Vol. 13, No. 11 (Washington, D.C.: International City Management Association, 1981), p. 11.

[57] National Research Council, *Toward an Understanding of Metropolitan America* (San Francisco: Canfield Press, 1975), p. 109.

[58] Advisory Commission on Intergovernmental Relations, *State-Local Relations Bodies: State ACIRs and Other Approaches* (Washington, D.C.: U.S. Government Printing Office, 1981), p. 3; and Jane Roberts, Jerry Fensterman, and Donald Lief, "States, Localities Continue to Adopt Strategic Policies," *Intergovernmental Perspective*, 11 (Winter 1985), p. 29.

[59] Patricia S. Florestano and Vincent L. Marando, "Urban Problems as Viewed from State Commissions: A Research Note," *Urban Affairs Quarterly*, 15 (March 1980), pp. 337–338.

[60] National Research Council, *Toward an Understanding of Metropolitan America*, p. 109.

[61] Bollens and Schmandt, *The Metropolis*, p. 58.

[62] National Research Council, *Toward An Understanding of Metropolitan America*, p. 108.

[63] Daniel R. Grant, "Urban Needs and States Response: Local Government Reorganization," in *The States in the Urban Crisis*, Alan Campbell, ed., (Englewood Cliffs, N.J.: Prentice-Hall, 1970), pp. 59 and 83.

[64] Advisory Commission on Intergovernmental Relations, *State Community Assistance Initiatives: Innovations of the Late 1970s* (Washington, D.C.: U.S. Government Printing Office, 1979), pp. 15–36.

[65] Fred Teitelbaum, "The Relative Responsiveness of State and Federal Aid to Distressed Cities," *Policy Studies Review* (November 1981), p. 320. "Distressed cities" in this study referred to those municipalities identified as in severe hardship by the Brookings Institution's "central city hardship" index. See: Richard P. Nathan and Charles Adams, "Understanding Central City Hardship," *Political Science Quarterly*, 91 (Spring 1976), pp. 44–52.

[66] Wright, *Understanding Intergovernmental Relations*, p. 389.

[67] For a good review of state practices in this area, see Patricia S. Florestano and Vincent L. Marando, *The States and the Metropolis* (New York: Marcel Dekker, 1981).

[68] John Meyer, W. Richard Scott, and David Strang, "Centralization, Fragmentation, and School District Complexity," *Administrative Science Quarterly*, 32 (June 1987), pp. 188–201.

[69] Catherine Lovell, *Federal and State Mandating on Local Governments: An Explanation of Issues and Impacts*, National Science Foundation Grant #DAR 77-20482 (Washington, D.C.: National Science Foundation, 1977).

[70] Advisory Commission on Intergovernmental Relations, *State Mandating of Local Expenditures* (Washington, D.C.: U.S. Government Printing Office, 1978).

[71] Rodney E. Hero and Jody L. Fitzpatrick, "State Mandating of Local Government Activities: An Exploration" (Paper presented at the 1986 Annual Meeting of the American Political Science Association, Washington, D.C., August 28–31, 1986), p. 18.

[72] R. B. Rainey, et al, *Seattle: Adaptation to Recession*; Barbara R. Williams, *St. Louis: A City and Its Suburbs*; Daniel Atesch and Robert Arvine, *Growth in San Jose: A Summary Policy Statement* (all published in Santa Monica, Calif.: Rand Corp., 1973).

[73] Bollens and Schmandt, *The Metropolis*, p. 60.

[74] Carl W. Stenberg, "Federalism in Transition, 1959–79," *Intergovernmental Perspective*, 6 (Winter 1980), pp. 6–7.

[75] Lovell, *Federal and State Mandating on Local Governments*, p. 82.

[76] National League of Cities, *Municipal Policy and Program Survey* (Washington, D.C.: National League of Cities, 1981), as cited in Advisory Commission on Intergovernmental Relations, *Regulatory Federalism*, p. 175. But see also Jeffrey L. Pressman, *Federal Programs and City Politics: The Dynamics of the Aid Process in Oakland* (Berkeley Calif.: University of California Press, 1975), p. 85.

[77] Thomas Muller and Michael Fix, "The Impact of Selected Federal Actions on Municipal Outlays," in *Special Study on Economic Change, Vol. 5: Government Regulation: Achieving Social and Economic Balance*, Joint Economic Committee, U.S. Congress (Washington, D.C.: U.S. Government Printing Office, 1980), pp. 327, 330, and 368.

[78] Albert J. Richter, "Federal Grants Management: The City and County View," *Municipal Year Book, 1977* (Washington, D.C.: International City Management Association, 1977), pp. 183–184.

[79] U.S. Bureau of the Census, *Statistical Abstract of the United States, 1990*, p. 290, Table 476.

[80] Robert Gleason, "Federalism 1986–87: Signals of a New Era," *Intergovernmental Perspective*, 14 (Winter 1988), p. 12.

[81] Stenberg, "Federalism in Transition, 1959–79," p. 7.

[82] Gleason, "Federalism 1986–87," p. 12. In addition to the sixteen federal grants-in-aid that dealt only with local officials, forty-five federal grant programs went to both state and local governments.

[83] U.S. Bureau of the Census, *Statistical Abstract of the United States, 1990*, p. 290, Table 476.

[84] John Herbers, "The Cavalry is Not Coming to Save the Besieged Cities," *Governing*, 3 (September 1990), p. 9. See also: Gary J. Reid, "How Cities in California Have Responded to Fiscal Pressures Since Proposition 13," *Public Budgeting and Finance*, 8 (Spring 1988), pp. 20–37.

[85] Robert W. Gage, "Intergovernmental Change: A Denver Area Perspective," *Intergovernmental Perspective*, 14 (Summer 1988), p. 15.

[86] See: Joseph F. Zimmerman, *The Federated City: Community Control in Large Cities* (New York: St. Martin's Press, 1972); Milton Kotler, *Neighborhood Government* (Indianapolis Ind.: Bobbs-Merrill, 1969); and Alan A. Altshuer, *Community Control: The Black Demand for Participation in Large American Cities* (New York: Pegasus, 1970).

[87] Howard W. Hallman, "Guidelines for Neighborhood Management," *Public Management* (January 1971), pp. 3–5.

[88] Advisory Commission on Intergovernmental Relations, *Citizen Participation in the American Federal System*, A-73 (Washington, D.C.: U.S. Government Printing Office, 1979), p. 4.

[89] John Herbers, "Neighborhood Activists Are Gaining Credence as a Political Force," *New York Times*, as reprinted in *The Arizona Republic* (August 12, 1979).

[90] Frank X. Steggert, *Community Action Groups and City Government* (Cambridge, Mass.: Ballinger, 1975), pp. 6–8.

[91] Advisory Commission on Intergovernmental Relations, *Residential Community Associations: Private Governments in the Intergovernmental System?* A-112 (Washington, D.C: U.S. Government Printing Office, 1989), p. 1

[92] *Ibid.*, p. 5.

[93] Betty A. Zisk, Heinz Eulau, and Kenneth Prewitt, "City Councilmen and the Group Struggle," *Journal of Politics*, 27 (August 1965), p. 633.

[94] *Ibid.*

[95] Thomas R. Dye, *Politics in States and Communities*, 3rd ed. (Englewood Cliffs, N.J.: Prentice-Hall, 1977), p. 300.

[96] John Rehfuss, "Citizen Participation in Urban Fiscal Decisions," *Municipal Year Book, 1979* (Washington, D.C.: International City Management Association, 1979), p. 87. Rehfuss surveyed all municipalities with 10,000 people or more, and all counties with 50,000 people or more. He obtained responses from 1,817 governments, a response rate of 57 percent.

[97] Monsignor Geno Baroni, quoted in Herbers, "Neighborhood Activists."

[98] The following typology is drawn from Lori M. Henderson, "Intergovernmental Service Arrangements and the Transfer of Functions," *Municipal Year Book, 1985* (Washington, D.C.: International City Management Association, 1985), p. 194.

[99] *Ibid.*, p. 201. The 1972 survey is in Advisory Commission on Intergovernmental Relations, *The Challenge of Local Government Reorganization*, A-44 (Washington, D.C.: U.S. Government Printing Office, 1976).

[100] Henderson, "Intergovernmental Service Arrangements," pp. 199–200.

[101] *Ibid.*, pp. 196–198, 201.

[102] G. Ross Stephens, "State Centralization and the Erosion of Local Autonomy," *Journal of Politics*, 36 (February 1974), p. 67.

[103] See, for example, Advisory Commission on Intergovernmental Relations, *The Condition of Contemporary Federalsim: Conflicting Theories and Collapsing Constrants* (Washington, D.C.: U.S. Government Printing Office, 1981), pp. 68–70; Jeffrey M. Stonecash, "Fiscal Centralization in the American States: Increasing Similarity and Persisting Diver-

sity," *Publius*, 13 (Fall 1983), pp. 123–137; and Jeffrey M. Stonecash, "Fiscal Centralization in the American Status: Findings from Another Perspective," *Public Budgeting and Finance*, 8 (Winter 1988), pp. 81–89.

[104] Henderson, "Intergovernmental Service Arrangements," pp. 194–202, for 1983 data; Advisory Commission on Intergovernmental Relations, *Pragmatic Federalism: The Reassignment of Functional Responsibility* (Washington, D.C.: U.S. Government Printing Office, 1976), for 1975 data; and Advisory Commission on Intergovernmental Relations, *The Challenge of Local Government Reorganization*, for 1972 data. For a detailed treatment of all three studies, see: Advisory Commission on Intergovernmental Relations, *Intergovernmental Service Arrangements for Delivering Local Public Services: Update 1983*, A-103 (Washington, D.C.: U.S. Government Printing Office, 1985).

[105] Henderson, "Intergovernmental Service Arrangements," p. 196. All information in this paragraph is for 1983.

[106] *Ibid.*, p. 198.

[107] *Ibid.*, p. 202.

CHAPTER
13

TOWARD A BUREAUCRATIC ETHIC

The notion that the public bureaucracy stands in need of ethical sensitivity in order to serve the public interest is a fairly new one. Although the first code of ethics for public administrators was adopted in 1924 by the International City Management Association (ICMA), it was a code that reflected the anticorruption and antipolitics values of the municipal reform movement of the period, rather than a statement of professional ethics in the tradition established by the fields of education, engineering, law, and medicine, among other professions. Congress imposed a code of ethics on federal administrators in 1958, and twenty years later expanded the code of ethics and founded the federal government's Office of Government Ethics as part of the Ethics in Government Act of 1978. The Office of Government Ethics has yet to establish a reputation of zeal for investigating questions of ethical behavior by federal officials. The first state code of ethics was established in 1967; it was only in 1984 that the chief association of public administrators at all levels of government, the American Society for Public Administration,

saw fit to write and adopt a code of ethics for professionals in the public sector.

There were reasons for this lethargy, and the reasons had less to do with a willingness among public administrators to permit and condone unethical practices in their field than they did with a commonly held assumption by society (including public administrators) about what the proper role of public administration and government was. Prior to the abandonment of the politics/administration dichotomy and the principles of administration, the public administrator needed codes of morality no more than a hotel clerk does who is carrying out his or her daily duties. After all, of what use was morality to a person who did no more than execute the will of the state according to certain scientific principles? Provided that public administrators accomplished their given tasks efficiently and economically, they were by definition moral, in the sense that they were responsible. (In fact, the original ICMA and federal codes of ethics placed notable stress on efficiency as an ethical concept—a notion that many ethicists might find puzzling.) Morality, after all, necessitates ethical choice, and, as the literature was wont to stress, ethical choice simply was not a function of the functionaries of public administration.

PUBLIC ADMINISTRATION'S ETHICAL EVOLVEMENT

The Demise of the Politics/Administration Dichotomy

Three developments have been instrumental in the emergence of the concept that ethics are, in fact, pertinent to public administration. One, of course, was the abandonment of the politics/administration dichotomy. When this naive bifurcation was eliminated, when politics and administration were recognized as being part of the same parcel, it was also admitted implicitly that morality had to be relevant to the bureaucracy. Now the public administrator was forced to make decisions not only on the comfortable bases of efficiency, economy, and administrative principles, but also on the more agonizing criteria of morality as well. Public administrators had to ask themselves: what is *the* public interest?

The Emergence of Decision-Making Theory

The second development was the new role of decision-making theory in public administration. Herbert A. Simon had called for the rigorous analysis of decision-making behavior as central to the future study of administration; he simultaneously decimated as simplistic the "proverbs of administration" in his *Administrative Behavior*.[1] Simon argued that administrators made decisions on bases other than those of economy and efficiency. He contended that social and psychological factors had a significant effect on the decisions that decision makers made. And, before the appearance of *Administrative Behavior*, Harold Lasswell in *Psychopathology and Politics*[2] and Chester I. Barnard in *The Functions of the Executive*[3] had made essentially the same argument. The contention that decision makers made decisions on the bases of feeling, emotion, and mental sets, as well as on "rationality," implied that public administrators

could make highly questionable, even immoral, public policies that possibly would affect whole populations. This was a serious matter. Public administrationists became increasingly cognizant of the disquieting notion that a sense of ethics—a sense of the public interest—was a genuine need in the practice of public administration.

This concern was exacerbated by the appearance of a new body of literature that addressed the topic of morality in public administration in a different manner. Paul H. Appleby, in *Morality and Administration in Democratic Government*, took on the ethical problems posed by the tensions between pluralistic politics and bureaucratic hierarchy. In Appleby's view, the pressures of politics and hierarchy forced moral dilemmas "up" to the highest appropriate policy-making levels in legislatures and bureaucracies and simultaneously simplified the number of choices available to public bureaucrats, usually leaving them with only two options. This was a realistic appraisal of the moral situation of the public bureaucrat; it emphasized the lack of ethical subtlety that the bureaucrat was permitted in making decisions. Although a situation might have "gray" areas in reality, decisions usually had to be either "black" or "white."[4] Similarly, Norton Long explained the connections between moral choice and administrative decision making in the public bureaucracy by his survival thesis. In Long's opinion, all decisions made by public administrators could be explained by their desire that their agencies survive. Long perceived this situation as beneficial to the public interest more often than not, but his reasoning did not rest easily with many of his colleagues as reasoning that cultivated moral rectitude in government.[5] Likewise, Joseph Harris, in *Congressional Control of Administration*, implied that federal public administrators made their decisions primarily on the basis of satisfying a few men who headed powerful committees in Congress; his logic did not strike many as a sound rationale for promoting the public interest.[6]

Perhaps the most shattering analyses of the public administrator's relationship to the public interest were Gordon Tullock's *The Politics of Bureaucracy*[7] and Dwaine Marvick's *Career Perspectives in a Bureaucratic Setting* (1954).[8]

Although we reviewed their contributions in Chapter 5, a brief consideration of their works' implications for bureaucratic ethics is warranted. By arguing that all decision making in bureaucracies is predicated on the individual "reference politician" getting ahead in the hierarchy, Tullock implied that, among public administrators, what is good for the public, or even for the organization, is at best an incidental consideration. Marvick's empirical study of public administrators hypothesized that all individual behavior in public organizations was a matter of conscious or sublimated self-interest. Some participants had deep security needs that obstructed organizational innovation. Others needed simply the opportunity to "do their own thing" and had no commitment beyond protecting that opportunity. Still others were consciously willing and able to disrupt, disorient, and undermine the organization if they felt such behavior would advance their own career goals. In brief, research such as Tullock's and Marvick's was disconcerting not only to public administrationists, but to democratic theorists as well. As Ferrell Heady observed, with the experiences of France and Germany chiefly in mind, public bureaucrats "have obediently and even subserviently responded to whatever political leaders have gained power."[9]

The Counterculture Critique

A third development that has led scholars and practitioners in public administration to dwell more acutely on the meaning of the public interest is the emergence in America of the "counterculture." The term *counterculture* is here used to refer to that body of literature that criticizes the American administrative state as being inhumane, technocratic, impersonal, and "faceless." The counterculture's critique of the public bureaucracy is an especially fundamental one: It states that the typical public administrator is not *immoral* but *amoral*—that is, he or she has been so seduced in this thinking by the values, pressures, and propaganda of the technocratic state that he or she no longer is capable of comprehending what morality is or is not. Thus, even if public administrators wanted to do the "right"

thing—indeed, even if they thought that they were doing the right thing—they neither would be able to make the proper moral decision, nor would they recognize the right decision should they happen to stumble on it.

The counterculture's argument is essentially a linguistic one. It holds that the symbols and values of technological society prevent individual men and women from choosing the lifestyles that they in fact would probably choose if they were not propagandized by the technocracy to be aggressive, amoral, competitive, and even warlike "consumer hedonists." Herbert Marcuse, for example, stresses the symbolic aspects of this view. He contends that the media and institutions of society represent a profound kind of authoritarianism, one that co-opts protest via the continual repetition of certain phrases over the mass media that restrict, by their drilling meaninglessness, alternative thinking; for example, the former Soviet Union's unending repetition of the phrase "warmongering capitalist imperialism" over its media squelched the objective analysis of Western economic and foreign policies on the part of its citizens while it encouraged popular paranoia.[10]

Likewise Jacques Ellul states that citizens in technological societies dwell on "technique" to the exclusion of "reality"; thus, moral choices are "defined out" of administrative problems, and technical means become far more important than ethical ends.[11] Similarly, Theodore J. Roszak argues that "scientism" is inadequate as a way to analyze social problems because it "hexes" our thinking on moral issues. As Roszak states:

...we have produced the scientized jargon which currently dominates official parlance and the social sciences. When knowledgeable men talk, they no longer talk of substances and accidents, of being and spirit, of virtue and vice, of sin and salvation, of deities and demons. Instead, we have a vocabulary filled with nebulous quantities of things that have every appearance of precise calibration, and decorated with vaguely mechanistic-mathematical terms like "parameters," "structures," "variables," "inputs and outputs," "correlations," "inventories," "maximizations," and "optimizations."...the more such language and numerology one packs into a document, the more "objective" the document becomes—which normally means the less morally abrasive....

Thus to bomb more hell out of a tiny Asian country in one year than was bombed out of Europe in the whole Second World War becomes "escalation."... A comparison of the slaughter on both sides in a war is called a "kill ratio." Totaling up the corpses is called a "body count." Running the blacks out of town is called "urban renewal." Discovering ingenious new ways to bilk the public is called "market research." Outflanking the discontent of employees is called "personnel management."...On the other hand, one can be certain that where more colorful, emotive terms are used—"the war on poverty," "the war for the hearts and minds of men," "the race for space," "the New Frontier," "the Great Society,"—the matters referred to exist only as propagandistic fiction or pure distraction.[12]

Charles Reich dubs this situation "Consciousness II" and lists its characteristics as a critique of the administrative state: the reduction of personal freedom via the amalgamation and integration of the public and private interests of society; the value-neutral, even value-less, bureaucracy that is consistently biased in favor of existing policy; the autonomy of the administrative bureaucracy, which makes particular decisions untraceable to particular sources; the displacing of traditional private property, such as land owned by people, by "the new property" of people belonging to organizations—thus, the status and identification conferred by the organizations replaces private property in man's traditional structure of values; and, finally, law as an "inhuman medium" that relates to classes and categories in society, but not to individual people. These features combine to produce the major symptoms of the administrative state, the essence of which "is that it is relentlessly single-minded; it has just one value...technology as represented by organization, efficiency, growth, progress." The effect on the individual public administrator of this relentless single-mindedness is the development of "a profound schizophrenia." Not only is his or her working self separated from his or her private self by the creation of unwanted needs and status drives via advertising, but there also is a split between the public self and the private self, which is accomplished through the nourishment of his or her "liberal" feelings of elitist paternalism for the dispossessed as well as by the cultivation of his or her own needs for status and identity in a consumer-oriented society.[13]

PUBLIC ADMINISTRATION AND THE RECOGNITION OF THE PUBLIC INTEREST: TWO INTELLECTUAL ATTEMPTS

The counterculture critique of the moral dilemma of public administrators (*i.e.*, that they are amoral because of the obfuscation of their language and symbols and the fractionalization of their sense of identify) is a profound one. Public administrationists, while increasingly concerned with administrative ethics and decision making, have not yet addressed themselves to the necessary chore of defining a workable framework of moral choice for the public administrator.

Bureaucratic "Responsibility"

In fact, public administrationists have avoided this task by implying that a moral framework is really not needed when they examine instead the various ways in which "responsibility" and "accountability" are assured in public bureaucracies.[14] For example, some scholars, such as Carl Friedrich and Norton Long, contend that the normal scruples and professional commitments that public administrators glean from being socialized into the public service, along with the "representative elite" nature of their bureaucracies, act as internal constraints against the perpetration of antidemocratic policies.

Most public administrationists, however, argue that a plethora of external checks exist as well, assuring compliance with the public interest. Charles Hyneman and Herbert Finer, for instance, believe that legislative surveillance is an adequate check. J. D. Lewis and L. Von Mises contend that citizen participation in bureaucratic decision making accomplishes the task of matching bureaucratic behavior with the public interest. Henry J. Abraham makes a case for the use of the ombudsman (a figure in Scandinavian governments and elsewhere who has no official power but great personal prestige, which he or she uses to rectify unjust bureaucratic decisions on an individual basis) as an effective means for assuring administrative responsibility. Dwight Waldo, John M. Pfiffner, and Robert Presthus have stated that decentralization of the bureaucracy provides an effective means of implementing the public interest. Gordon Tullock and Harold Wilensky urge the use of publicizing bureaucratic information to insure accordance with the public interest. And K. C. Davis believes that judicial review of administrative decisions checks policies not in the public interest.

In a very real sense, however, these efforts miss the crucial point: public administrators do make political decisions, but that no effective moral and philosophic guidelines (as opposed to *mechanisms* for correcting "bad" decisions) exist for their making these decisions in the public interest.

Organizational Humanism

What some writers have called "organizational humanism" represents another kind of skirting of the issue; rather than denying the appropriateness of bureaucratic ethics, however, organizational humanism dances a baroque minuet around the problem of moral choice. In an unusually solid review of this literature, Robert B. Denhardt observes that organizational humanism contains at least three themes that are of particular utility to the development of a theory of bureaucratic ethics: treating members of an organization humanely leads to greater organizational efficiency; treating organizational members humanely promotes organizational change; and treating the individual in an organization in a humane way is in and of itself a desirable objective.[15]

Organizational humanism was spawned in the literature of human relations and organization development—literary traditions that constitute two of the significant streams of the open model of organizations that we reviewed in Chapter 3. It focuses on the individual in the organization and his or her personal development. As we shall see, organizational humanism verges on addressing the question of bureaucratic ethics, but like the literature of bureaucratic responsibility, ultimately draws short of it.

Some of the early studies in the open model of organizations brought out questions—often morally tinged questions—concerning the individual's role in the organization. Chester I. Barnard's recognition of the "informal organization"; the Hawthorne studies that focused on the importance of social and psychological rewards for workers;

Douglas McGregor's development of the "Theory Y" model of workers' personalities; and Robert Blake and Jane Mouton's notion of the "managerial grid," in which they argued that a high organizational concern for people and the team approach to management most closely corresponded with high organizational productivity—all these studies had the effect of teasing out the idea that the satisfaction and happiness of the individual person in an organization was an important element in organizational effectiveness.[16]

Chris Argyris is among the better-known writers who have developed the argument that organizations would improve themselves if they were able to develop the full human potentiality of their members. In *Personality and Organization*, for example, Argyris argued that the normal dynamic of organizations caused people to "dematurize" in organizations, and, if organizations changed their internal dynamics, more creative and contributing organizational members would result. Argyris conceived of learning as the primary means through which individual members could develop their human capabilities, and "learning" to Argyris meant learning not only about the organization, but about one's self; learning, in Argyris's mind, equated with the maturation of both the organization and the individual.[17]

In a perceptive critique of Argyris's work, Denhardt observes that by emphasizing learning, Argyris "implies a relationship involving shared meanings and raises the possibilities for creating not only conditions of trust, openness, and self-esteem, but also conditions of community."[18] But for whatever reason, Argyris chose not to extrapolate the implications of learning in organizations, which in Denhardt's view constitutes the "potentially radical implication of Argyris's work," because, by inference, Argyris's idea of learning ultimately forces the issue of developing a set of bureaucratic ethics. Fundamentally, Argyris is still "bound to an instrumentalist perspective," or one that places the organization's needs above that of the individual's happiness.[19]

Robert T. Golembiewski, on the other hand, goes a step further. Rather than arguing for the desirability of emotionally mature organizational members, as does Argyris, Golembiewski directly addresses the problem of morality within the organization and the prospects of freedom for the individual worker. Golembiewski asserts that "moral sensitivity can be associated with satisfactory output and employee satisfaction."[20] Golembiewski's major contribution is that he confronts the question of morality in organizations, arguing that organization development, particularly the laboratory approach (recall Chapter 3), represents an unusually useful method of bringing morality to organizations.

The literature that we have been covering so far is drawn largely from organization theory, and, with the occasional exception of Golembiewski, this literature was not written by nor directed to the world of public administration. With the advent of the "new public administration" in the early 1970s, however, this situation began to change. We reviewed the new public administration in Chapter 2 in terms of its effects on the intellectual evolution of the field. Although its impact was not particularly lasting and, as has been pointed out, it was "a movement from the beginning more fictional than real,"[21] the literature associated with the new public administration nonetheless has overriding tones of moral and ethical concerns, and thus has pertinence here. Writers in the tradition of the new public administration emphasized the paramountcy of equity over efficiency, and of participation by organizational members over hierarchy.[22]

One of the more interesting contributions to this literature has been written by Eugene P. Dvorin and Robert H. Simmons, who observe that "little of the literature of public administration reflects on the nature of public interest, and virtually none reflects belief in the dignity of man as the ultimate value." Conversely, they add, the other branches of the government do have operational definitions of the public interest. Both the legislative and adjudicative branches "have their myths and techniques by which they serve these myths." In the legislature, the operational concept is majority rule as the fundamental precondition of democracy. In the judiciary, the concept is *stare decisis*, or judicial precedent, by which the evolutionary development of legal principles is perceived as the basic method for obtaining a system of justice that reflects the public interest. In both of these examples there are, of course, flaws. As Dvorin and Simmons say, the "myths" of majority rule and *stare decisis* in reality "serve several functions—to meet

the psychoemotional needs of the society and to protect and defend both legislators and judges." Nevertheless, the point stands that these concepts do not pretend to be value-neutral, and they do go far toward defining the abstract notion of the public interest in workable terms that meet the needs of the legislative and adjudicative institutions of society. Not so, however, with the executive branch, which has no such operational definition.

Dvorin and Simmons urge that "radical humanism" be accepted as the public bureaucracy's functional concept of the public interest. In their words:

"Radical humanism" forwards the proposition that the ends of man are the ends of man....Radical humanism is radical because it is not willing to compromise its human values on any grounds....Radical humanism calls for the ultimate capitulation of operational mechanics and political strategies to a concept of the public interest based on man as the most important concern of bureaucratic power.[23]

This statement is fine as far as it goes. Regrettably, Dvorin and Simmons go no further, and a serious problem arises in terms of what "radical humanism" means when it is applied to particular administrative problems. The same may be said, in fact, for organizational humanism in general.

AN EXAMPLE OF APPLIED ETHICAL CHOICE IN PUBLIC ADMINISTRATION

Consider, for an example, a growing dilemma in that traditionally hidebound field of public personnel administration: hiring members of socially disadvantaged groups. There are two positions. One is that government should make special efforts, including the reduction of entrance standards, to hire members of those segments of American society that have endured various forms of racial, religious, ethnic, or sexual discrimination. The reasoning is that, because of cultural bias in testing, lack of educational opportunity, and general social prejudice, government owes those people who have suffered these injustices a special chance to get ahead. If this should entail some bending of the civil service regulations (as is done for veterans), so be it. Such rule-bending will, after all, only balance the social equities for those applicants who have had to suffer bigotry in the past, and this is only as it should be since government is the single institution most responsible for assuring equality of opportunity in society.

The other position is that no "lowering of standards" should be considered, regardless of the applicant's past tribulations. The logic for this viewpoint is that government owes the best governance possible to all the governed. To hire applicants who do not score as well on tests as other applicants, or who do not have comparable educational attainments, or who are just less qualified, irrespective of the tough breaks in their backgrounds, is to do a disservice to the populace generally, deprived groups included. Governmental economy, efficiency, effectiveness, and responsiveness will deteriorate to the detriment of us all, unless only the top applicants are hired.

(It must be noted here that both arguments, pro and con, have been simplified considerably in order to emphasize the ethical aspects of each. Other pertinent facets, such as the efficacy of tests in measuring administrative ability and the role of strict civil service standards in protecting applicants from disadvantaged groups against discrimination, were reviewed in Chapter 9.)

It is reasonably apparent from this example that organizational humanism does not offer much of a guide to the public administrator in formulating a decision in terms of promoting the public interest. Organizational humanism states that treating people humanely should be the ultimate end in bureaucratic decision making, but which option should the public administrator choose in the case cited? Is humanity best served by hiring or promoting a deprived group member who may not execute his or her duties especially well, or is humanity best served by not hiring (or by holding back) the same disadvantaged group member, thus never permitting him or her to try to realize his or her full human potential? This dilemma can be rendered even more exquisite by making the hypothetical deprived-group member in question an applicant to an agency designed to end discrimination against deprived groups, such as the Equal Employment Opportunity Commission; thus, to hire or not to hire him or her implies a lack of sincerity in ad-

vancing the cause of disadvantaged groups, depending on one's point of view. In any event, organizational humanism would seem to lack a viable framework of clear-cut referent points for a public administrator in making an ethical choice that is in "the public interest."

JUSTICE-AS-FAIRNESS: A VIEW OF THE PUBLIC INTEREST

What is needed for the public administrator is a simple and operational articulation of the public interest that permits him or her to make a moral choice on the basis of rational thinking. It is forwarded in this book that such a useful concept may exist in the form of a theory of justice offered by philosopher John Rawls.

Rawls extends the notion of a social contract formulated by John Locke, Jean-Jacques Rousseau, and Thomas Hobbes, and contends implicitly that the public interest can be discerned in most situations by applying two "principles of justice": (1) that "each person is to have an equal right to the most extensive basic liberty compatible with a similar liberty for others," and (2) that "social and economic inequalities are to be arranged so that they are both (a) reasonably expected to be to everyone's advantage, and (b) attached to positions and offices open to all." Should these principles come into conflict, the second is expected to yield to the first; thus, just as in organizational humanism, the dignity of the individual person is considered to be of paramount importance.[24]

Rawls's theory of justice goes further, however. His principles necessarily lead to the conclusion that inequalities of wealth, authority, and social opportunity

are just only if they result in compensating benefits for everyone, and in particular for the least advantaged members of society. These principles rule out justifying institutions on the grounds that the hardships of some are offset by a greater good in the aggregate. It may be expedient but it is not just that some should have less in order that others may prosper.[25]

In short, as Rawls observes, his principles in essence are a rigorous statement of the traditional Anglo-Saxon concept of fairness.

INTUITIONISM, PERFECTIONISM, AND UTILITARIANISM

The usefulness of Rawls's justice-as-fairness philosophy can be elucidated by contrasting it with other philosophies of the public interest. One is the *intuitionist* philosophy, expressed by Brian Barry, Nicholas Rescher, and W. D. Ross, among others.[26] Intuitionist theories expound a plurality of first principles, which may conflict when applied to particular situations but which offer no precise method for choosing the principle that should take precedence in cases of conflict. Such dilemmas are resolved by intuition, by what seems most nearly right. Intuitionist philosophies do not help the conscientious public administrator to make a rational decision in light of an explicit theory of the public interest, other than rendering him or her some solace in justifying present practices. In other words, public administrators already make decisions on the basis of intuitionist theories—that is, they do what seems to be to them most nearly right on an individual basis and given particularistic circumstances. The view here, however, is that this practice—an ethical "muddling through"—is increasingly inadequate for a society in which rapid change is the only constant.

A second major philosophical school that addresses the public interest is *perfectionism*. The first and sole principle of perfectionism is to promote, via society's institutions, the attainment of excellence in art, science, and culture. There are, however, two forms of perfectionism. In its relative form, as advocated by Aristotle, the perfectionist principle is one among many first principles, and thus overlaps with intuitionism. In its absolutist form, by contrast, there are no problems of ambiguity: the public administrator should always strive to support the upper intellectual crust of his or her society; any misfortune for society's least fortunate segments that accrues from the necessary allocation of resources and that results from implementing the perfectionist principle is morally justified by the benefits incurred by the best members that the society has. As Nietzsche put it so pithily, the deepest meaning that can be given to the human experience is "your living for the rarest and most valuable specimens."[27]

Perfectionism is a counterpoise to the egalitarian notions rife in a democratic society, and for that reason we shall not dwell on it as an appropriate ethical decision-making framework for American public administrators. Nevertheless, this is not to imply that perfectionism has not been used as an operating premise by American bureaucrats in making decisions. The National Science Foundation's traditional criterion for financing "pure" scientific research (which has been, with few exceptions, the only kind of research that the foundation has financed)—that science should be funded for the sake of science—would appear to be an implementation of the perfectionist principle, although this emphasis has been changing in recent years.

A third ethical framework for the determination of the public interest is *utilitarianism*, as represented by Jeremy Bentham, Adam Smith, David Hume, and John Stuart Mill.[28] Of the philosophies that have had the most influence on public administrators in terms of intellectual rigor and social appropriateness, utilitarianism holds first place in theory, if not in actual practice.

The reasoning of utilitarianism is both democratic in values and systematic in thought. It holds that a public policy will be in the public interest provided the policy increases the net balance of social satisfaction summed over all the individuals belonging to the society. In other words, if a public policy makes everybody slightly better off, even if some individuals are left slightly worse off in other ways as a result of that policy, then the policy is just and the public interest is served. An example of a utilitarian public policy would be one that increased the income of medical doctors by raising everyone's taxes and turning over these new revenues to doctors, thereby increasing everyone's net balance of health by inducing a greater net balance of individuals to enter the medical profession. Even though society's least well off individuals would lose money under this arrangement, the policy would nevertheless be just and in the public interest under a utilitarian theory because everyone's net balance of health would be increased, including that of the least well off. The logic behind this justification of such a public policy is that since individuals try to advance as far as possible their own welfare in terms of net increases, it therefore follows that the group should do the same, and the society likewise.

The ethical theory of justice-as-fairness, however, would hold that such a public policy was not just and not in the public interest because it reduced the welfare of the least well off people in society, even if it is for the net benefit for the whole society. With some alterations, our hypothetical policy could be made just under Rawls's principles; for instance, by not taxing the poor but still letting them take part in the overall health benefits that derive from the policy. It is on the same logic that the United States has a mildly "progressive" income tax structure which is supposed to tax the rich proportionately more than the poor, rather than a "regressive" income tax structure, which taxes the poor proportionately more than the rich, or even a "proportional" tax, which taxes the indigent and the wealthy at the same rate.

Although, as we noted earlier, utilitarianism is practiced more by chance than by choice among American bureaucrats, occasionally agencies will select utilitarianism quite consciously as their operational definition of the public interest. An example is provided by the U.S. Army Corps of Engineers, which has adopted cost-benefit analysis as its method of deciding which engineering projects are in the best interests of the nation. But the assumptions underlying the Corps' use of cost-benefit analysis are squarely set in a utilitarian philosophy, and can bring utilitarian consequences.

For instance, in 1983, the Corps of Engineers conducted a cost-benefit analysis of flood control for La Puerta del Norte, a frequently-flooded community of 150 families living in mobile homes near the Santa Cruz River in Pima County, Arizona. The Corps' study concluded that flood control projects for La Puerta del Norte would not be cost effective because the potential flood damage that could be wreaked on mobile homes would not be great in terms of dollar losses. If, however, La Puerta del Norte had consisted of expensive homes, then the Corps' analysis would likely have justified a flood control project because the Corps' cost-benefit analysis formula was predicated on estimating the potential dollar loss in property damage that might result from floods.[29] Thus,

costlier homes (and wealthier people) are favored over cheaper homes (and poorer people) in the Corps' cost-benefit analyses because the technique itself is based on utilitarian precepts.

APPLYING THE JUSTICE-AS-FAIRNESS THEORY

Intuitionism, perfectionism, and utilitarianism illuminate by contrast the usefulness of justice-as-fairness as an ethical framework for public administrators in making decisions that are in the public interest. But how would justice-as-fairness help the public administrator in deciding our original dilemma, that of hiring "less qualified" applicants from disadvantaged groups in society? It would, by the inevitability of its logic, argue for the hiring of these applicants on these grounds:

1. *Not* hiring them would be further depriving society's most deprived groups for the sake of the whole society.

2. Hiring them would facilitate the full realization of their "basic liberty" (or personal dignity) without encroaching on the basic liberty of others.

3. Hiring them helps assure that all positions and offices are open to all.

4. Hiring them helps assure that privileges innate to such offices continue to work toward the advantage of all in a reasonably equal way, because the privileges and positions are being extended to the least well off in society.

Moreover, of the ethical frameworks considered, only justice-as-fairness would by its logic permit the public administrator the decisional choice of making a special effort to hire members from disadvantaged groups. Utilitarianism would demand that the good of the whole be the first priority, regardless of consequences for society's least well off. Perfectionism, in effect, would say to hell with society's least well off since they are not considered at all in its value structure. Intuitionism, which most public administrators practice, permits the choice of hiring members of minority groups, but only as a coincidental happenstance and not by the force of its theory.

Justice-as-fairness offers the public administrator a workable way of determining the public interest. So, for that matter, do utilitarianism and perfectionism, but we are rejecting those frameworks in this book; the former because it logically permits the least advantaged persons in society to be disadvantaged further and thus is "unfair" and not in the public interest in all instances, and the latter because its antidemocratic values are incompatible with the dominant values of American society. The choice in this book of justice-as-fairness as an operating moral logic for the public administrator is, of course, a value choice by the author and should be recognized as

Etiquette, Image, and Ethics in Public Administration

Beginning in the late 1980s, it became clear that the United States' biggest bankruptcy—the failure of much of the savings-and-loan (S & L) industry—could not be staved off, and the American taxpayers would be the losers. Congress and a conservative White House had, at one and the same time, insured (with federal funds) the deposits of citizens who invested their money in savings-and-loan associations; radically deregulated the S & Ls, allowing them to invest their depositors' savings in extremely questionable pursuits; and significantly cut back on the federal government's oversight and inspection of the savings-and-loan associations.

The results of these policies were perhaps predictable, but not their colossal dimensions: Hundreds of S & Ls (also known, ironically, as "thrifts"), beginning in the late 1980s, declared bankruptcy, and the estimates of the final federal bill to the taxpayer to cover these losses run as high at $500 billion over thirty years.

How much is $500 billion? Five hundred billion dollars is enough to excuse every U.S. taxpayer earning less than $50,000 a year from paying income taxes for three years. Five hundred billion dollars is $50 billion more than the combined budgets (in 1987) of all fifty states. Five hundred billion dollars is $40 billion less, in current dollars, than the total cost of World War II, including service-connected veterans' benefits. Five hundred billion dollars is about 99.9 percent more than the federal government spends per year on caring for the nation's homeless.

Five hundred billion dollars is, in brief, a lot of money. To administer the S & L bailout, Congress in 1989 created the Resolution Trust Corporation (RTC), which was charged with selling or liquidating insolvent or mismanaged savings and loan associations. The RTC typically sends a team of twenty to 100 auditors unannounced to the thrift in question on a Friday, which works with the S & L's staff over the weekend to determine the level of its fiscal soundness, and completes its work by Monday. The S & L then is either reopened under new ownership, or liquidated, in which case its depositors receive federal insurance checks covering their lost deposits.

The following memorandum was written by the RTC's administrator of its East Region to his regional audit teams. It unwittingly captures the macabre interrelationships among the maintenance of business etiquette, the unremitting pressure to manage an agency's image in the public sector, and the ethical collapse inherent in the S & L debacle.

As representatives of the Resolution Trust Corporation we must be cognizant of the fact that we are under the watchful eye of the press, the public, the General Accounting Office, and other oversight agencies. Our actions and activities must be above reproach. In that regard there are a few things that I wish to remind you of or admonish you to consider as we move forward with resolution activity.

First, over the closing weekend we allow you to dress in 'casual attire.' This is often referred to as 'golf attire'—clothing that is comfortable, but not worn or ragged. Shorts are not deemed acceptable attire for thrift-closing activities. Of course, in the event we reopen the thrift on Saturday morning, business attire is required. Think about what you are going to wear and whether it would look appropriate on television.

Many of you have recently acquired RTC T-shirts with the slogan WANNA BUY AN S & L? on the front and 141 OR BUST on the back. [The RTC recently had established as a goal the resolutions of 141 S & Ls by the end of the month.] Obviously, there is a time and a place to wear these shirts. The closing, with the stress that the thrift's employees are under, is not the time or the place.

Second, we must treat the employees of the thrift with courtesy and respect. The staff remaining after the association has been placed in conservatorship are not at fault for its problems. They have been under a tremendous amount of pressure and now have the added burden of concern about their future employment.

Although it is certainly not a widespread problem, I have heard of a few instances when members of our closing team were rude or disrespectful to association employees. This behavior will not be tolerated. Closing managers are instructed to respond to such behavior by sending the employee home immediately and providing a memorandum to this writer stating that the individual should not be considered for future closing activity.

Third, the confidentiality of this transaction prior to the closing hour must be stressed. The resolution date is not disclosed to the public prior to the press release issued at the closing hour. Keep this in mind at all times. Further, hotel reservations for closing activity should not be made in the name of the Federal Deposit Insurance Corporation or the RTC, and you should not register with the corporate Diners Club card until after the closing has occurred.

Fourth, those of you who have attended closings prior to the creation of the RTC probably remember the days of pizza on closing night. Those days are gone. Due to the focus on our activities by the media, it would not be appropriate to read in the paper how we ate pizza on the taxpayers' money.

Closing activity is not one great big party. Certainly some of the cities where you may be sent are great places to visit. While you are there you will want to have a little fun. However, remember that we are in the spotlight, and do not embarrass the corporation.

Finally, think about our image when you rent a car for corporation business. It is not how much you actually pay for the rental car that is most important but how it looks. The public may not understand that a Lincoln Continental is the same price as a Pontiac Sunbird. Therefore, stick with a reasonable-size vehicle.

This memorandum is not all-inclusive as to issues of a sensitive nature that we must consider in the closing routine. However, I trust that it will cause you to consider the ramifications of your actions. We are constantly in the fishbowl and must act accordingly.

Craig A. Francis, Jr., Administrator, East Region, Resolution Trust Corporation, June 18, 1990

Sources: For the information contained in the explanation introducing the memorandum, the sources are Janet L. Fix, "Mind-Boggling Bill for S & Ls," *Philadelphia Inquirer* (September 9, 1990), and Michael Gartner, "Biggest Robbery in History—You're the Victim," *Wall Street Journal* (August 9, 1990).

such by the reader. But it is believed to be a reasonable one under the circumstances.

PRACTICING ETHICAL PUBLIC ADMINISTRATION

Whatever ethical standard a public administrator chooses, and however each public administrator elects to employ that standard, it is reasonably apparent that career public administrators take the practice of ethical administration seriously. A national survey of public administrators at all levels of government in the United States found that almost 70 percent believe that the interest in ethical issues among public administrators seemed to be "steadily growing over time"; close to 60 percent disagree that ethics is "meaningless because organizational cultures encourage a Machiavellian philosophy of power, survival, and expediency"; about two-thirds think that "ethical concerns can be empowering in organizations" (only 6 percent disagree), and two-thirds reject the position that "expressions of ethical concern...evoke cynicism, self-righteousness, paranoia, and/or laughter"; and 90 percent take issue with the statement that there "is no real need for codes of ethics in work organizations."[30] These responses appear to support the proposition that public administrators maintain a belief set that codes of ethics and ethical behavior in their profession are needed, good, and growing.

Nevertheless, practicing ethical administration in the public sector remains a challenging chore. Reflecting a fundamental theme of this book—that the task environment is far more penetrating of the public organization than of the private one—half of public administrators report that "supervisors are under pressure to compromise personal standards."[31] The lower that one descends through the strata of the public organization, and the more youthful and politically liberal the public administrator, the stronger this belief becomes. Much of this perception is enmeshed in the ongoing tensions between career and noncareer public executives, as described in Chapter 9. Sixty percent of the respondents doubted that the "ethical standards of elected and appointed officials are as high as those held by career civil servants" (only 25 per-

cent accepted the contention that the ethical standards of both groups are comparable), and almost three-fourths took umbrage at the idea that "senior management has a stronger set of ethical standards than I do."[32]

In light of these views, it is perhaps not surprising that public administrators, while more critical of the ethics of corporate culture than government (nearly 90 percent spurn the notion that "government morality in America is lower than business morality"[33]), nonetheless are relatively remorseless in their hostility to the ethical failures of government. Not only do public administrators appear to register more outrage than the average citizen over government scandals, but their despondency over these scandals is deepening over time.

For example,[34] more than 90 percent of the public administrators believed that the corruption involved in overcharging the Pentagon by private contractors in 1988 was "a scandal just waiting to happen." By comparison, 82 percent of the general public felt the same way. Over three quarters of the public administrators dismiss the notion that the administration of Ronald Reagan "did a good job in enforcing ethical standards." By comparison, only 43 percent of the citizenry reject this statement.

And public administrators are becoming increasingly depressed and alienated over public corruption. In 1977, a poll of federal administrators in the United States found that over 60 percent of the respondents disagreed with the view that "governmental practices today suffer from a 'moral numbness' following a decade of strife...,"[35] while only 28 percent of public administrators in 1990 disagreed with the statement that "society suffers a 'moral numbness' following a decade of scandals...."[36] Although the surveys differ slightly, the trend of professional opinion seems clear.

In sum, public administrators in the United States seem to believe that ethics in government is extraordinarily important; that they are under pressures to engage in unethical behavior; and that, compared with business, government still is the more ethical institution. Public administrators appear to be more critical of ethical lapses in government than are the taxpayers themselves, and they may become, with time, even more irate over those lapses.

These perspectives among public administrators are encouraging ethical auguries.

CONCLUSION: POLITICS AIN'T BEANBAG AND MANAGEMENT AIN'T FOOD STAMPS

It is fitting to close this book on what the public administrator should and should not do as a moral, amoral, or immoral actor in the public bureaucracy. One can learn the techniques of management science, the notions of organization theory, and the intricacies of policy formulation and implementation, but ultimately public administration is a field of thought and practice in which personal ethical choices are made. Those who enter the field, either as thinkers or practitioners (and, one hopes, some of both), are, not infrequently, required to make decisions about moral questions that have far-reaching social consequences. Public administration is a profession of large responsibilities, and moral choices and ethical obligations will always be an integral part of those responsibilities.

We observed in Chapter 2 that the academic field of public administration combined both political science and management, and thus is not only larger than either but different from both. What holds for the study of public administration holds equally for its practice.

Practicing politicians, in explaining their craft, state simply that "politics ain't beanbag." Like most *clichés*, the phrase when new was insightful, witty, and accurate, and it remains so. "Politics ain't beanbag" summarizes professional politics: individuals competing ruthlessly against other individuals for power in an arena in which few if any rules apply—a refined variant of the Hobbesian state of nature.

To this verity of political life we might add one that describes the practice of management: "management ain't food stamps." Managers, in other words, are charged with advancing organizations and policies, but they are not charged with advancing (or even maintaining) the welfare of individuals. Of course, it is often true that when certain kinds of organizations and policies progress, so do the fortunes and the welfare of those individuals associated with them or affected by them, and one can argue (persuasively) that society created organizations and policies to benefit itself and the people composing it. But these happy occurrences are incidental to the fundamental duty of managers. The prime directive of management is to look after the system.

Because public administration combines the professions of both politics and management, we have in some ways the worst of both worlds: individual political and managerial actors competing against others to advance their own ends and the ends of their own systems and clienteles. The profession of public administration thus becomes both unusually brutal ("politics ain't beanbag") and unusually insensitive to the welfare of the individual members of the public organization ("management ain't food stamps").

This condition can elide easily into a potentially nasty administrative structure. It is a condition unique to the practice of public administration, and public administrators should always be keenly aware that, as a consequence, their profession offers an unusually rich variety of opportunities to make moral or immoral decisions, to make ethical or unethical choices, to do good or evil things to people.

As one who both practices and thinks about public administration, this writer asks that, if you enter the field, you remember when making your choices to ask yourself how people will be helped or hurt by your decisions. Few questions are more important in any context, but in the context of the public life of the nation, none is more important.

Public administration is neither beanbag nor food stamps.

NOTES

[1] Herbert A. Simon, *Administrative Behavior: A Study of Decision-Making Processes in Administration Organization* (New York: The Free Press, 1947).

[2] Harold Lasswell, *Psychopathology and Politics* (New York: Viking Press, 1930).

[3] Chester I. Barnard, *The Functions of the Executive* (Cambridge, Mass.: Harvard University Press, 1938).

[4] Paul H. Appleby, *Morality and Administration in Democratic Government* (Baton Rouge, La.: Louisiana State University Press, 1952).

[5] Norton Long, *The Polity* (Chicago: Rand McNally, 1962).

[6] Joseph P. Harris, *Congressional Control of Administration* (Washington, D.C.: Brookings Institution, 1964).

[7] Gordon Tullock, *The Politics of Bureaucracy* (Washington, D.C.: Public Affairs Press, 1965).

[8] Dwaine Marvick, *Career Perspectives in a Bureaucratic Setting* (Ann Arbor, Mich.: University of Michigan Press, 1954).

[9] Ferrel Heady, *Public Administration: A Comparative Perspective* (Englewood Cliffs, N.J.: Prentice-Hall, 1966), p. 45.

[10] Herbert Marcuse, *One Dimensional Man: Studies in the Ideology of Advanced Industrial Society* (Boston: Beacon Press, 1964).

[11] Jacques Ellul, *The Technological Society* (New York: Knopf, 1964).

[12] Theodore J. Roszak, *The Making of a Counter Culture* (New York: Doubleday, 1969), pp. 142–144.

[13] Charles A. Reich, *The Greening of America: How the Youth Revolution is Trying to Make America Livable* (New York: Random House, 1970).

[14] The following works are germane to this paragraph: Carl J. Friedrich and Taylor Cole, *Responsible Bureaucracy* (Cambridge, Mass.: Harvard University Press, 1932); Long, *The Polity*; Charles S. Hyneman, *Bureaucracy* (New York: Harper & Row, 1950); Herbert Finer, "Administrative Responsibility in a Democratic Government," *Public Administration Review*, 1 (Summer 1941), pp. 335–350; J. D. Lewis, "Democratic Planning in Agriculture," *American Political Science Review*, 35 (April and June 1941), pp. 232–249, 454–469; L. Von Mises, *Bureaucracy* (New Haven, Conn.: Yale University Press, 1944); Henry J. Abraham, "A People's Watchdog Against Abuse of Power," *Public Administration Review*, 20 (Summer 1960), pp. 152–157; Dwight Waldo, "Development of a Theory of Democratic Administration," *American Political Science Review*, 46 (March 1952), pp. 81–103; John M. Pfiffner and Robert Presthus, *Public Administration*, 5th ed. (New York: Ronald Press, 1967); Gordon Tullock, *The Politics of Bureaucracy* (Washington, D.C.: Public Affairs Press, 1965); Harold L. Wilensky, *Organizational Intelligence: Knowledge and Policy in Government and Industry* (New York: Basic Books, 1967); K. C. Davis, *Administrative Law* (St. Paul, Minn.: West Publishing, 1951).

[15] Robert B. Denhardt, *Theories of Public Organization* (Monterey, Calif.: Brooks/Cole 1984), p. 92.

[16] Barnard, *The Functions of the Executive*, p. 120; Fritz Roethlisberger and William Dickson, *Management and the Worker* (Cambridge, Mass.: Harvard University Press, 1940), p. 562; Douglas McGregor, *The Human Side of Enterprise* (New York: McGraw-Hill, 1960), pp. 47–48; and Robert Blake and Jane Mouton, *The Academic Administrator Grid* (San Francisco: Jossey-Bass, 1981), p. 128.

[17] Chris Argyris, *Personality and Organization* (New York: Harper & Row, 1957); but see also Argyris's *Interpersonal Confidence and Organizational Effectiveness* (Homewood, Ill.: Dorsey Press, 1962).

[18] Denhardt, *Theories of Public Organization*, p. 99.

[19] *Ibid.*, pp. 99, 101.

[20] Robert T. Golembiewski, *Men, Management, and Morality* (New York: McGraw-Hill, 1967), p. 53.

[21] Denhardt, *Theories of Public Organization*, p. 108.

[22] Among the contributors who are associated with the new public administration and who emphasize bureaucratic ethics are: Larry Kirkhart, "Toward a Theory of Public Administration," in *Toward a New Public Administration: The Minnowbrook Perspective*, Frank Marini, ed. (San Francisco: Chandler, 1971), pp. 127–163; Todd LaPorte, "The Recovery of Relevance in the Study of Public Organization," in *ibid.*, pp. 17–47; Dwight Waldo, ed. *Public Administration in a Time of Turbulence* (San Franciso: Chandler, 1971); Frederick E. Thayer, *An End to Hierarchy! An End to Competition!* (New York: New Viewpoints, 1973); and David K. Hart, "Social Equity, Justice, and the Equitable Administrator," *Public Administration Review*, 34 (January/February 1974), pp. 3–10.

[23] Eugene P. Dvorin and Robert H. Simmons, *From Amoral to Humane Bureaucracy* (San Francisco: Canfield Press, 1972), pp. 60–61.

[24] John Rawls, *A Theory of Justice* (Cambridge, Mass.: Belknap Press of Harvard University Press, 1971), p. 60.

[25] *Ibid.*, pp. 14–15.

[26] See, for example: Brian Barry, *Political Argument* (London: Routledge and Kegan Paul, 1965); Nicholas Rescher, *Distributive Justice* (New York: Bobbs-Merrill, 1966); and W. D. Ross, *The Right and the Good* (Oxford: Clarendon Press, 1930).

[27] Friedrich Nietzsche, as quoted in J. R. Hollingsdale, *Nietzsche: The Man and His Philosophy* (Baton Rouge, La.: Louisiana State University Press, 1965), p. 127.

[28] See, for example: Jeremy Bentham, *An Introduction to the Principles of Morals and Legislation*, J. H. Burns and H. L. A. Hart, eds. (London: Athlone, 1970); Adam Smith, *The Wealth of Nations*, Edwin Cannan, ed. (New York: Modern Library, 1937); David Hume, *Theory of Politics*, Frederick Watkins, ed. (Edinburgh: Nelson, 1951); and John Stuart Mill, *Essays on Politics and Culture*, Gertrude Himmelfarb, ed. (New York: Doubleday, 1962).

[29] Laura Mumford, "Policy Analysis and the U.S. Army Corps of Engineers" (Paper submitted to a graduate course in public administration, December 11, 1984, School of Public Affairs, College of Public Programs, Arizona State University, Tempe, Arizona, Nicholas Henry, instructor).

[30] James S. Bowman, "Ethics in Government: A National Survey of Public Administrators," *Public Administration Review*, 50 (May/June 1990), p. 346. Bowman contacted 750 randomly selected members of the American Society for Public Administration, and obtained responses from 441, or a response rate of 59 percent.

[31] *Ibid.*, p. 347.

[32] *Ibid.*

[33] *Ibid.*, p. 346.

[34] The material in this paragraph is drawn from: Associated Press, "Poll: Americans Believe Bribery Rampant," *Tallahassee Democrat* (October 4, 1988).

[35] James S. Bowman, "Ethics in the Federal Service: A Post-Watergate View," *Midwest Review of Public Administration*, 11 (March 1977), pp. 7–8.

[36] Bowman, "Ethics in Government," p. 346.

APPENDIX

A

ANNOTATED INFORMATION SOURCES IN PUBLIC ADMINISTRATION AND RELATED FIELDS

This appendix annotates major bibliographies, guides, dictionaries, directories, and encyclopedias in public administration and related fields, including political science, management, American government, law, statistics, and the social sciences. Entries are listed under their organizing category alphabetically by title. Numbers appearing in the right-hand margin are the entries' Library of Congress call numbers, and should facilitate your locating the work. The appendix is organized as follows:

Contents of Appendix A

Browsing through library shelves often can produce the richest lodes of knowledge. The following list provides Library of Congress call numbers that are among the most useful to students of public administration:

Call Numbers Most Specific to Public Administration

- HD 216-244 (public land)
- HD 3611-4730 (state and industry, public works)
- HD 8000-8030 (state labor)
- HJ (public finance)
- HT 1-399 (cities and towns, planning)
- JF (constitution and administration)
- JK (U.S., constitution and government)
- JL (British and Latin America, constitution and government)
- JN (Europe, constitution and government)

401

- JQ (Asia, Africa, Australia, Oceania, constitution and government)
- JS (local government)

I. PUBLIC ADMINISTRATION

This portion of Appendix A deals with information resources that focus directly on public administration and its subfields, public budgeting and finance, public personnel administration and human resource management, and community planning. A final section lists sources dealing with educational programs, internships, and jobs in public administration.

Contents of Section I

A. General Works
B. Public Budgeting and Finance
C. Public Personnel Administration and Human Resource Management
D. Community Planning
E. Education, Internships, and Jobs

A. General Works

A Centennial History of the American Administrative State. Ralph Clark Chandler, ed. New York: The Free Press, 1987. A commemoration of Woodrow Wilson's seminal essay on public administration of 1887, the book's seventeen original chapters use that essay as a pivot point from which both the past and future of the practice and theory of public administration are addressed. A very useful work in that it provides a concise, thorough understanding of the field's historical development and its evolution of defining ideas.   JK 411 .C46

Basic Documents of American Public Administration 1776–1950. Frederick C. Mosher. New York: Holmes and Meier, 1976. Just as the title states, the book covers the basic early American documents of public administration. An excellent compendium.   JK 411 .B3

Basic Documents of American Public Administration Since 1950. Richard J. Stillman, II. New York: Holmes and Meier, 1982. Editor's introductions place each topic and document into perspective. The 1976 edition organizes documents under these 1982 headings: The Foundations, The Management Movement, Depression and New Deal, and the Post War Period. The book reveals postwar reforms in organization, personnel, budgeting, and accountability.   JK 411 .B32

Directory of Organizations and Individuals Professionally Engaged in Governmental Research. Austin, Tex.: Governmental Research Association, 1981. Notes national, state, and local agencies concerned with the improvement of governmental organizations, administration, and efficiency. Indexed by names of organizations and individuals.   JK 3 .G627

Documentation in Public Administration. New Delhi: Indian Institute of Public Administration, 1973–. (Previous title: *Public Administration Abstracts and Index of Articles, 1957–1972.*) Indexes articles from a few selected journals relating to public administration. Issued monthly without cumulations. The coverage is limited, but still useful for long abstracts of major articles and some emphasis on administration in developing areas.   Z 7164 .82D6

Guide to Library Research in Public Administration. Antony Simpson. New York: Center for Productive Public Management. John Jay College of Criminal Justice, 1976. Excellent, comprehensive guide to the literature. Opens with an overview of the field of public administration, discusses research and then details resources.   JF 1411 .S5

Guide to Public Administration. D. A. Cutchin. Itasca, Ill.: Peacock, 1981. An excellent review of the field, Cutchin's *Guide* covers concepts, theories, and facts; lists them alphabetically; provides annotated bibliographies of research sources and journals; and furnishes organization charts of agencies in the federal executive branch.   JA 61 .C87

Handbook of Information Sources and Research Strategies in Public Administration. Mary G. Rock. San Diego, Calif.: Institute of Public and Urban Affairs, San Diego State University, 1979. A guidebook to the major research sources and retrieval tools for public administration and public affairs information. Includes evaluation of basic texts and readers. Beginning researchers and practitioners will profit from its perusal.   JF 1351 .R63

Handbook of Public Administration. James L. Perry, ed. San Francisco: Jossey-Bass, 1989. A remarkably solid compendium, published in cooperation with the American Society for Public Administration, that covers the waterfront of the field and more. Forty-nine original chapters written by some of the leaders of the profession are "designed to meet the needs of the range of the professionals who work in government or who interact with public agencies."   JF 1351 .H276

Public Administration: A Bibliographic Guide to the Literature. Howard E. McCurdy. New York: Marcel Dekker, 1986. Some 1,200 books and articles are listed and annotated in thirty-three categories, focusing on the 181 most frequently cited books in the field. Essays on the evolution of public administration as both a scholarly field and a profession are included. The book is an update of the 1973 edition.   JF 1351 .M23

Public Administration Dictionary. Ralph Chandler and Jack C. Plano. New York: John Wiley, 1982. Terms are alphabetized within seven chapter headings, but the index gives a term's location. In addition to a definitional interpretation the authors include a section explaining the "significance" of the term.   JA 61 .C47

Public Administration in American Society: A Guide to Information Sources. John E. Rouse, Jr. Detroit, Mich.: Gale Research, 1980. The 1,700 annotated entries cover the literature of public administration, "a professional discipline with no fixed principles, ideology, or methodology." Author, title and subject index. Appendices describe the American Society for Public Administration and National Association of Schools of Public Affairs and Administration.   JK 421 .R63

Public Administration Series: Bibliography. Monticello, Ill.: Vance Bibliographies, 1978–. Bibliographies vary in length and quality. Cover a wide range of topics related to public affairs, local to international. Treatment may be empirical, theoretical, or practical.   JT 1351 .A1 B38

Public Administration: The State of the Discipline. Naomi B. Lynn and Aaron Wildavsky, eds. Chatham, N. J.: Chatham House, 1990. Jointly sponsored by the American Society for Public Administration and the American Political Science Association, this collection of twenty original chapters covers the academic side of public administration's house. Among the topics covered are organization theory and behavior, comparative public administration, intergovernmental administration, budgeting, human resource management, public policy, methodology, and implementation. A welcome addition to the literature.   JF 1351 .P8185

Public Affairs Service Bulletin. New York: Public Affairs Service, 1915–. This index, with annual cumulations, unifies a wide variety of sources concerned with public affairs. It lists books, pamphlets, periodicals, and government documents. Most articles include brief explanatory items.   Z 7163 .P9761B

Public Policy: A Yearbook of the Graduate School of Public Administration, Harvard University. Cambridge, Mass.: Harvard University Press, 1940–. Each volume contains several essays on various subjects, emphasizing public administration.   JA 51 .P8

Recent Publications on Government Problems. Chicago: Merriam Center Library, 1932–. Semimonthly. Lists and briefly annotates new acquisitions received by the pioneer Merriam Center Library, a resource center jointly sponsored by such public administration organizations as the American Planning Association, the American Public Works Association, the Public Administration Service, and the Council of Planning Libraries. Entries are arranged by subject. Good current awareness tool with an emphasis on local and regional issues. Selective indexing of journal articles. Annual cumulation by subject.   Z 1223 .Z7C4

Sage Public Administration Abstracts. Beverly Hills, Calif.: Sage, 1974–. A quarterly publication that lists and abstracts more than 1,000 publications in the field annually. Abstracts are indexed by author, title, and subject, and a year-end cumulative index is published.   JA 1 .S27

B. Public Budgeting and Finance

Budget in Brief, U.S. Washington, D.C.: Executive Office of the President, Office of Management and Budget. Abridged explanation of the budget. Describes federal budget plans in all major policy areas.   PR Ex 2.8/2

Budget of the U.S. Government. Washington, D.C.: Executive Office of the President, Office of Management and Budget. Presentation of the president's budget proposals and how they were formulated. Includes president's budget message, and general assumptions about the economy; analysis of the U.S. budget system; budget breakdowns by function (national defense, education, health, etc.). Lists the amount each agency receives.   PR Ex 2.8

Budget of the U.S. Government, Appendix. Washington, D.C.: Executive Office of the President, Office of Management and Budget. Most precise and detailed of all budget documents. Contains the specific language of every proposal for each agency, as well as the functions the agency performs. Also lists permanent positions in each agency by number and federal grade level.   PR Ex 2.8: Appendix

Budget of the U.S. Government, Special Analysis. Washington, D.C.: Executive Office of the President, Office of Management and Budget. Analyses of specific programs financed from the budget. Gives financial information on employment, health, income security, civil rights, crime reduction programs, research and development, environmental protection, and other aspects of the economy.   PR Ex 2.8/3

Budget Revisions (by fiscal year). Washington, D.C.: Executive Office of the President, Office of Management and Budget. Summary of the administration's revisions to the budget.   PR Ex 2.8/7

Catalog and Quick Index to Taxpayer Information Publications. Washington, D.C.: U.S. Department of the Treasury, Internal Revenue Service. Provides a reference to taxpayer information publications. Part 1 gives a list of taxpayer information publications; Part 2 provides an index to the subjects discussed in each publication; and Part 3 is a list of forms and schedules and the publications in which they are illustrated.   T 22 .44/3

Economic Report of the President. Washington, D.C.: U.S. Government Printing Office. Annual. President's report for the past fiscal year. Review of personal consumption, business fixed investment, housing, exports, wages, corporate profitability, monetary policy, energy and agricultural developments. Also gives information on world economy.

PR 33 .10

Facts and Figures on Government Finance. Washington, D.C.: Tax Foundation. 1941–. Biennial. Information about taxes, expenditures, and debt at federal, state, and local levels. Statistics also cover selected national economic series, social insurance programs, and government enterprise operations. Glossary and Index.

HJ 257 .T25

Terms Used in the Budgetary Process. Washington, D.C.: U.S. General Accounting Office, 1977. Glossary divided into three sections: a compilation of general terms; terms applicable to Zero-Based Budgeting; and economic terms used in connection with the budget. Arranged alphabetically within each section.

GA 1.2 B85/2

C. Public Personnel Administration and Human Resource Management

Directory of National Unions and Employee Associations, 1979. Washington, D.C.: U.S. Department of Labor, 1980. Comprehensive listing of unions, including information on structure and membership. Indexed.

L 2.3 2079

Human Resources Abstracts. Beverly Hills, Calif.: Sage, 1966–. Quarterly. (Previous title: *Poverty and Human Resources Abstracts.*) Information on human, social, and manpower problems and solutions, as they relate to public policy, is arranged by broad topic, with author and subject indexes. Cumulative index for each year. Includes books, reports, periodicals and government documents.

Z 7165 .U5P2 — Z 7164 .C4P115

Human Resources Yearbook. Craig T. Norback, ed., Englewood Cliffs, N.J.: Prentice-Hall. Annual. A yearly compendium of all aspects of personnel administration, both public and private.

HF 5549.2 .U5H85

Labor-Management Relations in the Public Sector: An Annotated Bibliography. N. Joseph Cayer and Sherry Dickerson. New York: Garland, 1983. Topical arrangement of scholarly articles, monographs, and books published since 1962 that deal with public sector relations. Appendices list organizations and journals publishing articles in this area.

HD 8005 .6.U5

Michigan Index to Labor Union Periodicals. Ann Arbor, Mich.: Bureau of Industrial Relations, Graduate School of Business Administration, University of Michigan, 1960–. Covers about 50 publications, issued monthly with annual cumulations.

Z 7164 .T7U6

Personnel Bibliography Series. U.S. Office of Personnel Management Library. Washington, D.C.: U.S. Government Printing Office, 1970–. A comprehensive annotated listing of books and articles on themes of relevance to public personnel administration. Each issue concerns a particular theme, such as "Scientists and Engineers in the Federal Government," or "Managing Human Behavior." Although the series began earlier, only titles beginning in 1970 are presently available.

PM 1 .22/2

Personnel Literature. U.S. Office of Personnel Management Library. Washington, D.C.: U.S. Government Printing Office, 1969–. A monthly annotated listing of a wide range of public personnel materials.

HF 5549 .A3 — Z7164 .C81U456 83

D. Community Planning

Geo Abstracts Regional and Community Planning. Norwich, England: Geo Abstracts, 1972–. Six issues per year. Subject arrangement of articles on planning theory and methodology, as well as economic, environmental, and social planning. Annual cumulative index in last issue is arranged by region and by author.

HT 390 .G4

Housing and Planning References. Washington, D.C.: U.S. Department of Housing and Urban Development, 1962–. Six times a year. Good coverage of the subject, including both U.S. government and nongovernment sources, periodicals and monographs. Major disadvantage is that it does not cumulate, although each issue is arranged by subject.

HH 1 .23/3

International Handbook on Land Use Planning. Nicholas N. Patricios, ed., Westport, Conn.: Greenwood Press, 1986. The first comprehensive treatment of land use planning techniques used around the globe.

HD 108 .6158

Land Use Planning Abstracts: A Select Guide to Land and Water Resources. New York: EIC Intelligence, 1974–. Annual. Abstracts key land use articles, conference proceedings, governmental reports, and special studies. Covers power plant siting, strip mining, transportation controls, and Western water problems. Also includes annual review of events in these fields and a statistical section with maps and graphs. Subject, geography, and author index.

HD 171 .A1L35

E. Education, Internships, and Jobs

Complete Guide to Public Employment. Ronald S. Krannich and Caryl Rae Krannich. Manassas, Va.: Impact, 1986. Projects employment prospects in the public sector, explains effective job search skills, details how to approach government in exploring job opportunities, and has special sections on "third sector" and international job opportunities.

JU 716 .U68

Directory of Graduate Programs in Public Affairs and Administration. Washington, D.C.: National Association of Schools of Public Affairs and Administration, 1972–. Published biennially, the *Directory* is a rich information resource on graduate programs in public administration in the United States and Canada.   JF 1338 .A2N28a

Directory of Public Service Internships: Opportunities for the Graduate, Post-Graduate, and Mid-Career Professional. Debra L. Mann, ed. Washington, D.C.: National Society for Internships and Experimental Education, 1981. Entries for programs throughout the United States include the name, address, phone numbers, contact person, administering agency, number of interns accepted, program objectives and design, eligibility, selection, and remuneration. Lists programs in federal, state, and local government, public policy and urban affairs.   JK 2480 .16N37 1981

Internships: 16,000 On-the-Job Training Opportunities for all Types of Careers. Cincinnati, Ohio: Writer's Digest Books, 1983. Views internship as experiential education and offers advice on applications. Subject breakdown includes Public Interest/Public Service Groups and Government/Public Administration.   L 901 .166 1983

The Student Guide to Fellowships and Internships. New York: E.P. Dutton, 1980. Written by students of Amherst College, this guide presents advice on applying for internships, including sample resumes. Each subject area opens with a general introduction followed by a listing of specific programs, with "The Inside Word" section giving inside advice.   LB 2338 .S843

II. RELATED TOPICS: POLITICAL SCIENCE, MANAGEMENT, LAW, AND STATISTICS

Political science and public policy, management and business administration, law and justice, and general statistical and databases are all highly pertinent to an understanding of public administration. This section covers information sources in these areas. Some statistical and data sources are listed under other headings that are directly applicable to them.

Contents of Section II

A. Political Science and Public Policy
B. Management and Business Administration
C. Law and Justice
D. General Statistical and Data Sources

A. Political Science and Public Policy

ABC-POL SCI: A Bibliography of Contents: Political Science and Government. Santa Barbara, Calif.: American Bibliographical Center, Clio Press, 1969–. Five issues per year. Students may use this title to keep up with the latest articles in political science, government, and public policy. It reproduces the tables of contents from about 300 journals, with indexes for authors and subjects. Index cumulates.   Z 674.5 .A45B45

Almanac of American Politics. Michael Baron. New York: E.P. Dutton, 1979–. Annual. Provides political information by state on governors, senators, representatives; district information (population, voter profile, economic base, tax burden); and political group ratings of representatives and senators.   JK 271 .A45 Year

American Political Dictionary. 6th ed. Jack C. Plano and Milton Greenberg. New York: Holt, Rinehart & Winston, 1982. Unlike an A to Z dictionary, words are alphabetical under fourteen chapter headings. Useful will be "Public Administration: Organization and Personnel" and "State and Local Government." In addition to definition, authors explain significance of terms.   JK 9 .P55 1982

American Politics Yearbook. Jarol B. Manheim. New York: Longmans, 1982–. Chapter 4 notes policy planning organizations and Part Three lists alphabetically "Policies and Issues," with citations to articles in the *New York Times*; departments, agencies, and interest groups involved; search terms for finding the subject in basic indexes and bibliographic references.   JK 1 .A49

Combined Retrospective Index to Journals in Political Science, 1866–1974. Arlington, Va.: Carrollton Press, 1978. Provides retrospective bibliographic access to many journals never previously covered. Supplies in one search citations that formerly would have required searching many different indexes, volume by volume. Entries in hierarchical subject arrangement under keywords. Chronological arrangement within categories. Author index in volume VII and VIII. Take time to locate pertinent categories using the listing at the front of the volume (*e.g.*, V. 3 "Public Administration"). Journal titles are entered by code numbers. Code list is at front and back of the volume.   Z 7161 .C18

Energy Abstracts for Policy Analysis. Oak Ridge, Tenn.: U.S. Department of Energy, Technical Information Center, 1975–. Monthly. *EAPA* abstracts and indexes for nontechnical literature contributing to energy-related analysis and evaluation. Publications covered are government reports, regional and state government documents, books, conference proceedings, periodicals, and papers. Abstracts are arranged by broad subject area. Corporate author, personal author, subject, and report number indexes are cumulated annually.   E 1 .11

Guide to Resources and Services. Ann Arbor, Mich.: Inter-University Consortium for Political and Social Research. Annual. Cooperative repository for survey, election, census, and roll call data. Information supplied to member units on magnetic tape. Guide notes holdings in "Community and Urban Studies," "Governmental Structures, Policies, and Capabilities," and "Legislative and Deliberative Bodies." — H 62 .A1158

International Bibliography of the Social Sciences: Political Science. London: Tavistock, 1952–. Annual. An extensive bibliography covering 5,000 books, journals, and national and international documents. One section is devoted to "Government and Public Administration." Published by the International Committee for Social Science Information and Documentation. Subject and author indexes. — Z 7164 .E2158

International Political Science Abstracts. Paris: International Science Association. 1951–. Bimonthly. Abstracts the leading U.S. and foreign scholarly journals, although not all articles in each journal are abstracted. Probably the best starting point for literature searches in the field of foreign and comparative government and political theory. Abstracts are in English for English language articles; foreign language publications are abstracted in French. Index, cumulated annually, is in English by subject and by author. — JA 36 .15

Lexicon of Historical and Political Terms. Robert R. Davis, Jr. Palo Alto, Calif.: R and E Research Associates, 1982. A brief guide intended to introduce the undergraduate to the terminology used by historians and political scientists. — JA 61 .D36 1982

Perspective: Monthly Reviews of New Books on Government/ Politics/International Affairs. Washington, D.C.: Perspective, 1972–. Eight times per year. Reviews in this publication are substantive and signed. The scope is international. Annual index for previous year appears in January/February issue of following year. — JA 1 .P47

Political Science Abstracts. (Formerly, *Universal Reference System.*) New York: IFI Plenum, 1966–. Annual supplements since 1967 update the base set of ten volumes. Volumes are organized around broad subjects (*i.e.*, volume IV covers "Administrative Management: Public and Private Bureaucracy"; volume IX, "Public Policy and the Management of Science.") Valuable because entries include not only books, pamphlets, and periodical articles, but chapters of books as well. A challenge to use because of its complicated arrangement and indexing system, but extremely worthwhile. — Z 7161 .U643

Statesman's Yearbook: Statistical and Historical Annual of the States of the World. New York: St. Martin's Press, 1864–. Annual. Published continuously for more than 120 years, the *Yearbook* covers international organizations and countries, A to Z. History; area and population; government and — JA 51 .S7

constitution; defense, international relations; economy; energy and natural resources; industry and trade; communications; justice, religion, education, and welfare; diplomatic representatives and books of reference are narrated for each country. Great for comparative studies.

United States Political Science Documents. Pittsburgh, Pa.: NASA Industrial Applications Center, University of Pittsburgh, 1975–. Annual. Detailed abstracts and indexing from selected major American journals publishing scholarly articles in the broad area of political science. Coverage includes public administration, political and policy sciences. Published annually in two volumes, indexes are available for author/contributor, subject, geographical area, proper name, and journal. Journal index valuable for comparisons of annual output among journals in like fields. *Political Science Thesaurus II* (Z 695.1.P63B4 1979) serves as terminology control volume for *USPSD*. — Z 7163 .U58H9

World Encyclopedia of Political Systems and Parties. George E. Delury, ed. New York: Facts on File, 1983. An A to Z study of 169 sovereign nations and eight dependent territories. Each entry discusses the system of government, including executive, legislative, judicial, and local; the political parties and political forces and each nation's prospects for continuing or attaining political stability through the mid-1980s. For addresses, phone numbers, and forms of addresses for country officials consult *Lambert's Worldwide Government Directory with Inter-Governmental Organizations.* (JF 37.L34 1983). — JF 2011 .D44 1983

B. Management and Business Administration

Business Periodicals Index. Bronx, N.Y.: H.W. Wilson, 1958–. Monthly except August. Subject index to business periodicals. Includes a book review index under author name. Quarterly and annual cumulations. Good for management, personnel, budget and finance. Easy to use with its A to Z entries. — Z 7193 .A66

Encyclopedia of Management. 3rd ed. Carl Heyel, ed. New York: Van Nostrand Reinhold, 1982. Theories noted in this volume transpose effectively into public sector administration. Definitions are followed by listings of associations, journals, cross references, and information sources. There are 203 authorities contributing to this 1,371 page volume. Indexed. — HD 30.15 .E49 1982

International Review of Administrative Science (*Revue Internationale des Sciences Administratives*). Brussels: Institut Internationale des Sciences Administratives, 1928–. Each quarterly issue has a "Bibliographical Section," which contains abstracts of recent books on administration, plus a list of periodical articles. — JA 26 .158

Management Contents. Northbrook, Ill.: Management Contents, 1975–. Biweekly. Tables of contents of over 350 business-management journals stressing decision making and forecasting.
Z 7164 .O7M283 4

Management Research. Amherst, Mass.: University of Massachusetts School of Business Administration, 1968–. Monthly. An annotated bibliography of considerable use, covering periodical articles dealing with administration, organization, social responsibilities, personnel policy, personnel testing and selection, motivation and performance, human behavior, human resources development, etc. Also contains a list of new books and editorial notes about periodical publications.
HD 28 .M397

C. Law and Justice

Basic Documents in International Law. 3rd ed. Ian Brownlee, ed. New York: Oxford University Press, 1983. Emphasizes documents of significance in international relations. Includes charters of organizations, laws of the sea, outer space, diplomatic relations, natural resources, human rights, self-determination, treaties, and judicial settlement of disputes.
JX 68 .B78 1983

Black's Law Dictionary. 5th ed. Minneapolis, Minn.: West, 1979. The latest edition of this classic in the field reflects new legal concepts and doctrines while retaining old English, European, and federal terms. Pronunciation guides have been added, as have a U.S. government organizational chart, the U.S. Constitution, and a listing of U.S. Supreme Court Justices and terms.
KF 156 .B53 1979

CIS/Annual: Abstracts of Congressional Publications and Legislative History Citations. Washington, D.C.: Congressional Information Service, 1970–. Monthly. In the *Abstract* volume, the section "Legislative History Citations" is arranged by Public Law number. Besides noting the hearings and committee prints, the entry reveals references appearing in *The Weekly Compilation of Presidential Documents.* (GS 4.114).
KF 49 .C62

Code of Federal Regulations. Agency regulations which have the force of law are arranged by subject in separate volumes (titles), each with its own index. A multi-volume extensive index is available, see KF 70.A3415x.
GS 4 .108

Congressional Bills and Resolutions. The U.S. Government Printing Office now issues current bills on microfiche with a *Cumulative Finding Aid* (GP 3.28:Congress #), which indicates, by bill number, the microfiche and grid location where the bill may be found.
Y 1.4 #

Congressional Hearings. Since 1970, Congressional hearings are available as part of the CIS Microfiche Collection, accessed through the *CIS Index.* Paper copies of pre-70 hearings are accessed
KF 40 .C56

through the *Monthly Catalog of U.S. Government Publications. CIS U.S. Congressional Committee Hearings Index* (KF 49.C6225x) is in publication and now available for the 79th through 91st Congresses.

Congressional Index. Chicago, Ill.: Commerce Clearing House, 1953/54–. Looseleaf; updated service indexes legislation by subject, author, and bill number. Includes summaries, statutes, and voting records.
J 69 .C6

Directory of Criminal Justice Information Sources. Thomas Ketterman. Washington, D.C.: U.S. Department of Justice, National Institute of Law Enforcement and Criminal Justice. Lists agencies that provide information on criminal justice, including telephone numbers, directors or head, and information on area of activity.
J 26 .2In3

Federal Register. Agency regulations, proposed and adopted, first appear in the *Federal Register,* published daily Monday through Friday, with monthly, quarterly, and annual indexes.
GS 4 .170

Finding the Law: A Workbook on Legal Research for Laypersons. Al Coco. Bureau of Land Management. Washington, D.C.: U.S. Government Printing Office, 1982. Prepared by a law librarian, who also teaches law librarianship, at the University of Denver. Excellent workbook on federal law with illustrations, definitions, and resource citations.
L 41 .153:2

Index to Legal Periodicals. Bronx, N.Y.: H.W. Wilson, 1908–. Monthly. Subject and author and book review indexes are accompanied by a table of cases. Urban headings: public finance, documents and records, public officials and employees, etc. Annual cumulations.
K .1213

Law and Legal Information Directory. Paul Wasserman and Marech Kaszubski, eds. Detroit, Mich.: Gale Research, 1980. Guides user to sources of information including organizations, associations, schools, libraries, research centers, periodicals, and publishers.
KF 190 .L35

Legal Thesaurus. Burton, William C. New York: Macmillan, 1980. Establishes nuances among terms and allows the writer to vary word usage. The index refers users to entry under which index terms appear.
KF 156 .B856

Major Legislation of the Congress. Washington, D.C.: U.S. Government Printing Office, 1979–. Monthly during sessions. Classified subject arrangement. Discusses issues surrounding major legislation under consideration. Summary issue published at end of each Congress.
LC 14 .18 Congress #

Shepard's Acts and Cases by Popular Name, Federal and State. Colorado Springs, Colo.: Shepard's, 1979–. Cases are listed alphabetically by popular name. Covers cases to October 1979. Cites sources in which act can be found. Updates by pamphlets.
KF 80 .S5 1979

Shepard's Code of Federal Regulations Citations. Colorado Springs, Colo.: Shepard's McGraw-Hill, 1981. The first edition follows the format of other Shepard's citations, noting citations to the other CFR (by title number); Presidential Proclamations and Executive Orders (by numbers); and Reorganization Plans (by years), then listing source of citation. Pamphlet updates.
KF 78 .S54

Shepard's United States Citations, Statutes. 6th ed. Colorado Springs, Colo.: Shepard's Citations, 1968. The statute edition of Supreme Court coverage involves tracing subsequent action on a specific law and judicial action construing that legislation. Helps determine the applicability of statutes and cases for use in specific situations. Supplement covers 1968–1974. Pamphlet updates.
KF 78 .S56

Sourcebook of Criminal Justice Statistics. U.S. Department of Justice, Bureau of Justice Statistics. Washington, D.C.: U.S. Government Printing Office, 1972–. Issued annually since 1972, the Sourcebook describes the criminal justice systems, traces public attitudes on crime, record crime rates, and analyzes arrestees, defendants, prisoners, and parolees.
J 29.9 SD-SB

Sources of Compiled Legislative Histories. Nancy P. Johnson. Littleton, Colo.: Rothman, 1979. Guides student to sources for study of legislative history of specific public laws. Sources may be government documents, periodical articles, or books. Covers 1st through 94th Congress; does not include all public laws enacted. Looseleaf format.
KF 42 .2 1979

Statutes-at-Large of the United States of America. Published at the end of each session of Congress since 1789, the volumes include public laws, reorganization plans, private laws, congressional resolutions and proclamations. Often the sole source of text of private and temporary legislation not included in statutory compilations. Organized by date of enactment of law. Indexed.
GS 4 .111

Subject Compilation of State Laws: Research Guide and Annotated Bibliography. Lynn Foster and Carol Boast. Westport, Conn.: Greenwood Press, 1981. Facilitates comparative studies of state laws by subject areas. Includes indexes.
KF 1 .F67

United States Code. These sixteen basic volumes plus annual supplements are arranged by subject laws that are currently in effect. Table translates *Statutes-at-Large* numbers to *U.S. Code* entries.
Y 1 .2/5

United States Reports. Bound volumes are issued for each court term and include full text of all decisions. Prior to issue of bound volume, opinions appear in pamphlet form as they are released.
JU 6 .8

D. Statistical and Data Sources

American Statistics Index. Washington, D.C.: Congressional Information Service, 1974–. Monthly. Guide and index to the statistical publi-
Z 7554 .U5A46

cations of the U.S. government. The index is by subject, geographic area, and category (*i.e.*, statistics by race, sex, and geographic area). Publications in the abstract sections are analyzed in detail with references to page and table numbers. This is a major and unique index in the field of statistics and one that should be consulted. Will prove useful in subject searches, since narrative publications that contain statistics are included. Annual and five year cumulations.
Z 7554 .U5A512

Bureau of the Census Catalog. Washington, D.C.: U.S. Bureau of the Census. Annual. Guides user to the wealth of publications resulting from Census activities. Data covers population, housing, governments, transportation, etc. Includes data products produced by the reformatting of Census statistics.
C 3 .163/3 Year

Regional Statistics: A Guide to Information Sources. M. Balanchandrian. Detroit, Mich.: Gale Research, 1980. Identifies by subject the sources of socioeconomic data for small areas. Includes publications of federal, state, chamber of commerce, and utility company offices.
HA 217 .B34 —— Z7554 .U5D34

Statistical Abstract of the United States. U.S. Bureau of the Census. Washington, D.C.: U.S. Government Printing Office. Annual. Statistical compilations from federal agencies are presented. Notation of information source leads researchers to additional information. The best single source for national data on every topic.
HA 202 .A388 —— C3 .134

Statistical Reference Index. Washington, D.C.: Congressional Information Service, 1980–. Monthly. Companion to *ASI*, this resource indexes statistics published by sources other than the federal government, such as publications from trade, professional, and nonprofit associations and institutions; business organizations; commercial publishers; independent research centers; state government agencies and university research centers. *SRI* covers business, industry, finance, economic and social conditions, government and politics, the environment, and population. Includes data on foreign countries. Issued in index and abstracts sections. Indexes are cumulated annually. Indexing is by subject and names, categories (geographic, economic, and demographic), issuing sources, and titles.
HA 214 .S8 —— Z 7554 .U557

Statistics Sources: A Subject Guide to Data on Industrial, Business, Social, Educational, Financial, and Other Topics for the United States and Internationally. 9th ed. Detroit, Mich.: Gale Research, 1984. Alphabetical subject approach for U.S.; information for other countries is under country name and subtopics. Entries appear under headings such as cities, SMSAs, and government.
HA 36 .S84 1984 —— Z7551 .S84 1984

World Handbook of Political and Social Indicators. 3rd ed. Charles Lewis Taylor and Davis A. Jodice. New Haven, Conn.: Yale University Press, 1983. 2 v. The authors quantitatively assess nation-
HN 25 .T39 1983

states for "Cross National Attributes and Rates of Change" (v. 1), and "Political Protest and Government Change" (v. 2). Useful data for the comparative researcher.

III. AMERICAN GOVERNMENT: FEDERAL, STATE, AND LOCAL

Section III covers information sources for the federal government, state governments, and local governments, including urban affairs. Federal budget resources are covered under Section I A of this appendix.

Contents of Section III

A. Federal Government
B. State Government
C. Local Government and Urban Affairs

A. Federal Government

Catalog of Federal Domestic Assistance. Washington, D.C.: Executive Office of the President, Office of Management and Budget, 1980. Compendium of federal programs that provide financial assistance to state and local governments, for-profit and nonprofit organizations, and individuals. Lists eligibility requirements, amount of money available, application procedures, and related programs. PR Ex2 .20

CIS/Annual: Index to Congressional Publications and Public Laws. Washington, D.C.: Congressional Information Service, 1970–. Monthly. Indexes by subject, personal name, and agency, all congressional publications (*i.e.*, House and Senate reports, documents, hearings, and committee prints). Abstract section actually analyzes the *contents* of the documents, giving page numbers for pertinent sections. May be used to some extent as an index to the documents themselves. Annual cumulative index and abstract volumes. K 49 .C62

Congressional Directory. Washington, D.C.: U.S. Government Printing Office. Gives brief biographies of each member of Congress, terms of service, committee assignments. Includes statistical tables on sessions of Congress and election results of recent congressional elections. Y 4 .P93/1

Congressional Quarterly Weekly Report. Washington, D.C.: Congressional Quarterly, 1971–. Current awareness tool provides narrative background for intent of legislation. Summaries of bills and voting records. *Congressional Quarterly Almanac* (JK 8.C66) cumulates same information on an annual basis. Includes special reports and presidential messages. JK 1 .C15

Congressional Record. Washington, D.C.: U.S. Government Printing Office. Daily during sessions. The fortnightly index that accompanies the daily record of congressional debates; includes an "Index to Proceedings" and a "History of Bills and Resolutions." Access is by subject, sponsor, and bill number. The final bound issue, published at the end of a session, includes a comprehensive status table for bills enacted into law. X/ Congress/ Session

Congressional Staff Directory. Charles B. Brownson. Washington, D.C.: Congressional Staff Directory, 1980. Contains information concerning Congress, with emphasis on the staffs of legislators and members of the committees and subcommittees. JK 1012 .C74

Directory of Federal Regional Structure. Washington, D.C.: National Archives of the United States, 1980. Provides a map showing the Standard Federal Regions and lists the key officials, addresses, and telephone numbers of the agencies. GS 4 .119 Year

Encyclopedia of Governmental Advisory Organizations. 5th ed., Linda E. Sullivan and Anthony T. Kruzas, eds. Detroit, Mich.: Gale Research, 1985. Guide to public advisory committees, boards, panels, task forces, commissions, etc. Grouped by subject, with subject and key word index. Each entry has information on history of the committee, membership, program, publications, and reports. JK 901 .E5

Federal Information Sources and Systems. A Directory Issued by the Comptroller General. Washington, D.C.: General Accounting Office, 1981. Directory of executive agencies with sources of fiscal, budgetary, and program-related data and information. GA 1 .22 IN 3/980

Federal Yellow Book. Teri Calabrese, ed. Washington, D.C.: Washington Monitor. Annual. Loose-leaf directory of federal departments and agencies; names, titles, room and telephone numbers of 25,000 principal federal employees. Updated throughout the year. JK 6 .F440

Government Periodicals and Subscription Service. Washington, D.C.: U.S. Government Printing Office. Alphabetical listing of government periodicals with prices. GP 3.9 36

Government Reports, Announcements and Index. Washington, D.C.: U.S. Department of Commerce, National Technical Information Service, 1964–. Biweekly. Indexes and abstracts government-sponsored research and development reports and other government analyses prepared by federal agencies, their contractors, or grantees. Indexes are by key word, personal author, corporate author, contract/grant number, NTIS order/report number. C 51 .9/3

Guide to U.S. Government Directories, 1970–1980. Donna Rae Larson. Phoenix, Ariz.: Oryx Press, 1981. A subject-indexed list of directories published by or for a government agency. J 83 .L37 —— Z 1223 .A12L37 1981

Guide to U.S. Government Directories, 1980–1984. Donna Rae Larson. Phoenix, Ariz.: Oryx Press, 1984. A subject-indexed list of directories published by or for a government agency.

J 83
.L37
—
Z 1223
.A12L37
1984

Historic Documents of (YEAR). Washington, D.C.: Congressional Quarterly, 1972–. Full text or pertinent excerpts of documents are preceded by background information, and, on occasion, relevant subsequent developments. Chronological by month, entries highlight development of policy from issues.

E
839.5
.H57

Index to U.S. Government Periodicals. Chicago, Ill.: Infordata International, 1970–. Quarterly. Indexes substantive articles of lasting research and reference value that have appeared in the major periodicals published by the U.S. government. Annual cumulations.

Z
1223
.Z915

Monthly Catalog of United States Government Publications. Washington, D.C.: U.S. Government Printing Office, 1895–. Monthly. Principal index for government documents. Lists all U.S. Government Printing Office publications by issuing agency, with monthly, cumulative semiannual and annual indexes. Multiple access points are available for recent years, authors, title, subject (Library of Congress subject headings), series/reports, stock number, and title keyword. *Cumulative Subject Index to the Monthly Catalog, 1895–1971* and *Cumulative Title Index to United States Public Documents, 1789–1976* make it possible to check quickly such entries for those years.

GP
3
.8

Official Congressional Directory. Washington, D.C.: U.S. Government Printing Office, 1898–. Annual. Contains biographical sketches of members of Congress, their addresses, party affiliation, terms of service, committee assignments, and names of administrative assistants. Also lists committee staff members; memberships of committees and boards; lists of principal administrative officers of executive departments and independent agencies; biographies of the President, Vice President, and Justices of the Supreme Court; lists of officials of international organizations, foreign diplomatic and consular officers in the U.S., U.S. officers abroad; and election statistics.

JK
1011
.U5
—
Y
4
:93/1
1
Congress/
Session
Year

United States Government Manual. Washington, D.C.: U.S. Government Printing Office. Annual. This annual "official handbook of the federal government" has descriptions of all government agencies, including a statement of purpose or authority for each, addresses, tables of organization, and lists of key officials. Similar information is provided for international organizations in which the United States participates.

JK
421
.A3
—
C
3
.134

U.S. Organization Chart Service. Washington, D.C.: U.S. Organization Chart Service, 1980. Personnel charts for U.S. government agencies as well as for the major contractors with the government.

HD
9711
.5.U6
.U5 vol.
1

Washington Information Directory. Mary M. Neumann, ed. Washington, D.C.: Congressional Quarterly. Lists top-level appointments in the government, all congressional assignments, plus revised and updated sources of information available in Washington. Agency and organization index, as well as subject index.

F
192
.3
.W33

B. State Government

Book of the States. Lexington, Ky.: Council of State Governments, 1935–. Biennial. Contains a mass of descriptive and statistical data concerning state governments, their organization, finances, programs and services, and intergovernmental relations. Elective and administrative officials of each state are listed in supplements.

JK
2403
.B6

Guide to State Legislative Materials. Mary L. Fisher. Littleton, Colo.: Fred B. Rothman, 1979. One-stop resource, noting for each state the availability of bills, hearings, debates, committee reports, legislative digests, journals and proceedings, slip laws, session laws, legislative reference services, bar association legislative recommendations, state attorney general opinions, executive orders, administrative regulations, legislative manuals, state law guides, and contact personnel.

KF
1
.G8

Monthly Checklist of State Publications. Library of Congress. Washington, D.C.: U.S. Government Printing Office, 1910–. Monthly. Published by the Library of Congress since 1910, the *Checklist* includes state publications arranged under state name, then by issuing agency. It includes only those items received from each state by the Library of Congress. Periodicals of state agencies are listed each year in the June issue and then cumulated in the December issue. The *Checklist* also includes publications of associations of state officials, regional organizations, library surveys, studies, manuals and statistical reports. There is an annual index arranged by subject.

LC
30
.9

National Directory of State Agencies. Arlington, Va.: Information Resource Press. Biennial. Includes listing of state agencies by both state and by function, giving names of individuals; full addresses and phone numbers for state services in all areas. *State Information Book* (JK 2443 .L84 1980) includes federal offices in each state.

JK
2443
.N37

State Government Research Checklist. Lexington, Ky.: The Council of State Governments, 1957–. Bimonthly. Accessions list of materials received by the States Information Center of the Council of State Governments. Concentration here is on research reports issued by legislative service agencies, state study commissions, the council itself, university bureaus of governmental research, and the Advisory Commission on Intergovernmental Relations.

Z
1223.5
.A1L51

C. Local Government and Urban Affairs

City Data: A Catalog of Data Sources for Small Cities. Stephen J. Carroll, et al. Santa Monica, Calif.: Rand Corp., 1980. More than 270 sources of data on the quality of life in small cities with a population of at least 2,500. Entries note source, contact, description, geographic coverage, frequency, years covered, caveats, form (machine readable, hard copy), availability, and comments. Q 180 .A1R416 R-2612- HUD

County and City Data Book. U.S. Bureau of the Census. Washington, D.C.: U.S. Government Printing Office. Quinquennial. The most convenient format for extracting statistics from the many different Census Bureau series, such as the Census of Government. Access by county, by SMSA, and by city for all places with a population over 25,000. Data comes from Census of population, manufacturing, retail trade, etc. Equally useful is the *State and Metropolitan Area Data Book.* (C 3.134/5:982) HA 202 .A36 C 3.134/ 2 C83 1982

County Year Book. Washington, D.C.: National Association of Counties, International City Management Association, 1975–78. Annual. A parallel publication to the familiar *Municipal Year Book.* Publication ceased in 1978. JS 301 .C67

Index to Current Urban Documents. Westpoint, Conn.: Greenwood Press, 1972–. Quarterly. Bibliographic guide to publications of over 280 of the larger U.S. cities, counties, and regions. Indexed by subject and geographic identity. Z7165 .U5I654 Z1223 .Z7I36

Metropolitan Area Annual. Albany, N.Y.: Graduate School of Public Affairs, State University of New York at Albany, 1966–. An annual reference volume with a section entitled "Metropolitan Area Bibliography," which lists recent books, articles, and pamphlets, plus a "Metropolitan Surveys" section listing studies in progress or recently completed on metropolitan problems. HT 334 .U5M56

Metropolitan Area Problems: News and Digest. New York: Conference on Metropolitan Area Problems, 1957–. Each bimonthly issue has a section entitled "Recent Publications on Metropolitan Area Problems," which contains a selective listing of books and articles. HT 101 .M47

Municipal Year Book. Washington, D.C.: International City Management Association, 1935–. Annual survey of detailed data for local governments in United States and Canada. Narrative sections discuss trends and issues. Directory section notes organizations, administrators, and officials. "Sources of Information" section identifies books, reports, monographs, reference sources, and periodicals for major municipal departments. JS 342 .A2152

Periodical Literature on United States Cities. Compiled by Barbara Smith Shearer and Benjamin F. Shearer. Westport, Conn.: Greenwood Press, 1983. Lists 4,919 articles in widely available journals for cities with populations exceeding 100,000. Arrangement is by name of city. Among subjects covered are "Housing and Urban Development" and "Government and Politics." Subject and author indexes. HT 123 .S464 Z 5942 .S464 1983

Sage Urban Studies Abstracts. Beverly Hills, Calif.: Sage, 1973–. Quarterly. Indexes same type of publications as *Sage Public Administration Abstract* and is particularly good for planning and land use. The cumulative index is arranged by author and by subject. HT 51 .S24

Urban Affairs Abstracts. Washington, D.C.: National League of Cities, 1972–. Weekly. Covers up-to-date, relevant urban literature. Quarterly and annual cumulations have an author and a geographic index. HT 123 .U7

Urban Affairs Annual Reviews. Beverly Hills, Calif.: Sage, 1967–. A series of "annual reference volumes designed to present critical analyses" in various fields of urban studies. HT 108 .U7

Urban America: A Historical Bibliography. Neil L. Shumsky and Timothy Crimmins, eds. Santa Barbara, Calif.: ABC-Clio Press, 1983. More than 4,000 entries dealing with urban life were selected from *America: History and Life,* v. 11 through v. 17. Sections cover both historical and contemporary American urban life; Canadian urban life; American Indian urban settlements; and historiography, methodology, bibliography, and teaching. Author index and extensive subject index. HT 123 .U725 1983

Urban Studies: A Guide to Information Sources. Thomas P. Murphy. Detroit, Mich.: Gale Research, 1980. Charting social progress by means of indicators has become an integral part of urban policymaking and evaluation. The author lists entries tracing the history, types, problems, use, and future of urban indicators. HT 167 .M87

IV. MISCELLANEOUS USEFUL MATERIAL

Section IV lists miscellaneous information resources, concentrating on the social sciences, that are of particular utility to students of public administration.

American Behavioral Scientist. Beverly Hills, Calif.: Sage, 1957–. Each monthly issue contains an insertion section entitled "New Studies: A Guide to Recent Publications in the Social and Behavioral Sciences." This consists of brief abstracts of articles selected from over 300 journals, plus significant new books. HM 1 .A45

Bibliographic Index: A Cumulative Bibliography of Bibliographies. Bronx, N.Y.: H.W. Wilson, 1938–. Three times per year. Bound cumulation in December issue. Subject and author index to bibliographies with 50 or more citations. Bibliographies may be published separately or as sections within books, pamphlets, or periodicals. Easy to use. *(Z 1002 .B595)*

Changing Attitudes on Governments and Taxes. Advisory Commission on Intergovernmental Relations. Washington, D.C.: U.S. Government Printing Office. Annual. A very useful survey sponsored each year by the ACIR on public perceptions of governmental services, policies, and taxes. Each new issue replicates past surveys going back to 1972. *(Y3 .Ad 9 8:17 Year)*

Civil Rights Directory. Washington, D.C.: U.S. Commission on Civil Rights. List of agencies with civil rights responsibilities. Includes federal, state, and private organizations; research and women's organizations; and state and local commissions on the status of women. *(CR 1 .10:15-3)*

Current Contents: Social and Behavioral Sciences. Philadelphia, Pa.: Institute for Scientific Information, 1969–. Weekly. Reproduces the tables of contents of over 1,300 journals, worldwide. Includes sections on Demography, International Relations, Management Sciences, Planning and Development, Public Administration, Transportation, and Urban Affairs. Index in each issue is by key words in the title of the article. *(H 1 .C92)*

Directory of Directories. 2nd ed. James M. Ethridge, ed. Detroit, Mich.: Gale Research, 1983. Directories are listed under broad subject areas and indexed by title and subject. Biennial with supplements. Section on "Law and Government (Including Military)" is useful. "Public Affairs and Social Concerns" concentrates on social work; good for locating foundation directories. *(AY 2001 .D52 1983)*

Dissertation Abstracts International: A. The Humanities and Social Sciences; B. The Sciences and Engineering; C. European Abstracts. Ann Arbor, Mich.: University Microforms International, 1861–. Monthly. Cumulative indexes make it possible to check for all dissertations completed from 1861 to 1972; five-year cumulations and annuals supplement these. Dissertations owned by your library will be located in the card catalog, treated as monographs. Dissertations not owned by your library can be purchased on microfilm from University Microfilms or requested through Interlibrary Loan. *(AC 801 .D542/ .D544 —— Z 5055 .U49D57)*

Effective Research and Report Writing in Government. Judson Monroe. New York: McGraw-Hill, 1980. Extolls skills necessary for effective written communication in the public sector field. Also useful is *Research and Report Handbook: For Managers and Executives in Business, Industry, and Government* by Ruth Moyer (HF 5719.M69). *(JF 1525 .R46M65)*

Guide to Grants: Governmental and Nongovernmental. Donald Levitan. Washington, D.C.: Government Research, 1985. Designed for the grants seeker in virtually every area. *(AS 911 .A2L4x)*

International Encyclopedia of Sociology. 15 v. Michael Mann, ed. New York: Macmillan and The Free Press, 1984. This work supplements the old *Encyclopedia of the Social Sciences*, published in the early 1930s. A synthesis and summary of the "state of the art" in all the social sciences. Consisting of original articles contributed by leading social scientists, it covers the disciplines of Anthropology, Economics, Geography, History, Law, Political Science, Psychiatry, Psychology, Sociology, and Statistics. There are a number of articles on organization theory, administrative science, and one on public administration by Dwight Waldo. *(HM 17 .I153 1984)*

Journal of Economic Abstracts. Chicago: American Economic Association, 1963–. A quarterly journal containing lengthy abstracts of articles in the major economic periodicals, both English and foreign. Supplemented by a five-volume *Index of Economic Journals* (Homewood, Ill.: Irwin, 1961–1962), which indexes, but does not abstract, economic articles published from 1886 to 1963. *(HB 1 .J6)*

London Bibliography of the Social Sciences. London: London School of Economics, 1931–. Annual Supplements. A major bibliography in the broad field of social science. Listing is by subject. Strong in legislative and administrative reports and official publications. International in coverage with periodic cumulations. *(Z 7161 .L84)*

Masters Abstracts. Ann Arbor, Mich.: University Microfilms International, 1962–. Quarterly. Selectively lists master's theses from cooperating universities. "Political Science, Public Administration," and "Urban and Regional Planning" listings. Annual cumulative subject and author indexes. *(Z 5055 .U5A54)*

PAC Directory: A Complete Guide to Political Action Committees. Compiled by Marvin Weinberger and David U. Greevy. Cambridge, Mass.: Ballinger, 1982. In addition to listing Political Action Committees (PACs), the directory notes contributions, names, and Standard Industrial Classification of company sponsors, and it indexes of PAC support. *(JK 1991 .W44)*

Psychological Abstracts. Arlington, Va.: American Psychological Association, 1927–. Monthly. Classified arrangement. Monthly, with semiannual and annual cumulative author and subject indexes. Use *Thesaurus of Psychological Index Terms* to find subject headings and related terms. Index refers you to abstract number in a specific volume and year. Full citation includes titles in italics. Includes books, pre-1980 dissertations, reports, and periodical articles. Good for personnel and training issues, applied psychology. *(BF 1 .P65)*

Research Centers Directory. Detroit, Mich.: Gale Research, 1982. University-related and non-profit research organizations are described in terms of their governance, research activities and fields, and publications and services. Updated supplement, *New Research Centers* (AS 8.N4). [AS 8 .R4]

Selected Rand Abstracts. Santa Monica, Calif.: Rand Corp. 1963–. Irregular. The Rand Corporation publishes in such areas as decision making, policymaking, urban planning and services, and transportation. [AS 36 .R284 — A 180 .A1R18/ Rand #]

Social Science Citation Index. Philadelphia, Pa.: Institute for Scientific Information, 1969–. Quarterly. Appears three times per year with annual cumulations. Covers approximately 1,400 of the most frequently cited international journals in the social sciences *in toto* and another 3,100 selectively. [Z 7161 .S65]

Social Sciences Index. New York: H.W. Wilson, 1974–. Quarterly. (Previously titled, *Social Science and Humanities Index, 1965–73,* and *International Index to Periodicals, 1907–1965.*) Author and subject index with annual cumulations. Indexes journals of a scholarly nature, and it is easier to use than such indexes as *Psychological Abstracts* or *Sociological Abstracts.* [AI 3 .S62]

Sociological Abstracts. San Diego, Calif.: Sociological Abstract, 1952–. Five issues per year. Includes abstracts of books and articles from all the major sociological journals. Particularly useful for its coverage of the literature of political sociology, public opinion, bureaucracy, political interactions, economic development, and research methodology. Author and subject indexes cumulate annually. Additional cumulated indexes cover 1953–1962, 1963–1967, 1967–1970. [HM 1 S67]

State of Black America. Washington, D.C.: National Urban League. Annual. A particularly authoritative compendium on the yearly status of black Americans. [E 185.5 .N317]

Using Government Publications. 2 v. Jean L. Sears and Marilyn Moody. Phoenix, Ariz.: Oryx Press, 1985, 1986. Volume I provides guidelines by subject and agency; Volume II is more specialized, and concentrates on statistical and other techniques. [J 83 .S4x]

Work Related Abstracts. Detroit, Mich.: Information Coordinators, 1979–. Monthly. Succinct abstracts from over 250 management, labor, government, professional, and university periodicals. Articles concerning public affairs are found throughout the twenty broad subject divisions, such as "Personnel Management," "Socioeconomic and Political Issues," and "Government Policies and Actions." Looseleaf. [HD 4901 .W68 — Z 7164 .L1W68]

SELECTED ANNOTATED JOURNALS RELEVANT TO PUBLIC ADMINISTRATION

The following list identifies and describes journals that are particularly germane to public administration on a general level. That is, it encompasses such areas as public policy analysis, public personnel administration, budgeting, and so forth, but it does not delve deeply into those journals identified with fields of tangential relevance to public administration, such as political science, economics, and sociology.

There are a number of new journals bearing on public administration that, while worthwhile, are not well known. These have been included, as have foreign journals published in the English language.

Journals are listed alphabetically by title. Brief descriptions accompany each title. Library of Congress call numbers appear in the right-hand margins for your convenience.

Academy of Management Journal. A high-quality publication on general management with a mathematical and behavioral orientation. HD 28 .A24

Academy of Management Review. A more youthful version of *Academy of Management Journal*, and also of high quality. The *Review* has a thematically oriented book review section, while the *Journal* does not. HD 28 .A242x

Administration. Devoted to Irish administration, with an occasional article on Western European administration. JA 26 .A35

Administration and Society. Formerly the *Journal of Comparative Administration*, its contents no longer bear any resemblance to those of its predecessor. An excellent journal covering the broad spectrum of public administration. JA 3 .J65

Administrative Management. A quantitatively directed journal with a technical emphasis. Issued monthly. HF 5500 .A203

Administrative Science Quarterly. Perhaps the foremost journal in administrative theory and in organization theory of special relevance to public administration. HD 28 .A25

American City and County. Formerly *American City Magazine*, this is among the best periodicals in the field of planning and urban management. Articles are straightforward and practical. HT 101 .A5

American Journal of Public Health. Concerns policy and administration aspects of public health in the United States. RA 421 .A41

American Journal of Sociology. Publishes occasional articles relevant to public administration theory and public policy. Excellent book review section. HM 1 .A7

American Political Science Review. Occasional articles on public policymaking and the political JA 1 .A6

aspects of public organizations. Book reviews on boundary topics.

American Review of Public Administration. JK 1 Formerly *The Midwest Review of Public Adminis-* .M5 *tration,* this quarterly ranks among the best public administration journals in the field after *Public Administration Review.*

American Sociological Review. Has articles rel- HM 1 evant to administrative behavior, bureaucracy, or- .A75 ganization theory, and social issues. Quality book reviews.

Annals of Public Administration. Published an- JF 1351 nually since 1981, the *Annals* provide overview .P817 articles on a wide variety of topics related to public administration.

Annals of the American Academy of Political H 1 *and Social Science.* Each issue concentrates on a .A4 specific area in the social sciences, and produces an extensive book review and notes section covering the social sciences.

Baseline Data Report. Published bimonthly by JS 39 the International City Management Association, the .U72x periodical covers a wide array of municipal issues. Formerly was *Urban Service Data Report.*

Behavioral Science. Five to ten well docu- H 1 mented articles appear in this academic, largely .B44 theoretical journal on human behavior. Each issue contains a section on computer applications in the field.

Brookings Review. An informative, slim quar- H 1 terly that synopsizes in article form recent books and .B76 studies published by the Brookings Institution on matters of public policy. Formerly called *The Brookings Bulletin.*

Bureaucrat, The. Articles on public administra- JK 1 tion, usually on a theme for each issue. Regular .B86 features include a public policy forum, professional development articles, and a humor column.

Business and Society Review/Innovation. A HD 60.5 journal that absorbed *Innovation* and began publi- .U5 cation in 1972. Published quarterly, it addresses the B855 "role of business in a free society."

California Management Review. A high-qual- HD 28 ity journal in the style of *Harvard Business Review,* .C18 but more concerned with data.

Canadian Public Administration. Devoted to JL 1 Canadian public administration and comparative .C35 analysis.

Citizen Participation. A bimonthly newspaper JK 1 on activities involving citizen participation in policy .C58x formation at all levels of government.

City and State. Devoted exclusively to state and J81261 local public administration, this publication concen- .C4 trates on financial issues and is published as a newspaper. Very informative.

Current Municipal Problems. A quarterly jour- JS 39 nal dealing with policy and administrative issues at .C85 the local level.

Data Access News. Issued six to eight times a HA 37 year, this bulletin covers various statistical bureaus .U5C565 of the federal government.

Decision Sciences. The journal for the Ameri- HD can Institute for Decision Sciences, this quarterly 30.23 focuses on quantitative management techniques. .D4

Dialogue. A quarterly journal published by the JA Public Administration Theory Network that at- 1 tempts to express the cutting edge of theory in public D52 administration.

Economic Development and Cultural Change. HC 10 Concerns research findings in development. .C453

Evaluation Review. A journal on evaluation HM 1 research in the public sector. Formerly was *Evalu-* E8 *ation Quarterly.*

Evaluation Practice. Practical articles on public AZ 191 program evaluation. Formerly was *Evaluation News.* .E93x

Federal Labor Relations Reporter. Published KF 5365 since 1979, the *Reporter* follows developments in .F43 the public sector labor force.

Financial Accountability and Management. A HJ 9701 quarterly journal published in Britain since 1985, .F55x specializes in the financial management of governments, public services, charities, and "third sector" organizations.

Futures. An international journal of forecasting HB 3730 and planning. .F8

GAO Review. Published quarterly by the U.S. GA 1 General Accounting Office, this is a journal of high .I5 quality, it focuses on the whole spectrum of accountability in government.

Governing (The States and Localities). A new JK monthly magazine focusing on the management of 2403 state and local governments. Unusually well done G686 and increasingly popular.

Government Accountants Journal. Published HJ 9801 quarterly by the Association of Government Ac- .F4 countants, the *Journal* focuses on problems of accountancy at all levels of government.

Government Data Systems. A magazine pub- JK 468 lished bimonthly on all facets of electronic data .A8G65 processing as applied by public administrators at all levels of government.

Government Executive. Published monthly, JK 1 and billing itself as "government's business maga- .G58 zine," this publication focuses on management issues and agencies exclusively at the federal level.

Government Finance Review. A bimonthly HJ 9103 journal on municipal finance published by the Gov- .G68x ernment Finance Officers Association. It supersedes *Governmental Finance* (1972–1984), which in turn had superseded *Municipal Finance.*

Government Publications Review. An international guide to government information and bibliographic resources. — Z 7164 .G7 G71

Government Union Review. Published since 1979 by the Public Service Research Foundation, the review traces labor management relations at the federal, state, and local levels. — HD 8008 .A1 663

Grants Magazine. A journal for grants seekers and grant makers aimed towards those interested in sponsored research. — H 62 .A1G72

Harvard Business Review. Concerns a variety of administrative processes. An outstanding journal of quality. — HF 5001 .H3

HR Magazine. The "HR" stands for "human resources." Formerly *Personnel Administrator*, it is published by the Society for Human Resources Management. — HF5549 .A2P39

Human Organization. A journal of applied anthropology that focuses on problems of urban and modernizing societies. — GN 1 .H83

Human Relations. A behavioral journal of excellent quality, often dealing with organization theory. — H 1 .H8

Indian Administrative and Management Review. Devoted to administrative aspects of policy and development in India. — HD 28 .I42

Indian Journal of Public Administration. Relates to administration in India, comparative analysis, and development administration. — JQ 201 .I55

Industrial and Labor Relations Review. Devoted to industrial relations in both public and private sectors. Substantial book review section. — HD 4802 .I53

Intergovernmental Perspective. A quarterly magazine published by the Advisory Commission on Intergovernmental Relations; discusses the problems of federalism. One of the most informative journals on this topic available. — Y 3 .AD 9/8, 11

International Development Review. Published quarterly by the Society for International Development. Short articles devoted to development. Comprehensive book review section. — HC 60 .I546

International Journal of Government Auditing. A journal that covers all aspects of government accounting and auditing. — JA 1 .A1

International Journal of Public Administration. A quarterly journal with a comparative bent. — JA 1 .A11593

International Organization. Occasional articles on international administration. — JX 1901 .I55

International Review of Administrative Sciences. Devoted exclusively to comparative public administration and international administration. — JA 26 .I58

Journal of Administration Overseas. Concerned with development administration. — JS 40 .J6

Journal of African Administration. Deals with problems of public administration in Africa. — JQ 1881 .A1J6

Journal of Applied Behavioral Science. Devoted to applied behaviorism and organization development. — H 1 .J53

Journal of Collective Negotiations in the Public Sector. A quarterly publication designed to help public managers and employees understand each others' perspectives. — LB 2842.2 .J68

Journal of Criminal Justice. Published bimonthly, the *Journal* focuses on systemic issues of justice. — HV 7231 .J62

Journal of Criminal Law and Criminology. Devoted to policy and administration of law enforcement. — HV 6001 .J68

Journal of Management Studies. A Scottish journal that concerns applied behavioral theory. — HD 28 .J6

Journal of Organizational Behavior Management. A quarterly journal devoted to behavior management in business, government, and service organizations; quantitatively oriented. — HD 58.7 .J68

Journal of Police Science and Administration. Published quarterly by the International Association of Chiefs of Police. — HV 7935 .J6x

Journal of Policy Analysis and Management. Published quarterly by the Association for Public Policy Analysis and Management, the journal replaced the *Journal of Policy Analysis* and *Public Policy* in 1981. The journal tends to publish articles of a substantive rather than a methodological nature. — H 1 .J552x

Journal of Public Administration Research and Theory. A journal begun in 1991, *J-PART* is dedicated to tying research in the field to theory, and is published in affiliation with the Section on Public Administration Research of the American Society for Public Administration. — JA 1 .J65

Journal of Public Policy. A quarterly journal first published in England in 1981. The journal covers a wide range of policy issues from cutback management to government regulation. — H 1 .J65

Journal of State Government. Called simply *State Government* until 1986, *The Journal of State Government* is published quarterly by the National Conference of State Legislatures and the Council of State Governments; articles are generally good, and cover a wide range of state issues. — JK 2403 .S7

Journal of Taxation. A monthly magazine with a news orientation aimed at financial professionals. — HJ 2360 .J6

Journal of the American Institute of Planners. Devoted to public planning. — NA 9000 .A45

Journal of the American Planning Association. A quarterly publication devoted to land-use planning in the public sector. — HD 87.5 .A46a

Journal of Urban Planning and Development. Published aperiodically by the American Society of Civil Engineers, the focus is somewhat technical. NA 9000 .A5786

Management Information Service Report. A monthly publication of the International City Management Association, which deals with local government. The publication is practitioner oriented. JS 308 .M35x

Management: The Magazine for Government Managers. Formerly *The Civil Service Journal, Management* is published quarterly by the U.S. Office of Personnel Management. The publication focuses on public personnel administration. PM 1 .11/2

Management Review. A monthly publication, first put out by the American Management Association in 1914. Includes a survey of books for executives, critical reviews of between ten and twenty recent works, and a listing of recent publications received from publishers. T 58.A2 .M37

Management Science. Oriented to mathematics, systems, and the scientific method in administration. HD 28 .I453

Minerva. A philosophic journal devoted to the relationships among government, higher education, and science policy. AS 121 .M5

Monthly Digest of Tax Articles. A publication that does precisely what its title claims; the meaning of the complete article is well preserved in each synopsis. HJ 236D .N65

National Civic Review. Published every month except August by the National Municipal League, the *Review* provides short but informative articles on a wide variety of urban problems. JS 39 .N3

National Journal. Founded by a group of editors and reporters in 1970 who left *Congressional Quarterly* because they felt it did not pay enough attention to bureaucratic decision making. The *Journal* is published weekly and designed as a monitor of all government actions. It analyzes details surrounding such actions, focusing mainly on the relationships among the various agencies. It also contains in-depth reports on federal programs, biographical information on government officials, and analyses of congressional districts. JK 1 .N28

National Tax Journal. Published quarterly by the National Tax Association and the Tax Institute of America, the *Tax Journal* is the nation's foremost periodical on issues of government finance and taxation. HJ 2240 .N32x

New England Journal of Human Services. A quarterly journal that focuses on problems of social work and welfare. HV 1 .N45

New Zealand Journal of Public Administration. Devoted to New Zealand administration. JA .N12

Organizational Behavior and Human Performance. A high-quality journal focusing on interaction in small groups, conflict resolution, and the social psychology of organizations. BF 638 .A107

Organizational Dynamics. A quarterly review on organizational behavior written mostly by academics but aimed at professional managers, primarily in the private sector. Published by the American Management Association. HD 28 .O76

Personnel. Short articles on personnel; published monthly by the American Management Association. HF 5549 .A2P38

Personnel Management. A journal that concerns public personnel administration, often with a comparative orientation. HD 28 .I463

Personnel Manager's Legal Reporter. A monthly newsletter about legislation and court rulings affecting personnel managers in the public and private sectors. KF 3302 .P475

Philippine Journal of Public Administration. Devoted to Southeast Asian administration, comparative analysis, and development administration. JA 26 .P5

Policy Sciences. Concerns public policy theory and methodology. H 1 .P7

Policy Studies Journal. One of two journals published by the Policy Studies Organization on a quarterly basis. The *Journal* has a political science orientation. H 1 .P72

Policy Studies Review. Published jointly by the Morrison Institute for Public Policy at Arizona State University and the Policy Studies Organization, *Policy Studies Review* is an excellent journal in the field of public policy analysis, and it has a distinctly public administration flavor. H 97 .P66

Political Quarterly. Devoted to public policy issues and public administration in England. JA 8 .P72

Public Administration. Devoted to British administration and comparative analysis. Lists recent British government publications. JA 8 .P8

Public Administration. Devoted to Australian administration. JA 8 .N12

Public Administration in Israel and Abroad. Articles on Israeli administration and comparative administration. JQ 1825 .P3P8

Public Administration Newsletter. Published by the Public Administration Division of the United Nations, the newsletter contains occasional articles in field of development administration, but it is devoted principally to reports of field projects conducted by UN officials in developing countries. JF 251 .P8

Public Administration Quarterly. Formerly *Southern Review of Public Administration*, a good new journal on public administration with a broad orientation. An employment listing is available. JA 1 .S68

Public Administration Review. The most significant American journal concerned with public administration. *Review* articles are of high quality; research notes are provided. JK 1 .P85

Public Administration Survey. A bimonthly publication of the Bureau of Governmental Research at the University of Mississippi. — JK 4601 .M57

Public Administration Times. A biweekly newsletter with employment opportunities. Published by the American Society for Public Administration. — JA 1 .P975

Public Affairs. A public affairs and public policy journal. — JK 6501 .P83

Public Budgeting and Finance. A good quarterly journal on questions of public finance and budgeting that is jointly sponsored by the American Association for Budgeting and Program Analysis and the Section on Budgeting and Financial Management of the American Society for Public Administration. — HJ 2052 .A2P8

Public Choice. A policy journal with a political economy orientation. — H 35 .P33

Public Finance. Devoted to comparative public finance. — HJ 109 .N4P8

Public Finance Quarterly. A journal emphasizing economic approaches to budgeting in the United States. — HJ 101 .P83

Public Interest, The. High quality articles with a neo-conservative orientation on public policy issues. — H 1 .P86

Public Management. Short articles devoted to urban administration. Published monthly by the International City Management Association. — JS 39 .P97

Public Personnel Management. Directed at personnel administrators at all governmental levels, each issue has ten to twelve brief articles with a practical orientation. It is published by the International Personnel Management Association. — JK 671 .P48x

Public Productivity and Management Review. Initiated in 1975, this quarterly combines case studies and articles by academics and practitioners that focus on questions of program evaluation and productivity. Formerly *Public Productivity Review.* — JF 1411 .P8

Public Welfare. Devoted to policy and administration of public welfare in the United States. — HV 1 .P75

Publius. A journal devoted to intergovernmental relations and federalism. — JK 1 .P88

Research Management. Concerns problems of managing research and development units in large organizations. — T 175.5 .R4

Review of Public Data Use. A quarterly journal designed to encourage the use of publicly available data for research or analysis as applied to local, regional, or national problems. — H 62 .A1R47

Review of Public Personnel Administration. Published three times a year, the *Review* began publication in 1980 and covers all aspects of the field, particularly at the state and local levels of government. — JF 1601 .R4

Sage Professional Papers in Administrative and Policy Studies. Twelve academic papers are published annually in three issues, devoted to the administrative sciences. — H 31 .S24

Science. The major science journal of the nation; extremely useful for articles and reports on public policy with regard to science. — Q1 .S35

Society. Applies social science research to contemporary social and public policy problems. Formerly called *Trans-action.* — H 1 .T7

State and Local Government Review. A good journal covering a variety of aspects of state and local government, with an emphasis on public administration. — JK 2403 .S684

Urban Affairs Quarterly. Devoted primarily to sociological and political treatments of urban areas. — HT 101 .U7

Urban and Social Change Review. A journal with a social services orientation that attempts to appeal to both practitioners and academics. — HT 101 .U672

Urban Interest, The. A highly readable journal that aids professionals in analyzing and solving urban problems. Published twice a year. — JS 39 .U75

Washington Monthly. A liberal-journalistic publication of high quality. It focuses on the injustices of the public bureaucracy, as well as on policy issues. — E 838 .W37

Western City. Articles on urban administration in the West. Published monthly. — TD 1 .W4

APPENDIX

C

SELECTED ACADEMIC, PROFESSIONAL, AND PUBLIC INTEREST ORGANIZATIONS, WITH DESCRIPTIONS AND ADDRESSES

The following national groups all have a direct relevance to public administration. Virtually all of them publish journals and newsletters on topics of interest; you may wish to contact some of them for their materials. The organizations, together with a brief description and the address of each one, are listed in alphabetical order.

Academy for State and Local Government. 444 North Capitol Street, N.W., Suite 349, Washington, DC 20001. Supported by seven major organizations representing state and local interests, the Academy publishes original research on state and local issues. Its former title was the Academy for Contemporary Problems.

Advisory Commission on Intergovernmental Relations. 1111 Twentieth Street, N.W., Washington, DC 20036. Founded in 1959, the ACIR publishes significant studies of the federal system.

American Association of School Administrators. 1801 North Moore Street, Arlington, VA 22209. The largest association of school administrators.

American Association of State Highway and Transportation Officials. 444 North Capitol Street, Washington, DC 20001. The major association of state transit officials.

American Correctional Association. 4321 Hartwick Road, Suite L-208, College Park, MD 20740. The major association of correctional officials.

American Institute for Decision Sciences. 33 Gilmer Street S.E., Atlanta, GA 30303. Perhaps the premiere organization of quantitatively oriented academics interested in decision making.

American Management Association. 135 West 50th Street, New York, NY 10020. The major association of private sector managers.

American Planning Association. 1776 Massachusetts Avenue, N.W., Washington, DC 20036. An important organization of public planning officials. Formerly the American Society of Planning Officials.

American Political Science Association. 1527 New Hampshire Avenue, N.W., Washington, DC 20036. The chief academic association of political scientists.

American Productivity Center. 123 N. Post Oak Lane, Houston, TX 77024. Conducts and publishes case studies on productivity and the quality of work life.

American Public Transit Association. 1201 New York Avenue, N.W., Washington, DC 20005. The major association of public officials interested in mass transit.

American Public Welfare Association. 1125 Fifteenth Street, N.W., Washington, DC 20005. The major organization of public welfare officials.

American Public Works Association. 1313 East Sixtieth Street, Chicago, IL 60637. The principal association of public works administrators.

American Society for Public Administration. 1120 G Street, N.W., Washington, DC 20005. The major organization of academics and professionals in public administration at all levels of government.

Brookings Institution. 1775 Massachusetts Avenue, N.W., Washington, DC 20036. A major academic think tank with important concerns in domestic public affairs.

Center for Community Change. 1000 Wisconsin Avenue, N.W., Washington, DC 20007. Provides technical assistance to communities.

Center for Science in the Public Interest. 1779 Church Street, N.W., Washington, DC 20036. A coalition of scientists interested in the impact of public policy on science and society.

Committee for Economic Development. 477 Madison Avenue, New York, NY 10022. A private group that studies issues relating to business and public policy.

Common Cause. 2030 M Street, N.W., Washington, DC 20036. An organization of more than 300,000 members dedicated to political reform.

Conference Board, Inc. 845 Third Avenue, New York, NY 10022. A business group that often addresses public issues.

Conference of Minority Public Administrators. 1220 G Street, N.W., Washington, DC 20005. The major national association of minority public administrators.

Congressional Quarterly Service. 1735 K Street, N.W., Washington, DC 20006. Publishers of *Congressional Quarterly* and other publications relating to congressional action.

Council of State Community Affairs Agencies. Hall of the States, 444 North Capitol Street, Room 251, Washington, DC 20001. The major association of state community affairs officers.

Council of State Governments. Ironworks Pike, P. O. Box 11910, Lexington, KY 40511. Publishers of *The Book of the States* and other publications relating directly to state governments.

Council on Municipal Performance. 30 Irving Place, New York, NY 10003. Conducts research on urban service efficiency.

Environmental Action, Inc. 1525 New Hampshire Avenue, N.W., Washington, DC 20036. Environmentalists who are interested primarily in solid waste disposal.

Freedom of Information Center. School of Journalism, University of Missouri, P. O. Box 858, Columbia, MO 65201. Conducts studies on the public's uses of federal, state, and local freedom of information acts.

Government Finance Officers Association. 180 North Michigan Avenue, Suite 800, Chicago, IL 60601. Major organization of state and local finance officials, with an emphasis on local government. Formerly the Municipal Finance Officers Association.

Governmental Research Association. 24 Providence Street, Boston, MA 02108. One of the granddaddys of the municipal research bureaus, the Governmental Research Association was established in 1914 and is a national organization of individuals professionally engaged in governmental research.

Institute of Public Administration. 55 West 44th Street, New York, NY 10036. A public affairs research group that was one of the first public interest organizations.

International Association of Chiefs of Police. P. O. Box 6010, 13 First Field Road, Gaithersburg, MD 20878. The major organization of police chiefs.

International Association of Fire Chiefs. 1329 Eighteenth Street, N.W., Washington, DC 20036. The major organization of fire chiefs.

International City Management Association. 1120 G Street, N.W., Washington, DC 20005. The major organization of city managers and other individuals interested in city management.

International Institute of Municipal Clerks. 160 North Altadena Drive, Pasadena, CA 91107. The major association of municipal clerks, who, in small towns, often function as the town manager.

International Personnel Management Association. 1617 Duke Street, Alexandria, VA 22314. The major organization of public personnel administrators at all levels of government.

Labor-Management Relations Service. 1620 Eye Street, N.W., 4th Floor, Washington, DC 20006. Sponsored by the U.S. Conference of Mayors, this organization specializes in research on local labor problems.

National Association for the Advancement of Colored People. 733 Fifteenth Street, N.W., Washington, DC 20005. One of the most prestigious political organizations of African Americans.

National Association of Counties. 440 First Street, N.W., Washington, DC 20001. The major organization of county officials, and publishers of research on county government.

National Association of Housing and Redevelopment Officials. 1320 Eighteenth Street, N.W., Suite 500, Washington, DC 20036. The major association of state and local officials concerned with community development.

National Association of Regional Councils, 1700 K Street, N.W., Washington, DC 20036. The major organization of Councils of Governments and related organizations.

National Association of Schools of Public Affairs and Administration. 1120 G Street, N.W., Suite 520, Washington, DC 20005. The accrediting body for master's degree programs in public administration and public affairs.

National Association of Towns and Townships. 1522 K Street, N.W., Suite 780, Washington, DC 20005. Major organization representing towns and townships.

National Center for Public Productivity. 445 West 59th Street, New York, NY 10019. The Center gathers and disseminates information about productivity in public service and publishes a catalog of research on productivity improvement in the public sector.

National Conference of State Legislatures. Hall of the States, 444 North Capitol Street, N.W., Washington, DC 20001. The national association of state legislatures.

National Governors' Association. Hall of the States, 444 North Capitol Street, Suite 250, Washington, DC 20001. The organization of American governors.

National Institute of Governmental Purchasing. 115 Hillwood Avenue, Suite 201, Falls Church, VA 22046. Promotes improved procurement practices in government.

National Institute of Public Management. 1612 K Street, N.W., Washington, DC 20006. A research organization in public administration.

National League of Cities. 1301 Pennsylvania Avenue, N.W., Washington, DC 20004. One of the major associations of urban governments.

National Municipal League. 55 West 44th Street, New York, NY 10036. One of the major and oldest associations dedicated to improving urban governments.

National Public Employer Labor Relations Association. 1620 Eye Street, N.W., 4th Floor, Washington, DC 20006. Promotes better labor relations management at all levels of government.

National Recreation and Park Association. 3101 Park Center Drive, 12th Floor, Alexandria, VA 22302. The major organization of public parks and recreation professionals.

National Society for Internships and Experiential Education. 122 St. Mary's Street, Raleigh, NC 27605. Promotes public service internships, especially in the area of the environment. Formerly the National Center for Public Service Internship Programs.

Policy Studies Organization. 361 Lincoln Hall, University of Illinois, Urbana, IL 61801. The Policy Studies Organization consists largely of academics with an interest in public policy analysis.

Public Administration Service. 1497 Chain Bridge Road, McLean, VA 22101. An organization conducting significant research on public administration questions.

Public Service Research Foundation. 8330 Old Courthouse Road, Suite 600, Vienna, VA 22180. The Public Service Research Foundation was founded in 1977 and is an independent, nonprofit public education group whose purpose is to increase research and public awareness regarding public sector employee and employer relations.

Rand Corporation. 1700 Main Street, Santa Monica, CA 90406. A major think tank concerned in part with public problems.

Tax Foundation, Inc. One Thomas Circle, N.W., Suite 500, Washington, DC 20005. A private association concerned with tax issues.

United States Conference of Mayors. 1620 I Street, N.W., Fourth Floor, Washington, DC 20006. The major association of American mayors.

Urban Institute. 2100 M Street, N.W., Washington, DC 20037. A research organization devoted to urban issues.

D

CORRECT FORMS OF ADDRESS FOR PUBLIC OFFICIALS

Information, like money, is one of those things of which there is never enough. When you need information on a public issue that is not publicly available, it often is a good idea to write and ask someone who knows. A correct form of address can add to the effectiveness of your request from a public official, so this Appendix lists the proper ways of addressing public officials.

Public Official	Form of Address	Salutation
alderman	The Honorable John (or Joan) Green	Dear Mr. Green: (or Dear Ms. Green:)
assemblyman	see representative, state	
associate justice, Supreme Court	Justice Green The Supreme Court of the United States	Dear Justice Green:
Cabinet officers (as secretary of state and the attorney general)	The Honorable John (or Joan) Green, Secretary of State; The Honorable John Green Attorney General of the United States	Dear Sir: (or Dear Madam:)
chief justice, Supreme Court	The Chief Justice of the United States	Dear Chief Justice Green:
commissioner	The Honorable John Green	Dear Mr. Green:
councilmember	The Honorable Joan Green	Dear Ms. Green:

Public Official	Form of Address	Salutation
former U.S. president	The Honorable John Green	Dear Mr. Green:
governor	The Honorable Joan Green Governor of ————	Dear Governor Green:
judge, federal	The Honorable John Green United States District Judge	Dear Judge Green:
judge, state or local	The Honorable Joan Green Chief Judge of the Court of Appeals	Dear Judge Green:
lieutenant governor	The Honorable John Green Lieutenant Governor of ————	Dear Mr. Green:
mayor	The Honorable Joan Green Mayor of ————	Dear Mayor Green:
president, U.S.	The President	Dear Mr. President:
representative, state (same format for assemblyman)	The Honorable Joan Green House of Representatives (state capitol)	Dear Ms. Green:
representative, U.S.	The Honorable John Green The United States House of Representatives	Dear Mr. Green:
senator, state	The Honorable Joan Green The State Senate (state capitol)	Dear Senator Green:
senator, U.S.	The Honorable John Green United States Senate	Dear Senator Green:
speaker, U.S. House of Representatives	The Honorable John Green Speaker of the House of Representatives	Dear Mr. Speaker:
vice-president	The Vice President United States Senate	Dear Mr. Vice President

APPENDIX
E

BECOMING A PUBLIC ADMINISTRATOR

Now that you have read about public administration, why not consider working in it, too? Public administrators are in one of the world's most rewarding professions: the people's interests are served, the job security is high, the pay is good, and the field of public administration is fascinating.

And the popular appeal of public administration seems to be on the upswing. As one writer in the *Los Angeles Times* noted, "That scruffy orphan of the Me Generation, that woebegone villain of the Ronald Reagan epoch, that doleful survivor of a kinder and gentler past—that pursuit we know as public service—stands ready for a comeback."

JOBS! JOBS! JOBS!

There is a relatively high probability that you can get a good job in government. Employment in the public sector has been going up almost every year for the past three decades, and today there are more than 17 million full-time and part-time public employees, or about one for every six workers. The U.S. Bureau of Labor Statistics projects an increase of 8.4 percent in general government jobs between 1988 and 2000. Most of the jobs are in local government (58 percent); state government accounts for almost a quarter of public employment, and the federal government for less than a sixth. The fastest growth rates in public employment are among the state and local governments, and opportunities are quite good at these levels.

The MPA: A Door Opener

The single best educational qualification for a management position in the public sector is the Master of Public Administration (MPA) degree— a point on which both employees and employers agree. MPA degree holders believe that the MPA has made them significantly more knowledgeable and confident upon entering government service, and four-fifths of them, according to a survey by George Grode and Marc Holzer, think that the MPA has been more beneficial to them as professionals than any other kind of master's degree.

The same research found that employers seemed to agree. Nearly three-quarters of the supervisors of these graduates stated that the performance of their employees who held MPAs was slightly to "clearly superior" to the performance of holders of other kinds of advanced degrees who were also under their supervision.

The success rate of MPAs in the public bureaucracy validates these views. Gregory B. Lewis studied a large sample of federal employees with graduate degrees and found not only that graduate degree holders as a class advanced significantly higher and faster in the federal service than those without such credentials, but also that MPAs held a higher federal rank, on the average, than did the holders of any other kind of advanced degree (with the exception of law degrees). MPAs also earned larger salaries than most, and were more likely to hold administrative positions of authority. (The other advanced degrees were in business administration, law, social science, and the ubiquitous "other.") Federal employees seem to recognize that the MPA is the coming degree; the number of MPAs working in the federal government has more than doubled in the eight years between 1974 and 1982, a far greater rate of growth than any other kind of degree.

For successful employment in the public sector, the Master of Public Administration degree is the credential of choice.

Professional Specializations: The Best Prospects

Dalton S. Lee and Cathy Osborn have explored which specialties in public administration are likely to offer the most opportunities for new public administrators. Lee and Osborn sent questionnaires to professors of public administration in those universities that are members of the National Association of Schools of Public Affairs and Administration (NASPAA), all state and territorial personnel departments, and a random sample of cities with more than 50,000 people. The most conclusive finding in the survey was that holding a Master of Public Administration degree greatly enhances one's chances of being hired by a government. In addition, however, the study found differing opinions among respondents about the best career areas in public administration. These opinions are ranked as follows from the most favorable career opportunities to the least favorable.

Minorities and Women: Better Possibilities

More minorities and women are hired and earn more money in the public sector than in the private sector.

Public Administration Educators	State Personnel Specialists[1]	Local Government Administrators
1. Budgeting	1. Policy analysis/ program evaluation	1. Policy analysis/ program evaluation
2. Finance	2. Program management	2. Planning
3. Policy analysis/ program evaluation	3. Budgeting	3. Program management
4. Urban management	4. Finance	4. Urban management
5. Personnel administration	5. Planning	5. Budgeting
6. Program management	6. Personnel administration	6. Finance
7. Planning		7. Personnel administration

[1]Urban management was not ranked by these respondents.

Twenty-seven percent of all federal full-time employees are minorities; 16 percent are black, and 5 percent are Hispanic. Forty-eight percent of federal white-collar workers are women. A fourth of all state and local employees (excluding those in education) are minorities, and 42 percent are women. It appears that state and local governments may do a better job in promoting minorities and women, and paying them more, than does the federal government and the private sector. See Chapter 9 for details.

MONEY! MONEY! MONEY!

Public sector pay rates have gone up from 4 to 9 percent almost every year since 1970, and, despite tax revolts in the states, pay rates for state and local employees have increased more rapidly than have pay rates for federal employees. With the enactment of the Federal Employees Comparability Act of 1990, however, federal salaries may begin to rise at a faster pace than their subnational counterparts.

Federal Public Administration

There are more than 3 million people working in the federal civilian work force. Nearly two-thirds of these employees (outside of the U.S. Postal Service) have administrative or policy responsibilities. In addition, there are 2.1 million service men and women in the armed forces, and perhaps 3 million civilian employees in the private sector who are working under federal contracts.

Federal salaries at the executive levels are good, and with the passage of the Federal Employees Comparability Act in 1990, salaries will likely get even better. The Act ties federal salaries to comparable positions in the nonfederal sector and to local costs of living. Cabinet and subcabinet officers had salaries ranging from $101,300 to $138,900 in 1991, and members of the Senior Executive Service made from $87,000 to $108,300. Entry level administrative salaries begin at the level of Grade 7 of the General Schedule (about $25,000 in 1988), although it is possible to enter at a higher grade.

State Public Administration

There are more than 4.1 million state employees, a figure that includes 1.8 million state employees in education. The Council of State Governments reports that there are over 120 categories of top state officials, ranging from directors of state lotteries to secretaries of education, to directors of emergency management. Limited data have been compiled about compensation rates for state public administrators. However, $80,000 to more than $100,000 (in 1990) seems to be the salary level for the top state administrative jobs in the more populous states, and in these states, salaries at all administrative ranks appear to be roughly comparable to federal pay rates. But even in the least populated states, it is rare to find the top major job salaries at less than $50,000. Southern states tend to pay their public administrators the least, followed by Eastern states; Western states generally have the highest rates of pay. It is increasingly common to find top administrators in state government (particularly in higher education) that are paid more than the governor.

Local Public Administration

Local governments employ more than 10 million people, a figure that includes nearly 5.6 million local employees in education. Considerably more is known about administrative salaries at the local level than at the state level. The top positions in local government are nearing an average salary of $55,000, and salaries are increasing by about 6 percent a year. However, in the largest cities, top urban administrators typically earn more than $100,000; typically, school superintendents and, to a lesser degree, police chiefs, in cities with more than 500,000 people are paid more than the city administrator. West Coast governments pay their public administrators the most; Northeastern cities pay the least—often a third less than in the Western cities. Entry level administrative positions in small cities (5,000–10,000 people) typically pay around $25,000, and it is not uncommon to enter municipal service in a small town as the head of an entire department.

It appears that the best salaries, including entry-level salaries, in the public sector are offered by the special districts, such as water districts, transportation districts, and other single function jurisdictions. These governments, many of which are also public corporations, pay better, on the average, than any other type of government.

GETTING A JOB IN GOVERNMENT

When perusing the job announcements and want ads, it is important to know which jobs are appropriate for public administration students. Being new to the field, some students may not even be sure what job titles are related to public administration. For the most part, trainee and intern positions are for the less experienced and may not lead to permanent positions. A "I" after a title, such as Analyst I, usually indicates an entry-level position. An Analyst II or Analyst III would indicate that more extensive education or experience was required.

At the federal level, Executive Order 12364 in 1982 reconstituted the Presidential Management Intern (PMI) Program, which was established by Executive Order in 1977. The goal of the PMI Program is to attract outstanding men and women who are completing master's degrees from a variety of academic backgrounds to the federal service. The PMI Program seeks out those who have a clear interest in, and commitment to, a career in the analysis and management of public policies and programs, so the MPA is the preferred degree.

Each year up to 200 interns receive two-year appointments to developmental positions throughout the executive branch of the federal government. These positions differ from most entry-level positions in terms of pay and the emphasis on career development. While most entry level positions begin at GS-7, PMI Program employees enter at GS-9, are promoted to GS-11 at the end of the first year, and are routinely converted to regular civil service appointments upon the successful completion of the internship at the end of the second year. Professional positions at the GS-11 level normally require a doctorate, three years of full-time graduate study, or specialized work experience equivalent to one or more years at the GS-9 level.

Entry into the PMI Program is competitive. Each educational institution is limited in the number of candidates it may nominate. In recent years, almost 500 master's degree students complete applications each year for the PMI Program.

Of course, the new federal examination for entry-level administrative positions is now in operation, and should not be overlooked. Begun in 1990, after a nine-year hiatus, it tests applicants for suitability in 118 position classifications. Your campus placement office can provide you with the schedule for the examination. The test admits around 5,000 of the examinees to the federal service each year.

Regardless of the level of government that you are interested in, summarize your abilities in a resumé format that presents your most important assets first. What things were you able to accomplish in your job and education? State your case in terms of projects that you have directed, designed, developed, implemented, researched, reported, managed, controlled, planned, organized, edited, or built. When stated in these terms, those new or returning to the job market are disadvantaged by using the traditional *chronological resumé*. They should use a *functional resumé* format that highlights their training, analytic skills, ability to get along with others, knowledge of organization dynamics, budgeting strategies, and management tools and so forth. Both a sample functional resumé and chronological resumé are found on pages 429–431. But do not be shy in asking for help in polishing up your resumé; your campus placement office can be a genuine asset in not only developing a presentable resumé, but often in helping you practice interviewing skills as well.

An excellent way to develop job contacts is to join the American Society for Public Administration, or ASPA. ASPA has local chapters in cities across the country composed of public administrators from all levels of government. Typically, ASPA chapters sponsor monthly luncheons and regional conferences where new contacts are easily made. To learn how to join, ask your course instructor, or write:

American Society for Public Administration
1120 G Street, N.W., Suite 500
Washington, DC 20005
ASPA's telephone number is (202) 393-7878.

An internship, paid or voluntary, can be an important step toward gaining needed relevant work experience for students lacking public sector experience. Often, schools of public administration or departments of political science work with governmental agencies in developing local internship opportunities in personnel, budgeting, planning, policy analysis, and so forth. A satisfactory internship can provide strong recommendations and strengthen one's resumé.

CONCLUSION

If you are interested in becoming a public administrator, two recommendations are paramount. First, join the American Society for Public Administration. Not only does it provide unique networking opportunities, but it publishes a biweekly newsletter, *Public Administration Times*, listing professional job openings around the country.

Second, consider entering an MPA degree program. Increasingly, these programs cater to the scheduling needs of students who already have jobs, and the MPA itself is regarded as an important qualification for entry and advancement in the public sector. To learn more about the Master of Public Administration degree, contact your local university or the National Association of Schools of Public Administration (NASPAA) and ask for its highly informative pamphlet, "MPA: The Master of Public Administration Degree," which is available at no charge. NASPAA also publishes *In the Public In-*

terest, a useful quarterly newsletter on employment trends in the public service with a special emphasis on internships. A detailed *Directory* of about 200 MPA programs is also available from NASPAA for $12.50. NASPAA's address is the same as ASPA's:

National Association of Schools of Public Affairs and Administration
1120 G Street, N.W.
Washington, DC 20005
NASPAA's telephone number is (202) 628-8965.

SOURCES

John Balzar, "Public Service Making a Comeback," *Los Angeles Times* (April 1, 1990).

Bureau of the Census, *Statistical Abstract of the United States, 1990* (Washington, D.C.: U.S. Government Printing Office, 1990).

"*Governing's* 1990 Salary Survey," *Governing*, 4 (December 1990), pp. 65–67.

George Grode and Marc Holzer, "The Perceived Utility of MPA Degrees," *Public Administration Review*, 35 (July/August 1975), pp. 403–412.

International Personnel Management Association, *Pay Rates in the Public Service: Survey of 62 Common Job Classes in the Public Sector* (Washington, D.C.: International Personnel Management Association, 1985).

Dalton S. Lee and Cathy Osborn, "Employment Prospects in Public Administration" (Unpublished manuscript, School of Public Affairs, Arizona State University, Tempe, Arizona 1984).

Gregory B. Lewis, "How Much Is an MPA Worth? Public Administration Education and Federal Career Success," *International Journal of Public Administration*, 9 (April 1987), pp. 397–415.

State Administrative Officials Classified by Function, 1985–86 (Lexington, Ky.: Council of State Governments, 1985).

The Municipal Year Book, 1990 (Washington, D.C.: International City Management Association, 1990).

SAMPLE FUNCTIONAL RESUME

KENNETH L. MATTHEWS
1234 East University Drive
Tempe, Arizona 85281
(602) 000-0000 (work)
(602) 000-0000 (home)

URBAN PLANNING AND ADMINISTRATION

Responsible for initiating the Town of Snowflake's first general plan. Generated background information, organized all meetings, wrote news releases for local papers, created land-use maps, and developed fiscal impact statements.

Successful Community Development Block Grant (CDBG) application for $110,000 (FY 93-94). Analyzed data processing needs and initiated purchases of computer system for Town. Skillfully performed a wide range of general administrative tasks.

POLICY ANALYSIS

Generated reports for the Office of Community Relations at Arizona State University for submission to the state legislature on such topics as the need for a west-side campus, and the transportation crisis in Maricopa County.

Collected data and analyzed policy for the Town of Snowflake on water and sewer rate structures and employee pay scales. Also restructured all town policies and programs to meet federal antidiscrimination legislation.

RESEARCH METHODS

Strong academic background in research methods, which included work in congressional voting behavior and immigration policy. Practical experience in conducting job attitude survey for the Town of Eager, community needs survey for the Town of Snowflake, and a multiplicity of analytic reports for the Office of Community Relations at Arizona State University.

WORK EXPERIENCE

1991-93 Research Assistant, Office of Community Relations, Arizona State University

1992 Administrative Intern, Town of Snowflake

EDUCATION

1991 Master of Public Administration, ASU, 4.00 GPA

1990 Bachelor of Arts, Political Science, University of Washington, 3.67 GPA, cum laude, Phi Beta Kappa

SAMPLE CHRONOLOGICAL RESUME

VIVIAN LOOK
5678 East University Drive
Tempe, Arizona 85281
(602) 000-0000 (work)
(602) 000-0000 (home)

OBJECTIVE:

To work in an area of public administration related to legislation or public policy. The ideal position would allow me to utilize my skills in research analysis, interpersonal relations, and communication, both oral and written.

EDUCATION:

School	Dates Attended	Degree	Major Coursework
Arizona State University Tempe, Arizona	1-92 to present	——	Public Administration
University of Michigan Ann Arbor, Michigan	9-88 to 8-89	MPH	Public Health
University of California	3-78 to 7-81	BS	Nutritional Sciences, Economics, Psychology

Other training: Food Services Division, Milwaukee Public Schools, Milwaukee, Wisconsin, 9-76 to 6-77. Administrative dietetic internship focusing on the management of school food service programs.

PROFESSIONAL WORK EXPERIENCE:

Administrative Intern, Maricopa County Office of Management Analysis, Phoenix, Arizona. 1-93 to present.

Under the direction of the Deputy County Manager, assist Management Analysts in conducting management audits of county departments to investigate efficiency and effectiveness of services provided. Assess present and future staffing requirements and make recommendations for improving the service delivery system. Perform other duties as assigned by the Deputy County Manager and Management Analysts. Other assignments have included assisting the Contracts Specialist in Materials Management in developing a master copier plan for use by the county during the next five years.

Research Assistant, School of Public Affairs, Arizona State University, Tempe, Arizona, 8-92 to present.

Under the direction of ASU faculty member and Director of the Center for Urban Studies, assist in research, class preparation, and other duties as assigned. Work on research projects has included assisting in computer-based management and analysis of educational enrollment data for the Phoenix Town Hall, citizen surveys for the city of Glendale, and library research on public choice theory.

Project Nutrition Consultant, Bureau of Nutritional Services, Arizona Department of Health Services, Tempe, Arizona, 10-89 to 8-92.

Served as the primary contact person from the Bureau of Nutrition for county and tribal health departments, as assigned. In this capacity, monitored local agency programs for compliance to program and contract requirements, provided assistance in program management, and served as an advocate for local projects, participating in negotiations when appropriate. At the bureau level, participated in planning, development, and review of policies and procedures and budget allocation process for state-subvened funds. As the lead consultant for the bureau's Laboratory Quality Assurance Program from 1-92 to 8-92, researched alternative methods of carrying out the program and completed comparative cost studies. Developed and presented final recommendations for improving the program and reducing costs, which were ultimately adopted by the agency.

Nutritionist, Health Division, Lane County Department of Health and Social Services, Eugene, Oregon, 7-84 to 7-88.

Special Vocational Educational Teacher, Springfield School District No. 19, Springfield, Oregon, 9-83 to 6-84.

Trainer/Nutritionist, Community Nutrition Institute, Washington, D.C. 10-82 to 6-83.

RECENT PROFESSIONAL ACTIVITIES AND HONORS:

1992 to present	Regents Graduate Academic Scholarship, Arizona State University, Tempe, Arizona Member, American Society for Public Administration, Arizona Chapter
1991-92	Co-editor, Legislative Newsletter, Arizona Dietitians for Legislative Action
1990-91	Community Nutrition Section Chairperson and Executive Board Member, Central Arizona District Dietetic Association
1988-89	U.S. Public Health Traineeship, University of Michigan, Ann Arbor, Michigan
1987-88	Member, Task Force on Dental Health, Nutrition, and Health Education, Western Oregon Health Systems Agency Member, Nutrition Task Force, Oregon Public Health Association

INDEX

SUBJECT INDEX